Specifications for Commercial Interiors

Professional Liabilities, Regulations, and Performance Criteria

Specifications for Commercial Interiors

Professional Liabilities, Regulations, and Performance Criteria

S.C. Reznikoff

Whitney Library of Design
an imprint of
Watson-Guptill Publications/New York

Copyright © 1979 by Whitney Library of Design

First published 1979 in New York by the Whitney Library of Design
an imprint of Watson-Guptill Publications,
a division of Billboard Publications, Inc.,
1515 Broadway, New York, N.Y. 10036

Library of Congress Cataloging in Publication Data
Reznikoff, S   C   1930-
  Specifications for commercial interiors.
  Bibliography: p.
  Includes index.
  1. Building laws—United States. 2. Architects—
Malpractice—United States. 3. Buildings—Contracts and
specifications—United States. I. Title.
KF5701.R49   343'.73'078   79-17340
ISBN 0-8230-7353-X

Manufactured in U.S.A.

First Printing, 1979

7 8 9/86

For my Mother, Husband, Son, and Daughter

ACKNOWLEDGMENTS

The interior architectural students at Arizona State University provided the stimulus for this book and gave continued suggestions and encouragement throughout the research and development stages.

A book of this scope would not have been possible without the assistance of many people. I am especially indebted to Erma Striner, director of the General Services Administration Design Action Center, for valuable research directives. Among the many federal agencies that supplied information and data are the National Bureau of Standards, the National Fire Academy, the Consumers Product Safety Commission, the Federal Supply Services, the Department of Health, Education, and Welfare, and the General Services Administration.

Richard Hopper, Carpet and Rug Institute; Hank Roux, Armstrong Cork Company; John Galloway, Dupont Company; Don Henning, IBD; Cliff Avery, ASID; Diane Bramman Worth, ASID; Richard E. Stevens, NFPA; Professors Mary Shipley and Richard Perrell, FCSI, are among the people who reviewed portions of the manuscript and made helpful suggestions. Fire Engineers Donald Belles and Edward Prendergast also offered expert guidance.

The National Fire Protection Association, the American Society for Testing and Materials, the Construction Specifications Institute, the Architectural Woodwork Institute, the Carpet and Rug Institute, the Carpet Cushion Council, the Wallcovering Manufacturers Association, the Hardwood Plywood Manufacturer's Association, and the Business and Institutional Furniture Manufacturer's Association are a few of the organizations that generously supplied information.

The scope of this book was greatly enhanced by people in private industry and those design firms that gave permission for the inclusion of their photographs, drawings, and specifications.

Barbara and Gary Powell, Bambi Wesche, and Lu Schildmeyer worked many evenings and weekends to prepare the typed manuscript, drawings, and charts.

Without the enthusiasm and encouragement provided by the editors and staff of The Whitney Library of Design, this book would not have been possible. Special thanks to Sarah Bodine who visualized the timeliness and importance of the material and gave invaluable editorial guidance. I am particularly grateful to Susan Davis whose editorial expertise guided the work to completion.

CONTENTS

LIST OF ABBREVIATIONS

AATCC   American Association of Textile Chemists and Colorists
AHA   American Hardboard Association
AHLI   American Home Lighting Institute
AIA   American Institute of Architects
ALSC   American Lumber Standards Committee
ANSI   American National Standards Institute
APA   American Plywood Association
ASAHC   American Society of Architectural Hardware Consultants
ASHRAE   American Society of Heating, Refrigerating, and Air Conditioning Engineers, Inc.
ASID   American Society of Interior Designers
ASTM   American Society for Testing and Materials
ASI   American Specification Institute
AWI   Architectural Woodwork Institute
BBC   Basic Building Code
BHMA   Builders Hardware Manufacturers Association
BIFMA   Business and Institutional Furniture Manufacturers Association
BOCA   Building Officials Conference of America
BRAB   Building Research Advisory Board
BRI   Building Research Institute
CCC   Carpet Cushion Council
CIA   Cork Institute of America
CPSC   Consumer Product Safety Commission
CRI   Carpet and Rug Institute
CS   Commercial Standards
CSI   Construction Specifications Institute
CTI   Ceramic Tile Institute
DOC   Department of Commerce
DOL   Department of Labor
DOT   Department of Transportation
DWI   Durable Woods Institute
EPA   Environmental Protection Agency
FAA   Federal Aviation Administration
FHA   Federal Housing Administration
FPL   Forest Products Laboratory
FPRS   Forest Products Research Society
FRA   Federal Railroad Administration
FS   Federal Specifications
FSPT   Federation of Societies for Paint Technology
FSS   Federal Supply Service
FTC   Federal Trade Commission
FTI   Facing Tile Institute
FTMS   Federal Test Method Standard
GSA   General Services Administration
HEW   Department of Health, Education, and Welfare
HMMA   Hardware Merchants and Manufacturers Association
HPMA   Hardwood Plywood Manufacturers Association
HPSC   Home Products Safety Council
HUD   Department of Housing and Urban Development
IBD   Institute of Business Designers
ICBO   International Conference of Building Officials
IDEC   Interior Designer Educators Council

IES   Illuminating Engineering Society
LCC   Life Cycle Costing
MA   Mahogany Association, Inc.
MCSC   Model Codes Standardization Council
MFMA   Maple Flooring Manufacturers Association
MIA   Marble Institute of America
MIL   Military Specifications
MPS   Minimum Property Standards
NADAF   National Association of Decorative Architectural Finishes
NAMD   National Association of Marble Dealers
NAMM   National Association of Mirror Manufacturers
NAMP   National Association of Marble Producers
NBC   National Building Code
NBHA   National Builders Hardware Association
NBS   National Bureau of Standards
NCIDQ   National Council for Interior Design Qualification
NEC   National Electrical Code
NFPA   National Fire Protection Association
NHLA   National Hardwood Lumber Association
NKCA   National Kitchen Cabinet Association
NOFMA   National Oak Flooring Manufacturers Association
NPDA   National Plywood Distributors Association
NPVLA   National Paint, Varnish, and Lacquer Association
NTMA   National Terrazzo and Mosaic Association
NWMA   National Woodwork Manufacturers Association
OSHA   Occupational Safety and Health Administration
PBS   Public Building Service
PHS   Public Health Service
PLIB   Pacific Lumber Inspection Bureau
PMA   Philippine Mahogany Association
PPW   Ponderosa Pine Woodwork
PRF   Plywood Research Foundation
PS   Product Standards
SBCC   Southern Building Code Congress
SGA   Stained Glass Association of America
SPA   Southern Pine Association
SPI   Society of the Plastics Industry, Inc.
SSA   Social Security Administration
SSBC   Southern Standard Building Code
TC   Tile Council of America
UBC   Uniform Building Code
UL   Underwriters Laboratories, Inc.
ULC   Underwriters Laboratories of Canada
USCS   United States Department of Commerce, Commercial Standards
USFA   United States Fire Administration
VA   Veterans Administration
WCLIB   West Coast Lumber Inspection Bureau
WFIA   Wood Flooring Institute of America

Mathematical Symbols
$>$ Greater than
$<$ Less than
Σ Summation of

INTRODUCTION

It may prove unsettling to take a backward look at some of the events that have brought the interior designer to this era of liabilities and regulations. Interior design has been a profession traditionally rooted in aesthetics and involved almost exclusively in residential work. *Contract design*, a term meaning the design of commercial and institutional spaces, evolved during the late fifties and early sixties. The prosperity of these years brought about a surge of commercial construction. Small and large corporations turned to designers for assistance in planning and furnishing interior spaces that would project a corporate image. An editorial by Harry Anderson in *Interior Design* magazine in 1961 proudly announced "the interior designer's role as sculptor of the corporate image through the interior environment that he creates for business is now well established and respected . . . the finest non-residential interiors are created by professionals trained in residential work because of their *instinctive sensitivity* to the requirements of the individual."[1]

Apparently the transition from the personalized residential role to the corporate image-maker was not too difficult for the interior designer. And it soon became evident that there were two major advantages in commercial work: one was economic gain and the other was professional status. Sherman Emery's 1965 editorial in *Interior Design* magazine expressed the professional identity problems of that period: "The tremendous growth in contract work in recent years can be measured in more than dollars and cents. For in addition to becoming a multi-million dollar business, it has greatly increased *the professional standing* of the designer. Designing a non-residential installation also carries with it the connotation of *professionalism* . . . it frequently requires working with an architect, and this helps to further the *professional image*."[2]

The past two decades have witnessed the dynamic evolution of the interior design profession. The formation of the *American Society of Interior Designers* (ASID) in 1974, resulting from the merger of the American Institute of Designers and the National Society of Interior Designers, created the largest single organization of professional designers in the United States. The *Institute of Business Designers* (IBD) was organized in the mid-1960s to meet the needs of the increasing number of designers specializing in commercial design work.

Professional membership in these major national organizations requires that design competence be measured by the successful completion of a qualifying examination. The *National Council for Interior Design Qualification* (NCIDQ), composed of members from concerned organizations, developed and administers the examination.

Commercial and institutional design currently represents a $10 billion industry and involves more than the creation of a corporate image. More is required of a designer than "instinctive sensitivity." The increase in federal regulations and the liability lawsuit trend have resulted in an increasing professional sense of responsibility and a concern for acquiring more information about the technical and behavioral sciences. With this new emphasis, designers have become better equipped to deal with critical commercial and institutional spatial needs. It has, however, become increasingly difficult for the practicing designer to maintain a working knowledge of the technical advances in performance testing and the accompanying federal regulations. The primary purpose of this book is to provide this needed information that will allow designers to establish a systematic approach to making responsible specification decisions and thereby to minimize the possibility of professional liability. The contents of the book are divided into three parts:

Part 1 establishes the bases for specification decisions. Chapters 1 and 2 provide information on current professional and product liability problems facing designers today. Chapter 3 compiles information from many diverse sources to present a summary of federal and state regulations. Chapters 4 and 5 deal with the establishment of performance criteria based on user needs and examines the concepts of performance testing. The application of life cycle costing methods is explained in Chapter 6.

Part 2 provides the designer with a survey of interior subsystems and materials. Specification guidelines for each subsystem include information on construction and quality control, performance standards and regulations, installation, maintenance, and methods of life cycle costing.

Part 3 deals with the format and contents of specification documents. The importance of coordinating working drawings, schedules, and specification documents is clarified.

Part 1
Liabilities and Regulations

1 PROFESSIONAL LIABILITIES

The last two decades in America have been called the "golden age of consumerism." During those years, Ralph Nader became the consumer's advocate. In a 10-year period, 20 pieces of consumer legislation were presented to Congress; of them, 16 were passed into law.

Because the professional designer of commercial spaces may not actually sell products to an individual consumer, the designer may think that consumer legislation has little effect on his or her practice. Actually the commercial designer has created a new type of consumer—a *captive consumer*. A captive consumer is a person or persons using offices and public spaces such as hospitals, stores, airports, and other non-live-in institutional space. They are considered "captive" because they have not been directly involved in the selection of the interior materials, furniture, and furnishings they are forced to use.

Each time a designer enters into a contractual agreement and specifies furnishings, floor, and wall coverings, or any other subsystem of a commercial or institutional space, he becomes liable, or *responsible*, for the performance of that system. The system should perform well under normal usage and under critical conditions that might occur. As in the case of fire, the material should not contribute excessively to flame spread or smoke development.

A spot check of newspaper headlines indicates the frequency of mishaps due to possible faulty interior specifications. In an eight-week period during the summer of 1977, the following events were reported:

June 1, 1977
Southgate, Kentucky

"DEADLY PLASTIC FUMES SUSPECTED OF ADDING TO KENTUCKY CLUB TOLL"
"State Police commission to conduct tests on vinyl chairs. . . ."

June 27, 1977
Columbia, Tennessee

"POISON FUMES KILL 42 IN JAIL IN TENNESSEE"
"Gases from foam padded cell believed to be the cause. . . ."

August 1, 1977
Phoenix, Arizona

"COUNTY OK'S FUNDS TO REPLACE UNLAID CARPET IN NEW BUILDING"
"There may be a lawsuit later because someone made a mistake in selecting the wrong carpet." Was it the architect? "We don't know and we can worry about the lawsuit after the damages are established. . . ."

In a 1978 study prepared by the Office of Professional Liability Research, a division of the Victor O. Schinnerer Company, it was found that malpractice suits against architects were increasing at a rate of 20 percent a year. The report also stated that the average value of claims against architects for alleged design and construction failure had tripled since 1960. Almost 30 percent of insured architectural firms were sued in 1976. Insurance premiums were reported to have grown from less than 1 percent of an architect's gross income to between 2 and 10 percent of his or her income.

DIFFERING VIEWS ON THE LIABILITY PROBLEM

During this decade of increasing liability lawsuits, we have witnessed the development of many differing views on the advantages and disadvantages of this trend. Justin Sweet, professor of law at the University of California and an authority on professional liability, observed that "Those who support such a trend argue that it is long overdue. They contend that professional persons have enjoyed a type of immunity from responsibility for their acts which is not accorded others. Those who favor such a trend contend that it has made professional persons exercise a higher degree of care than they would have without such legal accountability. They also argue that professionals often operate through highly organized and profitable associations which can and should respond for losses caused by their conduct in furnishing professional services. This trend can also be supported as a method of eliminating incompetent professionals who somehow manage to continue to practice because of the laxity of enforcement of licensing and registration laws."

Many professional groups feel that such increased liability in the long run hampers proper professional practice. Opponents of increased professional liability state that it has forced professionals into large organizations which have not always produced imaginative professional work. They also contend that increased liability has caused the rates for professional liability insurance to soar astronomically and places an unreasonable burden on the younger professional. They also contend that increased professional liability will inhibit professionals from using new or unconventional techniques for fear that they will be held liable if things go wrong. While some professionals are willing to accept legal responsibility for their negligence, they feel that in reality they will be held to a standard of perfection by judges and juries. If anything goes wrong, they fear they will be held responsible.[1]

BASES FOR MOST LIABILITY SUITS

The legal bases for most liability suits are professional negligence, misrepresentation or implied warranty, implied fitness warranty, breach of contract, strict liability, and liability without fault for design defects. In many circumstances, these legal bases overlap. For example, a designer's failure to condemn or reject defective work by a supplier or contractor may be classified as professional negligence and breach of contract.

Professional Negligence. Professional negligence usually involves an error of omission and is the basis of most liability lawsuits. Whenever a designer exposes others to unreasonable risks because of defective design, selection of inadequate or improper materials or equipment, and failure to condemn defective work, he can be sued for professional negligence. Many disputes have involved the performance failure of a certain product or material. In other cases, the problem stems not from product failure, but from negligence on the part of the designer to determine the right material for a particular use. A hospital, forced to replace carpeting a few months after installation because the designer was unaware of static buildup in critical areas, should rightfully seek retribution.

Implied Warranty or Misrepresentation. A designer's ability to perform design work is not directly stated in a contractual agreement, but it is *implied*, and therefore warrants, or promises, professional competence. Verbal opinions expressed by a designer can also be construed as implied warranties. The definiteness with which the designer's professional opinion is stated may be the deciding factor in a legal judgment. It should be noted that compliance with building and fire codes is usually an implied warranty in a professional design contract. Failure to comply with state and local codes may also be considered professional negligence.

Implied Fitness Warranty. This warranty involves the specification of a product or material that later proves unfit for the intended use. If the designer knew of the specific intended use and the client relied on the designer's knowledge, skill, and expertise, then the designer is responsible. However, if the client ordered the use of a certain product or material, based on the specification of a third party, the designer would not be held responsible. The American Society of Interior Designers advises that the designer "refrain from procuring furniture, furnishings and equipment in any capacity other than as an agent for the owner. If the Designer is considered to have purchased and RESOLD FF&E, then the Designer may incur liability under an express warranty, under implied warranties of merchantability and fitness for a particular use, as well as under strict products liability (liability regardless of fault or negligence) for any defects in the FF&E, as part of the 'chain of distribution.' "[2]

Breach of Contract. In addition to the stated written content of a contract, there may also be many *implied* responsibilities. In some cases, this may involve design errors that are responsible for additional construction costs, depreciation of property values, or loss of the owner's business profit. If a retail store is scheduled to open on a certain date and the opening is delayed because an area is unfinished or a counter was built according to inaccurate measurements specified by the designer, then the designer is responsible for the owner's loss of income caused by the delayed opening.

Breach of contract may also involve the general satisfaction of the client regarding subjective decisions, such as color choice. Although color selections may be approved at every phase of the design work, the client's inability to visualize the final installation may result in disagreement. Legal judgments regarding mechanical performance are usually objective, but decisions involving aesthetics are often necessarily subjective.

Strict Liability. Strict liability is a basis for suits developed during the mid-1960s. Strict liability, essentially concerned with negligence, is often the reason interior designers become involved as a third party in product liability suits. This is explained in greater detail in regard to product liability.

Liability without Fault for Design Defects. Most professional contracts attempt to clearly define the limits of responsibility for both the designer and involved contractors. If, however, any injury or damage does occur that is the direct result of the designer's drawings, design, or specification, the designer will be held responsible. If the designer or his employees gave instructions or directions that can be proven were the primary cause of the injury or damage, the design firm will be held responsible.

Although liability suits have increased against interior designers, no formal study has been made to determine the exact number of claims. A random sampling of the types of suits incurred by designers from 1976 through 1977 indicates that the majority of claims involved three major areas:

1. Professional negligence

   Defective design

   Inaccurate measurements

   Noncompliance with codes

2. Breach of contract

   Defective design delaying job completion

   Inadequate supervision of installations

3. Implied warranty

   Specification of furnishings unsuitable for intended use

The two most frequent causes for claims were *inaccurate measurements* and the *specification of chairs unsuitable for intended use*.

HOW TO LESSEN THE POSSIBILITY OF LIABILITY SUITS

There are six specific things that you can do to protect yourself from the possibility of liability suits:

Perform within Your Area of Expertise. Many designers undertake project responsibilities that fall outside the acceptable area of practice generally understood by courts of law to be the prerogative of the interior designer. Structural alterations, rewiring, heating, and air-conditioning changes do not fall within the realm of interior design practice. So if a project requires the specification of large interior plants and greenery, for example, the designer would be well advised to enlist the aid of an interior landscape consultant who could also provide a complete maintenance program for the life of the plants.

Use Concise Contracts and Specifications. Contracts should carefully list all the areas of responsibility, both of the designer and of the owner/client. Although the law does not hold designers to a standard of perfection in the performance of professional services, applicable legal standards can be unintentionally, but dramatically, altered by the terms of the professional's contract. Courts will construe common words and phrases in contracts according to their common meaning. Therefore, every word in a contract should be read and interpreted literally and not according to the custom usage, or slang, of the construction or design profession. When a contract contains provisions which connote a standard of perfection, the successful defense of a professional liability claim arising out of those provisions becomes very difficult, if not impossible.

The following is a common example of a contract provision which seems to indicate that the designer's performance must reach unrealistic levels of attainment:

> The Design Professional shall prepare complete drawings and specifications for the project.[3]

According to various dictionary definitions for the word "complete," this contract requirement would obligate the designer to prepare drawings and specifications which were not lacking or incomplete in any respect; i.e., they must be perfect. Even though the law only requires design professionals to prepare drawings and specifications in accordance with the ordinary standard of care of the profession, i.e., without negligence, a court could interpret the above contract provision to hold that a substantially higher standard of performance had been agreed to by the parties. To avoid this particular problem, the use of substitute language patterned after the following would be helpful:

> The Design Professional shall prepare drawings and specifications setting forth in sufficient detail the requirements for constructing the Project.

In fact, the above statement is all that the parties normally intend since the drawings and specifications are not an end in themselves. They are the documents by which the designer conveys the design requirements to the contractor so that the project can be constructed. Therefore, designers should avoid contract terms which are absolute in their meaning unless that result is exactly what is intended by the parties.

Professional contracts should also clarify the meaning of estimated costs and project completion dates in regard to unforeseen circumstances beyond the control of the designer.

Comply with Codes and Regulations. Determine the authorities who have jurisdiction to regulate a particular proj-

ect. A designer who specifies upholstery or drapery fabric that does not comply with local fire codes may face a legal suit if the installation fails to pass a fire safety inspection that results in delaying completion of the project. Ignorance of a code or regulation is not a legal defense. Refer to Chapter 3 for more information on code compliance.

Secure the Services of Reputable Contractors and/or Workrooms. Be familiar with previous work of consultants and contractors; their skill and expertise should be consistently evident. Reliability in regard to meeting installation and job deadlines is an important aspect to consider.

Keep Accurate Records. There are many complicated details that demand attention during the course of a project. The areas of concern where the designer's responsibility is most frequently in question are changes of orders, directive instructions given during the course of the project, and rejection of defective work. Verbal discussions with clients and verbal instructions given to contractors should be subsequently recorded in written form.

Secure Liability Insurance and Legal Counsel. Two professional organizations, the American Society of Interior Designers and the Institute of Business Designers, have provided their memberships with a group professional liability insurance policy. Many policies cover errors, omissions, and negligent acts as a result of drawings, plans, specifications, schedules, and shop drawings. The coverage may not include implied warranties and inaccurate estimates of probable cost or cost estimates being exceeded. Coverage is usually extended only to work performed within the "customary" area of interior design performance; i.e., no structural alterations or other work normally performed by other professions. Legal counsel should be obtained on all contractual and insurance matters.

2 PRODUCT LIABILITY

A major problem affecting manufacturers, retailers, wholesalers, and distributors is the abundance of product liability lawsuits. Although designers may consider this an exclusive concern of manufacturers, evidence points to the fact that designers and specifiers not infrequently become involved in product liability suits because of *strict liability* tort laws which extend responsibility to those outside the chain of distribution. It is therefore important to understand current product liability laws and the ensuing product liability insurance problems which directly affect the availability and cost of interior systems.

Product liability is primarily concerned with negligence. It is considered the "duty" of the manufacturer to provide products that will not expose the consumer to undue risk, bodily injury, death or property damage as a result of the construction, design, installation, and assembly of the product. Also included in product liability actions is the manufacturer's failure to warn against a danger or hazard in the use or misuse of the product and failure to provide adequate instructions for the use of the product. Violation of *express warranty* may also be involved. An express warranty is a guaranty of performance and includes all advertising claims made by the manufacturer.

PRODUCT-RELATED INJURIES

Each year the U.S. Consumer Product Safety Commission publishes a list of product-related accidents. The list is long and includes everything from carpet to sporting and recreational equipment. A sampling from the 1976 survey indicates the large number of reported injuries involving chairs and other furnishings (see Table 2.1).

In a recent survey, published in *Human Behavior Magazine©*, it was found that 40 percent of the consumers questioned expressed a *caveat emptor* (buyer beware) attitude.

50% believed manufacturers shirked their responsibility to buyers

75% thought manufacturers were more interested in making a profit than in serving the customer

55% concluded the quality of products was not being improved

32% favored the federal government testing of competitive brands and the establishment of standards

75% favored a federal Consumer Protection Agency

These opinions undoubtedly contributed to the large increase in product liability claims. A 1977 Department of Commerce-sponsored survey of 21 member companies of the American Textile Manufacturers Institute, Inc., with sales over $100 million, showed that from 1971 to 1975 claims varied from a 1971 low of 64 new claims with an aggregate value of $28 million to a high in 1974 of 128 claims with an aggregate value of $52.5 million.

BASES FOR EVALUATING PRODUCT LIABILITY ACTIONS

Courts of law attempt to determine the contents and validity of the complaint against a product by examination of the following areas of concern: statute of limitations, useful life of the product, misuse or subsequent product modification, state of the art, duty to warn, punitive damages, and strict liability.

Statute of Limitations. Statutes of limitations establish prescribed time periods during which certain types of claims must be filed. These limitations vary from state to state. A typical situation involving a 12-year-old hotel will serve to illustrate the problem. When the hotel was new an interior designer for the project specified 200 chairs for the dining area. The chairs were used consistently for the 12 years, perhaps 7 to 10 times a day. One evening during routine cleaning, an employee dropped one of the chairs which imperceptibly weakened the structure of the chair. The next morning a customer sat on the chair which collapsed, and the customer was injured. The legal suit that followed provoked many perplexing problems. How long is a manufacturer or a designer responsible for the performance of a product? Research has found that 4 percent of all product liability claims involve products 25 years old. Insurance sources report that in 1974 and 1975 there were four claims on products manufactured 50 years prior to the injury. Between 1973 and 1976 there were 20 claims against products 20 years or older. Products in use for approximately six years accounted for the largest number of claims.

Many current statutes allow product-related claims to be filed against the manufacturer at the time of the injury, regardless of the age of the product involved. This procedure has provoked much concern for statute of limitations reform. If the mechanisms of statutes of limitations are to be changed from a time-of-injury to a time-of-sale basis, the best approach may involve making the statute applicable only to certain types of products. Product-related injuries are rare after 10 years have elapsed from the time of sale. However, capital goods, such as

TABLE 2.1 PRODUCT-RELATED INJURIES

	Estimated Injuries
Chairs, not upholstered	105,977
Chairs, upholstered	1,897
Couches/sofas	17,324
Bars and bar stools	6,430
Tables	85,592
Glass tables	4,421
Furniture, not otherwise specified	11,781
Carpeting	1,184
Window shades/blinds	2,933

furniture, which frequently lasts a long time, seem more susceptible to such claims. Consideration should be given to allow the statute to regulate only durable industrial goods or to assign different lengths of time to different categories of products.

Another approach which has been suggested would be to allow the statute to run from the date of sale only if the product had been used without problems in the intervening period. Suggested limitation periods have ranged from 4 to 12 years. If this approach were to be adopted, certain claims, such as those resulting from long periods of improper maintenance and use, rather than from the defective condition of the product when sold, would be eliminated. However, where the evidence indicates that improper maintenance was the cause of the injury, courts have generally refused to impose liability upon the manufacturer.

Limiting the duration of time for which a manufacturer could be liable for its products would undoubtedly reduce the number of claims, eliminate much of the current uncertainty, and perhaps allow manufacturers to price their products more accurately. However, such results could also be accomplished by the use of the "useful life" approach.

Useful Life. To some extent the courts have recognized the concept of *useful life*, citing the adage that "a manufacturer or seller is not required, under the law, to produce or sell a product that will never wear out."[2] The courts have also refused to impose liability where the evidence indicates that the accident in question was caused by normal wear and tear of the product. Thus the institution of useful life defense has been suggested. Under such a defense, a manufacturer would incur no liability after the product's useful life had expired.

Misuse or Subsequent Modification. Misuse is often cited as a defense by the manufacturer. If the seller or the consumer made alterations or modifications to a product and these subsequently became the substantial cause of the incident giving rise to the claim, then the manufacturer is not held responsible. This also applies to the installation of a product that was not operated in compliance with the directions or specifications of the manufacturer. Misuse of a given product may involve the injured party or a third party. Manufacturers claim that misuse is considered "unforeseeable" at the time that the product is manufactured.

State of the Art. Many groups of manufacturers have complained that courts have judged the danger of their products according to the current state of technology and knowledge, even if the product was as safe as others at the time of sale. Although courts admit evidence known as *industry custom* with respect to a product, it is not a final determinant of the issue of proper design, since the entire industry may be remiss in its design.

Duty to Warn. Manufacturers feel that duty to warn should apply only to products that are dangerous beyond what the ordinary consumer would expect. The courts consider what is known as "common knowledge"; i.e., a manufacturer of shoes that become slippery when wet is not liable because it is common knowledge that shoes tend to become slippery when wet. This, combined with unrealistic consumer expectations of product performance, plays a large part in product liability.

Punitive Damages. Punitive damages are awarded as an additional remedy to supplement compensatory damages in actions where the defendant's conduct shows intentional or reckless disregard of the rights of the consumer. The basic purposes behind the doctrine are to punish manufacturers for their misconduct and to deter them and others from engaging in such conduct in the future.

Strict Liability. Strict liability was initiated to alleviate problems of the consumer's burden of proof. It shifts the focus from the conduct of the manufacturer to the performance of the product. In design defect cases, the alleged defective design is considered the result of a conscious choice, whether the problem developed through the manufacturing process or was the result of a design defect. The difference between negligence and strict liability, in either a design or manufactured defect, is the element of conscious choice or knowledge on the part of the manufacturer or designer that the product was potentially dangerous. Strict liability is a much more serious charge than simple negligence, which may only involve a worker omitting a bolt during the assembly of a product.

HOW DESIGNERS CAN MINIMIZE PRODUCT LIABILITY ACTIONS

Specify Products Manufactured for the Intended Use. Manufacturers of commercial and institutional interior systems claim that a large percentage of product liability actions result from designers' specification of products that are unsuitable for the intended use. Some manufacturers have become actively engaged in educating designers about their role in preventive measures to lessen the number of product liability claims. In some cases manufacturers insist on supplying the designer with a written statement relieving the manufacturer from responsibility for the life of the product if improper specifications are made. They point out that their product liability insurance rates, which have increased 320 percent in the last several years, are reflected in increased wholesale prices to designers and clients.

3 REGULATIONS AND STANDARDS

Just as in all other aspects of life, government regulations and standards have become necessary to protect people from unsafe living and working conditions. This chapter will survey federal, state, and local legislation; detail building codes as well as the authorities with jurisdiction; and discuss risk management procedures for compliance.

FEDERAL REGULATIONS

Though many people consider federal regulations an intrusion on the rights of individuals and private enterprise, few of us understand that the origin of those regulations dealing with product performance and fire safety is the result of the federal government's power to regulate commerce among the states. The rationale of this approach is the need to protect the safety of the general public and maintain a steady flow of interstate commerce. For example, if the practices of the petroleum industry are unsafe, tragic accidents could result that would close down operations of a major part of that industry. This shutdown could trigger an economic chain reaction affecting transportation, employment, the building industry, which might jeopardize the nation's entire economic structure.

Laws are passed periodically, as Congress sees the need for uniform regulations in certain areas of industry. The enforcement of these laws is delegated to various federal agencies and departments. Each agency is authorized to develop further regulations within the limits of authority granted it by a specific act of Congress. Even though the regulations may not be actual congressional legislation, they have the binding force of law. Violation of a regulation can result in criminal penalties ranging from sizable fines to incarceration.

Table 3.1 summarizes the various federal agencies and departments that regulate areas pertinent to professional designers. The agencies and departments that *enforce* standards and regulations are noted. The identities and functions of these agencies can change without notice. Their function depends on current need.

STATE AND LOCAL LEGISLATION

State laws dealing with public safety represent an exercise of the powers that are "reserved to the states" in the Tenth Amendment of the federal Constitution. Local authority to enact ordinances and laws is based on powers granted by the constitution of each state. Over the past few years the increasing federal concern for public safety has resulted in preempting certain areas of state and local regulatory authority. The general policy concerning overlapping areas of concern has been handled in the following manner:

State laws on the same subject are superseded by federal law.

State laws not conflicting with federal laws remain valid.

State law does prevail if the state law is more stringent than the federal law. This often occurs in the area of fire protection.[1]

CODES

Many federal, state, and local regulations result in systematized bodies of law known as "codes." Adequate standards of practice and uniformity of workmanship are ensured by code enforcement; however, it should be noted that codes only provide for minimum levels of performance. Although codes represent the experience and knowledge of many professionals and are continually evolving through the consensus of many groups, codes often cause resentment among designers. Such regulations are considered interference, harassment, and, above all, time-consuming trivia. We all lose sight of the fact that the major concept of code development is safety. Most codes have come into existence after the fact—after a major tragedy involving the loss of human life. Modern investigative methods attempt to determine the cause of the product or structure failure, and the data gained is incorporated into codes that hopefully will prevent similar tragedies.

STANDARDS AND MODEL CODES

Standards establish criteria of excellence, or "models," that provide a means of comparison for measuring quality. Safety standards can be classified as "mandatory" or "voluntary." Some mandatory standards are established by government and enforced by law; others are enacted as statutes. Voluntary standards, or "model codes," are recommended but not enforced as law, unless adopted by federal, state, or local authorities. The four major model building codes listed below have each developed accompanying fire prevention codes. More complete information on code agencies can be found at the end of this chapter.

	Model Building Codes	Fire Prevention Codes
NBC	National Building Code, American Insurance Association, Engineering & Safety Service	American Insurance Association Fire Prevention Code
UBC	Uniform Building Code, International Conference of Building Officials	Uniform Fire Code
BOCA	Building Officials and Code Administrators International	BOCA Basic Fire Prevention Code
SBC	Southern Building Code Congress International	Southern Standard Fire Prevention Code

In addition to these four major model codes there are three other nongovernmental fire prevention groups involved in developing fire safety codes and standards. Aside from being involved in testing procedures, these three large groups are

TABLE 3.1 FEDERAL AGENCIES

Federal Departments	Duties	Acts of Congress	Date
DOC Department of Commerce			
NBS National Bureau of Standards	Testing of Materials. Promotes enforcement and adoption of uniform building codes.	Public Law 177 Act to establish NBS	1901
FEMA Federal Emergency Management Agency	Includes Civil Defense and Federal Disaster Administration and U.S. Fire Administration.	Reorganization Plan No. 3	1978
USFA United States Fire Administration	Service, education and training. Supports state and local fire safety training (National Fire Academy). Maintains a fire data system.	Federal Fire Prevention and Control Act	1974
HEW Department of Health, Education, and Welfare	Fire safety standards for health-care facilities.		
PHS Public Health Service	Sets standards for private and public nonprofit hospitals/ nursing homes.	Hill Burton Act Title IV of Public Health Service Act	1974
SSA Social Security Administration	Medicare and Medicaid. Requires compliance with fire safety standards.	Social Security Act Title 18-19	1965
HUD Department of Housing and Urban Development	*Enforces* standards for one- and two-family dwellings and nursing care-type housing.		
FHA Federal Housing Administration	Establishes and *enforces* minimum building standards.	Housing and Community Development Act	1974
DOL Department of Labor	*Enforces* mandatory standards for safety and health of employees.		
OSHA Occupational Safety and Health Administration	Established 1970. Develops and *enforces* mandatory standards for safety, educational and training programs for state and federal programs.	Title 29—USC Section 651	1970
DOT Department of Transportation	*Enforces* standards and regulates construction of private and commercial vehicles. Conducts research.	National Traffic & Motor Vehicle Safety Act	1966
		Transportation Safety Act	1974

Federal Departments	Duties	Acts of Congress	Date
FAA Federal Aviation Administration	*Enforces* standards for safety in aircrafts and airports.	Federal Aviation Act	1958
FRA Federal Railroad Administration	Sets standards for equipment and operations of trains/ railroads.		
CPSC Consumer Product Safety Commission	*Enforces* and regulates standards for products sold to consumers. Collects injury data. Conducts public educational programs. Administers the Flammable Fabrics Act.	Consumer Product Safety Act Public Law 92-573	1972
		Flammable Fabrics Act	1967
EPA Environmental Protection Agency	*Enforces* and regulates standards in regard to air, water and noise pollution. Publishes reports on criteria for noise levels.	Noise Control Act PL 92-574-HL-11021	1972
FTC Federal Trade Commission	*Enforces standards for:* 1. Misleading advertising of products 2. Misleading labeling of goods 3. Assists CPSC in enforcing the Flammable Fabrics Act.	Wool Products Labeling Act	1939
		Textile Fabric Products Identification Act	1951
		Fur Products Labeling Act	1951
GSA General Services Administration	Provides supplies and buildings for federal agencies. Performance standards. Systems approach to design.	Federal Property and Administrative Services Act Section 206	1949
FSS Federal Supply Service	Buys supplies and contracts for services for federal agencies.		
PBS Public Building Service	Responsible for supervising the design, construction, operation and maintenance of federal buildings.		
VA Veterans Administration	Regulates and sets standards for VA hospitals and health-care facilities. Conducts research on flammable fabrics. Sets standards for tests methods.		

Note: The identities and functions of federal agencies can change without notice. Their function depends on current need.

responsible for codes and standards based on consensus of their membership.

NFPA: National Fire Protection Association

ANSI: American National Standards Institute

ASTM: American Society for Testing and Materials

Frequently local authorities will adopt one of the major model building codes and, in addition, all or parts of the codes and standards of the three groups listed above.

Codes and standards may be classified as either "descriptive" or "performance" in character. Many are a combination of both approaches. Descriptive standards define exact materials or forms, whereas performance standards describe what a system should accomplish, regardless of its form or material content. The incorporation of standards into specifications is discussed in Chapter 16.

Building codes are primarily concerned with (1) the construction requirements of building and (2) hazardous materials or equipment used in the building.

Fire codes and standards are an integral part of building codes. It has been estimated that 75 percent of all codes deal with fire protection. Fire protection codes are concerned with minimizing fire hazards and may be classified as follows:

Fire prevention: Concerned with occupancy hazards, sources of ignition, and combustible fuel loads in buildings. Interior designers are most often involved with preventive-type fire codes that classify furnishings and interior finishes as potential fuels that contribute to the spread of fire.

Fire control: *Active:* Installation and maintenance of sprinklers, alarms, and extinguishing systems.
Passive: Construction elements that control the spread of fire, i.e., fire doors and fire walls.

Classification of Buildings

Because building classification is the basis of most fire prevention regulations, interior designers should be aware of the various established categories.

1. *Occupancy classification*

Apartments	Industrial
Assembly	Institutional
Business	Mercantile
Educational	Residential
Health Care	Storage

2. *Fuel load classification.* Based on the amount of combustibles in a building (per square feet of floor space):

a. Low hazard

Apartments	Museums
Churches	Nursing care facilities
Dormitories	Office buildings
Hospitals	Prisons
Hotels	Residences
Institutions	Schools
Libraries	Theaters

b. Moderate hazard
Auto parking
Retail shops

c. High hazard. Occupancy involving processing, mixing, storage, and/or dispensing of flammable or combustible liquids:
Airport hangars
Paint shops
Service stations
Varnish and paint works
Warehouses
Woodworking shops

d. Unusual structures. This class includes buildings or structures that do not fit into the above categories:
Mobile homes
Towers
Underground structures
Waft structures
Windowless buildings

Surveying the above list, designers might assume they are, for the most part, concerned with low- and moderate-hazard classifications. It should be noted, however, that regardless of the fuel load, a building classified as low hazard could easily be reclassified as high hazard because of variances in occupancy load.

Variances in Occupancy Load Classifications

Classifications vary depending on occupancy load and type of occupancy.

Occupancy Load. This refers to the maximum number of people expected to be in a building at any given time. As the occupancy load increases, the fire prevention requirements increase.

Places of Assembly	
Capacity	**Classification**
50 – 300	Low risk
300 – 1000	Moderate risk
1000+	High risk

The use of occupancy loads in calculating means of egress from open office areas will be discussed in Chapter 13.

Type of Occupancy. This is another classification factor. Safety standards increase when the occupants are children or elderly people; higher standards are also applied to physically disabled people.

LACK OF CODE UNIFORMITY

One of the most confusing aspects of codes and standards is the lack of uniformity between federal agencies, states, counties, and municipalities. The feasibility of ever attaining complete and total uniformity seems unlikely. There have been major efforts to unify codes on the national level. Approximately 85 percent of the states now have accepted model codes. Federal agencies such as the Department of Health, Education, and Welfare (HEW) and the Department of Housing and Urban Development (HUD) have adopted the Unified Building Code, and all the standards and codes of the National Fire Protection Association (NFPA) and the American National Standards Institute (ANSI).

Counties and municipalities present quite a different problem. Some cities, such as Houston, have large oil refineries,

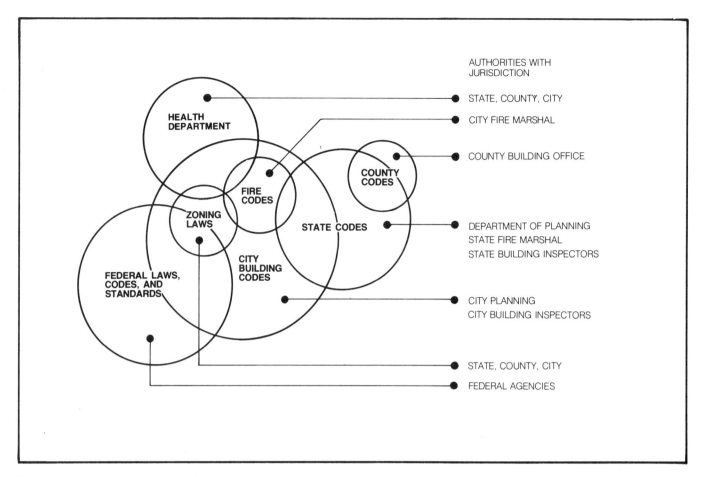

Figure 3.1 Overlapping code structures.

which create particular hazards. Chicago, New York, and other large cities require special codes and standards that relate to highrise buildings and population density. A small Midwestern town in the path of tornadoes may require special storm protection standards. The fact that codes have evolved through modification for particular geographic and population needs is understandable. Figure 3.1 shows the overlapping code structures and the authorities with jurisdiction that may be encountered at the local level.

Authorities with Jurisdiction

The following list clarifies the jurisdictional areas of the major codes and standards authorities that designers may encounter.

Federal. Federal laws, codes, and standards apply to federal buildings or structures built with the assistance of federal funds, such as hospitals, schools, and nursing homes. In some cases the federal agency will be required to obtain a local building permit and comply with additional state, county, or city standards. This occurs only when the local standards are more stringent than the federal standards.

State. State codes and standards regulate state-owned buildings, state hospitals, schools, and occasionally large places of assembly such as coliseums and exhibition centers. States rarely impose regulations on incorporated municipalities. Counties or small towns without codes or standards may be governed by state standards.

County. County building and fire safety regulations usually apply only to unincorporated rural areas.

Municipality. Municipality building and fire safety codes may be administered through one planning office or through several agencies such as the office of the city fire marshal, health department, or zoning commission.

Zoning. Zoning ordinances exist at the county and city levels. Zoning ordinances usually involve land use, type of building, occupancy, as well as building and fire safety standards.

Health Departments. Health departments primarily enforce code regulations involving sanitation, levels of occupancy, health, and safety. Their areas of concern include the food preparation facilities of restaurants, hospitals, schools, prisons, nursing homes, and day care centers. Floor, wall, and ceiling finishes are expected to perform well under heavy sanitation maintenance requirements. Many states divide enforcement responsibilities between state, county, and city health departments.

Insurance. Insurance interest should always be consulted by the designer. Having plans reviewed in the early design phase may reduce not only fire hazard problems, but also insurance rates on the building. Consultation may involve an individual insurance company already ensuring the building or an insurance group such as Factory Insurance Association or Factory

Mutual Insurance Association. Because insurance is subject to state regulations requiring standardized fire rating, many insurance agents rely on rating bureaus. The most important insurance-supported rating bureau is the Insurance Services Office.

RISK MANAGEMENT: PROCEDURES FOR CODE COMPLIANCE

In the programming phase of the design project when studies are being made to determine the feasibility of achieving the stated requirements of the project, it would be advisable to evaluate the fire safety factors of the proposed or existing building. Experts in building fire safety from the local fire department or insurance agencies should be consulted if any major deficiencies are discovered.

General Checklist for Fire Safety

1. What is the occupancy classification of the building?

2. What is the accepted occupancy load?

3. What types of occupancy are allowed?

4. Has a structural fire resistance rating been established?
    a. Floors
    b. Walls: interior and exterior
    c. Ceilings

5. Is the electrical wiring adequate for the proposed use?

6. What are the existing fire control and prevention methods in the building?
    a. Alarms
    b. Extinguishers
    c. Smoke detectors
    d. Sprinklers

Seek Interpretation on Levels of Compliance

To prevent costly changes in completed project plans, designers should contact the offices of the authorities with jurisdiction early in the design phase. After having the proposed project checked for compliance, designers may wish to seek interpretations on levels of compliance. *Levels of compliance* are alternate methods of achieving fire safety. The alternatives are based on infinite variances. Two variances on occupancy loading have already been discussed in this chapter. Other variances may include the use of sprinklers. A lower flame-spread rating may be allowed on a particular wall finish if sprinklers have been installed in that area of the building (see Life Safety Code 101 in Chapter 5). The same may apply to floor coverings in critical areas such as corridors that serve as access to exits. In another case, a special feature, such as a raised dance floor, may be allowed if seating capacity is reduced.

Clarify Terminology

Terms such as ''finishes'' and ''furnishings'' may take on different meanings depending on the project installation and on the particular code in use. In some jurisdictions, carpet is considered a furnishing if it is installed over a finished floor. If installed directly over concrete, it is classified as interior finish (see definition of interior finishes in Glossary, under Chapter 5). If a regulation defines carpet as a floorcovering finish with no mention of its use as a wall covering, do not specify carpet as a wallcovering without clarification. Because something is

not mentioned in a code *does not mean that it is permitted.*

Another area of confusing terminology involves movable partitions that are an integral part of office landscape systems. In some jurisdictions these partitions may be classified as furnishings, while in other jurisdictions they may be considered temporary walls.

Seek Clarification on Questionable Regulations

Designers generally shirk from questioning regulations or they totally avoid areas of uncertainty. Here are two suggested approaches:

1. Check on current regulations that have been adopted by the authorities in your jurisdiction. Do not assume that the current editions of codes and standards that are in your office are the same as those adopted by the local authorities.

2. Seek variances when outdated regulations are identified and try to initiate interest in modifying outdated regulations.

Proof of Compliance

Although professional contracts usually hold the owner/client responsible for filing documents required for the approval of authorities, the implied (and actual) responsibility for compliance rests with the designer.

Proof of Compliance Checklist. There are four points that should be considered on every job:

1. Submit a complete set of project working drawings, schedules, and specifications in duplicate to the various authorities involved. The number of sets needed for submittal will depend on the complexity of the project and local regulations. Every design firm should have a staff member knowledgeable about code requirements and regulations who can answer questions posed by the authorities with jurisdiction. If changes are required, an addendum should be attached to the contract documents. (Addenda will be discussed in Chapter 16).

2. Seek information on approved or qualified laboratories recommended by the authorities with jurisdiction. Some cities and states have established their own testing facilities. Federal agencies provide a listing of approved testing laboratories that are located throughout the United States. The National Fire Protection Association (NFPA) also provides a listing of laboratories that perform flammability testing.

3. If a particular material must be tested to prove compliance with safety performance requirements, always require written proof of the test results. Some jurisdictions require photographic documentation of the test results. More information on documenting test results is discussed in Chapters 15 and 16. It should be noted that even though a material has been tested and rated, the authority does not have to accept the use of the material in your project. Factors that influence these decisions may involve total fuel loads, occupancy loads, and any number of variances.

4. Keep records on the approval from on-site inspectors. After building permits are issued, field inspectors visit the project site to make sure that all work is being executed according to the approved drawings and specifications. The inspections are coordinated with each phase of the

work, i.e., after electrical wiring has been installed, after interior finishes are completed, and a final inspection prior to occupancy. Inspection record cards are usually provided by building permit departments.

Risk Management Summary

1. Evaluate the building and project area for fire safety.

2. Seek interpretation on levels of compliance.

3. Clarify code terminology.

4. Seek clarification on questionable regulations.

5. Secure proof of compliance on all materials testing and on-site inspections.

6. Whenever possible, specify safety performance beyond code requirements.

BUILDING CODES AND STANDARDS

Here is a list of the ten organizations that have established codes and standards:

AInsurA American Insurance Association
85 John Street, New York, NY 10038
(212) 433-4400

ANSI American National Standards Institute
1430 Broadway, New York, NY 10018
(212) 868-1220

ASTM American Society for Testing and Materials
1916 Race Street, Philadelphia, PA 19013
(215) 569-5400

BOCA Building Officials & Code Administrators, International
1313 East 60th Street, Chicago, IL 60637
(312) 324-3400

HUD Superintendent of Documents
U.S. Government Printing Office
Washington, DC 20402

ICBO International Conference of Building Officials
5360 South Workman Mill Road
Whittier, CA 90601
(213) 699-0541

MCSC Model Code Standardization Council
(This document can be purchased from either AInsurA, BOCA, ICBO, or SBCC.)

NFPA National Fire Protection Association
470 Atlantic Avenue, Boston, MA 02210
(617) 482-8755

NBS Superintendent of Documents
U.S. Government Printing Office
Washington, DC 20402

SBCC Southern Building Code Congress, International
3617 8th Avenue, South, Birmingham, AL 35222
(205) 252-8930

The following codes and standards may be obtained from the associations listed above. Request the most *current editions*.

Building Codes	Order From
Basic Building Code	BOCA
Uniform Building Code	ICBO
Accumulative Supplement to the 1973 Uniform Codes	ICBO
Standard Building Code	SBCC
Standard Building Code	SBCC
Standard Building Code	SBCC
National Building Code	AInsurA
One- and Two-Family Dwelling Code	MCSC
One- and Two-Family Supplement	MCSC
Life Safety Code (NFPA 101)	NFPA

Electrical Codes	
Lightning Protection Code (NFPA 78)	NFPA
Handbook of the National Electrical Code	NFPA

Housing Codes	
Basic Housing-Property Maintenance Code	BOCA
Basic Industrialized Dwelling Code	BOCA
Standard Housing Code	SBCC
Uniform Housing Code	ICBO
Standard for Mobile Homes (NFPA 501-B)	NFPA

Sign Codes	
Uniform Sign Code	ICBO

Fire Codes	
Basic Fire Prevention Code	BOCA
Uniform Fire Code	ICBO
Uniform Fire Code Supplement	ICBO
Standard Fire Prevention Code	SBCC
National Fire Codes (Contains all NFPA codes and standards in 16 volumes)	NFPA
National Fire Codes	NFPA
Supplements to National Fire Codes (3 volumes)	NFPA
National Fire Prevention Code (NFPA 1)	NFPA
Fire Prevention Code	AInsurA

Standards	
Uniform Building Code Standards	ICBO
ASTM Standards in Building Codes (2 volumes)	ASTM
ANSI Standards Catalogue	ANSI
ASTM Standards Catalogue	ASTM
NFPA Standards Catalogue	NFPA
Standards for the Design and Installation of the Fire Suppression System for Life Safety (BOCA 100)	BOCA

Standard for the Installation of Sprinkler
Systems (NFPA 13)   NFPA

Miscellaneous Government Standards
HUD Minimum Property Standards
    4900.1, Volume 1, MPS One- and
    Two-Family Dwellings   HUD
    4910.1, Volume 2, MPS for Multi-
    Family Housing   HUD
    4920.1, Volume 3, MPS for Care-Type
    Housing   HUD
    4930.1, Volume 4, Manual of Accept-
    able Practices   HUD

Publications List   AInsurA

Building Codes: Their Scopes and Aims   AInsurA

Ordinance for Nursing, Convalescent and
Old Age Homes   AInsurA

Codes and Code Administration: An Introduction to Building Regulations in the
United States   BOCA

BOCA Official Code Interpretations (per
each past one-year period)   BOCA

Administration of Building Regulations   BOCA

Perspectives for Code Administrators   BOCA

Readings in Code Administration   BOCA
    Volume 1
    Volume 2
    Volume 3
    Entire Set

Code Enforcement Guidelines for Residential Rehabilitation   BOCA

Analysis of Revisions to Uniform Building
Code   ICBO

Dwelling Construction under the Uniform
Building Code   ICBO

Plan Review Manual   ICBO

ICBO Research Recommendations   ICBO

4 QUALITY CONTROL: PERFORMANCE EVALUATION OF MATERIALS

After a review of the various liability factors, codes, regulations, and standards that are a vital part of professional practice today, the importance of knowing more about material performance and specification becomes increasingly evident. As professional designers, we are obligated to research, assimilate, and apply current material evaluation methods. Keeping pace with advances in material technology involves understanding human behavioral and physical needs, energy conservation, health and safety factors, economic feasibility, and functional effectiveness.

During the past decade, design education has primarily stressed the programming and developmental stages of the design process while often neglecting to provide the information necessary to transform design concepts into reality through knowledgeable specification of material components. As a result many designers are facing the increasingly difficult task of material quality control with little training in the area of material technology. This fact was verified in a recent survey conducted by the Cooper-Hewitt Museum. In order to determine the feasibility of a design data bank, researchers asked practicing designers what information they most frequently needed. The results showed that material and product information were the two highest ranking concerns.

Architects	Building materials	74.3%
	Product information	72.1%
Interior designers/	Product information	98.7%
space planners	Materials systems	73.2%

In many design offices material selection and evaluation are often based on past experience with a particular material component. Information from trade journals, manufacturers' representatives, and advertisements also serve as another basis for selection. On other occasions, decisions may be based on minimum performance requirements set forth in local codes and standards. All these methods have some degree of validity, but represent a disorganized approach to a very serious aspect of the design process. In addition, none of these methods provides a basis for evaluating new materials or subsystems that are constantly being produced.

LIABILITIES INVOLVED IN MATERIAL EVALUATION

The Office of Professional Liability Research, a division of Victor O. Schinnerer & Company, cited the following claim as an example of the consequences that can occur when specifications are prepared by a design professional who does not fully comprehend the characteristics of the material which he specified. Acting on a recommendation from the school district for which he was designing a school and gymnasium, a designer contacted a floor products company and received information in the form of advertising literature describing a particular sealant and finish for the gym floor. He also received a list of "satisfied customers." Since the school district had

successfully used this particular product to refinish old gymnasium floors, the designer did not investigate any further into the properties of the finish or its compatibility with new floors, but relied on the experience of the school district and the advertising literature in specifying the same sealant and finish for the new gym floor.

Several months after the sealant had been applied, the gymnasium floor began to buckle and crack. A subsequent investigation by a testing company and an expert on wood technology and utilization revealed that the specified finish possessed a peculiar adhesive effect which had caused the wood strips to become glued together. In the process of shrinking, the individual strips acted in the aggregate, causing rupture and buckling at those joints which were the weakest. The conclusion was that while the sealant and finish were an excellent choice for older gym floors which had settled and shrunk, it should have never been used on new floors. The entire gymnasium floor had to be replaced at a cost of $34,000. If the specifier had adequately researched and fully understood the characteristics of the material he had specified, the claim probably would not have resulted.

An article by attorney John S. Martel that appeared in *Guidelines for Improved Practice* further advises that "whenever a designer abandons a proven product in favor of a new product (see Glossary, Chapter 4), however justified the reason, the designer may be exposing himself to potential claims and lawsuits if the new product fails.

"When claims do arise from the failure of new products, the injured party may, and usually does, seek relief from the person who specified the product, the person who installed the product (the general contractor or subcontractor, or both), and the manufacturer of the product. If the injured party is the owner, he falls back on his own inexperience in construction matters and stresses his reliance on the expertise of his design professional. The contractor typically defends against such a claim by contending that he was never very enthusiastic about the specification, but nevertheless faithfully followed the plans and specifications provided by the designer in accordance with his contractual obligation. The manufacturer predictably contends that the product was not intended to be used in the manner specified by the design professional or that the new product must not have been applied as specified.

"Thus embattled on three fronts, the design professional is challenged with two basic allegations: (1) that he negligently selected or specified the new product, and (2) that he negligently 'supervised' the contractor's application of the new product."[1] Recommendations regarding procedures for the specification of new products will be found in Chapter 16.

Legally, the design professional is expected to use reasonable diligence and be informed about the latest developments in the profession. A designer's reliance on previous specifications would not constitute "reasonable diligence" under the applicable standard of "professional care," i.e., failure to "use the care ordinarily exercised in like cases by reputable members of his profession . . . and to use reasonable diligence and his best judgment in the exercise of his skill and the application of his learning, in an effort to accomplish the purpose for which he is employed."[2]

In order to avoid charges of negligence in the selection of material components, a rational and systematic method of accumulating information is badly needed. The approach employed should provide not only a basis for predicting material *performance*, but also a method of *documenting* a designer's "diligence" in accumulating information.

THE PERFORMANCE SYSTEMS APPROACH

A possible solution to the complicated problem of material evaluation and the need for a systematic approach to quality control was addressed at a 1972 international symposium jointly sponsored by the International Union of Testing and Research for Materials and Structures (RILEM), The American Society for Testing and Materials (ASTM), and the International Council for Building Research Studies and Documentation (CIB). The conference theme was "The Performance Concept in Buildings," and participants explored the areas of user requirements, design procedures, and methods of evaluating materials through performance requirements. Prior to and since this conference there has been much written about performance and systems concepts in relation to the design process.

Before evaluating the usefulness of these concepts in regard to material selection and specification, it is important to clarify their distinct differences and examine the advantages and disadvantages of their use. John Vilett, an architect and participant in the 1972 conference, pointed out that the widespread interest in the application of these concepts had resulted in some semantic confusion, and in common usage the performance and systems concepts are often considered inseparable or even synonymous.

We often refer to the performance of a single component or the performance of an entire system, which perhaps results in some confusion in terminology. Vilett cited this example: "One can speak of the performance of the entire building industry in terms of production rates, environmental quality, and provision of employment or one can also speak of the performance of a nail in terms of withdrawal resistance, shear strength, and corrosive resistance. The systems concept, however, is usually applied only to the larger scale of reference. Thus, the entire building industry can and should be viewed as a system, whereas a nail, although certainly a component of many building systems is not itself a system in any meaningful sense."[3]

The systems concept, on the one hand, emphasizes the whole rather than the parts. Emphasis is placed on the *interaction* between the components within the total system. *System analysis* is used to measure, identify, and control various kinds of interaction within the whole. The performance concept, on the other hand, is relevant to problems associated with *individual components* which have measurable physical properties and which have a direct influence on the users' environment. The emphasis is placed on the characteristics that a certain product or component must have, without making reference to how these characteristics are to be produced.

There may be situations and problems which call for the use of both the performance and systems approaches. For example, one might consider carpet a system made up of components such as yarn, latex, primary and secondary backing. An individual component of this carpet system could be evaluated in terms of performance; i.e., a careful analysis could be made of measurable qualities such as the physical strength, moisture retention, and abrasion resistance of the yarn. However, when the carpet is installed in a building it becomes a subsystem, or component, of the building and may require an additional systems analysis. If an evaluation of the acoustic performance of the installed carpet is required, one would have to identify, control, and measure the various kinds of acoustic interaction between the carpet, walls, and ceiling surfaces which are involved in shaping the total acoustic environment.

This example illustrates the fact that the performance and systems concepts actually complement each other and are often used in combination.

Although the performance concept was evolved for use in industry, its application to the areas of building and design has provided some useful means of informational processing for the designer. Designers are familiar with performance codes and standards and perhaps with performance specifications. In addition, most designers are currently using some of the preliminary phases of the performance approach in their daily practice. The definition of the design problem and the analysis of user requirements are methods used in most design approaches. To further implement and expand the designer's ability to evaluate materials, the performance approach offers additional methods of evaluation and documentation such as (1) establishment of performance attributes, (2) determination of material performance requirements, and (3) verification of material performance through various testing methods.

Phase 1: User Requirements and Performance Attributes

The first and most important consideration in the development of performance requirements for materials is the determination of the user needs. The performance requirement takes the form of a qualitative statement which identifies user needs through investigative methods based on the following questions:

Who is the user?

What are the user's needs?

Where do the needs exist?

When and for how long do the needs exist?

Performance attributes, or criteria, define the required health/safety, economic, and functional levels of performance which relate to the user's requirements. The performance attributes (Table 4.1) summarize the major areas of performance criteria that frequently result from a study of user requirements. Note that the criteria state the desired performance without establishing constraints on the methods used to accomplish the desired result.

Health/Safety Attributes. The major concern of the health/safety criteria is to provide protection from personal injury or death. These attributes impose the following component requirements:

1. Provide protection through the specification of materials that will not contribute to the spread of fire.

2. Provide surfaces that will not result in falls or injury from sharp projections.

3. Provide materials that possess azotic properties which will not produce or retain odors nor be subject to verminal and

TABLE 4.1 PERFORMANCE ATTRIBUTES*

| Health/Safety | Economic Effectiveness | | Functional Effectiveness |
	Durability/Stability	Maintenance	

1. Provide protection from personal injury and death:
  a. Fire
  b. Falls
  c. Azotic properties
  d. Sharp projections
 	
2. Provide anthropomorphic fit
 	
3. Provide glare-free illumination of work surfaces and work areas
 	
4. Provide acceptable reflectance levels
 	
5. Provide for use and make accessible to physically handicapped people
	1. Provide structurally sound components
	
	2. Provide resistance to tipping
	
	3. Provide resistance to damage
	
	4. Provide positive attachment of components
	  a. Resist vibration
	
	5. Provide color stability
	  a. Light fastness
	  b. Crockfastness
		1. Provide ease of maintenance and cleanability; stain resistance
		
		2. Provide ease of component replacement:
		  a. Upholstery
		  b. Luminaires
		  c. Telephones
		
		3. Provide for ease of component storage and reassembly
		
		4. Relocation does not impair performance of system
			1. Provide for flexiblity of modification
			
			2. Provide components that meet modular tolerances of the space
			
			3. Provide components that address *psychological* and *aesthetic* needs of the user:
			  a. Privacy
			  b. Sense of place
			  c. Color homogeneity
			  d. Visual compatibility
			  e. Appearance control
			
			4. Provide acoustical control
			  a. Airborne sound
			  b. Speech privacy potential
			  c. Impact sound transmission
			  d. Control sound generation
			
			5. Provide thermal control
			  a. Energy conservation

*These attributes are general in scope and do not represent any particular project.

organic deterioration. The material shall not support the growth of organism. (This is particularly important in health care and food service facilities.)

4. Provide furnishings designed for human dimensions (anthropomorphic fit) and not impair use by humans.

5. Provide illumination that will not produce glare on work surfaces and work areas.

6. Provide components that will have acceptable reflectance levels. This includes walls, floors, and furniture surfaces.

7. Provide components that allow accessibility to all physically disabled people (see Chapter 14 for more details on specification requirements for physically disabled people).

Economic Feasibility Attributes. Economic considerations include (1) durability and stability and (2) operational and maintenance factors that represent the user's immediate and long-range requirements.

Durability and stability:

1. Provide components that are structurally sound.

2. Provide furnishings and wall dividers that will resist tipping.

3. Provide positive and firm attachment of components which will prevent vibration.

4. Provide components that will maintain color stability and resist fading, crocking, and abrasion.

Operational and maintenance factors:

1. Provide components that will permit ease of maintenance.

2. Provide components that will not involve costly operational methods. This includes replacement of upholstery, luminaries, and relocation of office systems.

3. Provide components that will not involve costly storage and reassembly problems.

4. Provide components that can meet requirements of relocation without impairing performance. This is particularly important in furniture systems.

Functional Effectiveness Attributes. This category includes some criteria that could possibly be included in the category of health and safety. For example, acoustic control of the environment may be considered vital to health as well as a functional requirement.

1. Provide components that allow flexible modification.

2. Provide components that meet modular tolerance of the space and are capable of interfacing with other components. Many commercial spaces are designed on modular grids and components should be adaptable in size and scale.

3. Provide components that address psychological and aesthetic needs of the users. Components should provide a degree of privacy and allow the user to establish personal identity within the space—a sense of place. Components should also provide for appearance control when interfacing with other components through color homogeneity and visual and geometric compatibility.

4. Provide components that will aid in controlling impact and airborne sound. Components should control sound generation and provide speech privacy potential in open and closed spaces.

5. Provide components that include thermal control and energy conservation.

Phase 2: Determining Material Performance Requirements

After the performance attributes have been established for a

<table>
<tr><td></td><td colspan="7">Health-Safety</td><td colspan="5">Durability</td><td colspan="4">Maintenance</td><td colspan="5">Function</td></tr>
</table>

Performance Attributes / Components	Fire	Falls	Sharp projections	Azotic	Anthropomorphic fit	Glare free	Handicapped use	Structurally sound	Positive attachment	Color stability	Crockfastness	Light fastness	Cleanability	Component repair	Component storage	Relocation ability	Flexibility	Privacy	Color homogeneity	Acoustical control	Thermal control
Carpet	•	•		•				•	•	•	•	•	•	•					•	•	
Resilient tile		•				•		•	•	•		•	•	•					•	•	
Drapery	•		•						•	•	•	•	•	•		•	•	•	•	•	•
Wallcovering	•		•			•			•	•	•	•	•	•					•	•	•
Seating	•	•	•	•	•		•	•	•	•	•	•	•	•	•	•	•		•	•	
Desks	•		•		•	•	•	•	•				•	•	•	•	•	•	•		
Space dividers	•		•	•	•				•			•	•	•	•	•	•	•	•	•	
Others:																					

*Where a component intercepts (•) with a performance attribute a performance requirement is established.

Figure 4.1 Matrix of components and performance attributes.

<table>
<tr><td></td><td colspan="7">Health-Safety</td><td colspan="5">Durability</td><td colspan="4">Maintenance</td><td colspan="5">Function</td></tr>
</table>

Performance Attributes / Test Methods	Fire	Falls	Sharp projections	Azotic	Anthropomorphic fit	Glare free	Handicapped use	Structurally sound	Positive attachment	Color stability	Crockfastness	Light fastness	Cleanability	Component repair	Component storage	Relocation ability	Flexibility	Privacy	Color homogeneity	Acoustical control	Thermal control
Calculation Method	•		•			•				•	•	•								•	•
Physical simulation of actual use	•	•	•		•		•	•	•				•	•	•	•	•	•		•	•
Observation: User response criteria		•		•		•												•	•	•	

Figure 4.2 Matrix of test methods and performance attributes.

particular project, the designer may proceed to evaluate individual materials and components in relation to the established user requirements. A sample matrix of components and performance attributes is shown in Figure 4.1. The matrix provides a simple systematic method for accomplishing this evaluation. The process of selecting materials and components to be included on the matrix is usually based on the following factors:

1. Components that make up a large percentage of the project cost may benefit from a careful performance evaluation.

2. Components that present the potential for technical improvement may be included.

3. Components that have a direct impact on the user's working environment in terms of his ability to be comfortable and productive. For interior specification purposes this means interior surfaces, finishes, and furnishing components that *directly interface* with the user.

The sample matrix (Figure 4.2) illustrates that a performance requirement is established each time a component and attribute intercept (see Glossary, Chapter 4) on the matrix. For example, it becomes clear that almost all the components are required to provide fire safety, but the performance requirement for storage primarily involves furnishings.

The designer considering a component for specification now has a more systematic and rational basis for evaluating performance and establishing preliminary performance and specification checklists.

Phase 3: Proof of Material Performance

At the completion of phase 2 the designer may decide to evaluate two or more particular components in relation to the established performance requirements. If it appears that one of the components meets the necessary criteria, then the problem of verifying the performance claims made by the manufacturer must be considered. The designer can require special performance tests (see Glossary, Chapter 4) or use those that are standard in the industry. Millions of dollars are spent each year evaluating performance test methods. To assure that tests will have validity and provide results, the following criteria have been established:

1. The test methods should simulate, as much as possible, conditions typical of real use.

2. The test should provide reliable and quantitative results.

3. Results should be repeatable and reproduceable. Tests conducted on a given material in the same laboratory, under the same conditions, should not vary widely but provide a continuous scale of measure.

4. The test method should be economically suited to wide use. The size and cost of some testing equipment, as well as the time required for the test, must be considered, as well as the sample size or quantity required for testing.

5. The test results should be reported in terms that can be understood by groups of people who will make use of the test findings. Architects, interior designers, and code officials must be able to apply test results in their practices.

Performance testing methods are normally grouped in three categories:

Calculation Method. This type of test is used where compliance with specified requirements can be uncontroversially established by means of numerical and/or graphical calculations in accordance with accepted engineering practice and applicable codes.

Physical Tests. These tests are used where compliance with specified requirements can best be established by means of physical tests which simulate the required use condition. For example, the structural soundness of a partition can best be evaluated in an actual erection/installation test situation.

Observation Method. This method is used where compliance with specified requirements can only be established by observing the component under specified conditions. Open office systems often require this type of test to evaluate and establish traffic patterns within the space.[4]

Where visual evaluation is specified, the evaluation should be based on unanimous agreement of a panel of three independent observers.

The test methods matrix (Figure 4.2) illustrates which test methods are commonly used to evaluate different performance requirements. Designers should be aware that performance testing presents many unsolved problems. The difficulty of predicting a material's performance under various use conditions is sometimes impossible to determine in a laboratory situation. Areas of special concern, such as fire safety, may require the use of several test methods in order to fully understand how a material will function in a fire situation. It is, therefore, important that a designer specify exactly *how* and *where* a component will interface with other components. When requesting technical data from a manufacturer, the designer should state the intended use of the material in *written* form. This will document efforts to obtain complete information on the material performance and/or limitations.

DOCUMENTING MATERIAL EVALUATION

Legal authorities strongly advise that efforts to acquire information about material performance be transacted in writing.

Matrix forms and checklists can also serve as evidence of a conscientious effort to investigate the product's reliability. The designer's prospects for success in establishing compliance with standards governing professional liability will be in almost direct relationship to the *quantity* and *quality* of the documentation of professional concern.

The development of a performance checklist can be very useful in summarizing all the information accumulated through the performance evaluation process. The checklist shown in Table 4.2 lists components that intercepted with fire safety on the component and performance matrix (Figure 4.1). Items such as carpet, drapery, wallcovering, seating, desks, and space dividers can be listed with the necessary fire safety requirements and test methods. Information contained in column B, Requirements, would be determined by the designer under prescribed federal regulations or local codes. Column C contains the test methods which would be prescribed by codes, standards, regulations, or special tests required by the designer. Performance test methods for each component subsystem are explained in subsequent chapters. It should be noted that the installation location of some components is important because many code requirements vary with the proposed use of the material. (See the NFPA Safety Code 101 in Chapter 5.)

Other checklists could be devised that would serve to measure individual components against all the performance requirement categories, i.e., health and safety, maintenance, durability, and functional effectiveness. The example shown in Table 4.3 is based on a performance test plan used by the General Services Administration.

It is obvious that these forms can aid the designer in evaluating particular components that are being considered for use. They can also provide an accurate record of performance requirements for each design project, and as the project proceeds these checklists could prevent oversights in relation to compliance with various code requirements. In addition, these checklists can form the basis for developing specification outline guides, which will be discussed in Chapter 16.

TABLE 4.2 PERFORMANCE CHECKLIST
FOR FIRE SAFETY Criteria: Health/Fire Safety

Fire Performance Requirements
for Job Project No. _____

Component	Requirements	Test Method	Approved Yes/No	Comments
Carpet: Location in project*	Surface ignition	FF 1-70	X	
_____ Corridor	Smoke density ≤ 150	NBS 708	X	
_____ Public area	Flame spread ≤ 25 unsprinklered	ASTM E-84	X	
_____ Semipublic area	Flame spread ≤ 200 sprinklered	ASTM E-84		
_____ Other				
Wallcovering:				
_____ Corridor				
_____ Public area	(Column B)	(Column C)	(Column D)	
_____ Semipublic area				
_____ Other				
Drapery:				

*Consult the NFPA Life Safety Code for Interior Finishes. Note variances in finish location.
Column B — List required federal regulations, local codes or requirements of the designer.
Column C — List test method required by federal or local codes and/or by designer.
Column D — Result of test to be provided by manufacturer or test laboratory.

TABLE 4.3 PERFORMANCE TEST PLAN — CARPET

Matrix Yes/No	Carpet Requirement/Criteria*	Test		Test Results	Approved Yes/No
		As Spec.	Alt.		
	Airborne sound:				
	SPP $\geq$ 60 in open planned areas				
	NIC' + (NC $\leq$ 40) $\geq$ 60 in open planned areas				
	SPP $\geq$ 70 in rooms				
	NIC' + (NC $\leq$ 35) $\geq$ 70 in rooms				
	Mask vertical footfall sounds with NC $\leq$ 40				
	Fiber type, weight, density and relationship				
	Resistance to forces:				
	Tuft bind $\geq$ 7#				
	Pill resistance $\geq$ 4.0				
	Resist 2#/" width strip force				
	Horizontal adhesive strength $\geq$ 40 psf				
	Vertical adhesive strength $\geq$ vacuum cleaner force				
	Support wheel load of 1500#				
	Resist 100 psi static load				
	Resist shrinkage — no joint opening				
	Colorfastness:				
	Crock rating $\geq$ 4.0				
	Wet cleaning rating $\geq$ "good"				
	Colorfastness to light rating $\geq$ 4.0				
	Fire safety:				
	Flame spread $\leq$ 75 unsprinklered				
	Flame spread $\leq$ 200 sprinklered				
	Specific optical density of smoke $\leq$ 450				
	Critical specific optical density $\leq$ 16 in 30 seconds				
	Meet DOC standards for surface flammability				

*This chart may be extended to include all the requirements of a project.

Application Guidelines

1. Seek out and use the latest information on all materials. Reliance on previous experience with a material may not always prove beneficial because the product may have been improved or altered in some way since the last time you specified it for a project.

2. Carefully research and analyze all items before specification, particularly if you are not familiar with them through previous experience.

3. Document all evidence of your evaluation process.

4. Avoid using dimensions of components on *preliminary* drawings. The use of schematic-type drawings can prevent the use of too much detail that could cause potential conflict with specification requirements developed later.

5. Start component evaluation early in the design process. The phases discussed in this chapter are summarized in Table 4.4.

TABLE 4.4 SUMMARY OF DESIGN PHASES

Phase	Design Process	Component Evaluation
1	Schematic design	Develop performance attributes based on user requirements.
2	Design development	Based on attributes, develop matrix and establish material performance requirements. Develop checklists.
3	Contract document	Select specification methods.

5 QUALITY CONTROL: FIRE PERFORMANCE TESTING

The National Bureau of Standards estimates that there are 12,000 fire-related deaths annually in the United States. A large percentage of these deaths have been the direct result of design and construction deficiencies. Research has shown that decorative materials, furnishings, and interior finishes have also been a contributing factor in many fires.

Designers' Role in Fire Protection

Fire protection experts agree that the first 5 or 10 minutes of a fire are the most critical. The initial materials ignited can either contribute to the growth of the fire or prevent its spread to other areas of the building. All the interior components specified by the designer become crucial elements in the early phase of a fire. Floor and wallcoverings, drapery, and furnishings are the primary elements providing fuel to sustain the growing fire. It is important for designers to acquaint themselves with all available knowledge concerning the nature of *potential fire hazards* and to apply this information effectively in the specification of materials and systems.

POTENTIAL FIRE HAZARDS

Many factors contribute to the definition of the term "fire hazard" (see Glossary). The classification of a material as hazardous involves a knowledge of its combustibility, heat release, flame-spread rate, smoke release, and toxicity plus the environment in which the material is installed, i.e., the interaction with other materials in a given space.

Interior Finishes

Little research was directed to interior finishes as potential fire hazards until three major hotel fires in 1946 claimed the lives of 199 people. The fires occurred in Chicago, Illinois; Dubuque, Iowa; and Atlanta, Georgia. Evidence gathered from the fires indicated combustible interior finishes were definitely one of the contributing factors in the rapid flame spread. Prior to that time little was known about the potential hazards of interior finishes and furnishings.[1]

During the last 10 years that evidence has been verified in many other fires throughout the country (see Table 5.1).[2]

Release of Toxic Gases

One of the most disastrous fires in recent years took place in 1977 at the Beverly Hills Supper Club in Southgate, Kentucky. Designed to accommodate approximately 500 occupants, the facilities were crowded with over 1,000 when the fire erupted. Witnesses to the blaze described the "pungent odor of burning plastic." Medical reports showed that most of the victims died of smoke inhalation. Authorities requested tests on plastic chairs used in the supper club. Figure 5.1 illustrates the spread of the fire and the intensity of dense black smoke.[3]

Although it is known that plastics represent a potential hazard in the event of fire, plastics have become a way of life. The first commercial use of plastics dates back to the 19th century when in 1868 eyeglass frames were made of cellulose ni-

TABLE 5.1 FIRE FATALITIES

Location	Year	Facility Type	Death Toll
Marietta, Ohio	1970	Nursing home	32
Minneapolis, Minn.	1970	Apartment house	12
Tucson, Arizona	1970	Hotel	28
Texas Twins, Pa.	1971	Nursing home	15
Rosecrans, Wisc.	1972	Home for aged	10
Springfield, Ill.	1972	Nursing home	10
Pleasantville, N.Y.	1973	Retirement home	10
New Orleans, La.	1973	Cocktail lounge	32
Wayne, Pa.	1973	Nursing home	15
Brookhaven, Miss.	1974	Nursing home	15
Columbia, Tenn.	1977	Prison	42
Danbury, Conn.	1977	Prison	5
Southgate, Ky.	1977	Supper club	164

Source: National Fire Protection Association.

trate. Today any person reaching out in any direction would find within arm's length a product containing plastics. In the event that plastics were removed from the market the plastics industry estimates over 500,000 workers would be unemployed. In addition, 1 billion acres, which includes all the agricultural land in America, would be needed to graze wool-producing sheep to replace the synthetics the textile industry now uses. Another 40 million acres would be needed for cotton crops. Fire hazards notwithstanding, the only solution apparently seems to be to rely on improved testing methods and responsible use, based on knowledge of potential dangers.

Research has determined that plastics present three major hazards in a fire exposure situation:

1. *Heat*: A comparison of heat release data shows that plastics produce more intense heat than cellulose, resulting in a greater fire severity. One pound of polystyrene releases 18,000 BTU; one pound of pine wood releases 8,000 BTU.

2. *Smoke*: Plastics produce great amounts of dense black smoke. The toxic or flammable gas contents are released quickly at various stages of the combustion process.

3. *Rapid combustion*: Plastics burn more rapidly than natural products and thereby cause a more rapid flame spread.

A fire that occurred in the New York British Overseas Airways Corporation (BOAC) Terminal in 1970 has been termed the "shortest large-loss fire in the history of mankind." The fire started in the west gallery of the new BOAC terminal and within 30 minutes had spread the entire length of the 330-ft (100-m) area, resulting in $2½ million damage. The only com-

MAKING OF A HOLOCAUST

1 When fire breaks out in the Zebra Room, employees try to extinguish it. Fire department not called for about fifteen minutes.

2 Corridors and air ducts spread smoke through the building, and fire travels through airspace between ceiling and roof.

3 Patrons panic, stampede and fight their way through pitch-black smoky corridors. Scores suffocate.

4 In the crowded Cabaret Room, many guests are overcome by toxic smoke as they struggle to reach the exits. A few die while still seated at their tables.

Figure 5.1 Beverly Hills Supper Club fire. Reproduced with permission of Newsweek/Ib Ohlsson.

bustible materials in the all steel and glass structure were 600 seats near the gate entrances. The area was totally carpeted with a blend of 80 percent wool and 20 percent nylon installed over a felt pad. Investigations showed that the fire did not start in the seating, but evidence clearly indicated that the foamplastic seat cushions were the major fuel source and were responsible for the rapid flame spread. The carpet, probably because of the large wool content, did not play a major role in the flame spread.

In the past several years industry has made tremendous strides in reducing the potential hazards of foam upholstery. Flame-retardant upholstery components will be discussed in Chapter 11.

Designers should remember that all burning substances emit some degree of toxic gases. The primary cause of death in most fires is carbon monoxide, which is the principal toxic substance emitted from any burning material used in furnishings and finishes. Table 5.2 illustrates the principal toxic combustion products (other than carbon monoxide) emitted from a few nonplastic materials.

While it is possible to measure the exact amount of toxic gases emitted by a particular material in a controlled laboratory condition, the combination of many materials and furnishings in a building often makes accurate analysis impossible. Because of this factor, engineers predict it will be many years before a solution is found to the problem of toxic gas release.

TABLE 5.2 TOXIC GASES

Substance	Pulmonary Irritants	Other Toxic Gases
Wood/cotton	Acetacdehyde	Acetic acid
Newspaper	Formaldehyde	Methane, formic acid
Wood/silk	Ammonia	Hydrogen sulphide Hydrogen cyanide

TRENDS IN FIRE PERFORMANCE TESTING METHODS

A representative of the Federal Trade Commission once remarked that no single test could predict the reaction of materials when exposed to the wide range of fire conditions. This comment only hints at the broad range of problems involved in the field of fire research.

Of concern to many fire engineers are the inherent limitations of conventional laboratory testing methods. Testing one sample under one condition does not adequately predict performance in fire exposure. *Fire exposure* implies that materials will be exposed not only to the variety of temperatures that occur in a fire, but also to the heat released from all the other components contained in a compartment fire. Figure 5.2a shows the time-temperature profiles that frequently occur from the growth phase to the fully developed phase of a fire system.[4] Contrast this to the standard time curve that is employed in laboratory testing (Figure 5.2b). There appears to be a large variance between furnace-generated heat and actual fire conditions.

The Fire System

Fire performance testing is based on knowledge gained from the study of fire systems. In order to understand the unique problems of flammability testing, it is important to review the stages in the development of a fire system. Figure 5.3 illustrates three major fire stages:

Stage 1: Fire engineers refer to the time of *ignition* and the initial fire growth as stage 1. If the fire remains in the area of ignition (in this case, a trash basket), it is considered a stage 1 fire.

Stage 2: This is considered the *growth* stage when the entire compartment or room becomes involved in the fire. During this stage generated heat may cause the fire to *flashover* (see Glossary for this chapter) to an adjoining space or corridor.

Stage 3: During this state flashover has occurred and the *fully developed* fire begins to rapidly spread throughout the building.[5]

Table 5.3 presents a more detailed overview of the fire system and the physiological effects produced in each fire stage.

Standard Flammability Testing

Flammability testing may be broadly classified according to the stage of the fire system which the test seeks to evaluate:

Ignition/Growth Stages. Ideal fire performance testing involved with the first two stages of the fire development should measure material characteristics that *contribute* to the development and spread of fire. Combustibility, i.e., the ease of ignition, flame-spread qualities, and the amount of heat and smoke released by a material, is of major importance.

Fully Developed Fire Stages. Testing that deals with the fully developed fire is concerned with (1) the endurance of the building structure and (2) the physical endurance of humans exposed to the heat, flame, oxygen depletion, smoke, and toxic gases.

Flammability testing methods used to evaluate materials in the various stages of fire development may be classified as follows:

Calculation Prediction Methods. These performance tests are based on known release-rate data. The amount of heat and smoke released by materials under varied fire exposure conditions is documented and used as a basis for testing. The test method is employed in controlled laboratory conditions.

Full-Scale Simulation Methods. This test method measures material performance under simulated fire exposure. Efforts to simulate fire conditions range from "room burns" to full-scale burn-outs in buildings slated for demolition. The full-scale burn-out of a building offers valuable reference points for predicting what might happen in a similar circumstance. The probability, however, of a similar condition occurring is highly unlikely. Since weather conditions such as temperature and

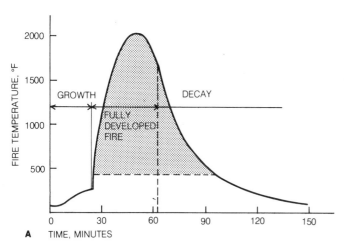

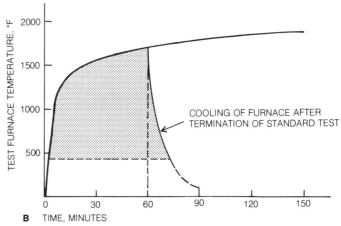

Figure 5.2 Time-temperature profiles. Reprinted from the April 1974 issue of Progressive Architecture, *copyright 1974, Reinhold Publishing Company.*

TABLE 5.3 EFFECTS OF COMBUSTION

Pyrolysis	Causes / Materials	Effects	Prevention
1. Fire origin			
a. Combustion; simultaneous ignition	Ignition, flash-over. Heat flux. Paper, interior finishes	Heat-produced smoke and flame	Codes—Regulations Fixed heat 165°F sprinklers
b. Smoldering	Wiring, paint rags or cans in confined space	Heat-produced gases and smoke	Central shutdown fans
2. Fully developed fire			
a. Heat	Products of combustion spread fire	Increased heart rate, dehydration, blockage of respiratory track	Holding rooms or areas within the building
b. Flame	Burning of materials in presence of oxygen	1st, 2nd, 3rd degree burns from heat	Sprinklers
c. Oxygen depletion	Oxygen depleted by fire	Diminished muscular skill, faulty judgment	
d. Smoke	Produced by materials burning—plastics, wood, etc.	Obscuration, panic, irritation of eyes	Compartmentalization to control combustion, dilution, exhaust fans
e. Toxic gases	All material and combined materials—plastics	Asphyxiation and death from CO, NO_2, HCN	Codes on combined use of materials—fuel loads
f. Volatile gases	High temperature "back drafts" when fed by oxygen	Asphyxiation—death	135°F sprinklers
3. Spread of fire			
a. Lateral	Through ducts, ceiling, plenums and doors	Means of escape blocked by smoke and fire	Code-rated materials. Vertical divisions. Compartmentalization
b. Vertical	Duct risers, shafts, stairs, elevators and open windows		
4. Expansion of contained fire			
a. Explosion	Breakage of containing members—windows and doors.	Expansion of fire	Fire rating of building structure
b. Deformation and collapse of structure			

SIDE ELEVATION (ROOM) SIDE ELEVATION (ROOM) SIDE ELEVATION (CORRIDOR)

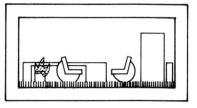
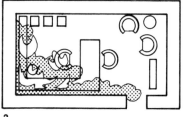
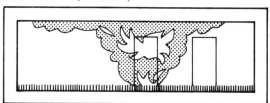

FLOOR PLAN (ROOM) FLOOR PLAN (ROOM) FLOOR PLAN (BUILDING)

1

2

3

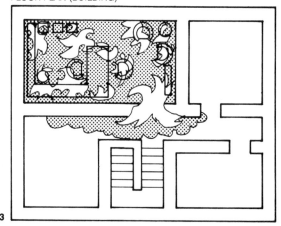

Figure 5.3 Stages of fire development. Source: National Bureau of Standards, NBSIR 78-1436.

TABLE 5.4 PRODUCT FLAMMABILITY PERFORMANCE

Test	Number	Measurement
Federal standard	DOC. FF-1-70	Pass
Steiner Tunnel Test	ASTM E-84	
Flame spread		Under 75
Fuel contribution	UL 992	Under 4
Smoke density	NBS 708/NFPA 258	Under 200
Radiant panel	NBS IR 75-950	
Radiant flux	NFPA 253	.45 watts/sq cm

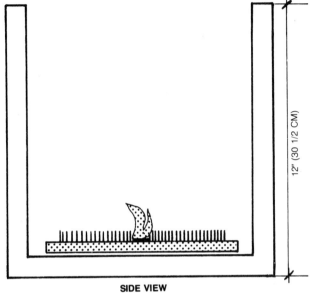

SIDE VIEW

12" (30 1/2 CM)

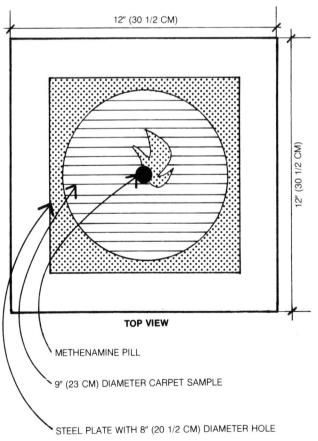

12" (30 1/2 CM)

TOP VIEW

METHENAMINE PILL

9" (23 CM) DIAMETER CARPET SAMPLE

STEEL PLATE WITH 8" (20 1/2 CM) DIAMETER HOLE

Figure 5.4 Methenamine Pill Test, FF-1-70. Source: National Bureau of Standards, NBSIR 78-1436.

wind direction are factors in a full-scale fire, accurate evaluations are difficult.

Combination Laboratory and Full-Scale Methods. The National Bureau of Standards constructed a fire research building in 1974, which incorporates a 40-ft (14-m) corridor lined with full-sized burn rooms. This facility has been successfully used to develop new data on the potential hazards of flame spread in corridors.

Current Flammability Testing: Interior Finishes

Designers are often puzzled by the long lists of flammability performance tests shown on many interior finish products. An illustration of this point, taken from a typical product sample, is shown in Table 5.4. The remainder of this chapter will survey the tests listed in Table 5.4 and explain the application of tests index rating systems.

Methenamine Pill Test

DOC. FF-1-70

DOC. FF-2-70

This test (Figure 5.4) was developed by the National Bureau of Standards and adopted by the Department of Commerce in 1970.

Purpose. This test seeks to prevent the use of highly flammable fiber floorcoverings capable of spreading flame in phase 1 fire exposure. The ease of surface ignition and surface flammability are evaluated. Some authorities require tests on both the front and back carpet surfaces and occasionally on carpet padding. DOC. FF-1-70 applies to carpet. DOC. FF-2-70 applies to rugs.

Test Procedure. A carpet sample 9 in. (22.9 cm) square is placed on the bottom of a 1 ft (30.5 cm) draft-protected square enclosed cube, which is open at the top. The sample is held in place by a 9-in. metal plate which has an 8-in. (20.3-cm) hole in the center. A timed Methenamine pill is placed in the center of the carpet and lighted. The surface flame should not show considerable spread. If the sample burns to within 1 in. (2.5 cm) of the metal plate, it fails the test. The test is repeated 8 times, and 7 out of 8 samples must pass to qualify for test approval.

Rating System. The samples are given a pass/fail rating.

Official Adoption. Since 1971 this test is required by law for all carpet produced in the United States. DOC. FF-2-70 is required on domestic and imported rugs.

Steiner Tunnel Test

ASTM E-84

NFPA 255

UL 723

Developed by A. J. Steiner for the Underwriters Laboratories, Inc. after World War I, this test (Figure 5.5) was adopted by ASTM and NFPA as official standards in 1958.

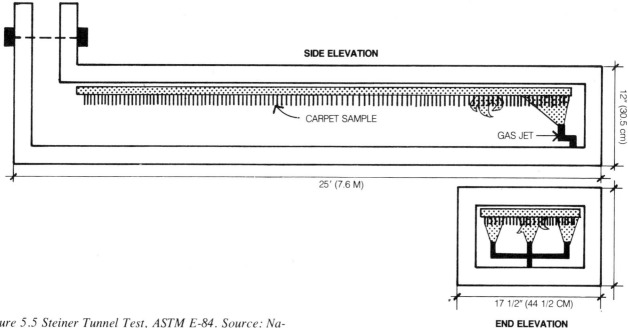

SIDE ELEVATION

CARPET SAMPLE

GAS JET

12" (30.5 cm)

25' (7.6 M)

17 1/2" (44 1/2 CM)

END ELEVATION

Figure 5.5 Steiner Tunnel Test, ASTM E-84. Source: National Bureau of Standards, NBSIR 78-1436.

Purpose. The test was devised to test the comparative surface burning characteristics of *building materials* and interior finishes. The test is designed to simulate a phase 2, or fully developed fire exposure, and provides data on flame spread, fuel contribution, and smoke density.

Test Procedure. A sample 24 ft (7.5 m) long and 20 in. (50.8 cm) wide is placed on the ceiling of a 25-ft (7.6-m) long tunnel. A double jet gas burner at the end of the tunnel provides about 5,000 BTU per minute during the test, which is 10 minutes in duration. Air is induced into the tunnel to pull the gas flame upstream for about 4 ft (121.9 cm). The distance of the burn along the test sample is measured to determine the flame-spread rating.

Rating System. All materials are rated on a scale ranging from 0 to 100. Cement-asbestos board which will not burn is arbitrarily given a rating of zero (0) and red oak flooring is rated at 100 (moderate burning rate).

Classification	Flame-Spread Range
A	0– 25
B	26– 75
C	76–200

Official Adoption. This test method is currently required in most states. It is used in the ASTM model code and the NFPA 101 Life Safety Code. Among federal agencies adopting this test method are HEW, GSA, FHA, and the test is required to meet the standards of the Hill-Burton Act that regulates fire safety in health care facilities.

Objections to Test. The carpet industry has long opposed the application of the ASTM E-84 test method for carpet for the following reasons: (1) the test was primarily designed for wall and ceiling finish materials. The tunnel test requires carpet to be tested in an upside-down position which causes many fibers to melt and drip at an early stage in the test process. (2) Research has proven that temperatures during a fire are much higher at the ceiling level than at the floor level. (3) It has been difficult to establish repeatable data when testing carpets in this method.

The Chamber Test

UL 992

This test method was developed as an alternative to the Steiner Tunnel Test.

Purpose. This test seeks to determine the flame spread and flame propagation of carpet.

Testing Procedure. A carpet sample 2 by 8 ft (.6 by 2.4 m) is installed on the floor of the chamber. A gas flame is then applied to the carpet for 12 minutes with a controlled air draft of 100 ft (30 m) per minute.

Rating System. Calculations are based on the length of the flame spread and time of flame travel. A rating index from 0 to 25 is used.

Class B	0–4
Class C	5–8

Objections. Rating index divides material into two groups, which makes a continuous classification scale difficult, and the index has not been proven relevant to fire hazards.

Official Adoption. Used by several states and some federal agencies, such as HEW and FHA.

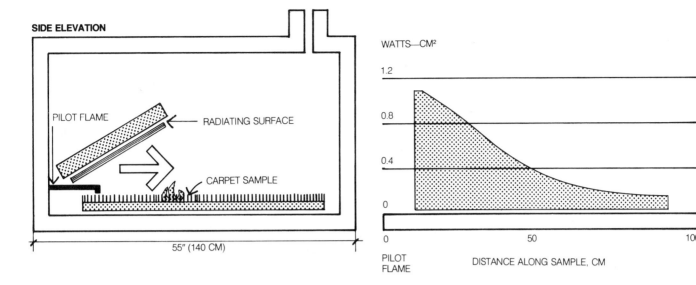

SIDE ELEVATION

PILOT FLAME

RADIATING SURFACE

CARPET SAMPLE

55″ (140 CM)

WATTS—CM²

1.2

0.8

0.4

0

0   50   100

PILOT
FLAME

DISTANCE ALONG SAMPLE, CM

Figure 5.6 Flooring Radiant Panel Test. Source: National Bureau of Standards, NBSIR 78-1436.

Figure 5.7 Flooring Radiant Panel Test Index. Source: National Bureau of Standards, NBSIR 78-1436.

Flooring Radiant Panel Test

ASTM E648

NBS IR 75-950

NFPA 253

The first research on this test method (Figure 5.6) was conducted by the Armstrong Cork Company in 1966. The National Bureau of Standards had considerable influence on the development of the test and the establishment of the Critical Radiant Flux Index rating. Many early tests were conducted at the NBS facilities which allowed full-scale corridor testing. The test is highly recommended for testing floorcovering systems for the following reasons:

1. It measures radiant exposures which are very important in full-scale corridor tests.

2. The total flooring system is tested, as used, and on a horizontal plane.

3. Reproducibility and repeatability are excellent.

4. The test apparatus is simple and compact; the test sample is small.

5. The test procedure is simple and provides a continuous scale of performance in the range of 0.1 to 1.0 watts/cm² radiant exposure.

Purpose. In the past decade many lives have been lost in hotel and nursing home fires. Both building types use corridors as a means of egress. This test specifically deals with the measurement of flame spread in a corridor or exitway which is under the influence of a fully developed fire in an adjacent room. The fully developed fire within the room transmits heat and radiant energy to the ceilings and walls of the corridor which ignite the carpet, thus blocking the only means of escape.

Test Procedure. Sample size is 39 in. (99.1 cm) long by 8 in. (20.3 cm) wide and is mounted horizontally. The sample receives radiant energy from an air gas-fueled radiant panel

mounted above the sample at an angle of 30°. After the sample is preheated a gas-fired pilot burner ignites the flooring system.

Rating System. The distance burned is measured and converted into a flux number which becomes the flame-spread index. The units used are watts per square centimeter. Critical radiant flux is the minimum energy necessary to sustain flame in the flooring system. In this test, the higher the number, the more resistant the material is to flame propagation. The lower the number, the greater the tendency of a subsystem to spread flame (Figure 5.7).

Critical Radiant Flux Recommended Limits. The National Bureau of Standards recommends the following: (1) 0.22 watts/cm² within corridors and exitways of all commercial buildings; (2) 0.45 watts/cm² within corridors and exitways of hospitals and nursing homes.

Official Adoption. All major federal agencies have adopted the test. This includes HEW, Veterans Administration, Public Building Service, Department of Defense, and the Department of Transportation. NFPA adopted the test as a standard in 1978.

Smoke Density Chamber

NBS 708

NFPA 258-1976

This test was developed by the Fire Research Section of the National Bureau of Standards in 1966.

Purpose. This test was devised to measure the smoke potential of solid materials. Because the density of smoke often prevents escape in a fire situation, the light obscuration characteristic of generated smoke is also measured.

Test Procedure. The chamber is a closed cabinet 2 by 3 by 3 ft (61 by 91.4 by 91.4 cm). A sample 3 in. (7.6 cm) square is

TABLE 5.5   MAJOR FLAMMABILITY TESTING OF INTERIOR FINISHES

	ASTM E-84 Steiner Tunnel	FF 1-70 FF 2-70	NFPA 253 Flooring Radiant	NBS 708 Smoke Density
Purpose of Test	Flame spread Fuel contribution Smoke contribution	Ease of ignition Surface flammability	Flame spread in corridors	Smoke density
Procedure Sample size	20″ × 25′ on ceiling of chamber	9″ × 9″ placed under 9″ × 9″ steel plate.	39″ × 8″ mounted in holding frame	3″ × 3″ flaming or smoldering condition
Test chamber	25′ long chamber	Draft controlled, hooded-mirror	Radiant panel at 30° angle	Chamber: 2′ D 3′ W 3′ H
Heat applied	Pilot source at one end. Standard draft condition	Methenamine pill lighted by match	Chamber preheated. Pilot heat source. No forced air	2.2 BTU per ft
How results measured	Based on red oak standard flame spread of 100. Flame spread: A = 0-25 B = 26-75 C = 76-200	7 out of 8 samples must pass Rated: pass/fail	Red oak = 0.35-0.4 Wool = 0.4-0.75 Vinyl = excess of 1.1 Measured in watts per square cm	Photometric light measures optical density of smoke
Federal agencies adoption	HEW, Hill Burton GSA, FHA	Federal law 1971—all carpet produced in USA must pass FF1-70	HEW, VA, DOT, GSA	NBS, HEW, GSA, FHA

supported vertically in a holder while exposed to heat under two conditions: flaming and nonflaming (smoldering). A photometric meter measures light density.

Rating System. Smoke quality is reported in terms of maximum optical density. The index range is between 0 and 800 units, which covers most building finish materials. Most federal agencies require a smoke density rate of 450 or less (flaming).

Official Adoption. Many states and federal agencies have adopted this method, including HEW.

Corner Test. This test has been used occasionally over the past 20 years. It is considered a very expensive test procedure which is difficult to control and evaluate. Factory Mutual and Underwriters Laboratories, Inc. have conducted experiments with this method.

Purpose. This test simulates real use conditions of interior finishes on walls and ceilings.

Test Procedure. This test method makes use of a corner construction, usually 8 ft (2.4 m) tall. Extensions on either side of the corner may extend from 4 to 8 ft (1.4 to 2.4 m) and a ceiling may also be attached. Material to be tested is applied to the walls and ceiling. A wooden crib (a wooden slat box usually 2 ft (61 cm) square filled with wood excelsior is used as an ignition source) is placed on the floor close to the corner walls.

Rating System. Materials are allowed to burn out and efforts are made to determine the extent of flame spread. No formal index has been published.

Official Adoption. Some cities have evolved their own version of the corner test, such as the Phoenix Corner Test. A corner test has not yet been officially adopted by the National Fire Protection Association.

Table 5.5 summarizes the major test methods used to evaluate interior finishes.

APPLICATION OF FIRE TESTING

Fire tests are valuable in determining the potential hazards of materials. It should be noted that many test methods establish different index ratings for the particular fire characteristic being evaluated. In some tests a high index rating indicates a greater hazard; in others it represents a lower hazard. The three tests presented in Table 5.6 illustrate the differences.

Codes and Standards Application

When referring to codes and standards, designers should also be aware that the same index rating may be used by more than one test method. Tunnel tests, such as NFPA 255, UL 723, and ASTM E-84, classify the flame spread of interior finishes in the following manner:

Class A	0–25
Class B	26–75
Class C	76–200

The 101 Life Safety Code published by the National Fire Protection Association classifies the flame-spread requirements for interior finishes according to occupancy and the index rating of the NFPA 255, "Method of Test of Surface Burning Characteristics of Building Materials" (see Table 5.7).

In an example from the Veterans Administration requirements (UM-44c) for floorcoverings, the flame-spread ratings of both the ASTM E-84 and the UL 992 are listed in Table 5.8.

Code Officials' Application

When a code official informs a designer that an interior finish or a component presents a fire hazard and cannot be used in a particular project, the designer often finds it difficult to under-

TABLE 5.6 TEST INDEX RATINGS

ASTM E-84 Steiner Tunnel Test	UL 992 Chamber Test	NFPA 253 Flooring Radiant Panel
Class A 0-25		0.45 w/cm²-Nursing homes
Class B 26-75	Class B 0-4	0.22 w/cm²-Commercial
Class C 76-200	Class C 5-8	
The higher the index rating, the greater the hazard.	The higher the index, the greater the hazard.	The higher the index rating, the *less* the hazard.

TABLE 5.7   NFPA INTERIOR FINISH REQUIREMENTS

Occupancy	Exits	Access to Exits	Other Spaces
Institutional, existing, completely sprinklered: hospitals, nursing homes, residential-custodial care	A or B No restrictions on floor surface	A or B No restrictions on floor surface	A, B or C
Institutional, new: hospitals, nursing homes, residential-custodial care	A	A	A B in individual room with capacity not more than 4 people
Residential, new: hotels	A or B	A or B	A, B or C
Residential, existing: hotels	A or B	A or B	A, B or C
Residential, new: apartment buildings	See table A-11-3		
Residential, existing: apartment buildings			
Residential: dormitories	A or B	A or B	A, B or C
Residential, new: 1- and 2-family, lodging or rooming houses			A, B or C
Residential, existing: 1- and 2-family, lodging or rooming houses			A, B or C
Mercantile: Class A*	A or B	A or B	Ceilings—A or B Existing walls—A, B or C
Mercantile: Class B*	A or B	A or B	Ceilings—A or B Existing walls—A, B or C
Mercantile: Class A or B sprinklered*	A, B or C	A, B or C	A, B or C
Mercantile: Class C*	A, B or C	A, B or C	A, B or C
Office	A or B	A or B	A, B or C
Office-sprinklered	A, B or C	A, B or C	A, B or C
Industrial	A or B	A, B or C	A, B or C
Storage	A, B or C	A, B or C	A, B or C
Unusual structures	A, B or C	A, B or C	A, B or C

*Exposed portions of structural members complying with the requirements for heavy timber construction may be permitted.

Notes:
Class A Interior Finish: flame spread 0-25, smoke developed 0-450.
Class B Interior Finish: flame spread 26-75, smoke developed 0-450.
Class C Interior Finish: flame spread 76-200, smoke developed 0-450.
Automatic Sprinklers — where a complete standard system of automatic sprinklers is installed, interior finish with flame spread rating not over Class C may be used in any location where Class B is normally specified, and with rating of Class B in any location where Class A is normally specified, unless specifically prohibited elsewhere in this Code.

Reprinted by permission from NFPA 101, *Life Safety Code*, copyright © 1976, National Fire Protection Association, Boston, Mass.

TABLE 5.8 VETERANS ADMINISTRATION (UM 44C) FLOOR COVERING REQUIREMENTS

Location within Building	Surface Flame-Spread Rating— Maximum Range, Floors
Enclosed stairways and other vertical openings	0-75 (4)
Corridors or hallways and other exits	0-200 (8)
Public rooms and entrance spaces	0-200 (8)
Lobbies and corridors between exit stairway and exterior	0-200 (8)
Service rooms, enclosing heat-producing or other mechanical equipment, and all other fire hazardous areas	0-75 (4)

Notes: 0-75; 0-200 = ASTM E 84 limits. ( ) = Index number for UL Standard No. 992.

TABLE 5.9   PANELS FOR USE IN OPEN OFFICE PLAN

| Panel No. | Surface Area, ft^2 | Product Material | Ease of Ignition* | Fire Characteristics of Product | | | |
				Flame-Spread Rating†	Potential Heat,‡ BTU/ft^2	Smoke Density,§ D_m	Carbon Monoxide Max., ppm ¶
1	8	A	1	100	8,000	100	3,000
2	18	B	2	75	4,000	300	5,000
3	6	C	4	25	10,000	350	2,000
4	6	D	1	200	16,000	450	5,000
5	12	E	3	50	6,000	200	6,000

Notes: All panels are of the same design, except for the surface area.
Fire characteristic test methods:
*Fictitious: number of combined methenamine tablets needed to cause sustained burning.
†ASTM E-84 (25' tunnel).
‡ASTM STP 464, pp. 127-52, per ft^2 of surface area.
§NBS Smoke Density Chamber, flaming mode.
¶Measured in NBS Smoke Density Chamber, flaming mode.

ALTERNATIVE 1
× (FLAME SPREAD IN CABINETS IS 200)

ALTERNATIVE 2
△ (FLAME SPREAD IN CABINETS IS 25)

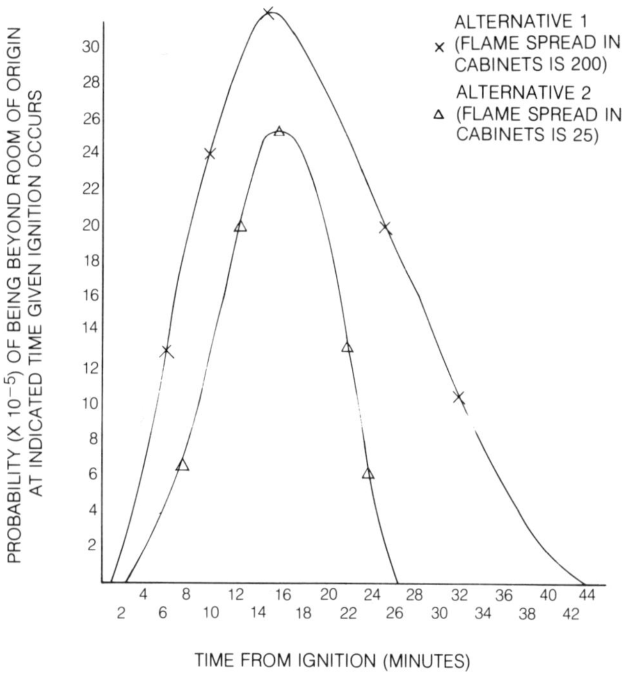

Figure 5.8 Distribution for two types of kitchen wallcovering, given ignition in kitchen.

TABLE 5.10 FLAME-SPREAD RATING OF INTERIOR FINISHES (ASTM E-84)

Alternative	Walls	Ceiling	Cabinets
1	200	200	200
2	200	200	25

stand the reason for the product rejection.

A researcher, interested in understanding the decision-making process used by code officials, devised a hypothetical situation in which a designer submitted the fire performance test results, shown in Table 5.9, to a code official for approval of a panel system to be used in an open office plan. On the basis of the tests submitted, officials were asked to evaluate the panel systems.

The presentation of this problem to code officials produced some interesting insights about the decision-making process used in evaluating fire safety factors. The majority of officials began by selecting the test methods thought to be the most appropriate for evaluating the office panels. Many chose the flame-spread factor (ASTM E-84) while others chose the ease of ignition (FF 1-70). Some were concerned with the heat potential (ASTM STP 464), although many would have preferred more information on rate of heat produced, rather than the total heat potential.

Another important criteria in the decision process involved the size and use of the panel, i.e., how the panel would interface with other materials in the space.[6]

This simple experiment can perhaps help designers to identify with code officials who are faced with many complex decisions regarding the approval of products.

Designers' Application

Making fire safety decisions is perhaps even more complicated for designers because of the additional concerns about function, costs, and aesthetics. As a result of research in the area of fire safety systems, the U.S. Department of Housing and Urban Development has projected the need for a designers' "application handbook."[7] This handbook would assist designers by providing information on evaluating the alternatives and probabilities involved in fire safety decisions. For example, a designer planning a kitchen interior may establish two sets of kitchen interior finish parameters (Table 5.10). Having selected the wall and ceiling finish, the designer would then have to decide between cabinets 1 and 2. Cabinet 1 has a flame-spread rating of 200 and costs $1,500. Cabinet 2 has a flame-spread rating of 25 and will cost $2,500.

The less expensive cabinet would meet the minimum requirements for the particular project, but in the event of fire would present a high probability of spreading the fire beyond the kitchen. Figure 5.8 illustrates that a fire occurring in the kitchen with cabinet 2 would only present a small probability of spreading beyond the kitchen.

Before making a decision between increased fire safety and cost factors, designers may also consider the possibility of other alternatives. There are often unspecified combinations of factors that may achieve equivalent levels of fire safety such as:

1. Smoke density potential versus use of smoke detectors.

2. Flame spread versus amount of fuel loading in the area.

3. Flame spread versus availability of public fire protection.

4. Heat content of materials versus use of sprinklers.

In order to make alternate decisions, it is evident that designers must be familiar with product test results indicating the smoke density potential, rate of heat release, and heat content of a particular material. It is also evident that designers making *responsible design decisions* is no less difficult than code officials making product approval decisions.

RISK MANAGEMENT CHECKLIST

1. Early in the design process try to determine the fire hazard potential of the project.

2. Determine the performance test method that will provide the level of fire protection required for the project.

3. Keep informed of new test methods as they are developed.

4. Make every effort to use concise fire terminology in specifications. ASTM has established guidelines regarding the use of certain terms as adjectives and nouns (see "flame resistant" and "flame resistance" in the Glossary).

5. Attend fire safety seminars provided for designers. The National Fire Protection Association conducts Life Safety Code Seminars each year. For information contact:

National Fire Protection Association
Educational Technology Unit
470 Atlantic Avenue
Boston, MA 02210

The United States Fire Administration conducts courses for architects and interior designers on fire-safe building design through the National Fire Academy. For additional information contact:

National Fire Academy
U.S. Fire Administration
P.O. Box 19518
Washington, D.C. 20036

6 QUALITY CONTROL: VALUE MANAGEMENT

Specification decisions should not be finalized without giving consideration to the concept of value management. The preceding chapters have reviewed methods of quality control through systems classification, performance evaluation, and testing methods. This chapter will examine value management as a method of determining the cost effectiveness of components, specifications, and performance criteria. Life cycle costing (LCC) is used to implement the principles of value management and provide formulas for obtaining the optimum total cost of components.

Since the mid-1960s, federal agencies and some areas of industry have effectively used life cycle costing methods. The publication of the *PBS Building Systems Program and Performance Specification for Office Buildings* by the General Services Administration in 1971 established life cycle costing as a standard of evaluation for interior systems in all federal buildings. In the past several years, the GSA Design Action Center has shown concern for the total working environment of federal employees by having interior designers serve on federal design teams. Perhaps for many designers this was their first introduction to the concepts of value management and life cycle costing.

The idea of trying to predict cost effectiveness is certainly neither new nor revolutionary. At one time or another everyone makes major decisions based on what is believed to be sound value judgments. Buying an automobile provides an excellent example of how life cycle costing can be effectively employed. When a new car is purchased, the owner is assured that the quality was controlled through performance testing. The warranty states that major expensive repairs will not be the owner's responsibility, at least not for the first several months. However, if soon after the warranty expires, the automobile begins to require expensive and frequent repairs, the owner may decide to replace the automobile for economic reasons. To determine the total ownership cost during the life cycle of the automobile, the following equation might be developed:

$$LCC = (AP_I + L + IN) + OC + PM + CM + R$$

where
- LCC = Life cycle cost
- AP_I = Acquisition price plus interest
- L = License
- IN = Insurance
- OC = Regular operating cost, such as oil and gas
- PM = Preventive maintenance, such as tune-ups
- CM = Corrective maintenance: repairs, including parts and labor
- R = Replacement cost which includes depreciation factors; residual value (trade-in)

Once these life cycle costs are established, the owner can determine the return on investment factors (ROI), and this infor-

mation can also provide a basis for making a decision on the purchase of another automobile.

ADVANTAGES OF USING LIFE CYCLE COSTING

Life cycle costing used as a method of quality control provides an accurate record of initial costs and the logistics of future costs. Obviously this approach can be a very valuable tool for the designer when specifying commercial and institutional installations. Instead of specifying the least expensive office system to meet a proposed budget, a designer would be wise to point out the advantages of life cycle costing to the owner. A client may not be aware of savings that can be realized in operational and maintenance areas. The General Services Administration provides this example of the LCC considerations that would determine federal specification decisions:

	Supplier A (Millions of $)	Supplier B (Millions of $)
BP	$48.00	$45.00
OMP	3.90	3.90
E	29.70	34.00
LRC	.07	.07
SAC	1.30	2.00
AP	**$83.00**	**$85.00**

where
- AP = Award price
- BP = Bid, or initial, price
- OMP = Operating and maintenance price
- E = Energy cost
- LRC = Luminaire relamping cost
- SAC = Space adjustment cost

The following formula was used to compute the figures above:

$$AP = BP + OMP + E + LRC + SAC[1]$$

This example illustrates that even though supplier B had the lowest initial cost, the energy and space adjustment cost factors were greater than those projected by supplier A. Therefore supplier A would be awarded the contract.

PEOPLE COST

Another important aspect that can affect long-range cost is the factor known as "user or people cost." GSA's Public Building Service reports that value management should include user costs over an extended period of time. Research has shown that people cost can account for as much as 92 percent of the total life cost of a facility; operating and maintenance cost for the same period might amount to only 6 percent, and the initial cost spread over the same period, only 2 percent.

The people cost concept is based on the knowledge that working environments do affect human performance. Therefore a design solution that results in improved production and efficient work flow will provide the owner/client with a return on investment. The following equation for projecting people cost was presented by J. T. Malarky at a 1972 symposium on "The Performance Concept in Building":

600 people × $5 per hour × 2,100 hours per year × 10 years = $63,000,000

Based on this hypothetical calculation, the total cost of ownership for an office facility for a 10-year period[2] would include the initial cost, operating cost, and people cost:

Initial cost	$ 4.5 million
Operating cost	4.2 million
People cost	63.0 million
Total cost:	$71.7 million

All design firms are familiar with the process of budget proposal. In some cases, a firm may decide to present an additional comparative cost analysis between the choice of one system as opposed to another, i.e., open office landscaping versus closed office planning. This may prove very helpful to the client in making initial cost decisions, but unless the analysis includes all the life cycle factors it represents only a partial view of the true ownership cost. Life cycle costing should be employed whenever possible because it adds another dimension to the design effectiveness, in the sense that it allows the designer another means of answering the user's immediate and long-range needs.

ELEMENTS OF LIFE CYCLE COSTING

To understand the actual application of life cycle costing it is important to review the factors that are considered in the process of evaluating components on the basis of total life cost. Figure 6.1 illustrates the major LCC elements and their interrelationships. This portion of the chapter will present more detailed information on each of the LCC elements and provide equations for calculating total costs. These equations were developed by the U.S. Federal Supply Service (FSS) and the General Services Administration for use in federal life cycle costing procurement. The equations are general in scope and designers may add or delete items depending on the circumstances of each particular project. All equations may not apply to every interior component, and designers should be aware that some interior subsystems would not benefit from LCC evaluation. The criteria used in the selection of items for LCC consideration are discussed later in this chapter.

Acquisition or Initial Cost

This involves the immediate known cost elements, such as the number of components needed, discounts for quantity or prompt payment, and shipping expenses. Other factors that could add to the initial cost are the expense of assembly if the components arrive unassembled, storage space if the items arrive prior to the completion of the project, and transportation of the components from the storage facility to the project site. Installation cost, including labor and materials, is added to the initial cost factor. The installation of equipment, such as open office systems, may require a brief training period to acquaint personnel with the optimum use of the system. This training cost would be absorbed into the initial cost factor. In the case

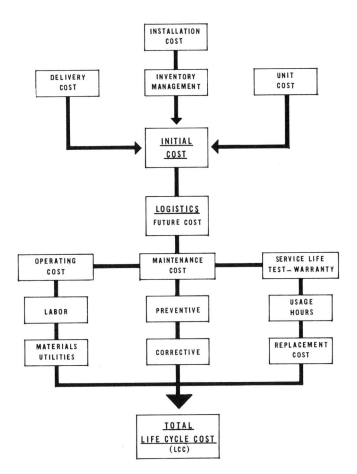

Figure 6.1 Life cycle costing.

of large institutional installations, the owner/client may incur additional administrative expense due to inventory management, i.e., the addition of new items to the inventory due to the new installation. There may be special costs unique to a specific item, such as unusual storage or handling. Inventory management is particularly important in installations such as hotels, motels, schools, hospitals, and nursing homes. A hotel scheduling many meetings and receptions on the same day must maintain an accurate inventory record of tables as well as stacking and folding chairs. Each commercial and institutional project will present different situations and result in different means of arriving at the acquisition cost. The following equations summarize initial cost and inventory management factors.

Initial Cost

$$IC = (P_I \times N_I) + A + I + S - D$$

where
- IC = Initial cost
- P_I = Unit price per item
- N_I = Number of items
- A = Assembly
- I = Installation
- S = Shipping
- D = Discount offered

Inventory Management

$$I_{im} = IMCF \times NI$$

where I_{im} = Initial inventory management cost

         IMCF = Initial management cost factor. This cost factor covers the general and administrative cost directly attributable to the addition of new items.

         NI = Number of new items

$$R_{im} = (RMCF \times NI) \times \frac{PIUP}{12}$$

where R_{im} = Recurring item management cost

         RMCF = Recurring management cost factor. This covers the general administrative cost on a yearly basis.

         PIUP = Projected inventory usage period. This is the number of months an item will have to be maintained in inventory.

The Logistics of Future Costs

This represents a most important aspect in the life cycle cost evaluation process. This method of predicting future costs is based on recurring costs, such as operations, maintenance, and inventory management. These records, often provided by industry, are based on previous systems in use. However, records should be carefully analyzed to determine if all the conditions and maintenance factors are similar to those in the proposed use. The performance and expected service life of a component are evaluated and the final cost involved in the removal and replacement of nonrepairable items is also calculated. Although accuracy in logistic cost prediction is preferred, a degree of reasonable accuracy is sufficient. Once the logistics costs are tabulated, a comparison can be made to current dollar values and cost increases.

Service Life

The service life of a component has to do with the reliability, prediction, and verification of how long a particular component will remain in useful service. There are four stages in the service life of a component. The first two stages, development and production, are controlled by the manufacturer who predetermines the reliability factors. After a system is installed, the operational stage becomes the real test of reliability. The owner aids in continuing the reliability factors by providing appropriate maintenance. The fourth and last stage is reached when the system is no longer repairable and must be discarded.

Prior to specification, a designer must determine if the reliability predicted by the manufacturer can be verified. Reliability verification involves the following procedure:

1. *Definition of System Failure.* If a system has never been used before, the manufacturer will be asked to provide a definition of failure that is applicable to the system. Contract statements regarding failures must be clearly stated in terms of the specific system; i.e., the failure of an office chair may be defined in terms of mechanical parts that malfunction and are beyond repair, such as a swivel joint. The designer or owner may prefer to establish the definition of failure based on previous experience with a particular system.

2. *Prediction of Failure.* The service life rationale is based on the premise that failures are predictable. Components or systems under evaluation are usually classified as "repairable" and "nonrepairable." In the area of interior specifications, office systems and specially constructed institutional furniture would be considered repairable. Many other items specified by designers would be considered nonrepairable or nonreusable. Interior components such as drapery, carpet, wallcoverings, and some types of upholstered seating may be repairable, but in most cases it would be considered uneconomical to do so. Some commercial facilities such as hotels and motels have a third classification that could perhaps be termed "consumables," i.e., items with an extremely high failure rate such as bedding components, dishes, silverware, and glassware. Aside from a high failure rate, these items are also subject to a high theft rate.

When a specification is written for a repairable item, a designer may wish to use an equation known as a "figure of merit" to predict or evaluate the Mean (average) *Time Between* Failures (MTBF). The figure of merit for nonrepairable items is known as the mean *Time To* Failure (MTTF). The important difference between the two equations is the fact that MTBF, on the one hand, measures the extended service life beyond a first or second failure and also projects the expected usage period. The MTTF equation, on the other hand, measures the total service life of a nonreusable component only to the first failure that terminates its useful life.[3]

a. *Service Life* (Reliability Prediction)

    (1) Figure of Merit: Nonrepairable components

$$UP = \frac{UL}{MTTF}$$

where   UP = Unit price or unit life cycle cost during the entire useful life of the nonrepairable component.

         UL = Unit logistics cost or all life cycle cost which would include all cost (operational, maintenance, initial cost, installation, item management, replacement); not on yearly basis, but for the projected life span.

         MTTF = Mean time to failure expressed in units of service life. Example: light bulbs expressed in hours or lumens of expected life.

    (2) Figure of Merit: Repairable components

$$EF = \frac{EU}{MTBF}$$

where   EF = Expected number of failures in projected usage period

         EU = Expected usage (hours) of each component

         MTBF = Mean time between failures

(3) Expected Usage:

$$EU = PIUP \times H$$

where
- EU = Expected usage (hours) of each component
- $PIUP$ = Projected inventory usage period (months)
- H = Hours operation/months per installed component

3. *Reliability Acceptance Testing.* Essentially the same criteria used in performance testing are applied in reliability acceptance testing. The component is usually tested in a situation simulating the actual use condition. If the component has not previously been in general use, laboratory testing is accepted for evaluation purposes. A specification based on life cycle costing should state which test methods will be acceptable.

4. *Warranties.* It is usually advisable to obtain some form of warranty protection if possible, but it is not absolutely essential. Warranties are not always applicable to all components. There are three major types available:

   a. Repair warranties apply to the operational aspects of a component. This type of warranty is usually held by the manufacturer and repair is dependent on the number of hours, months, or years the component has been in use. This warranty may or may not include temporary component replacement while repairs are in progress.

   b. Replacement warranties promise to replace defective components at no cost or offer a large discount on the replacement unit.

   c. Service function warranties may only apply to one component within the total system. For example, if the paint finish on a piece of office equipment begins to chip or crack the manufacturer will be responsible for replacing the finish. If this cannot be accomplished, the entire item may be replaced.

Warranties are usually made available through the manufacturer or the supplier/wholesaler. Even though a supplier may be more geographically convenient for repair warranties, the manufacturer may represent a more reliable source for repairs. Every warranty will stipulate certain installation, operational, and maintenance requirements which, if neglected, would invalidate the warranty agreement. The designer may recommend that the client obtain a "service contract," which, for an additional fee, will provide warranty protection, but it should be remembered that this expense should be included as an element in life cycle costing.

To evaluate the feasibility of warranty costs, the following factors should be determined:

1. Determine the price of a component with and without a warranty.

2. Evaluate the relative cost of buying a service contract in comparison with having the repairs done by people on staff (in house).

3. Determine shipping costs involved in returning the component to the manufacturer for repair. If it appears that the cost will be prohibitive, investigate the possibility of a supplier warranty with the stipulation that the supplier post a bond to assure his reliability.

4. Verify that all details of the warranty coverage are clearly defined in the contract.

Life cycle costing logistics include the final cost factors involved in the removal and replacement (R&R) of a system when it has reached the end of its service life. Consideration should be given to any possible residual value that can be obtained from salvageable component parts.

Recurring Operational Costs

It is important to identify what operational cost will be associated with a particular subsystem. Operational costs usually include the number of people required to operate the component, the average hourly wage, the expected service life of the component, and the amount and cost of utilities used in the operation of the system. For example, the operational cost of an ambient task office system would include the electric power consumed and the labor cost to relamp the luminaires. There is also the recurring cost of training new personnel in the use and maintenance of the office system. If a particular system, such as a computer, requires a special form of environmental control, this added expense should be included in the operational cost. The operation of a piece of equipment such as a vacuum cleaner would be calculated as a part of maintenance cost. The following equations explain the process used in calculating operational costs.

Operating Costs

$$MC = W \times N \times OH \times L$$

where
- MC = Manpower cost, including any manpower resource involved in the operation or monitoring of the system
- W = Average hourly cost of an operator
- N = Number of operators
- OH = Average number of operating hours per month
- L = Operating Life or Projected Inventory Usage Period (PIUP)

$$PEM = E \times C \times OH \times L$$

where
- PEM = Power, energy, or material consumed per hour, including the cost of any material consumed in the operation
- E = Units of energy, power, or material consumed per hour (watts per hour)
- C = Cost of one unit of energy
- OH = Average number of operating hours per month
- L = Operating Life or Projected Inventory Usage Period (PIUP)

Recurring Maintenance Costs

The calculation of maintenance costs takes into consideration the expected usage of the component (hours per month), expected failures during this usage period, and the required preventive and corrective maintenance that will be necessary to keep the component in working condition.

Preventive maintenance is performed on a regular basis throughout the useful life of a component. Corrective maintenance is performed when a system or component begins to fall below its expected level of performance and needs repair. Carpeting, for example, should receive regular preventive maintenance such as vacuuming and spot cleaning until the level of appearance demands corrective cleaning procedures. The desired maintenance or performance level is based on the owner's requirements and is included in the calculation of maintenance costs. A component may be maintained at a 100 percent perfect level (first), an 85 to 80 percent excellent level (second), or an 80 to 70 percent good level (third). All indications of maintenance level failure which are used in maintenance equation c are assumed to be subject to detection, isolation, removal, and replacement ("ith" maintenance level may be used to indicate any desired performance level).

Downtime is a term often associated with maintenance problems. It refers to the period of time involved in making extensive repairs or the time required for complete replacement of a component. The loss of income due to product failure or the added expense of equipment rental is considered as an element of life cycle costing over and above the normal cost of maintenance.

(a) Corrective Maintenance Equation. This equation applies to repairable and nonrepairable components.

$$LC = (LS_R)(LR_1) + \sum_{i=1}^{n} (LS_i)(LR_i)(P_i/100)$$

where

LC = Labor cost per failure

LS_R = Labor standard (hours) to detect, remove, and replace

LS_i = Labor standard (hours) to repair at ith maintenance level

LR_1 = Labor rate at the first maintenance level

LR_i = Labor rate at the ith maintenance level

n = Number of maintenance levels used in components repair

P_i = Percentage of removals repaired at ith maintenance level

i = ith maintenance

Labor standard information should be obtained from records of previous repair work.

(b) Repair Material Cost per Failure

$$MC = \sum_{i=1}^{n} [(MCS_i)(P_i/100)]$$

where

MC = Material cost per failure

MCS_i = Material Cost at _____ maintenance level

P_i = Percentage of removals to be repaired at _] _____ maintenance level (owner fills in desired maintenance level)

(c) Transportation Cost per Failure

$$TC = 2W \ [\ SPRL + SPMR + (ARS)(PW/W)\ ](1 - P_1/100)$$

where

TC = Transportation cost per failure

W = Weight of item

$SPLR$ = Standard packing labor rate

$SPMR$ = Standard packing material rate

ASR = Average shipping rate

P_1 = Percentage of repair actions at _____ maintenance level (owner fills in desired maintenance level)

PW = Packaged weight of item

(d) Preventive Maintenance Equation

$$PMC = (PIUP)(PMH)(PMR)$$

where

PMC = Preventive maintenance cost per item

$PIUP$ = Projected inventory usage period (months)

PMH = Preventive maintenance hours (monthly)

PMR = Preventive maintenance hour rate

(e) Preventive Maintenance Manhours per Month (PMR)

$$PMH = \sum_{i=1}^{m} (F_i)(R_i)$$

where

F_i = Manhours to accomplish preventive maintenance level ith

m = Number of different preventive maintenance actions performed

R_i = Number of times preventive maintenance action performed per month (at ith level)

(f) Total Maintenance Cost per Item

$$TMC = (EF - 1)(LC + MC + TC) + PMC$$

where

TMC = Total maintenance cost

EF = Expected failure rate

LC = Labor cost per failure

MC = Material cost per failure

TC = Transportation cost (item return to factory for repair)

PMC = Preventive maintenance cost

The expression $(EF - 1)$, the expected failure rate, is decreased by one on the assumption that equipment would be junked after the last failure rather than repaired.

APPLICATION OF LIFE CYCLE COSTING

Before deciding if life cycle costing methods will be economically feasible for a particular project, designers are advised to consider the following evaluation checklist.

1. *Initial Cost.* This should be calculated with a degree of accuracy before other logistics are considered. Determine all the elements that will be included in the initial costs:
   _____ Purchase price
   _____ Unit price
   _____ Discount offered
   _____ Shipping/delivery costs
   _____ Unusual handling
   _____ Assembly costs
   _____ Storage costs
   _____ Installation costs
   _____ Personnel training
   _____ Inventory management
   _____ Other

   After this list is completed, an individualized equation can be developed for initial cost factors.

2. *Capital Investment.* Having completed the initial cost factors, it is possible to determine which components represent a large capital investment. A listing of these items would indicate which would possibly benefit from an evaluation of return on investment (ROI).

3. *Percentage of Total Cost.* Another means of verifying that a component may benefit from life cycle costing is to consider what percentage of the total project cost it represents:

Component	**Percentage of Total Cost**
_____	_____
_____	_____
_____	_____
_____	_____
_____	_____

In large institutional projects this evaluation method can be very useful. Hotel installations provide a good example of this concept. The total cost of furnishing one guest room may average $2,000. Of that total cost, furniture may represent 70 percent, carpet 13 percent, drapery 10 percent, and miscellaneous items such as linens, 7 percent. Although it would appear that drapery is only a small percentage of the total cost of the guest room, it should be remembered that this does not reflect the *total project cost*. Total drapery cost is as follows:

$203/room $\times$ 300 rooms = $60,900 (TPC)

In all multiple installation situations (including hospitals and nursing homes), the total project costs should not be overlooked.

4. *Logistic Information.* Having narrowed the component list, the designer can now proceed to determine the availability of data that will allow further logistic evaluations. The logistic summary in Table 6.1 indicates where information might be obtained in order to complete LCC evaluations.

5. *Administrative Cost of LCC Applications.* Based on the availability of logistic data, the designer and client must determine if the time and cost involved balance the benefits to be obtained from LCC. Evaluate the following factors:

   a. Importance of LCC factor in obtaining project contract
   b. Research time involved
   c. Administrative staff necessary to conduct and tabulate research
   d. Administrative staff salary rate

6. *Repairable and Nonrepairable Components.* Based on measurable service life (MTBF or MTTF) and reliability testing factors, the designer may further classify the components into two groups: repairable and nonrepairable.

   a. Repairable items: Key LCC factors to consider:
      (1) Projected inventory usage period
      (2) Maintenance factor
      (3) Total life cycle cost
      (4) Requirement that manufacturer support proposed values
      (5) Requirements for reliability/maintainability testing

   b. Nonrepairable items: Key LCC factors to consider:
      (1) Statement of minimum acceptable service life
      (2) Formula for computing service life
      (3) Definition of failure
      (4) Requirement that manufacturer support proposed service life
      (5) Determine method of validating claimed service life

TABLE 6.1 LCC ELEMENT SUMMARY CHECKLIST; SOURCES OF LOGISTIC INFORMATION

	A	B	C	D
1. Purchase price	X			
2. Delivery cost	X			
3. Testing cost	X		X	
4. Installation cost		X		
5. Inventory management cost			X	
6. Personnel training costs	X		X	X
7. Service life and/or MTBF	X		X	X
8. Operating labor	X		X	X
9. Operating materials and utilities	X	X	X	X
10. Preventive maintenance cost	X	X	X	X
11. Corrective maintenance cost	X	X	X	X
12. Desired maintenance level			X	
13. Dismantling cost	X		X	
14. Residual value			X	X
15. Other (list)				

A — Obtain from manufacturer.
B — Contractor should provide.
C — Obtain from client.
D — Documented through designer's past experience.

Note: This table offers only suggestions regarding possible sources of logistic information. Sources may vary in each situation.

7. *Component Selection Matrix.* In order to determine which logistic elements are associated with particular components, a matrix may be developed for each project. For example, inventory management for continued replacement of nonrepairable items in hotel installations may represent a major logistic factor. Furniture and other repairable components may offer larger long-range savings through evaluation of operational and preventive maintenance costs. Figure 6.2 illustrates a component selection matrix based on items most frequently specified for interior use.

8. *Equation Application.* After the logistic elements have been matched to the components, the designer may proceed to apply the appropriate equations and complete the life cycle costing of particular components. The following is an example of the process that may be used to calculate maintenance costs for repairable components:

   a. Compute service life equation (Figure of Merit)
   $$EF = EU \times MTBF$$
   b. Compute expected usage (in hours)
   $$EU = PIUP \times H$$
   c. Compute corrective maintenance equation *a*.
   d. Determine material cost per failure from maintenance equation *b*.
   e. Compute transportation cost per failure if item must be returned to factory for repair, based on maintenance equation *c*.
   f. Determine preventive maintenance, equation *d*.
   g. Compute the preventive maintenance manhours per month, with maintenance equation *e*.
   h. Determine the total maintenance cost per unit by computing maintenance equation *f*.

9. *General Considerations.* Experts on value management and life cycle costing suggest the following general guidelines:

   Include: a. Nonrepairable items should be included if they account for an annual expenditure of $100,000.
   b. Repairable components which account for $300,000 annual expense.
   c. Standard commercial components (not custom made).

   Exclude: a. Items and components which are one of a kind. No comparative data would be available.
   b. Items for which noncompetitive bidding has

LOGISTIC ELEMENTS / COMPONENTS	Repairable	Non-Reuseable	Item Management	Service Life	Testing Costs	Warranty Costs	Operating Labor Cost	Operating Materials	Preventive Maintenance	Corrective Maintenance	Dismantling Costs	Residual Value	Replacement Cost	Downtime Costs
Office Systems	●			●	●	●	●	●		●	●	●	●	●
Seating – non Uph.	●		●	●	●	●	●		●		●		●	●
Seating – Uph.	●	●		●	●	●	●	●	●		●		●	●
Desks	●		●	●	●	●		●				●	●	●
Drapery		●	●	●			●	●	●		●		●	●
Carpet		●		●	●	●	●	●	●	●	●		●	●
Wall Coverings		●		●	●	●			●		●		●	●
Bedding		●	●	●	●	●	●		●		●		●	●
Luminaires		●	●	●	●	●	●	●	●	●	●		●	●
Tables	●		●	●	●				●	●			●	●

Figure 6.2 Component selection matrix.

been predetermined. Some large firms have prearranged purchasing agreements with manufacturers (hospitals, universities, and hotels).

10. *LCC Summary Cost Equation.* This equation contains three major cost categories:

$$LCC = A + I + R$$

where   A = Acquisition costs: the sum of the unit costs for the component, materials, data, and services

   I = Initial logistics costs: one-time logistic costs which are identifiable and would be incurred

   R = Recurring costs: operation, maintenance, and management of the component, including preventive and corrective maintenance.

Part 2
Interior Systems

7 FLOOR SYSTEMS: RUGS AND CARPETS

On the federal, state, and local levels carpeting is one of the most heavily regulated interior floor systems. The carpet industry, in addition, has established many self-regulatory standards of performance which have led to a wider acceptance of carpeting, not only in offices, but in schools and hospitals. Because of the many performance guidelines that have been established, one would assume that designers would have little difficulty in writing specifications for carpeting. On the contrary, the number of liability suits involving carpet seems to be increasing. In most instances, it is not the quality of the carpet that is questioned, but the fact that the carpet specified was not suited to a particular use. Such specifications often indicate scanty knowledge regarding the performance quality of various fibers, carpet construction, installation methods, and padding requirements. Maintenance and life cycle costing factors are frequently ignored.

The fact that designers are supplied with an overwhelming amount of carpet statistics perhaps accounts for the problem. Lacking the time to sort and study the material, designers are inclined to place their confidence in one particular fiber or carpet construction that proved successful in previous installations. This failsafe method of repeatedly specifying the same type of carpet for all projects without analyzing the particular variances in each installation can result in costly errors.

To discuss this broad subject in a clear and organized manner, this chapter is divided into three sections. The first deals with rugs, the second with woven and tufted carpet, and the third establishes specification programming for carpet.

RUGS

Rugs receive heavy scrutiny from the federal government in regard to flammability factors. The federal *Standard for the Surface Flammability of Small Carpets or Rugs* (FF 2-70) (see Chapter 5 for a detailed description of flammability test FF 2-70) defines a rug, or small carpet, in the following manner:

> any type of finished product made in whole or part of fabric or related material and intended for use or which may reasonably be expected to be used as a floor covering which is exposed to traffic in homes, offices or other places of assembly or accommodation, which may or may not be fastened to the floor by mechanical means such as nails, tacks, barbs, staples, adhesives, and which have no dimension greater than 1.83 m (6 ft) and an area not greater than 2.23 m³ (24 ft²).

Products such as "carpet squares" with dimensions smaller than these but intended to be assembled upon installation, into assemblies which may have dimensions greater than these, are excluded from this definition. They are, however, included in this standard. Mats and hides with natural or synthetic fibers and other similar products are also included in this definition if they are within the defined dimensions, but resilient floorcoverings such as linoleum, asphalt tile, and vinyl tile are not included.

This standard applies not only to goods exported from the United States, but also to all goods imported into this country. One-of-a-kind rugs such as antique Orientals or hides are excluded from this regulation.

Failure of the Flammability Test. Any rug that fails to pass the FF 2-70 test criteria must be labeled: "Flammable (fails the U.S. Department of Commerce Standard FF 2-70): Should not be used near sources of ignition."[1]

Use of Fire Retardant. A fire-retardant treatment, as defined in the FF 2-70 standard, is any process to which a rug has been exposed which significantly decreases the flammability of that rug and enables it to meet the acceptance criterion of the standard. When a rug has received a fire-retardant treatment, it is washed prior to undergoing the FF 2-70 test. This is done to determine if the retardant will remain effective for a reasonable length of time. A rug successfully meeting the test requirements must display "a conspicuous, legible and permanent label containing the following information: DO NOT WASH IN HOME MACHINE OR DRY CLEAN—AVOID RUBBING OR BRUSHING WHILE DAMP."[2] Additional instructions on the label explain acceptable cleaning methods. More detailed information on flame retardants is presented in Chapter 11.

Oriental Rugs

The use of Oriental rugs in commercial installations is recommended only on a *very limited basis*. Executive offices, conference rooms, special reception areas, or private clubs are examples of semiprivate spaces where the specification of an Oriental rug may be feasible. The Oriental Rug Retailers of America offers this description of an Oriental rug: "a rug made of either wool or silk knotted entirely by hand by native craftsmen in some parts of Asia—from the shores of the Persian Gulf, north to the Caspian Sea and eastward through Iran, the Soviet Union, Afghanistan, Pakistan, India, China, and Japan." To become completely knowledgeable concerning Oriental rugs would require years of intensive study; therefore designers would be well advised to consult with an expert on the subject. When consulting with a dealer the designer should be aware of the various classifications of Oriental rugs.

1. Age
   a. Antique: over 75 years old
   b. Semiantique: below 75 years and used in native land
   c. New: made in the last 10 or 15 years

2. Country of Origin
   Near and Middle Eastern countries have produced large numbers of Orientals which are classified into four major groups:

   a. Persian
   b. Turkish
   c. Turkoman
   d. Caucasian

Only a few of the many rug types found in these four categories would prove suitable for commercial installations because of size and construction limitations.

3. Size
   The intended use of the rug dictates the size, i.e., a prayer rug, camel cover, or floorcovering. It should be noted that Orientals rarely are made in what we would consider "standard sizes." Oriental rug measurements are usually uneven, such as 4'5" × 5'5" (1.4 m × 1.7 m) or 11'5" × 14'5" (3.5 m × 4.4 m).

4. Design Style
   Two main design styles characterize Oriental rugs. One group is primarily based on geometric motifs, while the other major style is largely curvilinear and floral in character. Nomadic tribal movements account for the widely overlapping styles found in various provinces.

5. Construction
   a. Kelims: smooth surface with no pile and having the same appearance on both sides. Kelims are common in the Persian style.
   b. Sumak: Woven into a herringbone effect on the front surface without knotted pile. There are usually many loose yarn ends on the back.
   c. Knotted: The most popular production method which features pile on the front surface while the reverse side is smooth. The knots most frequently used are Persian and Turkish.

Specification Guidelines. Table 7.1 provides an overview of the major style characteristics of rugs from the Near and Far East. Recommendations concerning usage of particular types are based on sizes currently available.

Installation. Installation of Oriental rugs is not a complicated matter. Orientals may be placed over rigid floor surfaces or placed over smooth surfaced wall-to-wall carpet. A felt or foam padding that is thin and firm should be used under Oriental rugs to prevent slippage, wrinkling, and excessive wear.

Maintenance. Maintenance is an important factor in preserving the beauty of an Oriental rug. The following maintenance procedures are recommended:

1. Spot clean as needed.

2. Vacuum weekly in a crosswise direction.

3. Professionally clean only when absolutely needed. Excessive cleaning removes the natural oils from the wools.

4. Rotate and reverse at least once a year to distribute wear evenly.

Machine-Made Domestic Oriental Style Rugs. A designer may choose to specify a machine-made or contemporary hand-tufted rug that closely resembles an authentic Oriental style. Not only do they cost less, but the designer can also specify the exact size and color and can order duplicates if needed.

CARPETS

Carpets can be categorized as either woven or tufted.

Woven Carpet

Reviewing the list of mills that produce woven carpet in the United States (Table 7.2) clearly indicates that Velvets and Wiltons are the most available and most frequently used woven carpets in commercial work. Although woven carpets represent perhaps only 10 percent of the commercial carpet market,

---

TABLE 7.1 ORIENTAL RUGS: INDEX AND SPECIFICATION GUIDE

Place of Origin	Persian	Turkish	Caucasian	Turkoman	Chinese
General style					
Design motifs	Curvilinear floral design. Vases, birds. Medallion in center	Many prayer rugs. Mihrab altar design. Tulips. Reds, greens	Geometric figures of men, birds and animals. Dark reds	Rows of rectilinear octagons (guls). Dark reddish browns.	Typical Chinese symbols. Yang-yin. Cloud bands. Flowers, birds
Sizes: (In., mm not shown)	10' × 15' (3 × 4m)	3' × 5' (.91 × 1.5 m)	5' × 7' (1.5 × 2.13 m)	6' × 10' (4.87 × 3.04 m)	9' × 12' (2.74 × 3.65 m)
	13' × 24' (4 × 7.31 m)	6' × 10' (1.82 × 3.04 m)	6' × 10' (1.82 × 3.04 m)	15' × 24' (4.57 × 7.31 m)	8' × 5' (2.43 × 1.52 m)
		5' × 7' (1.5 × 2.13 m)	Most are small	Most are small	
Usage:					
Floor	Saruk—Bijar				
H	Herez			Bokhara	
M	Kerman/Tabriz				Peking style
L	X				
AC		X	X	X	
Wall		X	X	X	

Notes: H—Heavy traffic; M—Medium traffic; L—Light traffic; AC—Accent rug; Wall—Wall hangings; X—Majority of style types.

TABLE 7.2 DOMESTIC MILLS PRODUCING WOVEN CARPETS

Manufacturer	Axminster	Wilton	Velvet
Bigelow-Sanford		X	X
Burlington		X	
Bloomsburg Carpet			X
Commercial Carpet Corp.			X
Couristan, Inc.	X	X	X
Downs Carpet Co.		X	
Firth Carpets*	X	X	X
Gulistan Carpets			X
Harding Corp.			X
Karastan Rug Mills	X		
Lees Carpets		X	X
Magee Carpet Co.			X
Mohawk Carpet Mills*	X		X
Philadelphia Carpet Co.		X	X
Sabre Carpet Co.		X	X
Seamloc-Loma-Loom Carpet Co.			X
Alexander Smith Carpet*	X		X

*Division of Mohasco, Inc.

TABLE 7.3 CONSTRUCTION FEATURES: WOVEN CARPETS

	Axminster	Wilton/Velvet
Fibers	Wool/nylon/acrylics	Nylon/wool/acrylics
Dye method	Skein dyed	Skein dyed
Backing	Jute/manmade/cotton	Jute/manmade/cotton
Texture	Cut pile	Varied
Pitch	189*	216*
Face weight (oz/sq yd)	23 to 33*	18 to 64*
Widths	27″ (6.87 mm) to 12′ (3.65 m)* Some 15′ (4.57 m)	4′6″ to 12′* (6.37 m to 3.65 m)
Flame spread ASTM E-84	75	75

*These figures represent averages. Construction may vary according to designer specification.

they are frequently specified for large commercial installations that require an extremely dense pile and tightly woven construction. The construction of woven carpets also allows the designer to specify custom-designed, intricate patterns.

Originally most woven carpets were made of wool, but today a large percentage are produced in nylon, acrylics, and a variety of blends that are somewhat lower in price and provide an equally beautiful long-wearing carpet.

Axminster. The production of Axminster carpet requires a very sophisticated loom. There are perhaps not more than three or four such looms in the United States. The weaving process entails long spools of various colored yarns, carefully preset in a desired sequence and delivered to the weaving section of the loom at a precise moment in the pattern design sequence. The process of changing pattern production is very costly and time consuming. The Axminster carpet has a smooth cut-pile surface and can be woven in limitless colors and patterns. An identifying feature is the heavy ribbed backing that only allows the carpet to be rolled lengthwise.

Wiltons. The Jacquard loom used to produce Wiltons was developed in England. The process makes use of preprogrammed pattern cards that are perforated and used to regulate the feeding of the colored yarn into the carpet surface. Although color ranges are sometimes limited, the surface texture of Wiltons can vary from level cut pile to multilevel loop construction.

Velvets. Velvets are produced on a relatively uncomplicated loom. This carpet is available in many color combinations and textures. The simplicity of the loom does not allow for patterned designs, but beautiful color combinations are used to produce tweed effects that are frequently used in commercial installations.

Table 7.3 further explains construction differences between woven carpets.

Tufted Carpet

The tufting process has been responsible for the tremendous growth of the carpet industry in America. This fast and relatively inexpensive process, combined with the use of synthetic yarns that have been developed in the last 20 years, has made carpet a standard floorcovering in most commercial and institutional installations. It has been estimated that tufted goods represent over 95 percent of the carpet produced in the United States. European countries are now also beginning to produce tufted carpet.

Figure 7.1 illustrates the basic construction differences between tufted and woven carpet. Tufting is basically a sewing process. Needles, threaded with yarn, punch back and forth through a premade backing material and produce a looped or cut tufted surface. Tufting machines, averaging 12 ft (3.6 m) in width, can produce hundreds of yards per day. After the yarn is punched through the primary backing, latex is applied to the underside, securely binding the tufts in place. A secondary backing of either jute or a manufactured fiber is applied to give better dimensional stability.

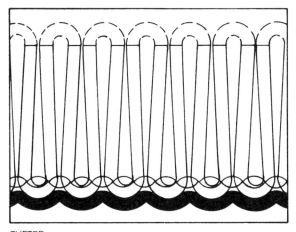

TUFTED

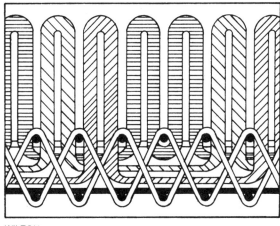

WILTON

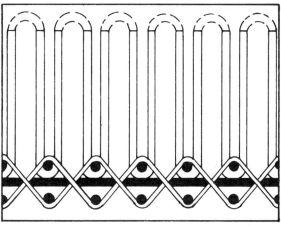

VELVET

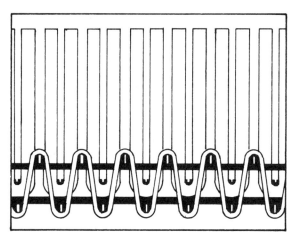

AXMINISTER

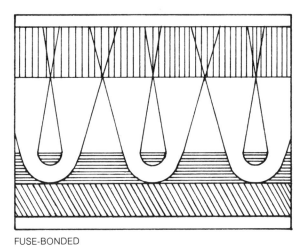

FUSE-BONDED

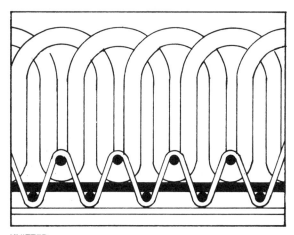

KNITTED

Figure 7.1 Types of currently manufactured carpet.

CARPET SPECIFICATION PROGRAMMING

The remainder of this chapter on carpeting will provide a systematic approach to the specification of commercial and institutional carpet.

Phase 1. Evaluation of Performance Criteria (Questionnaire)[3]

Phase 2. Selection of Generic Fibers

Phase 3. Analysis of Yarn Construction and Weight

Phase 4. Selection of Carpet Construction

Phase 5. Determinating Coloration Factors

Phase 6. Evaluating Durability Factors

Phase 7. Specification of Appearance Retention

Phase 8. Criteria for Health, Safety, and Comfort Factors

Phase 9. Traffic Classification

Phase 10. Criteria for Padding Selection

Phase 11. Estimating Yardage Requirements

Phase 12. Installation Criteria

Phase 13. Maintenance Programming

Phase 14. Life Cycle Costing

Phase 1: Evaluation of Performance Criteria

The following questionnaire will aid designers in assembling information to formulate specification criteria:

General

1. Type of traffic expected:
    Light _____ Medium _____ Heavy _____

2. Will carpet be used on stairs?
    Yes _____ No _____

3. Will there be concentrated traffic patterns?
    Yes _____ No _____

4. One-way traffic?
    Yes _____ No _____

5. Is plushness desired?
    Yes _____ No _____

    Degree:
    Minimum _____ Moderate _____ Extreme _____

6. Are employees walking on floors as part of daily work (i.e., retail, manufacturing, showroom, hospital)?
    Yes _____ No _____

7. Will carpet be exposed to direct sunlight?
    Yes _____ No _____

8. What kind of lighting will be used in the area?
    Incandescent _____ Fluorescent _____ Natural _____

9. Has a budget been established?
    Yes _____ No _____

Health, safety, and comfort factors

Flammability

1. Will carpet be used on walls?
    Yes _____ No _____

2. Will carpet be used in stair wells?
    Yes _____ No _____

3. Will carpet be used in exit ramps?
    Yes _____ No _____

4. Will carpet be used in a medical facility?
    Yes _____ No _____

5. Is Hill-Burton federal funding to be used?
    Yes _____ No _____

6. Will a fireplace or other open flame source be nearby?
    Yes _____ No _____

7. What is the occupancy load of the building?
    _____

8. Will sprinklers or other fire prevention equipment be used in the area?
    Yes _____ No _____

Static

1. Is static control a necessity?
    Yes _____ No _____

2. Is static control for human comfort _____ , computer tape _____ , memory transmission machines _____ , heart monitoring equipment _____ required?
    Yes _____ No _____

3. Will there be some method of controlling humidity above 20 percent at 70°F?
    Yes _____ No _____

4. Will electric typewriters and metallic office equipment be used?
    Yes _____ No _____

Acoustics

1. Are airborne noises important to consider, i.e., talking, machinery, typewriters, trays and dishes, cash registers, etc.?
    Yes _____ No _____

2. Will impact noise reduction be important, i.e., walking, rolling carts, dropping objects?
    Yes _____ No _____

3. Will area be used for public events or speeches?
    Yes _____ No _____

4. Will music listening be involved?
    Yes _____ No _____

5. Will a concentration of seating be prevalent?
    Yes _____ No _____

Installation

1. Type of floor: Wood _____ Concrete _____ Terrazzo _____ Other _____

2. Grade level: Below _____ Ground Level _____ Above _____

3. Type of building: New _____ Old _____

4. Is carpet presently on floor? Yes _____ No _____

    If yes, a. How old is it? _____
            b. Type of carpet? _____
            c. Type of backing (rubber, jute)? _____

d. Installation method (direct-glue, tackless)?
_____

5. Will old carpet be removed?
Yes _____ No _____

6. Will this disrupt operations?
Yes _____ No _____

7. Could a direct cement (no pad) installation be used?
Yes _____ No _____

8. Is pattern an important feature in the design criteria?
Yes _____ No _____

9. Will mechanical access to trench header ducts be required? Yes _____ No _____

10. Will partitions be fastened to the floor?
Yes _____ No _____

Will they be movable?
Yes _____ No _____

11. Will there be wheeled traffic?
Yes _____ No _____

If yes, a. Average weight of vehicle _____
b. Number of wheels _____
c. Size of wheels _____

12. Will wheeled traffic move directly from street to carpet (airport baggage carts, etc.)?
Yes _____ No _____

13. In office areas, will chairs have casters?
Yes _____ No _____

If yes, what type?
Regular _____ Carpet _____

Maintenance

1. Is there a daily maintenance program?
Yes _____ No _____

Other? Weekly _____ Biweekly _____ Bimonthly _____

2. Will maintenance program include emergency spot removal or daily stain removal?
Yes _____ No _____

3. Will smoking be permitted in carpeted area?
Yes _____ No _____

4. Will carpet be installed on street level?
Yes _____ No _____

5. Will carpet be exposed to "walk-off" from adjacent street areas, gutters, i.e., mud, snow, etc.?
Yes _____ No _____

Spillage

1. Are surroundings exposed to moisture?
Yes _____ No _____

2. Will food service be available in or directly adjacent to carpeted areas?
Yes _____ No _____

3. Will beverages be consumed in carpeted area?
Yes _____ No _____

If yes, hard drinks _____ , soft drinks _____ , coffee/tea _____ ?

4. Will carpet be used in a medical or clinical complex?
Yes _____ No _____

5. Will the area be exposed to possible flood situations?
Yes _____ No _____

Phase 2: Selection of Generic Fibers

Reviewing the project evaluation will reveal the major performance requirements, i.e., traffic and static levels, spillage, etc. For example, if spillage will be a problem in certain carpet areas, a carpet fiber should be selected that would have a low moisture-absorption rate. Table 7.4 provides information on the generic qualities of the fibers most frequently used in carpets today. After determining which fiber will best fulfill the majority of the project requirements, the designer can then proceed to evaluate the yarn construction of that particular fiber.

Phase 3: Analysis of Yarn Construction and Weight

Yarn weight and construction are determined in the following manner:

1. *Yarn count* refers to the fineness or coarseness of the finished yarn.
    a. Woolen count: This refers to the number of running yards in 1 ounce (oz) of finished yarn. This count system includes the number of plies of a yarn. Example: 3/60 count = 60 yards (yd) of 3-ply yarn per ounce.
    b. Denier count: This system makes use of metric measurements. The yarn weight is measured in grams based on a standard 9,000-meter (m) length of yarn. Example: a yarn denier of 1,225 means that 9,000 m of the yarn weighs 1,225 grams (g).

2. *Yarn plies* refers to the number of single yarns that are plied or twisted together. Simple ply yarns may be composed of three or more yarns. Manufactured fiber yarns such as nylon may be composed of long, unbroken lengths twisted together (continuous filament). Yarns, such as bulked continuous filament (BFC) nylon, may also be given added fullness in the finishing process.

Phase 4: Selection of Carpet Construction

The quality of carpet construction is based on density factors, such as stitches per square inch and gauge and/or pitch; pile height; and yarn weight or average pile density:

1. Density factors

    a. *Stitches or tufts per square inch* refers to the number of tufts within 1 sq in. (6.5 sq cm) of carpet. The more stitches per square inch the denser the carpet.

    b. *Gauge* represents the distance between rows of tufts across the width of a *tufted* carpet. If the gauge is listed as 5/32, tufts would be applied by 6.4 needles per inch.

    c. *Pitch* is the method used to determine the density factor in *woven* carpet. It refers to the distance between rows of tufts, but is counted on a 27-in. (68.6-cm) width of finished carpet. Therefore if the pitch listed is 316, it means that there are 316 rows of tufts in every 27-in. width.

    Table 7.5 defines the relationship between gauge and pitch.

TABLE 7.4 COMPARATIVE FIBER PERFORMANCE FEATURES

	WOOL	ACRYLICS	NYLON	OLEFIN
SPOTTING & SPECIAL CLEANING Removes discolorations and soil thereby giving added visible acceptability wear-life	May be cleaned on location. avoid alkaline detergents	VERY GOOD. Responds to standard methods. Usually complete on most acrylics	May be wet or dry cleaned. Readily spot cleans for stains. Cleans as for wool carpeting.	May be wet or dry cleaned. Readily spot cleans for stains. Cleans as for wool carpeting
STATIC ELECTRICITY	POOR	VERY GOOD	EXCELLENT With static control.	VERY GOOD
MOISTURE REGAIN At the standard relative humidity 70° F + 2. Wet cleaning is more effective on rapid drying fibers than on high moisture regain fibers. Fibers with a low moisture regain are more resistant to stains and have good texture retention.	POOR 16% absorptior	EXCELLENT 1.3 to 2.5% absorption	EXCELLENT 4% to 5% absorption	EXCELLENT
TOUGHNESS, FLEXIBILITY & ABRASION RESISTANCE Wear resistance determines the durability of a carpet and reduces fiber loss and damage during use.	VERY GOOD	VERY GOOD TO EXCELLENT	EXCEPTIONAL	OUTSTANDING FOR HEAVY DUTY
SOIL RESISTANCE Smooth fiber and filament surfaces eliminate crevices or indentations which entrap difficult-to-remove soil. Staple and textured yarns are less soil resistant than filament or smooth yarns.	GOOD TO EXCELLENT	GOOD TO EXCELLENT, CLEANS EASILY	GOOD TO EXCELLENT	GOOD TO EXCELLENT

Source: Interface Flooring Systems.

	WOOL	ACRYLICS	NYLON	OLEFIN
FLAME & HEAT RESISTANCE When a fiber is subjected to heat it will either burn and scorch or therm-melt. Cigarette burns fall in the category of "glow" burn damage. Flame resistance fibers will not support combusion and are termed safe fibers.	EXCELLENT Harsh at 212°F Scorches at 400°	FAIR Flame travel depends upon texture and construction sticks at 450° to 497° depending on type. Often blended with PVC to offer better resistence.	GOOD, melt burns. Melts at 428°	GOOD, melt burn Melts at 325°
SMOKE DENSITY	FAIR TO POOR	FAIR TO POOR	GOOD	GOOD
SURFACE FIBER COVERAGE Fine smooth fibers and filaments give least coverage. Any filament may be textured to produce loft so that yarn made from the fiber has more bulk or coverage for the same weight. Specific gravity fiber weight.	GOOD	VERY GOOD, EQUAL OR BETTER THAN WOOL	GOOD, EQUAL TO WOOL, depends on fiber cross section and textured finish.	GOOD
RESILIENCE OF PILE Elasticity of fiber permits rapid recovery from short term crushing, and recovery after 24 to 48 hours from large deformation from weighty objects or long term crushing	EXCELLENT	EXCELLENT Closely packed pile gives best service	GOOD TO EXCELLENT depends upon type and construction. Dense, cut-pile best	FAIR TO POOR

TABLE 7.5 GAUGE-PITCH RELATIONSHIP

Pitch (Woven)	Needle Ends per in. (2.54 cm)	Gauge (Tufted)
108	4.0	1/4
144	5.3	3/16*
173	6.4	5/32
180	6.6	—
189	7.0	9/64
216	8.0	1/8*
243	9.0	1/9
252	9.3	—
256	9.5	—
270	10.0	1/10*
356	12.8	5/64*

*Gauge density frequently used in commercial carpet.

2. Pile height

This is an important consideration in the overall evaluation of carpet construction. *Pile height* refers to the distance from the top of the yarn to the backing. When a carpet has a multilevel construction, the overall height is averaged. A lower pile height requires an increase in the stitches per inch. Pile height in woven carpets is referred to as "wire size."

3. Yarn weight or average pile density

Yarn weight is measured in ounces per square yard. Average pile weight refers to the amount of yarn in the *surface pile* of the carpet (face weight). This measurement does not include the primary backing, latex, or secondary backing. A carpet may have a total weight of 59.3 oz/sq yd and only have a face weight of 28 oz/sq yd. It is the face weight or actual surface yarn that is important. The average pile density is obtained with the following formula:

$$\frac{36 \times \text{finished pile weight (oz/yd)}}{\text{Finished average pile height}} = \text{Pile density}$$

a. Example: Information supplied by manufacturer on a particular carpet:

    Yarn size and ply: (1225, 1245)/2
    Machine gauge: 3/16 in. (144 pitch)
    Stitches per inch: 5.3
    Pile weight: 29.5 oz/sq yd (face weight)
    Finished pile height: 12/32 (.375) in.
    Total finished weight: 68.8 oz/sq yd (includes face weight + latex + backing)

Using this information a designer can calculate the average pile density:

$$\frac{36 \times 29.5 \text{ oz/sq yd}}{.375} = 2832 \text{ average pile density}$$

Many federal specifications extend the density figures to include "weight density" (WD).

b. Example:

Textures	Oz/sq yd	Average Pile Density(D)	Weight Density (WD)
Level loop	35	3600	126,000
Multilevel	40	3200	128,000
Plush	40	3000	120,000

The mathematical formula for calculating WD is:

$$\frac{\text{Face weight} \times \text{face weight} \times 36}{\text{Pile height}} = \text{WD}$$

Unless a designer is dealing with a federal specification, the Carpet and Rug Institute recommends that primary emphasis be placed on the average pile density factor.

Phase 5: Determining Coloration Factors

In selecting the dye method best suited to a particular specification criteria the designer will normally be concerned with the economy, soil-hiding factors, fade resistance, and aesthetics. Because some coloration methods may not be effective on all fibers, it would be advisable to consult with a textile expert.

Soil-Hiding Dyeing Methods. In the past few years an emphasis has been placed on dyeing methods that enhance the soil-hiding capacity of fibers. (A description of dyeing methods is included in the Glossary for this chapter.)

Fade Resistance. When specifying carpet that will be exposed to direct sunlight or extensive wet cleaning processes, it is important to require that tests be performed to determine colorfastness under the following conditions:

1. Intense sunlight

2. Atmospheric (ozone) fading

3. Wet cleaning

4. Abrasion (crocking) fading

Tests to determine textile colorfastness make use of the "Gray Scale" rating system. The amount of color change is determined visually and given the following rating (the term "break" refers to the amount of color change or fading):

5 No break
4 Slight break
3 Moderate break
2 Poor break
1 Severe break   See Table 7.6.

TABLE 7.6 SPECIFICATION GUIDE TO COLORFASTNESS TESTING METHODS

Performance Quality	Test Method	Rating Index
Light	1. Actual sunlight condition 2. Xenon arc weatherometer (AATCC 16 E test method)	Synthetics not below 4.0 on gray scale
Atmospheric ozone fading	Sample exposed to high ozone in high humidity condition. (AATCC 129/109 test methods)	Carpet should not have a shade change rating below 3.0
Wet cleaning	Test method described in DDD-C-0095A, Section 111-E-4. Sample put through cleaning process and rated. (AATCC 138-1972)	Carpet should show no change below 4.0
Crocking (abrasion fading)	Sample submitted to 20 friction cycles with a test cloth. Amount of color transferred from sample to test cloth is evaluated. (AATCC 8)	Results should not be below 4.0

TABLE 7.7 SPECIFICATION GUIDE TO DURABILITY TESTING METHODS

Performance Quality	Test Method	Rating Index
Tuft bind	Test for tuft permanent attachment to carpet back. Tuft pulled with minimum of 100 lb (45.36 kg). (ASTM D 1335) (DDD-C-0095A)	Test measured in pounds of pull tuft withstands. High rating 6-8 lb (2.72-3.63 kg)
Delamination strength	Measures permanent attachment of secondary backing to primary backing. Force used to determine if any separation will occur. (FTMS 191-5100)	Delamination strength should be a minimum of 2.5 lb per in. (warp direction) and withstand wheel load of 1500 lb
Dry breaking strength	4″ x 6″ (10.1 cm x 15.2 cm) sample subjected to pull force to determine breaking point. (FTMS 191-5100)	Sample should withstand 100 lb (45.36 kg)
Shrinkage	Sample is measured and then shampooed and dried to determine shrinkage. (FTMS 191-5100) (DDD-C-0095A)	Sample should not shrink beyond 5% in any direction

TABLE 7.8 SPECIFICATION GUIDE TO APPEARANCE RETENTION TESTING METHODS

Performance Quality	Test Method	Rating Index
Abrasion resistance	Test determines the amount of abrasion carpet will withstand. Taber abrader wheel is used. (ASTM D-1175)	Sample should withstand 6000 to 8000 cycles without showing excessive wear
Crush resistance	Test determines ability of carpet to recover thickness after subjected to heavy weight (furniture) or constant traffic. 50 lb/sq in. for period of 48 hr placed on carpet. (FTMS 501 A-3231)	Carpet should show an 85% recovery rate
Stain resistance	1. Ten major staining compounds are applied and cleaned immediately 2. Ten major staining compounds applied and left for 24 hr. (NBS-F 2)	Carpet should resist discoloration and show no noticeable staining (visual evaluation)
Pilling/fuzzing resistance	Carpet is placed in a cylinder and tumbled to determine amount of pilling and fuzzing that will occur in use. (DuPont Random Tumble Test 609)	Rated on scale between 5 to 1. Filament yarns should not rate below 4.0, staple yarns not below 3.0 (5 is highest rate = negligible)

Phase 6: Evaluating Durability Factors

Durability factors involve the physical strength of the carpet structure. It is advisable that designers require test results on the following components: tuft bind, delamination, dry breaking strength, and shrinkage (see Table 7.7).

Phase 7: Specification of Appearance Retention

The specification of factors that will *maintain the appearance level* of carpeting is as important as the actual construction qualities. A carpet may have to be replaced long before it has reached the end of its "useful life" because of the appearance level, i.e., the inability of the fiber to resist crushing, stains, and abrasion (see Table 7.8).

Crush and abrasion resistance: Designers should be aware that many factors, other than foot traffic, affect the ability of a fiber to withstand crushing and abrasion. The level at which a carpet is maintained (regular cleaning), the carpet density, and surface texture are all factors to consider in relation to crush and abrasion resistance (Table 7.9).

TABLE 7.9 ABRASION RESISTANCE OF SURFACE TEXTURES

Surface Textures	Recommended Use
1. Loop construction a. Level loop b. Cut and loop c. Ribbed loop	Usually high density. Good crush and abrasion resistance. Heavy traffic classification.
2. Cut pile construction a. Single level (plush) b. Shag c. Multilevel d. Saxony*	Moderate-high to light density. Moderate to light traffic classification depending on density.

*Saxony refers to carpet constructed of plied heat-set yarns.

Phase 8: Criteria for Health, Safety, and Comfort Factors

Flammability. The federal regulations involving carpet flammability are concerned with flame spread, surface flammability, ignition, radiant heat flux, and smoke development. The following testing methods are required in some jurisdictions. Refer to Chapter 5 for detailed descriptions of each test method.

ASTM E-84	Steiner Tunnel Test
UL 992	Chamber Test
DOC FF 1-70	Methenamine Pill Test
NBS IR 75-950 NFPA 253	Flooring Radiant Panel Test
NBS 708	Smoke Density Chamber

A summary of all carpet performance testing is provided in Table 7.17 at the end of phase 8 in this chapter.

Acoustics. Test results released by the Carpet and Rug Institute have shown that carpet provides valuable interior acoustic qualities in three major areas of concern:

1. Airborne sound absorption (NRC)

2. Impact Noise Reduction (INR) or
    Impact Insulation Class (IIC)

3. Surface noise reduction (NRC)

Airborne Sound. Airborne sound is defined as noise that radiates directly from machines, voices, radios, and other sources. Control of airborne sound is measured in terms of NRC (Noise Reduction Coefficient).

TABLE 7.10 ACOUSTICS TESTING METHODS OF AIRBORNE AND IMPACT SOUND

Performance Quality	Test Method and Purpose
Airborne sound	Reverberation room is used to test for floor sound absorption. Carpet installed with and without pad directly over concrete floor. ASTM C-423-60T. NRC rating system used.

TABLE 7.11 NOISE REDUCTION PROVIDED BY CARPET PADDING

PAD WT.	PAD MATERIAL	NRC
—	None	.35
32 oz.	hair	.50
40 oz.	hair	.55
54 oz.	hair	.55
86 oz.	hair	.60
32 oz.	hair jute	.55
40 oz.	hair jute	.60
86 oz.	hair jute	.65
31 oz.	⅜" foam rubber	.60
40 oz.	hair jute* foam rubber	.50
42 oz.	hair jute ⅛"* foam rubber latex	.60
44 0z.	sponge rubber	.45
86 oz.	sponge rubber ⅜"	.50

*Tested foam side down

Source: Carpet and Rug Institute.

TABLE 7.12 NRCs OF VARIOUS CARPET INSTALLED DIRECTLY OVER CONCRETE

• Specialized acoustical materials			.50 to .95 NRC
• Bare concrete floor			.05 NRC
• Tile or linoleum over concrete			.05 NRC

• Test carpet: identical construction, different manufacturers

	PILE WT.	PILE HT.	SURFACE	NRC
a.	44 oz.	.25"	loop	.30
b.	44 oz.	.25"	loop	.30
c.	44 oz.	.25"	loop	.30

• Identical constructions, different surfaces

	PILE WT.	PILE HT.	SURFACE	NRC
a.	35 oz.	.175"	loop	.30
b.	35 oz.	.175"	cut	.35

• Pile weight / height relationships in Cut Pile Carpet

	PILE WT.	PILE HT.	SURFACE	NRC	
a.	32 oz.	.562"	cut	.50	(lighter wt., higher pile)
b.	36.5 oz.	.43"	cut	.50	(heavier wt., lower pile)
c.	43 oz.	.50"	cut	.55	(heavier wt. higher pile)

• Increasing pile weight / height relationships in loop pile carpet

	PILE WT.	PILE HT.	SURFACE	NRC
a.	44 oz.	.25"	loop	.30
b.	66 oz.	.375"	loop	.40
c.	88 oz.	.50"	loop	.40

• Increasing pile weight (height constant) in loop pile carpet

	PILE WT.	PILE HT.	SURFACE	NRC	
a.	15 oz.	.25"	loop	.25	
b.	40 oz.	.25"	loop	.35	
c.	60 oz.	.25"	loop	.30	(added weight actually reduced NRC, possibly because of increased pile density)

Source: Carpet and Rug Institute.

TABLE 7.13 MEAN VALUE NRCs OF TYPICAL COMMERCIAL CARPET INSTALLED ON CONCRETE

Pile Height	NRC (mean)
⅛" (.125)	.15
³/₁₆" (.187)	.20
¼" (.250)	.25
⁷/₁₆" (.437)	.40

Source: Carpet and Rug Institute.

Impact Noise. This is the result of an object having impact on the structural surface of the building, such as footsteps on the floor above or furniture being dragged across the floor.

Surface Noise. Such noise is usually generated within the same room or area by objects scraping the surface of a desk or the floor (Table 7.10).

The following test was conducted to determine how the various weights and types of cushions increased the NRC of carpet. The carpet used in each case was a 40-oz [1.1-kilogram (kg)] loop pile construction with a .390-in. (9.9-mm) pile height (Tables 7.11-7.12).

Based on test results that show bare concrete to have a .05 NRC, the acoustic advantages of carpet cushion revealed outstanding results. This test showed that a sponge rubber cushion bonded to carpeting produced an NRC of only .30, but a 3/8-in., 31-oz (9.5-mm, 9-kg) foam rubber cushion installed separately produced a .60 NRC. It was found that hair-jute cushions coated with foam on one side produced a better NRC rating when installed with the foam side facing the floor. Hair-jute 56-oz (1.6-kg) cushion foam, coated on both sides, has produced ratings as high as .70 NRC.

Because the direct glue-down installation method is so frequently used in commercial installations, tests were conducted to determine the NRC rating of carpet installed directly over bare concrete without cushion (see Table 7.12).

Tables 7.12 and 7.13 illustrate the ability of carpet installed directly over concrete to control airborne sound. Although many factors affect an NRC rating, such as ceiling, walls, and other room components, the Carpet and Rug Institute was able to reach the following conclusions:

1. Variations in pile yarn fiber had little or no influence on sound absorption factors.

2. Cut pile seemed to achieve a higher NRC than loop pile construction. Increased pile height and weight also resulted in better sound absorption.

3. Carpet having a loop pile construction did not produce a higher NRC rating when the weight was held constant and the height increased (see Table 7.13).

Tests (Tables 7.14-7.15) were made to determine the impact noise rating of carpeting installed over concrete, both with and without carpet cushion. These tests indicate that the impact noise reduction was greatly increased in carpets having a heavier pile weight. Carpet cushion produced the following results:

1. Foam rubber cushions (weight for weight) produce the best impact noise reduction.

2. A mixture of hair and jute proved superior to all-hair cushions.

3. Cushions installed separately provided better impact noise reduction than cushion bonded to the carpet back.

4. Sponge rubber cushions that were generally not effective in reducing airborne noise performed well in the impact noise reduction tests.

The Kondaras Acoustical Laboratories (KAL) in Elmhurst, New York, advise that a rating (INR) of +10 to +15 should be about 80 to 90 percent satisfactory. Impact noise reduction ratings above +20 may or may not provide increased comfort, depending on the noise factors involved.

It should be noted that the Impact Insulation Class (IIC) is also listed in Table 7.15. The Federal Housing Administration (FHA) makes use of this numerical rating scale. To transpose INR to IIC, simply add 51 to the INR plus or minus number (INR + 5 = IIC 56).

Static Electricity.[4] The increased use of carpet combined with the increased use of electronic equipment in the contemporary commercial and institutional environment has been responsible for an increased awareness of electrostatic problems in the following areas: (1) hospitals: patient rooms and other areas where oxygen is used, and areas where heart monitors are in use; (2) commercial and industrial facilities: computer input terminals, data processing facilities.

Operating and service personnel in computer facilities are aware of problems arising from static. Apart from personal discomfort, computer users have commonly experienced static-caused operating troubles ranging from a transient malfunction to system shutdown. A static spark can have many different consequences because of the tremendous number of variables involved. Some of the more significant factors are the nature of the spark, its location, the path followed by the current, the machine state at the instant of discharge, and the susceptibility of the computer and its peripherals.

Although static problems are well recognized, their causes are not widely understood. Floorcoverings, particularly carpeting, and relative humidity are known generally to play an important role. However, the significance of shoe sole materials, furniture, and clothing is realized by very few, even among designers, specifiers, and managers who must make important decisions. As a consequence, situations come about in which carpeting is not used because it is believed to be the cause of the static electricity problems. A hard surface floor, although noisy, is specified because it is believed to be nonstatic.

Generation of Static Electricity. Static electricity generation in textile systems is primarily frictional or triboelectric in nature. This simply means that when two dissimilar materials which are in contact are separated, there is a tendency for a redistribution of charge between the two contacting surfaces; i.e., one surface becomes negatively charged and the other becomes positively charged. Determining which material will become negatively or positively charged is based on knowledge of the molecular structure of the two surfaces and on the relative position each holds in the triboelectric series. Figure 7.2 illustrates a typical triboelectric series. This table offers a basic ranking of materials in a dry condition without the addition of antistatic materials. Other common variances such as humidity, frictional speed and pressure, and temperature are not a consideration of the triboelectric series. The series simply points out that certain materials are positively or negatively charged. For example, if a person wearing shoes with PVC soles walked across a polyester or acrylic carpet, very little static electricity would be produced. If the carpeting was constructed of wool or nylon (which is positively charged), the negatively charged PVC soles would produce static electricity.

The same situation occurs when a person wearing a nylon shirt is seated in a chair upholstered in an acrylic fabric. Arising from the chair will cause static electricity if the shirt has been in direct contact with the upholstery. These surface charges induce a potential on the conductive human body, which can produce a spark when brought close to ground potential (finger to elevator button or doorknob). The potential

TABLE 7.14 IMPACT SOUND

Performance Quality	Test Method and Purpose
Impact sound	ISO R-140 Tapping Machine "Field and Laboratory Measurements of Airborne and Impact Sound Transmission." Machine set placed on floor above room. Microphone in room below measures sound transmitted. INR rating system used (−0 termed unsatisfactory; + number considered superior).

Test Findings: **IMPACT NOISE RATINGS (INR) — ON CONCRETE SLAB**

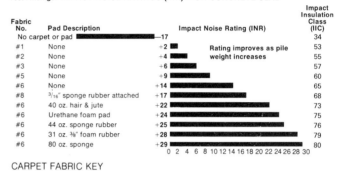

Fabric No.	Pad Description	Impact Noise Rating (INR)	Impact Insulation Class (IIC)
No carpet or pad		−17	34
#1	None	+2	53
#2	None	+4	55
#3	None	+6	57
#5	None	+9	60
#6	None	+14	65
#8	3/16" sponge rubber attached	+17	68
#6	40 oz. hair & jute	+22	73
#6	Urethane foam pad	+24	75
#6	44 oz. sponge rubber	+25	76
#6	31 oz. 3/8" foam rubber	+28	79
#6	80 oz. sponge	+29	80

Rating improves as pile weight increases

0 2 4 6 8 10 12 14 16 18 20 22 24 26 28 30

CARPET FABRIC KEY

CARPET	PILE WEIGHT, OZ	PILE HEIGHT, IN.
#1	20	.35-.15
#2	27	.20
#3	32	.56
#5	44	.25
#6	60	.25
#8	44 OZ WITH ATTACHED 3/16" SPONGE RUBBER PAD	

Source: Carpet and Rug Institute.

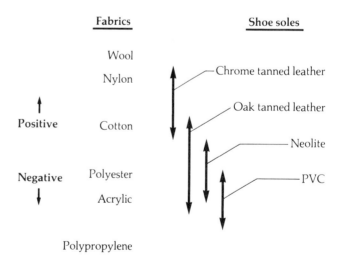

Figure 7.2 Typical triboelectric series. Reproduced with permission of W. G. Klein.

becomes even higher as the person walks away from the chair or floor area where the charging took place.

Conductors and Insulators. To understand performance testing for static potential and the application of static control methods used by the carpet industry, some basic terms should be clarified:

1. *Conductors* are the substances that do not offer undue resistance to the flow of electrical current. Conductors vary in the amount of resistance they produce.

2. *Insulator*, or nonconductor, is a term applied to substances that offer a very high resistance to the flow of electricity. Because all conductors offer some resistance and all insulators allow some flow of electrical current, the terms "conductor" and "insulator" are relative.

3. *Resistance* of a particular substance to the flow of electricity is measured in units known as "ohms." Substances with a resistance over 10^{13} ohms are usually considered insulators. At 10^8 ohms a 250-volt system would produce a current of only 2.5 microamperes, which is far below the normal level of perception. This relation between ohms and volts is universally considered safe, and the NFPA minimum standard for conductive flooring is stated in this way:

$$\text{Voltage} = \text{current} \times \text{resistance}$$
$$250 = 2.5 \times 10^4 \text{ ohms}$$

Safety criteria established by the IBM Corporation ranges from 1.5×10^5 ohms to 2×10^{10} ohms. This range provides safety from electrical shock hazards involving flooring, furniture, and carts used in computer facilities.

The most commonly accepted carpet static test used in this country is the AATCC 134, 1975, which is entitled the "Electrostatic Propensity of Carpets." This test measures static voltage levels of people walking on a carpet in a prescribed manner, wearing prescribed shoes, and with a prescribed 20 percent relative humidity (RH) and 70°F temperature. These testing criteria represent some of the common conditions under which carpet will be used.

Human sensitivity to static shock varies widely, but 2500 to 3000 electrostatic volts [2.5 to 3 kilovolts (kv)] is considered a safe level (1000 volts = 1 kilovolts). Figure 7.3 illustrates typical static voltages generated by walking on common floorcovering materials at 50 percent relative humidity and 20 percent relative humidity. (It should be noted that as the humidity lowers the static voltage increases.) These test conditions were measured by the AATCC 134 test method with Neolite shoe soles.

Computer Sensitivity. Although the sensitivity varies according to the type of equipment, many problems occur with inadequately shielded devices. Trouble can be caused by a relatively distant spark from across the room or by static discharges that occur directly on the frame of the equipment. Many undesirable consequences can result from static sparks, such as erroneous keyboard entries, change of data in MOS memory equipment, and upsets to terminal displays. Testing has established the critical voltage levels which may affect computer systems (see Table 7.16).

Referring to Figure 7.3 one can see the importance of maintaining the temperature and relative humidity levels in computer facilities. Many computer facilities have completely self-contained environmental systems which do not circulate air from the exterior and have a separate power source in the event of a general power failure. But the problem of smaller, "mini" computer systems that are used in general office situations remains difficult to control.

Carpet Static Control Methods. Many methods are available for the control of static levels in carpeting, but the designer must determine which method will best meet the needs of a particular installation. When reviewing these various methods designers should consider the following factors:

1. Is the control method durable?

2. Will the control method function at all relative humidity levels?

3. Will the treatment attract or increase soiling?

The available methods are described below:

1. *Provide a Conductive Path from Body to Ground:* In highly critical areas, for example, where explosives are being handled, a ground for the body is often provided by ankle or wrist grounding straps, but these would not be practical in office environments. It is possible, however, to make floorcoverings electrostatically conductive. This, together with many shoe soles currently in use, can provide a reasonable means of control.

2. *Select Material with the Smallest Triboelectric Propensity:* Figure 7.2 shows that polypropylene furniture upholstery and nylon clothing are far apart on the scale and could generate high static electricity. Ideally, all contacting materials should be basically the same, as in hospital operating rooms where traditionally everyone wears cotton. This is not practical in commercial situations, but the concept should be understood in relation to carpet specification. For example, the triboelectric scale illustrates that Neolite, oak tanned leather, and PVC soles, which constitute a large part of the shoe market, are all on the negative end of the scale. Since carpet fibers, such as polyesters, acrylic, and polypropylene, are also on the same negative end of the scale, they are thought to be inherently static free. If nylon was a commonly used shoe sole material, nylon would be considered inherently static free.

3. *Coat Surface with a Triboelectric Shifter:* A common form of antistatic protection for nylon carpet consists of treating the nylon carpet with chemical materials whose triboelectric position is close to that of common shoe sole materials. This approach is effective if properly done, and the effect can be enhanced by a contamination of the shoe

TABLE 7.16 VOLTAGE EFFECTS ON COMPUTER SYSTEMS

Voltage	Effects on Computer Systems
Below 2500	Usually none
2500-4000	Occasionally
4000-6000	Frequently
Above 6000	Almost always
Above 8000	Some equipment will have physical damage
Above 10,000	Common physical damage

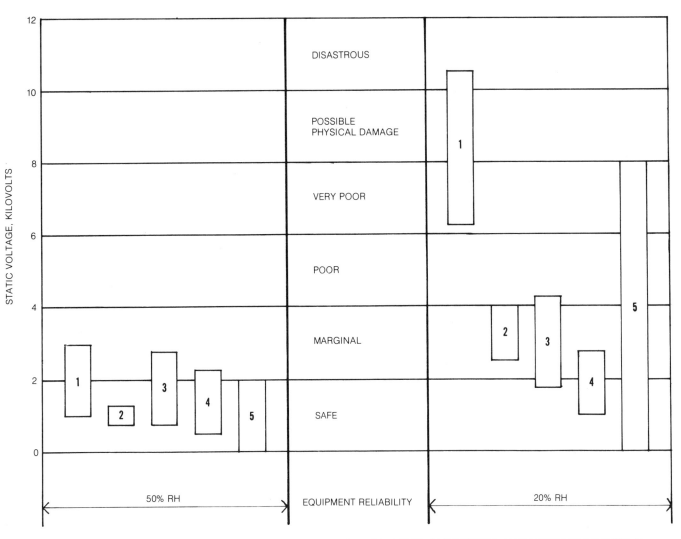

MATERIAL KEY; 1 REGULAR NYLON, 2 COMMERCIAL ANTISTATIC NYLON, 3 VINYL ASBESTOS TILE, 4 HIGH-PRESSURE LAMINATE, 5 ACRYLIC AND POLYESTER.

Figure 7.3 Typical static voltage generated by walking on common floorcovering materials.

soles with some of the chemical treatment which makes the shoe sole and the carpet even more similar electrically. These chemicals are not very durable, but are suitable for light commercial and residential use. Almost any antistatic treatment that coats the fibers will rub off on shoe soles and result in increased soiling of the carpet.

4. *Apply Electrostatically Conductive Finishes:* These finishes are generally ionic-humectant materials which attract and absorb moisture from the air and thus reduce the static electricity that is produced. This system has not proven terribly effective in very low humidity, but it tends to increase the soiling rate of carpet.

5. *Provide a Permanent Electrostatic Conductivity:* All relatively permanent antistatic systems used in carpets today employ elements in which the conductivity depends on metals or carbons. These elements may be metal fibers or polymeric fibers which have been made conductive by metal plating or carbon infusing. Metals such as copper, aluminum, and stainless steel have been successfully tufted with the fibers and woven into the backing. Carbon is infused into the core of the carpet fiber, and these carbon-infused fibers are spaced through the carpet. Each of these methods has its own particular advantage in terms of cost, manufacturing versatility, degree of static suppression, aesthetic effects, and longevity. For the exacting requirements of computer facilities and other static-sensitive areas, the carbon-infused polymeric fiber has distinct advantages. Predetermined spacing of these conductive elements throughout the carpet can be very effective. For example, a carpet with 10 conductive elements per inch, each with a resistance of 10^8 ohms/cm, will give much better static performance than a carpet with one conductive element per inch and a resistance of 1 ohm/cm. There are carpets on the market today that also employ a conductive backing in addition to the carbon-infused fibers on the surface and keep static electricity in the 2 kv range.

6. *Provide Adequate Humidity:* Static is not usually a problem in areas having a relative humidity of 50 percent or greater. Most floorcoverings generate voltage under 3 kv (regardless of shoe soles) in relative humidity of 50 percent. But it is not always possible to maintain the humidity at or near this ideal percentage. Many office areas, where mini computers are usually installed, can easily drop to 20 percent relative humidity. Other than by the installation of expensive humidification equipment, the control of humidity factors is not very reliable.

Furniture-Generated Static. The upholstery used on furniture does create electrostatic problems, but it appears that very few antistatic fabrics are specified because most designers are not aware of triboelectric factors. Authorities in the field of static control recommend that vinyls not be used on furnishings where static concerns are important.

Metal furniture is also not recommended. Wooden desks having metal trim and metal legs can be used safely with the addition of carbon on the base of the desk legs. Carbon coatings should also be specified for casters on chairs and carts that will be used in computer areas.

In summary, furniture-associated static in static sensitive areas is a problem for which there is no foolproof solution, but the problem can be minimized by avoiding plastic-coated furniture, keeping chairs as far away as possible from sensitive

equipment, and removing any piece of furniture known to be generating static electricity.

Antistatic Specification Guidelines

1. Specify carpet with a permanent method of static control. The specification should clearly state the required voltage level and the relative humidity and temperature factors.

   2500 volts at 20% relative humidity and 70°F

   These same requirements may also be stated in terms of kilovolts:

   2.5 kv at 20% RH and 70°F

   Many federal agencies specify a higher voltage level of 3000 volts, or 3 kv, which is considered the minimum safety level.

2. Carpet tiles are frequently specified for computer areas because they offer accessibility to in-floor electrical distribution systems.

3. Evaluate all ambient conditions, such as humidity, temperature controls, and type of furnishings that will be used in computer areas.

Sanitation Aspects of Carpeted Health Care Facilities.[5] For more than a decade the use of carpet in health care facilities has been a controversial subject. There have been many studies made in hospitals to establish the precise microbiological effects of carpet on the hospital environment. The results of these studies have been enlightening in terms of the tendency for carpet to serve as a dust trap and at the same time to lower bacterial counts.

Since the results of these investigations have been so universally positive in favor of carpet, the use of carpet in hospitals and nursing homes has increased significantly over the years and currently has attained an important status in the American contract market. By the mid-1970s, roughly 6 percent of the total commercial carpet produced was utilized by hospitals and nursing homes.

But before carpet was adopted, some unique problems had to be encountered: the determination of bacteria counts in carpet, estimating the probability of increased bacteria growth in carpet and the optimum cleaning and disinfecting cycles that would be required.

Bacterial Testing. Since tests were to compare the bacterial growth between resilient flooring and carpet, it was important to establish identical contamination potentials. The hospital areas to be used as test sites were carefully selected to offer varied levels of contamination. Both new and used carpet were seeded with bacteria. After an incubation period, it was found that the bacteria count had actually dropped in the first twenty-four-hour period after seeding. In all investigations where the bacteria mortality rate was categorized, it was found that carpet induced a higher mortality rate for bacteria than other surfaces such as resilient, cement, and wood flooring. Some researchers have attributed this to the catalyst containing formaldehyde used in the adhesive bonding of the carpet. While many studies found that vacuuming carpet reduced the number of bacteria present in the pile, it was found that the wet mopping process used on tile floors actually fostered pathogenic growth in dirt-clogged seams.[6]

Maintenance Factors. The fact that dust and soil are trapped in the pile of carpet would appear to be a negative factor, but because carpet serves as a dust trap it actually lowers the rate of airborne dust and bacteria. But carpet does present a unique maintenance situation in hospitals. Aside from having a porous, flexible surface, the three-dimensional construction necessitates a cleaning process for both the top and bottom levels of the pile. It has been found that carpet can be effectively disinfected by any aldehyde-containing disinfectant chemical compound when applied as a shampoo. The fact that carpet must be thoroughly saturated with this liquid compound can create problems such as drying time and carpet shrinkage.

Other Benefits of Carpet. There are several other reasons to choose carpet for hospital use:

1. The danger of slipping and falling in patient rooms and in corridors is greatly reduced. One study, conducted over an extended period of time, found that there were 17 percent fewer injuries after the installation of carpet. The direct glue-down method of installation has eliminated problems associated with the movement of wheeled carts and stretchers.

2. Research on the acoustic qualities of carpet in hospitals found that patients showed faster rates of recovery in areas free from noisy corridors, scraping chairs in adjoining rooms, and impact noise from other floors.

3. Carpet creates a noninstitutional atmosphere that promotes patient relaxation and eases tension. When patients are given the choice of a carpeted or uncarpeted room, the vast majority choose a carpeted room.

Conclusions. Summarizing the findings of the combined research indicates that the following advantages of carpet were substantiated by the majority of researchers:

1. Lower bacterial counts

2. Increased patient safety

3. Reduction in noise levels

4. Lower maintenance costs

5. Greater thermal qualities

6. Improved appearance

In spite of the merits of carpet in hospital environments, there is general agreement that several hospital areas *should not* be carpeted. These areas include operating rooms, intensive care units, utility rooms, and treatment rooms. All these areas are subject to heavy spillage, staining, and unusual soilage.

Specification Recommendations. The following critical factors should be considered when specifying carpet for health care facilities:

1. *Flammability*
   Specify that carpet has the following ratings:
   ASTM E-84, Steiner Tunnel Test, Class A
   Corridors: NFPA 253, Flooring Radiant Panel Test
   0.45 watts/cm² (unsprinklered)
   0.22 watts/cm² (sprinklered)
   Patient rooms: FF 1-70, Methenamine Pill Test

2. *Static Electricity*
   3 kv at 70°F and 20% RH

For more details on carpet construction, fibers, and installation suggestions, refer to the specification guidelines in Table 7.27

Phase 9: Traffic Classification

Before designers proceed to specify carpet padding, installation, or a maintenance program, the concept of traffic classification should be considered. The amount of wear that a floor surface will receive is calculated in the following ways:

1. The number of people who will *enter* or *leave* a given space per day following the same path as they enter or leave the space. For example, the foyers and halls of hospitals, schools, hotels, terminals, and commercial buildings receive *heavy* traffic. If this traffic is *constant*, night and day, and in addition, objects are wheeled across the floor surface, such as in hospitals and airports, then this would be considered *extra heavy* traffic.

2. The location of a space within the building also plays a part in the traffic classification. Aside from a foyer receiving heavy foot traffic, the floorcovering will be exposed to heavy soilage from tracked in dirt, mud, or water. Heavy traffic classifications should therefore include soilage and spillage factors. For example, a restaurant may not have the same amount of foot traffic as a hotel lobby, but the spillage factors would necessitate a classification in the heavy category.

Traffic classification is, to a large extent, judgmental on the part of the designer. Figure 7.4, provided by Monsanto Textiles Company, illustrates traffic classifications used to determine carpet requirements.

Phase 10: Criteria for Padding Selection

There are many reasons for specifying carpet cushioning.

1. *Acoustic qualities:* The Noise Reduction Coefficiencies which were discussed in Phase 8 illustrate that carpet padding is effective in substantially reducing airborne and impact noise. An evaluation of the other acoustic components that will be used in the space will indicate the amount of NRC the carpet padding should produce.

2. *Service life requirements:* The life span of a carpet can be extended by the addition of a padding underlay which may prevent (a) loss of thickness due to abrasion, (b) fraying and cutting of fibers by grinding action of embedded dirt, (c) pile crushing and packing. Carpet padding also increases the effectiveness of vacuuming processes by providing air circulation throughout the entire carpet structure.

3. *Thermal qualities:* The overall thermal environment will be improved by the heat transfer and insulating qualities of carpet padding.

4. *Installation factors:* Padding can often make installation less costly because it allows carpet to be installed over less than perfect surfaces without extensive repairs. Cracks, blow holes, and trowel marks will not be evident on the surface of the carpet that has a padding underlay.

There are four major categories of carpet padding available for

TABLE 7.17 TESTS SUMMARY OF CARPET PERFORMANCE ATTRIBUTES

Attribute	Tests	Minimal Federal Performance Requirements*
1. Flammability		
a. Flame spread	ASTM E 84	Flame spread <75 unsprinklered
	NFPA 255	Flame spread ≤200 sprinklered
	UL 992	Flame spread 4.0 unsprinklered
		Flame spread 8.0 sprinklered
b. Surface flamma-bility ignition	DCC-FF1-70	Charred portion not to exceed
	DDD-C-95(Rev)	within 2.54 cm (1.0″) of frame
	ASTM 2859-70T	edge
	DOC-FF 2-70	
c. Flooring radiant panel test	ASTM E-162-67	Commercial—0.22W/cm² (unsp)
	NBS IR-75-950	FF-1 70 (w/sp)
	NFPA 253	Health care—0.45W/cm² (unsp)
		0.22 w/cm(w/sp)
d. Smoke	NBS 708	Specific op density = 450/critical
	NFPA A 258/1976	16 @ 90 sec
2. Acoustics		
a. Airborne sound	ASTM C 423	SPP ≥60 in OPP/SPP ≥70 in RM
	PBS C.1	NIC′ + (NC 40) ≥60 in OPP
		NIC′ + (NC ≤35) ≥70 in RM
b. Impact sound	ASTM C 423-66	Mask vertical footfall with NC ≤
	PBS C.2	40
3. Colorfastness		
a. To light	AATCC 16E-1971	Rating of 4.0
b. To gas	AATCC 23-1972	Rating of 4.0
c. To ozone	AATCC 109-1972	Rating of 3.0
d. Crocking (W/D)	AATCC 8-1972	Rating of 4.0
e. Shampooing	AATCC 138-1972	Rating of 4.0
4. Electrostatic	AATCC 134-1975	Static level 3KV
5. Light reflectance	ASTM E 97	No more than 5%
	IES Transaction 33. P .378-1938	Not to exceed 15%
6. Azotic control	AATCC 112/30/90 100/103	High antibacterial level
7. Physical strength		
a. Tuft bind	ASTM D 1335-67 DD C 0095A	7 lb
b. Delamination	FTMS 191-5100†	Withstand wheel load of 1500 lb
c. Breaking	FTMS 191-5100	Withstand at least 100 lb
d. Shrinkage	DOC C 0095 A	Not to exceed 5% in any direction
8. Appearance		
a. Pilling/fuz	Dupont TRL 609	≥4.0
b. Stain resistant	PBS-F.2	No noticeable stain
c. Crush resistant	FTMS 501A/3231	85% recovery
d. Abrasion	ASTM D 1175 641 (Taber)	6000-8000 cycles

*Required by majority of federal agencies.
†FTMS—Federal Test Method Standard.

(L-M) denotes light-medium traffic
(H) denotes heavy traffic

CARPETED AREAS	TRAFFIC RATING
EDUCATIONAL+	
1. Schools & Colleges	
a. administration	L-M
b. classroom	H
c. dormitory	H
d. corridor	H*
e. cafeteria	H
f. libraries	L-M
2. Museums & Art Galleries	
a. display room	H
b. executive	L-M
c. lobby	H
MEDICAL+	
1. Health Care	
a. executive	L-M
b. patients room	H
c. lounge	H
d. nurses station	H
e. corridor	H*
f. lobby	H
COMMERCIAL+	
1. Banks	
a. executive	L-M
b. lobby	H
c. teller windows	H
d. corridors	H*
2. Retail Establishments	
a. aisle	H*
b. check-out	H
c. sales counter	H
d. smaller boutiques, etc.	H
e. window & display area	L-M
3. Office Buildings	
a. executive	L-M
b. clerical	H
c. corridor	H*
d. cafeteria	H
4. Supermarkets	H
5. Food Services	H
RECREATIONAL+	
1. Recreation Areas	H
a. club house	H
b. locker room	H
c. swimming pool	H
d. recreational vehicles	H
e. boats	H
2. Theaters & Stadiums (Indoors)	H
3. Convention Centers	
a. auditorium	H
b. corridor	H*
c. lobby	H
TRANSPORTATION+	
1. Terminals	
a. corridor	H*
b. administration	L-M
c. ticket counter	H
MULTI-RESIDENTIAL+	
1. Apartments, Hotels & Motels	
a. lobby/public areas	H*
b. corridors	H
c. rooms	L-M
RELIGIOUS+	
1. Churches/Temples	
a. worship	L-M
b. meeting room	H
c. lobby	H

+Major Construction Categories
*If objects are to be rolled over an area of carpet, the carpet should be of maximum density to provide minimum resistance to rollers. For safety, select only level loop or low, level dense cut pile.

Figure 7.4 Traffic classification. Reproduced with permission of Monsanto Textiles Co.

use by designers.[7] Each type may present slightly different qualities in regard to the amount of firmness provided, and the acoustic factors may also vary. For example, sponge rubber was found to have better acoustic qualities than a hair-jute pad when tested for impact sound transmission. Though installation requirements will vary, one of the four padding types will probably meet specification needs.

Felt. There are four types of felt padding:

Hair felt made of 100 percent animal hair.

Combination felt made of animal hair mixed with other fibers.

Fiber felt composed of 100 percent fibers.

Rubberized felt refers to any of the above which has a rubberized coating on one or both sides.

Performance Qualities. Felt offers a very firm, dense cushion which performs well in heavy, moderate, and light traffic classifications.

Manufacturing Process. Felt cushion is manufactured by garnetting the material, lapping, and needle punching through a substrate to form a dense heavy cushioning. Many federal specifications require that the animal hair shall be predominantly from washed cattle hair, which shall be the main fiber of the felt, but not to the exclusion of other fibers. The fiber content of all felt shall not be less than 90 percent cattle hair, except for the core material. Up to 9 percent adhesive is permitted for binding the interliner material. The animal hair shall be cleaned, washed, and sterilized by thorough drying and shall be free of loading materials and foreign matter. Rubberized jute and rubberized animal hair cushions shall be of needle-punched construction. A rubber coating shall be applied to both faces of the cushion. The rubber used may be either foamed or unfoamed rubber made from natural, reclaimed, or synthetic rubber. Rubber should not readily peel off when rubbed with fingers at a normal pressure.[8]

Widths. Available in widths up to 12 ft (3.7 m).

Weights. The grade of the carpet cushion is determined by weight per square yard. Felt is available in weights from 32 oz (995 g) to 86 oz (2,674 g) per square yard.

Sponge Rubber. Two types of sponge rubber padding will be discussed:

Flat sponge with a smooth or flat surface.

Waffled sponge with a rippled or waffle surface.

Performance Qualities. Sponge rubber will provide a degree of firmness depending on the formulation of the sponge and waffle pattern. Flat sponge is recommended for heavy traffic classification.

Manufacturing Process. Sponge rubber cushions are manufactured by combining natural and/or synthetic rubber with other chemicals, oils, and fillers in a pulverizing operation. Blowing and curing agents are then added to the compound. Flat sponge rubber is formed and expanded into a continuous sheet. Waffled sponge rubber is allowed to form and expand on a chain belt to achieve the desired waffled configuration. Both types have a synthetic fiber facing material laminated to the top side so conventional carpet products may readily slide across the rubber surface and allow stretching of the carpet during installation.

Widths. Sponge rubber is available in widths to 12 ft (3.7 m) in various wall lengths.

Weights/Thickness. Flat sponge rubber is available in thicknesses from 1/16 in. (1.6 mm), 1/8 in. (3 mm), to 5/16 in. (8 mm). Weights range from 41 oz (1,275 g) to 120 oz (3,732 g) per square yard. Waffled sponge is normally specified in terms of thickness.

Urethane Foam. Three types of urethane foam padding will be considered:

Prime urethane foam

Densified prime urethane foam

Bonded urethane foam

Performance Qualities. This is a light-weight cushion which can provide a degree of firmness depending on the resiliency achieved in manufacturing. It may be used in heavy-, medium-, or light-weight traffic.

Manufacturing Process. Each type of urethane foam discussed below is manufactured differently:

1. *Prime urethane foam* is manufactured by a chemical mixing process of polymeric materials. The foam is cut into continuous sheets of cushion and a facing is applied to one side.

2. *Densified prime urethane foam* is produced through a modified cell structure. Density is varied by controlling the cellular configuration. The foam is poured in large bins of devised density and slit into desired thicknesses to produce continuous rolls. A facing material is applied to one side.

3. *Bonded urethane foam* is manufactured from trimmed waste material left over from the manufacture of prime urethane. It is then granulated and bonded together through a compression and curing process into blocks, sheets, or rolls. Federal specifications will not allow fillers other than prime urethane. Designers should be aware that some quality of bonded foam may be composed of additives such as impregnated vinyl, fabric-backed foams, and foreign materials such as dirt, wood chips, and paper. No more than 1 percent debris should be permitted. The prime urethane should be ground or shredded to a particle size not exceeding 1/2 in. (12.7 mm). Coloring matter may be added, but the color should not bleed or cause any unsatisfactory performance of the padding or the carpet.

Widths. Urethane foams are available in 12 ft (3.7 m) widths and various roll lengths.

Weights/Thickness. Each type of urethane foam is specified by a different density and thickness:

1. Prime: Specified by density [pounds per cubic foot or ounces per square yard (kilograms per cubic meters or grams per square meters)]. Available in densities from 1.3

lb (.6 kg) to 6 lb (2.8 kg) per cu ft. Thickness varies from 1/4 in. (6.4 mm) to 3/4 in. (19.1 mm).

2. Densified prime: Specified by density averaging from 2.7 lb (1.2 kg) to 6 lb (2.8 kg) per cu ft. Thickness varies from .250 to .750 in. (6.4 to 19.1 mm).

3. Bonded: Density from 4 lb (1.8 kg) to 10 lb (4.6 kg) per cu ft. Thickness varies from 5/16 in. (7.9 mm) to 3/4 in. (19.1 mm).

Foam Rubber. This type of padding has the following characteristics:

Performance Quality. Foam rubber is a medium-weight padding that provides a degree of firmness under foot.

Manufacturing Process. It is manufactured from a latex rubber base, which can be natural, synthetic, or blended with additives to increase the cushioning and physical properties. Manufactured in flat sheets with a backing applied to one side.

Widths. Available in widths to 12 ft (3.7 m) in rolls of various lengths.

Weights. Available in weights from 28 oz (902 g) to 65 oz (1,800 g) per square yard. Thickness varies from 1/8 in. (3.2 mm) to 5/8 in. (15.9 mm).

Performance Testing for Carpet Padding. Designers should be aware that carpet padding is subject to standard flammability testing; several federal test methods standards have been established to evaluate physical performance.

Flammability. There are two tests to measure the flammability of carpet padding:

DOC FF 1-70 or DOC FF 2-70

ASTM E-84

Physical Performance Tests. These tests are covered under Federal Test Method Standards. The exact test methods used can be obtained in HUD and FHA Standard UM 72, 1979.

Weight	FTMS 191, Method 5040, 5041
Thickness	FTMS 601, Method 12031
	FTMS 191, Method 5030
Deflection	FTMS 601, Method 12151
	ASTM D-3574
	LC 001369
Compression	FTMS 601, Method 12131
Tensile strength	FTMS 601, Method 5100

Carpet Padding Specification Checklist. When specifying carpet padding the following physical aspects should be required:

1. Length	When definite length is specified, the delivered cushion shall not vary more than 1 percent.
2. Width	Width shall not vary more than 1 in. (2.5 cm).
3. Weight	Weight shall be as stated by manufacturer (within 5 percent). If weight exceeds 5 percent, it is not considered a defect.
4. Cuts/holes/tears	Holes and tears shall not exceed 1/2 in. (1.3 cm).
5. Lumps/high spots	The padding shall be free of lumps or high spots.
6. Thin or weak spots	The padding shall be free of these defects.
7. Imbedded or protruding foreign matter	This is considered a defect.
8. Seams	Seams shall be intact and smooth.
9. Edges	Padding edges shall be straight, parallel, and square.
10. Surfaces	All padding surfaces shall be flat and parallel.
11. Facing	Facing shall be as specified. Facing shall cover 98 percent of the surface area and not be tacky, nor have any loose areas. Facing shall be nonpeeling.

Padding Installation. Carpet cushion should be installed in the largest possible lengths with a minimum number of sections. Cushion should be placed flush with the edges of the tackless strips and installed with the scrim side facing upward. A slight stretch is required to flatten the wrinkles from the cushion.

Subfloors. When cushion is installed over concrete subfloors, it must be securely adhered to the subfloor with a cushion cement to prevent shifting. Cushion installed over wood floors may be stapled in place.

Seams. Cushion seams should be planned to prevent them from occurring directly under carpet seams. Sponge or foam cushion seams should be taped with a 2-in. (5.1-cm) wide nonpaper tape.

Recommended Carpet Cushion Weight. Designers frequently overspecify carpet cushion weights in commercial and institutional installations. Unlike residential installations that stress plushness, commercial carpet usually requires a firm cushion foundation because of the intense wear the carpet will receive. A cushion with excessive vertical displacement, such as waffled or rippled sponge rubber, places a strain on the carpet backing. This can result in accelerated wear and may necessitate restretching the carpet in areas that receive heavy traffic. Table 7.18 lists recommended cushion weights for medium and heavy traffic.

Phase 11: Estimating Yardage Requirements

Estimating the initial cost of carpet often involves a preliminary cost estimate before the project drawings are finalized. This can be accomplished by totaling the square feet of floor space to be carpeted. Because carpet is sold by the square yard, the square footage must be converted to square yards. Table 7.19 presents conversions in even numbers as a quick refer-

TABLE 7.18 DETACHED CARPET PADDING PERFORMANCE

Type	Class	Characteristics	Class 1‡	Class 2§	Test Method
1. Felt	a. Uncoated animal hair	Weight, oz/sq yd, min.	40.0 −5%	50.0 −5%	FTMS 191, Method 5040 or 5041
		Thickness, in., min.	0.25	0.375	FTMS 191, Method 5030
		Compression set, %, max.	15	15	FTMS 601, Method 12131
		CLD, 25% defl., psi, min.	30	30	FTMS 191, Method 5100
		Flammability*	Pass	Pass	DOC FF 1-70
			75 or less	75 or less	ASTM E-84
	b. Rubberized animal hair/jute	Weight, oz/sq yd, min.	40.0 −5%	50.0 −5%	FTMS 191, Method 5040 or 5041
		Thickness, in., min.	0.27	0.375	FTMS 191, Method 5030
		Compression set, %, max.	15	15	FTMS 601, Method 12131
		CLD, 25% defl., psi, min.	30	30	FTMS 191, Method 5100
		Flammability*	Pass	Pass	DOC FF 1-70
			75 or less	75 or less	ASTM E-84
2. Cellular rubber	a. Rippled	Weight, oz/sq yd, min.	48.0 −5%	64.0 −5%	FTMS 191, Method 5040 or 5041
		Thickness, in., min.	0.30	0.40	FTMS 601, Method 12031
		CLD, 25% defl., psi, min.	0.615	0.875	FTMS 601, Method 12151
		Compression set, %, max. @ 50% deflection	15	15	FTMS 601, Method 12131
		Tensile strength, psi, min.	8	8	FTMS 191, Method 5100
		Flammability*	Pass	Pass	DOC FF 1-70
			75 or less	75 or less	ASTM E-84
	b. Flat sponge	Weight, oz/sq yd, min.	56.0 −5%	64.0 −5%	FTMS 191, Method 5040 or 5041
		Thickness, in., min.	0.250	0.250	FTMS 601, Method 12031
		CLD, 25% defl., psi, min.	0.75	1.5	FTMS 601, Method 12131
		Compression set, %, max. @ 50% deflection	10	10	FTMS 601, Method 12131
		Tensile strength, psi, min.	8	8	FTMS 191, Method 5100
		Flammability*	Pass	Pass	DOC FF 1-70
			75 or less	75 or less	ASTM E-84
	c. Latex foam	Weight, oz/sq yd, min.	38.0 −5%	46.0 −5%	FTMS 191, Method 5040 or 5041
		Thickness, in., min.	0.25	0.25	FTMS 601, Method 12031
		CLD, 25% defl., psi, min.	1.0	2.0	ASTM D 1564
		Compression set, %, max. @ 50% deflection	15	15	FTMS 601, Method 12131
		Tensile strength, psi, min.	8	8	FTMS 191, Method 5100
		Flammability*	Pass	Pass	DOC FF 1-70
			75 or less	75 or less	ASTM E-84
3. Urethane foam	a. Prime	Density, lb/ft^3, min.†	2.2 −5%	3.0 −5%	ASTM D 3574
		Thickness, in., min.	0.375	0.375	ASTM D 3574
		CLD, 65% defl., psi, min.	0.7	1.0	ASTM D 3574
		Compression set, %, max. @ 50% deflection	15	15	ASTM D 3574
		Tensile strength, psi, min.	10	10	ASTM D 3574
		Fatigue height loss, max.	5.0	5.0	ASTM 1564
		Load deflection loss & max.	25.0	25.0	ASTM 1564
		Elongation, %, min.	100	100	ASTM D 3574
		Flammability*	Pass	Pass	DOC F 1-70
			75 or less	75 or less	ASTM E-84
	b. Densified	Density, lb/ft^3, min.†	2.2 −5%	3.0 −5%	ASTM D 3574
		Thickness, in., min.	0.313	0.25	ASTM D 3574
		CLD, 65% defl., psi, min.	0.85	1.30	ASTM D 3574
		Compression set, %, max. @ 50% deflection	10	10	ASTM D 3574
		Tensile strength, psi, min.	17	20	ASTM D 3574
		Elongation, %, min.	100	100	ASTM D 3574
		Flammability*	Pass	Pass	DOC F 1-70
			75 or less	75 or less	ASTM E-84
	c. Grafted and modified	Density, lb/ft^3, min.†	2.2 −5%	2.7 −5%	ASTM D 3574
		Thickness, in., min.	0.375	0.25	ASTM D 3574
		CLD, 65% defl., psi, min.	0.85	1.30	ASTM D 3574
		Compression set, %, max. @ 50% defelction	15	15	ASTM D 3574
		Tensile strength, psi, min.	12	17	ASTM D 3574
		Elongation, %, min.	100	100	ASTM D 3574
		Flammability*	Pass	Pass	DOC FF 1-70
			75 or less	75 or less	ASTM E-84
	d. Bonded	Density, lb/ft^3, min.†	5.0 −5%	6.5 −5%	L-C-001369
		Thickness, in., min.	0.375	0.375	L-C-001369
		CLD, 65% defl., psi, min.	4.0	5.0	L-C-001369
		Compression set, %, max. @ 50% deflection	15	15	L-C-001369
		Tensile strength, psi, min.	5	7	L-C-001369
		Elongation, %, min.	45	45	L-C-001369
		Particle size, in., max.	0.50	0.50	L-C-001369
		Debris	1%	1%	See Section 4, Type III d
		Flammability*	Pass	Pass	DOC FF 1-70
			75 or less	75 or less	ASTM E-84

*Either test may be used for compliance; in DOC FF 1-70 the laundering requirement does not apply.

†Apparent density will be corrected to urethane polymer density by performing the following test: Ash content, %, as determined in ASTM D 297, subtracted from 100%, and multiplied by apparent density, shall equal the minimum values listed in the above table.

‡Medium-light traffic.

§ Heavy traffic.

Source: HUD Standard for Detached Carpet Padding UM 72-1979.

TABLE 7.19 CARPET: SQUARE FEET TO SQUARE METERS CONVERSION TABLE

Ft^2	Yd^2	M^2	Ft^2	Yd^2	M^2	Ft^2	Yd^2	M^2
50	5.6	4.5	310	34.4	27.9	570	63.3	51.3
60	6.7	5.4	320	35.6	28.8	580	64.4	52.2
70	7.8	6.3	330	36.7	29.7	590	65.6	53.1
80	8.9	7.2	340	37.8	30.6	600	66.7	54.0
90	10.0	8.1	350	38.9	31.5	700	77.8	63.0
100	11.1	9.0	360	40.0	32.4	800	88.9	72.0
110	12.2	9.9	370	41.1	33.3	900	100.0	81.0
120	13.3	10.8	380	42.2	34.2	1,000	111.1	90.0
130	14.4	11.7	390	43.3	35.1	2,000	222.2	180.0
140	15.6	12.6	400	44.4	36.0	3,000	333.3	270.0
150	16.7	13.5	410	45.6	36.9	4,000	444.4	360.0
160	17.8	14.4	420	46.7	37.8	5,000	555.5	450.0
170	18.9	15.3	430	47.8	38.7	6,000	666.7	540.0
180	20.0	16.2	440	48.9	39.6	7,000	777.8	630.0
190	21.1	17.1	450	50.0	40.5	8,000	888.9	720.0
200	22.2	18.0	460	51.1	41.4	9,000	1,000.0	810.0
210	23.3	18.9	470	52.2	42.3	10,000	1,111.1	900.0
220	24.4	19.8	480	53.3	43.2	20,000	2,222.2	1,800.0
230	25.6	20.7	490	54.4	44.1	30,000	3,333.3	2,700.0
240	26.7	21.6	500	55.6	45.0	40,000	4,444.4	3,600.0
250	27.8	22.5	510	56.7	45.9	50,000	5,555.5	4,500.0
260	28.9	23.4	520	57.8	46.8	60,000	6,666.7	5,400.0
270	30.0	24.3	530	58.9	47.7	70,000	7,777.8	6,300.0
280	31.1	25.2	540	60.0	48.6	80,000	8,888.9	7,200.0
290	32.2	26.1	550	61.1	49.5	90,000	10,000.0	8,100.0
300	33.3	27.0	560	62.2	50.4	100,000	11,111.1	9,000.0

TABLE 7.20 CARPET SQUARE FEET CONVERSION

Ft^2		Yd^2		M^2
5000	=	555.5	=	450.0
600	=	66.7	=	54.0
50	=	5.6	=	4.5
5650	=	627.8	=	508.5

ence. Uneven amounts may also be determined from this table. Square feet may be converted to square meters by following the process shown in Table 7.20.

Any estimate based on project drawings must be considered preliminary because of the variances that may occur during the building process. Accurate measurements of the actual spaces must be made immediately prior to installation.

Measurement Techniques. Although designers frequently rely on the carpet contractor's expertise in matters of measurements and yardage estimates, the designer should understand measurement techniques and other factors that influence the total yardage requirements, such as carpet width, nap direction, and placement of seams.

Carpet measurements require that careful notations be made regarding projections, doorways, columns, and risers that will involve carpet cutting or seaming. To prevent miscalculations during installation, measurements are written without the foot (') or inch (") symbols, i.e., 4'6" is written 4⁶. Carpet measurements should extend 3 to 4 in. within each doorway to allow seam placement directly beneath the closed door. All doorways or openings leading to adjoining areas that may or may not be carpeted should be clearly labeled (see Figure 7.5).

Even during the most careful construction procedures, areas may not be squared; i.e., parallel walls may not be parallel. To check the squareness of a room the following method may be used:

Step 1: Starting at one corner of the room, point A, measure 3 ft along wall AB and mark this distance X (Figure 7.6a).

Step 2: Attach a chalkline at point X and extend it 5 ft and attach it to wall AD. Mark the point at which it intercepts with a Y (Figure 7.6b).

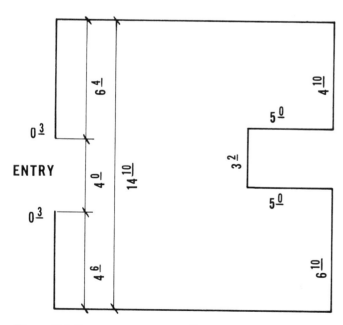

Figure 7.5 Carpet measurement diagram.

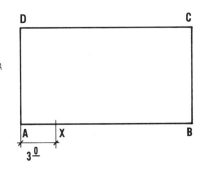

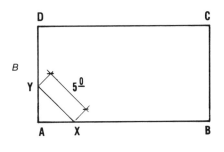

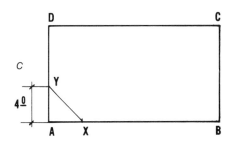

Figure 7.6 Measuring for squareness.

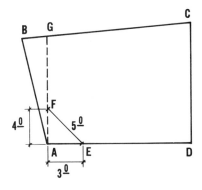

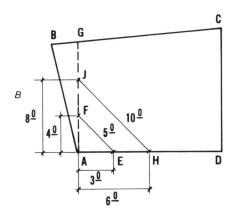

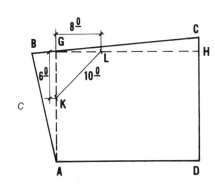

Figure 7.7 Measurement of irregular rooms.

Step 3: If the point between A and Y measures 4 ft in length, the corner may be considered square. If this measurement is more or less than the required 4 ft, then it can be assumed that one or both adjoining walls are not right-angled. This is commonly known as the "3-4-5 geometric method"[9] (Figure 7.6c).

Irregular-Shaped Areas. Many commercial installations involve complicated irregular shapes. To determine the required carpet yardage the area must be squared. The 3-4-5 method may be used to establish a right angle.

Starting in one angled corner, attach a chalkline from A through F to the opposite wall BC, establishing point G (Figure 7.7a). This results in a right angle between DAG.

The accuracy of the right angle DAG can be further verified by the use of a multiple such as 6-8-10 to establish point J on the AG line (Figure 7.7b).

To establish two additional right angle corners, the same 3-4-5 method is used from point G to point M along line CD. These corners may also be verified by the 6-8-10 method.

The remaining triangles of space may then be measured to determine the additional carpet needed for these irregular shapes[10] (Figure 7.7c).

Stairs. Two methods are used to carpet stairs. The cap and band method uses one piece of carpet for the riser area (D to E) and another carpet piece from the crotch (C) over the tread and lip (D). The second method employs one continuous piece of carpet and is known as the "waterfall" installation. The carpet is attached in the crotch area of the stairs (points A and B). (See Figure 7.8.)

Hanging or suspended stairs are usually carpeted completely around both sides. A wraparound measurement is made to determine the carpet yardage. An additional 3 in. should be allowed on the length and width measurements for seaming (Figure 7.9).

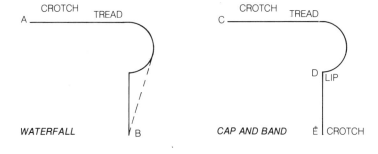

Figure 7.8 Stair installation methods.

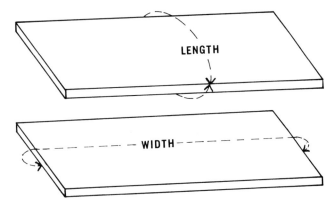

Figure 7.9 Suspended stair measurement.

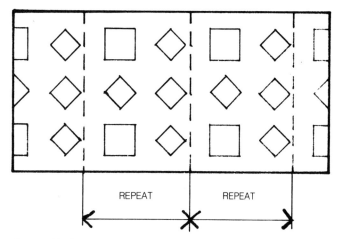

Figure 7.10 Set match pattern.

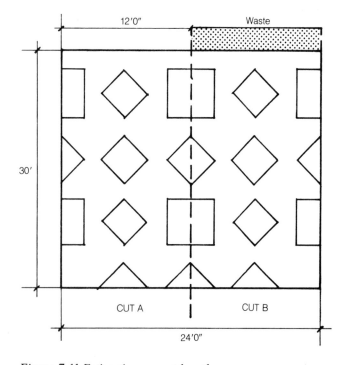

Figure 7.11 Estimating repeat length.

Patterned Carpets. Patterned carpets are composed of designs that are repeated at regular intervals in the length and width of the carpet. When the carpet is installed it must be side matched for perfect pattern continuity. Estimating the yardage needed for patterned carpets requires an understanding of the process of matching pattern repeats. A *repeat* is the distance from one design pattern motif to the next identical design pattern motif along the length of the carpet. Repeats may vary from 3 in. to 6 ft in length, and the size of the repeat determines the additional amount of carpet that will be required to match the repeats when carpet cut lengths are installed side by side.

The three major types of patterns produced in carpet today are the set match, the drop match, and the quarter drop match:

Set Match Pattern. This is composed of designs that are positioned or *set* side by side on the same level to form a straight line across the width of the carpet (see Figure 7.10). In estimating for a set match pattern always measure the matching pieces to be cut at the next highest multiple of the repeat length. For example, estimate for carpet 12′ in width with a set match pattern repeat measuring 3′ in length to be used in an area 24′ × 33′ (cut A) and a second area measuring 12′ × 33′ (cut B). A length of 33′ is the next highest multiple of 3′ over the required 30′ length that will allow for matching the pattern (Figure 7.11).

Drop Match Patterns. These patterns are such that every other repeat is dropped down one half its length to produce a diagonal match of patterns across the width of the carpet (see Figure 7.12). This design matches diagonally either up or down on half the length of the repeat or may be matched on the multiple of the repeat. This means that the carpet may be matched in the following ways:

1. Multiples of the repeat plus one-half of one repeat. Example: A drop match with a 3′ repeat could be side matched every 4′6″ (one repeat plus one-half repeat).

2. Multiples of the repeat only (depending on the length of the carpet and the number of widths required). Example: A drop match with a 3′ repeat could be matched every 9′ (three multiples) or every 10′6″ which would be three multiples plus one-half repeat.[11]

Quarter Drop Match Patterns. These are usually found in 27-in. width woven carpets. This pattern is made up of four blocks in every length repeat. Each repeat drops one block or one-quarter block of the repeat as shown in Figure 7.13. There are three methods used to accomplish a side match.

1. Multiples of the repeat plus one-quarter of a repeat. Example: If the repeat is 3′ in length one would estimate a side match in one multiple (3′) plus one-quarter of the repeat (9″) for a total of 3′9″.

2. Based on the same 3′ repeat, a second method would employ one multiple plus one-half of a repeat (3′ plus 18″).

3. A third method makes use of one multiple plus three-quarters of the 3′ repeat (3′ plus 27″).[12]

General Guidelines for Estimating and Specifying Patterned Carpet. The following points should be considered:

1. Obtain manufacturer's recommendations for the installation of patterned carpet.

2. When designing a custom patterned carpet, consult with the manufacturer regarding the pattern and repeat size that would be feasible in the proposed installation space.

3. Obtain the services of a carpet contractor who is experienced in the installation of patterned carpet. Visit several installations completed by the contractor under consideration.

Carpet Nap. Carpet nap refers to the carpet pile and the direction the pile tends to slant or lie (see Figure 7.14). The direction from which the nap is viewed affects the way in which the color is perceived (i.e., nap direction tends to produce shading effects). Looking into the nap tends to make the carpet look darker. Nap should be considered on stair and floor installations as follows:

Stairs. Carpet should always be installed with the nap running downward on the stairs. Aside from providing a more pleasing visual effect, this also provides longer wear. An exception is when a patterned carpet has an upward directional design, the pattern should point up the stairs.

Floors. Pile nap should run in the same direction; i.e., carpet cuts and side matches should be installed with the nap running in the same direction. If a carpet section is installed at a right angle to another section, the directional change and the seam will be obvious. When contractors submit seaming charts, the nap direction of each carpet section should be indicated.

Carpet Seam Placement. The placement of the carpet seams is perhaps one of the most important factors to consider in measuring and installation. The following guidelines should be followed in seam placement:

1. Avoid seam placement at pivot points where people using the space will change walking directions, e.g., in front of office equipment such as copy machines or near elevators.

2. Avoid seams that run across areas that receive heavy foot traffic, such as halls, meeting rooms, and reception rooms.

3. Do not plan seams that will run directly into a doorway, although seams placed horizontally across a doorway are sometimes unavoidable.

4. Request that carpet contractors submit a seaming diagram prior to installation. Seaming plan A shown in Figure 7.15 illustrates a good seam placement between cut A and B, but the nap direction of cut B will not create a good installation. The placement of the carpet seam between cut A and B in plan B runs directly into the doorway and also cuts across a direct traffic area.

5. Do not attempt to save on seaming or carpet by allowing carpet widths to be mixed. Carpet from a different roll width may also be from a different dye lot and vary in color.

Carpet padding is usually estimated in the same quantity as the carpet.

Phase 12: Installation Criteria
Each carpet manufacturer provides specific installation recommendations for his particular products; therefore, the information contained in this section is based on general recommendations provided by authorities in the industry.[13] Be-

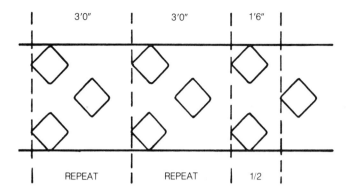

Figure 7.12 Drop match pattern.

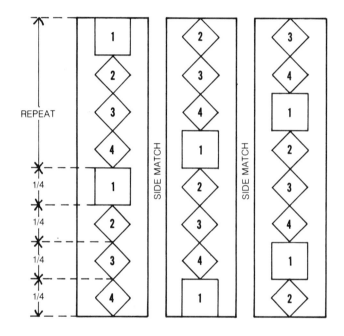

Figure 7.13 Quarter drop match.

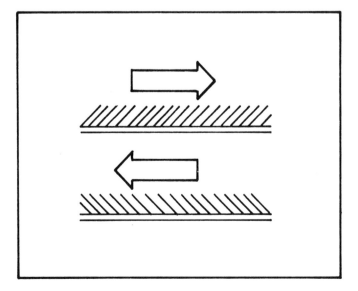

Figure 7.14 Carpet nap direction.

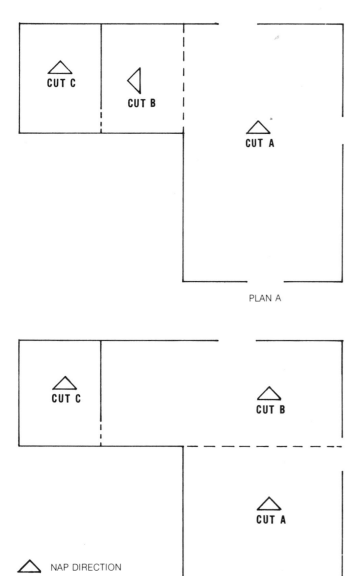

PLAN A

PLAN B

△ NAP DIRECTION

--- CARPET SEAM

Figure 7.15 Carpet seaming diagram.

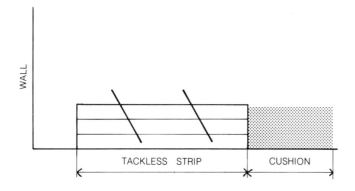

Figure 7.16 Tackless strip installation.

cause carpet specification documents contain installation instructions, designers should be familiar with installation terminology regarding the two basic methods of installation in use today: (1) carpet stretched over padding (tackless strip) and (2) direct glue-down.

Tackless Strip Installation. This method of installation involves *stretching* a carpet over a large area and attaching it with tackless strips. Tackless strips are made of water-resistant 3-ply plywood strips varying in thickness from 9/32 in. (7.1 mm) to 3/8 in. (9.5 mm). Strips are usually 1 1/2 in. (38.1 mm) wide and available in 4-ft (1.22-mm) lengths. These plywood strips contain two or three rows of angular rust-resistant pins positioned at a 60° angle and are long enough to penetrate through the carpet backing and provide a firm attachment. In commercial installations involving over 500 sq ft (46.5 m²), three rows of pins are usually specified (see Figure 7.16).

Tackless strips are installed around the perimeter of the area to be covered by carpet and are fastened to the floor a distance from the wall that is equivalent to about two-thirds of the carpet's thickness. Methods of securing the tackless strips to the floor surface depend, to a large extent, on the type of flooring involved:

Wood Floors	Strips may be attached with nails spaced close enough to assure holding power.
Cement Floors	Three methods may be used: 1. Adhesive applied according to the manufacturer's recommendations. 2. Drill and plug method 3. Nailing
Radiant-Heated Floors	Tackless strips usually attached with adhesive. Drill and plug or nailing method should only be used if pipe locations are known.

Tackless strip estimation is usually calculated at 2 1/2 linear feet of tackless strip for each square yard of carpet. Ten percent should be added for waste.

Seaming Methods. Although most carpets are produced in 12-ft (3.6-m) widths, almost every installation will involve seams. Three methods may be used to obtain a tight seam that will withstand the forces of stretching during the installation process as well as normal wear during the life of the carpet. It is recommended that carpet seams have a breaking strength of not less than 100 lb (46 kg).

Hand Sewing. This method requires skill and special equipment, such as curved needles for certain types of seams. Sewing should be done with a suitable carpet thread, such as a number 18 linen, and the completed seams should be ironed and coated with a latex adhesive to assure a flat seam. Hand sewing may not be feasible on some types of carpet construction, i.e., heavily sized backings, tightly woven carpets, and carpets having a double jute backing. Because this is a rather slow process, it is not used as frequently now as in the past.

Hot Melt Tape. A taped seam produces a flat, almost invisible seam that is very strong. This method makes use of a tape that is surfaced with an adhesive that bonds the carpet seams together when activated by heat. A small heating device (an iron) capable of reaching 425°F (218°C) is used to apply the tape. The Technical Services Department of Burlington's Carpet Division makes the following recommendations regarding the use of the hot melt tape method:

1. This method should only be used on fabrics for which it is recommended.

2. Seams should always be pretacked and fitted before the tape is applied.

3. The seam should be allowed to cool for at least ten minutes prior to stretching.

4. Tape should not be used on carpets containing yarns with a low melting point, a rubber or heavily latexed back, or a double-backed carpet where the secondary backing adhesion is not known.

5. This method is not recommended for use in conjunction with foam or sponge rubber underlays because they do not "accept" the tape; i.e., the seams become noticeable. Felt padding is recommended for a flat, less visible seam.[14]

Latex Tape. This method is very similar to the hot melt tape method except that latex becomes the binding agent that holds the seams together. A tape 2.5 in. (6.4 cm) wide is used at the back of the seam.

Carpet Stretching Methods. Occasionally designers are faced with a complaint about a carpet installation that may involve a stretching problem; i.e., the carpet is puckering or buckling due to expansion. A few weeks after completing a hotel lobby installation, one designer concluded that if the carpet expanded any further he would have enough extra carpet for an additional lobby. Improper stretching and changes in the temperature and humidity are all possible causes of the problem. The use of a carpet with a very heavy and dimensionally sound backing will not ensure against expansion, nor will the apparent tautness at the time of installation. Only stretching to the recommended "percent of stretch" in the warp (length) and filling (width) directions will prevent excessive expansion.

When specifying carpet, the designer should require the manufacturer to supply information on the amount of stretch in both the warp and filling directions. Because the carpet construction and the amount of lamination applied to the backing vary with each manufacturer and each carpet type, a different percent of stretch will be required for each carpet specified. For example, carpet with synthetic secondary backings usually requires extra taut stretching when installed over padding and the amount of stretch is usually 1 1/2 to 3 in. per every 12 ft (3.8 cm to 7.6 cm per every 3.6 m).

The information and percentage conversions in Table 7.21 were compiled by the Technical Services Department of Burlington's Carpet Division. The amount of stretch prescribed for each carpet is stated as a percentage, which must be converted into inches for the purpose of installation. Here is the procedure for using the conversion table:

1. Secure the specific stretch information from the manufacturer.

2. Refer to the chart for the percentage conversion. Start with the warp stretch and then the filling directional stretch.

Example. "A fabric [carpet] that has a recommended stretch of 3/4 percent in warp and 1 percent in the filling direction is to be installed in an area that measures 23′ × 47′4″ [7 m × 14.3 m]. The carpet should be installed with the warp of the carpet run-

ning in the longer direction. Consequently the warp measures 47′ in length (disregard the 4″) and the filling 23′.

"Referring to the chart, 3/4 percent stretch for 40′ [12 m] equals 3 5/8″ [9.2 cm]; 3/4 percent for 7′ [2.1 m] is about 5/8″ [16 mm], making the total required stretch 4 1/4″ [10.8 cm] in the warp direction. Referring to the chart for the filling stretch, 1 percent for 20′ [6.1 m] is 2 3/8″ [6 cm] and 1 percent for 3′ [.9 m] is about 3/8″ [9.5 mm], making a total of 2 3/4″ [6.9 cm] of stretch to be obtained across the width. The recommended stretches should be obtained in each direction because ease of stretch in just one direction can be gained at the expense of stretch in the other direction. The percent stretch is particularly useful when working on an unfamiliar fabric [carpet]."[15]

Carpet Molding Installation. The edges of carpet ending at doorways or connecting with resilient or hard-surface flooring should be anchored with metal binders (commonly known by their trade name: "Z" bars or "Gripperedge"). These metal binders should be specified on plans prior to installation.

Direct Glue-Down Installation. Direct glue-down installation involves three basic types of carpet products: (1) carpets with high-density foam backings, (2) carpets with a jute or non-woven synthetic secondary backing, and (3) carpets with a unitary backing, i.e., finished with latex, polyvinyl chloride, or polyurethane compounds.

This installation method evolved during the mid-1960s when carpet reached full acceptance as a floorcovering in large public areas receiving heavy traffic loads. Previously tackless strip installations had proven unsatisfactory in some of these areas because heavy traffic had caused the carpet to shift and pull the seams apart.

Before reaching a specification decision regarding this method of installation, one should review the advantages and disadvantages of direct glue-down application.

Disadvantages. There are four disadvantages to direct glue-down installation:

1. Direct glue-down installation makes no use of a separate carpet cushion, which could tend to increase the abrasion factor on carpet fibers and thereby shorten the useful life of the carpet.

2. The lack of a separate carpet cushion reduces the acoustic advantages normally associated with the use of a carpet.

3. The luxury factor normally associated with a soft carpet tread is lost.

4. Installation necessitates the use of a tight, low-surface carpet construction; therefore the variety of textures that may be specified is limited.

Advantages. There are three advantages to this method of installation:

1. Carpet is held firmly to the floor and does not shift or flex under heavy traffic. This has been particularly successful in areas where wheeled traffic is a factor, such as airports, hospitals, and food service centers.

2. This installation method allows access to floor areas containing electrical wiring. Total floor areas are often elevated to accommodate computer requirements.

3. Delamination and mildew problems are often eliminated.

TABLE 7.21 CONVERSION TABLE: PERCENTAGE OF STRETCH TO INCHES PER FOOT OF CARPET

	$\frac{1}{4}\%$	$\frac{1}{2}\%$	$\frac{3}{4}\%$	1%	$1\frac{1}{4}\%$	$1\frac{1}{2}\%$	$1\frac{3}{4}\%$	2%	$2\frac{1}{4}\%$	$2\frac{1}{2}\%$	$2\frac{3}{4}\%$	3%	$3\frac{1}{4}\%$	$3\frac{1}{2}\%$	$3\frac{3}{4}\%$	4%
1 ft.	$\frac{1}{32}$	$\frac{1}{16}$	$\frac{1}{8}$	$\frac{1}{8}$	$\frac{3}{16}$	$\frac{3}{16}$	$\frac{3}{16}$	$\frac{1}{4}$	$\frac{1}{4}$	$\frac{5}{16}$	$\frac{5}{16}$	$\frac{3}{8}$	$\frac{3}{8}$	$\frac{7}{16}$	$\frac{7}{16}$	$\frac{1}{2}$
2'	$\frac{1}{16}$	$\frac{1}{8}$	$\frac{3}{16}$	$\frac{1}{4}$	$\frac{5}{16}$	$\frac{3}{8}$	$\frac{7}{16}$	$\frac{1}{2}$	$\frac{9}{16}$	$\frac{5}{8}$	$\frac{11}{16}$	$\frac{3}{4}$	$\frac{3}{4}$	$\frac{13}{16}$	$\frac{7}{8}$	$\frac{15}{16}$
3'	$\frac{1}{16}$	$\frac{3}{16}$	$\frac{5}{16}$	$\frac{3}{8}$	$\frac{7}{16}$	$\frac{9}{16}$	$\frac{5}{8}$	$\frac{11}{16}$	$\frac{13}{16}$	$\frac{7}{8}$	$1.$	$1\frac{1}{16}$	$1\frac{3}{16}$	$1\frac{1}{4}$	$1\frac{3}{8}$	$1\frac{7}{16}$
4'	$\frac{1}{8}$	$\frac{1}{4}$	$\frac{3}{8}$	$\frac{1}{2}$	$\frac{5}{8}$	$\frac{3}{4}$	$\frac{13}{16}$	$\frac{15}{16}$	$1\frac{1}{16}$	$1\frac{3}{16}$	$1\frac{5}{16}$	$1\frac{7}{16}$	$1\frac{9}{16}$	$1\frac{11}{16}$	$1\frac{13}{16}$	$1\frac{15}{16}$
5'	$\frac{1}{8}$	$\frac{5}{16}$	$\frac{7}{16}$	$\frac{5}{8}$	$\frac{3}{4}$	$\frac{7}{8}$	$1\frac{1}{16}$	$1\frac{3}{16}$	$1\frac{3}{8}$	$1\frac{1}{2}$	$1\frac{5}{8}$	$1\frac{13}{16}$	$1\frac{15}{16}$	$2\frac{1}{8}$	$2\frac{1}{4}$	$2\frac{3}{8}$
6'	$\frac{3}{16}$	$\frac{3}{8}$	$\frac{9}{16}$	$\frac{3}{4}$	7.8	$1\frac{1}{16}$	$1\frac{1}{4}$	$1\frac{7}{16}$	$1\frac{5}{8}$	$1\frac{13}{16}$	$2.$	$2\frac{3}{16}$	$2\frac{5}{16}$	$2\frac{1}{2}$	$2\frac{11}{16}$	$2\frac{7}{8}$
7'	$\frac{3}{16}$	$\frac{7}{16}$	$\frac{5}{8}$	$\frac{13}{16}$	$1\frac{1}{16}$	$1\frac{1}{4}$	$1\frac{1}{2}$	$1\frac{11}{16}$	$1\frac{7}{8}$	$2\frac{1}{8}$	$2\frac{5}{16}$	$2\frac{1}{2}$	$2\frac{3}{4}$	$2\frac{15}{16}$	$3\frac{1}{8}$	$3\frac{3}{8}$
8'	$\frac{1}{4}$	$\frac{1}{2}$	$\frac{3}{4}$	$\frac{15}{16}$	$1\frac{3}{16}$	$1\frac{7}{16}$	$1\frac{11}{16}$	$1\frac{15}{16}$	$2\frac{3}{16}$	$2\frac{3}{8}$	$2\frac{5}{8}$	$2\frac{7}{8}$	$3\frac{1}{8}$	$3\frac{3}{8}$	$3\frac{5}{8}$	$3\frac{13}{16}$
9'	$\frac{1}{4}$	$\frac{9}{16}$	$\frac{13}{16}$	$1\frac{1}{16}$	$1\frac{3}{8}$	$1\frac{5}{8}$	$1\frac{7}{8}$	$2\frac{3}{16}$	$2\frac{7}{16}$	$2\frac{11}{16}$	$3.$	$3\frac{1}{4}$	$3\frac{1}{2}$	$3\frac{3}{4}$	$4\frac{1}{16}$	$4\frac{5}{16}$
10'	$\frac{5}{16}$	$\frac{5}{8}$	$\frac{7}{8}$	$1\frac{1}{8}$	$1\frac{1}{2}$	$1\frac{13}{16}$	$2\frac{1}{8}$	$2\frac{3}{8}$	$2\frac{11}{16}$	$3.$	$3\frac{5}{16}$	$3\frac{5}{8}$	$3\frac{7}{8}$	$4\frac{3}{16}$	$4\frac{1}{2}$	$4\frac{13}{16}$
20'	$\frac{5}{8}$	$1\frac{1}{8}$	$1\frac{13}{16}$	$2\frac{3}{8}$	$3.$	$3\frac{5}{8}$	$4\frac{3}{16}$	$4\frac{13}{16}$	$5\frac{3}{8}$	$6.$	$6\frac{5}{8}$	$7\frac{3}{16}$	$7\frac{13}{16}$	$8\frac{3}{8}$	$9.$	$9\frac{5}{8}$
30'	$\frac{7}{8}$	$1\frac{13}{16}$	$2\frac{11}{16}$	$3\frac{5}{8}$	$4\frac{1}{2}$	$5\frac{3}{8}$	$6\frac{5}{16}$	$7\frac{3}{16}$	$8\frac{1}{8}$	$9.$	$9\frac{7}{8}$	$.10\frac{13}{16}$	$11\frac{11}{16}$	$12\frac{5}{8}$	$13\frac{1}{2}$	$14\frac{3}{8}$
40'	$1\frac{3}{16}$	$2\frac{3}{8}$	$3\frac{5}{8}$	$4\frac{13}{16}$	$6.$	$7\frac{3}{16}$	$8\frac{3}{8}$	$9\frac{5}{8}$	$10\frac{13}{16}$	$12.$	$13\frac{3}{16}$	$14\frac{3}{8}$	$15\frac{5}{8}$	$16\frac{13}{16}$	$18.$	$19\frac{3}{16}$
50'	$1\frac{1}{2}$	$3.$	$4\frac{1}{2}$	$6.$	$7\frac{1}{2}$	$9.$	$10\frac{1}{2}$	$12.$	$13\frac{1}{2}$	$15.$	$16\frac{1}{2}$	$18.$	$19\frac{1}{2}$	$21.$	$22\frac{1}{2}$	$24.$
60'	$1\frac{13}{16}$	$3\frac{5}{8}$	$5\frac{3}{8}$	$7\frac{3}{16}$	$9.$	$10\frac{13}{16}$	$12\frac{5}{8}$	$14\frac{3}{8}$	$16\frac{1}{8}$	$18.$	$19\frac{13}{16}$	$21\frac{5}{8}$	$23\frac{3}{8}$	$25\frac{3}{16}$	$27.$	$28\frac{13}{16}$
70'	$2\frac{1}{8}$	$4\frac{3}{16}$	$6\frac{5}{16}$	$8\frac{3}{8}$	$10\frac{1}{2}$	$12\frac{5}{8}$	$14\frac{11}{16}$	$16\frac{13}{16}$	$18\frac{7}{8}$	$21.$	$23\frac{1}{8}$	$25\frac{3}{16}$	$27\frac{5}{16}$	$29\frac{3}{8}$	$31\frac{1}{2}$	$33\frac{5}{8}$
80'	$2\frac{3}{8}$	$4\frac{13}{16}$	$7\frac{3}{16}$	$9\frac{5}{8}$	$12.$	$14\frac{3}{8}$	$16\frac{13}{16}$	$19\frac{3}{16}$	$21\frac{5}{8}$	$24.$	$26\frac{3}{8}$	$28\frac{13}{16}$	$31\frac{3}{16}$	$33\frac{5}{8}$	$36.$	$38\frac{3}{8}$
90'	$2\frac{11}{16}$	$5\frac{3}{8}$	$8\frac{1}{8}$	$10\frac{13}{16}$	$13\frac{1}{2}$	$16\frac{3}{16}$	$18\frac{7}{8}$	$21\frac{5}{8}$	$24\frac{5}{16}$	$27.$	$29\frac{11}{16}$	$32\frac{3}{8}$	$35\frac{1}{8}$	$37\frac{13}{16}$	$40\frac{1}{2}$	$43\frac{3}{16}$
100'	$3.$	$6.$	$9.$	$12.$	$15.$	$18.$	$21.$	$24.$	$27.$	$30.$	$33.$	$36.$	$39.$	$42.$	$45.$	$48.$

Source: Technical Services Department, Burlington Carpet Division, Burlington Industries, Inc.

Direct Glue-Down Specification Requirements. Important factors that must be considered in the specification of direct glue-down installations include: (1) carpet construction, (2) abrasion resistance of fibers, (3) seaming, (4) preparation of subflooring, (5) adhesives, and (6) environmental conditions.

1. The carpet construction must provide a surface that will withstand the use of wheeled traffic and direct pressure against the subfloor without cushioning. The tightness of construction and the face weight of the tufted or woven carpet is very important. A low, level loop surface treatment will permit wheel traffic to move easily across the surface. The following are suggested face weights and gauges for use in direct glue-down installations (Table 7.24).

    The backing applied to the carpet should be one that will remain stable and provide a secure bond with the adhesive. Both jute and nonwoven synthetic backings have proven successful in this type of installation.

2. Fiber selection for this type of installation is very important. The abrasion resistance of a particular fiber should be carefully considered. Fiber blends are often used in direct glue-down applications. For example, a wool will offer better performance qualities when blended with a nylon. The fibers listed in Table 7.22 have been successfully used in direct glue-down installation.

3. Secure seaming is usually provided through the specification of a tight tuft bind construction that will prevent tufts from pulling loose at the seam edges. Prior to installation, seams are sealed with a latex-type glue.

4. Preparation of the subflooring assumes a greater importance in this type of installation because of adhesive application requirements. Surface irregularities, which normally would be concealed by the use of the cushion underlay, must also be corrected prior to installation. Listed below are some typical subfloor conditions that may be encountered:

    a. Concrete floors are classed as suspended (above ground), on-grade (directly in contact with the ground), and below-grade floors (slabs poured below ground level). (See Figure 7.17.) Moisture presents a major problem in dealing with concrete floors. On-grade and below-grade floors may have moisture continually rising through the slab. As the water passes through the slab, it mixes with the salts in the concrete and forms an alkaline mixture that can completely destroy the bonding ability of the adhesive. If the installed carpet has a synthetic backing that will not permit the moisture to evaporate, the carpet would gradually be destroyed by the alkaline solutions. Latex emulsion-type adhesives have been developed that may withstand a major portion of the alkaline solution. Various tests have been developed to determine the moisture level in concrete subfloors. One simple test method makes use of a rubber mat which is placed on the floor and left in the same position for several hours. If moisture collects under the mat, it indicates that a potential problem exists.

    b. Painted concrete floors will necessitate the removal of oil base paint prior to application of the adhesive.

TABLE 7.22 SPECIFICATION GUIDELINES: DIRECT GLUE-DOWN

Fiber	Face Weight	Gauge
Nylon	28 oz/yd^2	1/10
Acrylic	42 oz/yd^2	1/10
Wool	42 oz/yd^2	1/10
Olefin		
Spun yarn	33 oz/yd^2	1/10
Continuous fiber	28 oz/yd^2	1/10

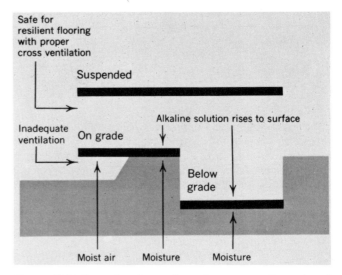

Figure 7.17 Ground moisture through concrete. Reproduced with permission of Armstrong Cork Co.

c. Radiant-heated floors must be maintained at a temperature level that will permit proper drying rates for the specified adhesive.

d. Existing resilient floors are often encountered in building renovation or remodeling projects. In some cases only minor repairs and a thorough cleaning may be necessary. If an asphalt floor must be removed by sanding, safety precautions should be taken to prevent inhaling the asphalt dust. Adhesive compatibility with various types of tiles should be verified.

e. Nonporous floors, such as terrazzo, ceramic, and quarry tile, usually require that the carpet have a porous-type backing, such as jute, that will allow the evaporation of the adhesive solvents. It may be necessary to fill grout lines and remove old wax and sealers. Manufacturers of the adhesives will provide detailed information on necessary floor preparation.[16]

5. Adhesives used for direct glue-down installations are grouped into four categories. Each type has different characteristics and application procedures.

    a. Natural latex
    b. Synthetic latex
    c. Solvent base rubber adhesive
    d. Alcohol solvent resins

Some latex-type adhesives have been specially developed for the installation of vinyl-backed carpets.

6. Environmental conditions may have an important effect on the success of the installation. The temperature of the carpet and the floor as well as the relative humidity are factors that can affect the stretch of the carpet and the drying rate of the adhesive. If the building has a central heating and cooling system, it should be in working order prior to the installation. Temperature in the areas to be carpeted should be maintained at between 70 and 80°F (21 and 27°C) for at least twenty-four hours before installation. Space heaters will not serve as a substitute because they will not heat the floors evenly. All the carpet should be spread in the area at least twenty-four hours before installation, and the temperature and humidity should be maintained at the same level for at least forty-eight hours after installation. Schools, churches, and similar institutions that shut down their heating or air conditioning for periods of time should be warned that the carpet may buckle due to the change in temperature.

Other Installation Considerations. The following factors should be included in a written carpet specification. The responsibilities of the contractor, owner, and designer must be clearly stated in contractual language (see Chapter 16) that prevents misunderstanding. A complete carpet specification example is included in Chapter 16. (The word "shall" is used in this section to designate a definite responsibility of the particular person involved.)

Delivery and Storage. The carpet contractor is usually responsible for the shipping instructions, receiving, and placement of the carpet on the job site. Carpet should be delivered to the job site or designated workroom in the manufacturer's bundles and the size, dye lot, and material content shall be clearly marked on each bundle. The contractor shall keep a written record of the carpet received.

In the event that special equipment is needed to lift carpet bundles to a highrise building installation, the contractor shall only be responsible for delivery to the first floor.

The owner of the building should provide locked storage for the carpet, padding, and necessary tools while the work is in progress. In addition, the owner should provide containers for scrap material. The owner should make access to the building and use of the elevators available for carpet installation during the normal working hours to prevent overtime charges. The owner should contact the general contractor regarding doors that should be trimmed and rehung prior to the carpet installation.

Excess Carpet. All carpet remnants 1 sq yd (.9 sq m) or larger should be left at the job site or packaged in appropriate wrapping, labeled, and delivered to the owner. These excess pieces are useful for replacement and repairs.

Responsibility of the Contractor. Aside from receiving and installing the carpet at the job site, the contractor shall be responsible for the following:

1. The contractor shall provide records that will verify his training and experience in carpet installation. This should include a list of previous work that is similar in scope. Names of people to contact for references should also be included. A minimum of five years' experience is required.

2. The contractor shall provide names of carpet manufacturers with whom he has worked in the past.

3. The contractor shall provide evidence that the work shall be performed by skilled installers and that the number of installers assigned to the job site will be adequate to complete the installation.

4. The contractor shall physically recheck all measurements provided in the specification. After completing the inspection and measurements, the contractor may make suggestions regarding another carpet width or type of installation that may eliminate unnecessary seams and yardage. This recommendation should be submitted to the designer for approval. A complete seaming diagram should also be submitted. No request for extra carpet will be considered when measurement or takeoff errors have been made by the installation contractor.

5. The contractor shall inspect all subfloors and test for moisture content. After inspection, the contractor should submit a written report on any conditions that would prevent the proper installation of the carpet. Once the carpet has been installed, it shall be understood that the contractor assumes responsibility for any unacceptable condition in the subfloor.

6. The contractor shall install all carpet as recommended by the manufacturer's installation manual. Carpet shall be installed wall to wall, using continuous lengths and as broad widths as possible. Cut edges shall be trued and appropriately treated to form nonraveling joints where exposed.

7. The contractor shall be fully responsible for the condition of the carpet until it has been finally approved. Upon completion of each floor, the installation shall be inspected by representatives of the owner and installer prior to approval by the owner. All dirt and carpet scraps must be removed from the surface of the carpet. All soiled spots or excessive adhesive on the carpet shall be removed with the proper spot remover. All pieces of loose face yarn must be removed with sharp scissors. The entire surface should be vacuumed with a heavy-duty machine.

8. The installation contractor shall guarantee in writing to relay or restretch the carpet, repair seams, joints, and edges one time if required after the original installation is completed. The guarantee shall be in effect for one year after the final approval of the installation. The owner shall provide the contractor with a two-week notice regarding the needed repairs.

9. The contractor shall be responsible for repair of any damage to wall surfaces, doors, or woodwork.

Responsibilities of the Designer. The designer shall be responsible for providing the contractor with drawings and specifications which clearly detail the location of the carpeted areas within the project and provide installation instructions. The time of the installation and the necessary completion date should be included in the contract specification. The designer should plan a preinstallation and postinstallation inspection.

Preinstallation Checklist. Four points need to be checked:

1. Has the carpet installation been properly scheduled? Be sure that all painting of doors and woodwork is completed;

all wall finishes and adjoining resilient or hard-surfaced floors have been installed prior to the carpet installation.

2. Is the heating and/or air conditioning equipment in operating condition so that proper temperature and humidity can be maintained during installation?

3. Has adequate storage been provided for the carpet and tools prior to installation?

4. Will the carpet installation take place on the prearranged date?

Postinstallation Checklist: Eight items need to be considered:

1. Check the carpet for wrinkles and buckling.

2. Do all seams run with the flow of traffic and not counter to the traffic flow?

3. Do seams appear to have been pulled too taut in the stretching process?

4. Check the nap direction of the carpet. All carpet should be installed in the same direction unless specified otherwise.

5. Check nap direction on stairs. Does the nap run downward on the stairs? Carpet backing should not show through tufting when curving over the stair structure.

6. Check installation for any evidence of patching.

7. If direct glue-down method was used, check for adhesive spots along the seam lines and be sure that seams are tightly sealed.

8. Is carpet securely attached to the metal moldings at doors and other areas where carpet adjoins another floor surface?

Phase 13: Maintenance Programming

In the past carpet maintenance was regarded as a semiannual or annual cleaning after the carpet had become very badly soiled. Extensive research and the development of new chemicals by those involved in the carpet industry have changed the whole approach to carpet maintenance. Carpet maintenance is now programmed on a regular basis to prevent abrasive soil particles from collecting between carpet fibers. Spills and spots are removed regularly to maintain the overall appearance of the carpet.

The level of appearance at which a carpet is maintained is based on the owner's requirements. A 100 percent appearance level is considered "brand new" or in original installation condition. A maintenance level of 85 to 80 percent is considered excellent, and levels between 80 and 70 percent are considered good. The majority of commercial and institutional installations are maintained at an 85 percent level of appearance.

Several specification factors may result in a lower carpet appearance level and increased maintenance costs:

1. *Color selection* should be carefully considered, not only for aesthetic reasons, but because of maintenance factors. Generally, carpets selected in the midvalue range will show less soil than very dark or very light colors. Carpet color selection should take into consideration the regional soil color. If the geographic area has a yellowish, sandy soil and the area to be carpeted will receive traffic directly from the exterior, a dark carpet would be difficult to maintain. Patterned or multicolored carpets often provide a

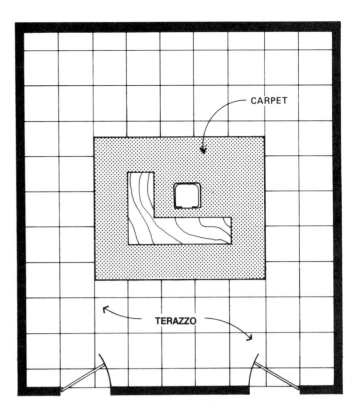

Figure 7.18 Carpet island.

good floorcovering for heavily traveled areas such as hotels, hospitals, theaters, and restaurants.

2. *Carpet construction* is also a serious factor to consider in relation to maintenance. A loosely constructed carpet with a low-fiber density allows soil and dirt to collect between the fibers and filter to the base of the carpet. The deeply embedded soil is difficult to remove and promotes carpet damage. Carpet specified for commercial installations should be tightly constructed with a high yarn density.

3. *Fiber selection* should be based on the traffic load and location of the carpet within the building. Where high spillage is expected, a fiber with a low moisture content should be specified. Many new so-called soil-hiding carpet fibers, though highly popular, may also produce maintenance problems. Maintenance experts caution against allowing long periods of time to elapse between cleaning these soil-hiding fibers because the soil, though not noticeable, is actually accumulating and causing carpet damage.

4. *Placement of the carpet* within the building may also be responsible for unnecessary maintenance expense. The installation of "islands" of carpet surrounded by large areas of hard-surfaced flooring will result in wax and dust being tracked onto the carpet from the hard-surfaced floor (see Figure 7.18). In the maintenance process there is also the danger of wax and cleaning solutions being splashed on the carpet.

Preventive Maintenance. Adequate preventive maintenance planning is based on knowledge of soil sources and the areas

TABLE 7.23 THE 20-DAY CARPET MAINTENANCE PLAN

The schedule covers 20 working days (exclude Saturdays and Sundays). It repeats 13 times per year, assuming 52 weeks usage of carpeting. Annual labor and material costs are shown per 1000 square feet. Rates of production for the activities are based on several years of experience in many types of installations and in a broad range of geographical locations. ODD and EVEN days refer to the day of the schedule not to the calendar date.

ACTIVITY	FREQUENCY	PRODUCTION RATE	EQUIPMENT
Trash pickup	Daily	2.2 minutes/1000 sq. ft.	Upright vacuum. Broom and dustpan optional
Vacuum track-off & funnel areas	Odd days	30 minutes/1000 sq. ft.	Upright vacuum
Vacuum corridors	Even days	15 minutes/1000 sq. ft.	Upright vacuum
*Vacuum office areas or other rooms	10th day	30 minutes/1000 sq. ft.	Upright vacuum
*Spot removal	10th day	43.3 minutes/1000 sq. ft.	Spot remover Chewing gum freezer Dry cleaning machine Absorbent compound
*Traffic area cleaning	20th day	11.4 minutes/1000 sq. ft.	Traffic lane cleaner Dry cleaning machine Absorbent compound
Overall cleaning	Only as needed	80 minutes/1000 sq. ft. does not include the moving of furniture	Traffic lane cleaner Dry cleaning machines Absorbent compound

*The PLAN indicates that once in every 20 days specific time is scheduled for each of these vital activities.

Copyright 1978 Racine Industrial Plant, Inc. Racine, Wisconsin 53403

that will receive the major soilage. Three common sources of carpet soilage are (1) airborne soil, (2) spillage, and (3) shoe surfaces. Maintenance authorities further classify soil into two categories:

1. Water-soluble soil, such as sugars and other food contents that can be dissolved by water and detergents.

2. Solvent-soluble soil, such as oils and airborne cooking grease, that can be dissolved by dry cleaning solvents and detergents.[17]

As soils build up in the carpet the oily content in these soils sticks or binds to the carpet fibers and is impossible to remove through the normal vacuuming process. At this point chemical and mechanical cleaning methods are required to break the oil bond and pull the soil away from the carpet fibers. This loosened soil must then be removed to prevent its being dispersed farther into the pile and becoming a source of resoiling. Effective carpet maintenance involves not only dissolving the soil, but completely removing all soil (other than permanent stains).

Major areas that require frequent or daily maintenance are defined as track-off and funnel areas:

Track-off Areas. These exist where carpet collects foot soil tracked in from outdoors or from hard-surfaced floors. Track-off areas at most building entrances average 90 sq ft (6′ × 15′). Internal doorways average 10 sq ft (2′ × 5′), and corridors 6 ft in width average about 40 sq ft (5′ × 8′) of track-off area. Preventive maintenance for track-off areas includes daily vacuuming, walk-off mats (both inside and outside), and regular spot and overall cleaning. The important objective is to prevent accumulated soil from being carried farther onto the remaining carpet areas.

Funnel Areas. These exist where foot traffic is squeezed into or through a concentrated area, such as elevators, doorways, stairways, corridors, and areas in front of drinking fountains and vending machines or counters. Funnel areas are estimated to be 12 sq ft (2′ × 3′) on either side of a door jamb and 2′ × 6′ in front of drinking fountains and vending machines. These area estimates are used to calculate necessary maintenance time and equipment used in the following 20-day maintenance plan.

An outstanding preventive maintenance plan shown in Tables 7.23 and 7.24 was developed by the Racine Industrial Plant, Inc. and schedules a 20-day cycle for regular mainte-

TABLE 7.24 CARPET MAINTENANCE CALENDAR

Carpet Maintenance Calendar

If carpeting is new, begin the 20 Day Plan immediately.
If it is not new, first give it a thorough overall wall-to-wall cleaning, then begin the 20 Day Plan.   From _____ To _____

SUNDAY	MONDAY	TUESDAY	WEDNESDAY	THURSDAY	FRIDAY	SATURDAY
	1 Vac track-off and funnel areas only Trash Pick-Up	**2** Vac corridors only Trash Pick-Up	**3** Vac track-off and funnel areas only Trash Pick-Up	**4** Vac corridors only Trash Pick-Up	**5** Vac track-off and funnel areas only Trash Pick-Up	
	6 Vac corridors only Trash Pick-Up	**7** Vac track-off and funnel areas only Trash Pick-Up	**8** Vac corridors only Trash Pick-Up	**9** Vac track-off and funnel areas only Trash Pick-Up	**10** Remove stains Vac offices Vac corridors Trash Pick-Up	
	11 Vac track-off and funnel areas only Trash Pick-Up	**12** Vac corridors only Trash Pick-Up	**13** Vac track-off and funnel areas only Trash Pick-Up	**14** Vac corridors only Trash Pick-Up	**15** Vac track-off and funnel areas only Trash Pick-Up	
	16 Vac corridors only Trash Pick-Up	**17** Vac track-off and funnel areas only Trash Pick-Up	**18** Vac corridors only Trash Pick-Up	**19** Vac track-off and funnel areas only Trash Pick-Up	**20** Traffic area cleaning by Dry Cleaning track-off and funnel areas Vac corridors Trash Pick-Up	

REPEAT 20 Day Schedule (13 times per year).

Copyright 1978 Racine Industrial Plant, Inc. Racine, Wisconsin 53403

nance. The schedule covers 20 working days (excluding Saturdays and Sundays). It repeats 13 times per year, assuming 52 weeks' usage of the carpeting. Annual labor is shown per 1,000 sq ft (92.9 m²). Rates of production for the activities are based on several years of experience in many types of installations and in a broad range of geographic locations. "Odd" and "even" days refer to the day of the schedule not to the calendar date.

Preventive Maintenance Activities and Equipment. There are three areas of concern here:

1. Vacuuming is usually performed with a heavy-duty upright-type machine equipped with brush agitators. Direct glue-down installations require a special "carpet groomer" agitator with two rows of brushes, rather than a brush and beater bar normally used on carpet installed over padding. Vacuuming equipment should be properly maintained and vacuum bags emptied frequently.

2. Spot removal should be accomplished as soon as possible after spills and spots occur. In very large carpet installations a special maintenance person may be required to handle only spot removal. Commercial spot cleaning kits are available and contain the chemical compounds necessary to remove most common causes of spotting.

3. Traffic lane maintenance involves daily vacuuming, spot removal, and corrective or restorative cleaning. Because traffic lanes receive heavy wear, corrective overall cleaning is required to maintain a level of appearance that will equal the surrounding areas of carpet.

Corrective Maintenance. The accumulation of oily soils on carpet fibers is one of the major reasons that corrective or overall cleaning must be performed. Prior to cleaning, carpeting should be preconditioned; i.e., carpet fibers should be carefully vacuumed to separate and loosen packed pile to allow the penetration of the cleaning agents.

There are several cleaning methods used for corrective maintenance, and selection of a particular method should be based on the manufacturer's recommendations, plus an understanding of the client's needs. For example, a wet method that requires several hours to dry before the area can be restored to use would be feasible in an office or school that is closed in the evenings and on weekends. In a hospital or other public facility that remains in operation day and night a wet cleaning method would be found to be impractical. The following cleaning methods are the most frequently used.

1. *Detergent solutions* should be selected with caution because some may contain harsh chemicals that could adversely affect carpet dyes. Unless recommended by the carpet manufacturer, detergent solutions should be tested on a small portion of the carpet. The following characteristics would be desirable in a detergent-type cleaning method:

   a. Ability to clean the soiled carpet.
   b. Prevent dulling of the carpet appearance.
   c. Prevent rapid resoiling.
   d. Avoid fading of the carpet dye.
   e. Provide a disinfectant.
   f. Avoid creating static electricity.
   g. Provide a reasonable drying time.

2. *Dry foam cleaning methods* provide a simultaneous vacuum pick-up to remove soil and the dry foam detergent. The detergents are contained in the dry foam that is deposited just ahead of the brush. Soil particles are loosened from the carpet fibers by agitation of the reel-type brush, suspended in the foam, and vacuumed back into the machine in one operation. This method prevents overwetting of the carpet, and cleaned areas are usually ready for use within one hour.

3. *Liquid dry cleaners* contain synthetic detergents and solvents that are sprayed over the carpet in a fine mist by a pressurized sprayer. The solution is allowed to penetrate into the carpet for about 10 minutes before a single disk floor machine lifts the soil from the carpet. The cleaned area may be ready for use within less than an hour.

4. *Hot water extraction cleaning* injects the pile with a hot detergent solution under pressure. The solution is immediately extracted along with the soil. This process is time consuming, and it may overwet the carpet and result in prolonged drying periods.

5. *Powder cleaners* are absorbent compounds consisting of an organic powder impregnated with detergents, solvents, and phenolic inhibitors. The powder is sprinkled over the carpet and brushed into the pile. These powders may be left on the carpet for a short period, during which the soil is attracted to the powder, and later the soil and the powder are vacuumed away. This method is ideal for interim cleaning and overall cleaning of areas that must remain in constant use, such as hospitals and hotels.

6. *Ultrasonic cleaning methods* employ high-frequency sound waves to attract soil away from the carpet fibers. This method has thus far been successfully employed in situations where the carpet can be removed and brought to a cleaning plant. On-site ultrasonic cleaning equipment is undergoing further research and development at the current time.[18]

Problems That May Occur from Improper Cleaning Methods. There are two major problems that can result from improper cleaning:

1. Fading and shrinking may result from carpet fibers being overwet for prolonged periods of time.

2. Carpet shading, or "pooling"—sometimes referred to as "browning"—may result from several factors. This problem usually occurs in dense cut pile carpet that may begin to pack and lie flat under pressure of constant foot traffic.

Job No. _____

Date _____

CARPET PERFORMANCE SPECIFICATION CHECKLIST

MATERIAL	PROPOSED USE	PERFORMANCE REQUIREMENTS								MAINTENANCE LEVEL		INSTALLATION METHOD	BUDGET
	Location	Local Codes	Fed. Regs.	Ozone Cond.	Static Control	Soil Color	Traffic Amount	Spills	Other	Prevent:	Correct:		
Fiber: Const:	Area:												
Fiber: Const:	Area:												

Figure 7.19 Carpet performance specification checklist.

Large spots or pools may also result from wet cleaning solutions not being adequately removed from the carpet.

Maintenance Manuals. Operational and maintenance instructions for products and components specified by the designer should be assembled into a manual and presented to the owner. Details concerning the development of a maintenance manual will be discussed in Chapter 16. Specification requirements for maintenance information from the manufacturer should include recommended brand names of cleaning solutions, spot removers, and equipment.

Phase 14: Life Cycle Costing

Estimating the life cycle cost of carpet involves establishing the initial cost factors as explained in Chapter 6. Recurring maintenance costs make up a major portion of total life cycle considerations. The cost schedule for 1,000 sq ft (92.9 m²) of carpet in Table 7.25 is based on the time factors established in the 20-day maintenance plan (frequency and production rate).

The worksheets in Table 7.26 developed by the Racine Industrial Plant, Inc. provide an effective method for arriving at the total yearly maintenance cost for 1,000 sq ft of carpeting based on an appearance level of 85 percent.

General Specifications Guidelines

Table 7.27 provides general guidelines for carpet specifications in various types of commercial occupancies. The recommended carpet weights are minimum and the maintenance levels will vary according to the actual use and maintenance provided. Figure 7.19 illustrates an additional type of carpet specification checklist that may be developed to aid designers in making decisions on performance requirements.

TABLE 7.25 COST SCHEDULE PER 1000 SQUARE FEET

ACTIVITY	ANNUAL HOURS	× HOURLY RATE	= ANNUAL LABOR COST	+ ANNUAL MATERIALS COST*	= ANNUAL TOTAL 1000 sq. ft.
Daily trash pickup	9.53	$5.00	$47.65	NA	$47.65
Vacuuming**	12.72	$5.00	$63.60	NA	$63.60
Spot removal***	9.39	$5.00	$46.95	$5.40	$52.35
Traffic area cleaning	2.28	$5.00	$11.40	$15.17	$26.57
ANNUAL TOTALS	**33.92**		**$169.60**	**$20.57**	**$190.17**

Some custodial personnel are required to cover 2400 square feet per hour for all maintenance. This equals 108.34 hours per year spent on each 1000 square feet. Industry figures show that about 52% of a custodian's time, or 56.3 hours, should be allowed for floor care. The 20 DAY PLAN requires only 33.98 hours per 1000 square feet vs. the 56.3 hours of time allowed by the industry formula.

If a higher appearance level is desired, additional time should be scheduled for vacuuming and traffic area cleaning, since these activities will produce noticeable results.

* Original equipment cost and depreciation not included.

** Assumes that 10% of carpeted area is in corridors, and also that TRACK-OFF and FUNNEL AREAS average 64 square feet.

*** Spots are easier to remove while they are fresh. However, prompt action is not always possible. It is more practical to schedule a specific time for spotting procedure. *Most spots can be removed quickly by using a dry cleaning machine, an absorbent compound, plus a general purpose spotting agent.*

TABLE 7.26   ESTIMATE YOUR TIME AND COST TOTALS

A. Vacuuming

1. Vacuuming of track-off areas:

    a) _____ track-off areas at internal doorways × 10 sq. ft. = _____ sq. ft. per vacuuming
    b) _____ track-off areas in corridors × 40 sq. ft. = _____ sq. ft. per vacuuming
    c) _____ track-off areas at outside entrances × 90 sq. ft. = _____ sq. ft.
    d) _____ total of a, b and c above × 129 times per year = _____ sq. ft. per year
    e) _____ sq. ft. per year ÷ 2000 sq. ft. per hour = _____ hours
    f) _____ hours × $ _____ per hour labor rate = $ _____ yearly track-off area vacuuming cost

2. Vacuuming of funnel areas:

    a) _____ internal funnel areas at doorways × 12 sq. ft. = _____ sq. ft. per vacuuming
    b) _____ funnel areas at fountains, vending machines, etc., × 12 sq. ft. = _____ sq. ft. per vacuuming
    c) _____ total of a and b above × 129 times per year = _____ sq. ft. per year
    d) _____ sq. ft. per year ÷ 2000 sq. ft. per hour = _____ hours
    e) _____ hours × $ _____ per hour labor rate = $ _____ yearly funnel area vacuuming cost

3. Vacuuming of corridors:

    a) _____ corridors × _____ sq. ft. per corridor = _____ sq. ft. per vacuuming
    b) _____ sq. ft. per vacuuming × 129 vacuumings = _____ sq. ft. per year
    c) _____ sq. ft. per year ÷ 4000 sq. ft. per hour = _____ hours
    d) _____ hours × $ _____ per hour labor rate = $ _____ yearly corridor vacuuming cost

4. Vacuuming offices:

    a) _____ total sq. ft. of offices × 13 vacuumings = _____ sq. ft. per year
    b) _____ sq. ft. per year ÷ 2000 sq. ft. per hour = _____ hours
    c) _____ hours × $ _____ per hour labor rate = $ _____ yearly office vacuuming cost

5. Sum of 1, 2, 3 and 4 above = _____ total yearly vacuuming cost

    a) _____ total sq. ft. of carpeting ÷ 1000 = _____ areas
    b) $ _____ total yearly vacuuming cost ÷ _____ areas = $ _____ yearly vacuuming cost per 1000 sq. ft.

B. Spot removal

1) 43.3 minutes per 1000 sq. ft. × 13 times per year = 562.9 minutes ÷ 60 = 9.39 hours × $ _____ labor rate = $ _____ yearly labor cost per 1000 sq. ft.
2) Spot remover $.83 + chewing gum remover $.23 + dry cleaning compound $4.34 = $5.40 yearly material cost per 1000 sq. ft.
3) $ _____ labor (#1 above) + $5.40 materials = $ _____ yearly spot removal cost per 1000 sq. ft.

C. Daily trash pick-up

1) 2.2 minutes per 1000 sq. ft. × 260 times per year = 572 minutes ÷ 60 = 9.53 hours.
2) 9.53 hours × $ _____ labor rate = $ _____ yearly trash pick-up cost per 1000 sq. ft.

D. Traffic area cleaning

1) 11.4 minutes per 1000 sq. ft. × 12 times per year = 136.8 minutes ÷ 60 = 2.28 hours × $ _____ labor rate = $ _____ yearly labor cost per 1000 sq. ft.
2) Absorbent compound 21.5 lbs. × 57.8/lb. = $12.42 + traffic lane cleaner $2.75 = $15.17 materials + $ _____ yearly labor cost = $ _____ yearly area maintenance cost per 1000 sq. ft.

E. Total

Totals from:
A. $_____
B. $_____
C. $_____
D. $_____
    $_____ Total yearly maintenance cost per 1000 sq. ft

TABLE 7.27 CARPET SPECIFICATION GUIDELINES: OCCUPANCY INDEX*

Occupancy Type	Traffic Class	Carpet Construction	Carpet Fiber	Carpet Face Weight oz	Density	Main-tenance Level, %	Installation Method	Padding	Maintenance Program
Schools									
Corridors	Heavy	WO/TU LL/PA	Nyl/OL BLD	28/46	4600 6600	85	DG	None	VAD/SP 20 DP
Exits									
Classrooms	Mod. heavy	TU/LL 12 lb tuft/BLD	Nyl/Acy BLD	28	3800 4600	85	DG	None	VAD/SP/20 DP
Offices	Light	WO/TU CP/LL	Nyl/Acy	22/28	3800 4600	85	ST	60/80 oz SPR	SP/20 DP
Cafeteria	Heavy	TU/WO LL/C&L	Nyl/OL/BLD	22/28	3800 4600	85-90	DG	None	VAD/SP/20 DP
Hospitals									
Corridors	Heavy	TU/WO/PA LL/C&L	Nyl/Acy W/BLD	28/32	4600 6600	85-90	DG	None	VAD/SP/CN
Lobby	Heavy	TU/WO/PA LL/CP	Nyl/Acy W/BLD	28/32	4600 6600	85-90	DG	None	VAD/SP/CN
Nurses Stations	Heavy	TU/WO LL	Nyl/OL Acy	22/28	4600 6600	90	DG	None	VAD/SP/CN
Patient Rooms	Mod. Heavy	TU/WO LL	Nyl/OL	22/28	3800 4600	90	DG	None	VAD/SP/CN
Offices	Light	TU/WO LL/CP/C&L	Nyl/Acy W/BLD	22/32	3800 4600	85	ST	60/80 FL .250 SPR	SP/20 DP
Hotels/Motels									
Corridors	Heavy	WO/TU LL/CP/PA C&L	Nyl/Acy W/BLD	28/36	3800 4600	85	ST	44/50 oz .275 FL SPR	SP/20 DP
Lobby	Heavy	WO/TU/PA LL/C&L	Nyl/Acy W/BLD	28/42	4600 6600	90	DG		VAD/SP/CN
Guest Rooms	Mod.	TU/CP	Nyl/Acy W/BLD	28/32	3800 4600	85	ST	40 oz FL 80 oz SPR	SP/CN
Meeting Rooms	Mod. heavy	WO/TU/PA CP/LL/C&L	Nyl/Acy W/BLD	28/32	3800 4600	85	ST	40 oz FL .275 SPR	SP/CN
Transportation									
Terminal	Extra heavy	WO/TU LL/PA	Nyl/W/BLD	28/36	4600 6600	85	DG	None	VAD/SP/CN
Corridors	Heavy	WO/TU LL/PA	Nyl/Acy W/BLD	28/46	4600 6600	85	DG	None	VAD/SP/CN
Office Buildings									
Executive	Light	WO/TU CP/C&L	Nyl/Acy W/BLD	32/46	3800 4600	90	ST	.325/.525 FL SPR	SP/20 DP
Clerical	Mod. heavy	WO/TU LL/CP/C&L	Nyl/Acy W/BLD	22/32	3800 4600	85	DG/ST	44-50 oz FL 60-80 oz SPR	SP/20 DP
Corridors	Mod. heavy	WO/TU/LL CP/PA	Nyl/Acy W/BLD	22/32	3800 5500	85	DG/ST	44-50 oz 60-80 oz FLAT SPR	VAD/SP/20 DP
Cafeteria	Heavy	WO/TU/LL PA	Nyl/OL Acy/BLD	22/28	3800 5500	85	DG	None	VAD/SP/CN
Banks									
Executive	Light	WO/TU/CP C&L	Nyl/Acy W/BLD	32/46	3800 4600	90	ST	.325 FL SPR 44-50 oz FL	SP/20 DP
Lobby	Heavy	WO/TU/CP LL/PA/C&L	Nyl/Acy W/BLD	28/32	3800 5500	90	ST	.325 FL SPR 44-55 oz FL	VAD/SP/20 DP
Tellers	Heavy	WO/TU/LL	Nyl/Acy W/BLD	22/28	3800 5500	85	DG/ST	44-50 oz FL	SP/20 DP
Computer Facilities	Mod. heavy	WO/TU/LL	Nyl/OL BLD	28/32	3800 4600	85-90	DG	None	VAD/SP/20 DP

*Abbreviations: Carpet construction: WO = woven; LL = level loop; CP = cut pile; PA = patterned; TU = tufted; C&L = cut & loop.
Fibers: Acy = Acrylic; Nyl = Nylon; W = wool; OL = Olfin; BLD = blend.
Installation: DG = direct glue; ST = stretched.
Carpet padding: FL = felt; SPR = sponge rubber.
Maintenance: VAD = vacuum daily; SP = spot clean; 20 DP = 20-day plan; CN = clean as needed.

Note: This table represents suggested *minimum* levels.

8 RESILIENT AND HARD-SURFACE FLOORING

Increased concerns about life cycle costing and the length of service provided by interior components have resulted in more frequent specification of resilient and hard-surface flooring in commercial interiors. With many new technical innovations in the resilient flooring industry, designers have a wide range of surface textures, colors, and materials from which to select.

RESILIENT FLOORING

Although some areas, such as open offices, may require a fiber floorcovering to aid in controlling acoustic factors, other commercial areas are well served by resilient flooring. Numerous performance criteria have been established to assure quality control in the areas of (1) health and safety, (2) construction, (3) physical strength, and (4) appearance. Table 8.1 provides a survey of some of the major physical characteristics and recommended uses for resilient materials.

Health and Safety Criteria
These criteria include such factors as flammability, light reflectance, and slipperiness.

Flammability. Resilient flooring is tested for flame spread and smoke obscuration in the following test procedures:

ASTM E-84

NFPA Standard 258

UL 992

NBS Smoke Chamber

Most federal specifications require a flame spread of 75 in un-

sprinklered areas and a 200 flame spread in sprinklered areas. Recommended optical density for smoke is 450 in both flaming and nonflaming conditions.

Light Reflectance. This affects the brightness and quality of light in an interior. Too much reflectance can be a source of glare and discomfort in areas where critical work is taking place, such as offices and schools. A person seated at a desk looking downward toward the task will view the floor as a secondary background. Research has established that the task surface (book or papers) should not exceed a reflectance factor of 30 to 50 percent, and the floor should not exceed a 50 percent reflectance level.

Other areas of concern are long hallways in hospitals or nursing homes where the reflectance level and the glare can distort the length or shape of the space and create difficulty for an ill or elderly person. A very glossy surface also creates special subfloor preparation problems; i.e., the surface must be very smooth to prevent any irregularities from showing on the tile surface.

Slipperiness. This is another health and safety factor that has been the subject of research by private industry, shoe manufacturers, insurance companies, and the National Bureau of Standards. National safety statistics have shown that falls in the home kill as many as 12,000 people and injure 6 million a year in the United States. Although the precise causes of the falls are not recorded, slippery floors are listed as a large contributor to these casualty rates.[1] Several laboratory tests have been developed to determine the factors that contribute to slipperiness, i.e., skid resistance or coefficient of friction between flooring and other materials such as footwear sole and heel materials.

TABLE 8.1 GENERAL PHYSICAL CHARACTERISTICS OF RESILIENT FLOORING

Material	Size	Gauges	Federal Specification	Load Limit (psi)	Construction and Recommended Use
Asphalt tile	9″ × 9″	1/8″ (0.125)	SS-T-312 Type I	25	Asbestos fibers, pigments, asphaltic binders. Use only marbleized pattern that penetrates entire thickness for commercial installation. Poor resilient quality.
Vinyl asbestos	9″ × 9″ 12″ × 12″	1/16″	SS-T-312 Type IV	25	Vinyl resins, asbestos fibers, plasticizors, color pigments and fillers. Semi-flexibility. Resistant to chemicals and moisture. Install all grades. Poor resilient quality.
Rubber tile	9″ × 19″ 12″ × 12″	1/8″ (0.125)	SS-T-312 Type II	200	Rubber compounds of synthetic butadiene-styrene type. Similar to vinyls in quality, but less durable and less resistant to grease and alkalis.
Vinyl sheet	6′ wide 90′	.090	L-F-00450 A L-F-475a Type II	100	Vinyl resin surface with a backing of asbestos-flex felt or resin-saturated rag fiber. Install all grades. Use only in light or moderate traffic. Low resistance to cigarette burns. Very resilient.
Vinyl tile	9″ × 9″ 12″ × 12″	.080 1/16″ 3.36″ 1/8″	L-F-475 a Type II SS-T-312 Type I	200	Blended composition of thermoplastic binders, fillers and pigments. Binders are polyvinyl chloride. Expensive in translucent type. Very resilient, but low resistance to cigarette burns.
Cork tile	6″ × 6″ 9″ × 9″ 12″ × 12″	1/8″ 3/16″ 5/16″		75	Pure cork particles bonded by baking process and thermosetting binders. May be finished or unfinished. Light to moderate traffic. Install on grade or suspended grade.
Vinyl cork tile	9″ × 12″	1/8″ (0.125)		150	Same as above, but may have thermoplastic binders and plastic film finishes.

The coefficient of friction between two surfaces is defined as the ratio of the force required to move one surface over the other to the total force pressing the two surfaces together. Thus:

$$\text{Coefficient of friction} = \frac{\text{horizontal force}}{\text{vertical force}}$$

The two types of friction that are considered in these test methods are static and dynamic (kinetic). *Static* friction is the amount of friction between two surfaces at the moment that one begins to move across the other. *Dynamic* friction occurs between two surfaces when movement is in progress without interruption. Laboratory equipment is designed to test flooring materials in a horizontal position, with the application of static friction or the use of dynamic friction in the form of a swinging pendulum. The test results are recorded as an "index of slipperiness" or a "skid resistance index." The specification of flooring that may result in falls is especially critical in lobby or vestibule areas (see barrier-free requirements in Chapter 14). The GSA specification for office buildings requires that resilient flooring be tested according to the ASTM D-2047 and have a slip resistance coefficient of greater than or equal to 0.5.[2]

Installation

The most important environmental factors to consider in the specification of resilient flooring are:

1. Moisture conditions in concrete subfloors and wooden on-grade floors and surface moisture that may occur in public baths, showers, and laundry rooms can create serious installation problems. The danger of moisture in concrete subflooring is discussed in Chapter 7. Table 8.2 lists the density classification of concrete slabs and recommended resilient floor application. Light-weight concrete may be structurally weak on the surface level and not support the adhesive bonding for resilient flooring. Serious problems can occur in wooden on-grade floors because the wood can absorb moisture through the sleepers, and if resilient flooring is installed over the wood, moisture could be trapped between the sleepers and the resilient material, thus causing the wooden floor below to deteriorate. For this reason, resilient flooring is not recommended for this type of installation. If, however, the wooden floor is constructed over a crawl space [at least 18 in. (45.7 cm) high] with good cross ventilation, the resilient flooring could be successfully installed.

   Surface moisture from spillage can best be counteracted by the selection of a resilient flooring with few seams, such as sheet material.

2. If direct sunlight is expected in areas having resilient flooring, designers should be aware that intense sunlight can blister, fade, shrink, and even make tile very brittle. Certain pigments, such as yellows and reds, tend to fade rapidly. In situations that present problems of this nature, designers should specify more neutral colors, such as tans and grays, which will resist fading.

3. Stain-producing chemicals may also present problems in making a specification decision. If very sanitary and clean conditions are required, the designer may consider sheet vinyl that is especially engineered for commercial use. Resilient floor tiles may also provide a very tight seam

TABLE 8.2 DENSITY CLASSIFICATION OF CONCRETE SLABS BY WEIGHT

Density	Type of Concrete	Lb per Cu Ft	Recommendations
Light	Expanded perlite vermiculite and others	20-40	Top with 1″ thickness of standard concrete mix
Medium	Expanded slag, shale and clay	60-90 90-120	Follow above recommendation or that given below
Heavy	Standard concrete of sand, gravel or stone	120-150	Approved for use of resilient flooring if troweled smooth and even

Source: Armstrong Cork Company.

through precision factory cutting.

Underlayments. Many types of subfloors require an underlayment to provide a smooth undersurface and prevent expansion and contraction of wood subfloors. There are two major types of underlayments:

1. Mastic types are made of a binder containing latex or polyvinylacetate resins. These should not be applied in thicknesses exceeding 1/8 in. (3.2 mm) and the subfloor should be free from paint, oil, and varnish.

2. Board-type underlayments may be hardboard, plywood, or particleboard. Generally, hardboard is used on renovation projects, and plywood or particleboard is used on new construction. Plywood should be specified in 1/4 in. (6.4 mm) thickness or heavier, interior type APA Underlayment Grade or exterior type APA CC (plugged). Particleboard underlayments are not recommended by all resilient flooring manufacturers. In fact, some manufacturers will not accept responsibility for flooring performance in the event of underlayment failure.

Adhesives. The specification of adhesives should be based on the manufacturer's recommendations. There are special types of adhesives used for resilient flooring.

Asphaltic. Used for the installation of asphalt and vinyl asbestos tile, these adhesives usually remain soft and tacky for long periods of time. Asphaltic adhesives are divided into two types:

1. Emulsion types are water-based and contain from 50 to 60 percent asphalt with no flammability or toxicity hazards. Standards of performance are established by federal specification MMM-A-115A. This adhesive may be used on suspended, above- and below-grade concrete flooring. Curing time required prior to installation is usually 30 minutes to 1 hour. Estimated coverage per gallon is between 150 to 200 sq ft (14 to 18.5 sq m).

2. Cut-back adhesives are solutions of asphalt in hydrocarbon solvents. Standards of performance are established by federal specification MMM-A-110A. This adhesive is trowel-applied and requires about 30 minutes' drying time

prior to installation. Superior to emulsions for vinyl asbestos tiles, it may be used on all concrete grades and plywood or hardwood suspended floors.

Brushable. These are higher viscosity adhesives that can be applied with a brush, roller, or trowel.

Resinous Waterproof. These adhesives usually contain alcohol as a solvent and have the same characteristics as linoleum paste. Although this type of adhesive is insoluble in ordinary water, it may be attacked by alkaline solutions. This makes it impractical for concrete surfaces on or below grade levels. Estimated coverage per gallon is about 150 sq ft (14 sq m).

Installation Inspection Checklist. Designers should not neglect to make adequate inspections before, during, and after installation. The following checklist is based on Construction Specifications Institute (CSI) recommendations.

Before:
1. Verify that proper provisions have been made for maintaining installation temperatures [70° F (21°C)].

2. Verify that conditions for storage of materials are satisfactory and that provisions for materials requiring acclimatization have been made.

3. Verify that substrate surfaces are dry, clean, sound, level, and conform with specified requirements.

4. Check that wood subfloors have been securely fastened with nonrising fasteners, and surfaces and joints have been treated to prevent "telegraphing" (when irregularities in a subsurface are noticeable on the surface of an applied finish).

5. Verify that all items scheduled to penetrate the flooring have been installed and that the area will be free from other work and traffic during the period required to install and complete installation.

During:
1. Check that joints and seams are tight, even, and aligned.

2. Verify that special inset patterns or borders are laid and that the desired laying pattern is followed.

3. See that materials requiring cutting and fitting are prepared in a neat, workmanlike manner.

4. See that materials requiring rolling are properly rolled and surfaces are free of air pockets, ripples, bubbles, and unevenness (asphalt and vinyl asbestos tiles do not require rolling).

After:
1. Check that floor surface is smooth and level with all tile joints tight, flush, and aligned.

2. Check that seams are sealed and matched in sheet material.

3. Witness conductivity tests and verify performance with requirements.

4. Check to see that base coverings are securely installed with sealed joints and properly aligned.

5. Verify that area is clean and all excess adhesive, scraps, soil, and stains have been removed.

6. See that final finishings, waxing, and polishing are accomplished.

7. After work is checked, see that work is protected from damage until accepted by owner.

8. Receive maintenance instructions and materials (if required); transmit to owner.[3]

Maintenance
Newly installed flooring should only be damp mopped without the use of excessive water until the adhesive has had time to thoroughly set (four to five days). The floor should be immediately protected with a light coating of water-based polish or finish.

Daily maintenance usually involves sweeping with a soft broom, treated cloths, or treated mops which will remove dirt and dust buildup. Washing of resilient floors may be required every two weeks in light traffic areas and more often in areas that receive heavy spillage, such as refreshment centers. This light-duty cleaning does not require the removal of the polish finish. Alkaline cleaners should not be used because the residue may dull the glossy finish.

Recommended polishes include water-resistant resin or polymer types. Polymeric floor finishes should not, however, be applied over waxy finishes because a streaky film may result, but waxy finishes can be applied over polymerics. Polymer finishes should be removed after every three or four applications to prevent excessive buildup. Paste waxes or liquid-solvent waxes, which contain solvents such as naphtha or turpentine, should not be used on resilient flooring. This flooring should also never be treated with lacquers, varnishes, or similar finishes because they will discolor and be difficult to remove.[4]

Protection against Indentation. Floor protectors are necessary to retain the beauty of resilient flooring. The concentrated weight of furniture legs can be more evenly distributed over the surface by using flat composite cups under the legs. Furniture that is frequently moved should be equipped with casters 2 in. (5.1 cm) in diameter with soft rubber treads at least 3/4 in. (19.1 mm) wide. Glides should have a smooth, flat base with rounded edges and a flexible shank. These should be 1 1/4 to 2 1/2 in. (3.1 to 6.3 cm) in diameter. The Resilient Tile Institute recommends a maximum loading of 75 lb per square inch (psi) for vinyl asbestos tile and 40 lb psi for asphalt tile. To prevent scratch-producing dirt buildup, protectors should be cleaned each time the flooring is washed.

Estimating Initial Costs
The initial cost must include cost of materials, such as adhesive, flooring material, and underlayments. In addition, the labor costs will be dependent on the preinstallation time needed for subfloor preparation. Installation labor costs are usually based on the number of square feet involved. To all these costs, the designer should add 15 to 20 percent for labor overhead and a profit surcharge of 10 to 15 percent.

Drawings and Specifications
The CSI recommends that the following be indicated on the working drawings:

1. The areas to be covered in resilient flooring should be clearly marked.

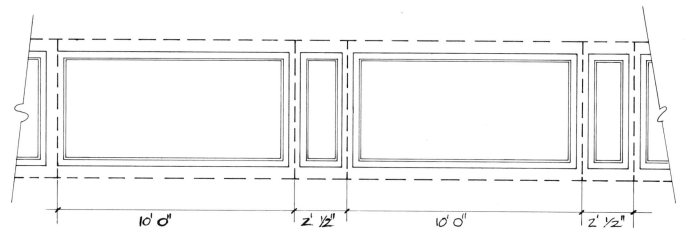

Figure 8.1 Working drawing for patterned resilient corridor flooring. Source: Architectural Interiors, Inc., Phoenix, AZ.

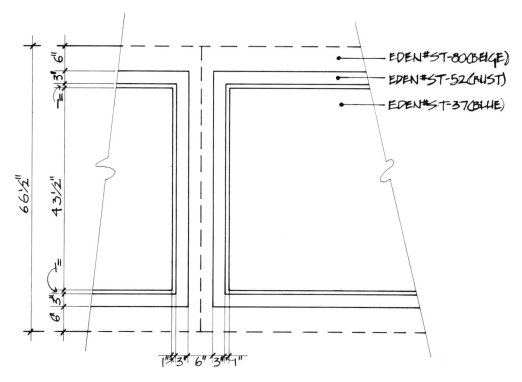

EDEN#ST-80(BEIGE)
EDEN#ST-52(RUST)
EDEN#ST-37(BLUE)

Figure 8.2 Detail drawing for patterned resilient flooring. Source: Architectural Interiors, Inc., Phoenix, AZ.

2. The type of flooring material and location of each different type must be shown on the drawings.

3. If two or more tile types or colors abut or if a resilient floor joins another floor finish, the joints between materials should be carefully shown. When the joining materials involve a difference in thickness, special design treatment, or trim, the details should be clearly shown on the drawings.

4. In the event that areas are to receive a custom-pattern design or special insert material, the design must be clearly indicated. Figures 8.1 and 8.2 illustrate detailed drawings

for a patterned resilient floor.

5. The locations and extent of any required base trim materials or special items, such as edge termination and saddles (inserts as interior openings), should be shown.

6. Coverings for stair treads, noisings, risers, runners, and stringers should be noted on the drawings.

The written specification for resilient tile in Figure 8.3 provides an example of the information that should be carefully specified.[5]

Figure 8.3 Specifications for resilient tile. Reproduced with permission of PAGS.

```
 1   SECTION 09650                                                     1
 2                                                                     2
 3   RESILIENT FLOORING-TILE                                           3
 4                                                                     4
 5                                                                     5
 6   PART 1 - GENERAL                                                  6
 7                                                                     7
 8   WORK SPECIFIED HEREIN                                             8
 9                                                                     9
10   ALL LABOR, MATERIALS, EQUIPMENT AND SERVICES NECESSARY TO        10
11   FURNISH AND INSTALL ALL RESILIENT FLOORING AND RELATED ITEMS     11
12   AS INDICATED OR SPECIFIED.                                       12
13                                                                    13
14   SUBSTITUTIONS                                                    14
15                                                                    15
16   IN ACCORDANCE WITH SECTION 01600.                                16
17                                                                    17
18   SUBMITTALS                                                       18
19                                                                    19
20   SUBMIT SAMPLES OF RESILIENT TILE, BASE, AND NOSINGS TO           20
21   ARCHITECT FOR REVIEW IN ACCORDANCE WITH SECTION 01340.           21
22                                                                    22
23   QUALITY ASSURANCE                                                23
24                                                                    24
25   MANUFACTURERS:                                                   25
26                                                                    26
27                                                                    27
28   PRODUCT DELIVERY, STORAGE AND HANDLING                           28
29                                                                    29
30   STORE ALL MATERIALS OFF THE GROUND UNDER WATERTIGHT COVER AND    30
31   AWAY FROM SWEATING WALLS AND OTHER DAMP SURFACES UNTIL READY     31
32   FOR USE.  ALL ROOMS, SUBFLOORS, TILES AND ADHESIVES SHALL BE     32
33   MAINTAINED AT A MINIMUM TEMPERATURE OF 70 DEGREES  F. FOR AT     33
34   LEAST 48 HOURS BEFORE COMMENCING WORK.  TEMPERATURE SHALL BE     34
35   MAINTAINED DURING INSTALLATION AND FOR AT LEAST 48 HOURS         35
36   AFTER COMPLETION.  REMOVE DAMAGED OR DETERIORATED MATERIALS      36
37   FROM THE PREMISES.                                               37
38                                                                    38
39   PROTECTION                                                       39
40                                                                    40
41   PROTECT FINISHED WORK INSTALLED BY OTHER TRADES PRIOR TO WORK    41
42   UNDER THIS SECTION.  ANY WORK DAMAGED BY WORKMEN OF THIS         42
43   TRADE SHALL BE REPLACED WITHOUT COST TO THE OWNER.               43
44                                                                    44
45   EXTRA MATERIAL                                                   45
46                                                                    46
47   PROVIDE 2 UNOPENED CARTONS OF RESILIENT TILE FOR OWNER'S         47
48   FUTURE USE.                                                      48
49                                                                    49
50   PROVIDE 40 LINEAL FEET OF RESILIENT BASE FOR OWNER'S FUTURE      50
51   USE.                                                             51
52                                                                    52
53                                                                    53
54   PART 2 - PRODUCTS                                                54
55                                                                    55
56   MATERIALS                                                        56
57                                                                    57
58   VINYL ASBESTOS TILE:  FS SS-T-312, TYPE IV, 12" X 12", 1/8"      58
59   THICK.  COLORS AS SELECTED FROM STANDARD PATTERNS AND COLORS.    59
60                                                                    60
61   RUBBER BASE:  MOLDED RUBBER COVE BASE (TOP SET) OR (CARPET)      61
62   AS MANUFACTURED BY                      OR APPROVED EQUAL, 4"    62
63   HIGH X 1/8" THICK.  COLORS AS SELECTED FROM DECORATOR PRICE      63
64   CATEGORY.  USE MATCHING PREFORMED CORNERS AND END-CAPS.          64
65                                                                    65
66   VINYL BASE:  VINYL COVE BASE (TOP SET) OR (CARPET) MANUFAC-      66
67   TURERS AS SPECIFIED ABOVE, 4" HIGH X 1/8" THICK.  COLORS AS      67
68   SELECTED FROM FULL COLOR RANGE OF MANUFACTURER.                  68
69                                                                    69
70   FLOORING ADHESIVES:  AS PER FLOORING MANUFACTURER'S RECOM-       70
71   MENDATIONS.                                                      71
72                                                                    72
```

EDGING STRIPS: 1/8" THICK, VINYL OR RUBBER, TAPERED OR BULL
NOSE EDGE, COLOR TO MATCH TILE OR AS SELECTED FROM MANUFAC-
TURER'S STANDARD COLORS.

BASE ADHESIVE:

UNDERLAYMENT:

MOLDED RUBBER STAIR NOSINGS SHALL BE AS MANUFACTURED BY
                         UNITS TO BE 1/4" THICK, SQUARE NOSE,
DOUBLE LOCK TYPE, COLOR AS SELECTED.

NOSING ADHESIVE:

PART 3 - EXECUTION

PREPARATION

INSPECT ALL SURFACES TO RECEIVE TILE BASE, AND TREADS AND
REPORT ALL DEFECTS THAT WILL AFFECT THE INSTALLATION. FILL
LOW AREAS WITH UNDERLAYMENT. THE WORK UNDER THIS SECTION
INCLUDES FILLING OF ALL JOINTS, CRACKS AND CHIPS IN SUBFLOOR
WITH CRACK FILLER OR UNDERLAYMENT AS REQUIRED TO PROVIDE A
TRUE, EVEN SURFACE TO RECEIVE TILE, AND SMOOTHING OF WALLS
WITH UNDERLAYMENT AS REQUIRED TO RECEIVE COVE BASE. CONCRETE
SURFACES TO RECEIVE TILE OR BASE SHALL BE DRY, FREE OF PAINT
AND OIL, AND SWEPT CLEAN BEFORE WORK COMMENCES. CONTRACTOR
SHALL BE HELD RESPONSIBLE FOR ANY DEFECTS IN THE SUBFLOOR
WHICH APPEAR IN THE FLOORING SURFACE AFTER COMPLETION.

INSTALLATION

AFTER PREPARATION OF SURFACES, APPLY ADHESIVE IN A THIN FILM
AND SPREAD EVENLY WITH A SERRATED TROWEL WITH NOTCHES 1/16" X
1/16", 1/8" APART.   LAY TILE IN A SQUARE PATTERN, WITHOUT
SPECIAL BORDERS, SYMMETRICAL ABOUT THE AXIS OF THE ROOM OR
SPACE.

DIRECTION OF GRAINING SHALL BE AS DIRECTED. LAY OUT WORK SO
THAT, AS FAR AS PRACTICABLE, NO PIECE OF TILE SHALL BE LESS
THAN 5" WIDE, PARTICULARLY AT DOORS.

ALL JOINTS SHALL BE TIGHT, IN TRUE ALIGNMENT, AND AS INCON-
SPICUOUS AS POSSIBLE. WHERE TWO COLORS MEET AT DOOR OPENINGS
OR WHERE TILE TERMINATES AT DOORS TO ROOMS HAVING EXPOSED
CONCRETE FLOORS, PROVIDE A 1" WIDE FEATURE STRIP DIRECTLY
UNDER THE DOOR. ARCHITECT SHALL HAVE THE OPTION OF SELECTING
DIFFERENT COLORS IN DIFFERENT AREAS OR ROOMS.

CUT AND FIT TILE SUFFICIENTLY CLOSE TO WALLS, COLUMNS, ETC.,
SO THAT JOINT WILL BE COVERED BY THE BASE, WHERE INSTALLED.
AT OTHER FIXED SURFACES, INCLUDING THRESHOLDS, PIPES, REMOV-
ABLE COVERS, FLOOR OUTLETS AND PERMANENT BUILT-IN CABINETS
AND EQUIPMENT, SCRIBE AND ACCURATELY FIT TILE AS REQUIRED.
PROVIDE TILE INSERTS AT REMOVABLE FLOOR OUTLET COVERS. RE-
MOVE EXCESS ADHESIVE FROM ALL SURFACES IMMEDIATELY. SEAL
JOINTS AT PIPES WITH WATERPROOF CEMENT.

PROVIDE UNDERLAYMENT AS REQUIRED TO BRING RESILIENT TILE SUR-
FACE TO THE SAME LEVEL AS ABUTTING CERAMIC TILE, OR OTHER
FLOORING.

INSTALL RUBBER STAIR NOSINGS PER MANUFACTURER'S INSTRUCTIONS.

BASE

AFTER PREPARATION OF WALL SURFACES, APPLY ADHESIVE TO BACK OF
BASE LEAVING TOP 1/4" FREE OF ADHESIVE. PRESS BASE FIRMLY
AGAINST THE WALLS SLIDING HORIZONTALY INTO PLACE, MAKING SURE

Figure 8.3 Specifications for resilient tile. (Continued)

```
 1    TOE IS TIGHT TO THE FLOOR AND AGAINST THE WALL.  ROLL THE       1
 2    ENTIRE SURFACE OF THE BASE WITH A HAND ROLLER, AND PRESS THE    2
 3    TOP OF THE BASE AGAINST THE WALL WITH A STRAIGHT EDGE.  RE-      3
 4    MOVE EXCESS ADHESIVE IMMEDIATELY.  INSTALL PRE-FORMED CORNERS    4
 5    AT ALL OUTSIDE CORNERS.  COPE AT INTERNAL CORNERS.  WHERE        5
 6    BASE TERMINATES AT PROJECTIONS INSTALL END CAPS.                 6
 7                                                                     7
 8    CLEANING AND WAXING                                              8
 9                                                                     9
10    CLEAN FLOORS BY A METHOD RECOMMENDED BY THE MANUFACTURER OF     10
11    THE FLOORING.  WAX THE TILE AFTER THE ADHESIVE HAS HAD AN       11
12    OPPORTUNITY TO REACH ITS FINAL, FIRM SET.  THIS PERIOD OF       12
13    TIME SHALL BE AT LEAST TWO DAYS AFTER LAYING THE FLOORING IN    13
14    THE SUMMER TIME AND AT LEAST FIVE DAYS AFTER LAYING THE         14
15    FLOORING IN THE HEATED BUILDING IN THE WINTER TIME.             15
16                                                                    16
17    APPLY ONE COAT OF CARNAUBA WAX TO THE TILE ACCORDING TO THE     17
18    MANUFACTURER'S INSTRUCTIONS AT THE RATE OF AT LEAST ONE GAL-    18
19    LON OF UNDILUTED WAX FOR EACH 3,000 SQUARE FEET OF TILE         19
20    SURFACE.                                                        20
21                                                                    21
22    AFTER THE CLEANING AND WAXING OPERATION, POLISH THE FLOOR       22
23    WITH AN ELECTRIC POLISHER TO A SMOOTH, EVEN AND HIGHLY RE-      23
24    FLECTIVE FINISH.  PROTECT THE FLOORING WITH HEAVY PAPER UNTIL   24
25    ACCEPTANCE OF THE WORK.                                         25
26                                                                    26
27                                                                    27
28    END OF SECTION                                                  28
29                                                                    29
30                                                                    30
31                                                                    31
32                                                                    32
33                                                                    33
```

HARD-SURFACE FLOORING

The second major type of flooring is composed of hard surfaces, such as marble, quarry tile, brick, and wood, both standard and acrylic. Because acrylic wood flooring involves a relatively new manufacturing process, it will be discussed in detail.

Marble

Marble is very expensive and requires special care, such as buffing and polishing. It is available in squares 11.7″ × 11.7″ (29.7 × 29.7 cm) and strips 3.9″ × 11.7″ × 0.36″ (9.9 × 29.7 × .9 cm). Larger sizes are also available, but because of the weight factor they become very difficult to install.

Quarry Tile and Brick

These materials are relatively expensive. Both are usually set within mortars and finished with grouted seams. Brick sizes are normally 2″ × 4″ × 8″ (5.1 × 10.2 × 20.3 cm), which are sliced thin for floor application. Quarry tiles range in size and shape from 1/2″ (1.3 cm) to 12″ (30.5 cm), in rectangular, square, hexagonal, and other shapes. The written specifications in Figures 8.4 and 8.5 give information on installation procedures.

Figure 8.4 Specifications for quarry tile. Reproduced with permission of PAGS.

```
 1      SECTION 09330
 2
 3      QUARRY TILE
 4
 5
 6      PART 1 - GENERAL
 7
 8      WORK SPECIFIED HEREIN
 9
10      ALL LABOR, MATERIALS, EQUIPMENT AND SERVICES NECESSARY TO
11      FURNISH AND INSTALL ALL QUARRY TILE AS INDICATED OR SPECI-
12      FIED.
13
14      SUBSTITUTIONS
15
16      IN ACCORDANCE WITH SECTION 01600.
17
18      QUALITY ASSURANCE
19
20      STANDARDS:  MATERIALS, PREPARATION AND INSTALLATION SHALL
21      CONFORM TO ANSI STANDARDS AS LISTED AND THE DETAILED INSTAL-
22      LATION INSTRUCTIONS OF THE MATERIAL MANUFACTURER INSOFAR AS
23      APPLICABLE.
24
25          INSTALLATION OF QUARRY TILE WITH WATER RESISTANT ORGANIC
26          ADHESIVES - ANSI A-108.4.
27
28          INSTALLATION OF QUARRY TILE WITH PORTLAND CEMENT MORTAR
29          - ANSI A-108.1.
30
31          INSTALLATION OF QUARRY TILE WITH DRY-SET PORTLAND CEMENT
32          MORTAR OR LATEX PORTLAND CEMENT MORTAR - ANSI A-108.5.
33
34      ACCEPTABLE MANUFACTURERS OF QUARRY TILE ARE:
35
36
37
38
39      SUBMITTALS
40
41      SUBMIT SAMPLES IN ACCORDANCE WITH SECTION 01340 FOR ALL WORK
42      UNDER THIS SECTION.   SUBMIT SAMPLES OF ALL MATERIALS SPECI-
43      FIED HEREIN OF THE SIZE SPECIFIED.
44
45      FURNISH MASTER GRADE CERTIFICATE FOR ALL TILE, BEFORE INSTAL-
46      LATION, BEARING THE CERTIFICATION MARK OF THE TCA, SIGNED BY
47      THE MANUFACTURER STATING THE TYPE AND QUALITY OF THE
48      MATERIAL.
49
50      FURNISH MANUFACTURER'S PRINTED INSTRUCTIONS FOR USE OF LATEX
51      PORTLAND CEMENT AND MORTAR.
52
53      EXTRA STOCK:   PROVIDE 2 CARTONS OF QUARRY TILE FOR OWNER'S
54      FUTURE USE.
55
56      PRODUCT DELIVERY, STORAGE, AND HANDLING
57
58      DELIVER TILE TO THE JOB IN UNOPENED CARTONS SEALED WITH A
59      GRADE SEAL BEARING NAME OF MANUFACTURER AND THE WORDS "STAND-
60      ARD GRADE" PRINTED THEREON.
61
62      MANUFACTURED MORTARS AND GROUTS SHALL CONTAIN HALLMARK CER-
63      TIFYING COMPLIANCE WITH REFERENCED STANDARDS AND BE TYPES
64      RECOMMENDED BY TILE MANUFACTURER FOR SPECIFIC APPLICATIONS.
65
66      ADHESIVES SHALL BE IN CONTAINERS LABELED WITH HALLMARK CER-
67      TIFYING COMPLIANCE WITH REFERENCED STANDARDS.
68
69      ORGANIC ADHESIVE CONTAINERS TO BEAR HALLMARK OF EITHER ADHE-
70      SIVE AND SEALANT COUNCIL OR TCA CERTIFYING COMPLIANCE WITH
71      ANSI 1-136.1.
72
```

Figure 8.4 Specifications for quarry tile. (Continued)

DELIVER MASTIC GROUT READY FOR USE.

DELIVER DRY-SET MORTAR IN SEALED, MOISTUREPROOF CONTAINERS.

STORE MATERIALS UNDER COVER IN MANNER TO PREVENT DAMAGE OR
CONTAMINATION.

JOB CONDITIONS

SET AND GROUT TILE IN PORTLAND CEMENT MORTAR WHEN AMBIENT
TEMPERATURE IS AT LEAST 50 DEGREES F. AND RISING.

COMPLY WITH MINIMUM TEMPERATURE RECOMMENDATIONS OF MANUFAC-
TURER'S FOR BONDING AND GROUTING MATERIALS IN OTHER THAN
PORTLAND CEMENT MORTAR.

PROTECT ADJOINING WORK SURFACES BEFORE TILE WORK BEGINS.

PART 2 - PRODUCTS

MATERIALS

ALL TILE SHALL BE OF DOMESTIC MANUFACTURE, STANDARD GRADE
MEETING THE REQUIREMENTS OF SPR R-61 OF THE U.S. DEPARTMENT
OF COMMERCE AND SHALL COMPLY WITH ANS A-137.1. TCA CERTIFICA-
TION MARK SHALL APPEAR ON EACH CARTON LABEL.

QUARRY TILE SHALL BE COLOR AS SELECTED. SIZE OF TILES SHALL
BE 6" X 6" X 1/2". BASE SHALL BE 5" HIGH, COVERED WITH BULL-
NOSE TOP. WHERE SHOWN, FURNISH TILE WITH ABRASIVE GRAIN
SURFACE.

GROUT MATERIAL SHALL BE HYDROMENT, COLOR AS SELECTED.

PORTLAND CEMENT SHALL CONFORM TO ASTM C-150, TYPE I.

SAND SHALL CONFORM TO ASTM C-144.

MORTAR SHALL BE ONE PART PORTLAND CEMENT, 6 PARTS DAMP SAND
BY VOLUME.

BOND COAT SHALL BE PORTLAND CEMENT PASTE ON A PLASTIC BED, OR
DRY-SET MORTAR ON A CURED BED OR LATEX PORTLAND CEMENT MORTAR
ON A CURED BED.

LATEX PORTLAND CEMENT MORTAR SHALL CONFORM TO ANSI A-118.4.

DRY-SET MORTAR SHALL CONFORM TO ANSI A-118.1.

ORGANIC ADHESIVE SHALL BE FLOOR TYPE CONFORMING TO ANSI
A-136.1.

EXPANSION JOINTS:

SEALANT: TWO COMPONENT COMPLYING WITH FS TT-S-0227; TYPE II
FOR JOINTS IN VERTICAL SURFACES; TYPE I FOR JOINTS IN HORI-
ZONTAL SURFACES.

BACK-UP: FLEXIBLE AND COMPRESSIBLE TYPE OF CLOSED-CELL FOAM
POLYETHYLENE OR BUTYL RUBBER, ROUNDED AT SURFACE TO CONTACT
SEALANT, AS SHOWN IN TCA DETAILS, AND AS RECOMMENDED BY
SEALANT MANUFACTURER. IT SHALL FIT NEATLY INTO THE JOINT
WITHOUT COMPACTING AND TO SUCH A HEIGHT TO ALLOW A SEALANT
DEPTH OF 1/2 THE WIDTH OF THE JOINT. SEALANT SHALL NOT BOND
TO THE BACK-UP MATERIAL.

PART 3 - EXECUTION

INSTALLATION

PAGS 978   09330 - 2

INSTALL ALL QUARRY TILE IN PORTLAND CEMENT MORTAR IN ACCORD-
ANCE WITH ANS A-108.1, AND TCA METHOD F-112-78.

INSTALL ALL QUARRY TILE USING WATER-RESISTANT ORGANIC ADHE-
SIVES IN ACCORDANCE WITH ANS A-108-4 AND TCA METHOD F-116-78.

INSTALL ALL QUARRY TILE IN DRY-SET MORTAR OR LATEX PORTLAND
CEMENT MORTAR IN ACCORDANCE WITH ANS A-108.5 AND TCA METHOD
F-113.78.

THESE SPECIFICATIONS, INSOFAR AS ANY PORTIONS ARE APPLICABLE,
ARE HEREBY MADE A DIRECT PART OF THIS SPECIFICATION AS THOUGH
REPEATED HEREIN.

LAY OUT FLOORS SO THAT NO TILE LESS THAN ONE-HALF SIZE
OCCURS. ALIGN ALL JOINTS IN BOTH DIRECTIONS.

GROUT TILE JOINTS FLUSH WITH FACE OF TILES MAKING A NEATLY
FINISHED SMOOTH SURFACE. INSTALL SPECIFIED GROUT IN STRICT
ACCORDANCE WITH MANUFACTURER'S PRINTED INSTRUCTIONS.

EXPANSION JOINTS

PROVIDE EXPANSION JOINTS IN ALL CERAMIC TILE SURFACES IN
ACCORDANCE WITH TCA METHOD EJ-411-78.

EXPANSION JOINT WIDTH SHALL BE 1/4" MINIMUM. JOINTS THROUGH
TILE AND MORTAR DIRECTLY OVER STRUCTURAL JOINTS IN THE BACK-
ING MUST BE AT LEAST THE WIDTH OF THE STRUCTURAL JOINT.

PREPARATION:

TILE EDGES TO WHICH THE SEALANT WILL BOND MUST BE CLEAN AND
DRY. SAND OR GRIND AS NECESSARY TO OBTAIN OPTIMUM SEALANT
BOND.

PRIME TILE EDGES WHEN RECOMMENDED BY THE SEALANT MANUFAC-
TURER. TAKE CARE TO KEEP PRIMER OFF TILE FACES.

INSTALLATION:

SET BACK-UP WHEN MORTAR IS PLACED OR UTILIZE REMOVABLE WOOD
STRIP TO PROVIDE SPACE FOR BACK-UP AFTER MORTAR HAS CURED.

INSTALL SEALANT AFTER TILE WORK AND GROUT ARE DRY. FOLLOW
SEALANT MANUFACTURER'S RECOMMENDATIONS.

CLEANING AND PROTECTION

CLEAN TILE AFTER GROUTING AND PROTECT FROM OTHER TRADES.
CURE ALL QUARRY TILE FLOORS FOR A MINIMUM OF 3 DAYS.

END OF SECTION

Figure 8.5 Specifications for brick flooring. Reproduced with permission of Henningson, Durham, and Richardson, Phoenix, AZ.

Part 1. GENERAL

A. The Contractor shall furnish all labor, materials, tools, equipment, and perform all work and services for all interior brick flooring as shown on drawings and as specified, in accordance with provisions of the Contract Documents, and completely coordinated with work of all other trades.

B. Although such work is not specifically indicated, furnish and install all supplementary or miscellaneous items, appurtenances and devices incidental to or necessary for a sound, secure and complete installation.

(Specifier: Delete or modify as necessary.)

1.02 Quality Standards:

A. ASTM C-62 and C-216 for brick.

B. ANSI and TCA standards for setting and grouting

C. Other manufacturers desiring approval comply with Section 01640.

1.03 Submittals:

A. Brick samples for color selection.

B. Test reports verifying compliance with ASTM standards.

1.04 Product Delivery, Storage and Handling:

A. Deliver to site on covered pallets.

B. Store cementitious materials protected from wetting.

1.05 Job Conditions:

A. Verify suitability of substrate to accept installation.

B. Installation of materials constitutes acceptance of substrate and responsibility for performance.

Part 2. MATERIALS

A. Brick Pavers: Comply with ASTM C-62 grade SW for all physical properties. In addition, units to comply with ASTM C-216, type FBS regarding appearance.
(Specifier: Insert type, size.)

B. Colors and finishes as selected by designer.

C. Setting Adhesives: thin set mortar or adhesive by UPCO or other TCA licensed manufacturer.

D. Grout: Premixed water resistant type for grouting of brick pavers, by UPCO or other TCA licensed manufacturer. Grout color as selected.

E. Sealant: Gungrade or self-leveling polyurethane, minimum shore A Durometer of 40. Color as selected.

F. Surface Sealer: (Specifier selection)

Part 3. EXECUTION

A. Install in accord with ANSI and TCA recommendations. Cut and drill without marring surfaces. Grind, cut and joint carefully around or against trim or penetrations. Lay so fields or patterns center in areas. Avoid pieces smaller than 1/2 brick. Install with caulked joints not over 20 ft. (6 m) o.c.

B. Clean surfaces as required to remove materials which will adversely affect installation. Fill depressions, cracks or holes with latex mortar or grout.

C. Mix mortar or adhesive in accord with manufacturer's instruction. Spread skim coating and comb with notched trowel. Coat paver backs with mortar or adhesive. Set into place and tap to assure adhesion. Set with nominal 1/4 inch (6 mm) joints.

D. Force grout between units to assure complete filling of joints. Remove surplus grout and leave faces clean.

3.01 Sealing:

A. Provide sealant joints where pavers abut vertical surfaces and over substrate expansion or control joints. Apply surface sealer.

3.02 Protection:

A. Protect with taped in place polyethylene.

B. Provide additional protection where traffic may damage pavers.

3.03 Final Cleaning:

A. Remove protective coverings and rubbish. Clean entire surface. Protect adjacent surfaces from damage due to cleaning operations.

B. Leave installation clean. Do not wax.

Wood

Wood flooring is available in strips, as well as parquet, which can be set into many intricate patterns (see the specification data in Table 8.3). Standard wood floorings require refinishing and polishing to maintain surface qualities. These maintenance factors have a definite affect on the total life cycle cost.

Acrylic Wood

Acrylic wood flooring has many of the same qualities of resilient flooring. This wood product was developed in the mid-1950s when experimentation was conducted with peacetime use of radiation. This process was developed as an alternative to using natural wood as a flooring material because of its vulnerability to stains, scratches, mechanical damage, and chemical deterioration.

Manufacturing Process. The wood [slates $6'' \times 5/16'' \times 1''$ $(15.2 \times .8 \times 2.5$ cm)] is first vacuumed in a large canister to remove air trapped within the pore network of the wood. A liquid containing plastic, dyes, and fire retardants is then forced into the pores by pressure. When the wood emerges soaked in this liquid, it is then transferred to another canister and lowered into a 20-ft (6-m) pool of water with Cobalt 60, the radiation source, at the bottom of the canister. The water serves to cool and reduce the heat reaction and provides a biological shield which absorbs the radiation. The canister moves along a track at the bottom of the pool, passing the ray of the cobalt. When the product is taken from the canister, it is warm and dry. It is then polymerized by radiation, trimmed, and made into blocks for flooring.[6] Figure 8.6 illustrates the process.

The process can be used successfully on most domestic woods, but is not effective on some exotic foreign woods. Acrylic wood is available in various sizes, ranging from square blocks to random planks.

Physical Properties. Eight qualities characterize acrylic wood flooring:

1. Coloration of the surface cannot be worn off because the plastic contains dyes which permeate the entire wood.

2. The grains and wood tones are enhanced.

3. The surface has a very high abrasion resistance.

4. The wood has a very high density. That of oak, for example, can increase from 35 to 60 percent.

5. The compression strength of the wood is also increased, which decreases, but does not eliminate, the natural tendency of wood to contract and expand.

6. It gains a high degree of fire resistance.

7. It has a high resistance to bacterial growth.

8. The wood has added acoustic qualities.

Installation. Designers should specify that installation be according to the manufacturer's recommendations. The following information is provided to acquaint the designer with typical installation factors that must be considered prior to specification.[7]

On Concrete Subfloors. Designers should require that concrete subfloors should meet the following criteria:

1. Concrete subfloor shall be of good workmanship, structurally sound and finished to proper elevation to accept the acrylic wood floor. Finish shall be by wood or mechanical float to a true level approved by the manufacturer.

2. Use of concrete curing compounds or surface sealers is prohibited. If used, these must be removed by sanding.

3. In cases where the subfloor is not level or otherwise unacceptable, the contractor may use corrective measures, such as machine grinding or leveling with material recommended by the manufacturer for such corrective work, and the contractor shall assume full responsibility for proper and permanent bonding of fill and leveling methods.

4. All grime, dirt, oil, or grease shall be removed by thorough scouring and grinding, if necessary.

5. The floor shall be mechanically scarified prior to installation, especially if the slab has been steel-troweled to a smooth finish.

6. Moisture in the floor must be controlled as follows: drying time may vary depending on climatic and site conditions, but the minimum shall not be less than one week per 1-in. (2.5-cm) thickness for suspended slabs and two weeks per 1-in. thickness for on-grade or below-grade installations, under favorable conditions such as free air circulation in temperate weather and heat and ventilation in colder weather. Floors with moisture membranes under the tiles are recommended and may require longer drying times.

7. Moisture content testing may be accomplished by:
    a. Commercial moisture meter designed for such testing.
    b. Calcium chloride sealed under glass at 10 or 12 well-distributed locations.
    c. Test drilling 1/4-in. (6.4-mm) diameter holes to 3/4-in. (19.1 mm) the thickness of the slab.

8. Concrete floors on-grade or below-grade shall be on washed gravel fill and a membrane of waterproof and fungus-resistant reinforced kraft paper coated with a layer of polyethylene and 1-in. thick fiberglass edge insulation shall be installed in accordance with the manufacturer's instructions.

On Wood Subfloors. These subfloors must meet the following criteria:

1. Wood subfloors shall be plugged and sanded exterior grade plywood. When placed over sheathing, 1/2-in. (2.7-mm) plywood shall be used. When placed over wood joist, 3.4-in. (19.1-mm) plywood shall be used with all sides supported by joists or cripples.

2. All irregularities of joints in the plywood shall be sanded smooth.

3. The plywood shall be nailed on 6-in. (15.2-cm) centers.

TABLE 8.3 SPECIFICATION DATA FOR WOOD FLOORING

PRODUCT DESCRIPTION AND PATTERN	PANEL SIZE	GRADE	SPECIES	APPROX. WT. (lbs. per m. sq. ft.)
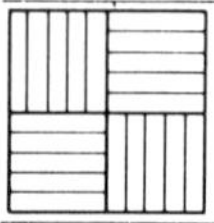 STANDARD Pattern Unfinished—Paper-Faced	5/16" x 19" x 19" 16 equal alternating squares 5/16" x 12" x 12" 4 equal alternating squares	Premium Select Rustic	Cherry—Maple Red Oak—White Oak—Cedar—Pecan—Walnut Rhodesian Teak Angelique (Guiana Teak) Panga-Panga	1250 1250
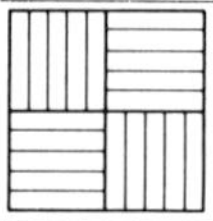 STANDARD Pattern Unfinished—WebBack or Mesh-Back	5/16" x 19" x 19" 16 equal alternating squares 5/16" x 11" x 11" 4 equal alternating squares	Premium Select Rustic Select & Better (Par & Better) Rustic	Red Oak—White Oak Pecan Red and White Oak	1250 1250
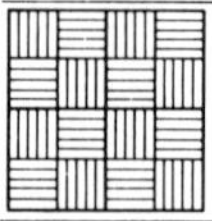 STANDARD Pattern Unfinished—WebBack (For Industrial Use)	5/16" x 19" x 19" 16 equal alternating squares 9/16" x 19" x 19" 16 equal alternating squares	Select & Better (Par & Better) Select Rustic & Better Rustic	Maple—Red Oak White Oak Pecan	1250 to 2650
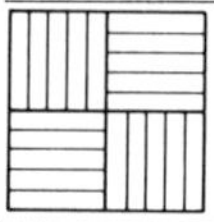 STANDARD Pattern Unfinished WebBack (For Industrial Use)	11/16" x 11" x 11" 4 equal alternating squares ¾" x 12-11/16" x 12-11/16" 4 equal alternating squares	Select & Better (Par & Better) Industrial & Better (Rustic & Better)	Red Oak—Maple	1250
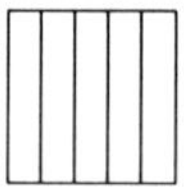 STANDARD Pattern Factory-Finished (Available in various colors)	5/16" x 6⅜" x 6⅜" 5/16" x 6½" x 6½" individual unit	Choice Natural & Better Natural Cabin	Oak—Walnut Pecan—Maple	1300
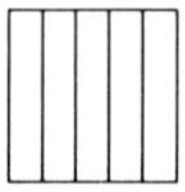 STANDARD Pattern Factory-Finished Foam-Back Tile	5/16" x 6½" x 6½" individual units . . . ⅛" foam, 2 lb. density	Natural & Better Natural Cabin	Oak—Pecan Maple	1300
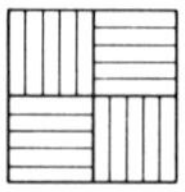 ANTIQUE TEXTURED (Factory-finished and Unfinished)—Kerfsawn Various colors available	5/16" x 6⅜" x 6⅜" individual squares 5/16" x 6½" x 6½" individual squares 5/16" x 11" x 11" 4 equal alternating squares	Select Natural & Better Select & Better (Par & Better)	Red Oak & White Oak Red Oak & White Oak	1250
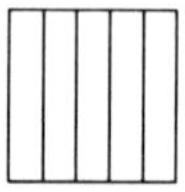 ANTIQUE TEXTURED (Factory-finished and Unfinished)—Wire brushed Various colors available	5/16" x 6⅜" x 6⅜" 5/16" x 6½" x 6½" individual squares	Natural & Better	Oak	1300
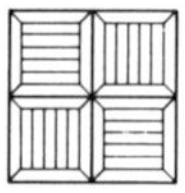 MONTICELLO Pattern Unfinished—Paper-Faced	5/16" x 13¼" x 13¼" 4 equal alternating squares	Select & Better (Par & Better)	Angelique (Guiana Teak) Red Oak—White Oak Panga-Panga—Black Walnut	1250
 HADDON HALL Pattern Unfinished—Paper-Faced	5/16" x 13¼" x 13¼" 4 equal squares	Select & Better (Par & Better)	Angelique (Guiana Teak) Red Oak—White Oak Panga-Panga—Black Walnut	1250
 HERRINGBONE Pattern Unfinished—Paper-Faced	5/16" x 14⅛" x 18⅛" (Approximate overall) 2 - "V" shape courses wide and 11 slats long	Select & Better (Par & Better)	Angelique (Guiana Teak) Red Oak—White Oak Panga-Panga—Black Walnut	1250
 SAXONY Pattern Unfinished—Paper-Faced	5/16" x 19" x 19" 4 equal squares on diagonal and 8 equal half squares	Select & Better (Par & Better)	Angelique (Guiana Teak) Red Oak—White Oak Panga-Panga—Black Walnut	1250
 CANTERBURY Pattern Unfinished—Paper-Faced	5/16" x 13¼" x 13¼" 4 equal alternating squares with diagonal center slats	Select & Better (Par & Better)	Angelique (Guiana Teak) Red Oak—White Oak Panga-Panga—Black Walnut	1250
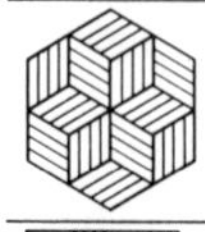 RHOMBS Pattern Unfinished—Paper-Faced	Hexagonal Shape 5/16" x 15⅛" x 15⅛" 12 equal Rhomboids	Select & Better (Par & Better)	Red Oak & White Oak	1250
 BASKET WEAVE Pattern Unfinished—Paper-Faced	5/16" x 15-1/5" x 19" 4 runs of 3 slats and 5 slats alternating	Select & Better (Par & Better)	Angelique (Guiana Teak) Red Oak—White Oak Panga-Panga—Black Walnut	1250
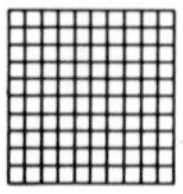 ITALIAN & DOMINO Pattern Unfinished—Paper-Faced	5/16" x 19" x 19" 400 equal size pieces butt-jointed	Premium Par & Select	Black Walnut Angelique (Guiana Teak) Maple—Red Oak White Oak	1250

Reproduced with permission of the American Parquet Association.

Acrylic/wood conversion process

Thoroughly dried wood is sealed in an evacuation chamber, and vacuumed to remove air trapped within the pore network of the wood (1).

A liquid substance containing the acrylic monomer, methyl methacrylate, dyes, and fire retardants, is then forced into the voids (2) of the pore structure until the wood is impregnated (3).

The canister and its contents are then irradiated by controlled exposure to Cobalt 60 gamma ray source (4). This causes the liquid plastic to polymerize into a solid substance, resulting in the hard, dense acrylic/wood composite (5).

Figure 8.6 Acrylic/wood conversion process. Reproduced with permission of Interiors *magazine.*

Working Conditions. The following conditions must be considered:

1. Flooring work shall not be installed until all masonry, plastering, tile, marble, and terrazzo work is completed and overhead work is finished.

2. The subfloor shall be dry, free from foreign materials, and broom clean. Temperature shall be maintained at 65°F (18°C) or higher for at least one week before, during, and 72 hours following installation.

3. When laying in-line flooring, it is recommended that the strips be laid with individual fillets butting end-to-end, offset by one-half fillet width.

Materials. The following conditions must be considered:

1. All materials shall be stored at the job site for enough time so that they can come up to equilibrium with site conditions. Cartons shall be opened at least 48 hours prior to installation. In installations where the air conditioning can be expected to be turned on and off, it is important that the material be properly acclimated so as to minimize humidity stress effects after installation.

2. The adhesive shall be recommended by the manufacturer. Epoxy type shall be used on concrete slabs on-grade or below-grade. Latex type shall be used for installations on wood subfloors or on concrete suspended slabs. Since plank flooring has a tendency to cup, it is recommended that the strongest mastic be utilized for these installations. Extra care should be taken to make sure of proper mastic coverage and to roll the strip and plank flooring properly into the mastic to assure good bonding so that the material will be able to resist stresses which might be encountered due to high humidity conditions and water expansion.

3. The adhesive shall be spread uniformly in accordance with the manufacturer's instructions. Flooring shall be installed within the allowable time as specified.

4. Individual parquet blocks shall be placed to match adjoining blocks, properly seated in the adhesive by tamping or rolling with a 100-lb (46-kg) roller. In-line flooring and strip flooring shall be butted together, but not too tightly, and tamped or rolled as described above.

5. An expansion void of 1/4 to 1/2 in. (6.3 to 12.7 mm) shall be provided at the walls to allow for expansion.

After Installation. Cleaning and buffing should include the following points:

1. It is recommended that the newly installed floor, after a 12-hour setting time, be cleaned and buffed before use to enhance its appearance.

2. Clean floor of all dust, grit, and abrasive particles by general sweeping, followed by a dry mop-type sweeper.

3. For a richer, deeper appearance, it is recommended that a coat of liquid buff be applied. Apply it lightly, approximately 1,000 sq ft (95 sq m) per gallon, and remove excess with dry rags. Floor may be buffed immediately; however, for best results, it is recommended that buffing be delayed for 8 hours.

4. Buff as follows:
    a. Buff with standard green pad.
    b. Buffing with standard tan pad will produce a long-lasting, lustrous finish.
    c. To produce a high-gloss finish, buff with standard white pad after completing above steps.

5. Upon completion of work, all materials, tools, equipment, and rubbish shall be removed from the site.

9 INTERIOR WALL FINISHES

Most building codes classify interior finishes as the materials used on the surface of walls, partitions, or ceilings. This chapter will survey the finishes most commonly specified by the designer, such as pliant wallcoverings, surface coating systems, and paneling.

PLIANT WALLCOVERINGS

Pliant wallcoverings are flexible materials such as papers, vinyls, foils, fabric, felt, cork, carpet, and thin wood veneers. Table 9.1 provides a summary of these finishes, their recommended use, their advantages, and their disadvantages.

Vinyl wallcoverings are designed for extreme serviceability and durability and are therefore frequently specified for commercial and institutional interiors. Vinyl wallcoverings are rated for flammability both by the Underwriters Laboratories and by other testing agencies. The ASTM E-84 Steiner Tunnel Test is used to determine the flame-spread and smoke development factors. Other performance criteria have been established by federal specifications and a voluntary standard.

1. *Federal Specification CCC-W-408* establishes minimum performance requirements and classifies these coverings into three types:
   a. Type I: Light duty with a total weight of 7 oz/sq yd (minimum 5 oz face coating weight).
   b. Type II: Medium duty with total weights of 13 oz/sq yd (minimum 7 oz face coating weight).
   c. Type III: Heavy duty with a total weight of 22 oz/sq yd (minimum 12 oz face coating weight).

   These three types are further classified:
   d. Class 1: Regular support backing not normally treated to prevent mildew.
   e. Class 2: Mildew resistant.
      Most vinyl-coated products are manufactured with mildew-resistant backings (class 2). This federal specification also establishes criteria for (1) abrasion

resistance, (2) cracking, (3) color fastness, (4) cold cracking, (5) heat aging, and (6) hydrostatic resistance and shrinkage.

2. *Federal Specification CC-T-191b* establishes requirements for abrasion, break and tear strength, and adhesion of the backing.

3. *Federal Specification D 1308-57* describes methods for testing stain resistance to household chemicals.

4. *Proposed Voluntary Standard* (TS 198) was developed in 1977 by the Chemical Fabrics and Film Association and the Wallcovering Manufacturers Association, which would establish a nationally recognized performance criteria for all wallcovering. Recognizing that certain wallcoverings are designed primarily for decorative effects, while others are designed to achieve a high degree of serviceability, the six proposed classes are based on serviceability and performance in the following areas:
   Colorfastness
   Washability
   Scrubability
   Stain resistance
   Crocking resistance
   Abrasion resistance
   Breaking strength
   Tear resistance
   Blocking resistance
   Coating adhesion
   Cold cracking resistance
   Heat aging resistance
   Shrinkage

Table 9.2 lists the six classes and the performance criteria for each. It should be noted that this standard does not establish any performance criteria for decorative class I type and only

TABLE 9.1 PLIANT WALLCOVERINGS

Covering	Use	Advantages	Disadvantages
Paper	Decorative	Many different patterns and colors. Moderate cost.	Subject to soiling, abrasion and fading. No flammability criteria.
Vinyl	Light, medium or heavy	Can be cleaned, resistant to fading, abrasion and tested for flammability. Many textures available.	No major disadvantages. Installation cost varies according to surface preparation.
Foils	Decorative	Add high reflectance levels, unusual decorative effects.	May create glare in certain areas. Conductor of electricity. Surface subject to abrasion and scratches; expensive installation costs.
Fabric	Decorative	Available in wide sizes and unlimited lengths. Can be installed over wide range of surfaces. Moderate cost.	Must be treated for soil resistance, may require extra backing.
Felt	Decorative, acoustic	Large widths available. Good for acoustic control.	Must be backed with paper. Tends to fade and difficult to spot clean.
Wood veneers	Moderate, heavy	Fire resistant, may be finished on site to desired finish, easy maintenance.	Expensive, special installation requirements.

minimum criteria for class II types of wallcoverings. The current classification method that is based on federal specification CC-W-408 (types I, II, and III) would be equivalent to class IV, V, and VI of this proposed standard.

Installation

Important considerations in the installation of wallcoverings involve the following factors:

1. Type and condition of wall surface

2. Type of adhesive

3. Environmental conditions

4. Installation procedures
   Seams
   Adhesive application
   Panel sequence

Table 9.3 provides information on wall preparation, types of adhesives, installation procedures, and recommended seams. Figure 9.1 illustrates the three types of seams most frequently used. The lapped seam is commonly used for vinyl wallcoverings and is double cut through both thicknesses, leaving a perfectly fitted seam. The exact procedure is described in the wallcovering specification guide (PAGS),[1] which is given later in this chapter in Figure 9.2. This specification guide also provides the designer with information on all areas of concern that should be included in a vinyl wallcovering specification.

Specification for other types of wallcoverings should follow this general guide. Designers may also require that the contractor install test panels (at least three) that can serve as a standard of required quality for the remainder of the work. Estimates and specifications should also include instructions about providing extra rolls or bolts of wallcovering for the owner's use in the event that repairs are required.

Estimation

The formula for estimating the quantity of wallcovering material needed for a given project is based on the number of square feet on the roll. Many wallcoverings are packaged in single rolls of 36 sq ft (3.4 sq m) or double rolls of 72 sq ft (6.7 sq m).

Measurements of the interior space are made in feet, noting the number of windows, doors, and other major architectural features, such as bookcases. For example, in estimating the wallcovering needed for a 12' × 12' (3.6 × 3.6 m) room with 8-ft (2.4-m) ceilings, two windows, and a door, proceed in this manner:

1. Measure the length of each wall and total.

   $$12' + 12' + 12' + 12' = 48'$$

2. Multiply the distance around the room by the ceiling height to determine the total number of square feet.

   $$48' × 8' = 384 \text{ sq ft}$$

3. Allow a 20 percent margin for waste.

   $$384 \text{ sq ft} + 20\% = 460.8 \text{ sq ft}$$

4. Calculate the actual areas for doors, windows, and other architectural features. Allow 15 ft as an average size per door and for every two windows.

   $$2 × 15 \text{ sq ft} = 30 \text{ sq ft}$$

5. Subtract the area for doors, windows, and other architectural features.

   $$460.8 \text{ sq ft} - 30 \text{ sq ft} = 430.8 \text{ sq ft}$$

This last figure represents the total number of square feet of wallcovering that is required to complete the space, and from it

TABLE 9.2   CLASSIFICATION CRITERIA: VOLUNTARY STANDARD TS 198

	Class I	Class II	Class III	Class IV	Class V	Class VI
	Decorative	Decorative & serviceable	Decorative with good serviceability	Decorative with full serviceability	Medium commercial serviceability	Full commercial serviceability
Minimum colorfastness		23 hours	46 hours	46 hours	200 hours	200 hours
Minimum washability		100 cycles	100 cycles	100 cycles	100 cycles	100 cycles
Minimum scrubbability			50 cycles	200 cycles	300 cycles	500 cycles
Minimum abrasion resistance			500 cycles (#8 Greige duck)	1000 cycles (#8 Greige duck)	300 cycles (#0 Emery paper)	1000 cycles (#0 Emery paper)
Minimum breaking strength			20 lb (89 N)	30 lb (133 N)	55 lb (245 N)	95 lb (423 N)
Minimum crocking resistance			10 cycles	10 cycles	20 cycles	20 cycles
Minimum stain resistance			Reagents 1-9	Reagents 1-12	Reagents 1-12	Reagents 1-12
Minimum tear resistance				5-point scale (w/o weight)	25-point scale (with weight)	50-point scale (with weight)
Maximum blocking resistance					2-point scale	2-point scale
Minimum coating adhesion					6-lb/2-in. strip (27-N/5-cm strip)	6-lb/2-in. strip (27-N/5-cm strip)
Minimum cold cracking resistance					Pass	Pass
Minimum heat aging resistance					Pass	Pass
Minimum shrinkage					2.5%	2.5%

Source: The Chemical Fabrics and Film Association.

TABLE 9.3 WALLCOVERING INSTALLATION PROCEDURES

Covering	Sizes	Adhesives	Seams	Surface Preparation and Installation
Papers	18-27" wide. Single or double roll 30-36 sq ft per roll.	Wheat paste or cellulose paste. Apply to paper back	Butted or wired	Clean and smooth surface. Wash to prevent bacteria growth after paper application. Apply with soft, wide brush working from center of panel outward. Matching patterns should be cut from alternating rolls.
Vinyls	54" wide by 30 yd in length. 405 sq ft per bolt.	Apply paste to fabric back	Overlap and double cut	Prime and seal all surfaces. Apply panels in exact order as cut from roll, using rolls in consecutive order. Use stiff bristle brush or flexible broad knife to eliminate air pockets. Wrap covering 6 in. beyond outside corners and 3 in. at inside corners.
Foils	18-27" wide. Double and triple rolls.	Premixed vinyls with low water content. Apply to wall	Butted smooth with oval seam roller	Wall surfaces must be painted with oil base enamel undercoat or wall primer. Prewash walls to remove bacteria. Surface must be very smooth. Apply with soft brush. Work from center out to edges. Puncture air bubbles and press down immediately. Wash finished panels with warm, clean water and soft cloth to avoid scratching. Avoid contact with electrical sources. When matching random patterns, reverse every other strip.
Fabric	36-54" any length. Sold by yard.	Wheat or cellulose. Apply paste to wall	Butted or wired	Clean and smooth surface. Apply antibacteria primer. Staple fabric along top as hanging to handle weight of wet fabric. Staples may be removed later. If not paper backed, do not stretch too tightly or pull out of shape. Use same corner installation as vinyl.
Felt	54-72" wide. Sold by yard.	Wheat paste applied to wall	Butted or wired	Felt should be paper backed for later removal. Wall should be clean and smooth and washed with antibacteria solution. Apply nap in same direction. Do not overstretch when applying.
Cork	Up to 36" wide. 36-45 ft lengths.	Wheat or vinyl	Butted	Clean and smooth surface. May require lining paper. Cork does not require matching. Follow manufacturers' installation recommendations.
Wood veneer	10-24" wide, up to 12 ft long.	Recommended by material supplier	Butted	Follow manufacturers' recommendations. Wood may be pre-finished or finished on site. Temperature control usually necessary prior to and during installation.

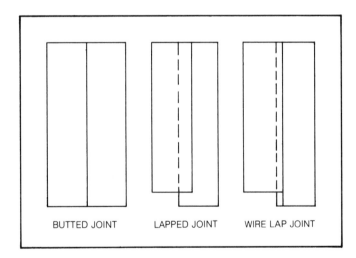

BUTTED JOINT   LAPPED JOINT   WIRE LAP JOINT

Figure 9.1 Wall covering seams.

the number of rolls of wallcovering that will be needed can be determined.

If the selected wallcovering is packaged in standard rolls containing 36 sq ft:

$$430.8 \div 36 \text{ sq ft/roll} = 11.97, \text{ or } 12 \text{ single rolls}$$

The amount needed would be 12 single rolls, or 6 double rolls. In the event that the wallcovering is packaged in rolls containing 30 sq ft (2.8 sq m), the project would require more wallcovering.

$$430.8 \div 30 \text{ sq ft/roll} = 14.4, \text{ or } 15 \text{ single rolls}$$

In this case the project would require 15 single rolls, or 7 double rolls plus 1 single roll.

Designers should remember that uneven figures should always be increased to the next highest number. If the wallcovering is only packaged in double rolls, the figures may have to be increased to the next highest even number; i.e., 6.4 rolls would be increased to 8 double rolls.[2]

Vinyl Wallcovering. Because commercial vinyls are packaged in 30-yd (28-m) bolts, which range from 52 to 54 in. (132.1 to 137.2 cm) in width, the estimation may be made in square feet, linear feet, or yards. The most common method used to calculate yardage is explained below in regard to fabric wallcoverings, but if the designer wishes to make the calculation in square feet, you can determine the square footage of a bolt in the following manner:

$$13.5 \text{ sq ft/yd} \times 30 \text{ yd} = 405 \text{ sq ft/bolt}$$

Using the same square footage requirements from the previous problem:

$$430.8 \div 405 \text{ sq ft/bolt} = 1.06 \text{ bolts, or } 2 \text{ bolts}$$

SECTION 09950

VINYL WALL COVERING

PART 1 - GENERAL

WORK SPECIFIED HEREIN

ALL LABOR, MATERIAL, EQUIPMENT AND SERVICES NECESSARY TO PRO-
VIDE THE VINYL WALL COVERING AND RELATED ITEMS AS INDICATED
OR SPECIFIED.

SUBSTITUTIONS

IN ACCORDANCE WITH SECTION 01600.

SUBMITTALS

SUBMIT SAMPLES OF EACH COLOR AND TYPE OF VINYL WALL FABRIC IN
ACCORDANCE WITH SECTION 01340. SAMPLES TO BE ONE-HALF YARD,
FULL WIDTH OF MILL RUN OF EACH PATTERN AND COLOR.

SUBMIT AFFIDAVITS CERTIFYING THAT MATERIALS PROVIDED AND IN-
STALLED ON THE PROJECT ARE EXACTLY AS TESTED.

QUALITY ASSURANCE

CERTIFICATION. VINYL FABRIC AND ADHESIVE SHALL HAVE BEEN
TESTED TO PROVIDE A UL CLASS "B" FIRE HAZARD CLASSIFICATION.

PRODUCT DELIVERY, STORAGE AND HANDLING

DELIVER AND STORE ALL WALL COVERING IN UNDAMAGED CONDITION AS
PACKAGED BY THE MANUFACTURER, WITH MANUFACTURER'S SEALS AND
LABELS INTACT. EXERCISE CARE TO PREVENT DAMAGE DURING DELI-
VERY, HANDLING AND STORAGE. STORE ALL MATERIALS FLAT IN A
CLEAN, DRY AREA WITH MAINTAINED TEMPERATURE ABOVE 40 DEGREES
F. MAINTAIN AREAS TO RECEIVE WALL COVERING AT A CONSTANT
TEMPERATURE OF 45 DEGREES TO 50 DEGREES F. FOR AT LEAST 3
DAYS BEFORE, AND ALL DURING, THE APPLICATION PERIOD.

PART 2 - PRODUCTS

MATERIALS

VINYL WALL COVERING. MANUFACTURER: L.E. CARPENTER CO., NEW
YORK, N.Y.

PATTERN: AS SELECTED

        TOTAL WEIGHT/LIN. YD.
        FABRIC/SQ. YARD
        VINYL/SQ. YD.
        THICKNESS (AVERAGE)
        FLAME SPREAD
        FUEL CONTRIBUTED
        SMOKE DEVELOPED

ADHESIVE. AS RECOMMENDED BY THE FABRIC MANUFACTURER, STRIP-
PABLE TYPE.

PRIMER. AS RECOMMENDED BY THE FABRIC MANUFACTURER.

SEALER. AS RECOMMENDED BY THE FABRIC MANUFACTURER.

PART 3 - EXECUTION

INSPECTION

Figure 9.2 Specifications for vinyl wallcovering.
(Continued)

```
 1  SURFACE TO RECEIVE WALL COVERING SHALL MEET THE MINIMUM RE-
 2  QUIREMENTS ESTABLISHED BY THE WALL COVERING MANUFACTURER.
 3
 4  GYPSUM WALLBOARD SHALL HAVE ALL FASTENERS RECESSED, WITH ALL
 5  JOINTS AND FASTENER DEPRESSIONS TAPED AND SPACKLED AND
 6  SANDED.
 7
 8  INSTALLATION
 9
10  PRIME AND SEAL SUBSTRATES PER FABRIC MANUFACTURER'S RECOMMEN-
11  DATIONS FOR THE TYPE OF SUBSTRATE TO BE COVERED.
12
13  FOLLOW THE ADHESIVE MANUFACTURER'S DIRECTIONS FOR MIXING AND
14  APPLYING ADHESIVE.
15
16  USE FABRIC PANELS IN EXACT ORDER AS THEY ARE CUT FROM ROLLS;
17  USE ROLLS IN CONSECUTIVE ORDER.  APPLY PASTE TO THE FABRIC
18  BACK USING A ROLLER OR PASTE BRUSH.
19
20  HANG SMOOTH, NON-MATCH PATTERNS BY PASTING STRIPS ON THE
21  WALL, OVERLAPPING THE EDGES, AND "DOUBLE-CUTTING" THROUGH
22  BOTH THICKNESSES.  USE A 0.04 OR 0.06" ZINC OR ALUMINUM STRIP
23  BETWEEN WALL AND MATERIAL WHEN CUTTING, TO AVOID GOUGING THE
24  WALL.
25
26  USE STIFF-BRISTLED BRUSH OR FLEXIBLE BROAD KNIFE TO ELIMINATE
27  AIR POCKETS AND TO SECURE THE WALL COVERING TO THE WALL SUR-
28  FACE.
29
30  FILL SPACES ABOVE AND BELOW DOORS AND SIMILAR AREAS IN
31  SEQUENCE FROM THE ROLL, NOT LATER WHEN ALL FULL-LENGTH PIECES
32  HAVE BEEN INSTALLED.
33
34  REMOVE EXCESS PASTE FROM EACH SEAM AS IT IS MADE AND BEFORE
35  PROCEEDING TO NEXT SEAM.  USE SPONGE DAMPENED WITH PLAIN WARM
36  WATER, BUT NOT WRINGING WET.  WIPE SEAM CLEAN WITH DRY CLOTH
37  TOWEL.
38
39  EXAMINE EACH SEAM CAREFULLY WHEN COMPLETED.  TRIM ADDITIONAL
40  SELVAGE WHERE REQUIRED TO ACHIEVE A COLOR AND PATTERN MATCH
41  AT SEAMS.
42
43  REMOVE HARDWARE, ACCESSORIES, PLATES, AND SIMILAR ITEMS TO
44  ALLOW FABRIC TO BE INSTALLED.  UPON COMPLETION OF EACH SPACE,
45  REPLACE THE ABOVE ITEMS.
46
47  INSTALLED FABRIC SHALL BE SECURE, SMOOTH, CLEAN, WITHOUT
48  WRINKLES, GAPS OR OVERLAPS.
49
50  WRAP WALL COVERING 6" BEYOND OUTSIDE CORNERS AND 3" AT INSIDE
51  CORNERS' CUTTING AT CORNERS WILL NOT BE ACCEPTED, NOR WILL
52  HORIZONTAL SEAMS BE ACCEPTABLE OTHER THAN AT INDICATED OR
53  REQUIRED FOR PATTERN CHANGE.
54
55  PROTECTION
56
57  PROTECT FINISHED WORK INSTALLED BY OTHER TRADES PRIOR TO WORK
58  UNDER THIS SECTION.  REPLACE ANY WORK DAMAGED BY WORKMEN OF
59  THIS TRADE WITHOUT COST TO THE OWNER.
60
61
62  END OF SECTION
63
64
65
66
67
68
69
70
71
72
```

Fabric Wallcovering. Estimating the fabric yardage for wall-coverings involves the following procedures:

1. Measure the width of each wall in feet and transpose to inches.

2. Number of widths = wall width (inches) ÷ width of fabric (inches)

3. Length of panels = height of wall (inches) + 3 in. for adjustment

4. Inches of fabric needed = length of panel × number of panels

5. Total yards needed = inches of fabric needed ÷ 36 in.

For example, if fabric was to be applied to one wall of a foyer and the wall was 18 ft wide and 9 ft tall, the designer should determine the number of fabric widths (48 in. wide) needed to cover the wall. After transposing the wall width to inches (18 ft = 216 in.), proceed in this manner:

216 ÷ 48″ = 4.5 widths of fabric, or 5 widths

The length of each panel or width is determined by transposing the wall height to inches and adding the needed 3 in. for adjustment.

9′ = 108″ + 3″ = 111″

To calculate the total inches of fabric required:

111″ × 5 (widths) = 555″

To transpose the inches into the required yardage, simply divide by 36 in.

555″ ÷ 36″ = 15.41 or 16 yd

If the fabric had a pattern, the length of the repeat would have to be considered because this would increase the required yardage. Methods of calculating pattern repeats are discussed in Chapter 10.

Estimating Labor Costs

Labor costs will vary depending on the preinstallation wall preparation that may be required; the complication of the installation, such as openings, projections, or an intricate patterned material; and the total number of square feet involved.

Labor is charged by the square foot. For example, the labor cost may be $.50/sq ft, or $18 per single roll. The labor charges for vinyl and foils are always higher than those for standard wallcovering. Labor for installing wood veneers can run as high as $3 to $4/sq ft because of the meticulous work involved.

The time involved in the installation depends on the project requirements, but it has been estimated, for example, that the experienced paperhanger may reasonably be expected to install about 250 sq ft, or 7 single rolls, per day.

In addition to the materials and labor cost, designers should remember to add an average of 10 to 20 percent overhead on the materials and labor.

Maintenance

Maintenance requirements vary according to the materials used and the abuse received by the wall surfaces. Table 9.4 summarizes recommended maintenance procedures.

Examples of Specification Guides

The PAGS specification guide for vinyl wallcovering (Figure

TABLE 9.4 WALLCOVERING MAINTENANCE

Material	Recommended Procedures
Papers	Wipe with soft cloth. Do not apply water, which may cause some inks to run.
Vinyls	Ordinary soilage may be removed with mild soap and water. A soft bristle brush may be used to remove soilage from deeply textured surfaces. Do not use abrasive cleaners, steel wool or solvent-type cleaners. In areas of moderate use, a general cleaning of the surface once or twice a year should be sufficient to maintain original condition. Some difficult stains can be removed with rubbing alcohol or naphtha.
Foils	Wipe with very soft cloth. May be washed with warm water. Care should be taken not to scratch the surface.
Fabrics	Should be treated with soil-resistant chemicals prior to installation. Surface may be vacuumed to remove collected dust. Stains may be removed with dry-cleaning fluids or mild soap and water if the fabric is washable.
Felts	May be vacuumed. Do not apply water or any cleaning solutions which may cause spotting or removal of color. Felts may fade if installed near direct source of light.
Carpet	Requires very little maintenance. May be vacuumed to remove collected dust. If stained, use cleaning method recommended by the manufacturer.
Leather	May be polished with paste floor wax. Some stains can be removed by brushing. Do not use water. Follow directions of supplier.
Cork	Should be vacuumed. May be washed with mild soap and water.
Wood veneers	May be polished to maintain luster. Hard paste wax is recommended.

9.2) may be easily adapted for use by adding or deleting lines. For example, lines 29 through 30 can state a more specific flammability requirement. If more than one pattern of wallcovering is to be used, lines 51 through 59 can be altered to include further instructions.

Other examples of specifications are shown for cork (Figure 9.3) and flexible wood (Figure 9.4) wallcoverings.

COATING SYSTEMS

Designers frequently specify paint by color and finish without consideration for the total coating system, i.e., the surface material, surface condition, method of application, curing process, and projected durability under varied use. To understand the complicated selection of paint coating systems, it is necessary to understand the generic classification of interior paint materials and their recommended application.

Coating systems are classified according to the vehicle or binder used to manufacture the coating, or classification can be based on the recommended use and finish provided.

1. *Vehicles and binders* determine the content and consistency of coating systems. Vehicles form the liquid portion of a paint, and binders are the film forming oils or resins.

2. *Primers* are classified as wall, wood, or masonry-type primers that are applied as a first coat of a paint, varnish, or lacquer system in order to improve the bond of the finish coats.

3. *Finish coats* provide the final protective coating to the surface. The finish is described as gloss, semigloss (eggshell), or flat.

4. *Transparent finishes* provide protection for wood or other surfaces that do not require an opaque finish. Transparent finishes may include varnishes, shellacs, stains, and lacquers.

Figure 9.3 Specifications for cork wallcovering. Reproduced with permission of Henningson, Durham, and Richardson, Phoenix, AZ.

```
00010  .npt,1,ar,6
00020  .pp
00030  09953-
00040  .lmar=11
00050  .rmar=75
00060  .lnr,b,3
00070  ./revised 77/10/10
00080  .t,c
00090  HENNINGSON, DURHAM & RICHARDSON
00100  .ul
00110                    DIVISION 9 - FINISHES
00120                    -------------------
00130
00140  .ul
00150              09953 - CORK WALL COVERING
00160              --------------------------
00170
00180  .ul
00190  1.  GENERAL
00200  ----------
00210
00220      A.  The  Contractor  shall  furnish  all  labor,  materials,
00230  tools, equipment, and perform all work and services necessary for
00240  all cork wallcovering work as shown on drawings and as  specified
00250  in  accordance  with  provilons  of  the  Contract Documents, and
00260  completely coordinated with Work of all other trades.
00270
00280      B.   Although  such  work  is  not  specifically  indicated,
00290  furnish  and  install  all  supplementary  or  miscellaneous items
00300  incidental  to  or  necessary  for  a  sound,  secure  and complete
00310  installation.
00320
00330      C.  Materials  must  have  Class A (under 25) flame, fuel, and
00340  smoke ratings.
00350
00360  .ul
00370  2.  ACCEPTABLE MANUFACTURERS (QUALITY STANDARDS)
00380  ----------------------------------------------------
00390
00400      A.  Manufactured by Laminating Services, Inc.
00410
00420      B.   Other   manufacturers  desiring  approval  comply  with
00430  Section 01640.
00440
00450  .ul
00460  3.  SUBMITTALS
00470  -------------
00480
00490      A.  Samples:  12 in.  sq.  sample of cork.
00500
00510      B.  Certificates:  Verifying flame spread rating.
00520
00530  .ul
00540  4.  JOB CONDITIONS
00550  ------------------
```

```
00570        A.    Verify     acceptability    of    substrate    to    accept
00580 Installation.
00590
00600        B.    Install    a    test    section    with    adhesive    to    verify
00610 compatibility and adhesion.
00620 ./           *****
00630 ./ Specifier:  Change type and color as required.
00640 ./           *****
00650
00660 .ul
00670 5.  MATERIALS
00680 _____
00690
00700        A.   Cork:   Cordova,   No.   409 EBAN, laminated to cloth, with
00710 acrylic surface coating.   Class A flame spread rated.
00720
00730        B.   Adhesive:   Vin-L-Fab 415 or Pliant wood 460.
00740
00750 .ul
00760 6.  INSTALLATION:   In accord with manufacturers recommendations.
00770 _____
00780
00790                     END OF SECTION
```

Figure 9.4 Specifications for flexible wood wallcovering.
Reproduced with permission of Henningson, Durham, and
Richardson, Phoenix, AZ.

```
00010  .npt,1,AR,6
00020  .pp
00030  09960·
00040  .LMAR=11
00050  .RMAR=75
00060  .lnr,b,3
00070  ./revised 79/03/05
00080  .t,c
00090  HENNINGSON, DURHAM & RICHARDSON
00100  .ul
00110                      DIVISION 9 - FINISHES
00120                      -------------------
00130
00140  .ul
00150            09960 - FLEXIBLE WOOD WALL COVERING
00160            ---------------------------------------
00170
00180  .ul
00190  1.  GENERAL
00200  ----------
00210
00220      A.  The Contractor  shall  furnish  all  labor,  materials,
00230  tools,  equipment,  and  perform  all  work  and services for all
00240  flexible  wood  wall  covering  as  shown  on  drawings  and   as
00250  specified,   in   accordance  with  provisions  of  the  Contract
00260  Documents, and completely coordinated  with  work  of  all  other
00270  trades.
00280
00290      B.   Although  such  work  is  not  specifically  indicated,
00300  furnish and install all  supplementary  or  miscellaneous  items,
00310  appurtenances and devices incidental to or necessary for a sound,
00320  secure and complete installation.
00330
00340  .ul
00350  2.  ACCEPTABLE MANUFACTURERS
00360  ---------------------------
00370
00380      A.  Material specified is manufactured by U.S.  Plywood.
00390
00400      B.   Other  manufacturers  desiring  approval  comply  with
00410  Section 01640.
00420
00430  .ul
00440  3.  SUBMITTALS  (See Section 01340)
00450  -------------
00460
00470  .   A.  Samples  of  materials, with  finish,  for  Architect
00480  selection.
00490
00500      B.  Shop  Drawings  of  blue  print layout of flitch to show
00510  pattern and placement around penetrations.
00520
00530      C.  U/L  certificate  of  flame  spread,  certifying Class A
00540  rating and fuel and smoke ratings.
00550
```

```
00570 4.    PRODUCT DELIVERY, STORAGE AND HANDLING.  Deliver in unopened
00580 _____
00590 packages,  plainly  marked  with  identifying  labels.  Store and
00600 handle to preclude damage.
00610
00620 .ul
00630 5.   JOB  CONDITIONS.  Verify   suitability   of substrate to accept
00640 _____
00650 installation.     Installation     assumes     responsibility    for
00660 performance.
00670
00680 .ul
00690 6.   MATERIALS
00700 _____
00710
00720      A.   Weld wood Architectural Flexwood.
00730
00740      B.   U/L Class A flamespread rating.
00750 ./                           *****
00760 ./          (Specifier:  Insert types and locations)
00770 ./                           *****
00780 ./
00790
00800
00810
00820
00830
00840      C.   Adhesive:  U.S.  Plywood No. 710.
00850
00860      D.   Wall Primer:  As recommended by material supplier.
00870
00880      E.   Finish Materials:  As recommended by material supplier.
00890
00900 .ul
00910 7.   INSTALLATION.  Prime   wall   surfaces.  Test wall for moisture
00920 _____
00930 and smoothness, fill and sand as required.
00940
00950 .ul
00960 8.    FINISHING.
00970 _____
00980
00990      A.   Sand surface, with grain, using 00 sandpaper.
01000
01010      B.   Apply finish to achieve desired finish.
01020
01030      C.   After finish is dry, apply paste wax.
01040
01050      D.   Protect until acceptance of building.
01060
01070                         END OF SECTION
```

TABLE 9.5 VEHICLE AND BINDER CLASSIFICATION

Vehicles/Binders	Description	Frequent Use
1. Alkyds	This binder is made from oil-modified resins. Good color retention, easy to apply and moderately priced.	Fast-drying enamels. Should not be used on masonry without alkali-resistant primer.
2. Latex emulsions	Made from synthetics that can be varied to produce various degrees of hardness, gloss and flexibility. Odorless, fast drying, easy to apply, blister and peel resistant.	Walls and masonry
3. Urethanes	Plastic binder used to produce hard-wearing varnishes.	Floor surfaces
4. Vinyl	Plasticized copolymers of vinyl chloride and vinyl acetate used for making varnishes. Usually applied with spray process.	Wooden furniture, paneling
5. Epoxy	Used to produce gloss enamels which offer excellent resistance to chemicals.	Brick, wood and metal
6. Oleoresinous	Composed of oils that are modified with various resins. Produce a hard, glossy finish.	Gym floors
7. Phenolic resins	Modified with oils. Produce hard-wearing sealers and varnishes.	Floors

TABLE 9.6 CLASSIFICATION OF INTERIOR PRIMERS

Primer	Description	Frequent Use
Wall Primers		
Latex	Quick drying, offers excellent alkali resistance. Provides for ease of equipment cleaning.	Drywall, brick, metal
Alkyd	Made from odorless alkyd, somewhat slow drying.	May be applied over partially cured plaster and metal.
Alkali	Alkali-resistant content based on butadine-styrene copolymer or chlorinated rubber.	Masonry, but do not use on below grade.
Wood Primers		
Enamel undercoat	Provides a low gloss and hard film which prevents penetration of the enamel paints that may be applied as top coats.	Excellent on surfaces which require smooth finish.
Paste wood fillers	Made from transparent and coarse pigment held together with a binder.	Used on open-grain woods. Provides added color and smoothness.
Clear wood sealer	Transparent pigment often added to reduce penetration and improve sealing.	Often used under clear wood finishes.
Masonry primers		
Cement grout	A thin mortar applied with a brush or trowel.	Used to provide a smooth surface to rough masonry.
Block fillers	Composed of either latex or a solvent-thinned epoxy-ester. Relatively thick and applied with a brush or roller.	May be applied to damp surfaces. Provides resistance to alkali.

Tables 9.5 to 9.8 provide a survey of the types of coatings and finishes formulated for interior use.

Estimating Coverage Capacity

The coverage capacity of paint is dependent on factors, such as "hiding power," percentage of volume solids, application methods, and type of surface receiving the coating.

Hiding Power. This refers to the ability of the coating system to cover or conceal the previous surface color. Some colors contain pigments that have little hiding power, and designers may have to specify more coats to compensate for this fact. Table 9.9 lists the pigments frequently having low hiding power. The recommended number of coats will depend on the surface texture and may vary when applying a light color over a dark color. Designers should remember that a series of thin coats is much more effective than one thick coat which may result in improper drying or curing.

Volume Solids. Paints having 100 percent volume solids (no thinners) will cover more surface and provide a thicker film. This film (when dry) is referred to as the "dry film thickness" (DFT) and the measurement is expressed in mils (1/1000 in.). When reference is made to the dry film thickness, the measurement always refers to the total coating system, not the thickness of one coat.

Because federal and industrial specifications frequently require a dry film thickness measurement (usually 5 mils), designers should be familiar with the terminology involved. Manufacturers usually list the amount of volume solids contained in each gallon and provide information on the number of DFT mils that can be obtained from the particular coating system. The mils, however, can vary depending on the amount of square feet that will be covered by the paint. For example, if the paint is 100 percent volume solid, the DFT mils may be listed in this manner:

Coverage per Gallon

1200 sq ft = 1 mil DFT

600 sq ft = 2 mils DFT

300 sq ft = 4 mils DFT

If the paint is 50 percent volume solid (thinned 50 percent), the mils of dry film thickness will be considerably altered:

Coverage per Gallon

600 sq ft = 1 mil DFT

300 sq ft = 2 mils DFT

In the event that a designer wishes to specify the dry film thickness, the required mils should be specified as the total thickness. For example, if the surface requires a primer, two coats of paint, and a dry film thickness of 5 mils, do not specify 2 1/2 mils per coat. The specification should state "5 mils dry film thickness applied in two coats."

Application Methods and Type of Surface. These also play a large part in estimating the coverage capacity. The spreadability and the coverage can vary considerably among spray, roller, and brush application methods. Rough textures and porous surfaces usually increase the amount of coating material required. Table 9.10 shows some *average* coat require-

TABLE 9.7 CLASSIFICATION OF INTERIOR FINISH COATINGS

Finishes	Descriptions	Frequent Use
Gloss Enamels		
Enamels	Usually alkyd enamels which are very resistant to yellowing and alkaline cleaners.	Brick, wood, particle board, metal, plywood
Floor enamels	Alkyd enamels that are abrasion resistant, but will blister and peel if wet.	Masonry and wooden floors
	Alkali-resistant enamels that are abrasion resistant, but provide poor resistance to solvents.	
	Epoxy or urethane enamels are abrasion resistant, not affected by water or solvents.	
	Latex floor paint provides good abrasion resistance.	
Dry fallout spray gloss	Similar to gloss enamels, but dries very rapidly.	Walls
Semigloss		
Semigloss enamel	Alkyd-based product with good gloss retention, also grease and alkali resistance.	Drywall, brick, wood, particle board, metal, plywood
Semigloss latex	Has moderate hiding power, ease of application and clean-up, rapid cleaning, low odor.	Drywall, plaster, wood, plywood
Dry fallout spray semi-gloss	Provides a moderate gloss level.	Walls and ceilings
Flat Finishes		
Alkyd flat	Superior to latex paints in hiding power and washability. Odorless, but should be used in well-ventilated areas.	Drywall, brick, wood, metal, plywood
Latex flat	Good hiding power, spreadability, odorless. Requires special primers prior to application on porous surfaces. Do not apply during temperature extremes.	Plaster, drywall, brick, masonry

TABLE 9.8 CLASSIFICATION OF TRANSPARENT FINISHES

Finishes	Description	Frequent Use
Varnishes		
Flat or satin	Flatting agent added which makes it less glossy in finish than glossy varnishes. Mar resistance is inferior to gloss varnish.	All types of wood surfaces
Counter or bar varnish	Dries very hard and is resistant to alcohols. Made from polyurethanes and polyesters.	Bar tops
Penetrating sealers	Very thin varnishes that are applied and removed while the surface is still wet. Fair resistance to marring.	All types of open-grained woods
Conversion varnish	Produced with alkyd and urea formaldehyde resins. Has good resistance to abrasion and allows a higher gloss buildup because of its solid content.	
Shellac	Often termed a "wash" coat on wood surfaces before final sanding. Fast drying, light colored, but has a poor resistance to abrasion, water or alcohols.	Wood, plaster, drywall, brick, plywood
Lacquers		
Standard	A coating material with high nitro-cellulose content that is modified with resins and plasticizers. Good durability, but little resistance to chemicals. Dries quickly and is easy to repair. Increases flammability of surfaces.	Wood furniture and paneling
Catalyzed	Superior to standard lacquer in resistance to chemicals.	Wood furniture and paneling
Vinyls		
Catalyzed	This is a clear converting catalyst vinyl coating. Fast drying and highly resistant to abrasion.	Wood furniture and paneling

TABLE 9.9 PIGMENT HIDING POWER

Pigment	Hiding Power	Coats Semigloss	Coats Flat
Gold	Fair	2	2
Yellow	Poor	3	3+
Green	Fair	2	2
Blue	Fair	2	2
Pink	Poor	3	3+
Off-white	Fair	2	2

TABLE 9.10 AVERAGE COAT REQUIREMENTS FOR INTERIOR SURFACES

Woodwork	Oil gloss paint	2-3 coats
	Semigloss paint	2-3 coats
Plaster	Alkyd flat	2-3 coats
Drywall	Alkyd flat	3 coats
	Vinyl latex	3 coats
Masonry	Vinyl latex	3 coats
Wood floor	Enamel	3 coats

TABLE 9.11 LABOR HOURS REQUIRED FOR BRUSHWORK APPLICATION

Paint	Sq Ft per Hour per Coat
Calcimining (ceilings)	200-250
Enameling	100-150
Flat painting	120-180
Shellacking	120-180
Staining	120-180
Varnishing	120-180
Trim: filling, spackling (given in linear ft)	50-75
Floors, filling, putting	120-180
Floor staining	150-200
Floor shellacking	150-200
Floor varnishing	140-200
Floor waxing	140-200
Floor polishing	100-150
Machine sanding	100-200

ments for new interior paint work on various types of surfaces.

The spreading capacity of paint is difficult to calculate because of the variances in surfaces and particular products; therefore manufacturers' specifications regarding the estimated coverage per square foot (per gallon) should be consulted.

Estimating Labor and Material Costs

To determine the labor cost and materials needed, designers should calculate the amount of surface to be covered. Major interior surfaces are measured in the following manner:

Square Feet	Linear Feet
Floors	Trim length
Walls and ceilings	Piping length
Doors (number, kind)	
Windows (do not deduct for glass)	

After the square and linear feet are determined, it is necessary to calculate the labor cost per square foot. The time required to paint 1 sq ft varies, depending on the location of the surface (floor, ceiling, walls) and the intricacy of the work. In addition, surface preparation, such as sanding, sealing, priming, or patching, will add to the total labor cost. Research has shown that the amount of surface that a painter can cover is also affected by the method of application. For example:

$$\text{Brush} = 50\text{--}200 \text{ sq ft/h}$$

$$\text{Roller} = 100\text{--}300 \text{ sq ft/h}$$

$$\text{Sprayer} = 300\text{--}500 \text{ sq ft/h}$$

Table 9.11 shows the *average* labor hours required for the brushwork application (one coat) of various coating systems. These figures should be doubled if two coats are required.

Painting Inspection Checklist

Careful inspection before, during, and after painting application can result in quality control and prevent project delays caused by improper color matching or application.

Upon Delivery

1. Verify that the specified paints (brands) have been delivered and that the containers are properly labeled and undamaged.

2. Check the area designated for the paint and materials storage. Be sure that there is adequate ventilation and fire protection equipment in the immediate vicinity. If possible, the paint workshop (mixing or thinning area) should be located outside the main building.

Before Application

1. Verify that the areas to be painted are completed and the general area is free from dust-generating conditions; i.e., other workers will not be sawing or creating other sources of dust.

2. Before work proceeds, require that the painting contractor clean, prepare, and paint a sample 5' x 5' area which can serve as a standard of performance for the entire job.

3. Clarify and review the color selections and means of application with the contractor.

During Application

1. Inspect each surface prior to the installation of *each* coat. This assures that the proper curing time has been allowed and the surface textures meet specification requirements.

2. Verify that color schedules are being followed; i.e., colors are being applied in designated areas.

3. Verify that temperature and relative humidity are within the limits recommended by the manufacturer.

4. Be sure that surrounding areas, which are not to receive paint, are protected.

After Application

1. Be sure that the clean-up of the painted area includes removal of all empty paint cans, drop cloths, and other equipment.

2. Make certain that touch-up and restoration of areas damaged during the installation or clean-up are competently completed.

3. Check that storage areas are cleared and cleaned.

Drawings and Specifications

Methods of showing finish locations on drawings and schedules are discussed in Chapter 15. Drawings must show the designated areas that are to receive specific colors and finish coats. This information is also contained in the color and finish schedules, which accompany the drawings and are also attached to the written specifications.

The written specifications contain instructions on the following:

1. Storage and protection of equipment, materials, and surfaces

2. Surface preparation

3. Quality assurance

4. Methods of application

5. Color and finish schedules

6. Products or substitutions

7. Cleaning and final inspection

The painting specification guideline in Figure 9.5 is general in scope and allows the designer to substitute or provide additional requirements.

WALL PANELING

Because there are over 150 varieties of wood veneers available on the commercial market and because these veneers can be provided in a variety of cuts (rotary, plain sliced, or quartered), designers may find that there are approximately 450 different surface veneers available for consideration. In addition, there are 3 basic varieties of core construction and about 10 varieties of panel finishes.

The following guidelines based on information from the Hardwood Plywood Manufacturers Association (HPMA) and the Architectural Woodwork Institute (AWI) should help to clarify and simplify specification decisions regarding wall paneling.

Specification of hardwood plywood paneling involves consideration of the following factors:

1. Flitch selection

2. Species selection

3. Matching of veneer

4. Panel construction

5. Panel finish

6. Flame resistance

7. Acoustical treatment

8. Panel selection

9. Installation

Flitch Selection

The term *flitch* refers to a given section or piece of a log. All the slices or cuts taken from this log are kept in sequence and this entire sequence is referred to as a "flitch" (Figure 9.6). The flitch for any given wall paneling project is selected by the designer, or the selection may be made by the manufacturer of the paneling. If the manufacturer is to make the flitch selection, based on the designer's requirements, the designer must supply information on the (1) general color range desired, (2) the grain characteristics, such as swirl or straight, (3) the height and approximate linear footage required, (4) type of wood, and (5) the desired method of matching. See the comparative table of wood species in Table 9.12.

One of the advantages of allowing the manufacturer to make the final flitch selection is the fact that they can predict the flitch yield and therefore more accurately adhere to a proposed budget. If a designer wishes to visit a local veneer supplier and make a selection from the showroom floor, the supplier should be questioned regarding the flitch yield. The manufacturer and supplier may not always agree on the amount of yield; i.e., the supplier may quote a 3 to 1 ratio (3,000 sq ft of flitch will be required to produce 1,000 sq ft of panel) and the manufacturer may quote a 4 to 1 ratio.

Species Selection

To simplify species selection for the designer, the comparative table of wood species in Table 9.12 has been prepared showing pertinent characteristics of some 34 species of domestic and foreign woods used in the Architectural Woodwork Industry. The table can quickly confirm or deny the wisdom of a species selection by the architect or conversely lead him or her to a proper selection after study of the characteristics.

The key to the table is the column listing *Principal Uses*—both exterior and interior. Careful analysis of this list will immediately narrow the selection appreciably for each type of application.

From this point, consideration is given to *Appearance*, which should be compared with *Finishing* characteristics for both paint and transparent finishes. These two columns have been prepared to assist in the area of aesthetics by describing, as briefly as possible, the appearance of the wood in its natural state.

Relative Cost has been broken into both *Lumber* and *Plywood* headings. The reason for cost variations in the two products is obvious when the physical differences are considered. Generally, the prices of veneered products reflect the high labor and equipment cost and relatively low material cost

Figure 9.5 Painting specification guidelines. Reproduced with permission of PAGS.

```
 1    SECTION 09900                                                 1
 2                                                                  2
 3    PAINTING                                                      3
 4                                                                  4
 5                                                                  5
 6    PART 1 - GENERAL                                              6
 7                                                                  7
 8    WORK SPECIFIED HEREIN                                         8
 9                                                                  9
10    ALL LABOR, MATERIALS, EQUIPMENT AND SERVICES NECESSARY TO    10
11    COMPLETE ALL PAINTING AND FINISHING REQUIRED FOR SURFACES AS 11
12    INDICATED OR SPECIFIED.                                      12
13                                                                 13
14    SUBSTITUTIONS                                                14
15                                                                 15
16    IN ACCORDANCE WITH SECTION 01600.                            16
17                                                                 17
18    SUBMITTALS                                                   18
19                                                                 19
20    PREPARE SAMPLES AT THE JOB AS REQUIRED UNTIL COLORS ARE      20
21    SATISFACTORY.   PAINT COLORS WILL BE AS SPECIFIED BY THE     21
22    ARCHITECT WHO, BEFORE ANY WORK IS DONE, WILL FURNISH COLOR   22
23    CHIPS AND A SCHEDULE SHOWING WHERE THE VARIOUS COLORS SHALL  23
24    GO.                                                          24
25                                                                 25
26    BEFORE SUPPLYING ANY MATERIAL TO SITE, THE PAINTING SUBCON-  26
27    TRACTOR AND THE PAINT MANUFACTURER'S AREA REPRESENTATIVE     27
28    SHALL PREPARE A COMPLETE SCHEDULE SHOWING THE MATERIALS PRO- 28
29    POSED TO BE USED FOR EACH TREATMENT SPECIFIED, AND SUBMIT    29
30    SAME TO ARCHITECT FOR REVIEW/APPROVAL.                       30
31                                                                 31
32    PRODUCT DELIVERY, STORAGE AND HANDLING                       32
33                                                                 33
34    DELIVER ALL PAINT TO SITE IN MANUFACTUTER'S LABELED AND      34
35    SEALED CONTAINERS.   LABELS SHALL GIVE MANUFACTURER'S NAME,  35
36    BRAND, TYPE, BATCH NUMBER, COLOR OF PAINT AND INSTRUCTIONS   36
37    FOR REDUCING.   THIN ONLY IN ACCORDANCE WITH PRINTED DIREC-  37
38    TIONS OF MANUFACTURER.                                       38
39                                                                 39
40    STORE ALL MATERIAL USED ON THE JOB IN A SINGLE DESIGNATED    40
41    SPACE.   SUCH STORAGE PLACE SHALL BE KEPT CLEAN.   MAKE GOOD 41
42    ANY DAMAGE TO IT OR TO ITS SURROUNDINGS.   REMOVE ANY OILY   42
43    RAGS, WASTE, ETC., FROM THE BUILDING EVERY NIGHT AND TAKE    43
44    EVERY PRECAUTION TO AVOID ANY DANGER OF FIRE.   IN NO CASE   44
45    SHALL AMOUNT OF MATERIALS STORED EXCEED THAT PERMITTED BY    45
46    LOCAL ORDINANCES, STATE LAWS, OR FIRE UNDERWRITER REGULA-    46
47    TIONS.                                                       47
48                                                                 48
49    ENVIROMNENTAL CONDITIONS                                     49
50                                                                 50
51    DO NOT APPLY EXTERIOR PAINT IN DAMP, RAINY WEATHER OR UNTIL  51
52    THE SURFACE HAS DRIED THOROUGHLY FROM THE EFFECTS OF SUCH    52
53    WEATHER.   DO NOT APPLY VARNISH OR PAINT WHEN TEMPERATURE IS 53
54    BELOW 50 DEGREES F.   AVOID PAINTING SURFACES WHEN EXPOSED TO 54
55    HOT SUNLIGHT.                                                55
56                                                                 56
57    PROTECTION                                                   57
58                                                                 58
59    BEFORE PAINTING, REMOVE HARDWARE, ACCESSORIES, PLATES, LIGHT- 59
60    ING FIXTURES AND SIMILAR ITEMS OR PROVIDE AMPLE PROTECTION OF 60
61    SUCH ITEMS.   ON COMPLETION OF EACH SPACE, REPLACE ABOVE     61
62    ITEMS.   USE ONLY SKILLED MECHANICS FOR REMOVING AND CONNECT- 62
63    ING ABOVE ITEMS.   PROTECT ADJACENT SURFACES AS REQUIRED OR  63
64    DIRECTED.   ANY DAMAGE DONE SHALL BE REPAIRED BY THE PAINTING 64
65    CONTRACTOR AT HIS EXPENSE.   A SUFFICIENT SUPPLY OF CLEAN DROP 65
66    CLOTHS AND OTHER PROTECTIVE COVERING SHALL BE PROPERLY DIS-  66
67    TRIBUTED AND MAINTAINED.                                     67
68                                                                 68
69    FINISHING OF THE FOLLOWING LISTED ITEMS AND MATERIALS WILL   69
70    NOT BE REQUIRED AND SHALL BE PROTECTED:                      70
71                                                                 71
72         STAINLESS STEEL, BRASS, BRONZE, COPPER, MONEL, CHROMIUM, 72

      PAGS 978              09900 - 1
```

ANODIZED ALUMINUM; SPECIALLY FINISHED ARTICLES SUCH AS PORCELAIN ENAMEL, PLASTIC COATED FABRICS, AND BAKED ENAMEL.

FINISHED PRODUCTS SUCH AS CERAMIC TILE, WINDOWS, GLASS, BRICK, RESILIENT FLOORING, ACOUSTICAL TILES, BOARD AND METAL TEES; OTHER ARCHITECTURAL FEATURES, SUCH AS "FIN-ISH" HARDWARE, FURNISHED IN ALUMINUM, BRONZE OR PLATED FERROUS METAL, PREFINISHED PANELS, OR OTHER ITEMS THAT ARE INSTALLED PREFINISHED.

COLOR SCHEDULE

THE ARCHITECT WILL PROVIDE A COMPLETE SCHEDULE OF COLORS. COLORS MAY BE SELECTED FROM VARIOUS MANUFACTURER'S STANDARDS. THE PAINT MANUFACTURER SUPPLYING THIS PROJECT SHALL MATCH THESE COLORS. WELL IN ADVANCE OF COMMENCING WORK, THE PAINT-ING CONTRACTOR SHALL OBTAIN THE SCHEDULE FROM THE ARCHITECT, AND PROCEED TO PREPARE DUPLICATE SET OF SAMPLES OF TREATMENTS FOR ALL MAJOR SURFACES.

PART 2 - PRODUCTS

PAINT MATERIALS

BRANDS OF PAINT, VARNISH AND STAINS ARE SPECIFIED HEREIN. BASIC PAINTING MATERIALS SUCH AS LINSEED OIL, SHELLAC, TUR-PENTINE, THINNERS, DRIERS, ETC. SHALL BE OF HIGHEST QUALITY, MADE BY REPUTABLE MANUFACTURERS AS SPECIFIED, HAVE IDENTIFY-ING LABELS ON CONTAINERS AND SHALL BE APPROVED BY ARCHITECT. ALL PAINT MATERIALS SHALL BE FACTORY FRESH.

AS PART OF THE LIST OF PROPOSED SUBCONTRACTORS, THE PAINTING SUBCONTRACTOR SHALL INDICATE THE NAME OF THE MANUFACTURER WHOSE MATERIAL HE PROPOSES TO USE.

PART 3 - EXECUTION

PREPARATION OF SURFACES

INSPECTION OF SURFACES: DO NOT BEGIN PAINTING ON ANY SURFACE UNTIL IT HAS BEEN INSPECTED AND IS IN PROPER CONDITION TO RECEIVE THE PAINT AS SPECIFIED. SHOULD ANY SURFACE BE FOUND UNSUITABLE TO PRODUCE A PROPER PAINT FINISH, NOTIFY THE GENERAL CONTRACTOR IN WRITING. APPLY NO MATERIAL UNTIL THE UNSUITABLE SURFACES HAVE BEEN MADE SATISFACTORY. AFTER ACCEPTANCE OF SURFACE, BY APPLICATION OF FIRST COAT OF PAINT, ASSUME RESPONSIBILITY FOR AND RECTIFY ANY UNSATISFACTORY FINISH RESULTING.

IF, AFTER TREATMENT, THE COMPLETED FINISH (OR ANY PORTION THEREOF) BLISTERS, CHECKS, PEELS, OR OTHERWISE SHOWS INDICA-TION OF DAMPNESS OR OTHER IRREGULAR CONDITION OF SURFACE, THE PAINTING CONTRACTOR SHALL, AT HIS OWN EXPENSE, REMOVE THE APPLIED TREATMENT AND REFINISH THE PART AFFECTED TO THE SATISFACTION OF THE ARCHITECT. (THE PAINTING CONTRACTOR SHOULD DETERMINE DRYNESS OF ALL MOISTURE-HOLDING MATERIALS BY USE OF A RELIABLE ELECTRONIC MOISTURE METER.)

WOOD: SANDPAPER TO SMOOTH AND EVEN SURFACE AND THEN DUST OFF. AFTER PRIMING OR STAIN COAT HAS BEEN APPLIED, THOROUGHLY FILL ALL NAIL HOLES AND OTHER SURFACE IMPERFECTIONS WITH PUTTY TINTED WITH PRIMER OR STAIN TO MATCH WOOD COLOR. SAND ALL WOODWORK BETWEEN COATS TO A SMOOTH SURFACE. COVER KNOTS AND SAP STREAKS WITH A THIN COAT OF SHELLAC.

STEEL AND IRON: REMOVE GREASE, RUST AND RUST SCALE AND TOUCH-UP ANY CHIPPED OR ABRADED PLACES ON ITEMS THAT HAVE BEEN SHOP COATED. WHERE STEEL OR IRON HAVE A HEAVY COATING

Figure 9.5 Painting specification guidelines. (Continued)

OF SCALE, REMOVE BY DESCALING, OR WIRE BRUSHING, AS NECES-
SARY, TO PRODUCE A SATISFACTORY SURFACE FOR PAINTING. WHEN
AREA WILL BE EXPOSED TO VIEW, SANDPAPER THE ENTIRE TREATED
AREA SMOOTH, FEATHER THE EDGE OF SURROUNDING UNDAMAGED PRIME
COAT AND SPOT PRIME IN A MANNER TO ELIMINATE EVIDENCE OF
REPAIR.

GALVANIZED METAL: THOROUGHLY CLEAN BY WIPING SURFACES WITH
SURFACE CONDITIONER AND PRIME WITH GALVANIZED IRON PRIMER AS
RECOMMENDED BY PAINT MANUFACTURER.

CONCRETE AND CONCRETE MASONRY: PREPARE SURFACES TO BE
PAINTED BY REMOVING ALL DIRT, DUST, OIL AND GREASE STAINS AND
EFFLORESCENCE. THE METHOD OF SURFACE PREPARATION SHALL BE
LEFT TO THE DISCRETION OF THE PAINTER PROVIDED THE RESULTS
ARE SATISFACTORY TO THE ARCHITECT. BEFORE FIRST PAINT COAT
IS APPLIED, SPOT PRIME ANY NAILS AND OTHER EXPOSED METAL
OCCURRING IN THE SURFACES WITH AN OIL-BASE MASONRY PRIMER AS
RECOMMENDED BY PAINT MANUFACTURER.

PLASTER SURFACES: FILL CRACKS, HOLES OR IMPERFECTIONS IN
PLASTER WITH PATCHING PLASTER AND SMOOTH OFF TO MATCH
ADJOINING SURFACES. BEFORE PAINTING ANY PLASTER, SURFACES
SHALL BE FIRST TESTED FOR DRYNESS WITH A MOISTURE TESTING
DEVICE. APPLY NO PAINT OR SEALER ON PLASTER WHEN THE
MOISTURE CONTENT EXCEEDS 12% AS DETERMINED BY THE TESTING
DEVICE. TEST SUFFICIENT AREAS IN EACH SPACE AND AS OFTEN AS
NECESSARY TO DETERMINE THE PROPER MOISTURE CONTENT FOR
PAINTING. IF THE MOISTURE CONTENT IS BETWEEN 8% AND 12%,
PRIME WITH ALKALI RESISTANT PRIMER. IF 8% OF LESS, PRIME
WITH SPECIFIED PRIMER. REMOVE THE DRY SALT DEPOSITS FROM ALL
PLASTER SURFACES BY BRUSHING WITH A STIFF BRUSH BEFORE PAINT-
ING.

WORKMANSHIP

PERFORM ALL WORK USING ONLY EXPERIENCED, COMPETENT PAINTERS
IN ACCORDANCE WITH THE BEST STANDARDS OF PRACTICE IN THE
TRADE. HAND BRUSH OR ROLL WORK EXCEPT WHERE OTHERWISE PER-
MITTED OR DIRECTED. OLYMPIA PRODUCTS ARE TO BE BRUSH
APPLIED. WHEN COMPLETED, THE PAINTING SHALL REPRESENT A
FIRST-CLASS WORKMANLIKE APPEARANCE. APPLY ALL PAINT
MATERIALS UNDER ADEQUATE ILLUMINATION.

TINT ALL PRIMERS AND UNDERCOATS TO APPROXIMATELY THE COLOR OF
THE FINISH COAT WITH EACH COAT BEING SUFFICIENTLY DIFFERENT
FROM THE WORK IN PLACE TO PERMIT EASY IDENTIFICATION.

FINISH EDGES, TOPS AND BOTTOMS OF ALL DOORS SAME AS DOOR
FACES. BOTH SIDES AND ALL EDGES OF DOORS TO BE FINISHED
SIMULTANEOUSLY.

PRIME COATS SPECIFIED HEREIN WILL NOT BE REQUIRED ON ITEMS
DELIVERED WITH PRIME OR SHOP COATS ALREADY APPLIED, UNLESS
OTHERWISE SPECIFIED.

APPLICATION

STAIN OR PAINT ONLY WHEN SURFACES ARE CLEAN, DRY, SMOOTH AND
ADEQUATELY PROTECTED FROM DAMPNESS. EACH COAT OF PAINT SHALL
BE WELL BRUSHED ON, WORKED OUT EVENLY AND ALLOWED TO DRY AT
LEAST 24 HOURS BEFORE THE SUBSEQUENT COAT IS APPLIED.

FINISHED WORK SHALL BE UNIFORM, OF APPROVED COLOR, SMOOTH AND
FREE FROM RUNS, SAGS, CLOGGING OR EXCESSIVE FLOODING. MAKE
EDGES OF PAINT ADJOINING OTHER MATERIALS OR COLORS SHARP AND
CLEAN, WITHOUT OVERLAPPING. WHERE HIGH GLOSS ENAMEL IS USED,
LIGHTLY SAND UNDERCOATS TO OBTAIN A SMOOTH FINISH COAT.

EACH COAT OF MATERIAL APPLIED MUST BE INSPECTED AND APPROVED
BY THE ARCHITECT BEFORE THE APPLICATION OF THE SUCCEEDING
SPECIFIED COAT; OTHERWISE NO CREDIT FOR THE CONCEALED COAT

PAGE 978   09900 - 3

```
 1    WILL BE GIVEN, AND THE CONTRACTOR SHALL ASSUME THE RESPONSI-      1
 2    BILITY TO RECOAT THE WORK IN QUESTION.   PAINTING CONTRACTOR      2
 3    SHALL NOTIFY THE ARCHITECT WHEN EACH COAT IS COMPLETED.           3
 4                                                                      4
 5    AT COMPLETION, TOUCH-UP AND RESTORE FINISH WHERE DAMAGED AND      5
 6    LEAVE FINISH SURFACES IN GOOD CONDITION.                          6
 7                                                                      7
 8                                                                      8
 9    PART 4 - SCHEDULES                                                9
10                                                                     10
11    SCHEDULE OF FINISHES                                             11
12                                                                     12
13    REFER TO THE "FINISH SCHEDULE" ON THE DRAWING FOR DESIGNATED     13
14    FINISHES OF AREAS, WHICH ARE LISTED IN ACCORDANCE WITH SCHE-     14
15    DULE FOLLOWING.   ITEMS LISTED ARE ACCEPTABLE PRODUCTS OF SOME   15
16    MAJOR  MANUFACTURERS.    RESPONSIBILITY FOR RECOMMENDING,        16
17    SCHEDULING AND USING  THE PROPER PAINT FOR THE JOB CONDITIONS    17
18    RESTS WITH THE MANUFACTURER AND PAINTING SUBCONTRACTOR.          18
19                                                                     19
20                                                                     20
```

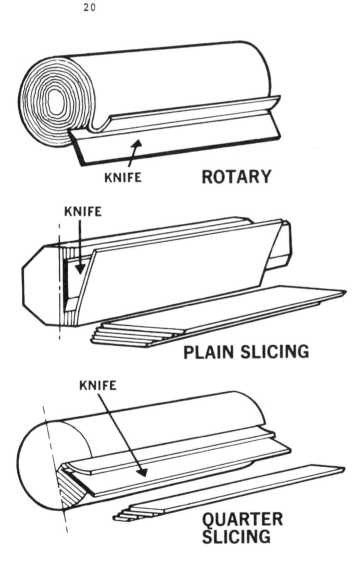

KNIFE   **ROTARY**

KNIFE   **PLAIN SLICING**

KNIFE   **QUARTER SLICING**

Figure 9.6 Methods of cutting flitches. Reproduced with permission of Hardwood Plywood Manufacturers Association.

TABLE 9.12 COMPARATIVE TABLE OF WOOD SPECIES

SPECIES	BOTANICAL NAME	PRINCIPAL USES	APPEARANCE COLOR	FIGURE	GRAIN	RELATIVE COST Lumber	RELATIVE COST Plywood
ASH, White	Fraxinus, American	Trim, Frames & Cabinets	Creamy White to Light Brown	High	Open	100	175
BASSWOOD	Tilia, American	Decorative Molds Carving turnery	Creamy White	No figure	Closed	85	—
BEECH	Fagus grandifolia	Semi-exposed Cabinet Parts	Light to Pinkish	Medium	Closed	80	Not Gen. Available
BIRCH, Yellow, "Natural"	Betula alleghaniensis	Trim, Frames Panelling & Cabinets	White to Dark Red	Medium	Closed	100	100
BIRCH, Yellow, "Select Red" (Heartwood)	Betula alleghaniensis	Trim, Frames Panelling & Cabinets	Dark Red	Medium	Closed	150	150
BIRCH, Yellow, "Select White" (Sapwood)	Betula alleghaniensis	Trim, Frames Panelling & Cabinets	Creamy White	Medium	Closed	130	120
BUTTERNUT	Juglans cinerea	Trim, Frames Panelling & Cabinets	Pale Brown	High	Open	300	500
CEDAR, Western Red	Thuja plicata	Trim, Panelling Exterior & Interior	Reddish to Pinkish Brown nearly White Sapwood	Medium	Closed	100	100
CHERRY, Black	Prunus serotina	Trim, Frames Trim	Reddish Brown	High	Closed	160	200
CHESTNUT, Wormy	Castanea dentata	Panelling and Panelling & Cabinets	Greyish Brown	High	Open with Worm Holes	150	NA
FIRE, Douglas Flat Grain	Pseudolsugu menziesii	Trim, Frames Panelling	Reddish Tan	High	Closed	100	80
FIR, Douglas Vertical Grain	Pseudolsugu menziesii	Trim, Frames Panelling	Reddish Tan	Low	Closed	100	NA
MAHOGANY, African Plain Sawn	Khaya ivornsis	Trim, Frames Panelling & Cabinets	Reddish Brown	Medium	Open	250	250
MAHOGANY, African Quarter Sawn	Khaya ivornsis	Trim, Frames Panelling & Cabinets	Reddish Brown	Low	Open	350	350
MAHOGANY, Tropical American, "Honduras"	Sweitenia macrophylla	Trim, Frames Panelling cabinets & Bar tops	Rich Golden Brown	Medium	Open	200	300
MAPLE, Hard "Natural"	Acer saccharum	Trim, Frames Paneling & Cabinets	White to Reddish Brown	Medium	Closed	75	150
MAPLE, Hard, "Select White" (Sapwood)	Acer saccharum	Trim, Frames Panelling & Cabinets	White	Medium	Closed	90	150
MAPLE, Soft "Natural"	Acer saccharum	Trim, semi-exposed Cabinet parts	White to Reddish Brown	Low	Closed	75	Not Gen. Available
OAK, Red Plain Sawn	Quercus ruba	Trim, Frames Panelling & Cabinets	Reddish Tan to Brown	High	Open	90	130
OAK, Red Rift Sawn	Quercus ruba	Trim, Frames Panelling & Cabinets	Reddish Tan to Brown	Low	Open	200	250
OAK, Red Quarter Sawn	Quercus ruba	Trim, Frames Panelling & Cabinets	Reddish Tan to Brown	Low	Open	200	250
OAK, White Plain Sawn	Quercus alba	Trim, Frames Panelling & Cabinets	Greyish Tan	High	Open	100	165
OAK, White Rift Sawn	Quercus alba	Trim, Frames Panelling & Cabinets	Greyish Tan	Low	Open	200	250
OAK, White Quarter Sawn	Quercus alba	Trim, Frames Panelling & Cabinets	Greyish Tan	Low figure accented with flakes	Open	200	250
PECAN	Carya species	Trim, Panelling & Cabinets	Reddish Brown with Dark Brown stripes	Medium	Open	100	200
PINE, Eastern or Northern White	Pinus strobus	Trim, Frames Panelling & Cabinets	Creamy White to Pink	Medium	Closed	100	NA
PINE, Idaho	Pinus monticola	Trim, Frames Panelling & Cabinets	Creamy White	Low	Closed	100	Not Gen. Available
PINE, Ponderosa	Pinus ponderosa	Trim, Frames Panelling & Cabinets	Light to Medium Pink	Medium	Closed	100	125
PINE, Sugar	Pinus lambertiana	Trim, Frames Panelling & Cabinets	Creamy White	Low	Closed	110	Not Gen. Available
PINE, Southern Yellow	Pinus echinata	Trim, Frames Panelling & Flooring Cabinets	Pale Yellow	High	Closed	65	Not Gen. Available
POPLAR, Yellow	Lirodendron Tulipifern	Trim, Frames Panelling & Cabinets	Pale Yellow to Brown with Green Cast	Medium	Closed	85	NA
REDWOOD, Flat Grain (Heartwood)	Sequoia Sempervirens	Trim, Frames Panelling	Deep Red	High	Closed	110	NA
REDWOOD, Vertical Grain (Heartwood)	Sequoia Sempervirens	Trim, Frames Panelling	Deep Red	Low	Closed	120	NA
ROSEWOOD, Brazilian	Dalbergia nigra	Solid Trim Incidental to Veneered Panelling	Intermingled Reds Browns, and Blacks	High	Open	NGA	780
SPRUCE, Sitka	Tideland spruce Picea sitchensis	Trim, Frames	Light Yellowish Tan	High	Closed	100	NA
TEAK	Techtona grandis	Trim, Frames Panelling & Cabinets	Tawny Yellow to Dark Brown	High	Open	400	400
WALNUT, Black	Juglans nigra	Trim, Frames Panelling & Cabinets	Chocolate Brown	High	Open	300	300
WALNUT, Nogal	Juglans nigra neotropica	Trim, Frames Panelling & Cabinets	Chocolate Brown	High	Open	200	NA

NOTE: Regional distribution differences may affect availability and cost relationship.

(A) Rated from 1 to 4 as follows:
1. In warehouse stock in good quantities and fair assortment of thicknesses and lengths.

Reproduced with permission of the Architectural Woodwork Institute.

	PRACTICAL SIZE LIMITATIONS		AVAILIBILITY OF MATCHING PLYWOOD (A)	HARDNESS	DIMENSIONAL STABILITY (B)	FINISHING		REMARKS
Thick	Width	Length				Paint	Transparent	
1½"	7½"	12'	3	Hard	10/64	Not normally used	Excellent	Excellent where strength is required bold grain.
1½"	7½"	10'	4	Soft	10/64	Excellent	Excellent	Best for mouldings no grain.
1½"	7½"	12'	4	Hard	14/64	Excellent	Good	North American Beech not generally used as show wood.
1½"	7½"	12'	1	Hard	12/64	Excellent	Good	One of the most common used.
1½"	5½"	11'	2	Hard	12/64	Not normally used	Excellent	Rich Colour.
1½"	5"	11'	2	Hard	12/64	Not normally used	Excellent	Uniform Appearance.
1½"	5½"	8'	3	Medium	8/64	Not normally used	Excellent	Beautiful and Rich.
3¼"	11"	16'	1 & 3	Soft	10/64	Not normally used	Good	Decay resistant, rough texture favorite.
1½"	5½"	7'	2	Hard	9/64	Not normally used	Excellent	Rich Colour.
¾"	7½"	10'	4	Medium	9/64	Not normally used	Excellent	Very limited supply.
3¼"	11"	16'	1	Medium	10/64	Fair	Fair	Good supply.
1½"	11"	16'	4	Medium	6/64	Good	Good	Very limited supply.
2½"	11"	15'	3	Medium	7/64	Good	Excellent	Fine hardwood.
2½"	7½"	15'	3	Medium	5/64	Not normally used	Excellent	Limited supply.
2½"	11"	15'	3	Medium	6/64	Not normally used	Excellent	One of the world's finest cabinet woods.
3½"	9½"	12'	3	Very Hard	12/64	Excellent	Good	Plentiful supply, excellent properties.
2½"	9½"	12'	3	Very Hard	12/64	Not normally used	Excellent	Uniform appearance.
3¼"	9½"	12'	4	Medium	9/64	Excellent	Not normally used	Good utility hardwood.
1½"	7¼"	12'	1	Hard	11/64	Not normally used	Excellent	Excellent architectural wood, low cost widely used.
1¹⁄₁₆"	5½"	10'	3	Hard	7/64	Not normally used	Excellent	Excellent architectural wood, limited supply.
1¹⁄₁₆"	5½"	8'	1	Hard	7/64	Not normally used	Excellent	Excellent architectural wood, limited supply.
1½"	5½"	10'	2	Hard	11/64	Not normally used	Excellent	Wide Range of grain patterns and colour.
¾"	4½"	10'	3	Hard	7/64	Not normally used	Excellent	Limited availability.
¾"	4½"	10'	3	Hard	8/64	Not normally used	Excellent	Pronounced flake, very limited use and supply.
1½"	5½"	12'	3	Hard	11/64	Not normally used	Good	Subject to regional availability, attractive.
1½"	9½"	14'	3	Soft	7/64	Good	Good	True white pine, wide range of applications for general usage.
1½"	9½"	14'	4	Soft	8/64	Good	Good	True white pine, wide range of applications for general usage.
1½"	9½"	16'	3	Soft	8/64	Good	Good	Most widely used pine, wide range of applications for general usage.
3¼"	11"	16'	4	Soft	7/64	Good	Good	True white pine, wide range of applications for general usage.
1½"	7½"	16'	4	Medium	10/64	Fair	Good	An economical hard pine.
2½"	7½"	12'	3	Medium	9/64	Excellent	Good	Ideal interior hardwood excellent paintability.
2½"	11"	16'	1 & 3	Soft	6/64	Good	Good	Superior exterior wood hign natural decay resistance.
2½"	11"	16'	3	Soft	3/64	Excellent	Excellent	Superior exterior wood high natural decay resistance.
—	—	—	3	Very Hard	7/64	Not normally used	Excellent	Exotice figure, high cost.
3¼"	9½"	16'	4	Soft	10/64	Fair	Fair	Limited general available.
1½"	7½"	10'	2	Hard	6/64	Not normally used	Excellent	Outstanding wood for most applications, high cost.
1½"	4½"	6'	1	Hard	10/64	Paint not normally used	Excellent	Fine domestic hardwood extremely limited widths and lengths more readily available in veneer.
¾"	9½"	9'	4	Medium	12/64	Not normally used	Good	Good substitute for juglans nigra where better widths and lengths required.

2. In warehouse stock in fair quantity but not in thicknesses other than ¼" and ¾"; or sizes other than 4'-0" x 8'-0".
3. Produced on a special order only.
4. Not generally available.

(B) These figures represent possible width change in a 12" board when moisture content is reduced from 10% to 5%. Figures are for plain sawn unless indicated otherwise in species column.

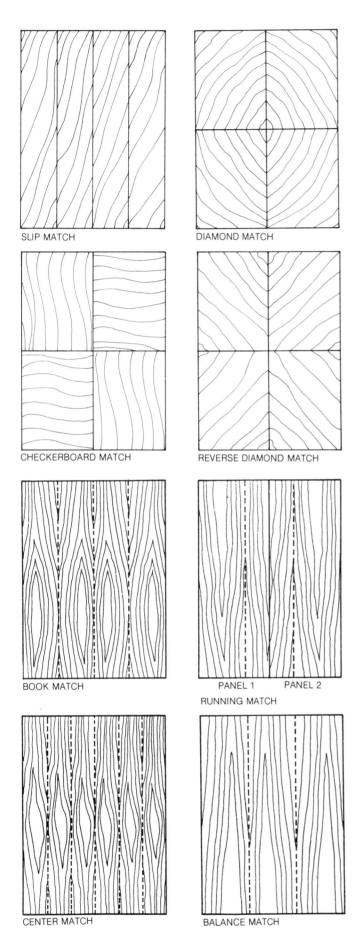

SLIP MATCH

DIAMOND MATCH

CHECKERBOARD MATCH

REVERSE DIAMOND MATCH

BOOK MATCH

PANEL 1   PANEL 2
RUNNING MATCH

CENTER MATCH

BALANCE MATCH

Figure 9.7 Veneer matching. Source: Hardwood Plywood Manufacturers Association.

in their manufacture. However, the price of lumber in most species may not reflect similar cost factors. In spite of their physical differences, the two products are always compatible, and both are essential to complete design freedom in contemporary buildings.

Practical Size Limitations schedules the maximum practical dimensions (not average) of each of the species in thickness, width, and length, considering reasonable quantity requirements. The thickness and width can be increased by laminating or edge bonding at the mill, while the length restrictions are handled by either a scarf or butt joint in the field. Where significant quantities of hardwoods are to be used, with constant dimensions in both width and length, such as vertical board paneling, consideration should be given to the use of more narrow members in order to reduce the cost of waste. However, the lead time afforded in the construction of a new building is usually adequate to procure quality materials in the quantity needed to satisfy the largest projects.

The *Availability of Matching Plywood* is relatively expressed from 1 (most readily available) to 4 (unavailable).

End use determines the importance of *Hardness* in selecting a species for each particular type of application. Counters, door frames, wall treatments in high-traffic areas are obvious uses of wood products where hardness and resistance to abrasion must be considered. In many other applications these factors, generally, are not of great importance.

Dimensional Stability is of much value in helping to select woods for use where humidity conditions may vary widely and where design or fabrication of a wood product does not allow free movement or the use of plywood. The column figures indicate extreme conditions and show the maximum amount of movement possible in a 12″ (30.5 cm) wide piece of unfinished wood where its moisture content changes from 10 to 5 percent, or vice versa. The possible change in dimension demonstrates that unfinished interior woodwork must be carefully protected prior to finishing by keeping it in rooms where relative humidities are between 25 and 55 percent. The column also shows the variation between species and between flat grain and edge grain, where such cuts are available commercially.

Remarks is a general information–type column that could either reinforce or weaken the reasons for your tentative selection. By the time this comes into play, your choice will probably be down to two or three species, and information contained under this heading will surely simplify your final decision.[3]

Matching of Veneer

Veneers are matched twice—once in production and again during installation. Matching is accomplished within each panel and from panel to panel. Within individual panels, the process of matching or arranging the veneer sheets involves alternating and turning over the sheets (like pages of a book) and hence the name "book matched" or "book leaf." This production method produces three types of match:

1. *Balance match* is composed of any number (odd or even) of veneer sheets clipped to an equal width for balanced arrangement within each panel.

2. *Running match* is when each panel face is arranged from as many veneer sheets as necessary for the specified panel width. When a portion of a veneer sheet is left over, it is used to start the next panel face.

3. *Center match* is composed of an even number of veneer sheets that are equal in width (approximate) arranged so

that a veneer point occurs in the center of the panel. This tends to reduce the usable veneer and increases the cost (see Figure 9.7).

Other methods may be specified for the arrangement of veneer sheets, such as a random effect (no match), diamonds, herringbone, checkerboard, or any other pattern the designer may desire.

Three basic methods are used to match panel to panel:

1. *Blueprint match* is accomplished by making an elevation drawing of the walls or wall to be paneled and numbering in sequence the desired number of panels. Panels are then fabricated in the required sizes and the proper sequence for the entire space. This includes all spaces above and below windows, doors, and bookcases. This produces a perfectly matched room.

2. *Sequence match* is produced by securing as many panels of the same size as are required. These panels are then numbered in sequence from left to right. Doors, if specified, may be furnished from the same flitch, but will not be matched in sequence with the panels.

3. *Warehouse matched sets* are premanufactured sets which are numbered in sequence. Sizes are usually 48″ × 96″ (121.9 × 243.8 cm) or 48″ × 120″ (121.9 × 304.8 cm). The sets vary from 6 to 12 panels. If more than one set is required, no match can be expected. Doors cannot be matched and it may be necessary to make wall adjustments near corners or wall ends.

Panel Construction

Paneling construction is composed of three components: thickness, core, and size.

1. Thickness usually recommended for paneling ranges from 3/4 in. (19.1 mm) to 1/4 in. (6.4 mm) for installations that may require curving of the wood.

2. There are three basic core types used for paneling and each has a distinct difference (see Figure 9.8). Table 9.13 points out the advantages and disadvantages of each.

Core types are given for the purpose of general comparisons; however, it should be remembered that panel cores can be altered to meet special project requirements. There are other core materials or combination of materials which can be used to achieve special properties. For example:

Treatment Desired	Material
Acoustics	Lead sheet
	Asbestos sheet
	Manufacturer's standard
	Acoustical panel
	Particleboard panel
Fire resistance	Chemically impregnated core
	Mineral core
	Asbestos sheet
Light weight	Aluminum honeycomb
	Kraft paper honeycomb
	Wood coils and grids

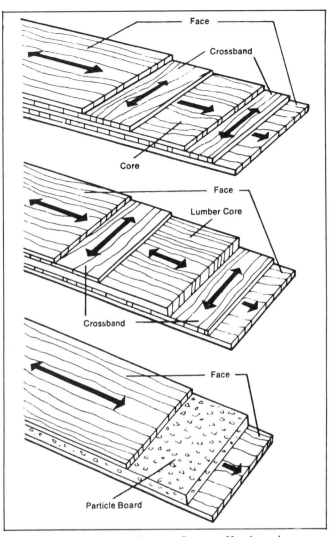

Figure 9.8 Plywood panel cores. Source: Hardwood Plywood Manufacturers Association.

TABLE 9.13 HARDWOOD PLYWOOD PANELING CORE TYPES

Core Type	Thickness	Advantages	Disadvantages
Veneer (all inner plies of hardwood/ wood veneer)	1/4″ (3 ply or less)	Inexpensive	Core imperfections may photograph through face veneer
	5/16″-1/2″	Inexpensive	
	Over 1/2″ (7 ply)	Best screw-hold power	Difficult to machine. Exposed edge shows core voids and imperfections. Most susceptible to warpage (doors)
Particle board (wood composition, also known as chipboard, chip-core)	1/4″ (infrequent) through 2″ (usually 3 plies)	Most stable. No core photographing. Least expensive (generally)	Poor edge screw-holding. Heaviest core
Lumber core (consists of strips of lumber 1 1/2″ to 4″ wide)	5/8″ through 2″ (usually 5 plies)	Easiest machined. Exposed edges are solid. Stable construction	Highest priced

Source: Hardwood Plywood Manufacturers Association.

TABLE 9.14 SELECTION GUIDE TO THE ARCHITECTURAL WOODWORK INSTITUTE'S FINISH SYSTEMS

	TRANSPARENT										OPAQUE					
	1 Standard Lacquer		2 Catalyzed Lacquer		3 Conversion Varnish Alkyd-Urea		4 Vinyl Catalyzed		5 Penetrating Oil Synthetic		6 Opaque Lacquer Standard		7 Opaque Enamel Synthetic		8 Opaque Vinyl Catalyzed	
SHEEN	C	P	C	P	C	P	C	P	C	P	C	P	C	P	C	P
Dull Rubbed Effect 16°-24°	X		X	X	X	X	X	X	X							
Medium Rubbed Effect 28°-36°	X		X	X	X	X	X	X								
Full Gloss 88°-96°	X		X	X	X	X	X	X			X		X		X	X
Semi-Gloss 28°-36°											X		X		X	X
Flat 16°-24°											X		X		X	X
EFFECT																
Open Grain	X		X	X	X	X	X	X								
Closed Grain	X		X	X	X	X	X	X								
Oil Finish									X							
Oil Finish (Simulated)							X									
PERFORMANCE																
Wear Resistance																
Water & Moisture Resistance	3		2	1	3	3	2	1	4		3		2		2	1
Print Resistance (8 oz. Duck) 2 PSI at room temperature	1		1	1	1	1	1	1	4		1		1		1	1
Abrasion Resistance Tabor Abrasor	3		3	2	3	2	2	1	5		3		2		2	1
Adhesion (Crosshatch)	2		2	2	2	2	1	1	2		2		2		1	1
Cold Check Resistance ASTM D1211-60	1		1	1	2	2	1	1	1		1		2		1	1
Impact Resistance (1 lb. steel ball — 17 inches)	2		2	1	2	3	1	1	1		2		3		1	1
Repairability	1		2	2	3	3	3	3	1		1		3		3	3
Chemical Resistance																
2% Caustic Solution	4		2	2	2	1	2	1	4		4		2		1	1
10% Sodium Hydroxide	4		3	2	4	3	3	2	4		4		4		3	2
10% Trisodium Phosphate	4		3	2	3	2	2	1	4		4		3		2	1
Glacial Acetic Acid	4		3	3	3	2	2	2	5		4		4		2	2
50% Sulphuric Acid	3		2	2	4	3	2	1	5		3		4		2	1
28% Ammonium Hydroxide	4		3	3	3	2	2	1	5		4		4		2	1
95% Ethyl Alcohol	4		3	2	3	2	2	1	5		4		3		2	1
Household Chemical Resistance																
Grease (Cooking Oil)	3		2	1	2	1	1	1	5		3		2		1	1
Hot Coffee	3		1	1	2	1	1	1	5		3		1		1	1
Orange Juice	3		1	1	1	1	1	1	4		3		1		1	1
Tomato Juice	3		1	1	1	1	1	1	4		3		1		1	1
Mustard	3		1	1	1	1	1	1	4		3		2		1	1
Nail Polish & Remover	5		4	3	3	2	2	1	5		5		5		1	1
Detergent (Soap)	4		2	1	2	1	1	1	5		4		2		1	1
Flame Spread																
Substantially affects (increases) Flame Spread	Yes		Yes	Yes	No	No	No	No	No		Yes		No		No	No

KEY

C = Custom   1 = Excellent
P = Premium   2 = Very Good
X = Availability   3 = Good
4 = Fair
5 = Poor

"DO NOT OVERSPECIFY" The esthetic considerations are generally the same for both Premium and Custom Grades. *The Performance of the finish constitutes the difference between Premium and Custom Grade.*

EXAMPLE 1 — Paneling on the walls of a high traffic corridor may be specified as Premium in view of the resistances required by nature of its location.

EXAMPLE 2 — Paneling on the walls of a Board of Directors Room may be specified as Custom since the need for resistance to wear and chemicals would probably be non-existent.

Panel Sizes. Plywoods can be obtained in any length, depending on the length of the flitch available and manufacturers' facilities. Small or long lengths can be ordered, when required. Through the processes of progressive and scarf-joint gluing, unlimited lengths and widths or panels may often be obtained by careful surface matching and joining of selected flitches. The tolerance for width dimension and length dimension should be plus or minus 1/32″ (0.8 mm). The tolerance for thickness for sanded panels should be plus or minus 3.64″ (1.2 mm). However, in architectural (premium) and other specially constructed grades, the tolerances may be kept to plus or minus 0″.[4] In some cases, panel sizes and thicknesses may be limited due to the availability of flame-retardant treated core sizes.

Panel Finish

It is usually advised that the designer have panels finished by the manufacturer because greater control is possible and the panels will be protected against moisture during transportation and storage prior to installation. If the project will involve a large amount of cutting and fitting, it may be necessary to finish on the site, but the designer then has to write very specific finishing instructions. In either case, the designer should request a sample of the finished panel before final specification. Table 9.14 lists types of transparent and opaque finishes recommended for paneling. This table also provides information on flammability and performance specification criteria.

Flame Resistance

Paneling is classified as an interior finish and must therefore be treated for flame-spread characteristics. Many species of wood have been tested, and it has been found that some untreated (without added flame retardant) woods produce a rather low flame spread. Table 9.15 lists approximate flame-spread rating of some typical veneer species. A more precise rating is dependent on core type (wood density) and manufacturing process.[5]

It has been found that the specific density of wood affects the flame-spread rating; i.e., the lower the density, the lower the flame spread. The following guideline may be used in the specification of wood paneling.

Flame Spread	Hardwood Plywood Paneling
25	1. Treated veneer core with a veneer density of 31.2 lb (14 kg) or less.
	2. Treated particleboard core with veneer density of 42.7 lb (19.5 kg) or less.
25–50	1. Treated veneer core with a veneer density of 43.7 lb (20 kg) or less.
	2. Treated particleboard core with a veneer density of 58.6 lb (27 kg) or less.
50–75	1. Treated (veneer, particleboard, or lumber) cores without species density limitations.

Fire resistance treatments are applied through impregnation of the cores and crossbands with waterborne salts of varying composition. (The treatment should never be applied to the panel surface because it makes proper finishing very difficult.) The impregnation method requires that the core be bonded with a waterproof-type adhesive.

Designers should order fire-resistant panels factory-finished or factory-sealed. When a complete finish is ordered,

TABLE 9.15 FLAME-SPREAD RATING OF FLAME-RETARDANT TYPICAL VENEER SPECIES

Flame Spread 25	Flame Spread 50	Flame Spread 75
Butternut	White Ash	White Oak
Chestnut	Avodire	Pecan
Cypress	Birch	Rosewood
African Mahogany	Cherry	Ebony
Prima Vera	Red Gum	East Indian Laurel
Redwood	Honduras Mahogany	
Fir	Lauan	
Limba	Tanguile	
	Hard Maple	
	Red Oak	
	Teak	
	Walnut	
	English Brown Oak	

Reproduced with permission of the Architectural Woodwork Institute.

make certain that the Underwriters Laboratories allows the panel to be labeled as "finished." Only experienced workers should install these panels because the edges, if cut, must be immediately resealed so that atmospheric humidity will not leach the salts from the core and leave a white deposit on the surface. Edges should be sealed with tung oil phenolic primers, tung oil phenolic spar varnish, or shellac.

Fire-retardant paneling does cost more than standard paneling, but savings may be realized on fire insurance reductions. In addition, it has been found that the treatment for fire resistance also provides resistance to decay from water, humidity, and termites.

Acoustical Treatment

The acoustic quality of hardwood plywood paneling can be increased by (1) modifying the panel construction or (2) selecting an appropriate method of installation.

Designers may specify panel modification in the following manner:

1. Require that face veneers be laid up in random 4-in. (10.2-cm) wide strips with a 1/8″ × 1/8″ (3.2 × 3.2 mm) routed grove 4 in. on center (oc). Edges should be shiplapped and groves either accented or colored to blend with the face veneer.

2. Require that panels be perforated with holes of varying dimensions, spaced as specified [3/16-in. (4.8-mm) holes spaced 1.2 in. (12.7 mm) on center.] These perforations, if kept to a minimum size, will absorb high-frequency sound and not disturb the overall grain or surface effect.

The following installation techniques may be effective in reducing noise (see Figure 9.9).

1. Placement of recessed or protruding battens between panels provides good sound diffusers.

2. Alternation of floating panels is also very effective.

Panel Selection

Grades of paneling are usually limited to "architectural," or premium grade, and custom grade. Custom grade assumes the use of standard or stock manufactured panels that are not sequence matched. The specification of premium grade allows the designer to select face veneers by species, specific grain and color, core construction and matching within the panel and between panels.

Installation

Installation requires a series of steps that include the following considerations:

Wall Subsurfaces. These fall into the following four categories:

1. *Stud walls* may require the addition of furring strips applied horizontally or vertically. If studs are straight and well seasoned, paneling may be applied directly to the studs.

2. *Plasterboard subwalls* may require an installation which combines adhesives and nailing. The nails must be long enough to penetrate both surfaces.

3. *Plaster walls* will receive a paneling application if the surface is not too rough or badly damaged. If the surface is damaged, furring strips should be applied horizontally.

4. *Concrete block walls* should be carefully checked for moisture prior to installation. Furring strips may be applied to the concrete wall either vertically or horizontally.

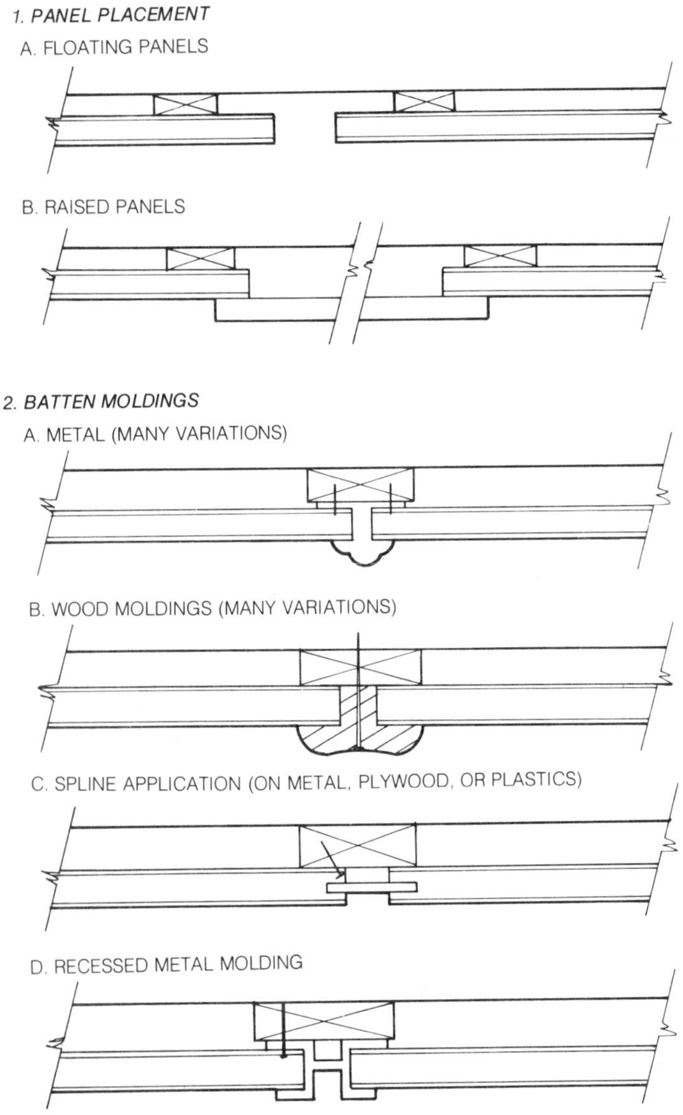

1. PANEL PLACEMENT

A. FLOATING PANELS

B. RAISED PANELS

2. BATTEN MOLDINGS

A. METAL (MANY VARIATIONS)

B. WOOD MOLDINGS (MANY VARIATIONS)

C. SPLINE APPLICATION (ON METAL, PLYWOOD, OR PLASTICS)

D. RECESSED METAL MOLDING

Figure 9.9 Panel installation for acoustic control. Source: Hardwood Plywood Manufacturers Association.

Storage and Handling. The Hardwood Plywood Manufacturers Association recommends the following procedures to assure safe handling and storage.

1. Panels should be allowed to remain in the room or in the place of application long enough to adjust to the temperature and humidity of the workroom in which the job is being assembled.

2. During periods of extreme humidity, it is best to wait until the panels have had a chance to dry out before attempting to install them.

3. Never erect a panel installation over fresh plaster. Wood is hygroscopic and will take on moisture from the plaster.

4. Never stand panels on end against a wall for any length of time. If it is not convenient to lay them flat, they should stand on their sides, with care being taken not to chip the edges.

5. To prevent moisture from penetrating through the panel to the face, back prime all panels erected over exterior plaster walls with one coat of pure white lead and linseed oil (three white to one linseed oil mixture) before applying to furring. Avoid getting any of the primer on the face of the panels as this will interfere with the finishing of the face.

6. Allow for expansion and contraction of panels. A great deal depends upon the extent of the paneled area, climate, and variables such as air conditioning and exposure to sunlight.

7. Panels stacked flat must not be placed directly on the floor, but should be placed on leveled 2 × 4s spaced not more than 16″ (40.6 cm) oc. An inexpensive cover sheet should be placed on top of the stack to keep the top panel from warping and to protect it from dust and natural or artificial light. Care must be taken that the panels are evenly stacked so as not to expose the face veneer along the edges at any point, since exposed faces are subject to color change.

Paneling may be installed by the use of adhesives, nails, or splints and molding.

Adhesive Applications. These may be made with (1) contact cement, (2) plastic resin, and (3) reclaimed rubber adhesive:

Contact Cement. This is applied to the back of the panel and permitted to partially set before application is made to the wall surface. This method of installation is suggested when nailing is not desirable.

Plastic Resins. These are usually supplied in powder form and are mixed with water to the consistency of heavy cream. This adhesive combined with nailing provides an extremely secure application. If nails are not desired, an electronic machine may be used to speed up the drying process of the resins.

Reclaimed Rubber Adhesives. These are applied in thick beads by a caulking gun directly to the wall surface. This method serves to fill in slight imperfections on the wall surface and allows a one-step installation.

Splints and molding methods of application are illustrated in Figure 9.10. Other mechanical devices are recommended for use with adhesives to assure a secure bond. These devices include metal Z clips and metal inserts (see Figure 9.11).

Edge Treatment. When an installation requires that ends be left exposed, several methods may be used to finish the edges. Table 9.16 illustrates edge treatments along with the advantages and comparative cost factors.

Inspection. The project must be inspected before, during, and after installation.

Before. Be sure to verify the following four points:

1. Check that architectural hardwood plywood paneling is of the required species and that the finish matches the reviewed samples.

2. Verify that panels are acclimated to building environment for a minimum of 48 hours prior to installation.

3. Check that panel surfaces are free of damage.

4. Check that panels match both in and among panels specified.

During. The following three items must be checked during installation.

1. Check that panels are aligned plumb and true.

2. Assure that panels are installed according to manufacturer's instructions.

3. Make sure that field cuts on flame-retardant treated cores are sealed.

After. Be sure to check the following points:

1. Make sure that damaged surfaces are restored to original condition.

2. Verify that the job site is left clean.

Guidelines for Specifying Architectural Paneling

The guidelines developed by the Architectural Woodwork Institute (Figure 9.12) include specification information on panel fire retardancy, flitch selection, and panel finish.[6]

TABLE 9.16 PANELING EDGE TREATMENTS

Type	Advantage	Cost
1. Exposed edge lumber core	May be stained to match	Inexpensive
2. Wood trim of matching specie	Applied on job site and finished with panel	Inexpensive
3. Edge routed by mill and hardwood strip of matching specie glued and inserted (variations)	Facilitates job cutting and conditions	Expensive
4. Matching veneer applied at edge of panel by manufacturer with edge-banding equipment	Can be finished with face veneer	Moderate
5. Matching hardwood lumber edge band inserted by manufacturer prior to application of face veneer	Edges may be routed, trimmed, etc.	Expensive

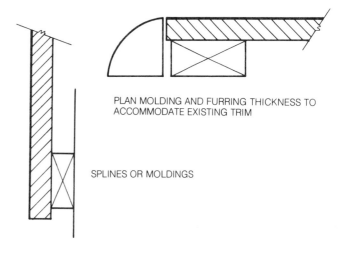

PLAN MOLDING AND FURRING THICKNESS TO ACCOMMODATE EXISTING TRIM

SPLINES OR MOLDINGS

Figure 9.10 Spines and moldings. Source: Hardwood Plywood Manufacturers Association.

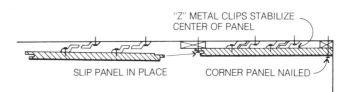

NAILED OR MECHANICAL APPLICATION

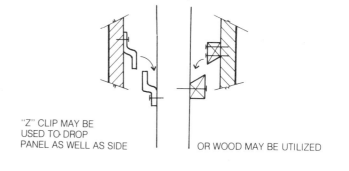

"Z" METAL CLIPS STABILIZE CENTER OF PANEL

SLIP PANEL IN PLACE   CORNER PANEL NAILED

"Z" CLIP MAY BE USED TO DROP PANEL AS WELL AS SIDE

OR WOOD MAY BE UTILIZED

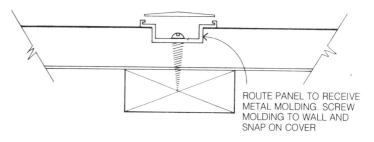

ROUTE PANEL TO RECEIVE METAL MOLDING. SCREW MOLDING TO WALL AND SNAP ON COVER

NOTE: IN MECHANICAL FASTENING, IT IS IMPORTANT THAT THE BASE AND CROWN MOLD ARE UTILIZED TO GIVE ADDITIONAL SUPPORT TO THE PANEL.

Figure 9.11 Mechanical devices used to install paneling. Source: Hardwood Plywood Manufacturers Association.

Figure 9.12 Guidelines for specifying architectural paneling. Reproduced with permission of the Architectural Woodwork Institute.

The many important requirements of an architectural paneling installation are most easily obtained with the use of the AWI Guide Specification.

This specification is a part of the AWI Quality Standards, and its use assures to the specifier the following operations and requirements that will help guarantee a completely satisfactory and well executed installation. Among the many items of work that are required by reference to the AWI Quality Standards, these are of major importance:

Moisture content of the wood, requirements for the appearance of exposed surfaces, the grades of lumber to be used, requirements for the treatment of joints and exposed edges in flush paneling, requirements for the treatment of exterior corners and applied mouldings, adhesive performance requirements, exacting tolerances for all workmanship, ratio requirement of 3 to 1 for raw veneer to finish wall paneling, compatibility of grain and color, requirements for backing or balancing sheets and edge treatment of High Pressure Laminate Paneling, shop assembly, sanding requirements, and specific requirements on how panels are to be raised. These and many other quality insuring factors are automatically required by the use of the AWI Guide Specification.

It is important to specify requirements for Fire Retardancy treating. Code requirements vary in different areas of the country and the extent of treating for each project must be carefully determined. *The following is the AWI Specification for Fire Retardancy treating.*

1.3 Requirements of Regulatory Agencies

A. Treat the following listed items as required by the _____(applicable building code) to obtain spread classifications noted:

Item	Location	Flame spread classification

Note to Specifier: If more than one flame spread classification is required, identify by item or area. Casework and trim are usually exempted from these requirements. Up to ten percent of the combined ceiling and wall surface area is also normally exempted, for unlabeled doors, interior trim and interior finish. Since fire retardant treatments will increase costs substantially and can affect the appearance of architectural woodwork, the applicable code should be studied thoroughly to make sure which, if any, items require the treatment.

The following is the recommended AWI specification for stile and rail panel work and all kinds of flush panel work made of lumber, plywood and high pressure laminate.

2.3 Panelwork

Note to Specifier: Include stile and rail panel work and all kinds of flush panel work made of lumber, plywood and high pressure laminates.

A. Flush Paneling, Wood Veneer

1. AWI quality grade: _____ (Premium grade or Custom grade)

2. Panel shall be: _____ thickness, using _____ ___ core. (Particleboard, Veneer or Lumber)

3. Face veneers: _____ (Species), _____ (Cut).
Note to specifier: Disregard following items 4 through 6 unless premium grade **was selected in 2.3A.1 above.**

4. Matching of adjacent pieces of veneer: _____ (Book match, Slip match or Random match)

5. Panel face assembly: _____ (Running match, Balance match or Center match)

6. Matching of adjacent panels:_____ (Specify one of the following: warehouse sets used full width, warehouse sets selectively reduced in width, sequence matched sets or blueprint matched.)

Note to specifier: Warehouse sets are usually available in 4' x 8' or 10' sheets, in sets of 6 to 12 pieces. Veneers are normally book matched and assembled in a running match. If blueprint matched panels and doors have been selected in paragraph 6 above and the architect either desires to or has already selected the flitch, then paragraph 7 below must be filled out accordingly.

7. Flitch selection: Allow _____ cents per square foot for face veneer - OR - Flitch _____ (Identification number) has been selected from _____ (Name of veneer company) at _____ (Address) containing _____ (Quantity) square feet of _____ (Length) veneer. The ratio of raw face veneer required to panel surface area shall be 3 to 1, unless otherwise specified.

Note to specifier: To determine the approximate amount of face veneer required, multiply the panel surface area by 3. The monetary allowance is for the cost of face veneer only, not the paneling. The above ratio may have to be increased to accommodate exacting requirements of appearance when the flitch contains a wide range of grain characteristics. *It is suggested that the selection be reviewed with someone competent to advise regarding adaptability of the flitch to specific job requirements.*

B. Flush Paneling, High Pressure Laminate.

1. AWI quality grade:_____ (Premium grade or Custom grade)

Note to specifier: AWI grade selection includes quality of workmanship and materials.

2. Laminate selection: _____ (High pressure laminate selection)

Note to specifier: Specify laminate manufacturer, pattern or color by name and number, and texture. If this is not possible, give woodworker choice of manufacturers and specify whether selection will be from solid colors, wood grains or patterns and also texture desired.

C. Stile and Rail Paneling: for Transparent Finish.

1. AWI quality grade:_____ (Premium grade or Custom grade).

Note to specifier: AWI grade selection determines quality of workmanship and material.

2. Solid wood:_____ (Species),_____ (Cut).

3. Plywood:_____ (Species), _____ (Cut).

4. Type of moulding: _____ (Solid or Applied).

5. Type of panel: _____ (Flat or Raised).

D. Stile and Rail Paneling: for Opaque Finish.

1. AWI quality grade:_____ (Premium grade or Custom grade).

Note to specifier: AWI grade selection determines quality of workmanship and material.

2. Solid wood: _____ (Species),

3. Plywood: _____ (Species),

4. Type of moulding: _____ (Solid or Applied).

5. Type of panel: _____ (Flat or Raised).

The following is the recommended AWI Specification for solid wood paneling.

Interior for Transparent Finish

Note to specifier: If both transparent and opaque finish are required for interior standing and running trim, the spaces to receive transparent finish should be listed here or scheduled on drawings and referred to here.

1. AWI quality grade:_____ (Premium grade, Custom grade or Economy grade).

Note to specifier: AWI grade selection includes quality of machining, sanding and materials.

2. Solid wood: _____ (Species),_____ (Cut).

3. Plywood: _____ (Species), _____ (Cut).

Note to specifier: If more than one specie is required for solid wood or plywood, they must be specified here and the spaces in which used noted.

Interior for Opaque Finish

Note to specifier: If both opaque and transparent finish are required for interior standing and running trim the spaces to receive opaque finish should be listed here or scheduled on drawings and referred to here.

1. AWI quality grade: _____ (Premium grade, Custom grade or Economy grade).

Note to specifier: AWI grade selection includes quality of machining, sanding and materials.

2. Solid wood: _____ (Species),

3. Plywood: _____ (Species),

Note to specifier: AWI Premium and Custom grades require particleboard, overlay plywood or hardwood plywood. Fir plywood is allowed only in Economy grade.

In the vast majority of paneling installations, it is desirable to have the paneling factory finished at the woodworker's plant. Wood in its dry unprotected state is hygroscopic and absorbs moisture when subject to dampness. The result is dimensional change and raised grain. Designing to allow free movement of the various parts, plus priming, sealing and finishing at the earliest possible time after the woodwork has been fabricated, results in the most satisfactory installation.

The following is the recommended AWI Specification for Factory Finishing of architectural paneling.

2.12 Factory Finishing

Note to specifier: Includes factory finishing of any and all architectural paneling items specified in this section. The advantages of factory finishing are most apparent for doors, paneling and casework, however, it may be desirable to have other woodwork items adjacent to these factory finished to maintain color and finish match.

A. Transparent Finish

1. Items: _____

Note to specifier: List here those architectural paneling and adjacent items and their locations which are to receive transparent factory finish.

2. AWI Factory Finish System # _____.

Note to specifier: Choose system and quality grade from selection guide for AWI Finish Systems Table (Test 1500-5). If more than one transparent type of finish is to be used on this project, use a separate subsection for each.

3. AWI quality grade: _____ (Premium grade or Custom grade).

4. Stain: _____ (None, Dark, Medium or Light).

5. Degree of Sheen: _____ (Dull rubbed, Medium rubbed, Full gloss).

6. Effect: _____ (Open or Close grain effect).

B. Opaque Finish

1. Items: _____

Note to specifier: List here the architectural paneling and adjacent items and their locations which are to receive an opaque factory finish.

2. AWI Factory Finish System # _____.

Note to specifier: Choose system and quality grade from selection guide for AWI Finish Systems Table (Test 1500-5). If more than one opaque type of finish is to be used on this project, use a separate subsection for each.

3. AWI quality grade: _____ (Premium grade or Custom grade).

4. Degree of Sheen:_____(Full gloss, Semi gloss or Flat).

C. Field Touch-up

Field touch-up shall be the responsibility of the installing contractor and shall include the filling and touch-up of exposed job made nail or screw holes, refinishing of raw surfaces resulting from job fitting, repair of job inflicted scratches and mars, and final cleaning up of the finished surfaces.

The AWI Guide Specification assures the owner of accurate costs as they are based upon exacting Standards which the industry recognizes and accepts as true Hallmarks of Quality.

10 WINDOW SYSTEMS

Designers can no longer consider interior window systems, such as blinds, shutters, shades, and drapery, as purely decorative treatments. With increasing concerns about energy conservation, light, and acoustic control, window systems assume an added importance in planning commercial interiors. This chapter will survey performance requirements, fabrication, estimation, installation, maintenance, and other factors that must be considered prior to making specification decisions.

PERFORMANCE CRITERIA

The majority of window components are not regulated by codes, but drapery fabrics that cover large expanses of wall are frequently required to meet certain flammability standards. For example, if drapery covers more than 10 percent of wall area, it is considered an interior finish by many codes.

Drapery Flammability Regulations

Drapery flammability regulations primarily involve fabric used in commercial, health care, and institutional installations. There are numerous state and city regulations in existence, but the most frequently quoted standards are those required in the City of New York, the City of Boston, and the State of California.

1. *The City of New York* requires that all flame-retardant chemicals used in the city be approved by a Board of Standards and Appeals. After the approval of the chemical is granted, a number is issued which must later appear on a notarized affidavit stating that the fabric has been treated with the approved flame retardant.
2. *The City of Boston* requires that a certificate of flame retardancy and a 15″ × 15″ (38.1 × 38.1 cm) sample of the treated fabric be sent to the Boston Fire Department. Complete details on the intended use must be provided along with a filing fee.
3. *The State of California* requires that all flame-retardant chemicals be approved by the State Fire Marshal. The state also requires that the treatments be applied in approved, licensed finishing companies. Certificates of flame resistance and a 12″ × 12″ (30.5 × 30.5 cm) sample must be submitted to the office of the State Fire Marshal. Designers may obtain a listing of approved pretreated fabrics, finishing companies, and chemicals recommended for particular fibers from the California State Fire Marshal's Office. Figure 10.1 illustrates a typical flame-retardance certificate.

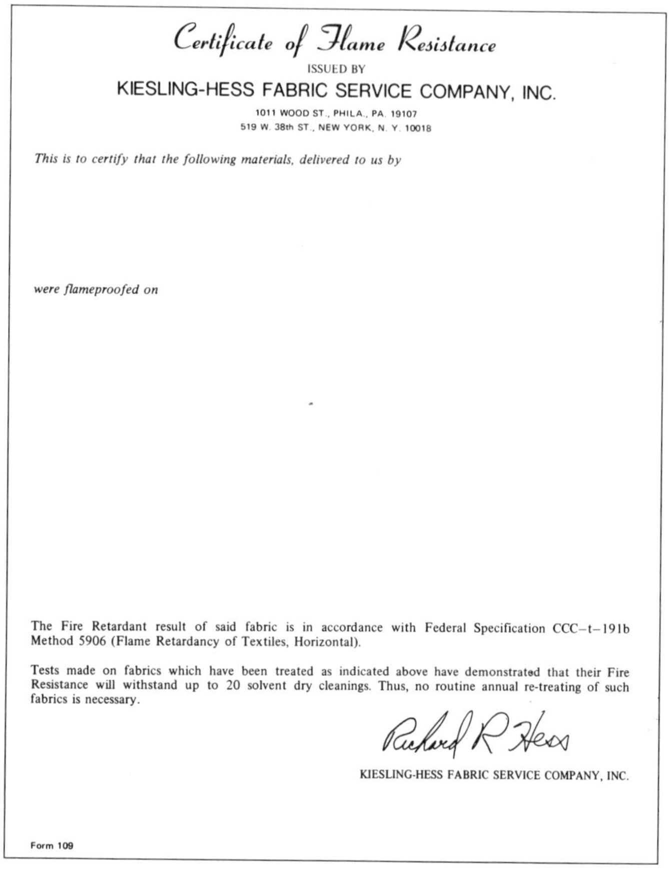

Certificate of Flame Resistance

ISSUED BY

KIESLING-HESS FABRIC SERVICE COMPANY, INC.

1011 WOOD ST., PHILA., PA. 19107
519 W. 38th ST., NEW YORK, N. Y. 10018

This is to certify that the following materials, delivered to us by

were flameproofed on

The Fire Retardant result of said fabric is in accordance with Federal Specification CCC–t–191b Method 5906 (Flame Retardancy of Textiles, Horizontal).

Tests made on fabrics which have been treated as indicated above have demonstrated that their Fire Resistance will withstand up to 20 solvent dry cleanings. Thus, no routine annual re-treating of such fabrics is necessary.

KIESLING-HESS FABRIC SERVICE COMPANY, INC.

Form 109

Figure 10.1 Certificate of flame resistance. Reproduced with permission of Kiesling-Hess Fabric Service Company, Inc.

Chapter 11 contains more detailed information on fabric flammability terminology and flame retardants. Fabrics that are considered inherently flame resistant, such as fiberglass, wools, and some modacrylics, do not require flame-retardant treatments. Some fabrics made for health care facilities contain a blend of saran, verel-modacrylic, and rayon, which is mildew-, rot-, and vermin-proof. This fabric blend will melt rather than support flame when a source of ignition is applied. Fiberglass responds to ignition in the same manner. Designers, however, should be aware that some dyes used on the surface of the fiberglass may burn and spread flame across the entire surface. Designers should require tests to ensure that the fire performance has not been impaired by methods of fabrication, weaving, or finishing.

Construction and Quality Control

Construction and quality control of interior window components is based on federal specifications that establish standards for a limited number of window coverings.

1. FS DDD-S251d *Shade, Roller, Window; Roller, Slat, Cord, and Accessories* describes performance requirements for one type of cloth window shade in stock widths up to 77 in. (195.6 cm) and lengths to 12 ft (3.6 m). Criteria are established for materials, such as cords, ring pull, rollers, roller diameter, slats, springs, brackets, and thread cotton. Dimensional criteria are established for length, hems, width, and roller coverage.

2. FS L-S-001787 (GSA-FSS) *Interim Federal Specification Shade, Window (Vinyl) with Roller, Slat, Ring Pull and Accessories and Vinyl Film (in Piece Goods)*, 1973, covers requirements for vinyl window shades and vinyl film in piece goods form. Criteria are established for tensile strength, elongation, tear strength, weight, volatility, specific gravity, color fastness, heat sealing, flame resistance, and resistance to cracking.

3. FS AA-V-00200B (GSA-FSS) *Interim Federal Specification Venetian Blinds*, 1973, covers two types of venetian blinds: type I, 2-in. (5.1-cm) slats, and type II, 1-in. (2.5-cm) slats. This specification establishes requirements for the slats, rails, head rails and braces, bottom rails and tape fittings, end caps, ladder tapes, breaking strength, color-fastness and dimensional stability, cords, operating hardware, tilting devices, installation hardware, and head rail intermediate supports.

Energy Conservation

Energy conservation can be substantially affected by the use and design of interior window coverings. Windows have six energy functions:

1. Provision of winter solar heat

2. Provision of year-round daylighting

3. Rejection of summer solar heat

4. Provision of air tightness during periods of heating and air conditioning

5. Provision of insulation

6. Provision of natural ventilation during temperate weather[1]

Specification of design components to save energy should be based on the importance of each window's function, the local climate, and the requirements imposed by the activities that will take place in the interior space. Evaluating the effectiveness of a particular installation must take the total window system into consideration:

1. *The site*, which includes shade trees, ground surfaces, orientation to the sun and wind.

2. *Exterior appendages*, such as sun screens, roll blinds, exterior shutters, awnings and architectural projections.

3. *The window framing components*, such as weather-stripping, type of operation, size, and window tilt.

4. *Window glazing methods*, which include applied films, mutiple glazing, reflecting glass, and glass block.

5. *Interior window components*, such as blinds, drapery, film shades, interior sun screens, opaque roll shades, and insulating shutters.

6. *The building interior components*, such as task lighting, colors and reflectance levels of interior surfaces, automatic switching, and fixture circulating (see Chapter 12 for more information on task lighting in relation to energy conservation).

Table 10.1 summarizes the advantages and disadvantages of various interior window components. The two most popular window treatments are blinds and drapery. Drapery is often favored because it adds textural contrast and is an excellent method for controlling noise in the interior environment.

Drapery Fenestration Data. An increasing number of contract fabric manufacturers are including fenestration data on fabrics designed for drapery. These data refer to the transmission of solar energy through glass to a building interior. The information provided by these data can be used to determine the heating and air conditioning needs of an interior. The selection of decorative fabrics to screen glass walls and wide glass areas requires a knowledge of how weaves, patterns, fabric weights, colors, and luster can influence the transmission of solar energy. When direct sunlight strikes a draped window, the fabric and glass act in combination to:

1. Transmit a portion of light and heat to the interior.

2. Reflect a part of the heat back to the outside atmosphere.

3. Absorb the remaining light as heat.

To minimize solar heat gain, the drapery exposed to sunlight should ideally have high reflectance and low transmittance.

Determining Fabric Fenestration Values. Consideration of visible and solar optical properties, shading coefficient, U-value, and air tightness should be included in a determination of fabric fenestration values.

1. Visible properties. Those functions of fabric construction—color and luster—which control the effect of glare and opacity on vision.
   a. Openness factor refers to the percentage of light transmitted through the interstices of the fabric. This factor correlates closely with the reduction of noise from interior sources.
   b. Visible transmittance refers to a numerical value useful in comparing different fabric qualities for glare and opacity.

2. Solar optical properties. Those functions of fabric construction—color and luster—which control the amount of heat energy passed through light.
   a. Solar transmittance refers to the amount of sunlight which passes through the fabric or penetrates through the yarns.
   b. Solar reflection refers to the amount of sunlight that is reflected from the fabric.
   c. Solar absorption refers to the amount of light neither transmitted nor reflected by a fabric, but absorbed as heat.

3. Shading Coefficient. A value derived from the three solar optical properties of a fabric; i.e., the total amount of heat transmitted by a window configuration divided by the total amount of heat transmitted by a single pane of double-strength glass. The *lower* the shading coefficient the greater the efficiency of the window system. The more efficient systems range from .40 to .60 in shading coefficient, the most effective have shading coefficients below .40. Table 10.2 illustrates a typical fenestration data listing for a particular fabric. The shading coefficient is listed for regular plate glass and heat-absorbing glass. In comparing the visible and solar optical properties, designers will notice that the fabric color has a definite affect on these properties.

TABLE 10.1 ADVANTAGES AND DISADVANTAGES OF INTERIOR WINDOW COMPONENTS

Component	Advantages	Disadvantages
Venetian blinds	1. Minimal space used to store blinds when open. Stack with minimal obstruction of window area. 2. Can be selectively tilted to direct sunlight to the ceiling or directly on the work surface. 3. Can be partially lowered to eliminate sunlight from only a portion of the room.	1. Difficult to clean. 2. Continued maintenance required to raise and lower, tilt and lift. 3. Maintenance required to replace lifting and tilting hardware, cord replacement. 4. Decreased effectiveness in reducing winter heat loss compared with shades or tight fitting drapery due to the cracks between each slat.
Film shades	1. Reduced summer solar heat gain and winter night losses with a reflective or selective film. 2. Reduced winter heat loss with shade configurations which provide insulating, trapped air spaces. 3. Reduced infiltration provided by obstructing flow of incoming air with a film shade sealed at edges. 4. Increased comfort near windows due to less body heat radiating to the inside film shade than to a cold window. 5. Elimination of ultraviolet radiation, thus less fading of carpets and furniture fabrics. 6. Reduced sky glare. 7. Daytime privacy and night visibility into public buildings for security surveillance.	1. Required management of shades by building occupants. 2. Difficult to install on other-than-right-angle window areas. 3. Lack of glare control from direct sunlight. 4. Lack of privacy at night. 5. Reduced winter solar heat gain through low emissivity film shades installed to reduce heat losses.
Opaque roll shades	1. Reduced solar heat gain in summer. 2. Privacy. 3. Glare control. 4. Self-storing. 5. Inexpensive.	1. Maintenance of spring mechanism. Springs jam with time and need replacement. 2. View out and shading at the same time is impossible. 3. Impeded ventilation from the top opening of double-hung windows when the shade is lowered.
Drapery	1. Improved comfort near windows is possible when the drapery is closed. 2. Glare control. 3. Privacy. 4. Decreased winter heat loss and summer heat gain. 5. Noise absorption. Noise within the room is absorbed by drapery rather than reflected from uncovered glass. Outside noise transmitted through glass is partially absorbed. The denser the weave and heavier the fabric, the more effective it is in reducing noise.	1. Periodic cleaning required. 2. Obstruction of view when closed. 3. Desire for airy, open drapery (casement) conflicts with thermal effectiveness of draperies in both summer and winter. 4. Possible breakage of glass when used in conjunction with heat-absorbing glass. The glass and the way it is set should be designed to withstand the additional heat buildup from sunlight being reflected back at the glass from closed drapery.

TABLE 10.2 FENESTRATION DATA FOR DRAPERY

Pattern		Fenestration Data			
Width:	48″				
Color:	Flax	Visual properties		Shading coefficients	
Contents:	63% Verel modacrylic, 17% rayon, 10% flax, 10% saran monofilament	Transmittance	.38	¼″ Regular plate glass	.50
		Openness factor	.28	¼″ Heat-absorbing glass	.46
		Solar optical properties			
Inherently fire safe		Transmittance	.32		
		Reflectance	.56		
		Absorption	.12		
Color:	White	Visual properties		Shading coefficients	
Contents:	63% Verel modacrylic, 27% rayon, 10% saran monofilament	Transmittance	.46	¼″ Regular plate glass	.49
		Openness factor	.32	¼″ Heat-absorbing glass	.46
		Solar optical properties			
Inherently fire safe		Transmittance	.36		
		Reflectance	.60		
		Absorption	.04		
Color:	Bronze	Visual properties		Shading coefficients	
Contents:	63% Verel modacrylic, 27% rayon, 10% saran monofilament	Transmittance	.30	¼″ Regular plate glass	.54
		Openness factor	.24	¼″ Heat-absorbing glass	.48
		Solar optical properties			
Inherently fire safe		Transmittance	.32		
		Reflectance	.48		
		Absorption	.20		

Source: Lazarus Fabrics.

Designers will occasionally see charts on which drapery material is characterized by a "fabric designator," consisting of a roman numeral with a capital letter subscript. The roman numeral refers to the weave and the subscript refers to fabric color or value:

a. I: Open weave
b. II: Semiopen weave
c. III: Closed weave

d. D: Dark
e. M: Medium
f. L: Light

These charts may also contain shading coefficient information in terms of a letter index. These letters range from A to J, with the shading coefficient decreasing from A to J (see Table 10.3).

Using this information, the window heat gain can be calculated by adding the solar heat gain and the conducted heat gain. The solar heat gain equals the amount of solar energy transmitted plus the amount of solar energy absorbed by the window system and dissipated into the building interior. The conducted heat gain equals the U-value multiplied by the inside/outside temperature difference.

4. U-value. The amount of heat conducted from the inside air (or heat conducted from the outside air) through the window configuration. A U-value of 0.65 means 0.65 Btus pass through each square foot of window configuration for every hour and for each Fahrenheit degree difference that exists between the inside and outside temperature. The *lower* the U-value, the greater the efficiency of the window system. For example, if two layers of drapery are used which are separated by an air space, the thermal per-

formance of the window would be improved. A U-value of 0.65 is possible for single glazed windows, assuming the same degree of air tightness for both layers of trapped air. In the event that the two layers of drapery would provide a higher degree of air tightness between the drapery and the window, a much lower U-value of 0.57 could be obtained.[2] If double draperies are used with insulating glass, a U-value of approximately 0.37 is possible.

5. Air tightness. The volume of air passing through an opening. This is measured by the cubic feet of air for a given time period, divided by the crack length. If drapery is installed against the wall or window frame at the sides and allowed to make contact with the floor or window sill, it serves to better insulate the window in the winter and provide shade in the summer. Though drapery can be fairly tight fitting on the sides, it is difficult to obtain an air-tight fit at the bottom and still allow for opening and closing the drapery. The manner in which the top is fabricated can aid in energy conservation by preventing conditioned air from circulating between the drapery and the glass. When room air comes in contact with cold glass and cascades back into the room through the bottom of the drapery, the efficiency is greatly impaired.

Additional Guidelines for Window Energy Conservation. Six more points must be considered for window energy conservation:

1. During the daylight hours in winter, draperies should be kept open for windows that receive direct sunlight, i.e., south-facing windows, east-facing windows in the morning, and west-facing windows in the afternoon. This allows sunlight to penetrate the interior and warm more

TABLE 10.3 FENESTRATION DATA AND FABRIC DESIGNATOR

COLOR	Openness Factor	Visual Transmittance	Solar Transmittance	Solar Reflectance	Solar Absorptance	Shading Coefficient 0°	Shading Coefficient 45°	Yarn Reflectance	Fabric Designator	Shading Coefficient Index Letter
WHITE	0.241	0.583	0.469	0.340	0.191	0.598	0.568	0.448	II$_M$	E
WHITE	0.141	0.566	0.418	0.392	0.190	0.548	0.521	0.456	II$_M$	D
WHITE	0.242	0.649	0.504	0.328	0.168	0.621	0.590	0.433	II$_M$	E
WHITE	0.0646	0.461	0.304	0.458	0.238	0.459	0.436	0.490	III$_M$	B
FLAX	0.131	0.479	0.335	0.422	0.243	0.492	0.468	0.486	II$_M$	C
FLAX	0.0628	0.376	0.277	0.424	0.299	0.463	0.440	0.452	III$_M$	B
WHITE	0.0744	0.411	0.289	0.434	0.277	0.464	0.440	0.469	II$_M$	B
FLAX	0.0529	0.365	0.270	0.402	0.328	0.470	0.447	0.424	III$_M$	C
FLAX	0.0136	0.408	0.289	0.425	0.286	0.468	0.445	0.431	III$_M$	B
FLAX	0.227	0.581	0.445	0.321	0.234	0.595	0.566	0.415	II$_M$	E
FLAX	0.0707	0.377	0.285	0.398	0.317	0.479	0.455	0.428	II$_M$	C
FLAX	0.169	0.582	0.430	0.315	0.255	0.591	0.561	0.379	II$_M$	E
WHITE	0.0563	0.376	0.278	0.475	0.247	0.438	0.416	0.503	III$_L$	B
FLAX	0.115	0.472	0.352	0.387	0.261	0.518	0.492	0.437	II$_M$	C
FLAX	0.122	0.492	0.373	0.355	0.272	0.544	0.517	0.404	II$_M$	D
WHITE	0.131	0.554	0.414	0.380	0.206	0.552	0.524	0.437	II$_M$	D
WHITE	0.140	0.528	0.411	0.341	0.248	0.569	0.541	0.397	II$_M$	D
FLAX	0.00889	0.322	0.255	0.406	0.339	0.461	0.438	0.410	III$_M$	B
WHITE	0.0185	0.473	0.355	0.418	0.227	0.504	0.479	0.426	III$_M$	C
FLAX	0.0106	0.380	0.271	0.464	0.265	0.440	0.418	0.469	III$_M$	B
FLAX	0.0119	0.312	0.263	0.445	0.292	0.445	0.423	0.450	III$_M$	B
WHITE	0.00908	0.365	0.292	0.475	0.233	0.445	0.423	0.479	III$_M$	B
WHITE	0.184	0.620	0.510	0.326	0.164	0.625	0.594	0.400	II$_M$	E
FLAX	0.181	0.591	0.516	0.318	0.166	0.632	0.600	0.388	II$_M$	E
WHITE	0.0204	0.478	0.364	0.430	0.206	0.503	0.478	0.439	III$_M$	C
FLAX	0.00802	0.415	0.319	0.441	0.240	0.475	0.451	0.445	III$_M$	C
FLAX	0.0138	0.253	0.205	0.465	0.330	0.407	0.386	0.472	III$_M$	A
WHITE)										
FLAX)										
WHITE)										
FLAX)										
WHITE)	AVAILABLE UPON REQUEST									
FLAX)										

massive materials and remote surfaces. This heat will then radiate to other interior surfaces rather than back to the glass.

2. In areas with little or no direct sunlight in winter, i.e., north-facing windows, east-facing windows in the afternoon, and west-facing windows in the morning, draperies should be drawn because they will be much closer to room temperature than the glass. During winter nights draperies on all windows should be drawn to reduce heat loss to the exterior. Also, draperies should remain closed as much as possible during summer days to reduce solar heat gains.

3. Drapery should be installed to allow the opened drapery to stack clear of the glass area so that more sunlight can enter the window.

4. Draperies should be designed to prevent conditioned air from blowing between the fabric and the glass. If an air register is directly above or below the window, deflectors may be necessary to direct the air into the room and not between the drapery and the glass.

5. Drapery heading may be designed to fit into a cove or recessed area to prevent air leakage above the drapery top.

6. Thermal liners may be used to promote better heat reflectance, but designers should be cautious about heat buildup which could damage the glass.

DETERMINING WINDOW MEASUREMENT AND HARDWARE INSTALLATION

Accurate measurements must be supplied to the fabricators of the window components for successful installations.

Shades

Shades are usually installed within the window jambs. Figure 10.2 illustrates the critical areas to be measured for the installation of spring roller shades. The following measurements must be noted:

Jamb: the width of the window opening into which the shade will be mounted. List this figure as the inside measurement.

Tip to tip: the width from the metal ratchet on the left to the tip of the pin on the right side of the shade roller [1/8 in. (3.2 mm) less than the jamb measurement to allow room for brackets].

Barrel width: the measurement of an existing roller, not including the tips.

Cloth: the measurement of the actual shade surface. The shade length is usually not specified unless the window is exceedingly long.[2]

Blinds

Blinds may be mounted within or beyond the window jambs. Since many blinds are custom fitted to the window, it is difficult to alter them if a mistake is made in the measurements. Designers should measure accurately to within 1/8 in. (3.2 mm), using a metal or wooden rule. The surface within the casing area (for inside installation) or outside the casing area should be examined for the best location of the bracket supports. Most brackets require a 1-in. (2.5-cm) width. If the installation is to be outside the jamb area, sufficient overlap of the blinds must be provided at the sides and bottom of the window opening. After the bracket position has been determined, the following measurements should be provided to the fabricator:

Inside Installation

1. *Width:* the length from jamb to jamb (C in Figure 10.3).

2. *Length:* the exact distance from the inside top of the window to the bottom ledge (A in Figure 10.3). If the blind is not to touch the bottom ledge, subtract 1/2 in. (12.7 mm) from the length measurement. If the blind is to extend to the floor, provide the measurement shown for length B in Figure 10.3. On any length, the measurement should include the distance from the floor to the top of the sill. This will allow the fabricator to estimate the required length of the operating controls.

Outside Installation

1. *Width:* the length between the points where the brackets will be located [for privacy, brackets should be located at least 3 in. (7.6 cm) beyond the edge of the window jamb].

2. *Length:* the distance from the top of the bracket location to the point where the blind is to reach. Most fabricators make blinds with a tolerance up to 1 in. (2.5 cm) longer than the given measurement.[3]

Drapery

Drapery hardware may be installed inside the window jambs and ceiling- or wall-mounted (see Figure 10.4). Specification of drapery hardware systems is based on the following criteria:

1. System type

2. Operational direction

3. Available lengths (or widths)

4. Drapery headings accommodated

5. Application

6. Bracket supports

7. Maximum fabric weight accommodated

Table 10.4 provides a survey of the characteristics found in typical drapery hardware systems designed for commercial use. Designers should be aware that these systems are made from heavy gauge steel and are engineered to withstand greater drapery weights than those designed for residential use. Calculating the finished weight of drapery is based on the weight per linear yard of the particular fabric. Table 10.5 shows various fabric weights and drapery sizes that could be used to arrive at a total of 32 lb (15.5 kg).[4] Hand-drawn hardware systems are usually installed in shorter widths and therefore accommodate less fabric weight. Some drapery construction makes use of a tape snapping system, which may also limit the weight allowed per drapery unit. Designers should verify weight limitations prior to finalizing fabric selection.

Critical measurement dimensions for drapery hardware involve: (1) the bracket placement and (2) method of installation. Bracket placement determines the length and width of the drapery, as well as the amount of glass surface that will be exposed when the drapery is fully opened. Figure 10.3 illustrates the dimensions that must be recorded for the installation contractor. Dimension line C is shown 4 in. (10.2 cm) above the glass area to indicate placement of standard pinched pleated drapery. This placement prevents exposing to view the fabrica-

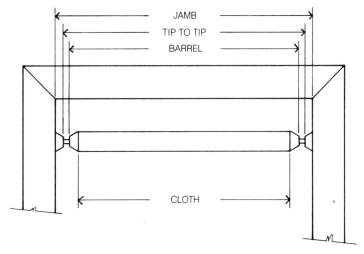

Figure 10.2 Measurement for spring roller shades.

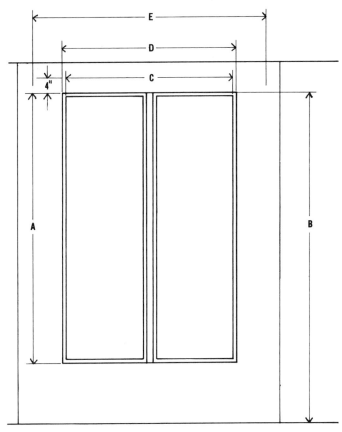

WINDOW MEASUREMENT

A OUTSIDE LENGTH	D CASING MOUNTING
B FLOOR LENGTH	E WALL MOUNTING
C INSIDE CASING MOUNTING	

Figure 10.3 Critical window dimensions.

TABLE 10.4 COMMERCIAL DRAPERY HARDWARE SYSTEMS

System	Operation	Lengths	Headings	Application	Support Brackets	Maximum Fabric Weights
Draw Cord System: Track is opened and closed by loop cord and tension pulleys	One-way draw Two-way draw Multiple draw	16 to 50' 24 to 60' 32 to 110'	Conventional pleated or snapped tape method	Recessed in coves or acoustic tiles. Ceiling mounted or wall mounted	Only required on wall-mounted hard-ware systems. Usually placed 48" apart along track	Ranges from 50 to 220 lb
Hand-Drawn System: Track is opened and closed with hand batons which are attached to lead carrier. No pull cords used	One-way draw Two-way draw	20 to 24' Up to 48'	Conventional pleated or snapped tape method	Recessed, ceiling or wall installation	Required on wall-mounted systems	Ranges from 48 to 96 lb

TABLE 10.5 VARIATIONS IN FABRIC WEIGHTS AND DRAPERY SIZES WHICH EQUAL A TOTAL WEIGHT OF 32 LB

Fabric Type	Weight per Linear Yd	Drapery Size 100% Fullness
Sheer or light-weight casement	5 oz	16' wide × 32' long 32' wide × 16' long
Lined sheers or medium-weight fabrics	10 oz	16' wide × 16' long 32' wide × 8' long
Lined medium-weight fabrics or heavy cotton velours and linens	20 oz	16' wide × 8' long

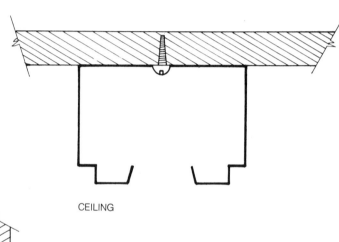

CEILING

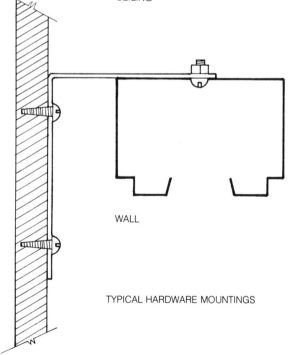

WALL

TYPICAL HARDWARE MOUNTINGS

Figure 10.4 Hardware installation.

tion components (pins and tape). The following formula may be used to calculate bracket placement in order to clear the glass area:

1. Add 12 in. to the total width of the window:

   $100'' + 12'' = 112''$

2. Divide this total by 6:

   $112'' \div 6 = 18\ 2/3''$

   (round out to next number, or 19'')

3. Extend bracket placement 19 in. on each side of the window, and the fully opened drapery will clear the entire window.

Dimensions that must be recorded on irregularly shaped windows are shown in Figure 10.5. Multiple drapery rods may be used in these installations, or hardware may be custom made or bent to fit the required dimensions.

Drapery hardware designed for ceiling or recessed installation does not require additional support brackets because the rod is usually attached at intervals along the entire length.

DRAPERY ESTIMATION

After the placement of the hardware has been determined, the designer may proceed to measure for the amount of drapery fabric required and specify the method of fabrication. Standard traverse drapery yardage (without pattern repeat) is calculated in the following manner:

1. *Finished length:* the distance from the top of the rod to the desired bottom of the drapery [allow 1-in. (2.5-cm) clearance at the floor].

2. *Cut length:* the distance from the top of the rod to the desired bottom of the drapery *plus hems and top headings.* These measurements may vary depending on the type of fabric and fabrication. Many designers add 18 in. (45.7 cm) for sheer drapery; 17 in. (43.2 cm) for unlined drapery; 13 in. (33 cm) for lined drapery. Example:

   Finished length = $84'' + 17'' = 101''$ cut length

3. *Finished width:* the distance of the rod from bracket to bracket *plus* the number of inches the brackets extend from the wall. This distance is known as the "return." To this measurement add another 6 in. (15.2 cm) for the center overlap (see Figure 10.6). Example: If the rod is 120 in. wide and the brackets extend 3 in. from the wall, the total finished width would be 132 inches:

   $120'' + 3'' + 3'' + 6'' = 132''$

4. *Number of widths required:* the number of fabric panels needed to span this distance is dependent on the desired fullness. One hundred percent fullness is 2 times the width; 150 percent fullness is 2.5 times the width. Some sheers may require 200 percent fullness, or 3 times the width.

   Finished width × 2.5 fullness ÷ width of fabric = number of widths

   Example:

   Finished width $132'' \times 2.5 = 330'' \div 48''$ fabric = 6.87, or 7 panels

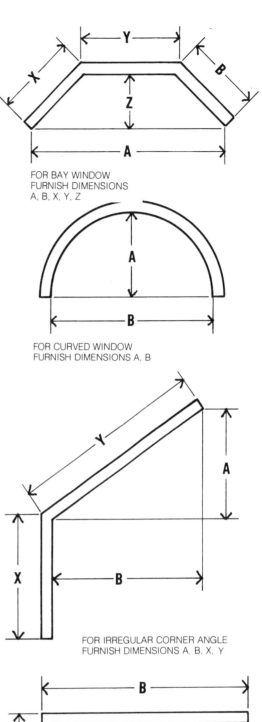

FOR BAY WINDOW
FURNISH DIMENSIONS
A, B, X, Y, Z

FOR CURVED WINDOW
FURNISH DIMENSIONS A, B

FOR IRREGULAR CORNER ANGLE
FURNISH DIMENSIONS A, B, X, Y

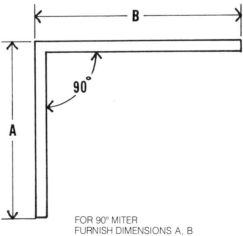

FOR 90° MITER
FURNISH DIMENSIONS A, B

Figure 10.5 Irregular window shapes. Source: Slim-Line Drapery Systems, Graber Company.

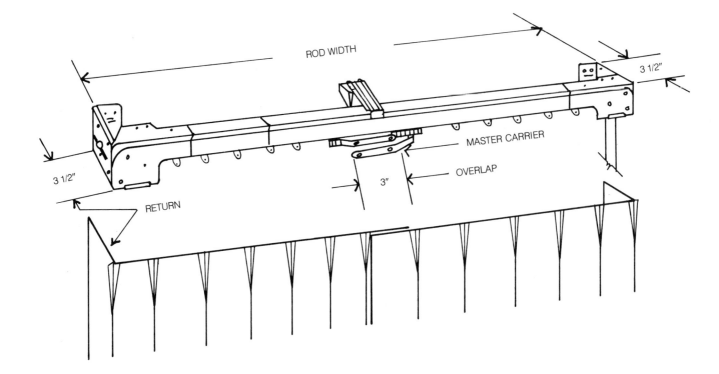

Figure 10.6 Center draw single traverse rod.

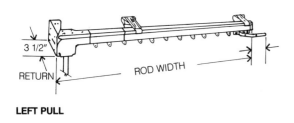

LEFT PULL

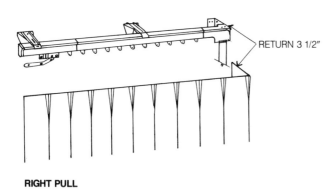

RIGHT PULL

Figure 10.7 Single one-way draw traverse rod.

The 7 panels would be equally divided into 3 1/2 panels placed on each side of the center draw.

5. *Number of yards required:* the number of panels is multiplied by the cut length to determine the total inches needed. This answer is then transposed into yards (divided by 36 in.). Example:

7 panels × 101″ = 707″

707″ ÷ 36″ = 19.63″, or 20 yd

If estimating for a one-way draw wall installation, proceed as follows:
a. Measure the length as in the above example.
b. Measure the width from the bracket to the end of the rod.
c. Add the required inches for bracket projections.
d. Add 3 1/2 in. (8.9 cm) for the return (see Figure 10.7).
e. Proceed as explained above.

Pattern Repeats

When the specified fabric has a pattern repeat, the required panel cut lengths and the total yardage will be increased. For example, in step 1 of the estimating procedure for a center draw drapery, the cutting length was calculated to be 101 in. (256.5 cm). If the fabric has a 24-in. (61-cm) repeat, the required cut length would be increased to accommodate matching the 24-in. repeats; i.e., four 24-in. repeats would only total 96 in. (243.8 cm); therefore five 24-in. repeats will be needed per panel [120″ in. (304.8 cm)]. The revised panel cutting length would now be 120 in.; therefore

120″ × 7 panels = 840″

It is suggested that one additional repeat length be added to this total to allow for matching the first panel cut; therefore the total yardage would be determined in this manner:

$$840'' + 24'' = 864'' \div 36'' = 24 \text{ yd}$$

Designers should measure the repeat to verify that the repeat size listed on the sample is accurate.

Institutional Cubicle Curtains

Most institutional cubicle curtains are fabricated to hang 14 to 16 in. (35.6 to 40.6 cm) above the floor. The tracks are either mounted on or suspended from the ceiling. To determine the height of the curtain, designers should measure from the track to the floor and deduct 14 to 16 in. Example:

109″	= distance from track to floor
− 16″	= clearance from the bottom of the curtain to the floor
93″	= finished length

The width is determined by measuring the track from left to right and adding 10 percent for fullness. Example:

148″	= actual track measurement
+ 14″	= percentage fullness
162″	= width

If the top of the curtains is to be fabricated with a mesh for ceiling ventilation, the specification should state that this is included in the finished length.

DRAPERY FABRICATION

There are four major types of drapery construction used in commercial installations. Figure 10.8 illustrates the style of headings employed by these four methods.

Pinch Pleat Systems

Pinch pleat systems are constructed with pleater tape and are attached to slide carriers with slip-on or pin-on hooks. This method requires more stacking space than other methods, and the hooks must be removed prior to cleaning. A standard traverse rod is used for installation.

Stack Pleat Systems

Stack pleat systems require one-half the stacking space needed for pinched pleats. Because this system employs a snap-tape fabrication method, the stack back widths and depths can be varied according to the snap spacings. Tape spacings are available in 7 1/2, 8 1/2, and 10 in. (19.1, 21.6, and 25.4 cm). (See Figure 10.9.)

1. 7 1/2-in. spacings produce a 14-in. (35.6-cm) stacking which is 3 3/4 in. (9.5 cm) deep. This tape spacing is recommended for draperies 54 in. (37.2 cm) in length.

2. 8 1/2-in. spacings produce a 12-in. (30.5-cm) stacking which is 4 1/2 in. (11.5 cm) deep. This spacing is recommended for draperies up to 108 in. (274.3 cm) in length.

3. 10-in. spacings produce an 11-in. (27.9 cm) stacking which is 5 in. (12.7 cm) deep. This is recommended for drapery over 108 in. in length or very heavy, bulky fabrics.

This fabrication method requires a special drapery rod which accommodates snap carriers. This and other snap-tape systems reduce installation time, and the tape need not be removed during cleaning.

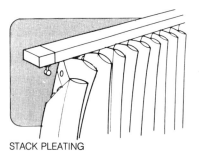
STACK PLEATING

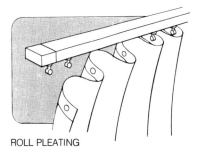
ROLL PLEATING

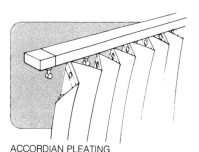
ACCORDIAN PLEATING

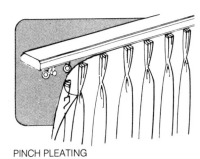
PINCH PLEATING

Figure 10.8 Drapery headings. Source: Slim-Line Drapery Systems, Graber Company.

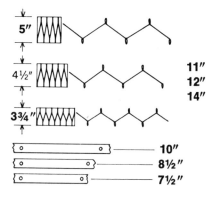

Figure 10.9 Stack pleating tape spacing. Reproduced with permission of Slim-Line Drapery Systems, Graber Company.

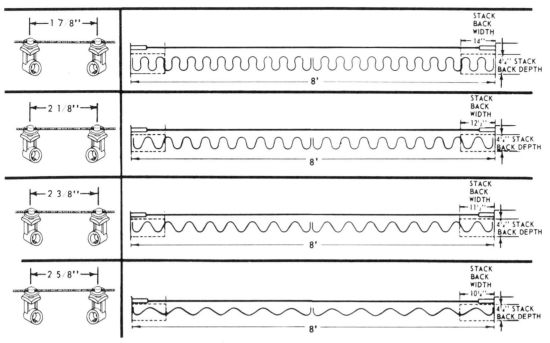

Figure 10.10 Roll pleat snap carrier placement. Reproduced with permission of The Kirsch Company.

Roll Pleat Systems[5]

Roll pleat systems provide a pleasing appearance from both the interior and exterior. Headings are fabricated with snap tape and are suspended under the track to prevent sagging. They require little stack space, and the use of a "butt"-type master carrier (instead of a center overlap carrier) eliminates a flat space in the drapery center. Figure 10.10 illustrates the butt-type installation and shows how the snap carriers can be spaced to vary the fullness and stack-back widths. When using 4 1/4-in. (16.6-cm) snap tape, varied carrier spacing produces the following drapery fullness:

Carrier Spacing	Percentage of Fullness
1 7/8 in. (4.7 cm)	120
2 1/8 in. (5.4 cm)	100
2 3/8 in. (6 cm)	80
2 5/8 in. (6.7 cm)	60

Accordion-Type Pleating Systems[6]

Accordion-type pleating systems provide a sharply tailored affect with a uniform exterior and interior appearance. This system is also fabricated with the snap-tape method and requires a rod system that employs the snap carriers. Figure 10.11 illustrates a butt-type center fabrication and shows the stacking width for center draw 88-in. (223.5 cm) wide drapery.

FABRICATION SPECIFICATION

Designers should provide the following information to drapery fabricators:

1. Specified fabric
   Name
   Number (mill number and purchase order number)
   Color
   Width
   Pattern repeat size
   Sample piece to verify correct shipment
   Total yardage required

2. Drapery measurement
   Width
   Stacking width
   Finished width
   Number of fabric widths
   Percentage of fullness
   Finished length
   Hems and headings
   Cutting length

3. Hardware
   Type
   Length of track
   Operational method
       One way
       Two way
       Multiple
       Cord operated
       Hand operated
       Motorized

4. Hardware installation
   Ceiling
   Wall
   Distance above casing
   Within casing
   Extension beyond window (inches on each side)

Hardware installation instructions should include a drawing of the window and wall with specific bracket locations clearly marked. Separate drawings should be made for each window and room (see Figure 10.12).

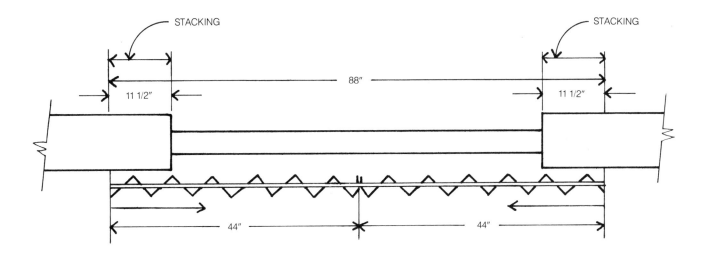

STACKING   STACKING

88"

11 1/2"   11 1/2"

44"   44"

Figure 10.11 Accordian pleating systems: drapery stacking.
Source: The Kirsch Company.

Drapery workrooms advise that designers make their fabric purchase orders as specific as possible, and a sample of the specified fabric should always be attached (see Figure 10.13). Workrooms are advised to inspect the fabric for defects before cutting because many fabrics may have flaws that will require reordering. To avoid costly delays, some designers specify additional yardage.

LIFE CYCLE COSTING OF WINDOW SYSTEMS

The initial cost factors plus energy conservation and the expected service life and maintenance are the major elements to consider in cost effectiveness of window systems.

1. Initial costs vary with the specific systems; e.g., material, installation hardware, and labor costs for drapery would be considerably higher than the initial cost of a roller shade installation.
    a. Materials
        (1) Blinds (vertical and horizontal) are priced by the linear and square foot.
        (2) Drapery fabric is sold by the linear yard.
        (3) Drapery hardware costs are based on the type and length of the system.
    b. Fabrication costs. Drapery workrooms normally base labor charges on the following:
        (1) The number of panels (widths)
        (2) Length of panel [if between 100 and 200 in. (254 and 508 cm) long]
        (3) Amount of handwork involved
        (4) Type of heading
        (5) Hook or pin application, pressing, and folding
        (6) Special fabrications, such as cornices, Austrian shades, or other special treatments
    c. Installation costs. Drapery fabricators will deliver and install completed drapery based on a labor fee per linear foot. Costs for installation of drapery hardware are based on the size and length of the system. Costs range from $3 to $8 per linear foot.

2. Expected service life. These estimates are based on normal usage and adequate maintenance:

Component	Service Life
Blinds	10 years
Shades	3 to 5 years
Drapery	5 years

3. Maintenance costs. These costs should include regular maintenance, such as vacuuming and periodic professional cleaning. Blinds and shades may also require parts replacement (springs, tapes, and pull cords).

4. Energy conservation. Computing energy savings includes consideration of the following:
    a. Initial cost of window system
    b. Expected service life
    c. Maintenance costs
    d. Initial fuel costs savings/unit area. A shading coefficient of .25 for a draped window could, for example, indicate a 75 percent reduction in the solar heat gained through an undraped configuration. Depending on the geographic location and window orientation, this could mean a sizable reduction in the capacity requirement of the heating or air conditioning equipment. The kilowatt hours used per day would be greatly reduced.
    e. Expected fuel savings/unit area (including fuel inflation rate) during the expected service life of the window system.

Figure 10.12 Drapery measurement sheet.

MEASURE SHEET

Name_____ Phone_____ Store_____

Address_____ Salesman_____

ROOM: FABRIC: LINING:

FABRIC	_____X_____	_____
LINING	_____X_____	_____
RODS	_____X_____	_____
LABOR	_____X_____	_____
INSTALL	_____X_____	_____
TRIM	_____X_____	_____
TRIM LAB.	_____X_____	_____
Total	_____	

LEFT   RIGHT

+ R & O   + R & O

FINISHED LENGTH

BELOW _____

PIN SETTING:
FINISH WIDTH: FINISH LENGTH: PAIR
                                              PANEL: CUTS: RETURNS:

ROOM: FABRIC: LINING:

FABRIC	_____X_____	_____
LINING	_____X_____	_____
RODS	_____X_____	_____
LABOR	_____X_____	_____
INSTALL	_____X_____	_____
TRIM	_____X_____	_____
TRIM LAB.	_____X_____	_____
Total	_____	

LEFT   RIGHT

+ R & O   + R & O

FINISHED LENGTH

BELOW _____

PIN SETTING:
FINISH WIDTH: FINISH LENGTH: PAIR
                                              PANEL: CUTS: RETURNS:

ROOM: FABRIC: LINING:

FABRIC	_____X_____	_____
LINING	_____X_____	_____
RODS	_____X_____	_____
LABOR	_____X_____	_____
INSTALL	_____X_____	_____
TRIM	_____X_____	_____
TRIM LAB.	_____X_____	_____
Total	_____	

LEFT   RIGHT

+ R & O   + R & O

FINISHED LENGTH

BELOW _____

PIN SETTING:
FINISH WIDTH: FINISH LENGTH: PAIR
                                              PANEL: CUTS: RETURNS:

Figure 10.13 Drapery work order form. Reproduced with permission of Booth's Drapery Service.

DRAPERY WORK ORDER

BOOTH'S DRAPERY SERVICE
223 E. INDIAN SCHOOL RD.
PHOENIX, ARIZONA 85012
(602) 277-4889

NAME		STORE		
ADDRESS		SALESMAN	DATE	CUSTOMER'S PHONE
ROOM		**NO MEASUREMENTS TAKEN UNTIL YOU HAVE COMPLETED THESE INSTRUCTIONS.**		

INSTRUCTIONS — DESCRIBE TREATMENT TO BE USED

LINED ☐ INTERLINED ☐ UNLINED ☐ FLOOR TO BE CARPETED Yes ☐ No ☐

SERVICE CHARGES	
LABOR	
HARDWARE	
INSTALLATION	

FABRIC

QUAN.	STOCK NO.	ITEM	COLOR	WIDTH	REPEAT	SOURCE	CODE	UNIT PRICE	
							TOTAL		
							TAX		

CORNICE OR VALANCE PATTERN PLEASE SKETCH

FABRIC SAMPLE

TOTAL (TAX INC.)

CUSTOMER'S SIGNATURE

APPROVED & ACCEPTED

FORM 103

DESIGNER'S CHECKLIST FOR DEFECTS IN BLINDS AND SHADES

The following checklists for defects in blinds and shades are suggested in federal specifications L-S-001787 (GSA-FSS) and AA-V-00200B (GSA-FSS).

Blinds: Classification of Defects

Examine	Defect
Finish (general)	Not color specified. Runs, wrinkles, grit, areas of no film, separation of color, or finish not smooth.
Construction and workmanship	Hardware components not deburred.
Slats	Not shaped as specified. Not flexible. Corners not rounded.
Rails or channel head	Does not conceal operating mechanism. Locking covers not furnished. Not U-shaped and size specified.
Bottom	Holddown brackets not furnished when specified. Not equipped with end caps.
Ladder tape (Type I)	Spacing of ladders not uniform.
Cords	Too short. Equalizer on pull cord not furnished or does not hold cord together. Exposed ends of cords not furnished with knots or tassels.
Tilting device	Not attached to left side of head rail (if applicable).
Tilting rod and support	Not secure to other components. Does not carry the weight of the blind. Does not hold the tape in alignment.
Lifting cord lock	Not furnished. Does not hold cord securely at any height.
Installation hardware	Not furnished.
Marking	Omitted, wrong location, incorrect, incomplete, or illegible.

Shades: Classification of Defects

Examine	Defect
Shade cloth	Pinhole (any). Cut, hole, or tear. Crease or wrinkle (when resulting in doubling or adhesion of surfaces). Wavy, rolled, or folded edges. Spot, stain, or streak. Objectionable odor. Color not as specified. Color nonuniform, shaded, spotted, or mottled. Any tacky areas.
Other material construction and workmanship	Pull with attached eyelet missing (when applicable). Pull not a matching color. Wood of roller not species required. Knot in roller over 1/4 in. (6.4 mm) in diameter or clustered knots. Hem not as specified. Plastic pull (when applicable) poorly constructed and not free of sharp or rough areas. Slope of grain in wood or roller exceeds 1 in. (2.5 cm) in 10 in. (25.4 cm). Roller not smooth and splinter-free. Brackets and screws missing (when specified). Metal or combination wood and metal rollers not used on shades over 72 in. (182.9 cm) wide. Material and coating of brackets, metal rollers, and ferrules and ends not as required. Metal components not free from burrs or rough edges. Any evidence of flimsiness (not firm) due to improper roller diameter used. Roller barrel extends more than 1/2 in. (12.7 mm) beyond end of shade cloth when shades are for use between jambs (i.e., inside mounting). Roller barrel extends more than 3/4 in. (19.1 mm) beyond end of shade cloth when shades are for use on face of window casing. Vinyl material not securely fastened to rollers.

DESIGNER'S CHECKLIST FOR DRAPERY

Designers should refer to the guide specification for drapery and drapery hardware in Figure 10.14 for suggested installation and postinstallation inspection criteria.

Figure 10.14 Guide specification for drapery and drapery hardware.

PART 1. GENERAL

1.01 Related Work Specified Elsewhere: _____

1.02 Quality Assurance:

    A. Acceptable Fabricators and Manufacturers

        1. Minimum of five years experience in drapery fabrication

        2. Manufacturer to be single source of hardware units including accessories, mounting brackets and fastenings.

    B. Requirements of Regulatory Agencies: Install drapery which meets flammability requirements of

    _____

    C. Fabric Shall be Tested to Provide:

        1. Fenestration data

    D. Fabric Shall be Inspected for Flaws Prior to Fabrication

        1. Color match to submitted samples

        2. Pattern alignment

1.03 Submittals:

    A. Samples: Two 12" x 12" fabric samples

    B. Shop Drawings:

        1. Drapery contractor shall take field measurements to verify openings scheduled to receive drapery.

        2. Where structural form requires cutouts, Contractor is responsible for developing detailed drawings showing special work.

        3. Details of abutments at corners and ceilings.

    C. Manufacturer's Specifications and Installation Instructions for Drapery Hardware.

    D. Maintenance Material:

        1. Operation and maintenance of drapery hardware

        2. Cleaning instructions from fabric mill

    E. Test Reports

        1. Certification of Flame Retardant treatment

        2. Certification of compliance with regulatory agencies

        3. Certification of shading coefficient

1.04 Product Delivery, Storage and Handling

    A. Fabricator shall deliver drapery items folded neatly, securely wrapped and clearly marked for size and installation location.

    B. Drapery Items shall be protected from snagging, soil and other damage. In the event that drapery items suffer damage, the fabricator shall clean, repair or replace at no expense to the owner or designer.

    C. Drapery items shall be delivered free of loose threads or lint. Drapery items shall not be delivered with horizontal creases.

    D. Drapery items or hardware shall be delivered to job site until the area is ready for installation.

1.05 Job Conditions:

    A. Examine substrates and conditions under which units are to be installed. Do not proceed until unsatisfactory conditions have been corrected.

    B. Environmental controls shall be in operation 48 hours prior to and after installation of drapery fabric.

1.06 Guarantee

    A. Drapery fabrication to be unconditionally guaranteed for ____ years against all defects in material or workmanship. All defects are to be replaced or corrected in not more than ____ weeks after notification of said defects, excluding normal wear and tear, without penalty to Owner.

PART 2. PRODUCTS

2.01 Drapery Hardware

    A. Channel track section manufactured by:

        1. Size and weight:

        2. Finish:

        (in accordance with Aluminum Association Specification No. AA-C22A 21).

        3. Permanently lubricated:

    B. Track to be equipped with following components:

        1. Pulley sets:

        One way draw: Two way draw:

        2. Master Carriers

        Butt carrier: Overlap carrier:

        3. Slides

        Snap tabs: Pin slides:

        4. Cord:

        Type:

        5. Cord Guide

        Tension pulley: Weighted Pull:

        6. Baton - hand operation:

        7. Support brackets and end brackets:

        8. Provide all end stops, splicers, installation anchorages and other necessary accessories.

2.02 Drapery

    A. Drapery fabric shall meet the following criteria:

        1. Weight (ounces per linear yard):

        2. Weave:

        3. Fiber content:

        4. Color:

        5. Repeat size:

        6. Soil resistant treatment:

7. Flame retardant treatment:

8. Shading coefficient (configuration):

B. Fabric shall meet or exceed the following Performance standards:

1. Flammability

NFPA Test No. 701

CCC-T-191b(5903)

CCC-W-408A

2. Abrasion

ASTM D 1175 64 T

3. Colorfastness

AATCC 16E-1971

2.03   Fabrication

A. Drapery is to be constructed with _____ heading system with _____ percentage of fullness.

B. Drapery shall be constructed of _____ panel widths with (center butt or center overlap) or one way draw (left or right).

C. Finished length:

Cut length:

Finished width:

Pattern repeat:

D. Drapery headings to be fabricated with _____ and is to measure ____ inches in depth. Bottom edge of heading is to be stitched through face fabric on sheers with lock stitch machine at 6-8 stitches per inch to meet federal specification #301.

E. Lined drapery shall have lining securely attached at heading to prevent any roll-up or separating of lining at heading.

F. Pleats are to be securely pinch tacked with a minimum of 12 stitch tacks of 40/3 thread or equivalent.

G. Bottom hems to be ____ inches full double turned and finished with a "blind stitch" machine at 2 to 1 ratio and not less than 50/3 thread. All bottom hems shall be true and square. Covered lead weights shall be placed in the corner of each panel.

H. Only first quality mercerized cotton, rayon or dacron thread shall be used in the fabrication of the drapery.

I. Side hems shall be ____ inches full double turned and finished with blind stitch machine at 2 to 1 ratio on medium drapery and sheers with no rack, roll or wrinkle. Needles shall not exceed #10 for sheer fabrics and #15 for medium weight fabrics.

J. Sheers shall be selvage edges trimmed and joined with a French seam method or reverse field method at no more than 1/8 inch width at

6-8 stitches per inch with 50/3 thread to meet federal specification #301.

K. Medium weight fabrics, such as linens, shall have selvage edges trimmed. Side seams shall have one row of lock stitches and all raw edges overlock stitched at not less than 10 stitches per inch and not lighter than 50/3 thread in loopers and needles with a minimum of 4 threads and not larger than the metric size 80 to meet federal specification #514.

L. Velours shall be fabricated with an anti-friction pressure foot and throat plate on needle feed and bottom feed. Drawn or puckered seams shall not be accpeted. Thread shall be 24/4 vat dyed, 100 percent mercerized.

M. Lining fabrics shall have lock stitches for seams at the rate of 6 to 8 stitches per inch. Selvage shall be notched and pressed back 1/2 inch to relieve pressure on the seams.

PART 3. EXECUTION

3.01   Inspection

A. Drapery shall hang in natural draping condition without creases.

B. Drapery contractor shall steam and hand dress all drapery at job site.

C. Drapery shall hang one inch above the finished floor or _____ inches below the window sill. All other measurements shall conform to drawings.

D. Seams shall be inspected for flatness and lack of puckering.

E. All patterns shall be perfectly aligned vertically and horizontally.

F. No needle holes shall leak light through blackout linings.

3.02   Installation

A. Install drapery tracks and accessories at locations indicated on the working drawings and in accord with manufacturer's instructions. Install level, plumb and secure, Cooperate with other trades for securing drapery tracks to substrates and finish surfaces.

B. Repair or replace damaged hardware parts as directed by the Designer, at no additional cost to the Owner.

C. Attach drapery to attached tracks installed by others. Fabricator is to add or decrease carriers as required for proper installation of the drapery.

3.03   Field Quality Control

A. All brackets are mounted to either concrete, wood, or hollow construction shall be tested to withstand a pull of ___ pounds.

B. All cords and operational components shall operate without application of undue force.

3.04   Adjust and Clean

A. All debris connected with the installation of the window system shall be collected and disposed of out of the area.

B. All blemishes to surrounding areas that are the result of installation are to be brought to the immediate attention of the designer.

C. All finger or tool marks or other blemishes are to be corrected and repaired by the Contractor without cost to the Owner.

D. Each room or area that is completed shall be cleaned up in consecutive order and made ready for use in a minimum time span.

3.05   Schedules

Attach window schedules, measurements and drapery work orders here.

END OF SECTION

11 FABRIC AND UPHOLSTERY FLAMMABILITY

Designers have traditionally specified upholstered furniture on the following basis:

1. Style

2. Comfort, based on knowledge of human factors

3. Functional and spatial needs

4. Construction performance: strength and durability

5. Cost factors

In recent years another consideration has been brought to the attention of designers, i.e., the potential flammability hazard of fabrics and filling materials used in upholstered furniture. Though a great deal of research had been done on the problem, little effort has been made to aid designers in applying the research findings to actual specification decisions.

This chapter will provide a review of recent research and new terminology that has resulted from efforts to establish a uniform national standard for producing more flame-resistant upholstered furniture. Prior to the 1972 adoption of the federal standard for the Flammability of Mattresses (FF 4-72) [reprinted in Appendix C], there had been no regulations of interior furniture. Table 11.1 lists the mandatory standards that became effective during the last decade. With the adoption of each standard, designers have expressed concern about federal intervention in design areas previously free of regulations. The proposed flammability standard for upholstered furniture, first announced in 1972, has provoked headlines in major city newspapers and many articles in professional magazines. The subject of death by fire is a highly charged subject, especially when linked to the antismoking campaigns of the late seventies.

The process involved in the development of a federal standard is complicated and often controversial. With the passage of the Consumer Product Safety Act in 1973, Congress also formed the Consumer Product Safety Commission

(CPSC) to (1) protect the public against unreasonable risks of injury associated with consumer products; (2) assist consumers in evaluating the comparative safety of consumer products; (3) develop uniform safety standards for consumer products and minimize conflicting state and local regulations; (4) promote research and investigation into the causes of product-related deaths and injuries.[1] Charged with these responsibilities and very carefully regulated procedures, the commission must establish priorities before taking action on a particular product by evaluating the frequency and severity of injuries associated with a product and projecting future injuries, deaths, and property loss.

BASIS FOR CONCERN: INJURY AND FIRE FATALITIES

Information on injuries and deaths from upholstered furniture fires is not all contained in computer banks. Some is never reported, while much comes to the public through the daily news media. Examples can be found in many local newspapers:

FIRE KILLS RESIDENT; HOUSE IS DAMAGED
A 54-year-old man died Monday in a fire that heavily damaged his north Phoenix home. The man was found in the den of his home. Fire investigators said the blaze started in a love seat in the den and was apparently caused by careless disposal of smoking material . . . the fire apparently smoldered for some time before spreading through the den, firemen said. The den and kitchen suffered fire damage, and the remainder of the house was heavily damaged by intense heat and smoke. The loss was estimated at $38,000.[2]

The Consumer Product Safety Commission gathers information on injuries and fatalities from many different sources:

National Fire Protection Association (NFPA)

TABLE 11.1 FEDERAL FLAMMABILITY STANDARDS (PRESENT AND PROPOSED)

End Use	Agency	Finding That Standard May Be Needed	Publication of Proposed Standard With Test Method	Adoption of Proposed Standard	Effective Compliance Date
Large carpets and rugs Larger than 24 sq ft	CPSC	Dec. 1968	Dec. 1968	April 1970	April 1971
Small carpets and rugs Less than 24 sq ft	CPSC	Dec. 1968	April 1970	Dec. 1970	Dec. 1971
Airplane carpet and upholstery	DOT	—	—	—	May 1972
Automobile upholstery and carpet	DOT	—	Dec. 1969, June 1970	Dec. 1970	Sept. 1972
Mattresses	CPSC	June 1970	Sept. 1971	May 1972	July 1973
Furniture upholstery	CPSC	Nov. 1972	Dec. 1976	—	Possible 1980-1981

Source: Frost and Sullivan, New York.

United States Fire Administration (formerly known as National Fire Prevention and Control Administration (NFPCA)[3]

National Household Fire Survey

Maryland State Fatality Study

Flammable Fabrics Accident Case and Testing System (FFACTS)

CPSC In-Depth Investigations

Death Certificates

National Electronic Injury Surveillance System (NEISS)

National Center for Health Statistics (NCHS)

From these sources, the CPSC estimated that 45,000 residential upholstered furniture fires occur each year in the United States. It was also estimated that an annual rate of 3,200 injuries and 800 deaths (from a range of 544 to 1,038 deaths) occur from residential upholstered furniture fires. It was found that approximately 1,700 of the injuries and 500 of the deaths were related to cigarette ignition of the upholstery. These estimates are based on data gathered from 1971 through 1976.

The CPSC further reports that economic losses due to the ignition of upholstered furniture are estimated to be about $540 million annually. These losses are the sum of estimated losses from deaths, injuries, and property damage. The estimates include hospital costs, rehabilitation costs, and losses in earnings. These figures do not include the total annual losses from pain and suffering.[4]

From a tabulation of all these figures, certain similarities began to appear in the fire incidents:

1. *Location and time of incidents.* The majority of fires occurred in the living room areas during the early morning hours between midnight and 6 A.M.

2. *Activity leading to ignition.* It appeared that most people became involved in these fire incidents after (a) falling asleep on the upholstered furniture while smoking a cigarette or (b) after leaving a lit cigarette smoldering on the furniture.

3. *Age of victims.* People directly involved in these upholstered furniture fires were mostly adults between the ages of 21 and 64.

4. *Involvement of intoxicants and disabilities.* Evidence strongly indicated that alcohol, drugs, and physical and/or mental disabilities sometimes played a part in these incidents, although not in the majority of cases. When intoxicants or disabilities were present, they involved adults in the above age range.

5. *Number of victims per incident.* Situations in which victims fell asleep with smoking materials tended to be single victim incidents; i.e., these adults were the victims of their own actions. Incidents in which cigarettes were left smoldering on the furniture tended to result in multiple victims. This involved injuries and deaths of children and elderly people, as well as the person responsible for leaving the cigarette on the furniture.

6. *Causes of injuries and deaths.* Burns, closely followed by smoke inhalation, caused the majority of injuries. Inhalation caused the majority of deaths.

7. *Property losses.* In situations where the victim fell asleep on the upholstered furniture with smoking materials, the property loss values were usually low ($300 or less). When the smoking material was left smoldering on the furniture, the property losses were usually extensive ($10,000 to $3,000,000).

8. *Material components of furniture involved.* In incidents where textile remnants were available after the fire for laboratory analysis, the results indicated that cellulosics predominated as the outer layer upholstery fabric. Cotton, rayon, and blends of these two fibers were most frequently involved. Research also found the fabric weight of the outer layer of upholstery averaged over 20 oz/sq yd. Cotton batting and combinations of urethane foam/cotton batting predominated as the inner layer of upholstery.[5]

If the commission, after carefully reviewing the data, decides that a standard or regulation is needed to protect the public from further unreasonable risks, they have been authorized to proceed in the following manner:

1. The commission publishes a "notice of proceedings" in the *Federal Register*. This notice serves as a public announcement to all concerned parties that a regulation is needed for a particular product and that research will begin on the development of a standard.

2. The commission is also authorized to publish a proposed standard. This proposed standard may be one that has previously been issued or adopted by a qualified public or private agency or organization.

3. The commission may also accept offers from agencies, organizations, or individuals who wish to propose a standard. Congress specifies that these must be submitted within 150 days after the "notice of proceedings" is published in the *Federal Register*.

4. The commission also encourages the general public and all interested people to participate in the development of a standard.[6]

5. If after considering the feasibility of all proposals submitted, the commission determines that no proposals have met the established criteria, the "development proceedings" may be terminated and the commission may then independently develop a standard. (See Appendix D for the text of the federal regulations.)

OPINIONS ON AND INVESTIGATIONS OF A FLAMMABILITY STANDARD

When news of the proposed standard was released, together with the injury data, some very definite opinions and viewpoints were provoked from consumers, the industry, and concerned designers.

Consumers

Many consumers felt that nothing should be done, while an equal number saw the need for a regulation. Nonsmokers felt that it was not the fault of the furniture, but the fault of the careless smoker. They thought it unfair that nonsmokers should have to bear the increased cost of furniture that would result from a federal standard. Other consumers felt that self-extinguishing cigarettes should be developed.

Industry

The textile and upholstered furniture manufacturers suggested that they be allowed more time to develop voluntary standards. They also proposed a system of labeling to inform the public about the flammability of upholstered furniture. Smoke detectors were also suggested as a protective measure. However, some industry representatives did not think that the injury data warranted a regulation that would impose costly testing, require recordkeeping, and necessitate an increase in the cost of retail furniture. They predicted that the consumer would be limited in the choice of fabrics and furniture design. Manufacturers favored a self-extinguishing cigarette as an alternative to a flammability standard for upholstered furniture. In 1975 the National Association of Furniture Manufacturers sought a court judgment against the Consumer Product Safety Commission because they felt that the commission had jurisdiction over cigarettes and should be enjoined to study the feasibility of producing self-extinguishing cigarettes, thus reducing flammability hazards associated with upholstered furniture. They further contended that any upholstered furniture flammability standard issued by the commission would be arbitrary and capricious because the commission had not considered self-extinguishing cigarettes as an alternative. In dismissing the suit, the court noted that an upholstery flammability standard had not (at that time) been issued by the commission; therefore the suit was premature. The following year (1976) Congress enacted the Consumer Product Safety Commission Improvements Act (Public Law 94-284) and omitted any reference to tobacco and tobacco products as sources of ignition. Section 3 of this act also specifies that tobacco and tobacco products are not to be considered hazardous substances under the Federal Hazardous Substances Act which is administered by the commission.[7] Thus, the CPSC was left without authority to regulate cigarette production.

Designers

Generally, designers have objected to the federal standard on the grounds that it would limit the use of certain textiles or necessitate the use of backings that would not enhance the aesthetic quality of the fabric. The estimated reduction in fabric selection may range from 10 to 14 percent. Designers, in the habit of specifying COM (customer's own material, or material not normally stocked by a manufacturer), may find that the COM material will require additional testing, which will increase the cost at the wholesale and retail level. Residential designers would be more affected by the standard than designers specializing in commercial and institutional work because most so-called contract fabrics used in commercial upholstery are ignition-resistant and therefore would not have difficulty in meeting test criteria.

DEVELOPMENT OF UPHOLSTERY FLAMMABILITY TESTING METHODS

When research began on methods of testing individual furniture components, several approaches were proposed. Since data indicated that the cigarette was a major source of ignition, many felt that this should be the ignition source used. Other authorities felt that a variety of sources should be considered, such as crumpled newspaper, matches, flaming trash basket contents, radiant heaters, and other flaming furniture in the same room. Other than differing opinions on the source of the ignition, the ultimate purpose of the test was considered, and the following alternatives were discussed:

Prevention of ignition	Ignition test
Prevention of flame spread	Flame-spread test
Prevention of heat contribution to growth of fire	Heat release test
Prevention of smoke development	Smoke generation test

In all these approaches several methods may be employed; the testing of an individual material (component testing); mockup testing (simulated combination of materials as used in the total furniture unit); and a full-scale test that simulates the full range of fire growth and development.

Some existing standards require a combination of mockup and component testing. Several manufacturers and the National Bureau of Standards (NBS) have conducted research with full-scale simulations, but none is required because of the cost factor.

Development of a Mandatory Test Method

The test method developed for a standard must be practical; i.e., it must be possible to produce a piece of upholstered furniture that will meet the test criteria. It must also relate to the hazard of the product tested and be reproducible and repeatable. In addition, the test must be simple, easy to understand, and inexpensive to perform.

The National Bureau of Standards, working with CPSC, determined the following hazards and products were involved:

1. Product: upholstered furniture (fabric and filling materials)

2. Hazard: smoldering combustion (fire, smoke, and heat)

3. Primary ignition source: nonflaming (cigarettes)

Component Testing: Fabric Classification. To make the testing procedure economically feasible, a fabric classification system was developed. Upholstery manufacturers may handle as many as 70 to 100 kinds of fabrics, and would find it impossible to test each type. The proposed standards would classify fabrics on the basis of their resistance to ignition by a cigarette. Two tests were devised to determine fabric classification. The first series of tests determines whether a fabric will ignite and support ignition without the influence of upholstery filling material. An individual fabric sample is placed on glass fiberboard (a nonflammable material) and tested by placing lighted cigarettes on the fabric surface. Figures 11.1 and 11.2 illustrate the device developed for fabric component testing.

Fabrics are classified by the char length produced by the lighted cigarette:

Class D	Any fabric that charred more than 3.1 in. (7.8 cm)
Class C	Fabrics that charred between 1.5 in. (3.8 cm) and 3 in. (7.6 cm)
Class B	Fabrics that charred 1.5 in. or more
Class A	Fabrics that charred less than 1.5 in.

Fabrics that show a char length of less than 1.5 in. are tested a second time over cotton batting that has not been treated with flame retardant. The samples that show a char length of 1.5 in. or more retain a class B rating; fabrics showing a char length of

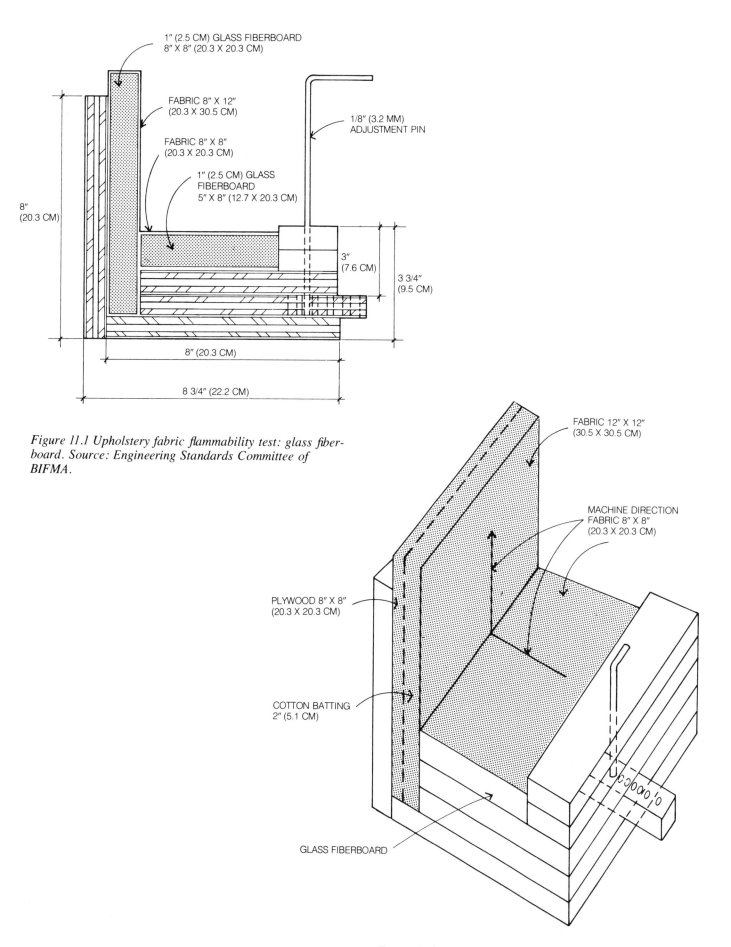

1" (2.5 CM) GLASS FIBERBOARD
8" X 8" (20.3 X 20.3 CM)

FABRIC 8" X 12"
(20.3 X 30.5 CM)

FABRIC 8" X 8"
(20.3 X 20.3 CM)

1" (2.5 CM) GLASS
FIBERBOARD
5" X 8" (12.7 X 20.3 CM)

1/8" (3.2 MM)
ADJUSTMENT PIN

8"
(20.3 CM)

3"
(7.6 CM)

3 3/4"
(9.5 CM)

8" (20.3 CM)

8 3/4" (22.2 CM)

Figure 11.1 Upholstery fabric flammability test: glass fiber-board. Source: Engineering Standards Committee of BIFMA.

FABRIC 12" X 12"
(30.5 X 30.5 CM)

MACHINE DIRECTION
FABRIC 8" X 8"
(20.3 X 20.3 CM)

PLYWOOD 8" X 8"
(20.3 X 20.3 CM)

COTTON BATTING
2" (5.1 CM)

GLASS FIBERBOARD

Figure 11.2 Upholstery fabric flammability test: cotton batting. Source: Engineering Standards Committee of BIFMA.

less than 1.5 in. are maintained as class A (Figure 11.3).

Using this method of classification, the following fabric types were found to be typical examples of each class:

Class A   Wools, wool blends, vinyl plastics, and heavy-weight synthetics (nylon, olefin, polyester, and acrylic)

Class B   Medium-weight synthetics and some light-weight or tightly woven cellulosics (cotton, rayon, and linen)

Class C   Medium-weight cellulosics

Class D   Heavy-weight cellulosics[8]

This testing confirmed that upholstery flammability was influenced by the following factors:

1. Cellulosic fiber content (cotton, rayon, linen) tended to present a smoldering-ignition hazard.

2. Smoldering potential increased as the fiber weight was increased.

3. The content of the filling used in the upholstery had an important effect on the smoldering potential of the entire furniture unit.

4. Thermoplastics (vinyl plastics, heavy-weight nylons, olefins, polyesters, and acrylics) rarely presented a smoldering hazard.

Mockup Testing of Total Furniture Unit. Based on information from the injury data, it was evident that upholstery ignited by cigarettes tended to smolder; therefore researchers determined it would be necessary to test finished products to accurately predict performance in a smoldering fire.[9] Previous testing experience with mattresses showed that individual components, such as fabrics and filling, may perform well when tested separately, but often display different burning characteristics when tested as a total unit.

To assure economic feasibility of the proposed testing method, a furniture mockup was devised by the National Bureau of Standards. A mockup must simulate the particular furniture being produced by the manufacturer doing the testing. In other words, it must be constructed with upholstery filling and a specific fabric assembled in the same configuration as the actual production furniture (see Figure 11.4). Mockup testing allows for various critical surface areas to be evaluated as well as the fabric and filling combinations. The number of surfaces that should be evaluated depends on the furniture design. Critical areas/surfaces may include (1) side cushion and crevice, (2) top of the armrest, (3) back cushion and crevice, (4) seat support system or deck supporting the loose seat cushions, and (5) the seat cushion surface and welt edges. If a sofa is manufactured with surface treatments such as quilting or tufting, each cushion type should be tested in a separate mockup assembly.[10]

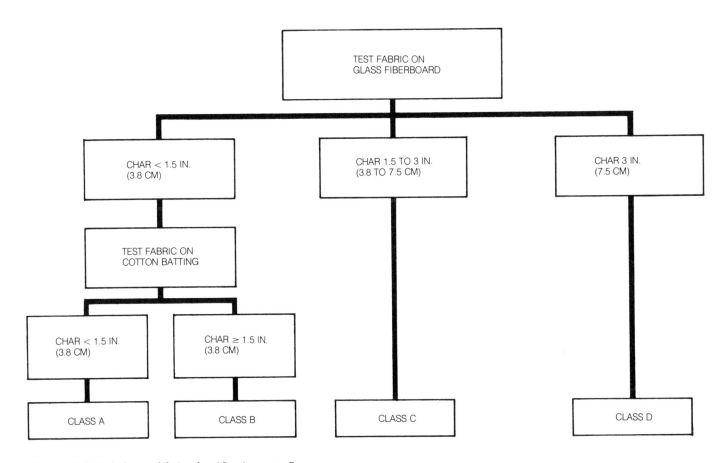

Figure 11.3 Upholstery fabric classification test. Source: Consumer Product Safety Commission.

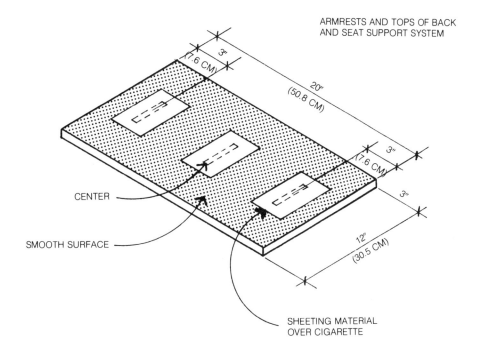

ARMRESTS AND TOPS OF BACK
AND SEAT SUPPORT SYSTEM

3"
(7.6 CM)

20"
(50.8 CM)

3"
(7.6 CM)

3"

12"
(30.5 CM)

CENTER

SMOOTH SURFACE

SHEETING MATERIAL
OVER CIGARETTE

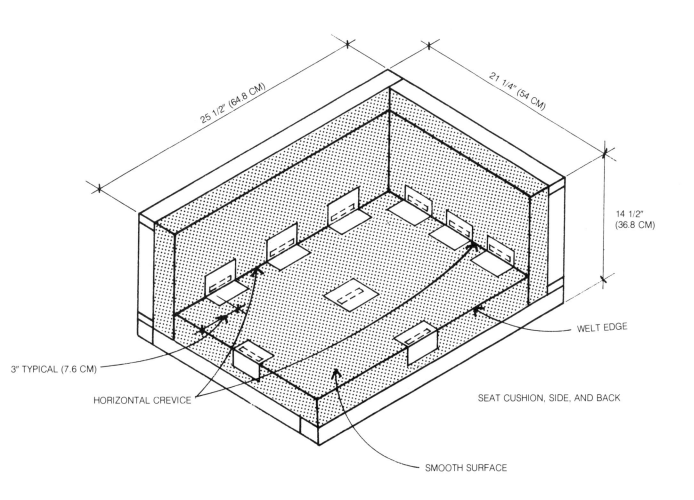

25 1/2" (64.8 CM)

21 1/4" (54 CM)

14 1/2"
(36.8 CM)

WELT EDGE

3" TYPICAL (7.6 CM)

HORIZONTAL CREVICE

SEAT CUSHION, SIDE, AND BACK

SMOOTH SURFACE

Figure 11.4 Upholstered furniture flammability mockup test.
Source: Engineering Standards Committee of BIFMA.

The fabric classifications, previously established, proved very useful in minimizing the number of fabric mockup tests that would be required. At first it appeared that any fabric of a particular class would serve as a representative of that classification, but later researchers found that fabrics from classes B and C showed a wide performance variation in mockup testing. Therefore it became necessary to select fabrics (from classes B and C) that would represent the low end or minimum performance qualities in order to provide a more stringent ignition test. Fabrics of those two classifications are termed "Standard Fabrics" (a Standard Fabric classification was not necessary for class A fabrics). In actual application, NBS recommends the following: "where mockups using B and C standard fabrics meet the acceptance criterion, other B and C fabrics respectively can be used in production furniture of that particular construction. If a mockup uses a class B or C fabric which is not a standard fabric for its class, production furniture is qualified for manufacture only with that fabric."[11] A mockup for a particular furniture style which meets all requirements with a standard class C fabric may be produced with any class C, B, or A fabric. On identical mockups, one type of class D fabrics was found adequate in random selection and testing.

Industry Testing Methods

Technology does exist that will allow manufacturers to safely use many existing fabrics and upholstery components that will comply with proposed and existing standards. Continuing research is developing methods to improve the ignition performance of upholstery fabrics and total upholstery units through the use of finishings, chemical treatments, fiber blends, fillings materials, heat barriers, and construction styling.

Flame-Retardant Treatments. The terminology associated with the burning behavior of textiles can be confusing because the terms are frequently misused. For example, "flame retardant" should only be used as a noun to define a chemical used to impart flame resistance. A fabric may be described by an adjective as "flame-retardant-treated," which means the fabric received a flame retardant. The term "flame-retardant-treated" does not apply to fabrics that are *inherently* flame resistant due to intrinsic properties of the material or the fiber-forming polymer. (See additional definitions in the Glossary for this chapter.)

Flame retardants are usually classified according to their permanence and effectiveness in providing resistance to open flame ignition. The majority of flame retardants provide the following degrees of durability:

1. Nondurable: a water-based chemical compound which is removed with water and requires frequent reapplication.

2. Semidurable: the application of a chemical compound that will make the fabric flame resistant and will resist water, but will not withstand dry cleaning solutions.

3. Durable: these chemical retardants will withstand dry cleaning and usually last the lifetime of the fabric.

Though most flame retardants offer resistance to open flame ignition, many do not provide protection from smoldering combustion, which is a major problem in upholstered furniture. The cotton industry has been conducting extensive research on means of providing smoldering resistance. Although phosphates and borates have been successfully used to retard flame and afterglow factors in cotton fibers, these chemical compounds were not effective in inhibiting smoldering.[12] The Southern Regional Research Center has developed a methyl borate system which appears to be effective on cellulosic fabrics. This process involves bringing the fabric into contact with the methyl borate vapors in an enclosed chamber. The vapors react with the moisture content of the cellulose fibers and form boric acid, which becomes deposited on and within the fibers being treated.[13] This process shows great promise because of the availability of borax as a raw material, but further research is needed to determine how this treatment will interact with soil-resistant chemicals, color fastness, and dye changes. The National Cotton Council of America estimates that it will cost between $100,000 and $300,000 to develop a full-scale treatment plant.

Changes in Fiber Content. Another method of achieving flame resistance is to blend thermoplastics with cellulosic fibers. When fabric weights contain at least 35 percent thermoplastic content, it has been found that the smolder potential is greatly decreased. Many fabric styles and looks formerly achieved only with cellulosics are now being produced with thermoplastics: examples include velvets, brocades, matélasse, and bulky Haitian-style fabrics.

Fabric Backcoating. In the past several years approximately 40 to 60 percent of upholstery-weight fabrics have been backcoated to increase dimensional stability, promote wear, and provide resistance to seam slippage. Increased research in the field of flame retardancy has prompted an interest in the application of flame retardants to backcoatings. The addition of sulfur to latex polymer backcoatings has proven successful in upgrading heavy-weight cellulosics, but industry anticipates some problems in the application of backcoatings to lighter-weight cottons because of the high application required per unit weight. It is estimated that the total industry cost of backcoating 50 percent of the class D–type fabrics would range between $12,400,000 and $12,300,000.

Upholstery Filling Material. Having confirmed that filling materials used beneath the fabric were a critical factor in controlling smoldering potential, the industry became concerned with the means of creating smolder resistance in the most commonly used fillers, such as cotton batting, polyester batting, polyurethane foam, and neoprene latex foam.

Batting. Boric acid is widely known as an effective means of controlling smoldering in cotton batting, but the increased cost and shortages of boric acid in recent years have forced researchers to try to find other methods of control. The methyl borate vapor process is one suggested alternative to using powdered boric acid. Another alternative under consideration is the substitution of polyester fiberfill for cotton batting.

Barriers. In the past several years various types of liners have been developed that serve as heat barriers between the upholstery fabric and the filling material. Liners have been produced from polyester/cotton materials, aluminum foil, and carboxylated chloroprene latex. The aluminum foil liner is made from a very thin layer of hole-punched aluminum, which has one side coated with a woven fiberglass and the other side covered with spun fiberglass.[14] This liner does not create undue stiffness when placed between the fabric and the filling.

Figure 11.5 Bus seat burn test. Reproduced with permission of E. I. du Pont de Nemours & Company, Incorporated, Elastomer Chemical Department.

The carboxylated chloroprene latex[15] is similar to Neoprene cushioning foam and is produced in various thicknesses for use as a liner, a fabric backcoating, or a complete encasement around the filling material. This interliner serves as more than a simple heat barrier by providing three types of retardant action when subjected to a heat source: (1) during the early stages of combustion this liner heats and releases water vapor, which serves to cool the fabric and filling material. (2) If the heat source continues, the liner releases chemical flame retardants, and (3) in a final stage of decomposition, the liner forms a char layer which helps to insulate the cushioning material from the heat and limits the flow of oxygen into the cushion. DuPont, the manufacturer of this liner, does not recommend it for use in installations that may be subjected to vandalism, such as public transit systems, public assembly seating, or institutional bedding. Figure 11.5 illustrates how slashing of bus seats affects the performance of liners.

Foams. It has been found that foam can be effectively treated with flame retardants to reduce the risk of open flame ignition, but research has shown that some chemicals that modify the open flame burning process may in fact compound the smoldering process in some foams. Highly flammable polyurethane treated with retardant functions well in open flame ignition tests, but tends to smolder. Without the retardant, the same foam displayed a resistance to smoldering. With or without a retardant, tests indicate that urethane produces large amounts of smoke.[16] (See results of theater chair burn tests in Figures 11.6 and 11.7.)

Private industry, as well as NBS, have conducted tests to determine the heat, smoke, and ignition characteristics of neoprene and polyurethene foams. Many of these tests have focused on rapid transit and public theater seating, using an open flame ignition source on the trash and litter that is frequently found in public areas. In two tests conducted at the

Test #1, Neoprene Foam

% Smoke Evolved vs. Time
Sensor 6 ft. Above Platform
Test Date: 6-20-75
Clock Start: 1:00

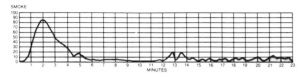

Test #2, HR Polyurethane Foam

% Smoke Evolved vs. Time
Sensor 6 ft. Above Platform
Test Date: 6-20-75
Clock Start: 12:00

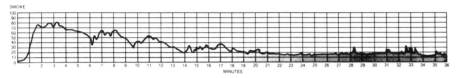

Test #3, Standard Polyurethane Foam

% Smoke Evolved vs. Time
Sensor 6 ft. Above Platform
Test Date: 6-20-75
Clock Start: 11:00

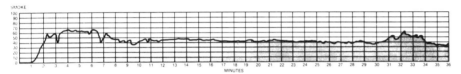

Figure 11.6 Theater chair burn test. Reproduced with permission of E. I. du Pont de Nemours & Company, Incorporated, Elastomer Chemical Department.

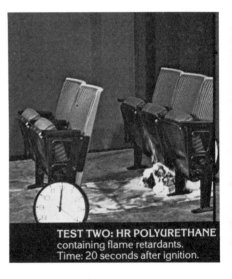

Figure 11.7 Theater seat burn test. Reproduced with permission of E. I. du Pont de Nemours & Company, Incorporated, Elastomer Chemical Department.

Time: 1 minute, 30 seconds.
Flame ignites center chair.

Time: 3 minutes, 00 seconds.
Center chair involved.

Major flames out. Time: 6 minutes, 00 seconds.
Damage: 1 chair involved, fabric melting and
smoldering on two adjoining chairs.

Test 1. Upholstery fabric was a woven vinyl treated with flame retardant.

Time: 1 minute, 30 seconds.
Flame ignites center chair.

Time: 3 minutes, 00 seconds.
Five chairs in two rows involved.

Major flames out. Time: 29 minutes, 30 seconds.
Damage: 5 chairs in two rows involved.

Test 2. HR polyurethane foam was treated with a flame retardant.
Upholstery fabric was woven vinyl treated with flame retardant.

Time: 1 minute, 30 seconds.
Flame ignites center chair.

Time: 3 minutes, 00 seconds.
Five chairs in two rows involved.

Major flames out. Time: 40 minutes, 00 seconds
Damage: All seven chairs involved.

Test 3. Upholstery fabric was woven nylon without flame retardant.

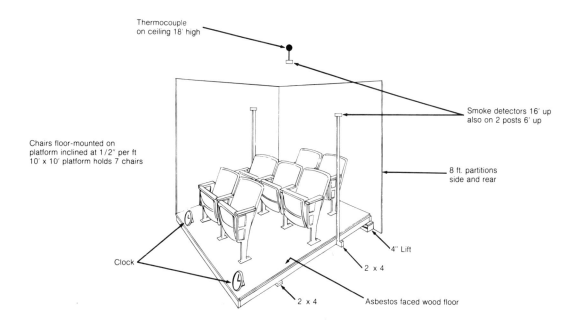

Figure 11.8 Theater seat test facility. Reproduced with permission of E. I. du Pont de Nemours & Company, Incorporated, Elastomer Chemical Department.

Bus Seat Test Facility

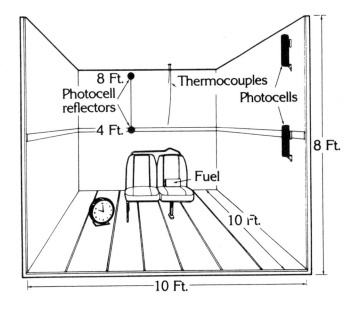

Figure 11.9 Bus seat test facility. Reproduced with permission of E. I. du Pont de Nemours & Company, Incorporated, Elastomer Chemical Department.

Factory Mutual Burn and Test Center, the test environment was carefully constructed to simulate the conditions found in theaters and rapid transit systems.[17] (See Figures 11.8 and 11.9.)

The testing of seats normally used in buses and rapid transit systems indicated a vast flammability difference between urethene (poly) and neoprene foam. Table 11.2 lists the seat construction, flame time, smoke peak (percentage of obstruction), and peak temperature. Figures 11.5 and 11.7 clearly show the hazardous potential of urethane upholstered seating in public seating areas.

Early in 1979 a fatal fire forced the closure of the underwater rapid transit system between San Francisco and Oakland, California. Sparks from an unknown source ignited one of the train cars, and victims described thick smoke and toxic fumes coming from the blazing plastic seats. One fireman died from smoke inhalation and 35 were hospitalized. This tragic accident confirms test findings that the standard polyurethane foam vinyl–covered seat ignites easily, burns rapidly at a high temperature, and produces a high level of smoke obscuration.

Interlaboratory studies conducted by the National Bureau of Standards also indicate that foam performance varies when used on vertical and horizontal surfaces of upholstered furniture. Table 11.3 shows the performance of filling materials tested in a vertical position. This illustrates that a barrier of foam or polyester over untreated cotton batting in the vertical position may not perform well with class D (11) fabrics. It also points out that some class D fabrics will ignite when used over flame-retardant-treated cotton batting, but class A (I) will not ignite when used over untreated cotton.[18]

Other major conclusions are summarized in Table 11.4, which rank orders the upholstery filling materials from safest (1) to the least safe (3-4), based on ignition probabilities in relation to the portion of the furniture involved. For these findings it would appear that foam is one of the most effective fillers for seat cushions.[19]

The total industry cost for upgrading smolder-resistance substrates is estimated to be between $18,100,000 and $33,100,000 for initial compliance efforts.

TABLE 11.2 IGNITION OF BUS SEATS (WITHOUT LINER)

Test	Seat Construction	Flame Time	Comments	Smoke Peak, % of Obscuration	Temperature Peak
1	Vinyl upholstery Urethene foam	13 minutes, 20 seconds	Seats totally consumed	100% at 10 minutes, 30 seconds	1000°F
5	Vinyl upholstery Neoprene	4 minutes, 30 seconds	Vinyl on back burned. Neoprene only slightly burned	67% at 8 minutes	250°F

Source: E.I. du Pont de Nemours and Company, Incorporated, Elastomer Chemicals Department.

TABLE 11.3 IGNITION PERFORMANCE OF UPHOLSTERY FABRIC MATERIALS: FILLING MATERIALS (VERTICAL)

Approximate UFAC Class	Fabric Class	Untreated Cotton Batting	1/2" Thick Foam or Polyester over Untreated Cotton Batting	Flame Retardant Treated Cotton Batting	Aluminized Fabric over Cotton Batting
Class I	A	N	N	N	N
	B	I	N	N	N
Class II	C	I	I	N	N
	D	I	I	I	N

I — Ignition   N — Nonignition

Source: Consumer Product Safety Commission.

TABLE 11.4 IGNITION PERFORMANCE OF FILLING MATERIALS

Furniture Component	Construction Material
Seat cushion	
Seat location	1. Foam (tight or loose) 2. Polyester fiberfill over foam 3. Tight cotton
Welt location	1. Tight foam 2. Polyester fiberfill over foam 3. Loose foam 4. Tight cotton
Side or back	1. Foam 2. Foam over cotton 3. Cotton
Top of arm or back	1. Polyester fiberfill over cotton 2. Foam 3. Foam over cotton 4. Cotton

Source: Consumer Product Safety Commission.

TABLE 11.5 CITY AND STATE UPHOLSTERY FLAMMABILITY REGULATIONS

End Use	Agency	Test Number	Method	Criteria
All upholstery material including carpet and drapery padding + 1/2" thick.	Port Authority of New York and New Jersey	CCC-T 19lb Method 5903 ASTM E 162-67	Open flame Radiant heat	Burn length 8" max. Afterflame 15" max.
Curtains, drapery and exterior upholstery	The Boston Fire Department	BFD 11-2	Open flame	Afterflame not to exceed 2 seconds. No flaming drop-off permitted. Self-extinguishing 0-15 seconds
Interior upholstery		BFD 11-3	Open flame	
Solid plastic-coated and laminated plastic furnishings		BFD 11-4	Open flame	
Upholstery coverings	The Commonwealth of Massachusetts	FPR 20	Open flame	Afterflame not to exceed 2 seconds; afterglow not exceeding 40 seconds
All upholstery material	State of New York	CCC-T 19lb Method 5903	Open flame	Burn length 8" max.
Resilient cellular material	State of California	CCC T-191 Method 5903	Open flame	Char length not to exceed 6-8". Afterflame not to exceed 5 seconds, afterglow 15 seconds. No flaming combustion. Char not to exceed 2"
Manmade filling		191-53		
Upholstery Fabrics		Cig. Ignition	Nonflaming	

Welt Cords. Numerous tests indicated that welt cording used at seam edges presented a flammability hazard because cigarettes dropped on upholstery became lodged against the welt cord.[20] Traditionally, welt cords have been constructed of untreated paper twist or cotton, but in 1978 many manufacturers began specifying smolder-resistance cords. At this time approximately 30 percent of upholstered furniture is being constructed with plastic (PVC) welt cords. Because designers have objected to the lack of resilience and stiffness of the PVC cording, research is being conducted on the feasibility of using treated paper, cotton, and other fiber cords such as polypropylene.

EXISTING REGULATIONS ON THE FLAMMABILITY OF UPHOLSTERED FURNITURE

Prior to the "Notice of Proceedings" issued by CPSC indicating the need for a flammability standard, several states and cities had issued regulatory standards on upholstered furniture and had already prompted many areas of industry to improve the flammability resistance of furniture components, such as fabric and substrate.

The state and city regulations exerting the most influence are listed in Table 11.5. Surveying these regulations indicates that the majority require component testing using an open flame source of ignition with components being rated by distance of flame spread or ability to self-extinguish within 0 to 15 seconds. The State of California Standard (Technical Bulletin No. 116 and 117, which is reprinted in the Appendix) requires mandatory testing of furniture, both with open flame and cigarette ignition sources. Finished furniture or mockup testing is voluntary, but labeling is mandatory. The state of California petitioned the commission to have their standard adopted as a federal standard. The commission denied the petition because it was felt that the effectiveness of a standard in predicting the ignition resistance of upholstered furniture was impossible without a mandatory mockup test method.

PROPOSED MANDATORY FEDERAL UPHOLSTERED FURNITURE FLAMMABILITY STANDARD

This mandatory standard would apply to all furniture manufactured, reupholstered, or imported for sale in the United States. Rather than design oriented, the proposed standard is performance-related in concept. A performance approach was proposed for the following reasons:

1. Complying products may be developed with maximum flexibility.

2. It allows for the use of new and improved materials dictated by current technology.

3. It prevents a major disruption by not requiring all manufacturers to use the same components.

Compliance Requirements

1. *Component* testing to establish the classification of fabrics based on their resistance to ignition from cigarettes burned on the fabric surface. Fabric manufacturers will assume major responsibility for this testing. Testing is required at intervals not exceeding 12 months.

2. *Mockup* testing to determine resistance of the entire furniture unit to ignition from cigarettes. Manufacturers and importers of furniture and reupholsterers of furniture for sale will be responsible for conducting mockup tests. They shall also be responsible for testing and classification of fabrics which are nonclassified, i.e., fabrics not normally intended for use as upholstery, but specified by designers cn a COM basis, or fabrics which the manufacturer had in inventory prior to the effective date of the standard.

3. *Labeling* required for compliance with this standard. Fabric manufacturers or importers of upholstery fabrics will be responsible for affixing a label which identifies (a) the

fabric classification (A, B, C, or D) and (b) the test number upon which the fabric was classified. The manufacturer or importer of furniture must also label each piece of furniture and identify (a) the fabric name, (b) fabric classification, (c) the mockup test number. All labels would state "Smolder resistant, CPSC Standard FF-6-78." Labels would also be required on non-compliance furniture produced or imported for a period of two years after the standard went into effect. This label would warn consumers that the furniture did not comply with the standard.

4. *Recordkeeping* required by all manufacturers and importers of furniture and upholstery fabric. Reupholsterers must also keep records on all furniture sold.

Effective Date of Standard

This standard would be effective 12 months after promulgation of the final standard. Other time factors would include:

1. Furniture manufactured or imported for a two-year period after the standard became effective would be allowed for sale. This provision was made to allow existing inventories of noncomplying furniture and fabric to be depleted without undue economic loss. Furniture would be labeled as noncomplying.

2. A three-year period would be allowed for manufacturers, suppliers, and trade organizations to develop and improve technology that would allow furniture to be constructed in compliance with the standard.

3. Fabrics produced after the proposed standard became effective would be tested and classified.

Enforcement of the Standard

The standard would be enforced by the inspection of the industry to assure that testing, labeling, and recordkeeping requirements were being observed.

PROPOSED VOLUNTARY UPHOLSTERY FLAMMABILITY STANDARDS

The majority of upholstery fabric and furniture manufacturers provided information to CPSC on industry efforts to improve the ignition resistance of furniture. Several organizations submitted voluntary standards as alternatives to a mandatory standard. The following organizations represented the upholstery industry:

1. Business and Institutional Furniture Manufacturer's Association (BIFMA)

2. Upholstered Furniture Action Council (UFAC)

3. American Textile Manufacturers Institute, Inc. (ATMI)

4. National Cotton Council of America (NCCA)

5. Fire Retardant Chemicals Association (FRCA)

A summary of the proposed voluntary standards will help designers understand the differences in approach.[21] The text of the California standards are included in Appendix B for those wishing to make a more detailed comparison.

Business and Institutional Furniture Manufacturer's Assocation

BIFMA proposed a voluntary standard. This standard includes an open flame test (CS 191-53) for components and a cigarette ignition resistance test for furniture assemblies (mockups). The assembly test is similar to the CPSC Draft Proposed Standard and the State of California Standard. BIFMA employed the Underwriters Laboratories to develop the test. There are no plans for monitoring the compliance of this voluntary standard.

Most of the commercial and institutional furniture now produced by members of BIFMA does comply with this standard. Most furniture complying with this standard would probably not ignite from a cigarette because a large percentage of thermoplastic fabrics are used in commercial furniture.

Upholstered Furniture Action Council

UFAC proposed a voluntary practices program. This program is based on constructive criteria with supporting component tests to remove or upgrade problem components in critical areas, such as welt cord (seam areas). This standard divides all fabric into two classes based on fiber content rather than ignition performance:

Class I: Fabrics containing 50 percent or more of thermoplastic fiber: polyolefin, nylon, polyester, acrylic, acetate, and triacetate, plus other fabrics which will comply to another test still under development. (Class I is equal to CPSC classes A and B.)

Class II: All other fabrics. (Equal to class C and D of the CPSC proposed standard.)

The testing for the standard would be done by the suppliers, not the furniture manufacturers.

In some instances, the commission felt this program underestimated the probability of ignition and could result in acceptance of hazardous furniture. And in some instances, this program overestimated the probability of ignition and added unnecessary cost and construction burdens to furniture manufacturers. The only measurement of compliance would be the number of "UFAC Recommended" labels sold.

American Textile Manufacturers Institute, Inc.

ATMI supports the voluntary concept of the UFAC program. They do, however, prefer fabric classification by performance rather than fiber content (UFAC). They have developed a modification of the CPSC fabric classification test and have been working on other test methods.

National Cotton Council of America

NCCA supported the concept of a voluntary program rather than a mandatory standard. Their research on smolder-resistance cotton batting and cellulosic upholstery fabrics shows promising results. They believe several more years are needed for research of the problem.

Fire Retardant Chemicals Association

FRCA supports the concept of a voluntary standard if a suitable one can be established. They believe component testing for both smoldering combustion and open flame ignition would produce safer furniture.

ECONOMIC CONSIDERATIONS OF A MANDATORY FLAMMABILITY STANDARD

Prior to publishing a proposed standard, the Consumer Product Safety Commission must consider the type and number of products that would be affected and the general economic impact on the following areas: (1) domestic business, (2) international trade, (3) projected industry cost to test and upgrade products, (4) projected elimination of products, (5) projected enforcement costs, (6) consumer cost.

Upholstered Products: Types and Quantity

For the purpose of identifying the types of furniture that would fall within the scope of the standard, the commission classified upholstered furniture into three major categories: residential, business and institutional, and juvenile. Also included are the market areas of rental, reupholstered, and imported furniture.

Residential Furniture. This represents the largest segment of the furniture market. Since the major number of reported upholstery fire incidents occur in residential situations, it is estimated that 85 to 90 percent of the furniture manufactured for residential use will be subject to the standard. Production figures in 1977 estimate the shipment of approximately 14 million chairs and 9.5 million sofas valued at $5.8 billion (retail).

Business and Institutional Furniture. This claims approximately 10 to 15 percent of the total furniture market. Most of this furniture is upholstered in heavy-weight thermoplastics and vinyl fabrics that would meet the proposed cigarette ignition standard. It had been proposed that this furniture classification not be included in the scope of the standard, but the CPSC felt this would complicate enforcement of the standard for the following reasons:

1. It would be impossible to distinguish between a product covered by the standard and one that was exempted, i.e., their basic similarity in function and design.

2. A product exempted from the standard may be purchased as a substitute for a product covered by the standard.[22]

Juvenile Upholstered Furniture. This is manufactured from the same types of components used in residential furniture; therefore it was reasoned that this furniture would present the same flammability hazards. Prior to the mattress flammability standard in 1972, the juvenile manufacturers petitioned the courts to exclude crib mattresses. This petition was based on the concept that since children do not smoke, it is not appropriate to include children's items under a standard dealing with cigarette ignition. The courts ruled that even though children do not smoke, an adult might drop a cigarette on a crib mattress. The commission denied an exemption request for the same reasons discussed in regard to business and institutional furniture.

Rental Furniture. This may or may not fall under the scope of the standard. Approximately $200 million was spent in 1977 on furniture rentals. The concept is based on rental cycles (usually seven to nine months) in which the furniture is rented and then returned to a warehouse for cleaning and repair and then rented again. The average rental life of this furniture is estimated to be two years, after which the furniture is sold through a return sales outlet. The commission has expressed concern over the label retention problem; i.e., all complying furniture would be labeled at the time of manufacture, but in the case of rental furniture, the labels may accidentally be removed during rental, which would prevent the resale of the furniture at a later date. (Under the proposed standard, furniture may not be sold or resold without a compliance label.)

Reupholstered Furniture. This would be covered by the standard if the reupholstered furniture is intended for resale. If a designer contracts with an upholsterer to recover and restructure a chair for personal use, with no intent to resell, the fabric selection would not be subject to the standard. But anyone who reupholsters for resale would be responsible for the testing, labeling (either complying or noncomplying), and maintaining the necessary records. Minor repairs that do not alter the fabric or filling content would not be included in the standard.

Imported Furniture. This is included in the proposed standard. All manufacturers and importers of upholstered furniture would be responsible for testing, labeling, and maintaining records.

Effects on Suppliers of Materials to the Upholstery Industry

Another large group of manufacturers directly affected by the proposed upholstery flammability standard are the suppliers of fabrics, cushioning, and padding materials. Fabric suppliers include (1) the fabric mills, (2) fabric finishers, (3) producers of plastic upholstery materials, (4) suppliers of other materials, such as leather, (5) suppliers of decorative trims. The cushioning and padding industry is composed of (1) suppliers of natural materials and (2) suppliers of synthetic materials.

These manufacturers would be involved in upgrading the upholstery components they produce and providing proof of each fabric's ability to resist ignition from cigarettes. Fabric manufacturers have already successfully proven the effectiveness of flame retardants on many textiles.

Figure 11.10 provides an overview of the materials and products that are necessary for the production of upholstered furniture.[23]

Projected Industry Costs

Major cost to industry will involve testing, recordkeeping, and research to upgrade various fabrics and fillers to meet standard requirements. The proposed federal standard would require fabric mills to conduct tests on their products, and the manufacturers of upholstered furniture would be required to conduct mockup tests of the total product.

Fabric Classification Testing Costs. It has been estimated that each fabric mill would be responsible for testing between 2,500 to 3,750 upholstery fabrics. Each classification test will cost approximately $16 to $17, which would represent a total cost of $4.4 to $6.9 million. It has also been estimated that about 1 percent of production furniture may be upholstered in fabric not intended as upholstery, and the additional testing of this fabric would bring the total testing cost to between $8 and $11 million. The proposed standard would require annual testing, but the commission projects a decrease in testing cost as some fabrics are dropped and others become exempt from re-testing.

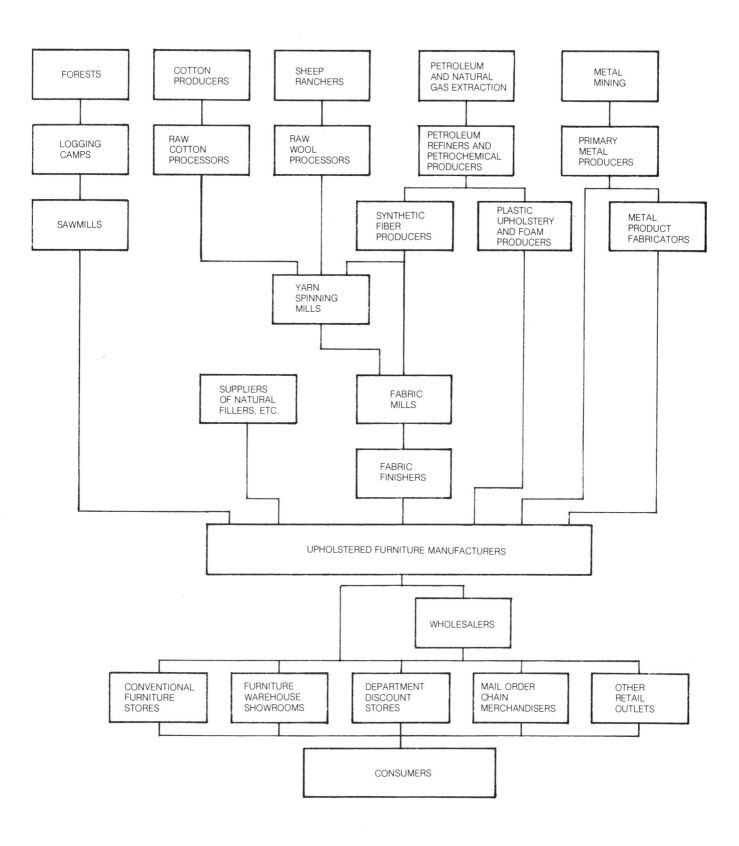

Figure 11.10 Typical flows of selected materials and products to and from upholstered furniture manufacturers. Source: Charles Smith, "Profile of Selected Groups Supplying Fabrics and Cushioning Materials to the Upholstered Furniture Industry," 1978.

Mockup Testing Costs. Manufacturers of upholstered furniture have compared the cost of doing the testing in their own plants or contracting with an independent testing laboratory. It was found that laboratories' testing would cost between $55 and $65 per test and amount to an annual total of $8 to $9 million the first year. The testing could be conducted in-house, but would involve building the testing facility, supplying storage areas, and adding qualified people to the staff to conduct the testing. Again the commission estimated that these testing costs will be lower in subsequent years as combinations of construction components are improved and fabrics are upgraded in flammability resistance.

Recordkeeping Costs. Industry has estimated that the cost may range from $1,000 annually for small firms to $10,000 annually for large firms. This cost includes the additional personnel and office space required. Total industry costs would range between $3 and $5 million per year. Firms having data processing equipment could probably reduce time and cost factors.

Consumer Cost
Ultimately the increased cost will be passed on the consumer. On a piece-by-piece basis, average manufacturing cost increases on a typical chair will be between $1.75 to $2.65 (wholesale), and the retail cost will increase from $3.50 to $5.30 per chair. On sofas the increased retail cost will range from $6.60 to $10. These figures represent a 2 or 3 percent increase, amounting to a total cost of between $57 to $87 million. Compared with the annual economic losses resulting from upholstery fires, the commission projects that the reduction in losses will more than compensate for the increased furniture costs. (See Table 11.6.)

Government Cost of Enforcement
The expense of establishing a new standard can be quite high. The federal agency responsible for the standard must also be responsible for conducting seminars and training sessions to educate the industry on matters of compliance. Additional training sessions must also be conducted for the agency field investigators. These seminars are estimated to involve 1,000 staff hours.

Inspections of test sites, mockup designs, and recordkeeping will require about 25 hours per inspection, and if laboratory testing of a random fabric sample is required, the time involved could total 34 hours.

Inspections during initial enforcement of a standard that do not show compliance usually involve 25 percent of the firms visited. These firms require an additional 30 hours of staff time, and if litigation is pursued, an additional 450 hours may be required.

TABLE 11.6 SUMMARY OF POSSIBLE COST INCREASES

Fabric classification testing costs	$ 8,000,000 to $10,900,000
Mockup testing costs	7,700,000 to 9,100,000
Costs of improving smolder resistance of substrates	18,100,000 to 33,100,000
Costs of backcoating 50% of D fabrics	12,400,000 to 17,300,000
Costs of using foil barriers on 10% of D fabric constructions	7,800,000 to 11,300,000
Recordkeeping costs	3,000,000 to 5,000,000
Total	$57,000,000 to $86,700,000

The commission estimates that the initial inspections will involve about one hundred firms. The total initial compliance program would require 3,500 hours of field time and approximately 1,150 hours of headquarter time.

DESIGNERS' GUIDELINES FOR THE SPECIFICATIONS OF UPHOLSTERED FURNITURE
The upholstery flammability standards discussed in this chapter have produced extensive research and information that can be applied by the designer in making specifications decisions. The following factors should be considered:

1. Care should be taken to use correct terminology when specifying for flammability resistance. In 1974 the Federal Trade Commission warned that certain cellular plastic products may present serious hazards in case of fire. These products were identified as polyurethane foam, polystyrene foam, polyvinyl chloride foam, ABS foam, cellulose acetate foam, epoxy foam, phenolic foam, polyethylene foam, polypropylene foam, urea foam, inomer foam, silicone foam, and foamed latex.

   The commission warned the manufacturers of these products to "cease and desist from using, publishing or encouraging others to use, publish or disseminate directly or indirectly, orally or in writing with reference to any test or standard, such descriptive terminology or expressions as 'Non-Burning,' 'Self-Extinguishing,' 'Non-Combustible,' or any other term, expression, product designation or trade name of substantially the same meaning." Manufacturers were also warned that any reference made to a numerical flame-spread rating must be accompanied by the following statement:

   > This numerical flame spread rating is not intended to reflect hazards presented by this or any other material under actual fire conditions.[24]

   In the opinion of the FTC, cellular plastics will produce a significantly higher flame spread in an actual fire condition. Therefore designers should be cautious about specifying these materials as furniture components. The manufacturer should be consulted regarding the intended use.

2. The specification of upholstered furniture for commercial and institutional use requires that designers be aware of particular installations that may present special fire hazards:
   a. Areas where smoking is permitted.
   b. Installation that may accommodate seating for extended periods of time (one hour or more):
      (1) Transportation seating: planes, buses, rapid transit systems.
      (2) Transportation terminals.
      (3) Cocktail lounges.
      (4) Restaurants.
      (5) Lounge areas in public buildings such as dormitories and hotels.
   c. Areas where the lighting level is low, such as cocktail lounges and many restaurants.
   d. Live-in accommodations that include bedding as well as seating, such as hotels, motels, dormitories, nursing or retirement homes.

3. Any of these commercial and institutional situations or a combination of all four factors (smoking, extended periods of seating, live-in, and low lighting levels) should require special upholstery flammability considerations:

   a. Fabric should be specified with a high thermoplastic content or a form of flame-retardant or heat barrier.

   b. Tufting or other decorative surface treatment should be limited to vertical surfaces. Tufting used on a horizontal seat and arm provides a critical area where a cigarette may lodge and burn unnoticed in a dimly lighted area (cocktail lounge or restaurant).

   c. Welt cording should be composed of a treated material or PVC because it also provides a crevice in which a cigarette may lodge. Specify welt cording only where necessary.

   d. Seams that are used across the horizontal seat area as a decorative treatment (square or diamond shapes) should be avoided because these seams tend to pull loose under heavy wear. This exposes the inner filling material to possible ignition from a cigarette.

   e. When possible, specify seating in which the back area and horizontal seat area are separated by 1 in. (2.5 cm). This will provide one less area or crevice in which a cigarette may lodge.

   f. Upholstery filling materials should be considered in relation to the fabric selected as the outer covering. Heat barriers, such as liners, should not be specified in seating that may be subject to vandalism (slashing or cutting) because this will render the liner ineffective.

The following summary based on tests made by the National Bureau of Standards gives *suggested* construction combinations that may be considered in specification decisions.

Summary of Findings: Constructions

To summarize the relationships among upholstery fabrics, filling materials, and constructions, descriptions of assemblies that are *expected* to provide acceptable cigarette ignition resistance are listed below (based on CPSC classification):

1. Class A (10–15 percent of the market) Most constructions and filling materials can be used.

2. Class B (25–30 percent of the market) Conventional urethane foam, polyester fiberfill, adequately treated cotton batting, and various barrier materials over untreated cotton can be used. Careful selection of the welt cord may be needed for additional protection in some foam-to-foam crevice locations.

3. Class C (20–25 percent of the market) If class C fabrics are upgraded by changes in fiber content, backcoating, or chemical treatment, construction materials could be used as described above for class A or B, as appropriate. Otherwide, class C fabrics generally perform well over urethane foam, treated cotton batting, and *polyester* fiberfill. The proper selection of welt cord, however, is critical to the performance of the welt edges of cushions and crevices. Barrier materials such as polyester, aluminum materials, and neoprene can also be used effectively.

4. Class D (25–35 percent of the market) Unless class D fabrics can be upgraded by changes in the fiber content, backcoating, or chemical treatment, very few acceptable construction techniques are available. Class D fabrics are the most prone to smoldering of all the classes, and exceptional interaction of the filling materials is required to overcome this characteristic. Polyester fiberfill as a substrate does not appear to be effective in preventing smoldering of some class D fabrics. More efficient heat barriers and heat-dissipating materials (such as aluminized barriers and PVC welt cords) used in immediate contact with class D fabrics at vulnerable areas of the construction appear to be viable alternatives, although the practicality of these systems has not been totally evaluated.[25]

SPECIFICATION CHECKLIST FOR FLAME-RESISTANT UPHOLSTERED FURNITURE

When specifying furniture from a particular manufacturer, request the following information:

1. The fiber content of the upholstery covering.

2. When the fabric is labeled as "flame resistant," request information on the type of flame retardant used.
   _____ Chemical (semidurable or durable)
   _____ Fiber blend
   _____ Backcoating
   _____ Other

3. What material is used in the welt cording?
   _____ Paper (treated or untreated)
   _____ Cotton cord (treated or untreated)
   _____ PVC
   _____ Other

4. When fabric is to be specified COM, determine the following:
   _____ Will the fabric accept a chemical retardant treatment?
   _____ Will the treatment adversely affect the soil resistance of the fabric?
   _____ Will any shrinkage occur?
   _____ Does the flame-retardant chemical meet the required standards of the authority with jurisdiction? Currently, some states and local authorities only approve certain chemicals applied in approved laboratories.

5. What filling materials are used in the following areas?
   _____ Horizontal areas (seats, arms, and top back)
   _____ Vertical areas
   _____ Deck area
   _____ Loose cushions

6. Will any of the above materials be treated with a flame retardant?

7. If a heat barrier is to be used, request information on the type and how it will be applied.
   _____ Type
   _____ Liner
   _____ Backcoating
   _____ Encased around filling

8. What will the addition of a flame retardant to the following components cost?
   _____ Upholstery fabric
   _____ Filling material
   _____ Welt cording

12 SPECIFICATION OF COMMERCIAL FURNITURE

In view of increasing safety concerns and the accompanying liability factors involved in the specification of furnishings, it is important that designers maintain quality control through performance evaluation of furniture components. This chapter will classify types of commercial furnishings, survey current performance testing, and provide guidelines for maintenance and life cycle costing.

COMMERCIAL FURNITURE CLASSIFICATION

Furniture manufactured for commercial installation is best classified by use rather than style. Four major categories can be established to include the following: (1) office furniture, such as (a) open office systems, (b) standard office furniture, and (c) executive office furniture; (2) seating; (3) tables; and (4) accessories.

Open Office Systems

Because open office systems entail more precise specification considerations than other types of office furnishings, more detailed information on it is given here. Open office systems are usually based on three methods of component assembly. (1) One system utilizes freestanding vertical screens with conventional office furniture. (2) The second type makes use of panels linked together to become self-stabilizing walls or dividers from which work surfaces and storage components are suspended. The panels vary in size from 30 to 78 in. (76.2 to 198.1 cm) in height and 22 to 48 in. (55.9 to 121.9 cm) in width. (3) A third method employs self-contained solid L-shaped wooden or steel units that serve both as storage components and dividers. The second and third systems approaches frequently incorporate lighting components. (See Figure 12.1.) Each system is usually composed of the following:

Workstations. These are semienclosed areas that may accommodate one or more people. The size of workstations is generally based on the functional needs of the occupant and may be classified as clerical, secretarial, accounting, legal, supervisory, word processing, middle management, and executive. Figure 12.2 shows some general configurations and average sizes of workstations and worksurfaces. It is usually recommended that a percentage of supervisory workstations be provided with a greater measure of privacy to accommodate discussion of confidential matters.

1. Work surfaces, primary and secondary level surfaces
    Panel supported
    Floor supported
  Tilted surfaces
    Panel supported
    Floor supported
  Mobile, pull-out surfaces

2. Storage components
  Filing units
    Panel supported
    Mobile
  Drawer units
  Shelf and overhead storage
  Wardrobes

3. Lighting components
  Integrated
    Ambient
    Task
  Freestanding lighting

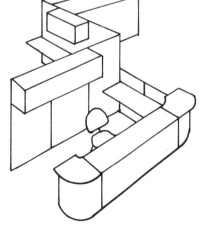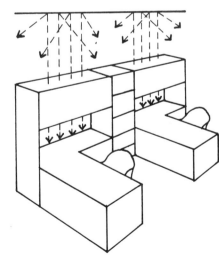

SYSTEM TYPE 1   SYSTEM TYPE 2   SYSTEM TYPE 3

Figure 12.1 Types of open office systems.

4. Utilities
   Internal raceways
   Overhead power connections
   Floor recessed
   Ganged outlet strips

5. Accessories
   Pin-up surfaces for display
   Modesty or privacy panels
   Coat racks
   Draw fittings
   Chalk boards

EVALUATING OPEN OFFICE SYSTEMS

In the past several years the abundant production of open office systems has created a perplexing problem for designers. Reaching a decision on which particular system will best meet the needs of a client is often complicated by the complexity of components and similarities between systems. For example, each manufacturer offers variations of the following components:

Workstation configurations

Acoustic controls

Accessories

Lighting components

Methods of integrating utilities

The problem is further complicated by the fact that a system designed by one manufacturer is rarely interchangeable with any other system; i.e., once a commitment is made to a particular system, a client may add to that system, but not mix components from another system. Other than complete re-installation and certain financial loss, a client is locked into a system for many years. Therefore, designers must give very serious consideration to the evaluation and specification of open office systems.

The performance approach discussed in Chapter 4 would prove very useful in establishing criteria on which to base a final specification decision. The development of a preliminary performance matrix points out major health/safety, durability, maintenance, and functional factors that should be evaluated when *comparing* open office systems (Figure 12.3). It may be necessary to develop a more detailed matrix for the evaluation of lighting and utility components, but designers should be aware that intensive research is being conducted which could make current methods of integrating lighting and electrical wiring obsolete. The flexibility of the electrical wiring system should be considered.

Performance Testing

Performance testing of open office systems has primarily been concentrated in the areas of user satisfaction, increased employee efficiency, ease of relocation, and the conservation of space and energy. Because much of this evaluation has been concerned with general user concepts and acceptance of open office systems, the research methods have involved behavioral observations, interviews, and questionnaires. Actual physical testing has been conducted on a limited number of critical components, such as vertical panels, work surfaces, and integrated lighting. Table 12.1 lists tests and minimal requirements established for the use of vertical panels by some federal agencies.

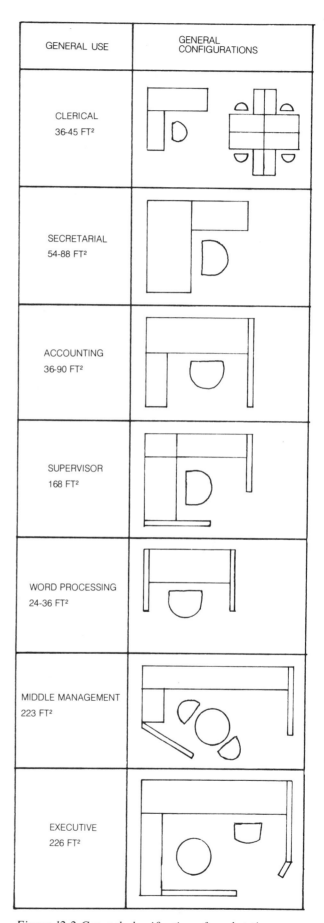

Figure 12.2 General classification of workstations.

Open Planned Office Components	Health-Safety						Durability					Maintenance				Function				
Performance Attribute	Flammability	Cause falls	Sharp projections	Anthropomorphic fit	Reflectance: glare	Handicapped use	Structurally sound	Positive attachment	Color stability	Lightfastness	Abrasion resistance	Cleanability	Component repair	Component storage	Relocation	Flexibility	Privacy	Color homogeneity	Acoustic control	Energy control
Vertical Panels	•	•	•		•	•	•	•	•	•	•	•	•	•	•	•	•	•	•	
Worksurfaces			•	•	•	•	•	•	•	•	•	•	•	•	•	•		•		
Filing	•	•	•	•		•	•	•	•			•	•	•	•	•		•		
Shelves and Storage		•	•	•	•	•	•	•	•			•	•	•	•	•		•		
Lighting					•	•	•	•	•			•	•	•	•	•				•
Seating	•	•	•	•	•	•	•	•	•	•	•	•	•	•	•	•		•		
Tables		•	•	•	•	•	•	•	•	•	•	•	•	•	•	•		•		
Other																				

Figure 12.3 Performance attributes of open plan office furniture.

Acoustics. Some tests were developed specifically to deal with open office problems; e.g., the acoustics tests PBS C.1 and C.2 evaluate the Speech Privacy Potential (SPP) between any two zones in a typical office area.[1] New terminology has also been developed to establish test parameters.

1. SPP: The voice level for which privacy is required. Through testing, the level was established at ≤60 db for conversation. The Speech Privacy Potential is derived from functional interzone planning criteria which specify the level of speech for which the system in use must provide confidential interzone privacy.

2. ISD: The Integrated Space Divider system which is composed of the following elements:
   a. Open Plan Privacy system (OPP) made up of panels providing privacy to seated people.
   b. OPP upgraded panel systems providing privacy to standing people.
   c. OPP support system (acoustical treatment on exterior walls).
   d. OPP privacy interface system (core walls).
   e. OPP room partitions, ceiling heights, doors.

3. ICB: The Integrated Ceiling and Background system which is composed of five subsystems:
   a. Acoustical materials
   b. Suspended ceiling system
   c. Luminaires
   d. HVAC terminals (air distribution system)
   e. Background noise distribution

4. NC: The background noise generated by the system-in-use condition. It is also considered "electroacoustic" because it includes noise from the luminaires in the ICB system. The NC background must fulfill its masking function without interfering with communication. NC_{40} is the single number rating used to describe the upper limit of background noise. If the NC rating is above 40, conversation will be obstructed.

5. NIC: Noise Isolation Class, which provides an index number for rating a measured set of noise reductions.

The PBS C.1 is considered a "subjective" test because it makes use of a jury of listeners rather than instruments to measure the acoustical quality of an open office space. The test area is made to simulate a typical open office situation with ceilings between 8'10" and 9'10" (2.6 and 3 m) in height, floors carpeted, and a speaker situated 6' (1.8 m) from a panel barrier. The PBS C.2 test is very similar except that the listeners are provided with a background-making sound device which they adjust to attain adequate SPP during the test.

Although most panel systems are currently listed with an NRC rating (refer to Chapter 7 for more information on NRC), designers should question the method used to determine the NRC rating; i.e., does the test method simulate actual use conditions?

Specification for acoustic levels in open office planning should include consideration of all the components of the space, such as the carpet, suspended ceiling, core walls, luminaires, and levels of background noise. The General Services Administration performance specification states the criteria in this manner:

The subsystem shall not impair the SPP (no less than

TABLE 12.1 PERFORMANCE ATTRIBUTES OF OPEN OFFICE PANELS

Attribute	Tests	Minimal Federal Performance Requirements
1. Flammability		
a. Flame spread	ASTM E-84	Flame spread ≤ 25 unsprinklered Flame spread ≤ 200 sprinklered
b. Smoke	NBS 708	Specific optical density ≤ 150
c. Potential heat	Test based on ASTM proceedings Vol. 61, 1961, pp. 1337-47	≤ 40,000 BTU
2. Acoustics		
a. Airborne sound	PBS-C.1 (Subjective) PBS C.2 (Objective test)	SPP ≤ 60 in open plan areas SPP ≤ 70 in rooms without doors NIC + (NC ≤ 40) ≤ 60 in open plan
b. Impact sound	Footfall test IB1-I 1-1965	Mask vertical footfall sounds W/NC ≤ 40
3. Stability		
a. Resist horizontal load	ASTM 72-74	Resist load of 50 lb Support 40 lb per linear ft of shelving
b. Resist tipping		
c. Resist impact	ASTM 72-74	Resist 30-lb impact. Horizontal force of 100 lb applied 5" above floor
4. Durability		
a. Abrasion	ASTM E 72-74	Resist abrasion
b. Color-fastness	Fadeometer	No color change after 50 hours at 150°F
c. Chemical resistance	FTM 141 A, Method 6081	Resist staining and damage

Figure 12.4 Task ambient furniture integrated lighting. Reproduced with permission of Knoll International.

TABLE 12.2 RECOMMENDED ILLUMINATION LEVELS FOR OFFICE TASKS*

Task or Area	Visual Difficulty (VDF)	Design Level (FC)	Average Level Range (FC)
Service or public areas	–	15	12-18
Circulation areas within office space, but not at workstations	–	30	24-36
Normal office work, reading, writing, etc.	1-39	50	40-60
Office work, prolonged, visually difficult or critical in nature	40-59	75	60-90
Office work, prolonged, visually difficult and critical in nature	60 & up	100	80-120

*See Table 12.3 for Visual Difficulty Ratings.

Source: GSA.

≤60) for any two zones in any space in the typical office area. No element in the ICB system shall impair the SPP (no less than ≤60). The ISD shall also perform as noted above. . . .[2]

Furniture-Integrated Lighting. The increased interest in conserving energy during the last decade prompted research into more efficient methods of lighting office environments. Previous theories about lighting had been based on the concept that a high quantity of light resulted in a better quality of light. Sy Shemitz was one of the first lighting engineers to begin working with the idea of localizing light sources directly over the work surface, thus eliminating the need for high levels of general lighting. Integrating task and general (ambient) lighting with the furniture components of a workstation became a viable alternative to the serious energy problems that developed in the midseventies (Figure 12.4). By the late seventies almost every manufacturer of office systems was utilizing the concept of task/ambient lighting. This was prompted, to a great extent, by the publicity surrounding the GSA Energy Conservation Demonstration Project which was installed in 1977. The GSA performance specification provided a criterion for low electrical energy consumption through the use of task-lit systems furniture. The specification established the following requirements:

Provide lighting system with low electrical energy consumption

Criterion: The lighting system's electrical energy consumption shall be less than 2 watts per square foot, for the total number of people within the project's square footage. (Energy per person = EPP.)

Total wattage of all luminaires in service in input watts divided by the net floor area in square feet equals watts per square foot.

$$\frac{\text{Square footage (12,000)}}{\text{Total number of people (68)}} = 176$$

$176 \times$ watts per square foot = EPP[3]

Designers not accustomed to the specification of office systems on the basis of energy conservation and watts per square foot have found it increasingly difficult to determine which lighting system should be specified. Aspects of lighting technology, normally handled by lighting engineers, have become the selling tool of furniture manufacturers and their representatives.

Since most systems with integrated lighting have pre-engineered illumination levels for workstation tasks and offer little or no opportunity for varying those levels, knowledge concerning recommended illumination levels for various tasks could perhaps aid designers in evaluating various systems.

Table 12.2 lists the illumination levels [in footcandles (FC)] recommended for various office tasks. Designers should be aware that the design criteria are based on the visual difficulty, length of time the task is performed, and the age of the person doing the task. These three factors are considered the Visual Difficulty Factor (VDF) for office tasks and are calculated in the following manner:

$$VDF = R \times T \times F$$

where   VDF = Visual Difficulty Factor

           R = Visual Difficulty Rating of Tasks, from Table 12.3

TABLE 12.3 VISUAL DIFFICULTY RATING OF TASKS

Task Description	Visual Difficulty Rating
1. Large black object on white background	1
2. Book or magazine, printed matter, 8-point and larger	2
3. Typed original	2
4. Ink writing (script)	3
5. Newspaper text	4
6. Shorthand notes, ink	4
7. Handwriting (script) in no. 2 pencil	5
8. Shorthand notes, no. 3 pencil	6
9. Washed-out copy from copying machine	7
10. Bookkeeping	8
11. Drafting	8
12. Telephone directory	12
13. Typed carbon, fifth copy	15

Source: GSA.

T = Duration of the particular visual tasks for day, hours

F = Multiplying factor for an aged person with uncorrectable eyesight problems. Use F = 1.5 for people over 50 years of age[4]

For a person spending five hours doing bookkeeping and an additional four hours doing shorthand, the Visual Difficulty Factors (Table 12.3) would be determined by multiplying the length of time by the VDF rating. For example,

$$5 \text{ hr} \times 8 + 3 \text{ hr} \times 4 = 52 \text{ VDF}$$

According to Table 12.5, 75 footcandles should be provided. If the person doing the work is over 50 years old, then the VDF should be modified to 52 × 1.5, or 78. This would change the required footcandles from 75 to a total of 100. The multiplying factor (F) cannot usually be applied in the early design phase because the personnel workstation assignments may not be known, but the specified office system should be able to provide for flexibility after installation.

Tables 12.2 and 12.5 also list recommended illumination levels (general lighting) for circulation areas within offices and other areas within an average office building. The last column on these tables gives the range that can be considered equivalent to the design levels when actually measured in the office after installation.

OFFICE ENERGY CONSERVATION

The following twelve principles for energy conservation through lighting of commercial offices recommended by GSA should provide additional design criteria which designers can use in specifying open office systems:

1. Design lighting for the task
   a. Provide the required illumination for visual tasks in the working areas only and appropriate lower levels in the general areas, such as corridors, storage, and circulation.

TABLE 12.4 LIGHTING COSTS USING TASK LIGHTING

Step 1: $1.25 \text{ w/sq ft} \times 10,000 \text{ sq ft} = \dfrac{12,500 \text{ w}}{1000 \text{ w/kw}} = 12.5 \text{ kw}$

Step 2: 12.5 kw × 2600 bh/y = 32,500 kwh

Step 3: 32,500 kwh × \$.0775 = \$2518.75 annual cost of electric energy for lighting

Lighting Cost Using Conventional Ceiling Systems:

The same three-step process can be used by simply changing the 1.25 w/sq ft for task lighting to the 5 w/sq ft normally consumed for ceiling systems. However, since that figure represents the only difference in the equation, ratios can be easily used as follows:

Ratio is 5 to 1.25 = 4

4 × 2518.75 = \$10,075 annual cost of electric energy for lighting

Air Conditioning Costs Related to Task Lighting:

Every watt of electric energy converted to heat = 3.413 BTU

1 ton of air conditioning = 12,000 BTU/year

Tons of air conditioning = $\dfrac{12,500 \text{ w} \times 3413 \text{ BTU}}{12,000}$ = 3.55 tons

A/C power (kw) = 3.55 × 1.2 (factor for kw/ton) or 4.72 kw

Step 2: 4.72 kw × 2600 = 11,092 kwh

Step 3: 11,092 × .0775 = \$859.65 annual cost for air conditioning using task lighting

Air Conditioning Cost Related to Ceiling Systems:

5 w/sq ft × 10,000 = $\dfrac{50,000}{1000 \text{ w/kw}}$ = 50 kw

$\dfrac{50,000 \times 3.413 \text{ BTU}}{12,000 \text{ BTU/ton}}$ = 14.2 tons

Step 2: 12 kw × 2600 = 44,369 kwh/yr

Step 3: 44,369 × .0775 = \$3438.60 annual cost for air conditioning using ceiling systems

Total Savings for Annual Energy Costs Alone: \$10,105.20

Total Savings per Square Foot Is Approximately \$1

Source: Knoll International.

TABLE 12.5 ILLUMINATION LEVELS FOR OTHER AREAS

Areas	Design Level (FC)	Range (FC)
Auditoriums	30	20-40
Cafeteria	30	20-40
Conference rooms	30	25-35
Corridors, lobbies and means of egress	15	10-18
Kitchen (average)	50	30-70
Mechanical rooms (general areas)	10	5-15
Storage areas (general storage)	10	5-15
Storage areas (fine details required)	30	25-35
Toilets	20	15-30

Source: GSA.

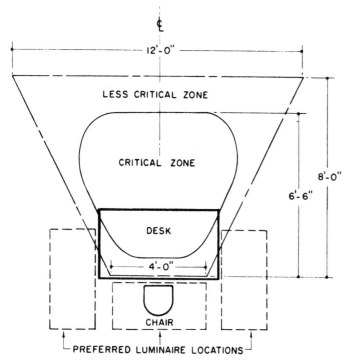

Figure 12.5 Nonuniform office lighting with direct luminaries. Source: GSA.

f. Reduce lighting requirements for hazards by:
   (1) Use of light fixtures close to and focused on the hazard.
   (2) Increased contrast of hazards; i.e., paint stair treads and risers white with black nosings.

g. Try to obtain variance from existing codes requiring specific lighting levels by varying the qualitative and quantitative requirements for a specific application.

3. Select the most efficient luminaires
  a. Consider the use of polarized lenses to improve the quality of lighting at task level.
  b. Consider the use of ballasts which can accommodate different types of High-Intensity Discharge (HID) bulbs.
  c. Consider the use of high-frequency lighting to reduce wattage per lumen output. Additional benefits are reduced ballast heat loss and longer lamp life.

4. Select the most efficient light sources
  a. Consider using 250-watt mercury vapor lamps and metal-halide lamps in place of 500-watt incandescent lamps for special applications.
  b. Use lamps with higher lumens per watt input:
   (1) One 8-ft (2.4-m) fluorescent lamp versus two 4-ft (1.2-m) lamps.
   (2) One 4-ft lamp versus two 2-ft (.6-m) lamps.
   (3) U-tube lamps versus two individual lamps.
   (4) Fluorescent lamps in place of all incandescent lamps, except for very close task lighting.

5. Select proper room characteristics
  a. Consider the use of landscape office planning to improve lighting efficiency. Approximately 25 percent less wattage per footcandle on tasks is possible.
  b. Use light colors for walls, floors, and ceilings to increase reflectance.
  c. Lower the ceiling or mounting height of luminaires to increase the level of illumination with less wattage.
  d. Select furniture and interior appointments that do not have glassy surfaces or give peculiar reflections (see Glossary).
  e. Avoid the use of glossy surfaces on the task and its surroundings.
  f. Use high-reflectance finishes on vertical surfaces; 50 to 60 percent reflectance is recommended on matte finished walls; 30 percent for carpet.

6. Provide proper controls for the luminaires
  a. Install switches for lights near the windows so that lights may be turned off in accordance with the amount of daylight available at any given time.
  b. Luminaires should be selectively switched according to possible groupings of working tasks at different hours.
  c. Use multiple lamp luminaires so that one lamp may be switched off during different times of the day.
  d. Design switch circuits to permit turning off unused or unnecessary lights.
  e. Evaluate the use of low-wattage (24 volts or lower) switching systems to obtain maximum switching capability.
  f. Provide times to turn off lights automatically in remote or seldom-used areas.

b. Reduce the wattage required for each specific task by a review of user needs and methods of providing illumination (see Table 12.4).

c. Consider only the amount of illumination required for the specific task, taking into account the duration, character, and user performance required.

d. Group similar tasks together for optimum conservation of energy per floor.

e. Consider the use of greater contrast between tasks and background lighting, such as 8 to 1 and 10 to 1.

2. Select proper lighting systems
  a. Illuminate tasks with fixtures built into furniture and maintain low-intensity lighting elsewhere.
  b. Consider wall washers and special illumination for features such as plants and murals in order to maintain proper contrast ratios without the use of overhead lighting.
  c. For horizontal tasks or duties, consider fixtures whose main lighting component is oblique, and then locate for maximum Equivalent Spherical Illumination (ESI) footcandle on the task. The concept of Equivalent Spherical Illumination was developed to express the effective illumination level on a visual task subject to veiling reflections. The ESI value is highly directional in concept and is very difficult to express without defining the exact angle from which the task is being viewed and the relative positions between the task and the luminaires (Figure 12.5). At present, the only practical method of calculating the true ESI values on the task is by using computer programs. Designers should consult lighting engineers on this matter.
  d. Avoid decorative floodlighting and display lighting.
  e. Use fixtures that give high-contrast rendition at task level.

7. Utilize daylight
   a. Use natural illumination in areas when a net energy conservation gain is possible without affecting the heating or cooling loads.
   b. Provide exterior reflectors at windows for more effective internal illumination.

8. Use thermally controlled luminaires
   If permitted by codes, use luminaires which will allow room air to flow through the lamp compartment.

9. Keep the luminaires in good working condition
   Use high utilization and maintenance factors in design criteria and instruct users to keep fixtures clean and change lamps frequently.

10. Design electrical wiring to allow for flexibility
    a. Arrange electrical floor and wall outlets to accommodate relocation of luminaires to suit changing furniture or systems layouts.
    b. Use multilevel ballasts to permit varying lamps that can be added or removed when tasks are changed in location.

11. Optimize all operational procedures
    Control overtime working hours and schedule maintenance work in various shifts during the working day or immediately following the closure of the offices.

12. In an office without integrated furniture lighting, lay out the luminaires for visual performance rather than uniform space geometry
    a. Within the limits of the ceiling configuration, locate the luminaires as close to directly over the task as possible without creating excessive reflections.
    b. Locate luminaires just beyond the ends and working edges of the desk. Avoid locating luminaires directly in front of the visual task. Try to avoid a trapezoidal ceiling area projection; i.e., if a line were projected from the working edge of the desk vertically to the ceiling, forming a line 4 ft (1.2 m) long centered on the worker, and a line were projected parallel to and 8 ft (2.4 m) forward of this line that is 12 ft (3.6 m) long, the sides of the trapezoid would connect the ends of these two base lines (see Figure 12.5). If luminaires are kept out of this zone, there will be less reflectance on the task surface and more effective use of the illumination.
    c. The use of a checkerboard arrangement with one tube fixture placed every 50 sq ft (4.7 sq m) can result in an energy consumption of 0.92 watts per square foot. The luminaire reflector-baffle assembly could be modified for use near walls to subdue scalloping effects[5] (see Figure 12.6).[6]

LIFE CYCLE COSTING

Aside from providing better lighting and achieving the necessary conservation of energy, task/ambient lighting also combats the rising cost of energy. Calculating the life cycle cost of open planned offices includes the initial cost plus the following factors:

1. Maintenance
2. Space adjustment
3. Energy consumption

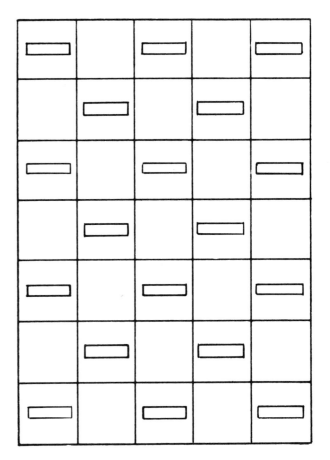

Figure 12.6 Checkerboard luminary placement. Source: GSA.

4. Luminaire relamping costs
5. Investment tax credits

Maintenance
The maintenance of office systems usually is based on a maintenance contract which can include parts repair and replacement (brackets and fasteners) and surface cleaning of panels and other surfaces. The maintenance calculation should *not* include (1) space adjustment costs; (2) janitorial services (floor cleaning); (3) relamping, reballasting, or cleaning of luminaires. Maintenance can be calculated on a yearly basis and extended to the entire expected service life of the system.

Space Adjustment Costs
Space adjustment costs include the annual cost of space changes based on the following formula:

SAC = area of change × rate of change × cost of change

The terms used in the formula are defined below:

Area of change is the estimate of the percentage of typical office space in which an office system will be installed or subject to change.

Rate of change is the estimated annual rate of planning change within the typical office space.

Cost of change includes the labor, material, equipment, and time needed to make the change. Materials or components which are left in position or stored for future use are not included in these figures. Labor costs should be itemized according to the type of assistance needed. For example, special trades such as electricians and telephone installers may be needed to deactivate power and telephones and make changes in the signal outlets. The hours and salary per hour must be included. The amount of time required varies between types of systems, but generally should average about 1/4 hr per linear foot for the furniture and panel components. If the change must be made during office hours, the downtime is important in regard to lost working time.[7]

Energy Consumption

The energy cost includes the heating and air conditioning costs (HVAC) and the cost of operating the luminaires. The air conditioning costs are directly related to the cost of lighting because the heat generated by lighting creates additional air conditioning costs. For example, for every 1,000 watts of lighting installed, an additional 341 watts of air conditioning is required. It has been estimated that 25 to 30 percent of air conditioning in office areas is consumed to off-set heat produced by lamps.

Annual air conditioning costs

1. Kilowatt hours per year = kilowatts × burning hours per year

2. Annual air conditioning costs = kilowatt hours × energy cost

Annual lighting costs

1. Kilowatts = watts per square foot × area ÷ 1,000 W/kW

2. Kilowatt hours per year = kilowatts × burning hours per year

3. Annual lighting costs = kilowatt hours × energy rate

The following case study was provided by Knoll International to illustrate the application of these principles. A hypothetical New York City firm having a typical office space of 10,000 sq ft (950 sq m), operating 12 hours per day (2,600 hours per year), and paying the New York City energy rate of $.0775 per kilowatt hour is considering the installation of task/ambient lighting at 1.25 watts per square foot. Table 12.4 shows how the energy saving would be calculated.[8]

GSA predicts, for purposes of life cycle costing evaluation, a doubling of electrical rates in five years and 5 percent increase per annum thereafter. To factor savings based on these predicted increases, multiply the savings by 1.78. The map in Figure 12.7 illustrates the variances that would occur in different parts of the country based on a difference in energy rates. Hauserman Inc. calculated these savings based on 3.02 watts/sq ft for conventional direct lighting and 1.65 watts/sq ft for task/ambient lighting. Illumination was based on 100 footcandles for both direct and indirect lighting systems.

To calculate the total initial cost savings for energy-related equipment, the following method could be used:

1. Air conditioning tonnage savings for _____ square feet = _____

2. Unit initial cost for air conditioning per ton _____

3. Savings on initial cost for air conditioning equipment_____ _____ (line 1 × line 2)

4. Air conditioning power reduction equivalent distribution equipment, such as transformers, switchgear, feeders, panel boards, and branch circuits that would be reduced in

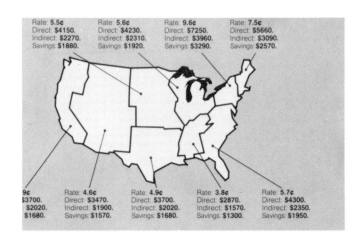

Figure 12.7 Comparative costs between direct and indirect lighting. Reproduced with permission of E.F. Hauserman Company © 1977.

size. Estimated at $150/kw (this is an approximate figure) = _____

5. Lighting power reduction for _____ sq ft = _____

6. Initial cost savings for electrical distribution equipment (for lighting equipment) that would not be required or could be reduced in size = _____ (line 5 × $150)

7. Grand total (lines 3 + 4 + 6) = _____ initial cost savings[9]

Luminaire Relamping Cost (LRC)

LRC represents the annual cost of maintaining the performance of the luminaire subsystems.

LRC = N B/R (C + i)

where   N = Number of lamps

B = Burning hours per year

R = Average rated lamp life (hours)

C = Cost per lamp (in dollars)

i = Labor cost per lamp for replacing lamps individually[10]

Investment Tax Credits

Another factor to consider in the life cycle costing of open office systems is the current tax structure which allows the owner to take a 10 percent write-off on panels and fixtures which could be considered furnishings and not part of the building structure. Depreciation would be based on seven years as personal property rather than the normal 20-year period of depreciation required for real estate. In some states task lighting may be used to obtain an investment credit as business equipment. The overall return on investment (ROI) can be sizable over a period of time. Designers may point out these factors to a client and suggest verification from a tax consultant.

SPECIFICATION GUIDELINES FOR OPEN OFFICE SYSTEMS

A matrix may prove the most useful means of comparing the various components provided by systems manufacturers. The example shown in Figure 12.8 may be expanded to include more manufacturers and components.

Manufacturer \ Components	Lighting							Storage				Type				Accessories			
	Raceway, horizontal	Vertical polls	Ganged outlet strips	Task lighting	Ambient lighting	Watts per square feet	UL approved	Files	Shelves	Cabinets: below/above	Racks	Free-standing panels	Panel hung components	Floor-standing comp.	Flame spread	Pin-up surfaces	Drawer fittings	Privacy panels	Coatracks

Figure 12.8 Systems component comparison.

The following checklist can be used when surveying available systems. Fire safety and barrier-free criteria for open office systems are provided in Chapters 13 and 14.

1. *Panels*
   a. What material is used in the core of the panel?
   b. Was a total panel mockup tested for flammability? How?
   c. For flame spread?
   d. For optical smoke density?
   e. Is the surface material treated with a flame retardant?
   f. What method was used to test the acoustic quality?
   g. Acoustic rating? NRC? NIC?
   h. Base of the panel? Adjustable? Connecting or free-standing?
   i. Are special tools needed to relocate the panels? Estimated time to relocate?
   j. Impact resistance? Test?
   k. Do the panels provide positive attachment for components?
   l. At points of attachment, do panels fully engage without rack or sway?

2. *Work Surfaces*
   a. Are all work surfaces capable of withstanding a vertical load placed at the leading edge and at midpoint between end supports of not less than 250 lb (115 kg)? Panel-suspended work surfaces should not separate from the panel under this weight.
   b. Have all work surfaces been tested to withstand the heat of lighted cigarettes without showing scorch marks?
   c. Are all work surfaces capable of being adjusted within a range of 26 to 31 in. (66 to 78.7 cm) surface height?
   d. Do all work surfaces provide adjustment of clearance between the floor and underside of 24 to 29 in. (61 to 73.7 cm)?
   e. Are work units capable of providing a knee space opening (width) of between 24 and 32 in. (61 to 81.3 cm)?

3. *Integrated Lighting*
   a. Can the illumination level be varied at an individual workstation?
   b. How flexible is the wiring?
   c. Does the system accommodate the use of more than one electrical machine per workstation? How many?
   d. How many workstations are fed off the same circuit?
   e. Are the workstations capable of providing more than one source of power?
   f. Is the secondary work surface provided with enough light? Task or ambient?
   g. Are lenses used on lighting fixtures?
   h. Will the luminaire accommodate varied types of lamps?
   i. Is the quoted wattage per square foot based on gross office space or workstation space?
   j. What is the reflectance levels of workstations components?
   k. What is the height of the ambient lighting sources? Above eye level?
   l. Is the system available without ambient components?
   m. What is the cost difference without ambient components?
   n. Does the task lighting prevent veiling reflections?
   o. Are switches located within reach of the user?
   p. Are all the electrical components approved by the Underwriters Laboratories?

4. *Storage Units*
   a. Are all operating hardware and pulls flush or fully recessed to prevent injury?
   b. Will hinged door components support a vertical force of more than 100 lb (46 kg) at the outer edge, when open?
   c. Do fully loaded drawers travel from the closed position to fully extended position without interfering with a neighboring drawer?

Figure 12.9 is a portion of a performance specification for a secretarial workstation and illustrates aspects of storage that should not be neglected when making specification decisions.[11]

SPECIFICATION OF GENERAL OFFICE FURNITURE

General office furniture is classified as desks, files, tables, credenzas, and other furniture that is not a component of open office systems.

Double Pedestal Desks

These desks are freestanding and usually have at least one file drawer and four storage drawers, and may be equipped to receive an extension that forms a secondary work surface.

Desk heights should be adjustable to accommodate people of different heights. Table 12.6 suggests appropriate height settings.[12]

Desks are not subject to any federal regulation or required testing, but private laboratories have developed methods of testing for structural strength, finish, drawer operation, and desk top serviceability. Table 12.7 shows test methods frequently used.

Based on many years of testing office equipment, the Buyers Laboratory offers the following suggestions for inspecting a desk:

1. Examine closely all finished surfaces; they should be free of objectional scratches, mars, dents, or blemishes.

2. Check for distortion of the pedestals that sometimes result when a desk is upended in shipping. Such distortion shows up in uneven spacing around the drawer fronts. Apart from appearance, this type of distortion can affect the operation of the drawers.

3. Run a pad of cheesecloth over all surfaces at or near the knee space. Any sharp edge or burred surface that scratches the cheesecloth is a hazard to clothing and skin.

4. Examine the glides at the bottom of the legs to be sure they can be turned without difficulty. On some desks it takes no more than a 6 in. (15.2 cm) drop in handling to bend the glide stems or damage the threads, making height adjustment difficult, if not impossible.

5. Make sure all drawers operate smoothly and with no interference between drawers, especially when they are only partly extended (the top edge of one drawer should not hit the lower edge of another drawer). This check is best

WORKSTATION
TYPE B
SECRETARIAL

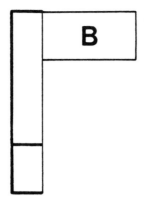

SPACE MAXIMUM
88 SQ FT

QUANTITY
7 WORKSTATIONS

All storage
(File, Closed,
Open, Box drawer
and Pencil drawer)
shall be at
maximum horizontal
or vertical dimen-
sions as space
allows. Values
in the specifica-
tions represent a
functional miminum
requirement

1.00 PRIMARY WORKSURFACE
1.01 Surface shall be a minimum of 1800 square inches.
1.02 Height shall be at task-level not to exceed 29"
      above finished floor.
1.03 Underside must accommodate components attachment.
1.04 Locate contiguous and perpendicular to leading
      edge of secondary worksurface.

2.00 SECONDARY WORKSURFACE
2.01 Surface shall be a minimum of 1296 square inches.
2.02 Height shall be at machine level not to exceed
      27" above finished floor.
2.03 Underside must accommodate components attachment.
2.04 Locate contiguous and perpendicular to primary
      worksurface.

3.00 BOX DRAWER STORAGE
3.01 Shall provide capacity of 2850 +/- 100 cubic
      inches with drawer depth not to exceed 6".
3.02 Locate contiguous to primary worksurface.

4.00 FILE STORAGE
4.01 Shall provide capacity of 180 +/- 15 filing
      inches of which not less than 125 will accommodate
      both letter and legal size.
4.02 Locate contiguous to primary and/or secondary
      worksurface.

5.00 PENCIL STORAGE
5.01 Shall provide 350 +/- 50 cubic inches.
5.02 Locate contiguous to primary worksurface.

6.00 CLOSED STORAGE
6.01 Shall provide capacity of 21,600 +/- 900 cubic
      inches.
6.02 Components shall open to allow full access to
      stored material.
6.03 Locate contiguous to secondary worksurface.

7.00 PAPER ORGANIZER
7.01 Shall provide 35 +/- 5 lineal inches with not less
      than 4 vertical dividers.
7.02 Locate in closed storage component contiguous
      to primary worksurface.

8.00 VERTICAL TACKABLE SURFACE
8.01 Width shall be equal to secondary worksurface.
      Width and height shall be from top of worksurface
      to underside of any component above or to top of
      privacy panel.
8.02 Locate contiguous to secondary worksurface.

9.00 MODESTY PANEL
9.01 Shall be width of worksurface and height shall be
      not less than 15".
9.02 Locate below primary and secondary worksurface.

10.00 PRIVACY PANEL   ✳
10.01 Shall provide for visual privacy on one side of
       workstation. Height shall be not less than 65"
       nor more than 80" above finished floor.

11.00 INTEGRATED POWER AND LIGHTING (See Article 4
       Specific Requirements and Performance Requirement
       Attribute I)
11.01 Shall provide not less than two convenience out-
       lets located above and contiguous to secondary
       worksurface.

*Post-use analysis revealed that visual privacy was desirable on three sides.

Figure 12.9 General services performance specification for office workstation. Source: GSA.

TABLE 12.6 RECOMMENDED DESK HEIGHTS

Height of Occupant	Approximate Desk Height
To 5'4"	28 1/2" (72.4 cm)*
5'4" to 5'9"	29" (73.7 cm)
5'9" to 5'11"	29 1/2" (74.9 cm)
5'11" to 6'1"	30" (76.2 cm)
6'1" and over	30 1/2" (77.5 cm)

*Glides may have to be removed.

TABLE 12.7 PERFORMANCE TESTING OF DESKS

Tests	Method	Acceptance Criteria
I. Structural strength		
Drop test	6" drop	No distortion or damage
Rack test	Tilted on two legs	No distortion or damage
Top loading	600 lb for 5 minutes	No deflection beyond 1/8" (3.2 mm)
Drawer tests	52 lb in file drawer	Withstand 50,000 openings and closings. Pull force not to exceed 3 3/4 lb. No distortion or deflection
II. Finish durability FSAA-D-00191d	Sand abrasion	No finish removal
	Bending of metal	No flaking, cracking or loss of finish adhesion
	Heat of cigarette	No scorch marks
	Chemicals applied	Withstand staining

made with the drawers loaded [about 50 lb (23 kg) for file drawers and 20 lb (9 kg) for storage drawers].

6. Examine the plastic laminate around the desk top to see that it is securely bonded to the top and edges. Also check for chipping that may have been caused by rough handling.

7. If the desk is equipped with an extension for typing, check the stability and attachment mechanism.

Filing Cabinets

Providing storage for paper materials still remains a necessary part of most office planning. The traditional means of storage has involved a vertical file cabinet with either four or five drawers. Five drawer files generally measure 57 to 60 in. (144.8 to 152.4 cm) in height and may present some problems for the user under 5'4" (162.6 cm) or a physically handicapped person. Another type of filing unit is the lateral file which allows side filing; i.e., the storage capacity is measured horizontally and the depth of the file cabinet is usually 15 to 18 in. (38.1 to 45.7 cm). These units can be stacked five high.

Specification of filing cabinets should involve a consideration of the filing needs of the client, available floor space, and the quality of workmanship in individual cabinets. In comparing vertical and lateral files, the following questions should be considered:

1. Are lateral files more economical than conventional files? Recent cost comparisons show that lateral files cost about $1.45 per linear filing foot while conventional files are $.98.

2. Do lateral files use less space? Depending on the space needs, lateral files can often fit into areas too narrow to accommodate conventional files. Used in two-drawer units, the top surfaces may also serve as a credenza, and three-drawer units are frequently used as space dividers.

Performance Testing of Lateral Files. The Business and Institutional Furniture Manufacturer's Association (BIFMA) adopted a *First Generation Voluntary Lateral File Standard* (LF-1-1978) in 1978. This standard is intended to provide manufacturers, designers, and users with a common basis for evaluating the safety, durability, and structural qualities of freestanding lateral files.

This voluntary standard recommends that manufacturers place caution labels on lateral files. These labels should contain operation and safety instructions regarding (1) cabinet leveling procedures, (2) loading techniques, (3) recommendations for weight distribution, and (4) general safety precautions.

The tests employed in this standard involve static and dynamic load applications and endurance of life test cycling. Figure 12.10 illustrates the stability test which is used to determine the stability level of the file in its least stable condition (with the top drawer extended). In this test the drawer is loaded with 2 lb per linear inch (0.91 kg per 25 mm) and a 10 lb (4.6 kg) horizontal force is applied to the normal hand pull location of the extended drawer. Test criteria require that the file withstand the pull force without tipping.

Figures 12.11 and 12.12 illustrate the file strength test which evaluates the ability of the file to support loads to which it will be subjected when in service.

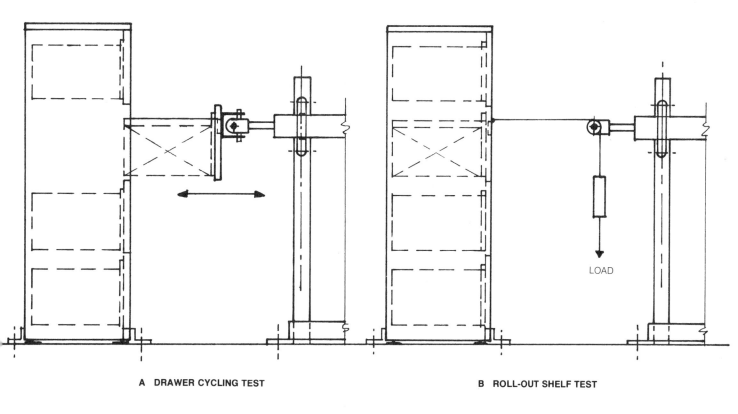

A DRAWER CYCLING TEST

B ROLL-OUT SHELF TEST

LOAD

Figure 12.10 Lateral drawer and roll-out shelf cycle test.
Source: BIFMA.

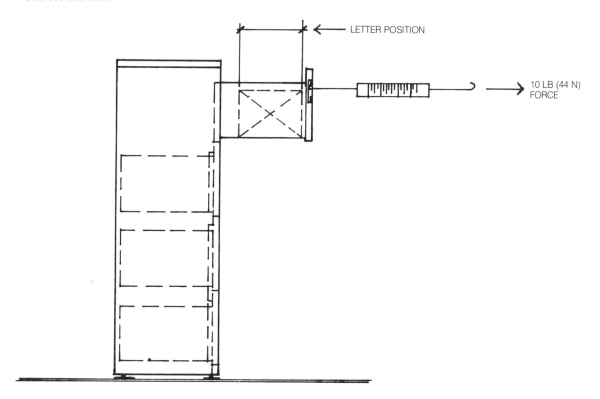

LETTER POSITION

10 LB (44 N)
FORCE

Figure 12.11 Stability test (dynamic load/force) lateral files.
Source: BIFMA.

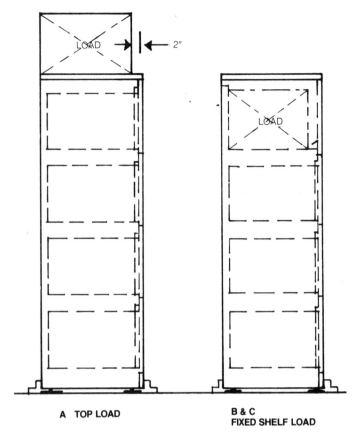

| A TOP LOAD | B & C FIXED SHELF LOAD |

Figure 12.12 Lateral file strength test (static load). Source: BIFMA.

Tables for Conference and Dining Areas

Conference tables are a necessary component in most offices. These tables are usually 30 in. (76.2 cm) in height and have various types of base supports which should not interfere with full capacity seating around the table. The number of people that must be accommodated during conferences is a major factor in the specification of the table size and shape. Because many situations will require very large tables, designers should determine the route by which the table will be delivered into the building; i.e., if the top surface is composed of one piece, check elevators, hallways, doorways, and windows to avoid installation problems.

Figure 12.13 illustrates some of the sizes and shapes used for conference tables.[13] The seating capacity listed for each size table is based on a 23-in. (58.4-cm) wide chair plus 4 in. (10.2 cm) allowance between each chair. When specifying a wider chair, the space should be adjusted accordingly. For example, if a 26-in. (66-cm) wide chair is used, it would be necessary to allow 30 in. for each chair (26″ + 4″).

Tables specified for dining areas require special performance criteria regarding (1) top surface construction and finish and (2) the weight and size of the table base. Table tops produced for dining facilities should have level, moisture-resistant surfaces. A well-constructed top is usually composed of three elements: (1) a plastic laminate surface which is highly resistant to burns, scratches, and impact; (2) a core of either plywood (7 to 15 plies) or particleboard [1 1/8 in. (2.8 cm) thick] which will resist warpage; (3) backing material to prevent warping caused by heat and humidity (Kraft paper or additional laminate).

Common problems associated with tables can be avoided through the proper specification of the base weight, size, and construction.[14]

1. Table instability (wobble and shake) is frequently the result of specifying a base size not in proportion to the top size. If the base and connecting column are too small or the gauge of steel used in the legs (spider) or column is not heavy enough, the table will tend to wobble and shake. Wood columns should never be specified for tables having tops larger than 36 in. (91.4 cm) in diameter.

2. Table tipping is a major cause of liability claims. Designers should be aware that many people (especially those who are elderly) use the table top for support when arising from a dining chair. The table will tip if the base leg spread is too narrow and not properly weighted. The table base (at floor level) should never be less than half the size of the table top. Carpet may also cause problems if the table legs do not have glides that can penetrate the carpet pile and form a stable support base. The carpet pile height should determine the length of stem glides used on the table legs (spider bases).

Custom Casework

Although there are many credenzas, counters, and storage components manufactured for commercial use, designers must often specify custom casework to meet particular design needs. To produce detailed working drawings and specifications that communicate pertinent facts regarding the desired casework, designers should provide the following information:

1. Drawings
   a. Include the location of all counters or cabinets that will be built-in on site.

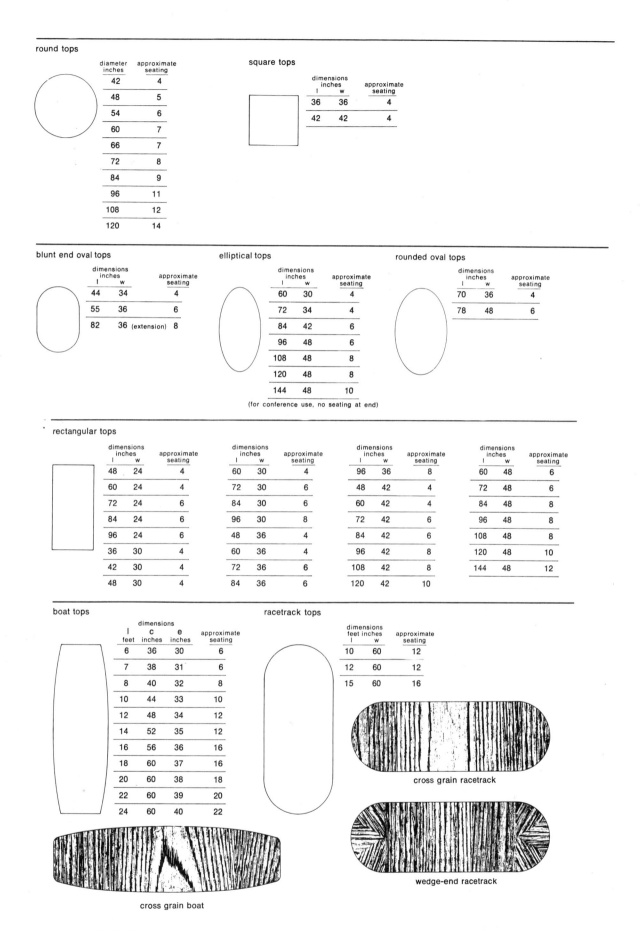

Figure 12.13 Size capacity of conference tables. Reproduced with permission of Vecta Contract.

PREMIUM GRADE

CUSTOM GRADE

Figure 12.14 Furniture face veneer.

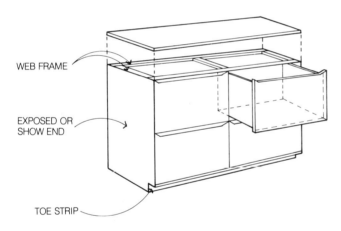

WEB FRAME

EXPOSED OR
SHOW END

TOE STRIP

Figure 12.15 Casework construction parts: exposed and semiexposed.

b. Each cabinet or counter must be identified by a number or some designation that will correlate to elevations, schedules, and the written specification.

c. Basic appearance and component arrangement must be clearly delineated in elevations and sections. Profile; critical parts; joinery; thickness of material; location and dimensions of drawers, doors, shelves, hardware.

d. If more than one species of wood is to be used on a particular piece of casework, the location should be shown on the details or on the finish schedule. The same applies to selected grades and finishes.

2. Schedules
   a. Hardware.
   b. Finishes and grade.
   c. Fasteners and adhesives.
   d. Any other items that need clarification.

3. Specification
   a. Definition of exposed, semiexposed, and concealed portions of casework.
   b. Shop assembly of all items.
   c. Hardware must be furnished and applied by the manufacturer or woodworker.
   d. Minimum thickness of all cabinet components and thickness of laminates. [Doors = 1 3/8″ (3.4 cm); case backs and drawer bottoms = 1/4″ (6.4 mm); shelves exceeding 36″ = 1″ (91.4 cm = 2.5 cm).]
   e. Quality of lumber grade and plywood for semiexposed portions.
   f. Gluing performance; types of core, edge treatment, and joint tolerances for high-pressure laminates.
   g. Method of fastening exposed members and tops.
   h. Method of case body joinery.
   i. Edge treatment of all exposed plywood members.
   j. Type of drawer construction (dust panels between drawers are not standard and if desired must be specified).
   k. Required joinery tolerances. (Premium = .007″; custom = .015″).
   l. Allowable warp and clearance for casework doors. Gap-flush overlay (Premium = .130″); warp (Premium = .027″).
   m. Design of casework appearance (flush, lapped, reveal overlay).
   n. Matched grain effect on exposed portions is not required and therefore must be specified (Figure 12.14).[15]

Casework Terminology. Figure 12.15 illustrates the exposed, semiexposed, and concealed portions of casework.

1. Exposed portions include all surfaces visible when doors and drawers are closed. Bottoms of cases more than 4 ft (121.9 cm) above the floor are considered exposed. All areas visible behind glass doors are also considered exposed.

2. Semiexposed portions are those concealed behind opaque doors, e.g., shelves, divisions, case backs, drawer sides, backs, bottoms, and the back side of doors.

3. Concealed portions are those that are not normally seen, such as sleepers, web frames, and dust panels.[16]

Design of Casework Appearance. There are three basic design categories in casework construction:

1. Exposed face frame (Figure 12.16)
   a. *Flush*

      This category is also known as "conventional flush" and is the most basic type. In this style the door and drawer faces are flush with the face frame.
      (1) Advantages: Allows use of different thicknesses of wood for doors and drawer fronts. Heavy-duty and conventional hardware may be used. Recommended for hard service areas because of the superior strength.
      (2) Disadvantages: More expensive because of careful fitting and aligning required for doors and drawers.
   b. *Lipped*

      Very similar in construction to the flush design. Advantages: More economical because fitting tolerance of doors and drawers are less critical.

2. Flush overlay (Figure 12.11)

   Provides a very sleek design with only door and drawer fronts visible on the face of the cabinet; permits a matched grain to be used across entire front [can be cut from one panel (Figure 12.9)]. Heavy-duty hardware can be used, but the absence of a face frame requires careful alignment.

3. Reveal overlay (Figure 12.11)

   A variation on the flush overlay, it presents a raised panel effect. It does not require a face frame and needs less careful fitting and alignment. The designer may use the "reveal" either vertically or horizontally.

Adhesives for Casework. Commercial Standard, U.S. Department of Commerce: Adhesives CS 35-61 classifies adhesives for the assembly of wood cabinets into three types:

Type I   Fully waterproof bond, exterior use. Typical adhesives are thermosetting polyvinyl acetate emulsions or resorcinolphenolics. Use in shower rooms or areas of high humidity.

Type II Water-resistant, interior use. Typical adhesives are thermosetting polyvinyl acetates, urea resins, and caseins. Use in damp climates.

Type III Nonwater resistant, but considered moisture resistant for interior use. Many wood adhesives fall into this category, e.g., the vinyl types, which are very popular for interior use because they dry clear for use on natural or stained work.

Casework Hardware. The hardware is usually furnished by the woodwork manufacturer and will be of standard quality unless the designer includes the following in the written specification:

1. Drawer slides _____ (brand and catalog number).

2. Shelf standards and brackets _____ (specify finish and brand name).

3. Sliding door track _____ (specify brand and catalog number).

4. Hinges _____ (specify brand and catalog number).

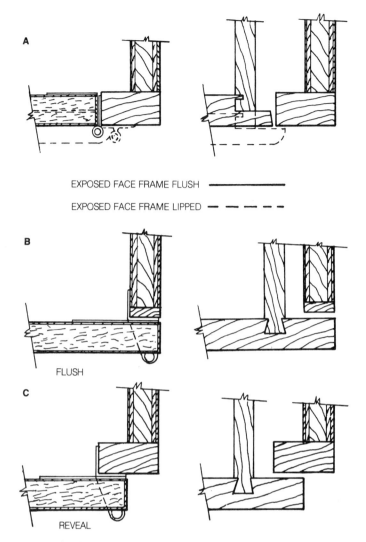

Figure 12.16 Casework design details. Source: Architectural Woodwork Institute.

TABLE 12.8 VISUAL TESTS FOR EXPOSED CASEWORK SURFACES

Defects	Premium	Custom
Orange peel — Slight depressions in surface, similar to skin of orange	3'*	6'*
Runs — Running of wet finish film in rivulets	None	None
Sags — Partial slipping of finish film creating a curtain effect	None	3'*
Finish sanding scratches	None	3'*
Blistering — Small swelled areas like a water blister on human skin	None	None
Glue spots	None	None
Checking, crazing or cracking — Crowfoot separation. Irregular line separation.	None	None
Filled nail holes	3'*	6'*

*Not noticeable beyond this distance viewed in the normal light in which casework is intended to be used.

Source: Architectural Woodwork Institute (AWI).

5. Catches _____ (brand and catalog number).

6. Pulls _____ (brand and catalog number). The desired location must be shown on the drawings.[17]

Table 12.8 explains various defects that are allowed in casework constructed of premium- and custom-grade wood. For more information on wood species and grades, see the AWI Comparative Wood Chart in Chapter 9.

Wood Joinery. Common methods of wood joinery used in architectural casework are illustrated in Figure 12.17.

Seating for Commercial Interiors

Seating is a major source of injuries and liability suits and should therefore be given careful consideration in regard to performance, durability, and stability. Commercial seating may be classifed as desk chairs, side chairs, assembly or auxiliary seating, permanent multiple seating, lounge seating, conference seating, and custom-designed multiple seating.

Desk Chairs. These may be either posture (tilt seat and back) or fixed seat and back; rotating or nonrotating; with or without arms. These chairs may be partially or fully upholstered and normally have casters for ease of movement. Figure 12.18 illustrates typical secretarial and clerical chairs. It should be noted that secretarial chairs are smaller in size than clerical chairs.

Construction: Swivel Arm Chairs (Nonposture). This type of chair is also known as a "fixed-back" chair in which the seat and back tilt as a unit; in a posture chair, the seam remains horizontal and only the back tilts. The fixed back swivel arm chair has two adjustments: one for seat height and the other to control the back tension or force required to tilt the seat and back unit backward. (Posture chairs have as many as four or five adjustments.) Figure 12.19 illustrates the major parts that should be considered when specifying a swivel arm chair.

1. Chair base is composed of a cross-shaped structure which supports the rest of the chair and to which casters are usually attached.

2. The *spindle* is a part of the structure which passes through the center of the base, supports the seat, and allows the chair to swivel. The spindle is partially enclosed in a *spindle housing* or hub which is set in the center of the base. The bearing surface in the housing is called the *spindle bushing.* The height of the chair seat is adjusted by turning the height adjustment *control handwheel* on the spindle thread. The upper end of the spindle is rigidly fastened to the *control iron* or chair control.

3. The *control iron* provides the chair tilting action and consists of three parts: (1) the *chassis* to which the spindle is attached; (2) the tilting mechanism; (3) the "spider arms" which support the seat.

4. The *tilting mechanism* controls the maximum angle of inclination of the chair seat and back as well as the back tension. Tilting mechanisms generally employ two major types of spring action. One type makes use of torsion bars and the other uses helical springs to control the back tension. Both types of tension mechanisms can be adjusted by the *back tension control.*

Spline Joint Used for gluing plywood in width or length. Since the spline serves to align faces, this joint is also used for items requiring site assembly.

Stub Tenon Joinery method for assembling stile and rail type frames that are additionally supported, such as web or skeleton case frames.

Conventional Mortise and Tenon Joint Joinery method for assembling square-edged surfaces such as case face frames.

Dowel Joint Alternative joinery method for serving same function as Conventional Mortise and Tenon.

Haunch Mortise and Tenon Joint Joinery method for assembling paneled doors or stile and rail type paneling.

French Dovetail Joint Method for joining drawer sides to fronts when fronts conceal metal extension slides or overlay the case faces.

Conventional Dovetail Joint Traditional method for joining drawer sides to fronts or backs. Usually limited to flush or lipped type drawers.

Drawer Lock-Joint Another joinery method for joining drawer sides to fronts. Usually used for flush type installation but can be adapted to lip or overlay type drawers.

Edge Banding Method of concealing plys or inner cores of plywood or particleboard when edges are exposed. Thickness or configuration will vary with manufacturers' practices.

Through Dado Conventional joint used for assembly of case body members—dado usually concealed by application of case face frame.

Blind Dado Variation of conventional dado with applied edge "stopping" or concealing dado groove. Used when case body edge is exposed.

Stop Dado Another method of concealing dado exposure. Applicable when veneer edging or solid lumber is used.

Exposed End Detail Illustrates attachment of finished end of case body to front frame using butt joint.

Exposed End Detail Illustrates attachment of finished end of case body to front frame using mitered joint.

Paneled Door Details Joinery techniques when paneled effect is desired. Profiles are optional as is the use of flat or raised panels. Solid lumber raised panels may be used when width does not exceed 10″. Rim raised panels recommended when widths exceed this dimension or when transparent finish is used.

Spline Joint

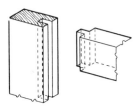

Stub Tenon

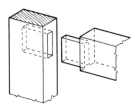

Conventional Mortise and Tenon Joint

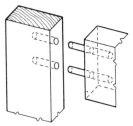

Dowel Joint

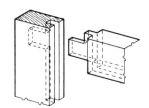

Haunch Mortise and Tenon Joint

Figure 12.17 Casework joints. Reproduced with permission of the Architectural Woodwork Institute.

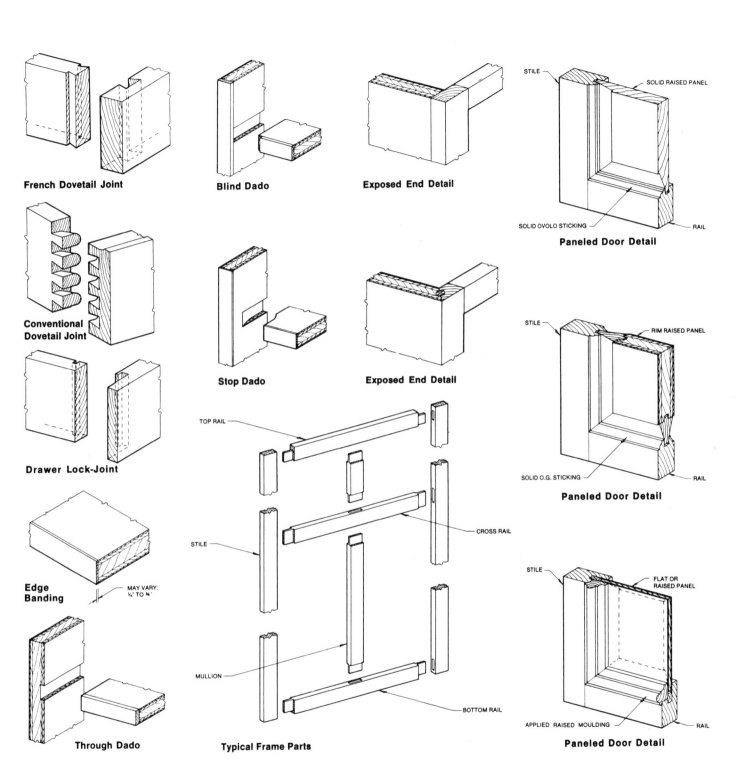

French Dovetail Joint

Conventional Dovetail Joint

Drawer Lock-Joint

Edge Banding

MAY VARY: ¼" TO ¾"

Through Dado

Blind Dado

Stop Dado

TOP RAIL

STILE

MULLION

CROSS RAIL

BOTTOM RAIL

Typical Frame Parts

Exposed End Detail

Exposed End Detail

STILE

SOLID RAISED PANEL

SOLID OVOLO STICKING

RAIL

Paneled Door Detail

STILE

RIM RAISED PANEL

SOLID O.G. STICKING

RAIL

Paneled Door Detail

STILE

FLAT OR RAISED PANEL

APPLIED RAISED MOULDING

RAIL

Paneled Door Detail

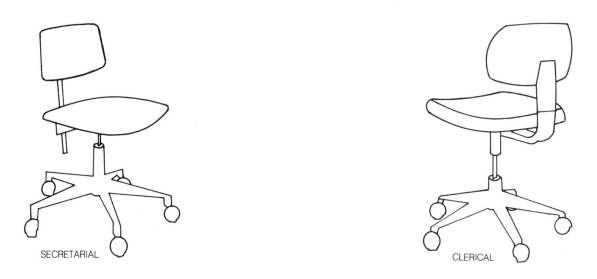

SECRETARIAL

CLERICAL

Figure 12.18 Secretarial and clerical desk chairs.

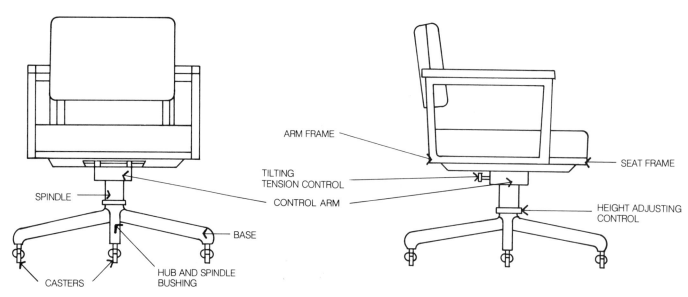

ARM FRAME

TILTING
TENSION CONTROL

CONTROL ARM

SEAT FRAME

HEIGHT ADJUSTING
CONTROL

SPINDLE

BASE

CASTERS

HUB AND SPINDLE
BUSHING

Figure 12.19 Construction features of a swivel arm chair.
Source: Buyers Laboratory.

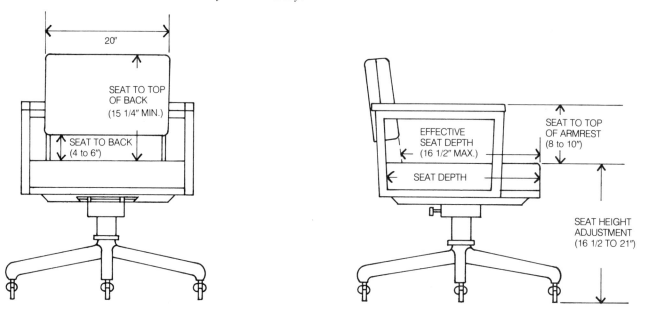

20"

SEAT TO TOP
OF BACK
(15 1/4" MIN.)

SEAT TO BACK
(4 to 6")

EFFECTIVE
SEAT DEPTH
(16 1/2" MAX.)

SEAT DEPTH

SEAT TO TOP
OF ARMREST
(8 to 10")

SEAT HEIGHT
ADJUSTMENT
(16 1/2 TO 21")

Figure 12.20 Swivel arm chair dimensions. Source: Buyers
Laboratory.

5. *Chair seats* usually consist of a steel or plywood *seat pan*, foam rubber, or other cushioning material (sometimes springs) and upholstery. In many seats a steel flange is fastened to the outer edge of the seat pan to add rigidity. Seat coverings are often fastened to the outer edge of the seat pan or the steel flange.[18]

Swivel Arm Chair Dimensions. When specifying chairs that will be used in offices, designers must be aware that individual requirements for seating comfort will vary widely, and therefore chairs engineered to offer the greatest flexibility of adjustment should be specified. The fact that people using the chairs will probably be seated for extended periods of time creates the problem of designing and/or selecting chairs that will prevent fatigue and backache. The following dimensions and flexibility should be considered:

1. Seat height should be adjustable to meet the needs of people with short or long legs; i.e., seat heights should not cause pressure on the underside of the thighs when the feet are placed squarely on the floor. Many office employees are forced to adjust the height of their chairs to accommodate the height of the desk or work surface, instead of adjusting for actual seating comfort. To accommodate the wide range of people who may be using the chair, the seat height adjustment may range from 14 1/2 to 21 in. (36.9 to 53.3 cm). Adjustment to lower than 14 1/2 in. may be necessary for some people. Desk heights should also be adjustable to coordinate work surfaces with seating heights. If a desk cannot be lowered enough for a short person, the seating should be raised, and a footrest may have to be provided to prevent extreme pressure on the underside of the thighs (see Figure 12.20).

2. Backrests and seat-to-back openings are an important consideration when specifying office seating. The height of the backrest area should not interfere with ease of movement, but should be high enough to provide adequate back support. The top of the back should be at least 15 1/2 in. (39.4 cm) above the top of the seat to provide adequate support for the back. The space from the seat to the back support is intended to prevent pressure against the lower end of the spine and may range from 4 to 6 in. (10.2 to 15.2 cm).

3. The seat shape should not constrict the movement of the seated person. Movement is essential when a person is seated for extended periods of time; therefore, padded seats which have slightly concave seat pans would be more comfortable than saddle-contoured seat pans which may constrict movement.

4. Seat cushioning should provide a firm support which would prevent excessive pressure on the bony projections of the buttocks. On unpadded flat seats, pressure may build up to as much as 60 lb psi (28 kg) at pressure points. Good seating should provide an even distribution of body weight over the seating area.

5. Seat depth should be carefully considered in regard to the pressure it will create on the legs. Too deep a seat presses on the legs below the knees and may also cause a person to sit forward and lose contact with the back support area. Recommended seat depths should not exceed 16 1/2 in. (41.9 cm) in depth. Firm padded seats may be more comfortable if the depth is limited to 15 in. (38.1 cm). Some authorities suggest a space of up to 3 in. (7.6 cm) between the rear of the calf and the front edge of the seat to allow adequate space for change of sitting position.

6. Armrests should not be too long or placed too high. The height of the armrest could cause uncomfortable pressure on the shoulder joints and also provide a constant annoyance by bumping into the desk or work surface. The recommended height between the top of the armrest and the seat is between 8 and 10 in. (20.3 and 25.4 cm). Extremely short or tall people may require armrest heights ranging from 6 to 11 in. (15.2 to 27.9 cm).[19]

Dimensions: Secretarial Posture Chairs. The major difference between a nonposture and posture chair is the fact that the backrest on a posture chair can be raised or lowered and the seat does not tilt when the back is tilted. On most posture chairs the back can be flexed and the pressure required to flex the back can be adjusted.

Adjustment Procedures. These are very important in obtaining the full use of a posture chair. The designer should make certain that the client or user is instructed in adjustment procedures. A chair should be adjusted to the particular user initially and again after about two weeks of use if the seating is found to be uncomfortable.

The secretarial posture chair generally has five adjustments: (1) seat height, (2) back height, (3) back angle, (4) back tension, and (5) back position. The seat height is adjustable to permit the user's feet to rest flat on the floor. The height may vary from 16 1/2 to 21 in. (41.9 to 53.3 cm) and is adjustable by turning the height control handwheel on the spindle thread.

The back top height should be adjustable within a range of 13 to 15 in. (33 to 38.1 cm) above the top of the seat. The height of the bottom of the backrest should range from 4 to 6 in. (10.2 to 15.2 cm) above the seat. The lower edge of the backrest should be set approximately 1 in. (25 mm) below a horizontal line through the top of the hip bone.

The backrest angle or the horizontal position of the chair back should be adjusted to permit the user to lean back about 10 or 15° from a straight/vertical line. The tension control should be set firmly for maximum support.

Side Chairs. These may be rotating or nonrotating; with or without arms; and normally with a nontilt fixed back. They are usually partially upholstered.

Assembly or Auxiliary Seating. This is designed to assemble easily and quickly and later be stored between uses. It is normally light-weight [9 1/2 to 15 1/2 lb (4.3 to 7 kg)] and may have only minimal upholstery. Because these chairs are stacked for storage, they are often constructed of fiberglass or plastic with tubular or rod-type legs of aluminum or other light-weight materials. Welded joints rather than bolted construction are recommended because the heavy use and frequent moving would loosen the bolts and weaken the entire chair structure. Accessories that may be attached to these chairs range from tablet arms and armrests to bookracks and ashtrays. The number of chairs that may be stacked in one group depends on the design and may vary from 15 to 45 chairs (unupholstered) on dollies, which are designed for storing and

Figure 12.21 Equipment for moving and storing seating. Reproduced with permission of Fixtures Manufacturing Corp., Kansas City, MO.

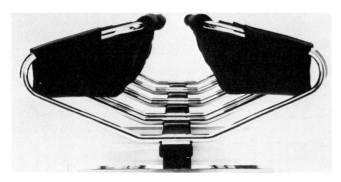

Figure 12.22 Zermatt cantilever assembly seating. Reproduced with permission of Vecta Contract.

transporting the chairs between uses (Figure 12.21). Special ganging devices are often used to interlock these chairs side by side during use because most fire codes require that stacking or folding chairs used in places of assembly be ganged to prevent injury to the occupants. In the event of a fire or other emergency, unattached seating would become disarranged or overturned and destroy aisles and passageways which would present an obstacle to safe egress of the occupants. The interlocking attachments range from plastic clips to metal hoods welded to the sides of the chairs.

Permanent Multiple Seating. This is primarily designed for use in large public areas such as theaters, transportation terminals, and public lobbies that are subject to heavy use. This seating is permanently joined together, either attached at the base or sides or attached to a long horizontal bar, which results in fewer vertical supports. The latter method of construction provides for greater ease of maintenance in areas that receive constant use. Figure 12.22 illustrates cantilever multiple seating supported by a horizontal bar. In specifying any multiple seating, designers should select units that will resist structural vibrations; i.e., the seating of a person at any point along the unit should not disturb others using the same unit.

Lounge Seating. This is usually upholstered sofas, chairs, and benches which are used in informal commercial or institutional reception and lobby areas that do not receive excessive use. Figure 12.23 shows upholstered lounge seating that is designed with ganging devices that allow the seating to be arranged in free-form arrangements. These units may also incorporate ganged tables and planters.

Conference Seating. This is designed for use around a conference table, and although these chairs have arms, they are designed to coordinate with the table height. To provide a more relaxed posture, the pitch or tilt of the back is greater than the pitch used in chairs designed for more concentrated tasks. These chairs often have a sled base or a center pedestal and pronged base which may or may not have casters. Since most conference rooms have carpet installed over padding, casters should be carefully selected to prevent damage to the floorcovering.

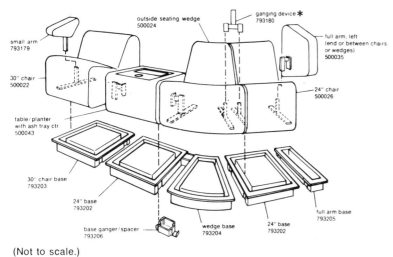

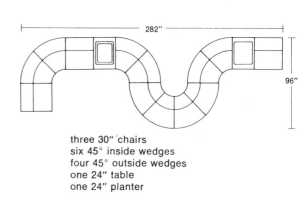

three 30″ chairs
six 45° inside wedges
four 45° outside wedges
one 24″ table
one 24″ planter

(Not to scale.)

Figure 12.23 Ganged lounge seating. Reproduced with permission of Tappo Seating System, Vecta Contract.

Custom-Designed Multiple Seating. This is frequently required in public areas, such as lobbies and restaurants. Figures 12.24 through 12.27 illustrate working drawings for restaurant banquettes and booths. Designers should provide detailed drawings containing information on the following:

1. Structural dimensions
2. Construction details
3. Location of springs, cushion components
4. Upholstery detailing (location of tufting, seaming, and welting)

Figure 12.28 shows a typical schedule or bill of materials that is required to further clarify the working drawings. This schedule includes:

1. Structural materials (wood, metal, or plastics)
2. Hardware, fasteners, and adhesives
3. Finishes on exposed and semiexposed areas

Figure 12.29 illustrates an upholstery schedule that should accompany furniture working drawings. That schedule includes:

1. Frame construction
2. Spring construction
3. Filling materials and liners
4. Fabric direction, construction, and trim

A written specification, shown in Figure 12.30, is necessary to assure accurate completion of the work, and should include a description of the following:

1. Quality of materials
2. Fabrication
3. Species of wood and grade required
4. Relationship with the other work in the specifications

Performance Testing of Seating. For many years private industry and independent laboratories have been involved in developing various methods for testing the structural integrity of seating components. These efforts reflect the manufacturers' concern about the increasing rate of product liability claims involving chair-related injuries (see Chapter 2).

Tests to determine the probable performance of office chairs are concerned with durability, structural strength, and stability. Chairs are tested by the application of dynamic and static leads, and all moving parts are evaluated on the basis of endurance or service life.[20]

Durability tests for secretarial posture chairs involve the three primary sources of motion performed by the chair, i.e., the swiveling of the seat, the flexing of the back, and the caster movement.

1. Back flexing tests mechanically flex the chair back to determine the number of flexes the structure will withstand. Acceptance criteria vary, but some tests require chairs to withstand up to 12,000 flexes. This criterion is based on the assumption that an average secretarial posture chair will receive about ten flexes per hour over a six-year use period.

2. Swivel cycling tests often seek to accelerate wear conditions by placing a heavy static (nonmoving) load on the seat of the chair while subjecting the swivel mechanism to an intensive amount of cycling per hour. Well-constructed chairs should withstand up to 200,000 revolutions without showing excessive wear.

3. Caster durability tests are conducted with varying static loads placed in the chair, and casters are normally expected to withstand 100,000 revolutions.

Structural strength tests are conducted to determine any weaknesses that may cause structural failure of the chair and injury to the occupant. Many of these tests are based on the Interim Federal Specifications No. AA-C-00275 (d) for aluminum office chairs and AA-C-00293 (a) for steel office chairs.

1. Back pull tests require that the chair back be slowly pulled to the rear with a force of 100 lb (46 kg) for steel chairs and 125 lb (56 kg) for aluminum chairs. Acceptance criteria are based on the amount of distortion caused by the test. Permanent distortion should not exceed 1/4 in. (6.4 mm).

2. Drop tests for seats are based on the application of a dynamic load to the seat surface. A sandbag weighing 175 lb (80 kg) for aluminum chairs and 225 lb (102 kg) for steel chairs is dropped from a height of 6 in. (15.2 cm) onto the seat. Distortion should not exceed 1/8 in. (3.2 mm) in aluminum chairs and 1/4 in. (6.4 mm) in steel chairs. In addition, the chairs should show no signs of fractures or internal or exterior breakage.

Stacking chairs are subjected to the same general types of tests, but the emphasis is on more varied use conditions. Dynamic loads are applied to the front edges of seats, and other tests are conducted to determine the potential hazards presented by the tipping or rocking of light-weight chairs.

In an effort to provide consistent performance and safety standards, the Business and Institutional Furniture Manufacturers Association submitted a proposal for a voluntary standard to the American National Standards Institute, Inc. (ANSI). In 1977 the standard was adopted as the "American National Standard Tests for General Office Chairs" (ANSI X 5.1–1977). The testing machine shown in Figure 12.31 was designed for testing office furniture.

MAINTENANCE OF FURNITURE MATERIALS

Consideration must be given to the maintenance of furniture materials which are specified for commercial interiors. Designers should obtain information from manufacturers about special maintenance requirements, and this information should be used in making specification decisions. For example, knowing that marble is very porous and easily etched by acids contained in wine or fruit juices would make marble a poor choice for a bar surface.

The most common materials used in furniture are metals, woods, plastics, stone, and glass. General maintenance for these materials is listed below.

Aluminum

Aluminum furniture and parts are produced in polished and satin finishes and are usually protected with a coat of clear lacquer. When the lacquer wears off due to prolonged abrasion, the exposed area usually oxidizes in the same color as the original material, and therefore recoating is not necessary.

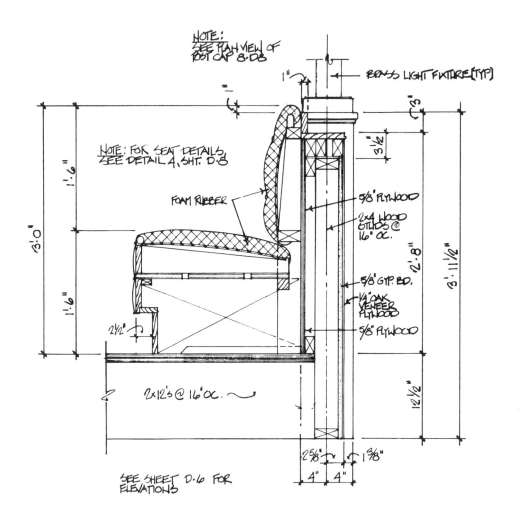

NOTE:
SEE PLAN VIEW OF
POST CAP 8·D8

BRASS LIGHT FIXTURE (TYP)

NOTE: FOR SEAT DETAILS
SEE DETAIL 4, SHT. D·8

FOAM RUBBER

5/8" PLYWOOD

2×4 WOOD
OTHERS @
16" O.C.

5/8" GYP. BD.

1/4" OAK
VENEER
PLYWOOD

5/8" PLYWOOD

2×12's @ 16" O.C.

SEE SHEET D·6 FOR
ELEVATIONS

VERTICAL SECTION OF BANQUETTE @ THE BALCONY [133] ⑤
SCALE: 1½" = 1'·0"

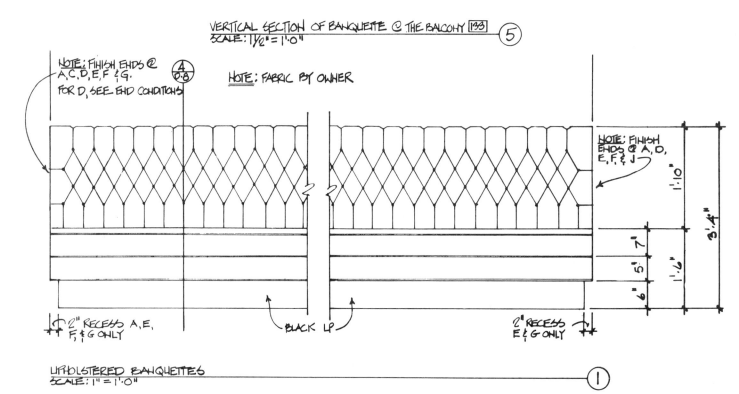

NOTE: FINISH ENDS @
A, C, D, E, F & G.
FOR D, SEE END CONDITIONS   ④
0.8

NOTE: FABRIC BY OWNER

NOTE: FINISH
ENDS @ A, O,
E, F & J

2" RECESS A, E,
F, & G ONLY

BLACK LP

2" RECESS
E & G ONLY

UPHOLSTERED BANQUETTES ①
SCALE: 1" = 1'·0"

Figure 12.24 Custom upholstered restaurant banquette seating. Reproduced with permission of Selje, Bond, Steward & Romberger, Phoenix and Los Angeles.

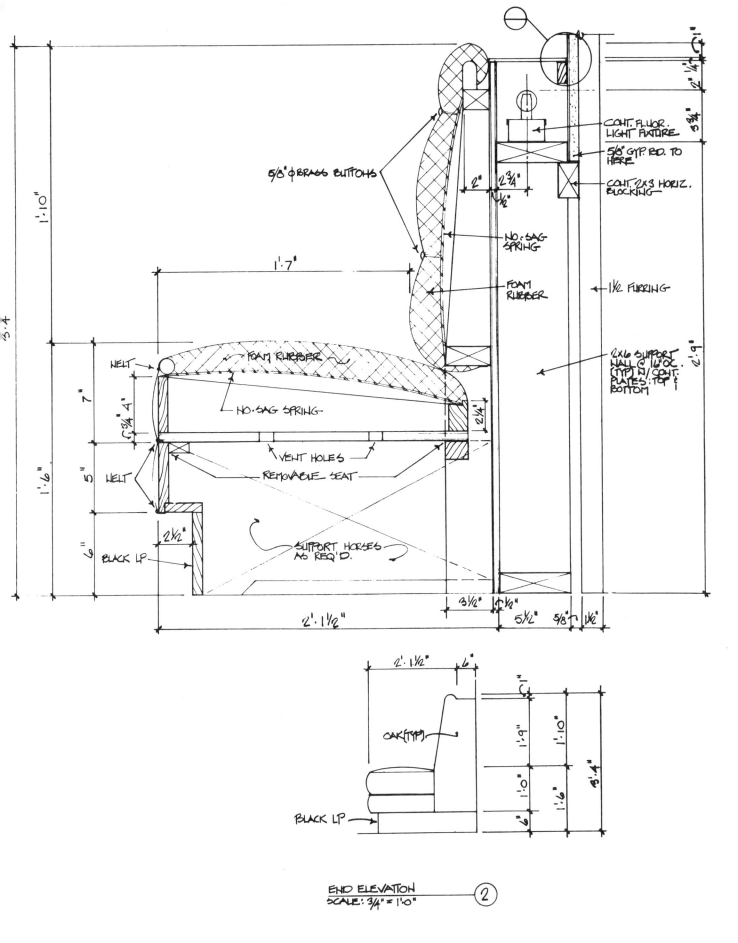

5/8"⌀ BRASS BUTTONS

CONT. FLUOR.
LIGHT FIXTURE

5/8" GYP. BD. TO
HERE

CONT. 2x3 HORIZ.
BLOCKING

NO·SAG
SPRING

FOAM
RUBBER

1½ FURRING

2x6 SUPPORT
WALL @ 16" O.C.
(TYP) W/ CONT.
PLATES TOP &
BOTTOM

1'·10"

3'·4"

1'·6"

1'·7"

WELT

7"

2¾"

5"

WELT

6"

BLACK LP

2½"

FOAM RUBBER

NO·SAG SPRING

VENT HOLES

REMOVABLE SEAT

SUPPORT HORSES
AS REQ'D.

2"   2¾"
½"

2¼"

2'·1½"

3½"   ½"
5½"   5/8"   1½"

1"
2½"
5¾"
2'·9"

2'·1½"   6"

OAK (TYP)

BLACK LP

1'·9"

1'·0"

6"

1"

1'·10"

1'·6"

6"

3'·4"

END ELEVATION
SCALE: 3/4" = 1'·0"   ②

*Figure 12.25 Custom upholstered restaurant banquettes. Re-
produced with permission of Selje, Bond, Steward &
Romberger, Phoenix and Los Angeles.*

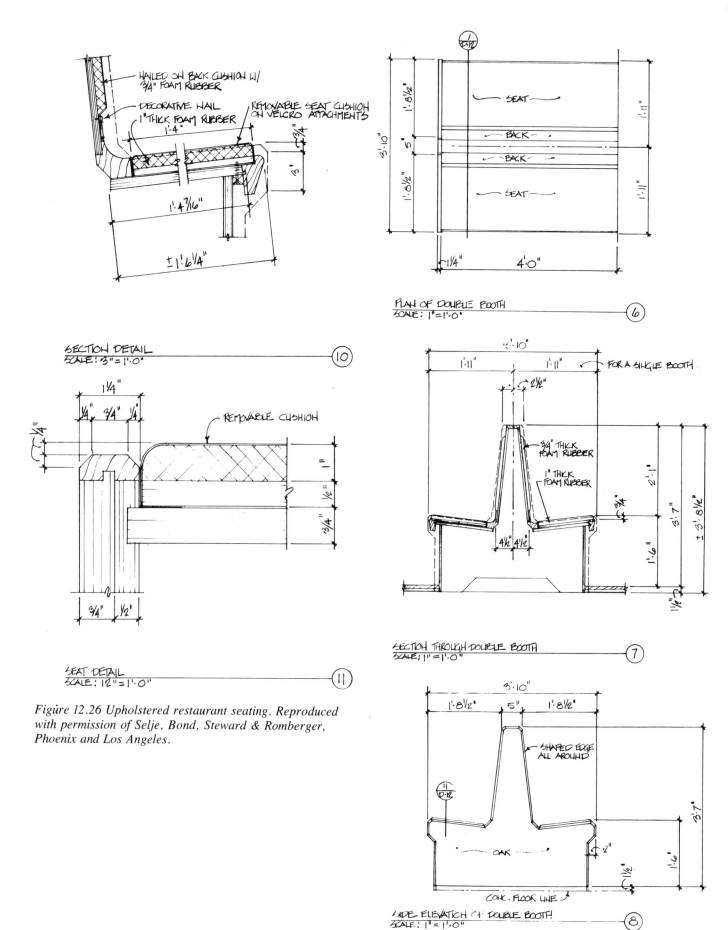

NAILED ON BACK CUSHION W/ 3/4" FOAM RUBBER

DECORATIVE NAIL 1" THICK FOAM RUBBER

REMOVABLE SEAT CUSHION ON VELCRO ATTACHMENTS

1'.4"

3/4"

3'

1'.4 7/16"

± 1'.6 1/4"

SECTION DETAIL
SCALE: 3" = 1'.0"   10

1 1/4"

1/4" 3/4" 1/4"

1/4"

REMOVABLE CUSHION

1"

1/2"

3/4"

3/4" 1/2'

SEAT DETAIL
SCALE: 1 1/2" = 1'.0"   11

Figure 12.26 Upholstered restaurant seating. Reproduced with permission of Selje, Bond, Steward & Romberger, Phoenix and Los Angeles.

PLAN OF DOUBLE BOOTH
SCALE: 1" = 1'.0"   6

1'.8 1/2"

5"

3'.10"

1'.8 1/2"

SEAT

BACK

BACK

SEAT

1 1/4"

4'.0"

1'.11"

1'.11"

3'.10"

1'.11"   1'.11"   FOR A SINGLE BOOTH

2 1/2"

3/4" THICK FOAM RUBBER

1" THICK FOAM RUBBER

3/4"

2'.1"

1'.6"

3'.7"

± 3'.8 1/2"

4 1/2" 4 1/2"

1 1/4"

SECTION THROUGH DOUBLE BOOTH
SCALE: 1" = 1'.0"   7

3'.10"

1'.8 1/2"   5"   1'.8 1/2"

SHAPED EDGE ALL AROUND

11
D.12

OAK

2"

1/2"

1'.6"

3'.7"

CONC. FLOOR LINE

SIDE ELEVATION OF DOUBLE BOOTH
SCALE: 1" = 1'.0"   8

Figure 12.27 Custom seating details. Reproduced with permission of Selje, Bond, Steward & Romberger, Phoenix and Los Angeles.

BILL SHEET OF ONE Booth			B. C. SMITH DESIGNERS BILL OF MATERIALS							SHEET _____ OF _____			Date Required _____ Deliver to _____

Part. No.	Parts per Article	Part Name	Finish			Rough			Species	Molding	Net Rough Footage	Fasteners, Adhesives	Finish and Grade	Remarks
			L	W	T	L	W	T						
1	2	End panel	43	46	3/4	44	47	3/4	Oak	⌐			Transp. Premium	
2	1	Top panel	44	5	3/4	45	6	3/4	Oak	⌐				

Note: Finish dimensions always shown in inches. L = length in direction of wood grain; W = width across the wood grain; T = thickness measurements before sanding; rough measurements = required lumber sizes before cutting; grade = quality of wood (premium, custom, or economy); finish = transparent or opaque (see Chapter 9).

Figure 12.28 Bill of materials for wood furniture construction.

Article No.	Part Name	Frame Construction			Spring/Support			Filling Padding	Liner	Fabric Direction		Trim and Construction				
		Solid	Open	Slip	No Sag	Coil	Other			V	H	Welt	Tuft	Channel	Buttons	Other
Banquette 1	Seat			X				4 lb Neoprene	Heat B.	X		PVC				
Banquette 1	Back	X			X			4 lb Neoprene	Heat B.	X		PVC	X		Brass	

Note: Filling or padding listed by pounds per cubic foot; liner = heat barrier; fabric direction = vertical or horizontal.

Figure 12.29 Upholstery schedule of custom-built seating.

Part I: GENERAL

1.01   RELATED WORK SPECIFIED ELSEWHERE:

_____

1.02   NOT FURNISHED, BUT INSTALLED:

_____

1.03   SUBMITTALS

    A. Shop Drawings:

        1. Submit shop drawings in accord with contract conditions for all wood and upholstered booths, identified with location, quality, grade, type of finish, wood species, fabric, upholstery details.

        2. Submit drawing of the installed positions with sections in 3 inch (76.2 mm equal 403.8 mm) scale.

        3. The manufacturer shall be responsible for details and dimensions not controlled by job conditions.

        4. Show all required field measurements beyond control of the manufacturer.

    B. Samples:

        1. Submit _____ samples, _____ inches x _____ inches of each species of wood, upholstery fabric, foam, welt cording.

        2. Identify each sample - species, cut, grade, fiber content.

    C. Quality Assurance

        1. Compliance with California Upholstery Standard _____.

        2. Certificate verifying flame spread, smoke development and density, of upholstery fabric and filling material.

        3. Certificate verifying type of flame retardant used on fabric and filling material.

    D. Maintenance

        Submit complete instructions for recommended repair and maintenance procedures.

1.04   DELIVERY, STORAGE, AND HANDLING

    A. Deliver, store, and handle seating units in manner to prevent damage and deterioration.

    B. Defer delivery to job until the installation and storage areas are completed and dry of all wet construction.

    C. Maintain relative humidity in storage areas not to exceed _____ percent.

    D. Protect all surfaces of seating booths subject to damage while in transit.

    E. Provide temporary skids under ajl large or heavy seating booths.

1.05   GUARANTEES

_____

Figure 12.30 Specification guide of upholstered booths.

PART II: PRODUCTS

2.01 QUALITY GRADE

Materials and fabrication: _____ grade for _____

finish in accordance with _____.

2.02 MATERIALS

A. Exposed wood for transparent finish (species
and cut) .

B. Solid wood for semi-exposed members (species)

C. Solid wood for concealed members (fill in
species or "any")

D. Fasteners _____. Adhesives _____

E. Filling-padding material (weight and density -
material)

F. Spring support (type and manufacturer)

G. Upholstery fabric (weight, fiber content, type
of flame and soil retardant)(Manufacturer, style
and color number)

H. Accessories (findings, such as buttons, welt
cording or other trim)

2.03 FABRICATION

A. All edge grain of exposed and semi-exposed plywood
shall be concealed. All upholstery fabric shall
be installed in the same direction with all
patterns on seat and back areas matching (unless
otherwise noted).

B. Welt cording shall be self covered. Seams of
the welt covering shall only appear on the
sides or rear of the seating units.

C. The removable seat cushion shall fit securely
in frame.

D. All buttons shall be securely attached and
anchored with #_____ cord.

PART III: EXECUTION

3.01 CONDITIONS OF SURFACES

A. Examine all grounds, stripping and blocking to
secure seating booths.

B. Do not install until all defects are corrected.

3.02 INSTALLATION

A. Install booths plumb and level without distortion.

B. All booths shall be installed in a rigid manner,
shim as necessary.

3.03 ADJUST AND CLEAN

A. All upholstered surfaces shall be free of spots
or damage.

B. All exposed wooden areas shall be free from
scratches, nicks or other damage.

C. All booths shall be protected from damage
until final acceptance.

END OF SECTION

*Figure 12.31 Machine for testing office chairs. Reproduced
with permission of BIFMA.*

Baked Enamel Paint on Metal

Many metal desks and files are finished by this process which fuses the finish to the surface by firing. This produces a very strong and resistive surface and only soap and water are required for cleaning.

Black Epoxy Finish on Metal

Epoxy enamel is a very tough plastic finish which is baked over a primer for good adhesion. This finish presents few maintenance problems. The sheen of the surface can be restored by polishing and waxing with products designed for automobile finishes. Touch-ups should not be attempted with lacquers because they will not adhere to the finish. An enamel touch-up paint used in auto repair would be more suitable.

Brass with or without Lacquer

Brass is frequently lacquered to prevent oxidation and staining. Cleaning fluids or abrasives should not be applied to lacquered surfaces because they tend to remove the protective coating. A paste wax should be applied every six months to help maintain the finish and prevent finger markings.

Bronze

This metal corrodes and rusts easily and needs a protective coating of either lemon oil or lacquer. The lemon oil coating must be renewed every six months. The lacquer is usually sprayed on and may be cleaned with a soft dry cloth. If the lacquer needs replacement, it should be professionally removed, the bronze item repolished and then relacquered. This is usually necessary every three to five years.

Chromium Plate

Furniture having this plating in either a brushed or a polished finish requires special care. It can be cleaned with automobile cleaners, polished, and waxed with a hard paste wax for protection from the atmosphere and moisture. In areas with high moisture the chromium should be cleaned and waxed frequently to prevent rust.

Pewter Finish on Metal

This process is a hand-antiqued finish which is protected with a clear lacquer. These surfaces should be cleaned with a soft dry cloth to prevent abrasion.

Plastic Coated Steel

This finish is a cellulose acetate coating that may be cleaned with any soap, detergent, or cleaner. The use of steel wool or other abrasives is not recommended.

Stainless Steel

This is one of the most durable and handsome of all metals. It is rustproof and maintains a high polish without any protective coating. Use automobile polish or ordinary household cleaners. Although small scratches may show on a new surface, they fuse with daily use and are not noticeable after a time.

Woods

Woods may be finished with lacquer, oil, wax, ebony, and numerous other methods to preserve the beauty of the wood.

Lacquer Finish on Wood

For best service, lacquer finishes on wood should be protected with a hard wax applied every three to four months during the first year of use. Dirt marks that may show on light woods can be removed with a very fine steel wool (No. 000). More serious scratches can be repaired with a crayon stick, but any really serious repairs must be handled by a professional wood refinisher.

Wax Finish on Wood

This finishing technique usually involves application of wax over a penetrating sealer which gives the wood protection and acts as a base for the wax. Reapplication of an ordinary paste furniture wax will clean and renew the surface.

Ebony Finish on Wood

A standard ebony finish consists of a series of black stain and black lacquer coats. This surface may be maintained in the same manner as lacquered wood except that a clear liquid oil-based polish is recommended. Do not use a paste wax because it will give a gray tone to the open pores. If scratch repairs become necessary. a black wax crayon should be used.

Glass

Commercial spray cleaners may be used to clean the surface. Deep scratches can sometimes be concealed with the use of "plastic glass," which is a synthetic material that hardens clear as glass.

Marble

Marble should not be specified for surfaces that will receive excessive wear. The surface may, however, be protected with a coating of clear wax. Marble must be kept very clean with frequent washing. Use clear lukewarm water on a clean cloth and rewax after each washing. Marble may be commercially refinished if the surface becomes deeply etched. To maintain the high luster, apply wax immediately. When specifying marble for a large table, make certain the center area of the marble has substantial support to prevent breakage.

Travertine

Follow the instructions for marble. After the application of a sealer, a sealer or buff wax may be used to add luster.

Slate

This surface produces a low luster with a deep black color after being oiled. No artifical colors or lacquers are used. The only maintenance required is the occasional application of mineral or household oil.

Plastic Laminates

This is frequently used on desk tops, cabinets, and counter tops. It is a very durable material which is impervious to many chemicals. It may be cleaned with any household cleaner and waxed. Woodgrain laminates show less small scratches and are almost maintenance free.

Plexiglass

This material has become very popular for table surfaces in the past several years, but designers should be aware that this material tends to show scratches. The surface should be dusted with a very soft cloth and washed with a mild soap and lukewarm water. Dry by blotting with a damp cloth or chamois. Do not use window cleaning solutions. The surface may be waxed with a good grade of automobile wax (not a cleaner-wax combination) and buffed with a clean cotton flannel or jersey cloth. After polishing, wipe with a clean damp cloth to ground any electrostatic charges which may attract dust particles. Scratches may be removed by sanding with 400 grit wet or dry sandpaper or a fine grit buffing compound.

Molded Plastic

For normal cleaning of molded plastic chairs use warm water and soap. After cleaning, the surface may be waxed with a furniture polish. Do not use a strong acid or alkali as a cleaner.

Natural Cane

Natural cane fiber, which has a hard, glossy outside surface in its natural state, provides its own protective coating. For added protection cane is frequently lacquered. These surfaces can be cleaned in the same manner that lacquered wood is cleaned. Designers will note that cane frequently will show slack or loosening during humid weather and return to its original taut condition as the air dries. Clients should be made aware of this condition prior to installation.

MAINTENANCE OF FURNITURE COMPONENTS

Mechanical components of furniture should be maintained on a regular basis to prevent injuries and prolong the service life of the furniture.[22]

Drawer Slides

Metal drawer slides do not usually require lubrication. When drawers receive very heavy wear, a small amount of light oil may be applied to the nylon rollers.

Swiveling or Turning Devices

The swivels and casters on office chairs are usually lubricated permanently, but if additional lubrication is needed, it would be necessary to disassemble the swivel and apply a small amount of light machine oil. Most manufacturers maintain replacement parts, should any difficulty arise.

Desks

Several component parts of the desk may require maintenance checks:

1. Drawers should be removed and cleaned with a flameproof cleaner, such as Carbona.

2. Pedestal channels may be wiped lightly with #10 oil on the roller bearings of large letter drawers. Drawers should be replaced in the same opening from which they were removed. (Number on the bottom to avoid misplacement.)

3. Desk alignment should be checked and corrected if necessary.

Filing Cabinets

1. Remove drawers, clean, and apply #10 weight oil lightly.

2. Tighten loose drawer handles.

3. Check and adjust locks.

4. Large groups or batteries of files should be bolted together to provide alignment. After bolting, the grouping can be shimmed on the floor to obtain evenness and provide square openings for the drawers so they will operate smoothly.

Chairs

Check regularly for loose bolts and weakened joints. If a chair is damaged, it should be removed from use to avoid injury.

LIFE CYCLE COSTING

The question of furniture life cycle costing often arises when a client is moving to a new facility and seeks advice regarding the continued use of currently owned equipment. Before any decision can be made, the designer should conduct a furniture inventory and note the condition of each piece. Figure 12.32 illustrates one method that can be employed.

Reaching a decision on which furniture should be replaced, repaired, sold, or donated may be dependent on the following factors:

1. Initial cost

2. Maintenance and repair cost

3. Moving cost

After these costs are compared with the cost of total replacement, additional alternatives, such as selling the furnishings at market value or the possibility of receiving a tax deduction by donating the furniture, may be considered.

In the event that new furniture is specified, the designer's choice of furniture finishes and construction will, to a large extent, lengthen the expected service life of furnishings. Assembly seating, such as stacking chairs, requires special life cycle cost consideration. The following equation may be used:

$$I + E + L + S + M = \text{total cost}$$

where
I = initial cost

E = equipment for handling (dollies)

L = labor cost for handling

S = space needed for storage (sq ft)

M = maintenance

The chair design will determine the number of chairs that can be stacked on one dolly. For example, if only ten chairs can be stacked per dolly and the dollies cost $40 each, a 500-chair installation would require 50 dollies. If other chairs were specified that could be stacked 20 per dolly, the client would realize a $1,000 initial cost saving.

Labor cost for handling the chairs can range from 4 to 7 cents per chair. Normally it takes three hours to set up 100 folding chairs and only one hour to set up 100 stacking chairs; therefore stacking chairs could result in sizable savings.

The space needed to store stacking chairs between use must also be considered in the total cost. If 500 chairs can be stacked and stored in 100 sq ft (9.5 sq m) and that commercial space costs $45 per square foot, the total storage cost would be $4,500 per year.

Maintenance costs can vary, depending on the quality of the chair and the design specified. Stacking chairs that are upholstered should have a bumper or other means of preventing damage to the upholstery during handling. Designers should also avoid specifying stacking chairs that are constructed with bolts because these tend to loosen and fall out during constant use.

This example of stacking chairs can also apply to folding or stacking tables or other furniture that is designed for multiple use.

SELJE BOND & STEWART
DESIGN CONSULTANTS

Project Number _____ Project Name _____

Date _____ Prepared By _____

LEGEND

L–Left	P–Poor
R–Right	G–Good
D. P.–Double Pedestal	E–Excellent
S. P.–Single Pedestal	D–Damaged

FURNITURE INVENTORY   Sheet_____ of _____

Item No.	Quantity	CASE GOODS										SEATING							FILING								OTHER	REMARKS	COND.				New Location
		Type Sec.		Type Exec		D. P.	S. P.	Creden.	Components Left	Right	Size	Finish	Swivel	Steno.	Guest	Lounge	Sofa	Frame	Uphol.	2	3	4	5	Letter	Legal	Lateral	Style & Mfr.			P	G	E	D	
		L	R	L	R																													

FORM No. P-329

Figure 12.32 Furniture inventory form. Reproduced with permission of Selje, Bond, Steward & Romberger, Phoenix and Los Angeles.

13 FIRE SAFETY CRITERIA FOR OPEN OFFICE PLANNING

Although designers are aware that the removal of fixed office walls, the development of the movable panel, and the elimination of the fixed office corridor have provided more efficient use of space, increased communication, and productivity, few are aware that these innovations have increased the potential for disaster in the event of fire or other emergencies.

Because walls and doors have traditionally contained and restricted the spread of fire within building enclosures and well-defined means of egress are necessary for the safety of the occupants, the increased use of open office plans has presented a new area of concern for fire safety engineers and code officials. Some of the first criteria for fire safety in open offices were developed by the General Services Administration. Though these GSA requirements apply to government offices, they do indicate a trend in safety concerns that will require a broader knowledge of fire safety terminology and new areas of design criteria.

Based on knowledge of fire behavior, the following factors should be considered in the design of an open office plan:

1. Fuel load

2. Occupancy load

3. Means of egress

4. Exit locations and arrangement

FUEL LOAD

Fuel load refers to the potential hazard of the contents in a particular occupancy. The contents are evaluated on the basis of (1) ease of ignition, (2) smoke potential, (3) explosive flash fire potential, and (4) the flame-spread characteristic of the material.

Designers should be aware that classifications such as high or low hazard (discussed in Chapter 3) are often dependent on the intended goal of a particular code. Some codes are primarily concerned with the safety of the occupants, while other codes may be concerned with the preservation of property. For example, an office with a high fuel load of papers and other combustibles may be considered a moderate hazard in terms of structural safety; i.e., a fire produced by these combustibles could be controlled by sprinklers and therefore not threaten the entire building. Life safety codes may classify the same contents as a high hazard because the potential for smoke and heat could endanger the lives of the occupants before the sprinklers could be activated.

The classification of office buildings established by GSA is based on fuel load in relation to life safety:

Group 1: *Low Intensity, Low Severity*
This group refers to occupancies with small amounts of combustibles that present no flash fire or explosive potential. A fire in this type of occupancy would not be expected to involve more than one area, i.e., not spread beyond the room of origin.

Examples:

a. Offices using all metal furniture.
b. Open office spaces having a fuel load of 6 lb (2.8 kg) per square foot or less.
c. File rooms where combustibles are contained in metal files.
d. Computer rooms.
e. Offices which use wooden furniture, provided the occupancy does not exceed one person per 200 sq ft (19 sq m) of floor area. [Example: 15 people per 3,000 sq ft (280 sq m)].

Group 2: *Full Intensity, Low Severity*
Areas where fire may be expected to spread beyond the room of origin, but the maximum expected severity would not exceed a one-hour fire (see Figure 5.2, standard time-temperature curve, in Chapter 5).

Examples:
a. Open office plans having fuel loads in excess of 6 lb per square foot.
b. Drafting rooms.
c. Offices using wooden furniture with an occupancy exceeding 200 sq ft per person. (Example: 30 people per 3,000 sq ft.)
d. Storage areas less than 500 sq ft (46 sq m).
e. Cafeterias and kitchens.

Group 3: *Full Intensity, Medium Severity*
Occupancies where fire severity may equal that produced in a two-hour fire. Fuel load in excess of 6 lb per sq ft.

Examples:
a. Libraries [shelving not exceeding 9 ft (2.7 m) in height].
b. Printing and reproduction areas.
c. Magnetic tape libraries.
d. Storage areas [exceeding 500 sq ft (47 sq m)].

Group 4: *Full Intensity, High Severity*
Occupancies having high fuel loads with flash fire or explosive potential.

Examples:
a. Library stack areas with shelving exceeding 9 ft in height.
b. Record and archive centers with open file shelving.[1]

Accurate classification of open offices according to the fuel loading is difficult because the amount of combustibles in an office may exceed the recommended 6 lb per sq ft during certain periods. For example, when extensive copy work and collation is taking place, table tops may be stacked with papers prior to filing or mailing. Recognizing that changes may occur in an office situation, the following examples of reclassification illustrate the flexibility allowed:

1. Drafting rooms using all metal furniture may be reclassified from group 2 to group 1.

2. Offices having metal furniture and metal files, but also containing large amounts of unfiled papers and books, may be reclassified from group 1 to group 2.

3. The addition of fire protection systems, such as sprinklers, can result in reclassification; i.e., group 2 may be reclassed as group 1, group 3 may be reclassed as group 2. Exception: group 4 occupancies would not qualify for reclassification.

4. When a building has a multiple occupancy on either the same or different floors, the building will be classified according to the occupancy having the greatest hazard.

Restricting Fuel Loads

Through careful specification the designer can limit the intensity and potential of fire by controlling the fuel load, smoke development, and flame-spread characteristics of the interior components. GSA requires that open offices meet the group 1 classification which specifies a fuel load not exceeding 6 lb per sq ft. These fire safety criteria may be accomplished in the following manner:

1. Limit the occupancy to a maximum of 3,000 sq ft (280 sq m) or 30 people.

2. Specify a complete, automatic sprinkler system to control flame spread.

3. Specify enclosed steel files and steel desks.

4. Specify noncombustible partitions and panels. [Wood-framed panels not exceeding 1,000 sq ft (95 sq m) are permitted in an unsprinklered area.]

5. Drapery should be noncombustible and treated with flame retardant.

6. Avoid furniture with large combustible surfaces, such as wooden or plastic wardrobes and bookcases.

7. Specify lounge chairs and couches with flame-retardant upholstery and a foam, such as neoprene.

8. Specify metal waste baskets.

9. Avoid the use of plastic artificial plants that would produce large amounts of smoke and/or drip when exposed to flame.

10. Provision of wood furnishings would not increase the fuel loading if the occupancy is limited to 15 people per 3,000 sq ft.

When these criteria cannot be met because of space limitations or the fact that a client may wish to use furnishings from another office, the designer may make a fuel load calculation to verify that the actual load of 6 lb per sq ft has been met.

Fuel Load Analysis

In order to determine the actual fuel loading of an office, the following factors are considered:

1. Enclosed combustibles, such as papers and books that are enclosed on all six sides by steel containers, such as all steel filing cabinets and steel desks.

2. Partially enclosed combustibles that are contained by steel on five sides, i.e., bookcases with glass fronts, top drawers of a metal frame desk having a particleboard or masonite top surface.

3. Free combustibles refers to papers or books exposed on top of horizontal surfaces which are 6 1/2 ft (198.1 cm) or less above the floor surface. This includes the contents of shelves with two or four sides attached to a movable partition or wall, drawers in a wooden desk, and the contents of waste baskets.

4. Furniture fuel load refers to the weight (in pounds) of all wood or cellulose furniture components. This is calculated to be 8,000 BTU per pound multiplied by the weight of the furniture. The plastic furniture components, such as urethane, polyvinyl chloride, polyester, and polypropylene, which may range between 6,000 and 22,000 BTU per pound, are multiplied by double their weight. For example, 20 plastic chairs weighing 15 lb each would equal 600 lb (280 kg) of fuel load. For example,

$$20 \times 15 = 300 \text{ lb} \times 2 = 600 \text{ lb}$$

The following items are not included in the calculation of fuel load:

1. Interior finish of walls and ceilings

2. Floorcoverings

3. Finish on metal desks that is less than .035-in. thick (veneer and vinyl desk tops)

4. Telephones, typewriters, or waste baskets

5. Ceiling height partitions

6. Filing cabinets with a UL rating of one-hour fire resistance

7. Coat racks

Though designers may not frequently make fuel load calculations, understanding the principle involved will create a better understanding of fire safety criteria. The calculation is based on the following equation:

Fuel load = A + B + C + D + E

where

A = weight of all wood or cellulose furniture in pounds

B = weight of all plastic furniture in pounds $\times$ 20

C = weight of books and papers enclosed in six-sided steel containers [multiply the volume of the container (cubic feet) by 28 lb per cubic foot].

D = weight of books and papers partially enclosed in five-sided steel containers (multiply by 28 lb per cubic foot).

E = weight of free combustibles (multiply the volume of books and papers on the horizontal surface by 28 lb per cubic foot). (To convert a surface area from square feet to cubic volume, divide the total square feet by 24.)

Additional Fuel Load Considerations

The following criteria for interior finishes are required by GSA for open office areas:

1. All interior finishes in an unsprinklered office must not exceed a flame-spread rating of 25. Smoke density is not to exceed a rating of 50. If the area is sprinklered, a flame-spread rating of 75 and smoke density rating of 100 are permitted.

2. Wall paneling in executive offices and conference rooms should not exceed 5,000 sq ft (470 sq m). The paneling should be treated with a flame retardant that is impregnated throughout the wood and have a flame-spread rating of 75 or less and a smoke density of 100 or less. In sprinklered areas these ratings should not exceed 200. The paneling should be installed in direct contact with a noncombustible wall, and furring strips should not be spaced further than 10 ft (3 m) apart (either vertical or horizontal).

3. Floorcoverings are required to have a smoke density not exceeding 450 and the critical optical density of 16 should not be reached in less than 30 seconds.

    Class A: Critical radiant flux (CRF) 0.50 w/per cm
    Class B: Critical radiant flux (CRF) 0.25 w/per cm
    Class C: Pass the FF-1-70

    Class A carpets are only required in health care facilities. Class B carpet is recommended in unsprinklered corridors which are exposed by or adjoining open office areas with a fuel load of 6 lb per square foot (group 1). Class C carpet may be used in offices and corridors protected by sprinklers. When carpet is installed by the direct glue-down process, the adhesive shall have a flash point of 140°F (60°C) or more.

OCCUPANCY LOADING

Another important factor in providing fire safety in open offices is the limitation of occupancy loads, i.e., the maximum probable number of people expected to use the space at any given time. Occupancy load restrictions depend on building use and may vary from 7 to 200 sq ft (.65 to 19 sq m) per person depending on local codes and the judgment of code officials. Some typical examples of occupancy restrictions (per person) follow:

	Psf
Class rooms	20
Apartments/hotels	200
Stores, street level	30
upper level	60
Assembly, fixed seats	15
nonfixed seats	7
Business, open office	100

These occupancy load restrictions are used to control fuel load and also determine the minimum size and number of exits needed to provide safe egress from a building in the event of an emergency.

MEANS OF EGRESS

Egress from a building may be accomplished through both vertical and horizontal exits. Horizontal exits are defined by fire codes as doors, ramps, and exit passageways or corridors. All

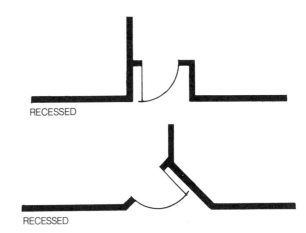

Figure 13.1 Corridor exit doors.

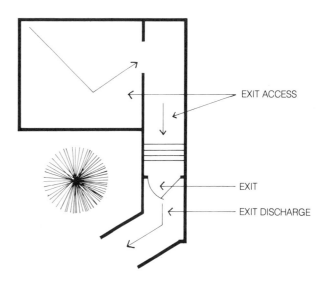

Figure 13.2 Means of egress.

doors that lead to a means of egress must swing in the direction of egress. Doors that open into corridors or exit passageways must be recessed to prevent obstruction (Figure 13.1). Most codes prohibit the use of sliding doors, and with any exit having two leafs, each must measure no less than 20 in. (50.8 cm) in width and no wider than 48 in. (121.9 cm) in width.

Vertical means of egress are primarily served by stairs which are protected from smoke and fire by enclosure and fire-rated doors at each entrance. In terms of fire safety the means of egress is divided into three sections (Figure 13.2):

1. Exit access refers to the path of travel from the point where a person is standing to the point at which the protected exit begins. (A *protected exit* is one that is equipped with a self-closing fire-resistant door.) Exit access also includes the path of travel through rooms, aisles, or corridors which lead toward the stairway or outside door.

2. Exit refers to the enclosed and protected passage leading to the outside. This includes enclosed stairways or horizontal exits.

3. Exit discharge leads from the end of the exit to the public way, i.e., sidewalks or steps leading from the exit door to courtyards or streets.

Calculation of Required Exit Capacity

The effectiveness of an exit is determined by whether it provides (1) adequate capacity, (2) adequate protection, and (3) adequate safety by proper placement and location. The first step in calculating the required exit capacity is to determine the building population or occupancy load. Because codes specify occupancy by the number of people per square foot, designers must determine the size of each area or the entire building in terms of gross or net area. The *gross area* is considered the total space without deducting for interior walls, closets, etc. The *net area* is the actual usable space after the deduction of interior walls, corridors, counters, bars, planters, or any large object that prevents a person from occupying that space. The net method is usually used for high-density occupancies, such as places of assembly. The gross method of calculation is normally used on lower-density occupancies, such as residential and office areas. Since many office buildings contain various types of occupancies, such as cafeterias and assembly rooms, the net method is frequently used. When a building or floor of an office building is multitenanted, designers should use the sum of all the occupancies in determining the exit capacity.

Once the net or gross area has been defined, the designer can proceed to calculate the expected occupancy load per square foot. For example:

Net floor area, psf		Code occupancy requirement, psf		Occupancy load (exit capacity)
Firm A	3000 ÷	100	=	30
Firm B	5000 ÷	100	=	50 (second floor)
Assembly	2000 ÷	15	=	134 (second floor)
				214

This example illustrates the method used to calculate the total number of people that the exits must accommodate (214). Most codes restrict office occupancy to 100 square feet per person, but designers should consult their local code requirements.

Exit capacity is measured by *units of width*. One unit width measures 22 in. (50.9 cm) and the units are increased by 12 in. (30.5 cm) increments to accommodate the occupancy load of the area served by the exit.

1 unit width = 22″ (50.9 cm)

1 1/2 unit widths = 34″ (86.4 cm)

2 unit widths = 44″ (111.8 cm)

2 1/2 unit widths = 56″ (142.2 cm)

Exit capacity per unit width is usually established by code. For example, most codes prescribe 100 people per unit width for horizontal exits; 60 people per unit width for ramps; and from 45 to 75 people per unit width for vertical exits.

After the designer has decided on the type of exits that will be needed (a two-story building will require a vertical exit in addition to horizontal exits), the following procedure would be used to determine the widths and number of exits needed. Using the occupancy figures from the previous example, we determine that a vertical exit must be established which can ac-commodate firm B and the assembly area located on the second floor (184 people).

Occupancy (second floor) 184 ÷ 45 people/unit
= 4.08 vertical units

In order to provide adequate exit capacity from the second floor, it would be advisable to provide five units of vertical exit. Rather than provide one large stairway (five units wide), the designer should provide two stairs 56 in. (142.2 cm) wide, or 2 1/2 units of width per stair.

To determine the size of the first floor main exit (horizontal), the following equation would be used:

Total occupancy 214 ÷ 100 people/unit = 2.14 horizontal units

In public buildings the main exit should accommodate not less than 50 percent of the total occupancy because people have a tendency to return to the exit through which they entered the building. This is known as *exit imprinting* and occurs in buildings where people are not familiar with other possible exits.

EXIT LOCATION AND ARRANGEMENT

After the number and sizes of exits have been determined, the designer must then proceed to arrange and locate exits in a manner that will minimize the possibility of blockage due to an emergency. GSA has established the following criteria for exit location in open office floor areas:

1. Every open plan floor area shall have at least two exits, remotely located from each other, separated by at least two-thirds the distance of the longest floor dimension (Figure 13.3).

2. In multitenanted floors, each tenant's space occupied by 50 or more people or containing 5,000 sq ft (470 sq m) or more shall have the same exit requirements. [Some codes require two exits for each 3,000 sq ft (280 sq m) of office space.]

3. Rooms within open floor plans or multitenanted spaces containing 50 or more people, such as conference or training rooms, shall have two exits remotely located from each other (Figure 13.3).[2]

Other critical areas of concern are the location of the exits within the central core area of commercial buildings. In many cases these exits are poorly planned in regard to fire safety criteria and the designer should make every effort to plan exits from individual tenant spaces that will allow safe egress in more than one direction. Figure 13.3 illustrates a multitenanted building which presents some egress problems. The exits from firm C, although remotely spaced, result in one exit which offers only one means of travel (a dead end). If a fire spread to the elevator corridor and beyond, the people in firm B would have no means of egress. Figure 13.4 illustrates a solution that could be used to provide protection in cases where the vertical means of egress are placed too close together. The addition of fire-rated automatic doors could prevent any single fire from involving all means of egress from a particular level.

Because continuous fire-rated corridors connecting exits are not used in open office planning, the following criteria should be established:

1. The space layout shall be planned to ensure maintenance of rational routes with well-marked secondary aisles. The space shall not create mazelike configurations inhibiting

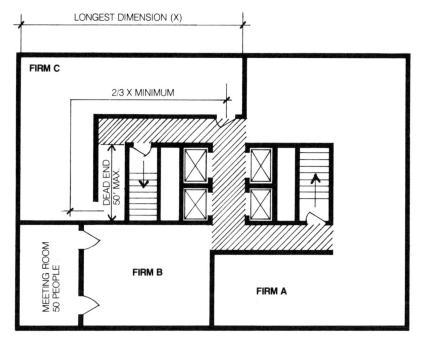

Figure 13.3 Multitenanted floor area.

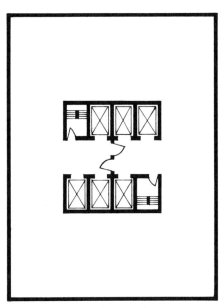

Figure 13.4 Corridor exit fire protection.
Source: NFPCA- National Fire Academy.

occupants' recognition of exit routes. Color dynamics and other innovative directional guidance may be needed in large installations.

2. The minimum width of any passageway within the open office plan shall not be less than 44 in. (111.8 cm) clear width that is not obstructed by columns, partitions, doors, or other objects (Figure 13.5).

3. Space divider and partition heights shall be limited to 5 1/2 ft (167.6 cm) in height so that occupants can quickly identify problems that may arise from fire in the area and identify the routes to reach exits. Higher partitions should be limited to the periphery areas. Freestanding dividers shall resist a momentary overturning force of 25 lb (13 kg) perpendicular to the face applied at a height of 60 in. (152.4 cm) above the floor. Panels must be arranged in a manner that will not interfere with egress.

4. Dead-end corridors which offer only one means of egress shall not exceed 50 ft (15.2 m) in length (Figure 13.3).[3]

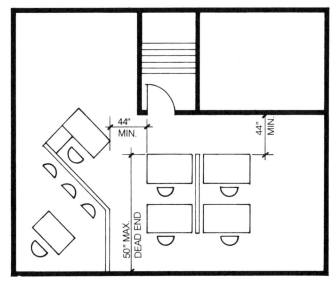

Figure 13.5 Open office exit access widths. Source: GSA.

Travel Distance to Exits
GSA has established the following travel distance criteria for open office plans:

1. Travel distance to exits shall not exceed 200 ft (61 m) in unsprinklered space and 300 ft (91.4 m) in sprinklered space measured from the center line of the path of travel from the most remote point subject to occupancy (Figure 13.6). If the most remote point is a room occupied by a maximum of 6 people who can exit from the room within a travel distance of 50 ft, measurements can start from the doors of such rooms (Figure 13.6).

2. Paths of travel leading to an exit may not pass through a secondary space subject to closure by doors, storage material, or other projections.

Exit Profiles and Rate of Travel
Establishing a profile of the expected movement of people

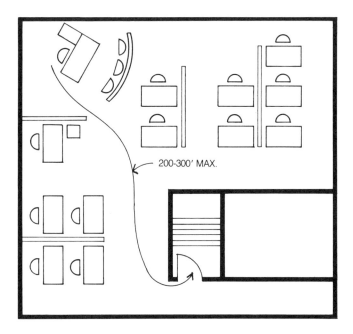

200-300' MAX.

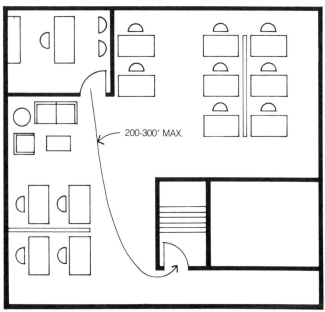

200-300' MAX.

Figure 13.6 Open office exit travel distances. Source: GSA.

toward an exit in an emergency situation can aid designers in planning the configuration of open office areas. An exit profile represents the concentration of people at various points in an exit path (Figure 13.7). The ability to predict the rate at which people will reach the first waiting point, usually a doorway from the office or a door at the entry of the stairs, can help determine the placement of workstations so that all occupants of the office can exit within a reasonable length of time. GSA requires that all people should not travel more than 15 seconds in a fire area and must relocate from the fire area within 90 seconds. The exit down to the exterior of the building, or a safe refuge, should be accomplished in not more than 5 minutes.

Research has established that the rate of travel in horizontal exit paths depends on the amount of crowding in the path.[4] With free movement, the average adult walking speed is between 250 and 300 ft (75 and 90 m) per minute. As crowding increases, the space per square foot per person may drop to 7 sq ft (.65 m) per person and the rate of travel decreases to about 150 ft (45 m) per minute. At 2 to 3 sq ft (.19 to .28 sq m) per person, movement is almost impossible, and this extreme crowding can result in panic. Figure 13.7 illustrates the points at which crowding usually occurs. The maximum flow rate through a doorway is 60 people per minute per unit width. If the number of people approaching the doorway is maintained at a rate of 60 per minute, then crowding will not occur. Based on this information, designers can readily see the importance of additional doorways and adequate spacing of workstations.

Vertical discharge is usually at the rate of 45 people per minute per stair unit width. A stairway two units wide [44 in. (111.8 cm)] could accommodate double the amount of people moving in a double row. The timed exit calculation used by GSA to exit people in five minutes is based on the following formula:

$$T = \frac{N}{(r)} + \frac{n}{(u)}$$

where

T = Time in minutes required for complete evacuation by stairs

N = Number of people exiting from floors above the first story

n = Number of people who can stand on the stairs at the same time [at 3 sq ft (2.8 sq m) per person] or the number of people on the floor, whichever is less

r = Rate of discharge on stairs in people per unit of exit width per minute

u = Number of 22-in. (55.9-cm) units of stair width.

OPEN OFFICE PLANNING FIRE SAFETY CHECKLIST

1. Where are the existing exits located?

2. Are exit doors the required width for the number of occupants that will be using the building? (Consult local codes.)

3. Do all exit doors swing outward to permit ease of exit?

4. Is exit lighting and directional signage properly placed?

5. What is the width and length of corridors?

6. Which corridors provide egress to the outside? Are there special fire regulations regarding these corridors?

7. What is the width of the stairs? Are floor numbers displayed at each floor level?

8. Are the stairs placed an adequate distance from the elevators?

9. Is there more than one stair exit provided? If so, are the two stairs adequately separated?

10. Is a door placed at the entry of the stairs to provide a smoke barrier?

11. Are the elevators equipped with a call mechanism?

12. Where is the design project located within the building in relation to the exits?

13. Does the building and project area provide accessibility to physically disabled people? (See Chapter 14.)

Figure 13.7 Exit profile.

14 SPECIFICATIONS FOR BARRIER-FREE PUBLIC INTERIORS

The material in this chapter is based on standards developed by federal agencies in order to comply with Public Law 90-480 and the American National Standard A 117.1-1961 titled "Specifications for Making Buildings and Facilities Accessible to, and Usable by, the Physically Handicapped."[1]

Due to an increased public awareness about accessibility problems, many buildings, though not government owned or financed, are being planned with barrier-free environments for physically disabled people. During the past decade this concern has been reflected in the numerous state and city codes dealing with barrier-free regulations that have been adopted.

A person confined to a wheelchair is the usual stereotyped image of the "physically disabled" person. The General Services Administration defines a physically disabled person as "any individual who despite a physical disability, can be expected, without assistance from another person, to visit and utilize a building."[2] Another federal agency further expands the definition to include the following categories:

1. Nonambulatory disabilities: those where people are confined to wheelchairs.

2. Semiambulatory disabilities: those which allow a person to walk with difficulty. This includes people who walk with crutches, braces, or walkers.

3. Disabilities of incoordination or palsy: due to brain or nerve damage.

4. Hearing disabilities: those which impair a person's ability to detect warning signals.

5. Sight disabilities: those which prevent people from perceiving signals or dangerous situations.

6. Temporary disabilities: due to injury, illness, or pregnancy.

7. General disabilities: due to aging which reduces a person's mobility, coordination, and perception.[3]

Reviewing this list, designers will agree that "barrier-free" does not merely imply ramps and adequate door widths, but expands to include a whole range of considerations. Aside from the obvious architectural barriers which have limited the free movement of physically disabled people, society is now becoming aware of the *psychological barriers* that physical space imposes upon those who are handicapped. When a handicapped person must enter by a service entrance or ask assistance in opening a door, he or she is made to feel humiliated and helpless. Millions of dollars are spent each year rehabilitating and training physically disabled people to function and contribute to society, but our buildings have made it impossible for them to move about, contribute, and enjoy the same privileges that able-bodied people take for granted. When reduced to the status of second-class citizens, those who are handicapped feel discriminated against.

The design of barrier-free public spaces involves concern for two major categories of users: visitors and employees. The general purpose of the building indicates the type of people who will be using the facility. Theaters, federal buildings (such as post offices), banks, libraries, and restaurants, will require clearly marked exit routes, rest rooms, and other accessibility factors for visitors not familiar with the building. Office buildings will require more detailed planning to accommodate both visitors and employees who are handicapped.

The following guidelines for the specification of barrier-free public interiors are arranged as a checklist for use during the planning phase. Federal requirements are starred (*) and the remaining criteria are recommended. Designers should remember that requirements are minimum; therefore every effort should be made to incorporate the additional recommended guidelines.

GENERAL REQUIREMENTS FOR INTERIOR ACCESSIBILITY

1. Walls and partitions
   *a. Provide fixed or nonfixed partitions that are sturdy and will withstand a 60-lb (28-kg) force applied from any direction.
   *b. Mount decorations, hardware, and equipment with the capability of withstanding but not necessarily supporting a 60-lb force applied from any direction.
   *c. Provide markings at heights of 36 in. (91.4 cm) and 60 in. (152.4 cm) on large expanses of glass.
   d. Avoid abrasive wall surfaces within 60 in. (152.4 cm) of the floor in heavy traffic areas.
   e. Avoid hazardous glare in corridors and stairways by specifying matted surfaces, low-glare lighting fixtures, and window coverings.

2. Windows
   a. Avoid strong contrast between window and wall surface. Provide drapery or window coverings that will eliminate glare in work areas and points of directional decision, such as lobbies, corridors, and intersection points.
   b. Provide window coverings that will prevent drafts and reduce radiant heat loss in areas where people will spend extended lengths of time.
   c. Provide long wand sticks for the manual operation of drapery and blinds.

3. Doors
   *a. Doors must have a clear opening of at least 32 in. (81.3 cm) when open and must be operable by a single effort. The weight required to open a door should be 5 but not exceeding 8 lb (2.3 to 3.7 kg). (Note: two-leaf doors are not recommended unless they open with a single effort or one of the leaves provides a clear opening of 32 in.)
   *b. The floor on both sides of the door must be level for at least 60 in. (152.4 cm) and the floor must extend at

least 12 in. (30.5 cm) beyond each side of the door.

*c. Thresholds shall be flush with the floor if possible. When a raised threshold is necessary, it must be beveled or ramped gradually on both sides of the door. (See Figure 14.1.)

*d. Vestibules: the inner and outer doors of a vestibule must be separated by at least 42 in. (106.7 cm) in addition to the door swing. Both doors must swing in the same direction. (See Figure 14.2.)

*e. Handles shall be mounted at a maximum height of 42 in. Panic bars shall be placed 32 in. above the floor. Kickplates at least 16 in. (40.6 cm) high are recommended for all doors. Door closers with a 4- to 6-second time delay are recommended.

f. Vision panels are desirable to all swinging doors. Safety glass should be placed a maximum of 36 in. (91.4 cm) above the floor.

g. Sliding doors should have top-hung self-lubricating tracks and bottom guides. Doors should be easy to operate. Nylon wheels or roller bearings on metal tracks are recommended.

h. Door openings should not be placed directly opposite a stairway.

*i. Provide protection for doors opening into corridors.

*j. Provide outswing doors to storage rooms, closets, and accessible restroom stalls.

4. Hardware

*a. Provide hardware, both latching and nonlatching, operable with a single hand that does not require wrist action or fine finger manipulation.

*b. Position operating hardware between 32 in. (81.3 cm) and 42 in. (106.7 cm) above the floor. A 36-in. (91.4-cm) center line is recommended.

c. Provide a clearance of 1 3/4 to 2 1/4 in. (44.4 to 57.4 mm) between operating hardware and door jambs. (A wider clearance is not recommended.)

d. Provide texture on door hardware for identification.

e. Use lever handles or panic hardware on all side-hung latched doors.

5. Floorcovering

*a. Firmly attach all coverings to base floor.

b. Flush mount floorcovering where it joins another flooring material. (See Figure 14.3.)

*c. Floors must be on a common level throughout a given story or be connected by ramps. Variations no greater than plus or minus 1/4 to 1/8 in. (6.4 to 3.2 mm).

*d. Floors must have nonslip surfaces. Friction coefficient: no less than .5 when wet or dry, measured by static means. (See page 88 for the discussion of resilient flooring in Chapter 8.)

e. Floors should withstand a load of 125 psi and deflection shall not exceed 1/2 in. (12.7 mm).

*f. Carpeting must be heavy-duty contract quality, high-density, tight-weave, low-looped pile. Padding when used should be dense and firm. Broadloom should be tightly stretched and carpet tiles should be securely in place.

*g. Floors of primary circulation paths shall have a hard surface, such as vinyl-asbestos tile, to permit ease of movement for wheelchairs. Travel distance over carpet to reach such a path should not exceed 50 ft (15.2 m).

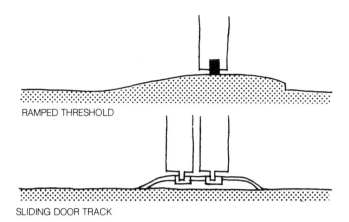

Figure 14.1 Thresholds. Unless otherwise credited, illustrations in this chapter were adapted from Design Criteria: New Public Building Accessibility, *PBS (PCD)..DG5.*

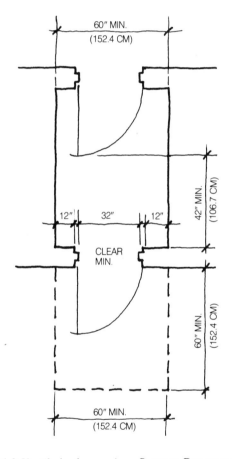

Figure 14.2 Vestibule door swing. Source: Department of Health, Education, and Welfare, Office of Facilities Engineering.

Figure 14.3 Flooring transition strip. Source: Department of Health, Education, and Welfare, Office of Facilities Engineering.

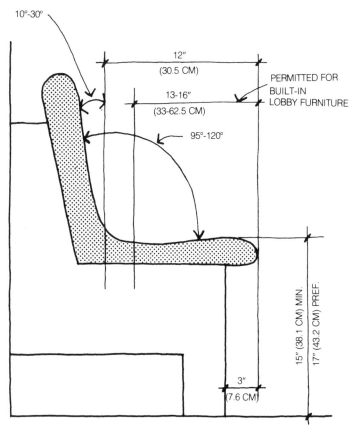

Figure 14.4 Built-in seating.

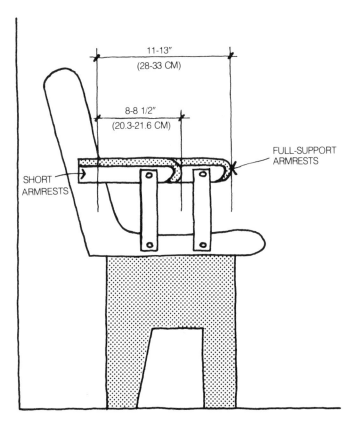

Figure 14.5 Assembly seating armrests.

h. Flooring materials should not produce sharp reflections or glossy surfaces.
i. Select single colors or muted patterns for floorcoverings. Highly contrasting patterns create visual confusion for people with visual impairments.

6. Furniture
    a. Furniture legs or supports should not present a tripping hazard.
    b. Furniture selected for public use should contrast (in value) with the background so it is distinguishable by people with sight disabilities.
    c. Seating depth may vary:
        (1) Lobby: minimum 12 in. (30.5 cm) for short-term seating.
        (2) Assembly seating: minimum 13 to 16 in. (33 to 40.6 cm).
        (3) Short-term seating: maximum 16 in. (40.6 cm) for use with backrest.
    d. Seat widths should be no less than 16 in. (40.6 cm).
    e. Fixed seating should be no less than 15 in. (38.1 cm) from the floor [17 in. (43.2 cm) preferred].
    f. Recommended seating angles vary according to use:
        (1) Backrest to seat angle: 95° to 120°.
        (2) Backrest to vertical angle: 10° to 30° measured from a vertical extended from base of seat. If the back has more than a 30° angle from the vertical line, a headrest should be provided. (See Figure 14.4.)
    g. Upper back support should be provided on lounge chairs and tilted lounge chairs that have more than a 30° angle from the vertical.
    h. Armrest widths should be no less than 2 in. (5.1 cm); 2 1/2 to 3 1/2 in. (6.4 to 8.9 cm) are preferred widths.
    i. The length of an armrest varies with use:
        (1) Casual seating: full armrest of 11 to 13 in. (27.9 to 33 cm).
        (2) Assembly seating and desk or table seating: short armrests about 8 1/2 in. (21.6 cm) long.
    j. The space between the armrests may range between 19 and 22 in. (48.3 and 55.9 cm). Assembly seating should not be wider than 20 1/2 in. (52.1 cm).
    k. Height of armrests are usually 8 1/2 in. (21.6 cm) above the seat. (See Figure 14.5.)
    l. Padding for upholstered furniture should be firm to prevent bottoming out of the seat area.
    m. Upholstery should be neither rough nor slippery. Material should be porous and of a medium weave. Welt cording should not be placed along front edge of seat cushions because it may hamper blood circulation.

Communication and Signage for Accessibility

The General Services Administration offers some very effective recommendations for communication or cuing systems to provide directional, emergency, and safety information. Cuing systems make use of changes or contrast in color, texture, and lighting to reinforce communication. An effective communication is based on four criteria: (1) unambiguity: distinct elevator lobbies for various floors; (2) consistency: room numbers and directional signs placed in the same location on each floor; (3) reinforcement of information through coded textural and color cuing: warning danger signals; (4) predictability factors such as having all room numbers on one side of the corridor.[4]

The following suggestions include areas of concern such

as general circulation; emergency safety information; the use of lighting, tactile, and sound cues; and signage design.

1. Circulation
    a. Provide for directional information to accessible areas, such as transportation points; drop-off zones; car parking for people who are handicapped.
    b. Provide information along accessible routes to the entry; to vertical access (stairs, ramps, elevators). For visitors provide directions at vertical access to various floors and levels.
    c. Signage to accessible interior circulation; to public facilities and conveniences (restrooms, assembly areas, lobbies, offices, and dining facilities).
    d. Mark accessibility of conveniences; e.g., indicate the provision of a chairbound water closet on the *exterior* rest room door.
    e. Number all rooms including conference rooms and dining rooms.
    f. Provide floor numbers at vertical access areas (stairs, elevators, or ramps).
    g. Provide warnings if there is a level change in corridors.

2. Emergency safety information
    a. Provide both visual and audible alarms when required by local codes. (Flashing light next to exit sign.)
    b. Emergency exit signage must be distinct from regular circulation information. Routes to accessible holding areas (for fire emergency) should be clearly marked.
    c. Mark areas not recommended for chairbound people during an emergency.
    d. Plaques bearing raised letters or numbers shall be used to identify rooms or offices. They shall be placed on the corridor wall on the latch side of the doorway approximately 60 in. (152.4 cm) above the floor. Letters should be 5/8 in. (15.9 mm) in height and should be raised at least 1/32 in. (.8 mm) above the surface.
    e. Doors leading to dangerous areas not normally used by the public, such as mechanical rooms, loading platforms, and fire escapes, should be identified by handles with knurled finish.

3. Signage design
    a. Uniform format, color, and wording.
    b. Use of short familiar phrases.
    c. Simple and clear graphic designs.
    d. Use black or dark color background with white or light letters; also size will help the sign be discerned from the surrounding background.

4. Wall graphics
    a. When used as directional signage, the graphic should reinforce cues for intersections and level changes.
    b. Provide value contrast at junction of walls and flooring. A difference of 20 percent in reflectance value is recommended.

5. Lighting
    Use lighting to emphasize important areas or hazards.

6. Tactile and textural cues
    a. Handrails should provide a change in texture to indicate approaching vertical level changes, intersections, or doorways.
    b. Flooring textures may be used to indicate an approaching level change or doorway.

7. Sound cues
    Changes in the floorcovering from soft to hard can be used to warn the blind of an approaching level change.

Horizontal Circulation through Interior Space
Corridors, ramps, and other horizontal passages that accommodate physically disabled people require additional space considerations.

Corridors
*1. Primary corridors allow for the passage of two wheelchairs side by side. These corridors should measure 60 in. (152.4 cm) in width.

*2. Partial or secondary corridors measure 54 in. to 60 in. (137.2 to 152.4 cm). In a very cramped situation a secondary passage may measure 42 to 44 in. (106.7 to 111.8 cm).

3. A full one-way passage should measure 36 in. (91.4 cm).

*4. Primary corridors are limited to a maximum distance of 100 ft (30.5 m) between rest stops.

*5. Rest stops are alcoves along corridors which are designed to allow parking for wheelchairs and seating. Parking for one wheelchair should measure 48 in. (121.9 cm) in length and 32 in. (81.3 cm) wide. Additional space must also be provided for approach, turning, and backing up. (See Figure 14.6.)

*6. Partial or secondary corridors are limited to a maximum of 50 ft (15.2 m) to a 360° turnaround area [60″ × 60″ (152.4 × 152.4 cm)].

7. One-way passages are limited to a maximum distance of 50 ft (15.2 m) to a 180°-wheel pivot turnaround. Distance to a 180° axle-pivot turn is 25 ft (7.6 m). A one-way passage that requires backing out is limited to 8 ft (243.8 cm).

8. A turn of 360° requires a diameter circle at footrest height. (See Figure 14.7.)

9. 180° turns require 75 in. (190.5 cm) by 64 1/2 in. (163.9 cm). (See Figure 14.8.)

10. A 90° turn requires 55″ × 66″ × 36″ (139.7 × 167.6 × 91.4 cm). (See Figure 14.9.)

11. Overall lighting should equal 10 footcandles. Major intersections should provide 15 to 20 footcandles.

Vertical Access in Interior Spaces
Means of accessible vertical egress—stairs, elevators—are critical in the event of a fire. The following requirements should be observed:

*1. Provide two types of vertical access at all change levels.

*2. Provide ramped access for level changes from 1/4 in. (6.4 mm) to the height of one step.

*3. Cue vertical changes greater than 1/2 in. (12.7 mm). It is recommended that level changes be avoided in heavy traffic areas. Also avoid level changes of less than three steps.

4. Stairs
    *a. Width should be 44 in. (111.8 cm).

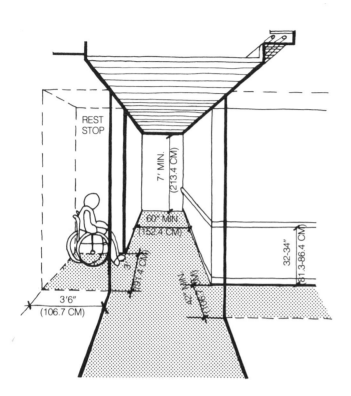

Figure 14.6 Corridors with rest stops.

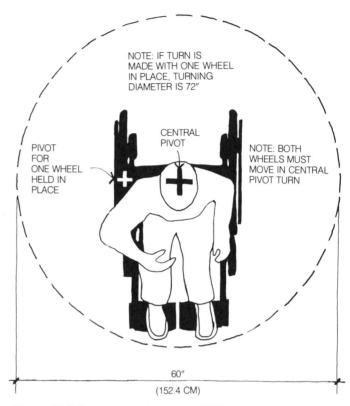

Figure 14.7 Turning requirements: 360° turn.

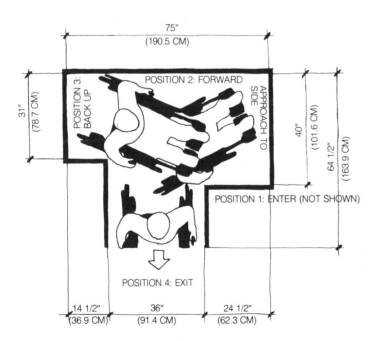

Figure 14.8 Turning requirements: 180° three-point turn.

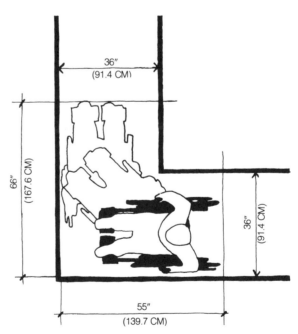

Figure 14.9 Turning requirements: 90° turn.

b. Risers should not exceed 7 in. (17.8 cm). All risers should be closed on stairs used for primary egress.
c. Tread areas of stairs should not be less than 10 in. (25.4 cm).
d. Maximum uninterrupted vertical rise should be 9 ft (2.7 m).
e. Approaches and landings should be level and have cuing (color, light, or texture) to warn of approach.

5. Handrails
    *a. Handrails 32 in. (81.3 cm) high measured vertically from the stair noising are required on both sides of the stair. Rails should be round or oval in section and measure between 1/2 and 2 in. (12.7 to 50.8 mm) in diameter and have a nonslip surface.
    *b. Handrails shall be continuous at landings and extend 12 in. (30.5 cm) beyond the edge of the beginning and final step.
    *c. Treads shall be finished in a nonslip material. Heavily patterned floor surfaces are not recommended on landings.
    *d. Stairs must be adequately lighted at all times. Minimum level of 5 footcandles is recommended.

6. Ramps
    A ramp with a gradient of 5 to 8 percent shall have the following:
    *a. The same width as the walk or corridor it serves—48 in. (121.9 cm) minimum.
    *b. Shall be kept to a maximum gradient of 8.33 percent, or 1-ft (30.5-cm) rise in 12 ft (3.6 m) of run.
    *c. The ramp shall be built of firm, fixed, nonslip materials. The ramp shall also not have grating or other openings.
    *d. Ramp shall be provided with a level platform at the top which shall measure 60″ × 60″ (152.4 × 152.4 cm) and a straight level clearance of at least 72 in. (182 cm) at the bottom of the ramp.
    *e. A level landing shall be provided at 30-ft (9-m) intervals and at all changes of direction and intersections with other ramps or doors. These landings shall be 60 in. (152.4 cm) in length.
    *f. Ramps shall be provided with handrails on one side (and both sides if possible). The rails must be smooth and extend out from the walls at least 1 1/2 in. (3.8 cm). Rails shall extend beyond the top and bottom of the ramp at least 12 in. (30.5 cm).
    *g. Ramps shall be provided with curbs 2 in. (5.1 cm) high or guard rails or walls at least 32 in. (81.3 cm) high where there is a drop in grade at the edge of the ramp.
    *h. Provide lighting for ramps at all times (5 footcandles minimum recommended).

7. Elevators
    *a. Elevators must be available at the level of the major building entrance which is used by physically disabled people. The elevators must give access to all levels of the building normally used by the public.
    b. Call buttons should be centered at 42 in. (106.7 cm) above the floor. A visible and audible signal indicating direction of travel is required.
    *c. Cab size must allow for movement of a wheelchair. A 180° turning of the wheel is recommended.
    *d. Door opening width must be a minimum of 32 in. (81.3 cm).
    *e. Doors shall be fitted with a door reopening device capable of sensing an object in the path of the doors and without requiring contact for activation.
    *f. Operation must be automatic and self-leveling within 1/2 in. (12.7 mm) of floor levels under normal use conditions.
    g. At least one wall of the car should be equipped with a handrail 32 in. (81.3 cm) above the floor.
    *h. All essential controls which are designed for unilateral vertical reach from a wheelchair shall be mounted at a maximum height of 60 in. (152.4 cm). Controls shall be usable by blind people and shall feature raised numerals and symbols.
    *i. An emergency telephone without dial shall be mounted at a maximum height of 48 in. (121.9 cm) above the floor.

8. Entrance lobbies
    a. Provide waiting areas with seating and space for wheelchair parking within the main lobby or adjacent to the main entry. A vestibule area is acceptable, but paths of egress should not be blocked. (See Figure 14.10.)
    b. The space should be provided for parking at least two wheelchairs. This space requires a minimum length of 48 in. (121.9 cm) and a minimum width of 32 in. (81.3 cm). Additional space should be provided for parking, backing, and approaching. Provide at least 24 in. (61 cm) between seating and passageway if seating is facing into the circulation area.
    c. A full primary two-way passage must be provided through the lobby area [60 in. (152.4 cm)]. This passage should connect the reception desk, elevators, and public conveniences (drinking fountains, telephones, restrooms) that are located near the lobby.
    d. *Floorcovering* in the immediate entrance area should not be a slick surface that may result in slipping and falling. Avoid the use of terrazzo, polished stone, or hand-crafted ceramic tiles with deeply grouted seams which could make wheelchair movement difficult.
    e. Provide a flush mount between hard-surfaced entry flooring and adjoining carpet. (See Figure 14.10.)
    f. *Furniture* in lobby areas must be designed for use by physically disabled people. Stability of construction in seating furniture is important.
    *g. Information or reception desks (counters) shall not exceed 36 in. (91.4 cm) in height. Exception: Some counters may be built higher if a section [at least 30 in. (76.2 cm) wide] is 36 in. high. If a counter is provided for writing, it should not exceed 34 in. (86.4 cm) in height. (See Figure 14.11.)
    h. Reception counters should be visible from the entrance doors.
    i. *Minimum lighting* levels for lobbies is 10 footcandles. Writing areas should provide 30 footcandles.

9. Exhibit and display areas
    a. Exhibits in lobbies shall not create barriers or obstruct normal passage paths.
    b. Display equipment (structures) should be able to

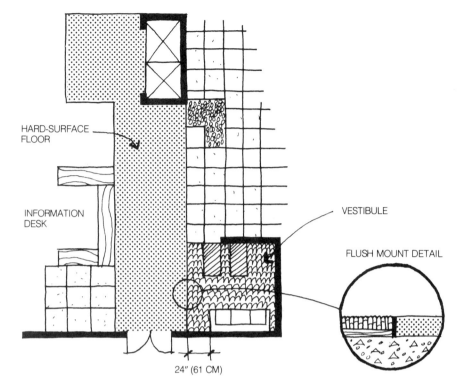

HARD-SURFACE
FLOOR

INFORMATION
DESK

VESTIBULE

FLUSH MOUNT DETAIL

24" (61 CM)

Figure 14.10 Vestibule floor surfacing.

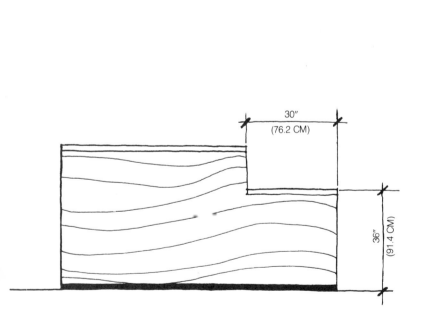

30"
(76.2 CM)

36"
(91.4 CM)

Figure 14.11 Lobby information desk.

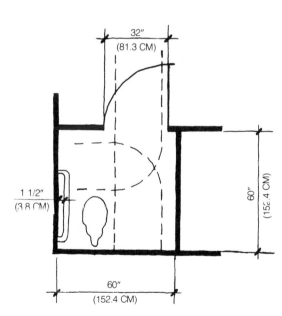

32"
(81.3 CM)

60"
(152.4 CM)

1 1/2"
(3.8 CM)

60"
(152.4 CM)

Figure 14.12 Side transfer toilet.

withstand 250 lb (150 kg) of force applied from any direction.

Toilet Facilities

Each floor of a building shall have at least one toilet facility available to physically disabled people of each sex. The following requirements must be provided:

*1. The floor of the toilet room shall be at the same level as the corridor floor.

*2. The layout of entrance foyers, doors, and privacy screens shall allow sufficient clearance for wheelchair passage.

*3. The floor space must contain a clearance of at least 60″ × 60″ (152.4 × 152.4 cm) for wheelchair turning.

4. At least one toilet stall shall be the side-transfer type. (See Figure 14.12.) This type of stall shall have the following measurements:
   a. A minimum width of 66 in. (167.6 cm) and a depth of at least 60 in. (152.4 cm).
   b. A 32-in. (81.3-cm) wide clear opening to one side of the front of the stall with an outswinging door.
   c. One water closet with seat 20 in. (50.8 cm) above the floor and the centerline located 18 in. (45.7 cm) from the side wall on which the grab bar is located and away from the door. If possible, a wall-mounted water closet is preferred.
   d. The wall-mounted bar shall be 1.5 in. (3.8 cm) in diameter and be placed 1.5 in. from the wall. It shall be located 33 in. (83.8 cm) from the floor. When multiple toilet sets are provided, the grab bars and toilets should be alternated between the left and right sides of stalls.

*5. At least one lavatory shall be wall mounted with a 29-in. (73.7-cm) minimum clearance underneath the apron of the fixture [10 in. (25.4 cm) from the face of the fixture] to provide wheelchair approach. Faucets shall be easily operated with no self-closing fixtures. Single lever or wrist blade types that do not require hand grip should be used.

*6. Toilet rooms for men shall have wall-mounted urinals with the rim 19 in. (48.3 cm) above the floor or shall have floor-mounted urinals which are at the same level as the main floor of the toilet room.

*7. Mirrors and shelves shall be mounted above accessible lavatories as low as possible, not exceeding 40 in. (101.6 cm) from the floor. Towel racks, soap dispensers, and all other accessories should be located no higher than 40 in. above the floor.

Drinking Fountains and Public Telephones

At least one telephone and one fountain shall be located at an accessible location on each floor of a building:

*1. The fountain shall be hand operated or hand and foot operated with up-front water and jet controls. A wall-mounted model with a 12-in. (30.5-cm) projecting bowl with a rim placed 30 to 36 in. (76.2 to 91.4 cm) above the floor. An alcove is desirable for the location of a fountain in a corridor. (See Figure 14.13.)

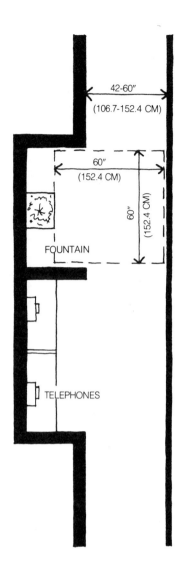

Figure 14.13 Public telephones and drinking fountains.

*2. Telephone dials, handsets, and coin slots shall be located no higher than 54 in. (137.2 cm) above the floor. Push button dials are preferred and cords should be 36 in. (91.4 cm) long. Directories should be mounted 30 to 34 in. (76.2 to 86.4 cm) above the floor. At least one telephone should be equipped with an amplifier for use by those with a hearing disability.

Open Office Barrier-Free Criteria

Open offices present special problems for physically disabled people because standard corridors are not established. Therefore accessibility factors require special attention.

1. Locate conference rooms and meeting rooms so that they are convenient to main circulation routes and vertical access.

2. Accessible conference rooms should be within 50 ft (15 m) of accessible restrooms, drinking fountains, and public telephones. Where duplication of conference facilities occurs, one room or area of each type should be accessible.

*3. Provide office work areas usable by physically disabled people without segregating them into one area. Allow additional linear wall space and/or floor space for storage usable by those who are handicapped in private office situations.

4. Provide two different means of access to built-up areas and elevated computer floors (vertical).

5. Workstation access aisles should have a clear width of at least 36 in. (91.4 cm) with a wheelchair turnaround area of at least 60″ × 60″ (152.4 × 152.4 cm) located at 50-ft (15-m) maximum intervals. (See Figure 14.14.)

6. Each workstation, reception area, and storage room should provide space for a wheelchair turn.

7. Provide for several interview spaces beside desks. This space should be large enough for a wheelchair [32″ × 48″ (81.3 × 121.9 cm)]. Light-weight furniture may occupy this space when not needed for interviewing handicapped people. (See Figure 14.14.)

8. The distance from an individual workstation to the nearest accessible rest room should not exceed 150 ft (45.7 m).

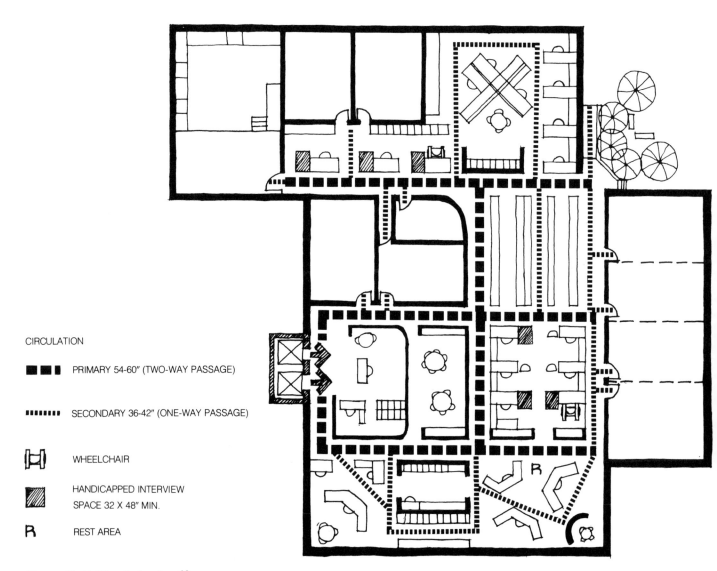

CIRCULATION

■ ■ ■ PRIMARY 54-60″ (TWO-WAY PASSAGE)

▪▪▪▪▪▪▪ SECONDARY 36-42″ (ONE-WAY PASSAGE)

⊞ WHEELCHAIR

▨ HANDICAPPED INTERVIEW SPACE 32 X 48″ MIN.

R REST AREA

Figure 14.14 Circulation in offices.

9. Vertical panels should provide an 8-in. (20.3-cm) open space between bottom of panel and the floor to permit detection by blind long-cane users.

10. A guide rope or other cue should be provided along vertical panels to aid blind employees. (See Figure 14.15.)

11. Wall panels should not have base supports that extend into a path of egress in an open office plan.

12. When several panels are connected in a linear assembly, there should be one stabilizing panel attached to the assembly at a 45° to 90° angle for each three panels.

13. The entire open office system, including the carpeting and permanent walls, should provide sufficient color and value contrast to permit identification of components and various means of egress by visually impaired people.

14. Work surfaces should have a minimum undersurface kneespace width of 32 in. (81.3 cm). A leg room depth of 20 in. (50.8 cm) should also be provided.

15. Work surfaces, storage units, typing tables, and conference tables should be capable of being adjusted incrementally in height. Other than typing tables, all work surfaces should have an adjustable height from 25 to 30 in. (63.5 to 76.2 cm) measured from the underside of the work surface. (See Figure 14.16.)

16. All horizontal work surfaces should be capable of supporting a 200-lb (90-kg) load at the outer edge without tipping.

17. Work surfaces should be provided with a nonglare top surface.

18. All edges and corners of furniture components should be rounded wtih a radius of 1/8 in. (3.2 mm).

19. When overhead storage is used, the work surface width should not exceed 25 in. (63.5 cm) if kneespace is provided. When kneespace is not provided, the top width should not exceed 20 in. (50.8 cm). The bottom of the overhead shelf should not be higher than 44 in. (111.8 cm) above the floor when a kneespace is provided; without a kneespace, the height should be 46 in. (116.8 cm).

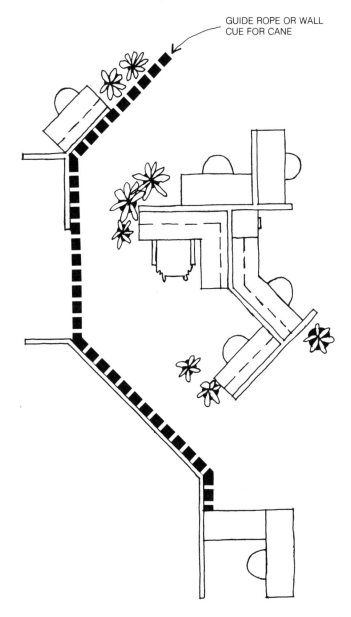

Figure 14.15 Circulation: passage through open office plan.

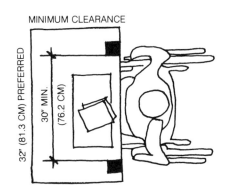

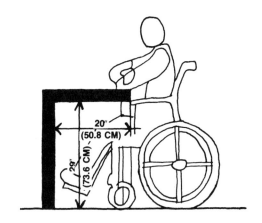

Figure 14.16 Work surfaces.

20. All doors and drawers should be operable with one hand. Use side-hung doors if they do not cause obstruction to movement within the space.

21. Provide a variety of file storage that is accessible to disabled people. A seated person may reach a filing system from 10 to 42 in. (25.4 to 106.7 cm) high; a standing person's reach is from 10 to 56 in. (25.4 to 142.2 cm) high. (See Figure 14.17.)

22. All hardware should be flush or recessed. Trim may only protrude 1/8 in. (3.2 mm). Latches and handles to overhead storage should be located at the bottom of the doors. All desk hardware should be located (if possible) at least 18 in. (45.7 cm) from the floor.

23. Hooks and hangers within wardrobes should be adjustable from 48 to 66 in. (121.9 to 167.6 cm).

24. Lighting levels at workstations should average 50 ESI footcandles for task illumination. Overall illumination for general circulation should average 10 footcandles.

25. Locate outlets to prevent potential hazards, such as raised mounts or multiple plug adaptors. Extension cords should not be allowed to run under work surfaces. All electrical power receptacles, switches, and telephone outlets which are housed in the furniture system should be located between 12 and 48 in. (30.5 and 121.9 cm) above the floor.

26. Controls on telephones shall not require wrist action or finger manipulation. Provisions should be made to add receiver volume controls to telephones when needed. Other handicapped aids should also be made available, such as teletypewriter, speaker system, and foot controls.

Accessibility to Public Spaces

Dining areas, dormitories, and spectator spaces require the following design considerations:

1. Dining areas
   a. Dining areas should be directly accessible to physically disabled people without having to enter through a service area or kitchen.
   b. Provide a variety of dining choices within the facility. Do not segregate handicapped people in one area.
   c. Access aisles between tables or booths should be at least 36 in. (91.4 cm) wide with wheelchair turning space of no less than 60″ × 60″ (152.4 × 152.4 cm) located at 50-ft (15.2-m) maximum intervals.
   d. *Food service* lines should allow a minimum clear aisle width of 42 in. (106.7 cm) between food service counters (or tray slides) and control railing. Outside rail height of tray slide should not be more than 34 in. (86.4 cm). (See Figure 14.18.)
   e. Vending areas should provide a turning space of no less than 60″ × 60″ (152.4 × 152.4 cm). (See Figure 14.19.)

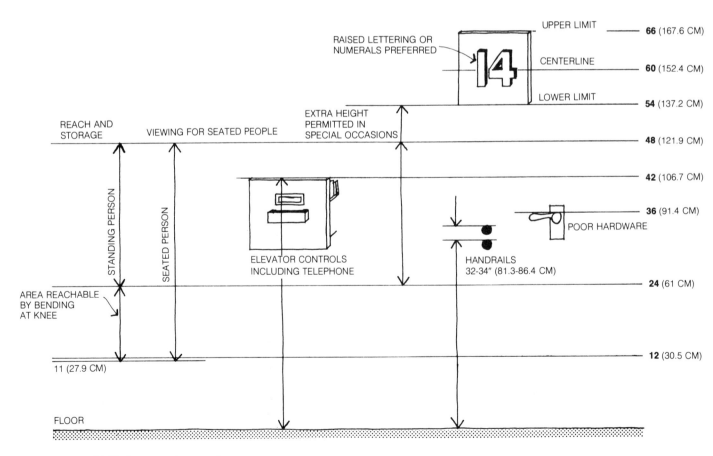

Figure 14.17 Comparative reach.

f. Undertable clearance should measure 29 to 30 in. (73.7 to 76.2 cm). Minimum clear knee recess width of 32 in. (81.3 cm) and a depth of 20 in. (50.8 cm) should be provided.

g. Booths, stand-up counters, and other such facilities are permitted when other alternatives are provided for those who are handicapped.

h. Dispensers for eating utensils, glassware, and drinking water should be available to people not going through the food service line. Drinking glasses should be provided with a support shelf while they are being filled from a tap dispenser.

2. Dormitories

a. Rooms should be large enough to allow placement of furniture with at least 52 in. (132.1 cm) between major elements. Clearance between the bed and a wall surface should be 38 in. (96.5 cm).

b. Clothing storage rods should be adjustable to 48 in. (121.9 cm) above the floor. To be fully accessible, closet should allow partial entry of a wheelchair.

c. Mattress top should be 22 in. (55.9 cm) above the floor.

d. Rooms should be adequately ventilated in bedrooms where wheelchairs may be recharged.

3. Spectator spaces

a. Lecture halls, auditoria, and theaters should have areas set aside for wheelchair users. Wheelchair stations should be level, be out of the traffic zone, and provide good visibility. (See Figure 14.20.)

b. The number of wheelchair stations varies with the capacity of the assembly space.

Assembly Space	Number of Wheelchair Stations
Up to 75	Minimum 1
76 to 500	Minimum 2
501 to 1000	Minimum 3
1001 to 1500	Minimum 4
Over 1500	Minimum 4 plus 1 for each 400 people over 1500

c. Seating should also be provided for semiambulant people. The amount of seating provided should equal a minimum of 1 percent of the total number of seats. Allow for a choice of seating location.

d. Accessible lounge seating should be provided for a minimum of two people in the entry areas.

*e. All sloping floors must be covered in nonslip materials. Floors that slope more than 1:20 shall be considered ramps. Ramps should be provided at level changes that exceed more than 1/2 in. (12.7 mm).

f. Where writing surfaces are provided for use in lecture rooms or assembly spaces, the equipment should not prevent ease of sitting or rising.

g. A means of vertical access should be provided to all podia or stages. This may be portable or temporary.

h. A minimum of 10 footcandles should be provided for general circulation areas. Foot lighting should be provided on stairways and aisles.

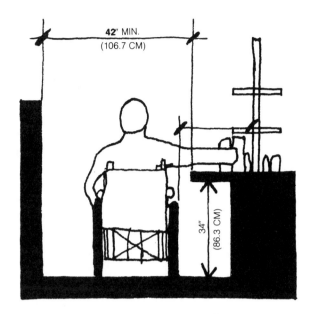

Figure 14.18 Food service.

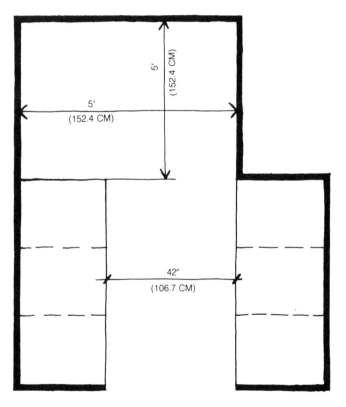

Figure 14.19 Vending machines.

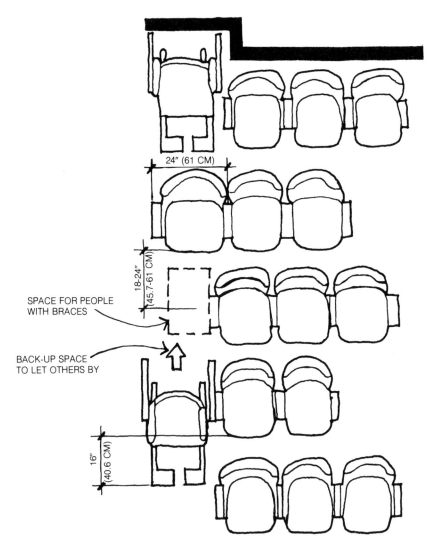

24" (61 CM)

18-24" (45.7-61 CM)

SPACE FOR PEOPLE
WITH BRACES

BACK-UP SPACE
TO LET OTHERS BY

16" (40.6 CM)

Figure 14.20 Assembly seating.

PROCEDURES FOR COMPLIANCE WITH BARRIER-FREE REQUIREMENTS

Designers involved in the design and specification of interior components for federal buildings or public spaces that must comply with Public Law 90-480 should obtain procedures for compliance from regional offices of the General Services Administration or the Office of Facilities Engineering of the Department of Health, Education, and Welfare. Currently these federal agencies employ a checklist for documenting compliances; and after a final inspection to certify that the facilities meet the requirements, a certificate of compliance is issued. State and local governing agencies should also be consulted on compliance procedures.

Exceptions and Waivers

The following exceptions are currently allowed by federal regulations:

1. The design, construction, or alteration of any portion of a building which need not, because of its intended use, be made accessible to, or usable by, the public or by physically disabled people.

2. The alteration of an existing building if the alteration does not involve the installation of, or work on, existing stairs, doors, elevators, toilets, entrances, drinking fountains, floors, telephone location, curbs, parking areas, or any other facilities susceptible of installation or improvements to accommodate physically disabled people.

3. The alteration of an existing building, or of such portions thereof, to which application of the standard is not structurally possible.

4. The construction or alteration of a building for which plans and specifications were completed or substantially completed on or before Setpember 2, 1969. However, any building constructed under the National Transportation Act of 1960, the National Capital Transportation Act of 1965, or Title III of the Washington Metropolitan Area Transit Regulation Compact shall be designed, constructed, or altered in accordance with ANSI standards regardless of design status or bid solicitation as of September 2, 1969.[5]

All exception and waiver requests submitted for approval shall be fully supported by documentation outlining the conditions which generated the request and the reasons for submittal.

Part 3
Specification Technology

15 COORDINATION GUIDELINES FOR CONTRACT DOCUMENTS

Specifications and drawings serve complementary functions, and as such the preparation of both should be pursued concurrently and should be closely coordinated in order to minimize misunderstandings, discrepancies, and oversights. The following claim example indicates the difficulties that could result from inadequate coordination.[1]

Example of Inadequate Coordination

In preparing a rendering for a college science building, the designers displayed the windows and glass curtain wall as tinted glass. The college authorities were quite pleased with the aesthetic appearance of the structure and commented favorably on the use of the tinted glass. The entire structure, especially the air conditioning system, was designed based on the assumption that tinted glass would be used. The outline specification which included tinted glass was prepared as part of the bidding agreement.

The project was discussed and delayed by the college officials for a period of time before contract documents were prepared. In working up the final contract documents, the designer inadvertently omitted all reference to tinted glass and specified 1/4-in. (6.4-mm) plate glass. As a result, 1/4-in. clear glass was ordered by the contractor, and by the time the oversight was noted by the designer on a visit to the project site, all the glass had been manufactured and delivered, and a substantial portion had been installed.

The designer suggested several alternate methods of resolving the discrepancy, but the college officials insisted on tinted glass. The total cost to the designer to remedy the situation was $27,827.

This case is a typical example of claims that result from poorly coordinated contract documents. If the drawings and specifications had been prepared with reasonable professional care, the omission that culminated in this claim would probably not have occurred. There was no question about the fact that tinted glass was required from both the functional and aesthetic points of view, but it was not specified simply because of an oversight.

Although drawings, schedules, and specifications are complementary parts of the contract documents, each serves a distinct purpose:

Drawings	Schedules	Specifications
Graphic	*Abbreviated Notes*	*Written*
Define QUANTITY	Simplify and CLARIFY	Define QUALITY
Generic materials	Generic materials	Standards of workmanship
Component location, form, and shape	Finishes, colors	Physical requirements

Drawings	Schedules	Specifications
Graphic	*Abbreviated Notes*	*Written*
Relationship to space	Room information: ceiling height, columns, casework, trim, doors, windows	Installation methods
Size and structure		Quality of finishes
		Warranty requirements

This brief listing clarifies the fact that drawings contain the graphic means of showing and identifying a material, but drawings should not include a description of the material or component. Drawings show the quantity of components; e.g., the number of chairs to be used, their location and size. The schedule further *clarifies* the chair finish or color. The *quality* of construction, finish, and upholstery is described in the written specification document.

COMMON COORDINATION PROBLEMS

The Construction Specifications Institute, Inc. (CSI) points out the following problems that commonly occur in contract documents.[2]

Duplication and Overlapping

Specification experts suggest that the information shown in drawings, schedules, and specifications should not be duplicated; i.e., information need not be repeated more than once in the contract documents. Since each document has been purposely established to cover distinct areas of information, there is no reason for duplication.

The use of trade names on drawings and schedules often accounts for discrepancies. In the event that a product substitution must be made, valuable time is spent changing the drawings and schedules. If an oversight occurs and the trade name is inadvertently left on a drawing, a bidder may interpret the conflicting duplication to mean that he may use either of the two products that are mentioned. When trade names are used, they should appear in the written specifications. All other references should indicate only the generic name of the material, such as resilient tile, paint, or carpet.

Another common source of duplication is the use of written notations on working drawings. Occasional notes may be necessary to identify a component, but the note should give a minimum of information. Too many notes make a drawing difficult to understand and often lead to duplication and confusion.

Omissions and Gaps

The claim regarding tinted glass discussed earlier in this chapter is a perfect example of a situation where the omission of information caused serious problems. Careful attention must be paid to gaps in information that can occur between the contract documents. For example, two types of carpet may be specified for a particular project, but the drawings and schedules neglect to show where the two types of carpet are to be installed.

Inconsistent Terminology

The two most frequent causes of inconsistencies result from improper terminology and graphic symbols. Terms should be defined and clarified in the scope of the specification and their use must be consistent throughout the contract documents. Some common terms that cause confusion are:

Room names:	Lounge, rest rooms, ladies room, comfort area Lobby, foyer, entry Cocktail area, bar, lounge
Floorcoverings:	Rug, carpet, mat, padding, cushion
Window coverings:	Drapes, draperies, curtains, blinds, shades
Furnishings:	Sofa, lounge, loveseat
Chairs:	Executive chair, secretarial chair, clerical chair, posture chair, desk chair, side chair, lounge chair, occasional chair
Casegoods:	Desk, work surface, console, credenza, cabinet, end table, lamp table, occasional table, conference table, coffee table, brunch table
Accessories:	Wall hanging, relief, sculpture, sculpture relief

The list could go on endlessly, but the importance of using consistent terminology cannot be overemphasized. Figure 15.1 illustrates some inconsistencies that frequently appear on schedules and drawings. On the "Floor Covering Legend," note that item "B—Carpet" would be more accurately termed a "rug." *Carpet* is defined as a floorcovering which is installed (stretched or glued down) wall to wall in a given area. Other inconsistencies appear on the "Paint and Wall Covering Legend." Notice that in some cases the manufacturer, style, and color numbers are mentioned and in other cases they are omitted. Indicating parts of the work to be done by a specific type of contractor or subcontractor should not be placed on the drawings or schedules. The "Drapery Notes" use the improper nomenclature "drapes." Since the directional draw of the drapery was not shown on the drawing, it should have been included in the schedule information.

These examples illustrate just a few of the common inconsistencies, duplications, and omissions that could later be used as evidence that a designer lacked professional competence. For example, in the event that a contractor installed carpet #303—Blue from the Carp Mills, but the color number the designer ordered had previously been changed, the contractor would not be held responsible. If the designer, in the written specifications, had requested and received current color numbers, but neglected to update the schedules, any complaint he might make against the contractor would probably be negated by the inconsistency in the schedule. The old belief that specifications have precedence over drawings and schedules is no longer the fact. All contract documents are considered equally legal and binding.

WALL AND PAINT FINISH LEGEND

NO.	MAT'L	MFG'R	NO.	COLOR	REMARKS
1	OAK			STAIN	BY J.J. LEE
2	VINYL	REZ.	461	BLUE	
3	FOIL	COPPER			BRIGHT LITS
4	VINYL	BRITE	33	BROWN	

FLOORCOVERING LEGEND

LET.	MAT'L	MFG'R	NO.	COLOR	
A	WOOD	JONES		WALNUT	PREWAXED
B	CARPET	CARP	303	BLUE	FELT PAD

DRAPERY NOTES
1. ROOM DRAPES
BY T.S.R. MILLS # 463 BROWN

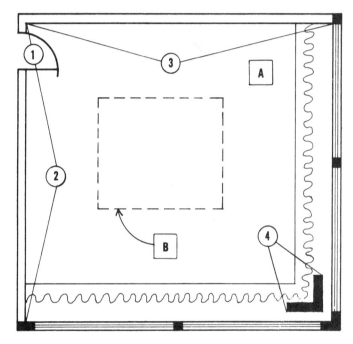

Figure 15.1 Room finish legends.

Inconsistent Use of Symbols

Although there is no universal standard for symbols, consistency can be controlled by developing a legend of symbols that will be used in a particular set of working drawings (see Figure 15.2). Symbols can be either geometric shapes or number codes, and often a combination of both is used. Symbols are useful when reference is made to a class of material, such as paint, carpet, or furniture. Figure 15.3 illustrates a furniture schedule which lists furniture by general type rather than specific number or trade name. If a symbol refers to a specific type of paint, i.e., semigloss latex, it could become ineffectual and cause revisions each time a specification change was made. Properly used, symbols can aid in avoiding confusing terminology. For example, in Figure 15.4, components have a coded reference note in place of a descriptive note for identification. Instead of labeling "conference chair" on a drawing, a coded reference, such as "317002," could link the chair directly to the specification. The number "31" could indicate chairs, of which several types are specified. The last four numbers indicate the specific conference chair described in the specification. If the designer decided to change the position of the chair or specify another type of chair in its place, he or she could simply remove the last four numbers and insert the proper number corresponding to the new selection.

Aside from avoiding confusing terminology, this method of coding forces the contractor and bidders to read the specifications. An excellent example of the coded reference is provided in Figure 15.5 and the accompanying color schedule. The finish schedule on the drawing links the coded numbers and letters to the drawing, and the additional written schedule relates the coded numbers and letters to the material. (See Table 15.1.)

Symbols used to indicate interior finishes and furnishings require very careful application. The finish schedule shown in the previous example made use of the directional symbols north, south, east, and west. This is very useful on a large project where it would be impossible to show individual rooms. On smaller projects where each room can be shown and in situations where the designer may wish to vary the wall finish within the same room, another symbol system would have to be devised. Often a geometric shape is used, with a letter or number to indicate a particular wall finish. Lines are extended from the geometric symbol to the exact area to which the symbol applies. In the example shown in Figure 15.1, it is easy to determine where finish (2) and (3) are to be applied. The column is clearly marked for another finish number (4).

This symbol method is also very useful in areas having irregular walls and spaces, but the designer must be exact in the placement of the line indicators. The examples shown in Figure 15.6 illustrate the confusion that may result from an inadequate concern for detail. If we compare the three examples, we can readily determine which drawings would result in inconsistencies and inaccuracies.

If a painting contractor attempted to determine which areas were to be painted in Exhibit A or B, he would find that some areas have an abundance of lines pointing to walls to show finish material, but other walls, such as the top fireplace walls and the window recesses, have no indication of finish requirements.

Although lines are frequently used to point out a certain detail in drawings, this interior finish symbol was designed to indicate large areas to be finished in the same material. When the line is used as a *pointer* (Exhibit A and B), it does not con-

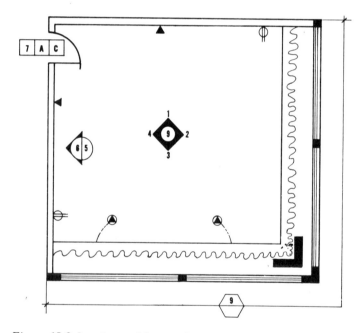

INTERIOR ARCHITECTURAL LEGEND

SYMBOL	DESCRIPTION
∿∿∿	DRAPERY
⬡ 9	ROOM NUMBER
6⟨5	ELEVATION NUMBER
4◆2 9	DRAWING NUMBER
7 / A / C	ROOM ELEVATIONS BY WALL NUMBER ROOM NUMBER DOOR NUMBER TYPE OF DOOR A. FULL HT. WALNUT BY MILL
⊖	B.S. BASE DUPLEX OUTLET
----	TELEPHONE CONDUIT
◀	B.S. BASE TELEPHONE OUTLET
●	B.S. FLOOR TELEPHONE OUTLET

Figure 15.2 Interior architectural symbols.

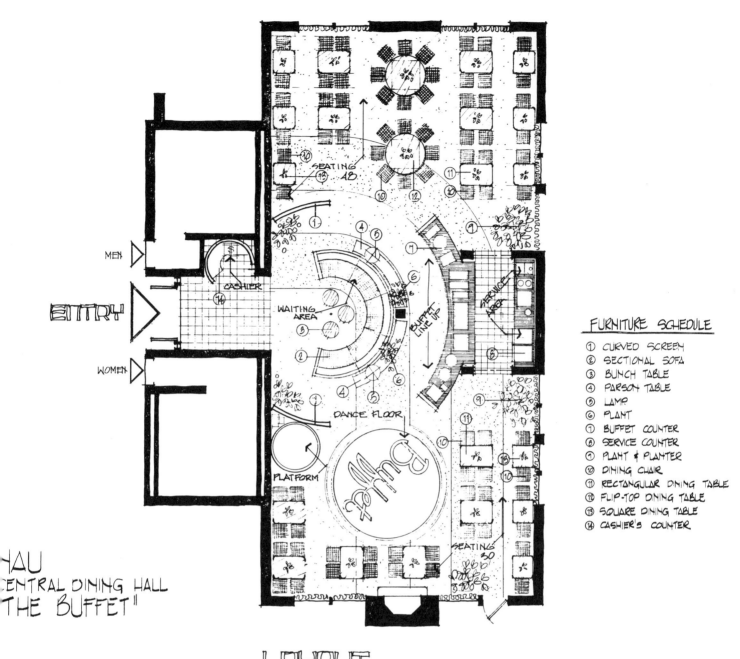

MEN

ENTRY

WOMEN

CASHIER

WAITING AREA

SEATING 18

BUFFET LINE UP

SERVICE AREA

DANCE FLOOR

PLATFORM

Buffet

SEATING 30

HAU
CENTRAL DINING HALL
"THE BUFFET"

LAYOUT
NEW BUFFET FLOOR PLAN
SCALE: 1/4"=1'-0"

FURNITURE SCHEDULE

1. CURVED SCREEN
2. SECTIONAL SOFA
3. BUNCH TABLE
4. PARSON TABLE
5. LAMP
6. PLANT
7. BUFFET COUNTER
8. SERVICE COUNTER
9. PLANT & PLANTER
10. DINING CHAIR
11. RECTANGULAR DINING TABLE
12. FLIP-TOP DINING TABLE
13. SQUARE DINING TABLE
14. CASHIER'S COUNTER

Figure 15.3 Furniture schedule. Reproduced with permission of B. Eric Bron & Associates, Phoenix, AZ.

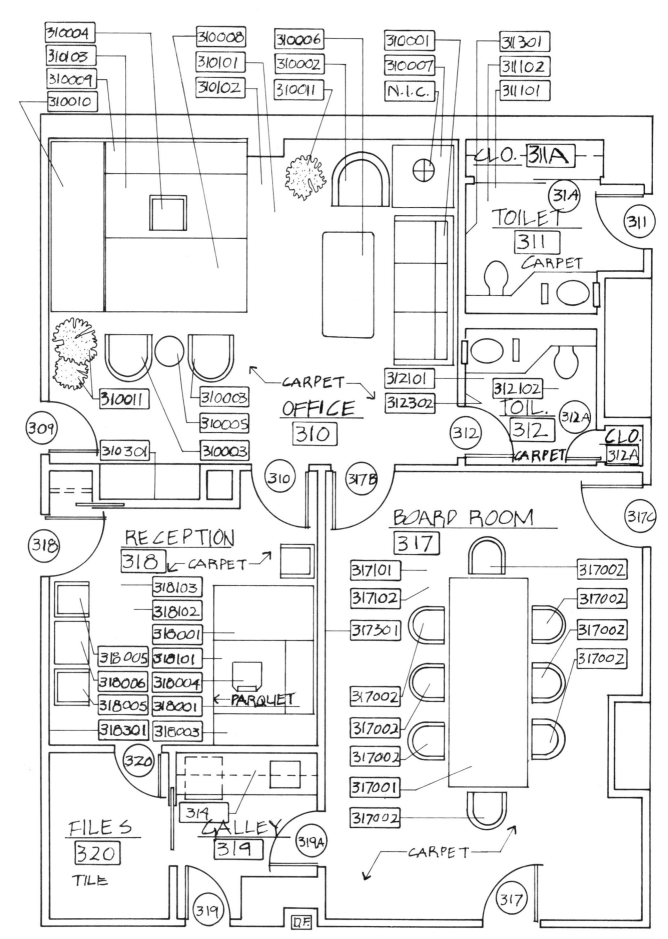

Figure 15.4 Coded furniture schedule. Reproduced with permission of Architectural Interiors, Inc., Phoenix, AZ.

TABLE 15.1   FINISH SCHEDULE

1. Base
   R   — (rubber) "Burke" #598-P dark brown
   Q/T — (quarry tile) "Summitville" Sunglo

2. Floors
   CP   — (carpet)
   CP   — 1 "Burke Industries" pattern: Oakglen
                              Color: Terra Copper #14085
   CP   — 2 "Burke Industries" pattern: Oakglen
                              Color: Heather #14071
   CP   — 3 "Burke Industries" pattern: Oakglen
                              Color: Ripe Avocado #14024
   C/C   — (colored concrete) "Davis Colors" Buff #5447
             (substitute if necessary — #5262)
   Q/T   — (quarry tile) "Summitville" Sunglo
             Grout color — Flashed Walnut
   C   — (concrete) Unfinished
   V/A   — (vinyl asbestos tile)
   V/A   — 1 "Kentile" pattern: Criterion
                       Color: Off-white (ground)
   V/A   — 2 "Kentile" pattern: Criterion
                       Color: Nocturne (border)
3. Walls
   V/W   — (vinyl wallcovering)
   V/W   — 1 "Vicrtex" pattern: Malmo, color: Arctic Dawn #1517
   V/W   — 2 "Vicrtex" pattern: Madagaska, color: Jungle Shells #1438
   V/W   — 3 "Vicrtex" pattern: Madagaska, color: Burnt Orange #1608
   V/W   — 4 "Vicrtex" pattern: Adagio, color: Crocus #8734
   V/W   — 5 "Vicrtex" pattern: Adagio, color: Mushroom #8733
   V/W   — 6 "Vicrtex" pattern: Adagio, color: Topazine #8735
   V/W   — 7 "Vicrtex" pattern: Adagio, color: Buff #8732
   V/W   — 8 "Vicrtex" pattern: Studio, color: Tawny Beige #1027
   V/W   — 9 "Vicrtex" pattern: Studio, color: Ember #5072
   V/W   — 10 "Vicrtex" pattern: Studio, color: Burnt Orange #1608
   V/W   — 11 "Vicrtex" pattern: Studio, color: Ginger #1071
   C/T   — (ceramic tile)
   C/T   — 1 "Monarch" color: White #192 (ground)
              "Monarch" color: Sand #135 (border trim)
              Grout color — White
   C/T   — 2 "Design Technics" pattern: #58 Size: 6 × 12"
              Glaze — #LZ4M on red clay
              (1% red iron, 1% rutile and 1/4% iron chromium)
              Grout color — match color of tile
   C/T   — (ceramic tile)
   C/T   — 1 "Monarch" color: White #192 (walls)
   C/T   — 2 "Monarch" color: Sand #135 (trim)
   G/C   — (glazed concrete)
   G/C   — 1 "Desco" white #65-25
   G/C   — 2 "Desco" yellow #12-7
   G/C   — 3 "Desco" terra cotta #70-1
   L/P   — (laminate plastic) "Nevamar" #W-8-73
                              Barrel Oak, textured finish

4. Doors* (see floor plans for the designated colors)
   Plochere #73
   Plochere #153
   Plochere #169
   Plochere #209

5. All asbestos panels shall be painted to match adjacent doors. If there
   are no adjacent doors, then paint — Plochere #169.

6. All steel door frames — Plochere #329

7. All concrete, plaster and gypsum board ceilings — Plochere #95, unless
   specified otherwise.

8. All toilet partitions — "Weis" #32.

---

*All mechanical room doors at housing — Plochere #209.
Source: B. Eric Bron & Associates, Phoenix, Arizona.

Figure 15.5 Coded room finish schedule. Reproduced with permission of B. Eric Bron & Associates, Phoenix, AZ.

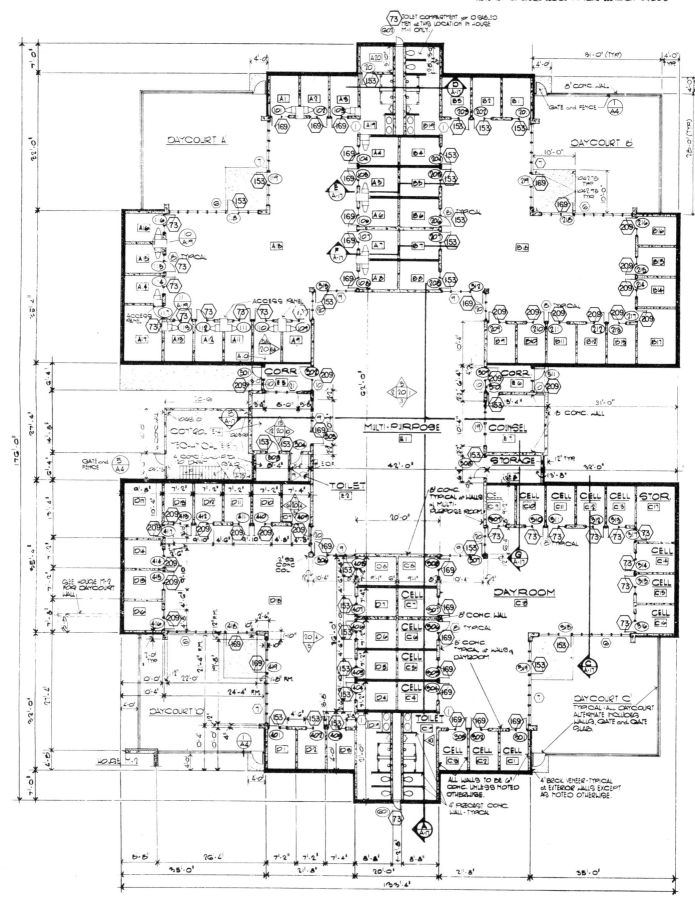

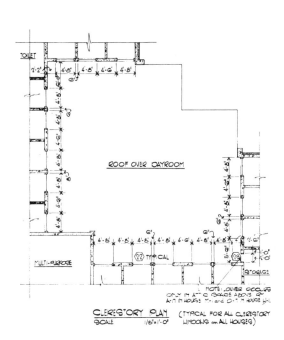

CLERESTORY PLAN (TYPICAL FOR ALL CLERESTORY
SCALE 1/8"=1'-0" WINDOWS on ALL HOUSES)

TOILET

ROOF OVER DAYROOM

MULTI-PURPOSE

STORAGE

⑫ TYPICAL

NOTE: LOUVER OCCURS
ONLY IN ATTIC SPACE ABOVE "A"
A-17 IN HOUSES "A" and "C-17" HOUSE "C"

```
           P-1
   P-7 ◀—CONCRETE DOUBLE T'S—▶ P-7
  ┌──────────┬──────────┬──────────┐
  │   P-7    │   P-7    │   P-7    │
  ├──────────┼──────────┼──────────┤
  │ WINDOWS  │   P-6    │ WINDOWS  │
  ├──────────┼──────────┼──────────┤
  │   P-6    │   P-6    │   P-6    │
  ├──────────┼──────────┼──────────┤
  │   P-1    │   P-1    │   P-1    │
  └──────────┴──────────┴──────────┘
```

TYPICAL MULTI-PURPOSE ROOM WALLS
(THIS DRWG. DESIGNATES WHERE COLORS OCCUR)
✳ REFER TO INTERIOR WRITTEN PORTION OF THE
COLOR SCHEDULE TO FIND ABBREVIATIONS.

⬡ PAINT COLOR FOR DOORS OCCURS IN THESE HEXAGONS
✳ NOTE: SEE WRITTEN PORTION OF THE COLOR SCHEDULE FOR GUIDE
TO ABBREVIATIONS & THEIR MEANINGS

COLOR SELECTION SCHEDULE

ROOM FINISH SCHEDULE

RM. NO	ROOM TITLE	FLOOR	BASE	WALLS NORTH	EAST	SOUTH	WEST	PAINT FIN	CEILING MAT'L	HGT	PAINT FIN	RMKS
A 1	CELL	C/C	R	P-4	P-1	P-1	P-1	F/V	C/PL	VARIES	F/V	
A 2	CELL	C/C	R	P-4	P-1	P-1	P-1	F/V	C/PL	VARIES	F/V	
A 3	CELL	C/C	R	P-4	P-1	P-1	P-1	F/V	C/PL	VARIES	F/V	
A 4	CELL	C/C	R	P-1	P-4	P-1	P-1	F/V	C/PL	VARIES	F/V	
A 5	CELL	C/C	R	P-1	P-4	P-1	P-1	F/V	C/R	VARIES	F/V	
A 6	CELL	C/C	R	P-1	P-4	P-1	P-1	F/V	C/PL	VARIES	F/V	
A 7	CELL	C/C	R	P-1	P-4	P-1	P-1	F/V	C/R	VARIES	F/V	
A 8	CELL	C/C	R	P-1	P-4	P-1	P-1	F/V	C/PL	VARIES	F/V	
A 9	CELL	C/C	R	P-1	P-1	P-2	P-1	F/V	C/R	VARIES	F/V	
A 10	CELL	C/C	R	P-1	P-1	P-2	P-1	F/V	C/PL	VARIES	F/V	
A 11	CELL	C/C	R	P-1	P-1	P-2	P-1	F/V	C/PL	VARIES	F/V	
A 12	CELL	C/C	R	P-1	P-1	P-2	P-1	F/V	C/PL	VARIES	F/V	
A 13	CELL	C/C	R	P-1	P-1	P-2	P-1	F/V	C/PL	VARIES	F/V	
A 14	CELL	C/C	R	P-1	P-1	P-1	P-2	F/V	C/PL	VARIES	F/V	
A 15	CELL	C/C	R	P-1	P-1	P-1	P-2	F/V	C/R	VARIES	F/V	
A 16	CELL	C/C	R	P-1	P-1	P-1	P-2	F/V	C/R	VARIES	F/V	
A 17	STORAGE	C/C	R	P-1	P-1	P-1	P-1	F/V	C/PL	8'-0"	F/V	
A 18	DAYROOM	C/C	R	P-1	P-1	P-1	P-1	F/V	A/T	9'-0"	☐	
A 19	TOILET	Q/T	Q/T	GC-1	GC-3	GC-1	GC-1	☐	C/PL	8'-0"	E	
A 20	STORAGE	C/C	R	P-1	P-1	P-1	P-1	F/V	C/PL	8'-0"	F/V	
B 1	CELL	C/C	R	P-3	P-1	P-1	P-1	F/V	C/R	VARIES	F/V	
B 2	CELL	C/C	R	P-3	P-1	P-1	P-1	F/V	C/R	VARIES	F/V	
B 3	CELL	C/C	R	P-3	P-1	P-1	P-1	F/V	C/R	VARIES	F/V	
B 4	CELL	C/C	R	P-1	P-1	P-1	P-3	F/V	C/R	VARIES	F/V	
B 5	CELL	C/C	R	P-1	P-1	P-1	P-3	F/V	C/R	VARIES	F/V	
B 6	CELL	C/C	R	P-1	P-1	P-1	P-3	F/V	C/R	VARIES	F/V	
B 7	CELL	C/C	R	P-1	P-1	P-1	P-3	F/V	C/R	VARIES	F/V	
B 8	CELL	C/C	R	P-1	P-1	P-1	P-3	F/V	C/R	VARIES	F/V	
B 9	CELL	C/C	R	P-1	P-1	P-5	P-1	F/V	C/R	VARIES	F/V	
B 10	CELL	C/C	R	P-1	P-1	P-5	P-1	F/V	C/R	VARIES	F/V	
B 11	CELL	C/C	R	P-1	P-1	P-5	P-1	F/V	C/PL	VARIES	F/V	
B 12	CELL	C/C	R	P-1	P-1	P-5	P-1	F/V	C/R	VARIES	F/V	
B 13	CELL	C/C	R	P-1	P-1	P-5	P-1	F/V	C/R	VARIES	F/V	
B 14	CELL	C/C	R	P-1	P-5	P-1	P-1	F/V	C/R	VARIES	F/V	
B 15	CELL	C/C	R	P-1	P-5	P-1	P-1	F/V	C/R	VARIES	F/V	
B 16	CELL	C/C	R	P-1	P-5	P-1	P-1	F/V	C/PL	VARIES	F/V	
B 17	STORAGE	C/C	R	P-1	P-1	P-1	P-1	F/V	C/PL	8'-0"	F/V	
B 18	DAYROOM	C/C	R	P-1	P-1	P-1	P-1	F/V	A/T	9'-0"	☐	
B 19	TOILET	Q/T	Q/T	GC-1	GC-1	GC-1	GC-3	☐	C/PL	8'-0"	E	
C 1	CELL	C/C	R	P-1	P-1	P-4	P-1	F/V	C/R	VARIES	F/V	
C 2	CELL	C/C	R	P-1	P-1	P-4	P-1	F/V	C/R	VARIES	F/V	
C 3	CELL	C/C	R	P-1	P-1	P-4	P-1	F/V	C/R	VARIES	F/V	
C 4	CELL	C/C	R	P-1	P-1	P-4	P-1	F/V	C/R	VARIES	F/V	
C 5	CELL	C/C	R	P-1	P-1	P-4	P-1	F/V	C/R	VARIES	F/V	
C 6	CELL	C/C	R	P-1	P-1	P-4	P-1	F/V	C/R	VARIES	F/V	
C 7	CELL	C/C	R	P-1	P-1	P-4	P-1	F/V	C/R	VARIES	F/V	
C 8	CELL	C/C	R	P-1	P-1	P-4	P-1	F/V	C/R	VARIES	F/V	
C 9	CELL	C/C	R	P-2	P-1	P-1	P-1	F/V	C/R	VARIES	F/V	
C 10	CELL	C/C	R	P-2	P-1	P-1	P-1	F/V	C/R	VARIES	F/V	
C 11	CELL	C/C	R	P-2	P-1	P-1	P-1	F/V	C/R	VARIES	F/V	
C 12	CELL	C/C	R	P-2	P-1	P-1	P-1	F/V	C/R	VARIES	F/V	
C 13	CELL	C/C	R	P-2	P-1	P-1	P-1	F/V	C/R	VARIES	F/V	
C 14	CELL	C/C	R	P-1	P-2	P-1	P-1	F/V	C/R	VARIES	F/V	
C 15	CELL	C/C	R	P-1	P-2	P-1	P-1	F/V	C/R	VARIES	F/V	
C 16	CELL	C/C	R	P-1	P-2	P-1	P-1	F/V	C/R	VARIES	F/V	
C 17	STORAGE	C/C	R	P-1	P-1	P-1	P-1	F/V	C/PL	8'-0"	F/V	
C 18	DAYROOM	C/C	R	P-1	P-1	P-1	P-1	F/V	A/T	9'-0"	☐	
C 19	TOILET	Q/T	Q/T	GC-1	GC-1	GC-1	GC-3	☐	C/PL	8'-0"	E	
D 1	CELL	C/C	R	P-1	P-1	P-3	P-1	F/V	C/R	VARIES	F/V	
D 2	CELL	C/C	R	P-1	P-1	P-3	P-1	F/V	C/R	VARIES	F/V	
D 3	CELL	C/C	R	P-1	P-1	P-3	P-1	F/V	C/R	VARIES	F/V	
D 4	CELL	C/C	R	P-1	P-3	P-1	P-1	F/V	C/R	VARIES	F/V	
D 5	CELL	C/C	R	P-1	P-3	P-1	P-1	F/V	C/R	VARIES	F/V	
D 6	CELL	C/C	R	P-1	P-3	P-1	P-1	F/V	C/R	VARIES	F/V	
D 7	CELL	C/C	R	P-1	P-3	P-1	P-1	F/V	C/R	VARIES	F/V	
D 8	CELL	C/C	R	P-1	P-3	P-1	P-1	F/V	C/R	VARIES	F/V	
D 9	CELL	C/C	R	P-5	P-1	P-1	P-1	F/V	C/R	VARIES	F/V	
D 10	CELL	C/C	R	P-5	P-1	P-1	P-1	F/V	C/R	VARIES	F/V	
D 11	CELL	C/C	R	P-5	P-1	P-1	P-1	F/V	C/R	VARIES	F/V	
D 12	CELL	C/C	R	P-5	P-1	P-1	P-1	F/V	C/R	VARIES	F/V	
D 13	CELL	C/C	R	P-5	P-1	P-1	P-1	F/V	C/R	VARIES	F/V	
D 14	CELL	C/C	R	P-1	P-1	P-1	P-5	F/V	C/R	VARIES	F/V	
D 15	CELL	C/C	R	P-1	P-1	P-1	P-5	F/V	C/R	VARIES	F/V	
D 16	CELL	C/C	R	P-1	P-1	P-1	P-5	F/V	C/R	VARIES	F/V	
D 17	STORAGE	C/C	R	P-1	P-1	P-1	P-1	F/V	C/PL	8'-0"	F/V	
D 18	DAYROOM	C/C	R	P-1	P-1	P-1	P-1	F/V	A/T	9'-0"	☐	
D 19	TOILET	Q/T	Q/T	GC-1	GC-3	GC-1	GC-1	☐	C/PL	8'-0"	E	
E 1	MULTI-PURPOSE	C/C	R	✳	✳	✳	✳	F/V	C	21'-8"	F/V	① ✳
E 2	TOILET	Q/T	Q/T	P-1	P-3	P-1	P-1	E	C/PL	7'-0"	E	③
E 3	MECHANICAL	C	R	P-1	P-1	P-1	P-1	F/V	C/PL	8'-0"	F/V	
E 4	CONTROL	CP-2	R	P-1	P-1	P-1	P-4	F/V	A/T	8'-0"	☐	
E 5	CORRIDOR	C/C	R	P-8	P-1	P-1	P-1	F/V	C/PL	8'-0"	F/V	
E 6	CORRIDOR	C/C	R	P-8	P-1	P-1	P-1	F/V	C/PL	8'-0"	F/V	
E 7	COUNSEL	CP-1	R	P-1	P-3	P-1	P-1	F/V	A/T	8'-0"	☐	
E 8	STORAGE	C/C	R	P-1	P-1	P-1	P-1	F/V	C/PL	8'-0"	F/V	
E 9-12	MECHANICAL	C	–	C	C	C	C	☐	C	VARIES	☐	②

① CEMENT PLASTER FURRED SPACE at PERIPHERY of CEILING.

② SEE SHEET 15 for FLOOR PLAN.

③ FURRED at PLUMBING WALL (EAST).

✳ LOWER PORTIONS OF WALL DIVIDED BY EXPANSION JOINTS: P-1
UPPER & CENTER PORTION OF WALL DIVIDED BY
EXPANSION JOINTS: P-6
SOFFITS OR THAT PORTION OF WALL AT FURRED SPACE: P-7

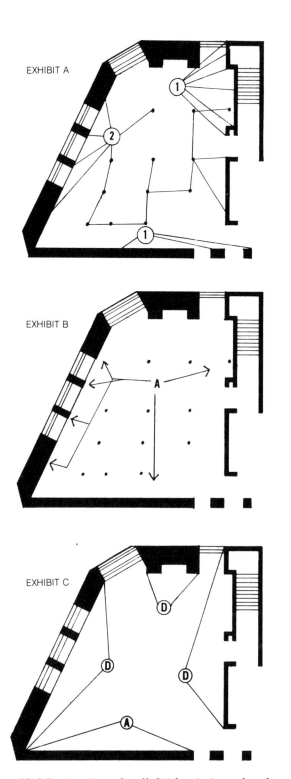

EXHIBIT A

EXHIBIT B

EXHIBIT C

Figure 15.6 Designation of wall finishes in irregular-shaped rooms.

vey the needed information. In Exhibit C the lines encompass the *entire width* of the area to be finished and therefore offer more precise graphic information. Figure 15.7 illustrates another method of indicating placement of wall finishes. If a wall is to receive two finishes, an elevation may be necessary (see Figure 15.8).

In a drapery symbol, the omission of a line indicating which direction the drapery should draw may result in installation difficulties. If drapery is to be installed over a sliding glass door, the drapery contractor may not be able to determine the slide direction of the door from the drawings, and as a result, the drapery may be made and installed incorrectly.

SCHEDULE EXAMPLES

Schedules are normally made for doors, windows, furniture, room finishes, colors, and any other project components needing clarification that can be provided by a schedule. A Room Finish Schedule would include the assigned room number and room name on smaller scale projects. Categories are established for the floors, bases, walls, ceilings, and trims. Vertical columns are established below these headings which indicate types of room materials, such as vinyl, carpet, tile, wood, plaster, and any other finishes that may be used. Blank columns are usually left between each category for ease in reading and also to accommodate additional finishes that may be required at a later date. (See Figure 15.9.) A legend is often placed in the upper right-hand corner of the schedule to indicate room materials and finishes. Abbreviations for the materials and finishes should be consistent with those used elsewhere in the documents. A symbol should also be established for "Applicable" and "Not Applicable" situations.

Other columns are established for the ceiling height. This height is stated in feet and inches (meters or centimeters). If a room has varied ceiling heights, the average height should be used, such as 11'0''. Another column is needed to indicate the drawing sheet number where the room elevations are to be found. The "Remarks" column is used for providing additional information, such as details concerning custom cabinetwork or columns in the centers of spaces. (See examples in Figure 15.10). The room finish and color schedule combination shown in Figure 15.10 makes use of circles to indicate the location of finishes. Directional symbols (N, S, E, W) are used in the upper left-hand corner. If the circle appears in the center of the square, all four walls are to receive the same finish.

It should be remembered that there is no one correct way to design a schedule. A schedule format that provided the needed information for one project may prove totally inadequate in another situation.

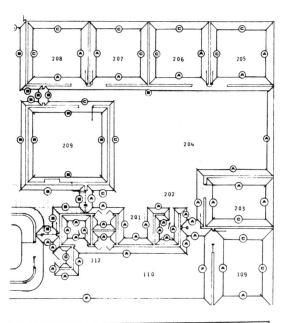

FINISH MATERIALS LEGEND

SYM.	MATERIAL	SYM.	MATERIAL
A	"DEER-O" ALPINE WHITE	G	"BALMORAL", WALL COVERING
B	"DEER-O" DAWN GRAY	H	"STAUFFER", STERLING GRAY #1704
C	"DEER-O" CHARCOAL GRAY	I	CERAMIC TILE
D	"EUROTEX"-ACOUSTICORD #587	J	
E	"VICRTEX" TASCO ORIENT GREY #370	K	WD. PANELING, WALNUT VENEER
F	"VICRTEX" STIL-L COARSE MOONSTONE 5006		

Figure 15.7 Room finish materials. Reproduced with permission of Peter A. Lendrum Associates, Architects, Engineers, Planners, Phoenix, AZ.

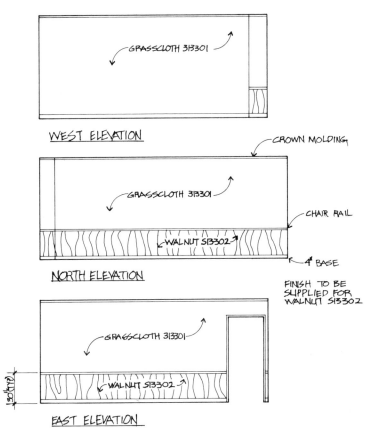

Figure 15.8 Wall elevations designating multiple finishes. Source: Architectural Interiors, Inc., Phoenix, AZ.

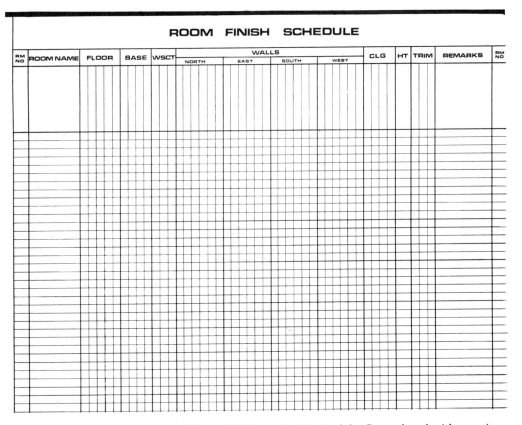

Figure 15.9 Room finish schedule. Reproduced with permission of Selje, Bond, Steward & Romberger, Phoenix and Los Angeles.

SUMMARY

Contract documents that lack coordination often result in job site confusion that causes faulty construction and installations. Changes of orders and other time delays are frequently directly related to simple oversights that could have been prevented by coordinating the drawings, schedules, and specifications. In addition, a uniform basis for bidding is often impossible to establish when the contract documents are unclear or incomplete.

To prevent some of these problems, a coordination checklist may be helpful.

1. Have all terms and symbols been clearly listed in the general conditions section of the specifications or included in the drawings or a legend?
2. Are components of the same generic type represented with the same symbols?
3. Are all terms consistent on the drawings, schedules, and specifications?
4. If a product substitution has been made in the specification, does it necessitate changes on the drawings or schedules?
5. Is the location of all wall, floor, and ceiling finishes clearly indicated?
6. Would some notes shown on the drawings be better placed in the schedules?
7. Has more than one person checked your drawings and schedules for inconsistencies?

ROOM FINISH SCHEDULE / COLOR SCHEDULE

(Room name key: N, E, S, W; • indicates wall)

	ROOM NAME	FLOOR: CARPET	FLOOR: V.A.T. [EXISTING]	BASE: 4" RUBBER · COVELESS	WALLS: GYP. BD. · PAINTED	WALLS: J.C. "A"	WALLS: J.C. "B"	WALLS: J.C. "C"	CEILING: EXISTING 2X4 SUSPENDED LAY-IN	CEILING: EXIST'G. GYP. BD.	clg ht	remark
201	COMMITTEE RM.	●		●		●			●			
202	RECEPTION	●		●	●				●			
203	OFFICE #1	●		●	●				●			
204	OFFICE #2	●		●	●				●			
205	OFFICE #3	●		●	●				●			
206	SECRETARY	●		●	●				●			
207	PRESIDENT	●		●			●		●			
208	TOILET		●							●		
209	MEN		●							●		
210	WOMEN		●							●		
211	CORRIDOR	●		●	●				●			
212	CORRIDOR	●		●	●				●			
213	BOARD ROOM	●		●	●				●			
214	WORK ROOM	●		●	●				●			
215	LUNCH ROOM	●		●	●				●			
216	ADMINISTRATIVE	●		●	●				●			

Figure 15.10 Finish and color schedule. Reproduced with permission of Selje, Bond, Steward & Romberger, Phoenix and Los Angeles.

16 SPECIFICATION FORMAT AND CONTENT

Specifications are used by designers to communicate the project requirements to the contractor. They are written descriptions of a technical nature which deal with materials, equipment, construction systems, standards, and workmanship. Being written documents, they are more readily understood than drawings by people not commonly associated with the construction industry. Hence, they become a potential source of liability. The courts among others often look to the specification to determine the message conveyed by the contract documents to those who must work with them. Review of numerous liability cases indicates that many of the claims arising out of faulty specifications come from the following major reasons:

1. Ambiguous or inadequate text to describe the items required to be specified by the designer. (Inability to determine from the written word what was actually intended.)

2. Lack of coordination between the drawings and the specifications. (Overlap or gaps in documenting the design requirements.)

3. Lack of understanding on the part of the specifier about the capabilities of the items specified. (Items specified were not able to meet design or performance requirements.

Any design professional who writes specifications would be well advised to place himself in the position of the general contractor's personnel who must use these documents to translate the concept into the accomplished project. Since the specifications set forth those project requirements which are most readily expressed in words, their meaning must be conveyed clearly, adequately, and unambiguously.[1]

TYPES OF SPECIFICATIONS

Specifications may be broadly classified as "closed" or "open." A *closed* specification is one that specifies an exact material or component by style number and trade name, thus eliminating the consideration of any other product. An *open* specification allows the consideration of multiple materials or components through the use of an "or equal" clause or the use of performance requirement standards. These specifications state the necessary means to achieve the requirements as well as the required end results, but do not refer to any particular material or component.

Closed Specifications

Manufacturer's and proprietary specifications fall into this category:

1. *Manufacturer's specifications* are written specifically for a manufacturer's product. Aside from providing information on the performance attributes and recommended installation methods for the particular product, these specifications serve to promote a product. Designers may find these specifications useful in making comparative studies of various materials and components. In the event that a particular product is specified, the designer may incorporate all or part of the manufacturer's specification into the final specification.

2. *Proprietary specifications* are those which specify a particular product by trade name. When the specification allows for no substitution of materials it is known as a "base bid" proprietary specification. The term *base bid* means that all people who wish to provide materials for the project must base their bid on the product named in the specification. Designers frequently employ this type of specification because of the following advantages:
   a. The designer is able to prepare detailed working drawings based on the component or material which has been selected for use.
   b. Based on these detailed working drawings, the designer is often able to clarify the project details for the client.
   c. Proprietary specifications are shorter in length and easier to write because manufacturers will often supply much of the needed data and installation information.
   d. The designer has full control over the materials and components that will be used on the project.
   e. Because the specification does not allow for multiple selections, competitive price analysis and other bidding procedures are expedited.

Open Specifications

The following items should be considered under this category:

1. *Proprietary specifications* may also be used as open specifications with the addition of the "or equal" clause, which allows other products to be considered for bid if the product can be proven equal in all aspects to the product named in the specification. Designers can readily see that there may be certain disadvantages to this method of specification:
   a. Controversy may develop concerning opinions about a product's equal quality.
   b. The designer or specifier becomes involved in a more time-consuming process of evaluating and selecting materials.
   c. This type of specification often results in material selection being diverted from considerations of quality to price comparisons. Because competitive bidding usually results in the lowering of prices, some manufacturers who may have provided reliable warranties and service may withdraw from the bidding.
   d. In order to avoid these difficulties, the Construction Specifications Institute recommends that the following procedures be outlined in the specification:
      (1) "State the requirements and procedures under

which proposed substitutions of materials and methods will be considered.

    (2) "State that all proposed substitutions must be submitted in writing before the close of the bid period. (About ten days or so should prove sufficient in most cases.)

    (3) "Inform the bidder that all acceptable substitutions—all 'equals'—will be approved in addenda which will be issued to all bidders."[2]

Another method of controlling "or equal" difficulties is to use a "modified or equal" type of proprietary specification. This method not only mentions the brand name of a product, but also establishes requirements and standards for the specified materials, thus eliminating opinions as a sole source of material evaluation.

The following clause is suggested for use with the "modified or equal" proprietary specification:

> The specified products establish minimum qualities that substitutes must meet to be considered acceptable. To obtain approval of unspecified products under the modified or equal provisions, bidders shall submit written requests at least ten days before the bid date. Requests received after this time will not be considered. Requests must clearly describe the product for which approval is requested, including all data necessary to demonstrate acceptability.[3]

2. *Descriptive specifications* do not employ the name of a particular product and are therefore considered open specifications. This type of specification involves a detailed description of the manner in which the material is to be constructed and the method of installation required. Although this specification is lengthy and more time consuming to produce, it may be necessary when a particular material or component is complex and difficult to show on the drawings. For example, other than indicating the carpet location within the project, it is difficult to indicate carpet construction details on the drawings or schedules. Therefore, it may be necessary to use a descriptive specification for this particular interior component.

A carpet descriptive specification would list the requirements for the following construction features:

Construction type (tufted, woven, or other)

Pile yarn (generic)

Gauge or pitch

Stitches per inch or wires

Pile height or wire height

Coloration method

Yarn size and ply

Width

Pile yarn weight and total weight

Primary and secondary backing

Descriptive specifications may also be written as reference standards; i.e., reference standards, which are also descriptive in character, may be used as a part of the descriptive specification. These standards are listed as additional construction or installation requirements.

American Society for Testing and Materials

ASTM _____ (number)

Federal Standard. FS _____ (number)

(Name of applicable) Building Code ( )

Designers and specifiers should be sure that reference standards do not contradict or duplicate other requirements stated elsewhere in the contract documents. More details on the use of reference standards will be discussed later in this chapter.

To write effective descriptive specifications, the specifier must be knowledgeable in the following areas:

    a. Material construction methods and the critical performance factors that will allow the component to function effectively.

    b. Minimal acceptable criteria for each type of material to be specified.

    c. Procedures for verifying whether a material or component complies with the described requirements. These procedures may include testing methods and established standards.

    d. Installation methods that would be suitable for each type of material and component.

3. *Performance specifications* establish the performance requirements without dictating the means by which the end results are to be achieved. Any material or system that meets the performance criteria could qualify for use. These specifications contain a qualitative statement regarding the performance requirement, the quantitative criteria, and the test methods that should be used to assure the desired results. For example, for a space divider subsystem, the attribute of "health and safety" is stated as follows:

Requirement: Provide fire safety
Criteria: (a) This subsystem shall have a maximum flame spread of 25. (b) If a fully sprinklered fire protection sprinkler system is provided, the flame-spread rating shall not exceed 200.
Test: Type—Calculation
Method: ASTM-E 84 "Surface Burning Characteristics of Building Materials."[4]

This type of specification does not require that the designer have an extensive knowledge about the generic qualities or construction aspects of any particular materials. *But the ability to establish concise performance requirements and the appropriate testing methods are essential in writing a performance specification.*

The Carpet and Rug Institute has suggested that either a descriptive or performance specification be used when there is to be open bidding on carpet. Because the performance specification tells the manufacturer how the carpet must perform without setting restrictions on how the carpet must be made, the manufacturer is allowed to use the most recent technology and newly developed fibers to meet the performance requirements.

Because material technology is becoming increasingly complex, many designers may choose to use a combination of descriptive and performance specifications to assure that the requirements will be fulfilled by the best materials currently available.

4. *Reference standards* are frequently used in proprietary, descriptive, and performance specifications. Making reference to an established standard serves to clarify material, workmanship, or installation requirements. Though standards originate from reliable sources (see Chapter 3) and are widely known and accepted as a basis for performance evaluation, it should be remembered that many standards represent only minimum levels of performance. Before including a standard in a specification, the designer should become familiar with the entire contents and scope of the particular standard, understand how to incorporate it effectively, and know how to assure compliance with the standard.

The Construction Specifications Institute (CSI) offers the following guidelines for the use of standards in specifications.[5]

a. Make certain that all contractors associated with the project have access to copies of the latest edition of the standards. Copies may either be attached to the specifications or made available through the designer's office.

b. Be aware that some standards may present "hidden choices"; i.e., the material mentioned in the standard may be classed in one or more types, and each type may have different performance criteria. For example, the voluntary wallcovering products Standard TS 198, 1979, which is discussed in Chapter 9, classifies wallcoverings in five major types. The classification criteria chart included in the standard clearly illustrates that the criteria for class II wallcovering is quite different than the criteria for a class V wallcovering. If reference is made to this standard without clarifying which wallcovering type is required in the project, the contractor may assume that a choice may be made.

c. Designers and specifiers should carefully examine the standard for requirements that may conflict with other more stringent requirements listed elsewhere in the specification. If conflicts or duplications are found to exist, a clause may be added to the specification which states that the more stringent requirement shall govern. It is recommended that in all cases of discrepancies between the specification and standards, the requirements of the specification shall remain in effect.

d. To properly incorporate the standard into a specification document, the standard must be listed by the full name and title, as well as the number and the approval date. If a standard is tentative (awaiting final acceptance by standards committees), it may be used as a reference, providing the designer lists it as "tentative" at the time the specifications are written. Contractors should be advised to refer to the latest edition of standards used in the specification.

e. Enforcement of the standard is accomplished through on-site inspections, careful analysis of prepared working drawings, samples, and established performance testing methods. Manufacturers should provide written proof of test results and construction processes required in the standard.

5. *Federal specifications* are developed for use by federal agencies to assure a uniformity throughout the governmental purchasing process. Because these specifications are written by experts in material technology and are frequently revised, they provide an excellent source of information for designers and specifiers. Designers will encounter four major types of governmental specifications: federal, interim federal, military, and departmental. Each type may be amended or revised whenever necessary, and when a federal agency identifies a particular need not covered by a current specification, an interim specification may be written. An Index of Federal Specifications identifies the specifications by letters and numbers.

The portion of the Federal Specifications reproduced in Figure 16.1 illustrates the classification and numbering system used for indexing. The letters and numbers found in the upper-right corner indicate the following:

DDD = The federal procurement group. These letters may appear in single, double, or triple form (the *same* letter is repeated).

S = Represents the first letter of the item specified (shades).

251 = Serial number refers to the location in the procurement group.

d = Designates that the specification has been revised four times. Each revision is given a letter symbol in alphabetic order.

```
                          DDD-S-251d
                          April 13, 1966
                          ─────────────────
                          SUPERSEDING
                          Fed. Spec. DDD-S-251c
                          July 12, 1962


            FEDERAL SPECIFICATION

   SHADE, ROLLER, WINDOW; ROLLER, SLAT,
   CORD, AND ACCESSORIES

 This specification was approved by the Commissioner,
 Federal Supply Services, General Services Administration,
 for the use of all Federal agencies.
```

Figure 16.1 Coded indexing numbers on federal specifications. Source: GSA.

```
AA-V-00200B(GSA-FSS)
June 5, 1973

INTERIM REVISION OF
Fed. Spec. AA-V-200A
November 6, 1965


INTERIM FEDERAL SPECIFICATION

VENETIAN BLINDS
```

Figure 16.2 Coded indexing of interim federal specifications. Source: GSA.

The interim specification shown in Figure 16.2 is indexed in the following manner:

AA = Federal procurement group.

V = First letter of the item specified (Venetian).

"OO" = These are used on all interim specifications. Placed on front of the serial number.

B = Represents the second revision.

(GSA-FSS) = The agencies issuing the interim specification. (General Services Administration and the Federal Supply Service.)

Examples of proprietary, descriptive, and performance specifications are shown in Figures 16.3 through 16.5. Table 16.1 summarizes the recommended usage of each specification type.

TABLE 16.1 RECOMMENDED USAGE OF EACH SPECIFICATION TYPE

Specification	Type	Recommended Use
1. Proprietary	Closed	a. Used when the designer wishes to have complete control over the product selection.
		b. Used in remodeling situations where exact colors and materials may have to be matched.
		c. Recommended when exact dimensions must be used to clarify the design concept to the client.
		d. Recommended when drawing, specification, and bidding procedures must be expedited due to project deadlines.
"Modified or Equal"	Open	a. Used when competitive bidding is required.
		b. Used when designer is prepared to make informed decisions on alternate materials.
		c. Recommended when adequate control can be placed on bidding periods and submittal requirements.
2. Descriptive	Open	a. Used when no trade names are allowed. This is often the case in government building projects.
		b. Recommended when a component or material is complex and requires detailed descriptive specification. Example: mechanical and electrical systems; carpet.
		c. Used when performance specifications are not feasible.
3. Performance	Open	a. Used when trade names are not allowed.
		b. Used when a designer has a unique design problem that may require an innovative new material or component. Example: ambient task lighting.
		c. Recommended for use when the desired performance level can be evaluated by valid standards and testing methods.
		d. Used when it is required that materials be selected on a performance basis.
4. Reference standards	Open	a. Recommended for use when the specifier wishes to write a less elaborate document through reference to standards.
		b. Used when a widely acceptable and familiar reference is needed to expand or implement a descriptive, performance, or proprietary specification.

Figure 16.3 Performance specification: GSA space divider subsystem.

```
E  PERFORMANCE SPECIFICATION                Third Edition
7  SPACE DIVIDER SUBSYSTEM                   November 1975
```

---

b SUBSYSTEM ATTRIBUTES

---

c) attribute: ACOUSTICS

REQUIREMENT: (1) <u>Control airborne sound transmission.</u>

Criteria: (a) Provide Speech Privacy Potential (SPP) of no less than 60 in the open plan areas of the Typical Office Space. Utilize 60" height system screens and system carpet.

Test: Type - System Prototype/System Field
Method - PBS-C.1

Criteria: (b) Criterion (a) above shall be met if the sum of the speech privacy Noise Isolation Class (NIC') plus a compatible NC-Background of 40 shall be no less than 60.

Test: Type - System Prototype/System Field
Method - PBS-C.2

Criteria: (c) Provide Speech Privacy Potential (SPP) of no less than 70 between any two adjacent rooms without interconnecting doors. Utilize system carpet and opaque partition (A70).

Test: Type - System Prototype/System Field
Method - PBS-C.1

Criteria: (d) Criterion (c) above shall be met if the sum of the speech privacy Noise Isolation Class (NIC') plus a compatible NC Background of 35 shall be no less than 70.

Test: Type - System Prototype/System Field
Method - PBS-C.2

Criteria: (e) Provide Speech Privacy Potential (SPP) of no less than 60 between any two adjacent rooms without interconnecting doors. Utilize system carpet and opaque partition (A60).

Test: Type - System Prototype/System Field
Method - PBS-C.1

Criteria: (f) Criterion (e) above shall be met if the sum of the speech privacy Noise Isolation Class (NIC') plus a compatible NC-Background of 35 shall be no less than 60.

REQUIREMENT: (2) <u>Control impact sound transmission.</u>

Criteria: (a) Footstep sounds transmitted to rooms located directly below shall be masked by an NC-Background not greater than 40. The system shall have the capability of masking footfall sounds transmitted to rooms located directly below with an NC-Background not greater than 35.

Test: Type - System Prototype/System Field
Method - Impact Sound Transmission Test by Footfall Method, IBI-1-I, 1965
Modification - The Offeror shall propose modifications to test method for prototype and field application in his Technical Proposal; use male walker with metal-tipped heels in addition to specified female walker.

Criteria: (b) Door slam sounds in this subsystem, transmitted to rooms contiguous vertically and horizontally shall be masked by an NC-Background not greater than 40. A door shall not occur in the partition between the contiguous rooms.

Test: Type - System Prototype/System Field
Method - The Offeror shall submit test in his Technical Proposal. Door slam shall be in accordance with PBS d.1.

REQUIREMENT: (1) <u>Provide resistance to horizontal loads.</u>

Criteria: (a) This subsystem's partitions and screens in use shall resist a uniformly distributed horizontal load of 5 pounds per square foot with no damage to this or any other subsystem. The maximum deflection of a partition under load shall not exceed 0.25". Screens may move horizontally but shall not overturn.

Test: Type - System Prototype
Method - ASTM E 72-68, Section 10
Modification - Apply load to a specimen 5' in length with no abutting partitions. Install and support in the Prototype as in use.

Criteria: (b) This subsystem's partitions in use shall resist a horizontal concentrated load of 50 pounds applied through a 1" diameter disc at the weakest point on the surface on either side, perpendicular to the faces, with the average residual indentation not exceeding 0.030". The average applied concentrated load to produce structural failure of the surface shall be not less than 150 pounds.

Test: Type - System Prototype
Method - ASTM E 72-68, Section 11
Modification - Apply load to a specimen 5 feet in length with no abutting partitions which shall be installed and supported in the prototype as in use. The load shall be applied 3 times. The rate of loading shall be such that the load is attained in not less than 1 minute nor more than 2 minutes.

Criteria: (c) No part of this subsystem or any other subsystem supported by this subsystem shall separate from its supports, fail, or cause failure in a manner that will endanger occupants, when subjected to seismic forces, as specified in the GSA Handbook, "Structural Engineering."

(d) This subsystem, in addition to resisting the seismic forces as specified above in the Project Buildings, shall be capable of resisting seismic forces similarly at any location in the 50 states as specified in the above handbook.

Test: Type - Subsystem
Method - Calculation/Structural Analysis
Modification - The coefficient "Z" shall be 1.5 instead of 1.0 for earthquake zone 3.

Criteria: (e) This subsystem's free-standing screens, in use, with or without bookshelf loading, shall resist an overturning force of 25 pounds perpendicular to its face. Horizontal movement but no overturning shall be allowed.

Test: Type - System Prototype
Method - Apply a horizontal force of 25 pounds perpendicular to the face of a free-standing screen 5'-0" long. Load shall be applied through a 1" diameter disc at one edge of the screen 5'-0" above finished floor. Perform the test 3 times on a screen without bookshelf. Repeat the test 3 times on a screen with a bookshelf attached to one side only loaded with 40 pounds per linear foot. Load shall be applied to face opposite book shelf.

REQUIREMENT: (2) <u>Provide resistance to impact.</u>

Criteria: (a) This subsystem's partitions and screens in use shall resist an impact of 30 foot-pounds with no damage to the surface or other part of this or any other subsystem. Displacement of this subsystem or any other subsystem, when measured immediately after impact, shall not exceed the accepted tolerance limits for that subsystem or any other subsystem. Maximum displacement measured at the time of impact shall not exceed 1/2". Screens may overturn but shall not be damaged.

Figure 16.3 Performance specification: GSA space divider subsystem. (Continued)

Test: Type - System Prototype
        Method - Strength Test of Panels/ASTM E 72-68,
        Section 13
        Modification - Apply impact 5 times to
        partition specimens 5 and 20 linear feet in
        length with no abutting partitions and to a
        specimen 5 linear feet in length abutted at
        both ends, all of which shall be installed and
        supported in the prototype as in use, and
        report all damages in th prototype; apply
        impact to specimen at lines of support and
        half-way between supports. Apply impact 5
        times at the center of a free-standing Type B
        screen 60" long.

Criteria: (b) No part of this subsystem or any other
           subsystem shall be damaged or have a
           displacement measured during and immediately
           after each door slam exceeding the specified
           tolerance limits for this subsystem.

Test: Type - System Prototype
        Method - Door Slam PBS - d.1
        Modification - Slam door located in center of
        a space divider with none abutting it for at
        least 30' of its length. Door shall be
        slammed with a force of 17 foot-pounds. Door
        shall swing through an angle of 30 degrees.

REQUIREMENT: (3) Provide resistance to point impact.

Criteria: Any component part of this subsystem, 1
           surface of which is exposed to view, shall
           withstand 9 inch-pounds of impact on its
           exposed surface without any indentation
           greater than 1/16" inch measured 24 hours
           after impact, and without any splitting,
           cracking, or other permanent damage.

Test: Type - Subsystem
        Method - Falling Ball Impact, Fed. Test Method
        Std. No. 406, Method 1074.
        Modification - Use 1/2-pound ball at 18".

REQUIREMENT: (4) Provide resistance to racking force.

Criteria: Free-standing screens shall support a
           concentrated load of 15 pounds applied
           perpendicular to its face 5'-0" above the
           finished floor at an end. The screen shall
           sustain 200 cycles of loading and unloading
           without delaminating, cracking, taking
           permanent set, or sustaining other damages.

Test: Type - Subsystem
        Method - Load one vertical edge of
        free-standing screen 5'-0" above finished
        floor with a 15-pound horizontal force
        perpendicular to its face. Fix the base of
        screen to the floor. Repeat load/unload cycle
        200 times. Report damage or permanent set.

REQUIREMENT: (5) Provide support for attached loads.

Criteria: This subsystem's screens, in use, shall
           support the load of 40 pounds per linear foot
           of shelf imposed on book shelves specified as
           a capability by this subsystem. Screens shall
           support loaded shelves on one or both faces of
           the screen. Any displacement of surface shall
           be within tolerances specified for this
           subsystem.

Test: Type - Subsystem
        Method - The Offeror shall propose test.

REQUIREMENT: (6) Provide resistance to vertical loading.

Criteria: This subsystem's mechanical unit enclosures
           shall support without damage a vertical load
           of 50 pounds per square foot with a 250-pound
           concentrated load at any point with deflection
           within this subsystem's specified tolerances.

Test: Type - System Prototype
        Method - Load mechanical unit enclosure with
        50 pounds per square foot and with a 250-pound
        concentrated load distributed over an area of
        one square foot located in the center span.
        Measure and report deflection.

REQUIREMENT: (7) Control friability.

Criteria: (a) Any component part of this subsystem
           constructed with acoustically absorbent
           material shall not lose more than 50% in
           weight in 10 minutes.

Test: Type - Subsystem
        Method - ASTM C 367, Paragraphs 7-12, Strength
        Properties of Acoustical Materials
        Modification - 4 of the specimens tested shall
        be edge pieces, 10 minutes.

REQUIREMENT: (8) Provide cohesive strength
              of laminated surfaces.

Criteria: Any component part of this subsystem's
           partitions and screens shall withstand a
           tensile force of 2 PSI applied normal to any
           face or surface with no delamination and no
           more than 1/8" increase in thickness measured
           10 minutes after the force is removed.
           Surfaces designed to be acoustically absorbent
           are excepted.

Test: Type - Subsystem
        Method - PBS-d.2

REQUIREMENT: (9) Provide cohesion/adhesion
              of surface coatings.

Criteria: All coatings under 0.005 inches thick on
           exposed surfaces of this subsystem shall not
           delaminate.

Test: Type - Subsystem
        Method - PBS-d.4

REQUIREMENT: (10) Control surface color stability.

Criteria: (a) The exposed surface of this subsystem, in
           use, when compared with the reference samples
           and with any other specimen subjected to this
           test, shall not differ in color by more than 3
           NBS units or by more than color tolerances
           proposed for the system and approved in the
           Prototype, whichever is greater. Variegated,
           irregular, or translucent finishes shall be
           evaluated visually for acceptability of color.
           change.

           (b) The exposed surface of this subsystem in
           use shall not exhibit any form of cracking,
           crazing, splitting, spalling, blisters,
           delaminations, breaks, discontinuities, or
           other form of surface deterioration when
           evaluated visually, subject to review by the
           Contracting Officer.

Test: Type - Subsystem
        Method - Colorfastness to Light, Fed. Std. No.
        501A, Method 5421.
        Modification - Exposure time shall be 40
        standard fading hours; use 3 samples for each
        color or texture; samples shall include joints
        and seams if the design calls for them.
        Colorimetric evaluation shall be by Fed. Test
        Method Std. No. 141A, Method 6123; all visual
        evaluations shall be made from a distance of
        36" at any angle, with the sample illuminated
        as in use, and shall be subject to the
        approval of the Contracting Officer.

REQUIREMENT: (11) Provide resistance to abrasion.

Criteria: Exposed surfaces of this subsystem shall lose
           no more than 250 milligrams per 1000
           revolutions. If vinyl is proposed, no
           exposure of the backing material shall occur.

Test: Type - Subsystem
        Method - Fed. Test Method No. 406; Method
        1091; Abrasion test for surfaces over 1/16"
        thick.
        Modification - Use CS 10 wheel; Paragraph 4.E
        does not apply.

        Method - Fed. Test Method No. 141a; Method
        6192, Abrasion test for surfaces less than
        1/16" thick.

Modification - Use CS 10 wheel; 1000 gram load, 1000 revolutions.
Method - ASTM-D-1175-71; Abrasion Test for Textile Surfaces; use rotary platform doublehead abraser; 1000 gram load; H 18 wheel; 1000 revolutions.

REQUIREMENT: Provide fire safety.

Criteria: (a) This subsystem shall have a maximum flame-spread rating of 25.

(b) If a fully automatic fire protection sprinkler system is provided as part of the system, as specified in the Structure Subsystem, the flame-spread rating shall not exceed 200.

Test: Type - Subsystem
Method - ASTM E 84, "Surface Burning Characteristics of Building Materials".

Criteria: (c) The maximum specific optical density shall not exceed 150 when tested under both flaming and non-flaming conditions of burning.

(d) The critical specific optical density of 16 shall not be reached under less than 30 seconds in both flaming and non-flaming conditions of burning.

Test: Type - Subsystem
Method - Interlaboratory Evaluation of Smoke Chamber, National Bureau of Standards Technical Note 708.

Criteria: (e) This subsystem shall not have a potential heat of more than 40,000 BTU per linear foot of horizontal projection, except that if a fully automatic fire protection sprinkler system is provided as a part of the system as specified in the Structure Subsystem, there shall be no limitation on the potential heat.

Test: Type - Subsystem
Method - Proceedings of ASTM, Vol. 61, 1961, pp. 1337-1347.

REQUIREMENT: (1) Provide stain resistance.

Criteria: (a) Stains of the following types shall not be visually evident on the exposed surface of this subsystem after cleaning. Evaluation shall be subject to the approval of the Contracting Officer.

    Pencil or graphite dust
    Coffee
    Tea
    Milk

    Cold drinks and carbonated beverages
    Chalk
    Heel marks
    Ten weight motor oil

Criteria: (b) Stains of the following types shall be removed with only a slightly visible trace remaining after cleaning. Evaluation shall be subject to the approval of the Contracting Officer. Surfaces designed to be acoustically absorbent are excepted.

    Grease pencil
    Ballpoint pen ink
    Water-based marker ink

Test: Type - Subsystem
Method - PBS-F.2
Modification - Stains shall be removed using methods and agents proposed by the Offeror.

REQUIREMENT: (2) Provide chemical resistance.

Criteria: (a) The exposed surface of this subsystem in use when compared with the reference samples and with any other specimen subjected to this test shall not differ in color by more than 3 NBS units. Variegated, irregular, or translucent finishes shall be evaluated visually for acceptability of color change. Surfaces designed to be acoustically absorbent are excepted.

Criteria: (b) The exposed surface of this subsystem in use shall not exhibit any form of cracking, crazing, splitting, spalling, blisters, delaminations, breaks, discontinuities, or other form of surface deterioration when evaluated visually, subject to review by the Contracting Officer.

(c) The component parts of this subsystem, the surface of which is exposed in use, shall not change in dimension sufficiently to impair the specified performance of the system in use.

Test: Type - Subsystem
Method - Spotting Resistance, Federal Test Method Std. No. 141A, Method 6081
Modifications - Use 60-minute exposure time; apply over joints, if applicable. Use the following reagents in accordance with ASTM D 543-67: distilled water (15), detergent solution (12), soap solution (37), and any additional cleaning agents specified in the maintenance manual. Colorimetric evaluation shall be Fed. Test Method Std. No. 141A, Method 6123; all visual evaluations shall be made from a distance of 36" at any angle, with the sample illuminated as in use, and shall be subject to the approval of the Contracting Officer.

```
 1        SECTION 09665                                                    1
 2                                                                          2
 3        RESILIENT FLOORING - SHEET                                        3
 4                                                                          4
 5                                                                          5
 6        PART 1 - GENERAL                                                  6
 7                                                                          7
 8        WORK SPECIFIED HEREIN                                             8
 9                                                                          9
10        ALL LABOR, MATERIALS, EQUIPMENT AND SERVICES NECESSARY TO        10
11        PROVIDE THE SHEET RESILIENT FLOORING AND RELATED ITEMS AS        11
12        INDICATED OR SPECIFIED.                                          12
13                                                                         13
14        SUBSTITUTIONS                                                    14
15                                                                         15
16        IN ACCORDANCE WITH SECTION 01600.                                16
17                                                                         17
18        SUBMITTALS                                                       18
19                                                                         19
20        SUBMIT SAMPLES OF SHEET VINYL FLOORING FOR REVIEW IN             20
21        ACCORDANCE WITH SECTION 01340.                                   21
22                                                                         22
23        PRODUCT DELIVERY, STORAGE AND HANDLING                           23
24                                                                         24
25        STORAGE OF MATERIALS:  STORE ALL MATERIALS OFF THE GROUND        25
26        UNDER WATERTIGHT COVER AND AWAY FROM SWEATING WALLS AND OTHER    26
27        DAMP SURFACES UNTIL READY FOR USE.  STORE MATERIALS FOR AT       27
28        LEAST 24 HOURS BEFORE COMMENCING WORK, AT A TEMPERATURE OF AT    28
29        LEAST 70 DEGREES F.  MAINTAIN TEMPERATURE DURING INSTALLATION    29
30        AND FOR AT LEAST 24 HOURS AFTER COMPLETION.  REMOVE DAMAGED      30
31        OR DETERIORATED MATERIALS FROM THE PREMISES.                     31
32                                                                         32
33        QUALITY ASSURANCE                                                33
34                                                                         34
35        INSTALLER SHALL BE TRAINED AND APPROVED BY THE MANUFACTURER      35
36        AS COMPETENT IN THE PERIMIFLOR INSTALLATION TECHNIQUE INCLUD-    36
37        ING THE USE OF THE SEAM-MASTER MACHINE.                          37
38                                                                         38
39        GUARANTEE                                                        39
40                                                                         40
41        GUARANTEE IN WRITING THAT SEAMS WILL NOT SEPARATE.               41
42                                                                         42
43        EXTRA MATERIAL                                                   43
44                                                                         44
45        DELIVER TO THE OWNER LEFT OVER REMNANTS OF SHEET VINYL FOR       45
46        USE IN FUTURE REPAIRS TO THE FLOOR.                              46
47                                                                         47
48                                                                         48
49        PART 2 - PRODUCTS                                                49
50                                                                         50
51        MATERIALS                                                        51
52                                                                         52
53        MANUFACTURER:  ARMSTRONG.                                        53
54                                                                         54
55        PATTERN:                                                         55
56                                                                         56
57        COLOR:                                                           57
58                                                                         58
59        GAUGE:  .090                                                     59
60                                                                         60
61        BACKING:  HYDROCORD                                              61
62                                                                         62
63        GRADE:  PERFECTS                                                 63
64                                                                         64
65        ADHESIVE:  PERIMIFLOR ADHESIVE S-200.                            65
66                                                                         66
67                                                                         67
68        UNDERLAYMENT:  S-235 LATEX FILLER.                               68
69                                                                         69
70                                                                         70
71                                                                         71
72                                                                         72
```

PART 3 - EXECUTION

PREPARATION

INSPECT ALL SURFACES TO RECEIVE SHEET VINYL AND REPORT ALL
DEFECTS THAT WILL AFFECT THE INSTALLATION. FILL LOW AREAS
WITH UNDERLAYMENT. THE SCOPE OF THIS SECTION INCLUDES FILL-
ING OF ALL JOINTS, CRACKS AND CHIPS IN SUB FLOOR WITH CRACK
FILLER OR UNDERLAYMENT AS REQUIRED TO PROVIDE A TRUE, EVEN
SURFACE TO RECEIVE SHEET VINYL. CONCRETE SURFACES SHALL BE
DRY, FREE OF PAINT AND OIL AND SWEPT CLEAN BEFORE WORK COM-
MENCES. CONTRACTOR SHALL BE HELD RESPONSIBLE FOR ANY DEFECTS
IN THE SUB-FLOOR WHICH APPEAR IN THE FLOORING SURFACE AFTER
COMPLETION.

INSTALLATION

PRIME THE FLOORS FOR PERMANENT ADHESION IN ACCORDANCE WITH
THE DIRECTIONS OF THE MANUFACTURER OF THE FLOOR COVERING.
SUB-FLOOR SHALL BE COMPLETELY DRY BEFORE APPLICATION OF
ADHESIVE. MAKE MOISTURE TESTS IN ACCORDANCE WITH FLOORING
MANUFACTURER'S RECOMMENDATIONS. INSTALL SHEET VINYL FLOORING
BY THE PERIMIFLOR SYSTEM. CUT SEAMS WITH 'SEAM MASTER' ELEC-
TRIC CUTTING TOOL. BOND THE SEAMS AND PERIMETER OF ALL
SHEETS TO THE SUBFLOOR WITH A 4" TO 6" BAND OF ADHESIVE, AND
ROLL A BAND OF CEMENT INTO ALL SEAM EDGES. REMOVE EXCESS
ADHESIVE FROM THE SURFACE BEFORE IT HAS SET, IN ACCORDANCE
WITH THE MANUFACTURER'S INSTRUCTIONS. WHERE INDICATED COVE
MATERIAL TO FORM INTEGRAL BASE. TERMINATE WITH J TRIM.

CLEANING

CLEAN FLOORS BY A METHOD RECOMMENDED BY THE MANUFACTURER OF
THE FLOORING. SEAL THE SHEET VINYL FLOORS AND BASE WITH TWO
COATS OF ARMSTRONG C-460 POLYMERIC SEALER IN ACCORDANCE WITH
MANUFACTURER'S RECOMMENDATIONS. AFTER THE CLEANING OPERA-
TION, THE FLOORING SHALL BE PROTECTED WITH HEAVY PAPER UNTIL
ACCEPTANCE OF THE WORK.

PROTECTION

PROTECT FINISHED WORK INSTALLED BY OTHER TRADES PRIOR TO WORK
UNDER THIS SECTION. ANY WORK DAMAGED BY WORKMEN OF THIS
TRADE SHALL BE REPLACED WITHOUT COST TO THE OWNER.

END OF SECTION

```
0090  HENNINGSON, DURHAM & RICHARDSON
0100  .ul
0110                      DIVISION 9 - FINISHES
0120                      ———————————————————
0130
0140  .ul
0150                        C9682 - CARPET
0160                        ———————————————
0170  ./            Acrilan (25 Flamespread)
0180
0190  .ul
0200  1.  GENERAL
0210  ——————————
0220
0230      A.  This  section covers furnishing of all labor, materials,
0240  tools, equipment, and performing all work and  services  for  all
0250  carpeting  as  shown  on drawings and as specified, in accordance
0260  with  provisions  of  the  Contract  Documents,  and  completely
0270  coordinated with work of all other trades.
0280
0290      B.  Although  such  work  is  not  specifically  indicated,
0300  furnish and install all  supplementary  or  miscellaneous  items,
0310  appurtenances and devices incidental to or necessary for a sound,
0320  secure and complete installation.
0330  ./                          *****
0340  ./   (Specifier:  These  manufacturers  are  only  ones  who
0350  ./    comply with  this  spec  at  time  of  writing.  Before
0360  ./    adding names, verify with interiors department regarding
0370  ./    color and pattern. Verify that "or equal" carpets have
0380  ./    same type construction and yarn face weights. Verify that
0390  ./    flame and smoke ratings comply with state laws.
0400  ./                          *****
0410
0420  .ul
0430  2.  ACCEPTABLE MANUFACTURERS
0440  ——————————————————————————
0450
0460      A.  Subject  to  compliance with specifications, products of
0470  following manufacturers are approved for use:
0480
0490      Alexander Smith
0500      Bigelow-Sanford
0510      Mohawk
0520      Lees
0530
0540      B.  Other  manufacturers  desiring  approval comply  with
0550  Section 01640.  Furnish samples, technical  data  and  laboratory
0560  test  reports  to  show  flame,  smoke,  static  and  handicap
```

00570 requirements.
00580 ./   * * * * *
00590 ./   (Specfier: Modify manufacturers when other types of
00600 ./   carpet are specified)
00610 ./   * * * * *
00620
00630 .ul
00640 3.   SUBMITTALS (See Section 01340)
00650 _____
00660
00670   A.   Written approval by Federal, State and local fire
00680 authorities, building officials, and other authorities having
00690 jurisdiction. Use tests approved by these authorities. In event
00700 that authorities require other tests, test carpet by such tests,
00710 in addition to test method specified. Submit certificates or
00720 letters   of   approval   from   authorities   having   ultimate
00730 jurisdiction.
00740
00750   B.   Certified copies of test reports to Owner.
00760
00770   C.   Samples, shop drawings and seaming diagrams for approval
00780 before starting work.
00790
00800   D.   Guarantee.
00810
00820 .ul
00830 4. PRODUCT   DELIVERY, STORAGE AND HANDLING. Deliver when areas
00840 _____
00850 of building are ready for carpet. Provide protection from loss
00860 or damage. Deliver with mill register numbers attached. Tag and
00870 mark accessory items for identification.
00880
00890 .ul
00900 5.   JOB   CONDITIONS.
00910 _____
00920
00930   A.   Install   after all other finishing operations are
00940 completed in area to be carpeted.   Verify suitability   of
00950 substrate to accept carpeting.
00960
00970   B.   Check moisture content by sealing an inverted glass
00980 tumbler to floor with putty for 24 hours. If moisture condenses
00990 inside glass, moisture content is too high. Delay installation
01000 until moisture is within acceptable limits.
01010
01020 .ul
01030 6. GUARANTEE
01040 _____
01050
01060   A.   Guarantee entire carpet installation complies with
01070 specifications and that damaged, defective, wrinkled, shrunken or
01080 stained carpet will be removed and replaced. Guarantee carpet
01090 will not shrink or show excessive wear for a period of five years
01100 from date of acceptance. Excessive wear is defined as wearing
01110 away of face yarns which reduces pile height by more than 10
01120 percent in any area, seam separation and/or pulling out of nap.

Figure 16.5 Proprietary (or equal) specification. (Continued)

```
01130
01140        B.  Guarantee  to  cover  entire cost of carpet replacement,
01150 including removal and disposal of defective carpet.
01160
01170        C.  Written guarantee to be jointly  signed  by  Contractor,
01180 Installer and Manufacturer.
01190 ./                           *****
01200 ./   (Specifier:  This carpet is current office standard for
01210 ./   institutions per fire and other codes, where 25 (Class A
01220 ./   flame spread is required. Modify if
01230 ./   necessary for other projects)  Verify smoke rating.
01240 ./                           *****
01250 ./           *****
01260 ./   Specifier:  Edit as required.  See State Requirements for
01270 ./   smoke.  If no State Requirements, use Federal Requirements.
01280 ./           *****
01290
01300 .ul
01310 7.  FIRE, SMOKE, STATIC, AND HANDICAP REQUIREMENTS
01320 ----------------------------------------------------
01330
01340        A.  All  carpet  (and  padding) shall comply with applicable
01350 state and local codes regarding flame  spread,  fuel  contributed
01360 and  smoke  developed  as  tested by ASTM E-84.  Flame spread not
01370 exceeding (25) 75 and smoke not exceeding 450 (250) (200) (75).
01380
01390 ./           *****
01400 ./   Specifier:  In health care facilities specify minimum
01410 ./   critical flux of 0.45 watts.  In facilities other than
01420 ./   health care specify minimum critical flux of 0.22 watts.
01430 ./           *****
01440        B.  Provide  carpet  with  minimum  critical  flux of (0.45)
01450 (0.22) per square centimeter as determined  by  Flooring  Radiant
01460 Panel Test (NBS) in all corridors and means of egress.
01470
01480        C.  In  other areas, provide carpet which meets requirements
01490 of Standard for Surface Flammability of  Carpets  and  Rugs,  DOC
01500 FF-1-70.
01510
01520        D.  Smoke  developed  for  all  facilities not exceeding 450
01530 when tested by NFPA Standard 258-76.
01540
01550        E.  To meet handicap requirements, provide  only  carpet  of
01560 high  density,  low  uncut  pile,  non absorbent fiber with total
01570 height of carpet and pad not exceeding 3/8 in. (0.95 CM).
01580
01590        F.  Static requirements, for all carpet, not  exceeding  3.5
01600 KV per AATCC test 134-1975.
01610
01620 .ul
01630 8.  MATERIALS
01640 --------------
01650
01660        A.  Carpet:  First  quality,  no  seconds  or  imperfects.
01670 Colors  as  selected  by  Architect.  Specified  carpet  is:
01680                                    meeting  minimum  requirements
```

.90 indicated.
.700
.1710   B.   Construction: Face yarns 3 or 4 ply anti-soiling 100
01720 percent solution dyed Acrilan.   Static control   of   copper
01730 filament, Zefstat or Brunslon, or integral static control.
01740 Carpet Velvet, woven thru back.
01750
01760   Rows per centimeters: minimum of 3.15
01770   Rows per inch: minimum of 8
01780   Pitch: 216.
01790   Wire size: .200
01800   Face yarn weight: minimum of 35 oz/sq. yd. (0.83 KG/Sq. M)
01810   Warp: Rayon
01820   Stuffer& Backer   Preshrunk Cotton, Jute or
01830   Polyester
01840   Filler: Jute
01850   Total weight: minimum of 68 oz/sq. yd. (1.61 KG/Sq. M)
01860   Colors: base manufacturer's standard line
01870   Width: 12 ft. (3.66 M)
01880
01890   C. Carpet edging: Where carpeting terminates at other
01900 types of floor finishes Carpet Transition Reducer No. 101 of
01910 thickness to match carpet, as manufactured by Mercer Plastics,
01920 Inc., Newark, N.J. Color as selected by Architect.
01930
01940   D. Joint filler: Non-crumbling, non-staining type approved
01950 by carpeting manufacturer.
01960
01970   E. Adhesive: Non-staining, non-bleeding strippable type as
01980 recommended by carpet manufacturer.
01990
02000 .ul
02010 9.   PREPARATION
02020 _____
02030
02040   A. Check conditions of areas to receive carpet. Fill and
02050 level, thoroughly clean, free of foreign matter. Fill all
02060 cracks, joints, holes or uneven areas with non-crumbling latex
02070 base floor filler, remove excess.
02080
02090   B. Before commencing work, test an area with glue and
02100 carpet to determine "open-time" and bond. Test for moisture.
02110
02120   C. Install using trained, skilled mechanics, with work
02130 supervised by an experienced superintendent.   Install   with
02140 minimum of cross seams or visible side seams. Lay so pile and
02150 pattern of adjacent pieces have same direction.
02160
02170   D. Where carpet terminates at a non-carpeted floor surface,
02180 install edge stripping.
02190
02200   E. Carefully check all dimensions and carefully fit and
02210 install carpet. Use a minimum number of seams located where
02220 indicated on approved seaming drawings. Do not piece carpeting.
02230 install in longest practicable lengths with seams arranged
02240 symmetrically about centerline of room or space.

Figure 16.5 Proprietary (or equal) specification. (Continued)

```
.2260        F.  In  corridors,  install  carpet  lengthwise.
02270
02280  .ul
02290  10.  INSTALLATION
02300  ────────────────────
02310
02320        A.  Installation  instructions  stated  herein  are based on
02330  Bigelow- Sanford installation data.  Carpet  manufacturer  submit
02340  complete written installation data prior to start of work.
02350
02360        B.  Prime all floor areas to receive carpet.
02370
02380        C.  Use  contact  adhesive about 6in.  (15.24 CM) wide along
02390  carpet edges where they butt to a wall, where carpet  terminates,
02400  and  along  all  cross  seams,  to  minimize possibility of later
02410  shrinkage from overwetting. Wherever contact  adhesive  is  used,
02420  hold  glue  back  at  least one inch.  Apply carpet glue over all
02430  remaining areas  where  carpet  is  applied.  Apply  both  contact
02440  adhesive  and  glue  at  rate,  and  using  tools, recommended by
02450  manufacturer.
02460
02470        D.  Unroll  carpet  face  up  and  cut  to lengths required,
02480  making  sure  that  pile-lay  runs  in  same  direction.  Check
02490  starting  wall  for  squareness.  Allow  for off-square wall. Chalk
02500  line entire length of area where seam falls.  Place  two  lengths
02510  in  proper  position  for  installing and trim selvedge.  Line up
02520  seam edge with chalk line.  Make sure that carpet lays perfectly
02530  flat  and  tension free.  Fold  or  roll both widths back 3 feet
02540  (0.91 M) from seam area for  entire  length  of  carpet.  Do  not
02550  crease.
02560
02570        E.  Apply  contact  adhesive along seam edges.  Spread carpet
02580  glue  from approximate center toward each end.
02590
02600        F.  When  sufficient  area has been covered with glue, drop or
02610  roll  first  width  into  place.  Apply coating of edge sealer to
02620  seam edge of first width.  Follow  procedure  on  each  succeeding
02630  seam.  Brush  or  roll  looseness and air bubbles away from seam,
02640  fold over remaining portion of first width.  Apply glue to  floor
02650  and  carpet.  Drop  and  roll  carpet  into  place.  Place within
02660  allowable open time of adhesive.
02670
02680        G.  Roll  back  dry  portion  of  second  width towards seam,
02690  spread glue and place carpet to 3 feet (0.91 M) from  where  next
02700  seam  will  fall.  Drop or roll second width into position, and fit
02710  seam in tightly.
02720
02730        H.  Brush  or  roll out looseness and air bubbles as carpet is
02740  placed,  repeat  procedure  on  continuing  widths.  Use suitable
02750  trimmer for trimming carpet.
02760
02770        I.  Bind all seams with seam cement.
02780
02790        J.  Remove any spillage of glue or adhesive from carpet face
02800  or  seam  using  remover provided by manufacturer.
```

```
 .23
 2820  .ul
 2833  11.   MAINTENANCE  INSTRUCTIONS.
 2843  --------------------------------

 2853       A.   Provide   Owner  with  3  copies  of  carpet  care  and
 2873  maintenance  instructions.   Advise  maintenance  personnel  regarding
 2883  care  and  maintenance  if  Owner  so  requests.
 2893
 2903       B.   Mill  to  demonstrate  cleaning  methods  on  job  site  after
 2913  carpet  installation  to  instruct  Owner's  personnel.
 2923
 2933  .ul
 2943  12.   CLEAN  UP
 2953  ------------

 2963
 2973       A.   After  installation  is  complete, clean  up  all  dirt  and
 2983  debris.   Clean  carpet  of  all  spots, remove  all  loose  threads  with
 2993  sharp  scissors.   Completely  and  thoroughly  vacuum.
 3003
 3013       B.   At  completion  of  work,  review  with  Owner  all  pieces  or
 3023  remnants  of  carpet.   Turn  over  to  Owner  all  such  pieces  that  he
 3033  may  require  for  repair.   Remove  all  other  scraps  from  site.
 3043
 3053  .ul
 3063  13.   EXTRA  MATERIAL
 3073  -------------------

 3083
 3093       A.  Furnish  Owner  with  minimum  of  10 square  yards  (8.36
 3103  Square  Meters)  of  each  type, pattern  and  color  for  maintenance
 3113  purposes.
 3123
 3133
```

SPECIFICATION FORMAT

The Construction Specifications Institute initially published *The CSI Format* in 1963, and since that time the *Format* has gained widespread acceptance throughout the building and design professions. The groupings that compose the *Format* are organized in the following order:

Bidding Requirements

Contract Forms

General Conditions

Specifications

The technical specification portions of *The CSI Format* are divided into *divisions* and *sections*. There are sixteen basic divisions which form the framework around which the specification is developed. Each division denotes a group of related sections which should appear in that particular division.

This specification format was developed to encompass the entire building construction. Therefore, the majority of divisions deal with areas beyond the scope of interior design work. However, it should be noted that the divisions are interrelated and several divisions (italicized on the divisions list below) deal with concerns of the interior specialist. In writing the specification sections for interior materials and components, the designer of interiors must understand how these sections relate to the overall specification format.

CSI Format, Specification Divisions

Division 1: General Requirements

Division 2: Site Work

Division 3: Concrete

Division 4: Masonry

Division 5: Metals

Division 6: *Wood and Plastics (Carpentry)*

Division 7: Thermal and Moisture Protection

Division 8: *Doors and Windows*

Division 9: *Finishes*

Division 10: *Specialties*

Division 11: *Equipment*

Division 12: *Furnishings*

Division 13: *Special Construction*

Division 14: Conveying Systems

Division 15: Mechanical

Division 16: Electrical

The division listing in Figure 16.6 shows the section contents that are usually used in each division. Those listed represent what is known as "broadscope" subjects, i.e., section headings. For example, in Division 9: Finishes, the section "Wallcoverings" would include "narrowscope" (terms developed by CSI) headings, such as vinyl wallcoverings, textile wallcoverings, and any other materials used to cover walls. The number preceding the narrowscope heading relates to the divi-

sion; e.g., the first two numbers 03 refer to division three, the last three numbers 100 refer to the narrowscope. (See Figures 16.7 and 16.8.)

Specification Sections Format

The section format is divided and outlined under three major headings or parts.

Part 1: General

Description (scope)

Quality Assurance

Submittals

Product Delivery

Storage and Handling

Job Conditions

Alternatives

Guarantee

Part 2: Products

Materials

Mixes

Fabrication

Manufacture

Part 3: Execution

Inspection

Preparation

Installation

Application/Performance

Field Quality Control

Adjust and Clean

Schedules

It is not always necessary to list all the article headings in each part. For example, "Mixes" in part 2 may not relate to an interior component; therefore it could be omitted.

The following list summarizes the general contents that are included in each specification part:

Part 1. General

a. Description
    This article includes the scope of the work and the interrelationship between work in this section and work in other sections. Also includes definitions and options.

b. Quality Assurance
    Paragraphs used to define the qualifications of the contractors, subcontractors, consultants, installers, and testing agencies. Types of required tests are described.

c. Submittals
    Details and instructions on submitting samples, shop drawings, test reports, maintenance plans, and operating instructions.

DIVISION 1—GENERAL REQUIREMENTS

01010 SUMMARY OF WORK
01100 ALTERNATIVES
01150 MEASUREMENT & PAYMENT
01200 PROJECT MEETINGS
01300 SUBMITTALS
01400 QUALITY CONTROL
01500 TEMPORARY FACILITIES & CONTROLS
01600 MATERIAL & EQUIPMENT
01700 PROJECT CLOSEOUT

DIVISION 2—SITE WORK

02010 SUBSURFACE EXPLORATION
02100 CLEARING
02110 DEMOLITION
02200 EARTHWORK
02250 SOIL TREATMENT
02300 PILE FOUNDATIONS
02350 CAISSONS
02400 SHORING
02500 SITE DRAINAGE
02550 SITE UTILITIES
02600 PAVING & SURFACING
02700 SITE IMPROVEMENTS
02800 LANDSCAPING
02850 RAILROAD WORK
02900 MARINE WORK
02950 TUNNELING

DIVISION 3—CONCRETE

03100 CONCRETE FORMWORK
03150 FORMS
03200 CONCRETE REINFORCEMENT
03250 CONCRETE ACCESSORIES
03300 CAST-IN-PLACE CONCRETE
03350 SPECIALLY FINISHED (ARCHITECTURAL) CONCRETE
03360 SPECIALLY PLACED CONCRETE
03400 PRECAST CONCRETE
03500 CEMENTITIOUS DECKS
03600 GROUT

DIVISION 4—MASONRY

04100 MORTAR
04150 MASONRY ACCESSORIES
04200 UNIT MASONRY
04400 STONE
04500 MASONRY RESTORATION & CLEANING
04550 REFRACTORIES

DIVISION 5—METALS

05100 STRUCTURAL METAL FRAMING
05200 METAL JOISTS
05300 METAL DECKING
05400 LIGHTGAGE METAL FRAMING
05500 METAL FABRICATIONS
05700 ORNAMENTAL METAL
05800 EXPANSION CONTROL

DIVISION 6—WOOD & PLASTICS

06100 ROUGH CARPENTRY
06130 HEAVY TIMBER CONSTRUCTION
06150 TRESTLES
06170 PREFABRICATED STRUCTURAL WOOD
06200 FINISH CARPENTRY
06300 WOOD TREATMENT
06400 ARCHITECTURAL WOODWORK
06500 PREFABRICATED STRUCTURAL PLASTICS
06600 PLASTIC FABRICATIONS

DIVISION 7—THERMAL & MOISTURE PROTECTION

07100 WATERPROOFING
07150 DAMPPROOFING
07200 INSULATION
07300 SHINGLES & ROOFING TILES
07400 PREFORMED ROOFING & SIDING
07500 MEMBRANE ROOFING
07570 TRAFFIC TOPPING
07600 FLASHING & SHEET METAL
07800 ROOF ACCESSORIES
07900 SEALANTS

DIVISION 8—DOORS & WINDOWS

08100 METAL DOORS & FRAMES
08200 WOOD & PLASTIC DOORS
08300 SPECIAL DOORS
08400 ENTRANCES & STOREFRONTS
08500 METAL WINDOWS
08600 WOOD & PLASTIC WINDOWS
08650 SPECIAL WINDOWS
08700 HARDWARE & SPECIALTIES
08800 GLAZING
08900 WINDOW WALLS/CURTAIN WALLS

DIVISION 9—FINISHES

09100 LATH & PLASTER
09250 GYPSUM WALLBOARD
09300 TILE
09400 TERRAZZO
09500 ACOUSTICAL TREATMENT
09540 CEILING SUSPENSION SYSTEMS
09550 WOOD FLOORING
09650 RESILIENT FLOORING
09680 CARPETING
09700 SPECIAL FLOORING
09760 FLOOR TREATMENT
09800 SPECIAL COATINGS
09900 PAINTING
09950 WALL COVERING

DIVISION 10—SPECIALTIES

10100 CHALKBOARDS & TACKBOARDS
10150 COMPARTMENTS & CUBICLES
10200 LOUVERS & VENTS
10240 GRILLES & SCREENS
10260 WALL & CORNER GUARDS
10270 ACCESS FLOORING
10280 SPECIALTY MODULES
10290 PEST CONTROL
10300 FIREPLACES
10350 FLAGPOLES
10400 IDENTIFYING DEVICES
10450 PEDESTRIAN CONTROL DEVICES
10500 LOCKERS
10530 PROTECTIVE COVERS
10550 POSTAL SPECIALTIES
10600 PARTITIONS
10650 SCALES
10670 STORAGE SHELVING
10700 SUNCONTROLDEVICES(EXTERIOR)
10750 TELEPHONE ENCLOSURES
10800 TOILET & BATH ACCESSORIES
10900 WARDROBE SPECIALTIES

DIVISION 11—EQUIPMENT

11050 BUILT-IN MAINTENANCE EQUIPMENT
11100 BANK & VAULT EQUIPMENT
11150 COMMERCIAL EQUIPMENT
11170 CHECKROOM EQUIPMENT
11180 DARKROOM EQUIPMENT
11200 ECCLESIASTICAL EQUIPMENT
11300 EDUCATIONAL EQUIPMENT
11400 FOOD SERVICE EQUIPMENT
11480 VENDING EQUIPMENT
11500 ATHLETIC EQUIPMENT
11550 INDUSTRIAL EQUIPMENT
11600 LABORATORY EQUIPMENT
11630 LAUNDRY EQUIPMENT
11650 LIBRARY EQUIPMENT
11700 MEDICAL EQUIPMENT
11800 MORTUARY EQUIPMENT
11830 MUSICAL EQUIPMENT
11850 PARKING EQUIPMENT
11860 WASTE HANDLING EQUIPMENT
11870 LOADING DOCK EQUIPMENT
11880 DETENTION EQUIPMENT
11900 RESIDENTIAL EQUIPMENT
11970 THEATER & STAGE EQUIPMENT
11990 REGISTRATION EQUIPMENT

DIVISION 12—FURNISHINGS

12100 ARTWORK
12300 CABINETS & STORAGE
12500 WINDOW TREATMENT
12550 FABRICS
12600 FURNITURE
12670 RUGS & MATS
12700 SEATING
12800 FURNISHING ACCESSORIES

DIVISION 13—SPECIAL CONSTRUCTION

13010 AIR SUPPORTED STRUCTURES
13050 INTEGRATED ASSEMBLIES
13100 AUDIOMETRIC ROOM
13250 CLEAN ROOM
13350 HYPERBARIC ROOM
13400 INCINERATORS
13440 INSTRUMENTATION
13450 INSULATED ROOM
13500 INTEGRATED CEILING
13540 NUCLEAR REACTORS
13550 OBSERVATORY
13600 PREFABRICATED STRUCTURES
13700 SPECIAL PURPOSE ROOMS & BUILDINGS
13750 RADIATION PROTECTION
13770 SOUND & VIBRATION CONTROL
13800 VAULTS
13850 SWIMMING POOLS

DIVISION 14—CONVEYING SYSTEMS

14100 DUMBWAITERS
14200 ELEVATORS
14300 HOISTS & CRANES
14400 LIFTS
14500 MATERIAL HANDLING SYSTEMS
14570 TURNTABLES
14600 MOVING STAIRS & WALKS
14700 TUBE SYSTEMS
14800 POWERED SCAFFOLDING

DIVISION 15—MECHANICAL

15010 GENERAL PROVISIONS
15050 BASIC MATERIALS & METHODS
15180 INSULATION
15200 WATER SUPPLY & TREATMENT
15300 WASTE WATER DISPOSAL & TREATMENT
15400 PLUMBING
15500 FIRE PROTECTION
15600 POWER OR HEAT GENERATION
15650 REFRIGERATION
15700 LIQUID HEAT TRANSFER
15800 AIR DISTRIBUTION
15900 CONTROLS & INSTRUMENTATION

DIVISION 16—ELECTRICAL

16010 GENERAL PROVISIONS
16100 BASIC MATERIALS & METHODS
16200 POWER GENERATION
16300 POWER TRANSMISSION
16400 SERVICE & DISTRIBUTION
16500 LIGHTING
16600 SPECIAL SYSTEMS
16700 COMMUNICATIONS
16850 HEATING & COOLING
16900 CONTROLS & INSTRUMENTATION

Figure 16.7 CSI narrowscope, division 9: finishes. Reproduced with permission of the Construction Specifications Institute.

NUMBER	TITLE
09100	**METAL SUPPORT SYSTEMS**
–10	Non-load Bearing Wall Framing Systems
–20	Ceiling Suspension Systems
–30	Acoustical Suspension Systems
09200	**LATH AND PLASTER**
–01	Furring and Lathing
–02	Gypsum Lath
–03	Metal Lath
–04	Plaster Accessories
–10	Gypsum Plaster
–15	Veneer Plaster
–20	Portland Cement Plaster
–25	Adobe Finish
09230	**AGGREGATE COATINGS**
09250	**GYPSUM WALLBOARD**
–60	Gypsum Wallboard Systems
–80	Gypsum Wallboard Accessories
09290–09299	(Reserved)
09300	**TILE**
–10	Ceramic Tile
–20	Ceramic Mosaics
–30	Quarry Tile
–31	Chemical Resistant Quarry Tile
–32	Slate Tile
–40	Marble Tile
–50	Glass Mosaics
–60	Plastic Tile
–70	Metal Tile
–80	Conductive Tile
09400	**TERRAZZO**
–10	Portland Cement Terrazzo
–11	Terrazzo Bonded to Concrete
–20	Precast Terrazzo
–21	Terrazzo Tile
–30	Conductive Terrazzo
–40	Plastic Matrix Terrazzo
09500	**ACOUSTICAL TREATMENT**
–10	Acoustical Ceilings
–11	Acoustical Panels
–12	Acoustical Tiles
–13	Metal Ceiling Systems
	Linear
	Leaf
	Pan
–20	Acoustical Wall Treatment
–25	Acoustical Units
–30	Acoustical Insulation and Barriers
09540–09499	(Reserved)
09550	**WOOD FLOORING**
–60	Wood Strip Flooring
–61	Gymnasium Type Hardwood Strip Flooring
–62	Gymnasium Type Steel Splined Flooring System
–70	Wood Parquet Flooring
–80	Plywood Block Flooring
–90	Resilient Wood Flooring System
–95	Wood Block Industrial Flooring
09600	**STONE AND BRICK FLOORING**
–10	Stone Flooring
–11	Flagstone Flooring
–12	Slate Flooring
–13	Marble Flooring
–14	Granite Flooring
–20	Brick Flooring
–22	Industrial Brick Flooring
–23	Reinforced Brick Masonry Slab

NUMBER	TITLE
09650	**RESILIENT FLOORING**
–51	Cementitious Underlayment
–60	Resilient Tile Flooring
–65	Resilient Sheet Flooring
–70	Fluid Applied Resilient Flooring
–75	Conductive Resilient Flooring
09680	**CARPETING**
–81	Carpet Cushion
–82	Carpet
–83	Bonded Cushion Carpet
–84	Custom Carpet
–90	Carpet Tile
09700	**SPECIAL FLOORING**
–01	Resinous Flooring
–10	Magnesium Oxychloride Floors
–20	Expoxy-Marble Chip Flooring
–21	Seamless Quartz Flooring
–30	Elastomeric Liquid Flooring
–31	Conductive Elastomeric Liquid Flooring
–40	Heavy-Duty Concrete Toppings
–41	Armored Floors
–50	Mastic Fills
–55	Laminated Plastic Flooring
09760	**FLOOR TREATMENT**
–70	Metallic-type Static Disseminating and Spark-resistant Finish
09800	**SPECIAL COATINGS**
–10	Abrasion Resistant Coatings
–11	Chemical Resistant Coatings
–15	High-Build Glazed Coatings
–20	Cementitious Coatings
–30	Elastomeric Coatings
–35	Textured Plastic Coatings
–40	Fire-Resistant Coatings
–45	Intumescent Coatings
–60	Anti-graffiti Coatings
–70	Coating Systems
–71	Protective Lining for Concrete Storage Tanks
–72	Interior Coating System for Steel Storage Tanks
–73	Exterior Coating System for Steel Storage Tanks
–74	Linseed Oil Protection for Concrete Surfaces
–75	Coating System for Steel Piping
09900	**PAINTING**
–10	Exterior Painting
–20	Interior Painting
–30	Transparent Finishes
09950	**WALL COVERING**
–51	Vinyl-Coated Fabric Wall Covering
–52	Vinyl Wall Covering
–53	Cork Wall Covering
–54	Wallpaper
–55	Wall Fabrics
–56	Asbestos Wall Covering
–60	Flexible Wood Sheets and Veneers
–70	Prefinished Panels
–90	Adhesives

Figure 16.8 CSI narrowscope, division 12: furnishings. Reproduced with permission of the Construction Specifications Institute.

NUMBER	TITLE
12100	**ARTWORK**
–10	Murals
–11	Photo Murals
–20	Wall Hangings
–30	Paintings
–40	Carved or Cast Statuary
–50	Carved or Cast Relief Work
–60	Custom Chancel Fittings
–70	Stained Glass Work
12200–12299	(Reserved)
12300	**MANUFACTURED CABINETS AND CASEWORK**
–01	Metal Casework
–02	Wood Casework
–03	Built-in Tables
–10	Bank Fixtures and Casework
–15	Library Casework
–20	Restaurant and Cafeteria Fixtures and Casework
–25	Educational Cabinets and Casework
–30	Dormitory Casework
–35	Medical and Laboratory Casework
	Nurse Server Cabinets
–40	Pharmacy Casework
–45	Laboratory Casework
–46	Wood Laboratory Casework
–47	Metal Laboratory Casework
–48	Laboratory Tops, Sinks and Accessories
–50	Hospital Casework
–55	Dental Casework
–60	Optical Casework
–65	Veterinary Casework
–70	Hotel and Motel Casework
–75	Ecclesiastical Casework
–80	Display Casework
–90	Residential Casework
–91	Kitchen and Bath Cabinets
12500	**WINDOW TREATMENT**
–01	Drapery and Curtain Hardware
–02	Drapery and Curtain Operators
–10	Blinds and Shades
–11	Vertical Louver Blinds
–12	Horizontal Louver Blinds
–13	Shades
–14	Lightproof Shades
–15	Woven Wood Shades
–20	Drapes and Curtains
–21	Lightproof Drapes
–22	Fabric Drapes
–23	Woven Wood Drapes
–24	Vertical Louver Drapes
–25	Curtains
12530–12549	(Reserved)
12550	**FABRICS**
–51	Drapery and Upholstery Fabrics
12560–12599	(Reserved)
12600	**FURNITURE AND ACCESSORIES**
–10	Landscape Partitions and Components
–20	Office Furniture
–30	Lounge Furniture
–40	Specialized Furniture
–41	Laboratory Furniture
–42	Hospital Furniture
–43	Classroom Furniture
–44	Restaurant and Cafeteria Furniture
–45	Ecclesiastical Furniture
–46	Hotel and Motel Furniture
–47	Dormitory Furniture
–48	Residential Furniture
–50	Accessories
–51	Ash Receptacles
–52	Lamps
–53	Desk Accessories
–54	Waste Receptacles

NUMBER	TITLE
12670	**RUGS AND MATS**
–71	Rugs
–72	Foot Grilles
–73	Mat Frames
–75	Floor Mats
–76	Floor Runners
–77	Matting
12680–12699	(Reserved)
12700	**MULTIPLE SEATING**
–01	Stacking Chairs
–02	Portable Folding Chairs
–03	Interlocking Chairs
–10	Auditorium and Theater Seating
–30	Stadium and Arena Seating
–40	Booths and Tables
–50	Multiple-Use Fixed Seating
–51	Pedestal Table Armchairs
	Single Unit
	Tandem Mounted
–60	Telescoping Bleachers
–70	Pews and Benches
–61	Telescoping Chair Platforms
12780–12799	(Reserved)
12800	**INTERIOR PLANTS AND PLANTING**
–10	Interior Plants
–15	Planters
12820–12999	(Reserved)

d. Product Delivery, Storage, and Handling
Instructions may include protective measures, such as temperature control at the site.

e. Job Conditions
Describe conditions that are necessary for the contractor or installer to perform the installation, i.e., humidity, temperature, ventilation, electric power.

f. Alternatives
Describe acceptable alternatives.

g. Guarantee
Required guarantees for the work included in this section.

Part 2. Products

a. Materials
In proprietary specifications list the materials, trade names, manufacturers, and reference standards. In an open specification list the performance requirements.

b. Mixes
Usually not applicable to most interior materials. May refer to paint mixes or adhesive mixes.

c. Fabrication and Manufacture
Describe the method of fabrication, such as tufted or woven carpet.

Part 3. Execution

a. Inspection
Describe the inspection procedure and the designer's requirements regarding the condition of the finished work.

b. Preparation
Include description of subsurface preparation, measuring and seaming requirements.

c. Installation/Application/Performance
Include instructions on the type of installation required, materials and equipment necessary to accomplish the installation.

d. Field Quality Control
Describe tests that will be performed after installation. State who will perform them.

e. Adjust and Clean
Describe the required adjustment and required cleaning after installation. This article also includes the necessary protection of finished work prior to final acceptance by the owner.

f. Schedules
Schedules that show the contractor where to install the interior materials are included here. Schedules may include paint, color, furniture, room finish, and any other necessary items.

SPECIFICATION DEVELOPMENT

The information contained in the specification must be assembled and coordinated with the drawings early in the design process. As work on the project proceeds, the designer may use several methods to assemble and organize the material that will later become a part of the final specification.

Specification Form

Figures 16.9 and 16.10 illustrate the recommended CSI format for specifications. Other specification examples shown in Figures 16.4 and 16.5 are based on computer technology; i.e., all lines are numbered and the format is not organized in paragraph form.

Specification Checklist. This may list all the materials under a particular division, thus allowing the designer to indicate the materials intended for use.

Outline for Final Specifications. These are more formal in nature. The specification format provides an overview of the divisions and sections that will form the final specification.

Specification Guides. These are provided by private industry, government agencies, trade associations, and manufacturers. These guides may prove useful, but they are general in scope and should be carefully reviewed prior to application. Master specification guides contain standard clauses that may be useful in the preparation of the final specification.

Examples of these three items are shown below:

Specification Checklist (Partial)
Division 6: Wood and Plaster
a. Architectural Millwork:
_____ Paneling
_____ Prefinished
_____ Natural hardwood
_____ Paint grade wood

b. Casework (AWI):   Construction Type:
_____ Premium grade   _____ Exposed face frame
_____ Custom grade   _____ Flush
_____ Economy grade   _____ Exposed

Face Frame:
_____ Lipped
_____ Flush overlay
_____ Reveal overlay

Division 9: Finishes
a. Floor Tile:
_____ Unglazed
_____ Natural clay
_____ Mosaics
_____ Quarry tile
_____ Glazed

b. Resilient Flooring:
_____ Vinyl asbestos tile
Thickness: 1/16" _____ 3/32" _____ 1/8" _____
Size: 9" × 9" _____ 12" × 12" _____
_____ Vinyl coated wood
_____ Vinyl coated cork

c. Wallcovering
_____ Vinyl, Type I _____ Type II _____ Type III _____
_____ Fabric
_____ Vinyl-coated paper

Figure 16.9 Sample specification format. Reproduced with permission of the Construction Specifications Institute.

Unbound margin ½ inch

Top margin minimum ½ inch to ¾ inch

Begin each section on a right hand page

Section (in all capitals) with the appropriate 5-digit number centered on the page

Fully spelled out section title in all capitals centered on page separated from section number by one blank line

Optional indication of master text source document

Separate part designation from section title with two blank lines

Part designation, all capitals, flush left

Separate article heading from part designation with one blank line

Article heading, all capitals, never followed on the same line with text

Separate article heading from paragraph with one blank line

Sublevels of paragraphs stacked with no space between

One paragraph or subparagraph may be submitted under a heading

Separate paragraphs from each other with one blank line

Separate part designation from item above with two blank lines

Bound side margin minimum ¾ inch to 1-¼ inches depending on type of binding

Optional project date on bound edge at page bottom

Bottom margin minimum ½ inch to ¾ inch

5-digit section number with hyphen and sequential section page number

Optional project identification number on unbound edge at page bottom

Optional sequential project manual page number preceded by the word "page" on the unbound edge at page bottom

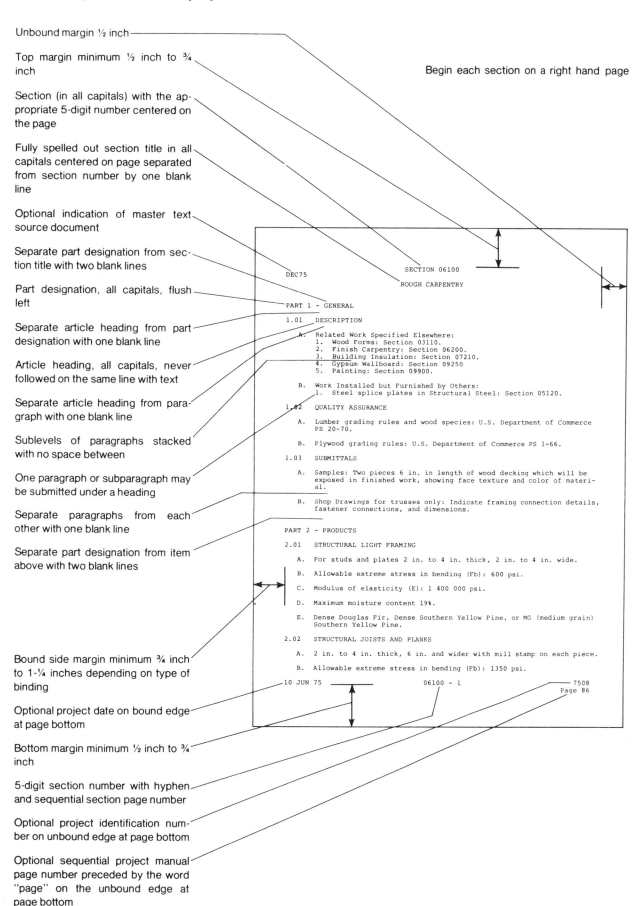

DEC75

SECTION 06100

ROUGH CARPENTRY

PART 1 - GENERAL

1.01   DESCRIPTION

 A. Related Work Specified Elsewhere:
  1. Wood Forms: Section 03110.
  2. Finish Carpentry: Section 06200.
  3. Building Insulation: Section 07210.
  4. Gypsum Wallboard: Section 09250
  5. Painting: Section 09900.

 B. Work Installed but Furnished by Others:
  1. Steel splice plates in Structural Steel: Section 05120.

1.02   QUALITY ASSURANCE

 A. Lumber grading rules and wood species: U.S. Department of Commerce PS 20-70.

 B. Plywood grading rules: U.S. Department of Commerce PS 1-66.

1.03   SUBMITTALS

 A. Samples: Two pieces 6 in. in length of wood decking which will be exposed in finished work, showing face texture and color of material.

 B. Shop Drawings for trusses only: Indicate framing connection details, fastener connections, and dimensions.

PART 2 - PRODUCTS

2.01   STRUCTURAL LIGHT FRAMING

 A. For studs and plates 2 in. to 4 in. thick, 2 in. to 4 in. wide.

 B. Allowable extreme stress in bending (Fb): 600 psi.

 C. Modulus of elasticity (E): 1 400 000 psi.

 D. Maximum moisture content 19%.

 E. Dense Douglas Fir, Dense Southern Yellow Pine, or MG (medium grain) Southern Yellow Pine.

2.02   STRUCTURAL JOISTS AND PLANKS

 A. 2 in. to 4 in. thick, 6 in. and wider with mill stamp on each piece.

 B. Allowable extreme stress in bending (Fb): 1350 psi.

10 JUN 75   06100 - 1   7508
                  Page 86

Figure 16.10 Sample specification format. Reproduced with permission of the Construction Specifications Institute.

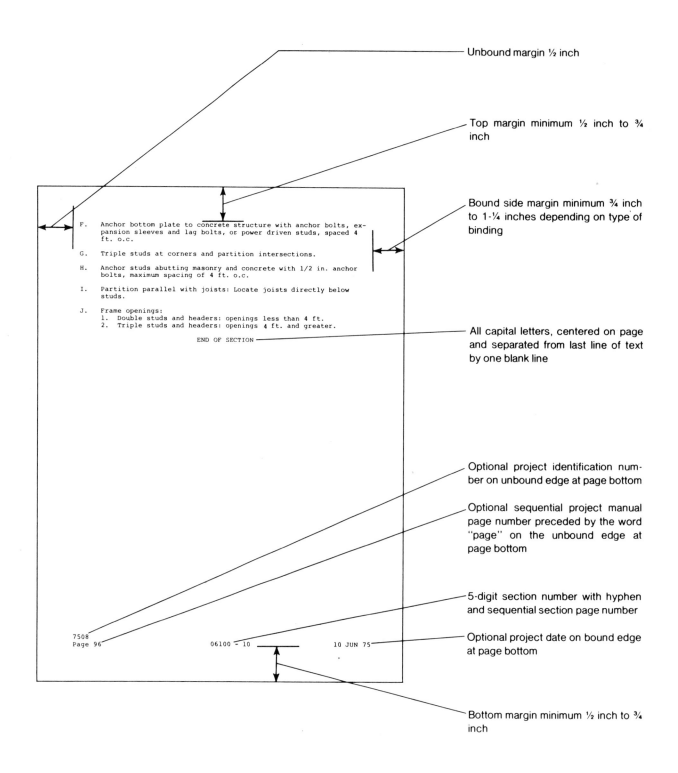

Unbound margin ½ inch

Top margin minimum ½ inch to ¾ inch

Bound side margin minimum ¾ inch to 1-¼ inches depending on type of binding

All capital letters, centered on page and separated from last line of text by one blank line

Optional project identification number on unbound edge at page bottom

Optional sequential project manual page number preceded by the word "page" on the unbound edge at page bottom

5-digit section number with hyphen and sequential section page number

Optional project date on bound edge at page bottom

Bottom margin minimum ½ inch to ¾ inch

The following text appears within the sample page illustration:

F.   Anchor bottom plate to concrete structure with anchor bolts, expansion sleeves and lag bolts, or power driven studs, spaced 4 ft. o.c.

G.   Triple studs at corners and partition intersections.

H.   Anchor studs abutting masonry and concrete with 1/2 in. anchor bolts, maximum spacing of 4 ft. o.c.

I.   Partition parallel with joists: Locate joists directly below studs.

J.   Frame openings:
     1.   Double studs and headers: openings less than 4 ft.
     2.   Triple studs and headers: openings 4 ft. and greater.

END OF SECTION

7508
Page 96   06100 - 10   10 JUN 75

SPECIFICATION LANGUAGE

Throughout this chapter specifications have been stressed as a means of communication. The general organization that is accomplished through divisions and sections is important, but if the written text is ambiguous or inadequate, the specification will not communicate.

The clarity of specifications depends on simple, direct statements, concise use of terms, and attention to grammar and punctuation. Specification sentences are usually structured in the indicative or imperative mood; in fact, the indicative mood is the traditional sentence structure found in most specifications. The imperative mood sentence begins with a verb, usually results in shorter sentences, and eliminates the repetitious use of "shall" in every sentence.

Indicative Mood

"The carpet shall be secured to the floor with adhesive."

"All soiled spots shall be removed from the surface."

"Materials shall be stored in an enclosed, dry area."

Imperative Mood

"Secure carpet to the floor with adhesive."

"Remove all soiled spots from the surface."

"Store materials in an enclosed, dry area."

Specification terminology must be carefully evaluated to avoid misunderstanding. Definitions of the following words should be considered:

Shall and Will: Often used incorrectly. "Shall" is used to designate a command; "will" implies a choice.

Either: If the specification states "either side of the column is to be painted," the contractor may assume that a choice may be made between either one side or the other.

Amount: "The amount of fabric."

Quantity: "The quantity of fabric." "Amount" is a term used to refer to money. "Quantity" refers to yardage and volume.

Any: "The Contractor shall assume the responsibility for *any* unacceptable work." This sentence implies that the contractor may select the work that is unacceptable.

All: "The Contractor shall assume the responsibility for *all* unacceptable work." This sentence leaves no doubt about the contractor's responsibility.

And/or: Avoid this word combination in specifications.

Etc.: Meaning: so forth. The implied uncertainty does not belong in a specification.

The Construction Specifications Institute recommends the following guidelines for the use of numerals in specification documents:

1. Numbers less than thirteen, such as twelve, ten, nine, five, one, should be written in words; higher numbers such as 15, 16, 20, should be in numerals.

2. Clock time and dates should be expressed in numerals, e.g., 2:10 P.M. or June 15, 1970.

3. Decimals should be expressed in numerals, e.g., 6.225. (For quantities less than one, a zero should be used before the decimal point.)

4. Numerals should be used for sums of money, e.g., $5.00.[6]

The following words should be capitalized when used in the specification document:

Agreement	Contractor	Client
Architect	Designer	Owner
Article	Engineer	Room Name
Clause	Government	Section
Contract	General Conditions	State

The designer should never underline anything in a specification because underlining implies that the remaining material can be ignored.

SPECIFICATION OF NEW MATERIALS

Once the designer is satisfied that a certain new product justifies selection over other, more standard products, steps must be taken to assure that it is properly specified and installed.

1. Commit the manufacturer to an appropriate specification, either by having him prepare the specification himself (which should later be checked and approved by the general contractor) or by obtaining his written approval of a specification prepared by you. In either case, provide the manufacturer with as much information as you can concerning the intended use of the product, including, where possible, copies of all relevant working drawings. This helps to establish express warranties of fitness of the product for the intended use. If you should fail to provide relevant data and a problem develops, the manufacturer will claim that he would not have made the recommendation or given approval had he been provided with the omitted data. For the same reason, it is important to submit any pertinent subsequent changes in drawings or specifications to the manufacturer and to obtain his assurance that the changes do not affect the appropriateness of the approved specification.

2. Write the specifications so that is shop drawings are to be prepared by the manufacturer, he is required to get the written approval of the installing contractors; and conversely, if they are to be done by the installing contractors, the written approval of the manufacturer is to be obtained.

3. Require the manufacturer, on projects where the new product plays a major role, to provide a field representative to observe or supervise the installation and to certify, upon completion, that the product has been installed according to the manufacturer's recommendations. The specifications can also require the installing contractor to obtain the manufacturer's written certification as a condition to your own certification as to the completion of the contractor's work.

4. The general or supporting conditions should contain provisions requiring contractors to thoroughly familiarize themselves with all specified products relating to their work and to submit written objections prior to bidding if they object to the proposed use of any product.

5. The specifications should require installing contractors to adhere strictly to drawings and specifications in the installation of all products unless written authorization for deviation is obtained from the designer, in which case the designer should obtain written approval from the manufacturer's field representative.

6. Finally, if proper installation of the new product is critical, the designer should arrange to make at least one visit to the site during installation to personally verify proper installation procedures.[7]

ADDENDUM AND CHANGE ORDER PROCEDURES

The importance of making clear and concise *written* additions, revisions, and deletions to specifications and drawings cannot be overemphasized. To avoid confusion, designers should never give oral instructions nor change orders.

An addendum is used to revise the original construction documents *during* the bidding phase, *before* the contract is awarded. The change order method is used *after* the contract is awarded.

The Construction Specifications Institute suggests that addendum may be used for the following changes:

1. In the date, time, and location for receipt of bids.

2. In the required quality of work.

3. In the sequence of installation or method of installation.

4. To include additional qualified products or additional standards affecting performance.

5. In scheduled completion dates.

This list could never be inclusive because the situations that may require an addendum are many.

Addendum Format

The format used for addendum is similar to that of the specifications and drawings. Figure 16.11 illustrates a typical addendum format, with the major elements numbered in this manner:

1. Name and address of designer

2. Project identification

3. Addendum number

4. Date of addendum

5. To whom addendum is addressed

6. Opening remarks and notice to bidders
   Sequence of addendum changes

7. Changes to prior addenda

8. Changes to bidding requirements
   a. Instruction to bidders
   b. Bid forms
   c. Other bidding requirements

❶ JONES AND SMITH, Architects: John Doe Bldg.
Washington, D.C.

❷ First National Bank of Brownsville: Project No. 11863

❸ ❹ ADDENDUM NO. 2: August 15, 1975

❺ To: All prime contract bidders of record.

❻ This addendum forms a part of the Contract Documents and modifies the original specifications and drawings, dated July 1, 1975, and Addendum 1, dated August 1, 1975 as noted below. Acknowledge receipt of this Addendum in the space provided on the Bid Form. Failure to do so may subject bidder to disqualification.

This Addendum consists of_____. (Indicate the number of pages and any attachments or drawings forming a part of the addendum.)

ADDENDUM NO. 1

❼ 1. Drawings, page AD 1-1. In line 3, number of the referenced Drawing is changed from "G-1" to "G-7."

❽ INSTRUCTIONS TO BIDDERS
2. Proposals. The first sentence is changed to read: "Proposed substitutions must be submitted in writing at least 15 days before the date for opening of bids."

❿ GENERAL CONDITIONS
3. Article 13, Access to Work. The following sentence is added: "Upon completion of work, the Contractor shall deliver to the Architect all required Certificates of Inspection."

❿ SUPPLEMENTARY CONDITIONS
4. Article 19, Correction of Work Before Substantial Completion. This Article is deleted and the following is inserted in its place: "If proceeds of sale do not cover expenses that the Contractor should have borne, the Contractor shall pay the difference to the Owner."

⓫ SPECIFICATIONS
5. Division 9
Gypsum Wallboard: Page 09250-5, following Subparagraph 2.01.C.2, add "3. Smooth shank nail:
    a. ASTM C 514
    b. Length: 1 3/8 inches."

6. Division 15
Refrigeration: Page 15650-10, Subparagraph 2.03.B2, Change total square feet of surface from "298" to "316."

Liquid Heat Transfer: Page 15700-17, Paragraph 2.04.C, Delete "as selected_____ or owner."

⓬ DRAWINGS
7. S-9, Beam Schedule. For B-15 the following is added: "Size, 12 x 26; Straight, 3_____#6; Bent, 2_____#8; Top Over Columns; 3_____#7."

8. M-1: At room 602 change 12 x 6 exhaust duct to 12 x 18; at room 602 add a roof ventilator. See print H-1R attached.

Figure 16.11 Sample addendum format. Reproduced with permission of the Construction Specifications Institute.

9. Changes to the agreement or other contract forms

10. Changes to the general conditions or supplementary conditions

11. Changes to the specifications—in proper sequence

12. Changes to the drawings—in proper sequence

Addendum drawings may accompany this document.

Change Orders

The two most frequent reasons for change orders involve, first, design changes that have been requested by the client, either to expand or reduce the scope of the work, and second, to correct omissions, errors, or discrepancies that appear in the contract documents. Other reasons for changes may result from the fact that certain specified materials are no longer available or the contractor may encounter structural conditions that necessitate rewording of installation methods.

When change orders do not involve major changes and revisions in the contract price or completion date, a field order is frequently used. These orders are used in emergency situations that require immediate attention.

Change orders are usually negotiated between the owner, contractor, and designer. After all have agreed on the proposed changes, the written change order should be signed by the owner, contractor, and designer. When these decisions involve financial changes, special attention must be paid to the method of crediting the owner for deductions, the unit price for determining the total price, and confirmation of costs that are incurred by the contractor.

OPERATIONAL AND MAINTENANCE MANUALS

The collection of all technical data on the maintenance and operation of specified components could prevent costly repairs, improper operation, and client dissatisfaction with the entire project.

The specification of open office systems, for example, requires that a training manual be made available to the users of the space. In addition to written material, manufacturers may be required to conduct training sessions with the client and staff involved.

An operations and maintenance manual should include all the warranties or guarantees not covered by the standard contract documents. It should also include the servicing and precautions recommended by the manufacturer in order to keep the guarantees in force.

It is usually the duty of the owner to decide who will be responsible for assembling and writing the manual. The contractor often must supply part of the information, such as parts lists, name of nearest service dealer, and other necessary data. The designer usually assembles and writes the description of the system and sequence of preventive maintenance.

The manual should follow the following order:

Part 1. The general description of the items to be covered in the manual. This should also include names and addresses of the contractors involved, the suppliers, and the dates that use and maintenance will begin. The example given below illustrates how the information may be organized.

Carpet
1. General description:
   a. Approximate area _____ sq ft
   b. Carpet type _____
   c. Manufacturer _____

2. Construction contractor requirements after acceptance:
   a. Contractor to guarantee installation for a period of one year after work acceptance.

3. Owner begins maintenance:
   a. Anticipated date _____
   b. Actual date _____

4. Names, addresses, and telephone numbers of involved contractors, suppliers, and installers.
   a. Carpet supplier _____
      Address _____
      Telephone number _____
   b. Installation contractor _____
      Address _____
      Telephone number _____

5. Names, addresses, and telephone numbers of other contacts for advice:
   a. Carpet manufacturer representative _____
      _____
      Address _____
      Telephone number _____
   b. Interior designer _____
      Address _____
      Telephone number _____

Part 2. Detailed information on the operation and maintenance of the items contained in the manual.

SUMMARY AND GENERAL GUIDELINES

The following recommendations may serve as a checklist during the preparation of specifications:

1. Inform all project personnel concerning the proposed content of the specifications while the project drawings are being prepared. This will improve their understanding about the nature of the specifications and how they relate to the design requirements and the working drawings.

2. Coordinate the preparation of the drawings and specifications throughout the construction phase so there will be no gaps in documentation and minimum overlapping of data.

3. *Begin preparing the specifications when work on the drawings is begun. Do not wait until the drawings are virtually complete.*

4. Do not "over" specify or "under" specify. Use just the right amount of text to communicate project requirements to the contractor.

5. Use standard specification language so that all parties will understand what is intended by the written word.

6. Review the text of all specifications carefully to ascertain whether (a) it really meets the intent of the design and (b) the items specified can meet the *performance requirements*.[8]

7. Beware of typographic errors in the final version of the specifications.

APPENDIX

A CONVERSION TABLE: ENGLISH TO METRIC UNIT MEASUREMENT*

ENGLISH MEASUREMENT	ACTUAL METRIC CONVERSION	SUGGESTED METRIC SIZE*
1/8″	3.18 mm	3.0 mm
1/4″	6.35	6.0
9/32″	7.14	7.0
5/16″	7.94	8.0
11/32″	8.73	9.0
3/8″	9.53	10.0
7/16″	11.11	11.0
15/32″	11.91	12.0
1/2″	12.70	13.0
9/16″	14.29	14.0
19/32″	15.08	15.0
5/8″	15.88	16.0
21/32″	16.67	17.0
11/16″	17.46	17.0
23/32″	18.26	18.0
3/4″	19.05	19.0
25/32″	19.84	20.0
13/16″	20.64	21.0
7/8″	22.23	22.0
1″	25.40	25.0
1-5/32″	29.39	29.0
1-1/4″	31.75	32.0
1-5/16″	33.34	33.0
1-13/32″	35.72	36.0
1-1/2″	38.10	38.0
1-9/16″	39.69	40.0
1-3/4″	44.45	44.0
2″	50.80	51.0
2-1/8″	53.98	54.0
2-1/4″	57.25	57.0
2-1/2″	63.50	64.0
3″	76.20	76.0
3-1/4″	82.55	83.0
3-1/2″	88.90	89.0
3-9/16″	90.49	90.0
3-3/4″	95.25	95.0
4-1/4″	107.95	108.0
4-1/2″	114.30	114.0
4-9/16″	115.89	116.0
4-3/4″	120.65	121.0
5-1/2″	139.70	140.0
5-3/4″	146.05	145.0

*Reproduced with permission of the Wood Molding and Millwork Producers.

B CALIFORNIA UPHOLSTERED FURNITURE FLAMMABILITY LAW

Flammability Law

19161. All mattresses manufactured for sale in this state, including any mattress manufactured for sale for use in a hotel, motel, or other place of public accommodation in this state, shall be fire retardant. On and after October 1, 1975, all upholstered furniture sold or offered for sale by a manufacturer or wholesaler for use in this state, including any upholstered furniture sold to or offered for sale for use in a hotel, motel, or other place of public accommodation in this state, shall be fire retardant and shall be labeled in a manner specified by the bureau. "Fire retardant," as used in this section, means a product that meets the regulations adopted by the bureau.

Flammability Regulations

1370. Flame Resistant, Flame Retardant. Filling materials and fabrics labeled as "Flame Resistant," "Flame Retardant" and words of similar import shall be tested in accordance with and shall meet the requirements of the State of California, Bureau of Furniture and Bedding Inspection Technical Bulletin No. 105 entitled "Requirements, Test Procedures and Apparatus for Testing and Flame Retardancy of Filling Materials and Fabrics," dated January, 1973.

1371. Mattresses. Mattresses shall meet the requirements set forth in the United States Government Standard for Flammability of Mattresses FF-4-72.

1372. Mattress Labeling and Requirements.

1373. Voluntary Notice. Each mattress may have a label attached to the top thereof stating: "Notice: This mattress is designed to resist combustion which may result from a smoldering cigarette."

1374. Flammability. Upholstered Furniture. (a) All filling materials contained in any article of upholstered furniture shall meet the test requirements as set forth in the most recent State of California, Bureau of Home Furnishings Technical Bulletin Number 117, entitled "Requirements, Test Procedures and Apparatus for Testing the Flame Retardancy of Filling Materials Used in Upholstered Furniture."
(b) In addition to the requirements of subsection (a) above, finished articles of upholstered furniture shall not ignite when tested in accordance with the most recent State of California, Bureau of Home Furnishings Technical Bulletin 116 entitled "Test Procedures and Apparatus for Testing the Flame Retardance of Upholstered Furniture."

1374.1. Exemptions. (a) Articles exempted from the provisions of Section 1374 of these regulations shall have a label attached to the surface area of the article, in plain view stating the following:

Notice

THIS ARTICLE DOES NOT MEET CALIFORNIA BUREAU OF HOME FURNISHINGS' FLAMMABILITY REQUIREMENTS-TECHNICAL BULLETIN 117. CARE SHOULD BE EXERCISED NEAR OPEN FLAME OR WITH BURNING CIGARETTES.

(b) The minimum size of the label shall be 2 × 3 inches and the minimum size of type shall be one-eighth inch in height. All type shall be in capital letters.

1374.2. Criteria for Exemption. Articles of upholstered furniture, other than juvenile furniture and furniture used for and in facilities designed for the care or treatment of humans, which meet any of the following criteria shall be exempt from compliance with the provisions of Section 19161 of the Home Furnishings Act: (a) Cushions and pads intended solely for outdoor use. (b) Any article which is smooth surfaced and contains no more than one-half (1/2) inch of filling material, provided that such article does not have a horizontal surface meeting a vertical surface.

1374.3. Labeling. The provisions of subsections (a), (b) and (c) of this section shall become effective January 1, 1978.
(a) Upholstered furniture conforming to the requirements of Section 1374(a) and 1374(b) of these regulations shall have a label permanently attached to the article, in plain view, stating the following:

Notice

THIS ARTICLE MEETS ALL FLAMMABILITY REQUIREMENTS OF CALIFORNIA BUREAU OF HOME FURNISHINGS BULLETINS 116 AND 117. CARE SHOULD BE EXERCISED NEAR OPEN FLAME OR WITH BURNING CIGARETTES.

(b) Upholstered articles conforming to Section 1374(a) but which may not conform to Section 1374(b) shall have a label permanently attached to the article, in plain view, stating the following:

Notice

ONLY THE RESILIENT FILLING MATERIALS CONTAINED IN THIS ARTICLE MEET CALIFORNIA BUREAU OF HOME FURNISHINGS FLAMMABILITY REQUIREMENTS. CARE SHOULD BE EXERCISED NEAR OPEN FLAME OR WITH BURNING CIGARETTES.

(c) Minimum size of the label for subsections (a) and (b) shall be 4 × 4 inches and the minimum size of the type shall be one-eighth inch in height. All type shall be in capital letters.

Upholstered Furniture Flammability Law Responsibility

Supply Dealer's Responsibility: Bulk Filling Materials and Fabrics

A. *Bulk Materials* The supply dealer must stamp on his invoice for the products he sells in the State of California on and after March 1, 1977, that the product meets the requirements of Bureau of Home Furnishings Technical Bulletin Number 117. Similar requirements are mandatory for the supply dealer's label.

B. *Fabrics* No certification is required that the fabric meets the provisions of law. This is a matter between the fabric mill and the supply dealer or manufacturer. The test for fabrics is a United States Government test for clothing textiles which has been in existence since 1953. This test requirement has merely been extended by the Bureau to include upholstery fabrics. The mills should use the same system for insuring compliance for upholstery fabrics that they have been using for clothing textiles since 1953.

Manufacturer's Responsibility: Completed Article. It is the responsibility of the manufacturer to insure that the materials used are in accordance with law and that the proper label be attached to completed articles of upholstered furniture.

Wholesaler's Responsibility: Completed Article. It is the wholesaler's responsibility to insure that all upholstered products have the required labels attached.

Retailer's Responsibility: Finished Article. It is the retailer's responsibility to insure that each and every upholstered article offered for sale by the retailer has the required labels attached.

TECHNICAL BULLETIN NO. 116

Requirements, Test Procedure and Apparatus for Testing the Flame Retardance of Upholstered Furniture

I. Upholstered furniture means any product as set forth in Section 19006 of the State of California Home Furnishings Act.

Requirements:
(1) An article of upholstered furniture fails to meet the provisions of law if any of the following conditions occur:
     (A) If obvious flaming combustion occurs.
     (B) If a char develops more than two inches in any direction from the cigarette, measured from its nearest point.
(2) Flame retardant properties shall be retained by the furniture under all normal conditions of temperature, humidity and use.

II. Test Materials
(1) Cigarettes. Cigarettes shall be made from natural tobacco and shall be 85± 2mm long with a diameter of 0.3± 0.02 inches and a weight of 1.1 gms ± 0.1 gms and shall attain an ember temperature of not less than 1,000°F. "Ember temperature" means the temperature at which the lighted portion of a cigarette burns. Filter tip cigarettes shall not be used.
(2) Furniture. The article of upholstered furniture tested shall be the finished product ready for sale to the consumer.

III. Preparation of Test Materials
(1) Furniture and cigarettes shall be conditioned for not less than 48 hours at a temperature of 65-80°F and a relative humidity of less than 55% immediately prior to test. Furniture shall be positioned so as to allow for maximum surface exposure to conditioning environment.

IV. General Requirements
(1) The furniture shall be tested under conditions of between 65-80°F temperature and at less than 55% relative humidity.
(2) Test shall be performed in such a manner that each differently-dyed area of the furniture fabric is included in the test locations.
(3) If a cigarette extinguishes before burning its full length the test is considered "no test" and must be repeated with a freshly lit cigarette on a different portion of the same type of location on the furniture.
(4) Location of the test cigarettes on the furniture shall be no less than 6 inches apart.
(5) All exposed horizontal surfaces (including smooth, tape edge, quilted, tufted or button locations plus all crevices created by the orientation of seat cushions and furniture sides and back panels) shall be tested.

(6) Horizontal surfaces include all surfaces which may be vertical in normal use but which are designed to become horizontal surfaces in special use, e.g., recliners, etc.

(7) Horizontal surfaces which are not wide enough to support a cigarette need not be tested.

V. Testing

(1) Each furniture surface shall be tested until either (a) three cigarettes have burned their full length, (b) three cigarettes have extinguished before burning their full length, or (c) one cigarette has resulted in failure as outlined in (I), (A) and (B).

VI. (1) Smooth Surface Test. Three burning cigarettes [well lighted but not burned more than 4mm (0.16 inch)] shall be placed directly on a smooth surface location on the test furniture. The cigarettes should burn their full lengths on a smooth surface without burning across a tuft or stitching of a quilted area. However, if this is not possible because of furniture design, then the cigarettes shall be positioned on the furniture in a manner which will allow as much of the butt ends as possible to burn on smooth surfaces.

(2) Tape Edge Test. Three burning cigarettes shall be placed in the depression created by the upholstered furniture and the tape edges, parallel to the tape edge. If there is no depression at the edge, hold the cigarettes in place along the edge and parallel to the edge with straight pins. Three straight pins may be inserted through the edge at a 45° angle such that one pin supports the cigarette at the top, one at the center and one at the butt. The heads of the pins must be below the upper surface of the cigarette.

(3) Quilted Location Test. Three burning cigarettes shall be placed on quilted locations of the test furniture. The cigarettes shall be positioned directly over the thread in the depression created by the quilting process. If the quilt design is such that the cigarettes cannot burn their full lengths over the thread, then the cigarettes shall be positioned in a manner which will allow as much of the butt ends as possible to burn on the thread.

(4) Tufted Location Test. Three burning cigarettes shall be placed on tufted locations of the test furniture. The cigarettes shall be positioned so that they burn down into the depression caused by the tufts and so that the butt ends of the cigarettes burn out over the buttons or laces used in the tufts.

(5) Crevices. If crevices exist, created by the orientation of seat cushions and side or/and back panels, then at least one cigarette shall be placed at the crevice location so that it burns between the seat cushion and the upholstered panel.

TECHNICAL BULLETIN NO. 117

Requirements, test procedure and apparatus for testing the flame retardance of resilient filling materials used in upholstered furniture.

SECTION A

Part I Resilient Cellular Materials

I. Requirements
   1. The average char length of all specimens shall not exceed 6 inches.
   2. The maximum char length of any individual specimen shall not exceed 8 inches.
   3. The average afterflame, including afterflame of molten material or other fragments dropping from specimens, shall not exceed 5 seconds.
   4. The maximum afterflame of any individual specimen, including afterflame of molten material or other fragments dropping from the specimen, shall not exceed 10 seconds.
   5. The average afterglow, including afterglow of molten material or other fragments dropping from the specimen, shall not exceed 15 seconds.
   6. Resilient cellular materials shall meet the above requirements both before and after aging for 14 days in a forced air circulating oven at 150°F.

II. Test Procedure
   1. Scope
      This procedure is intended for use in determining the resistance of resilient cellular materials to flame and glow propagation and tendency to char.
   2. Test Specimen
      Test specimens shall be rectangles of cellular materials 12 × 3 × ½ inches. A minimum of 5 specimens shall be tested.
   3. Apparatus
      3.1. Cabinet. A test cabinet fabricated in accordance with the requirements of Federal Test Method Standard No. 191 Method 5903.2 shall be used.
      3.2. Burner. The burner shall be in accordance with the requirements of Federal Test Method Standard No. 191 Method 5903.2.
      3.3. Gas. The test gas shall be Matheson Gas B.
      3.4. Specimen Holder. A stainless steel specimen holder fabricated in accordance with the requirements specified in Figure 117A shall be used.
   4. Procedure
      4.1. All specimens shall be tested, and conditioned for a minimum of 24 hours, at 70 ± 5 °F and less than 55 percent relative humidity.
      4.2. The specimen in its holder shall be suspended vertically in the cabinet in such a manner that the lower end of the specimen is 0.75 inches above the top of the burner.
      4.3. The burner flame shall be adjusted by means of a needle valve in the base of the

burner to give a flame height of 1.5 inches with air supply to the burner permanently shut off and taped.

    4.4. After inserting the specimen, the burner flame shall be applied vertically at the middle of the lower edge of the specimens for 12 seconds.

    4.5. The cabinet door shall remain shut during testing.

III. Definitions

    1. Afterflame. The afterflame time shall be the time the specimen continues to flame after the burner flame is extinguished, and shall include afterflame of molten drops of material.

    2. Afterglow. The afterglow time shall be the time the specimen continues to glow after it has ceased to flame, and shall include afterglow of molten drops of material.

    3. Char Length. The char length shall be the distance from the end of the specimen which was exposed to the flame, to the upper edge of the burned or charred or void area. In the measurement of char length all readily removeable portions of carbonaceous char shall be removed prior to measurement.

IV. Test Results

    1. The char length of each specimen shall be recorded to the nearest 0.1 inches and the after flame time and afterglow time to the nearest 0.1 seconds.

    2. Maximum and average char length, afterglow and afterflame shall be determined for each resilient cellular material.

Part II Shredded Resilient Cellular Materials (e.g. shredded polyurethane foams)

Shredded resilient cellular materials shall meet the following requirements.

1. The resilient cellular material used for shredding shall meet the requirements of Section A and D of this Technical Bulletin prior to shredding, or, a post flame treated shredded foam may be used.

2. All resilient cellular material shall be encased in a fabric/ticking, and the requirements of the following test procedure shall be met.

3. A 13 × 13 inch (finished size) pillow/cushion fabricated from the fabric/ticking and filled with the flame retardant foam, shall be used for testing.

4. The packing density of the shredded foam shall approximate that of intended use, but shall not be less than 2.0 pounds per cubic foot or greater than 4.5 pounds per cubic foot.

5. The pillow/cushion shall not lose more than 5 percent in weight when subjected to a 1.5 inch flame from a Bunsen Burner for 12 seconds.

6. The burner shall be positioned 0.75 inches below the center of the bottom lateral surface of the horizontally positioned pillow/cushion.

7. The pillow/cushion shall be supported in such a manner that a minimum 10 inch diameter circular portion of the lower fabric surface be directly exposed to the burner flame.

8. The pillow/cushion shall meet the test requirements both before and after aging for 14 days at 150°F in a forced air circulating oven.

9. The test gas shall be Matheson Gas B, and all pillow/cushions shall be conditioned for a minimum of 24 hours at 70 ± 5°F and less than 55 percent relative humidity.

10. The burner flame shall be adjusted by means of a needle valve in the base of the burner to give a flame height of 1.5 inches with air supply to the burner permanently shut off and taped.

11. The fabric/ticking used to encase the shredded resilient cellular material shall meet the requirements of Technical Bulletin 117, Section A, Requirements 1, 2, 3, 4 & 5, when tested in accordance with Federal Test Method Standard No. 191 Method 5903.2. The burner flame shall be applied vertically at the middle of the lower edge of the specimens for both 3 seconds and 12 seconds.

Part III Expanded Polystyrene Beads

Expanded polystyrene beads may be used in articles of upholstered furniture provided that a fire modified grade of expanded polystyrene, meeting the requirements of the following test procedure, is used.

A. Requirements

    1. Weight loss shall not exceed 5 percent in any of five consecutive tests.

    2. Materials shall meet the above requirement after aging for 48 hours in an air circulating mechanical convection oven at 150 ± 5°F.

B. Apparatus

    1. Oven: A mechanical convection air circulating oven capable of maintaining 150 ± °F.

    2. Laboratory hood: The test shall be conducted in a laboratory fume hood.

    3. Test basket: 3 inch deep, 8 inch square, wire mesh basket. (U.S. mesh No. 12 or finer)

    4. Aluminum foil: to catch molten material.

    5. Methenamine reagent tablets: Eli Lilly No. 1588.

    6. Tongs.

    7. Matches.

    8. Balance: capable or measuring to the nearest 0.1 gram.

C. Test Procedure

    1. All test material shall be conditioned for a minimum of 48 hours at 150 ± 5°F.

    2. A pre-weighed wire basket shall be filled to the 3 inch level with the aged material, and the weight of the test material determined.

    3. Place the test basket on a sheet of aluminum foil in a fume hood. The hood fan should remain off during the test.

    4. Hold a methenamine tablet with tongs and ignite with a match.

    5. Place the burning tablet *gently* on the top center of the test material.

    6. Continue the test until all flames are completely extinguished.

7. After cooling, reweigh the basket and record percentage weight loss. Molten material which remains in the basket or on the aluminum foil is not considered as weight loss.

8. A total of five test samples of each material shall be evaluated.

SECTION B

Part I Non–Man-Made Filling Materials

I. Non–man-made filling materials shall meet all the requirements under Section A of this technical bulletin, with the following modifications:

1. Specimens shall not be mounted in a specimen holder, but shall be vertically suspended into the flame. The upper ½ inch of the specimen may be used for suspension.

2. Specimens size shall be 12 × 3 inches and in the thickness in which the batting is to be used up to one inch. If the filler is to be used in thicknesses of greater than one inch, specimens shall be cut to one inch thickness prior to testing.

3. A standard wing tip shall be added to the burner for specimens greater than ½ inch in thickness. The long dimension of the wing tip shall be parallel to the batting thickness.

4. Non–man-made products shall not be aged for 14 days at 150 °F.

Part II Shredded and Loose Fill Materials: Feathers and Down

Feathers and Down may be used in articles of upholstered furniture provided that the following requirements are met:

1. The feathers and down shall be encased in a flame retardant fabric/ticking.

2. The fabric/ticking shall meet the requirements of Technical Bulletin 117, Section A, Requirements 1, 2, 3, 4, and 5, when tested in accordance with Federal Test Method Standard No. 191 Method 5903.2.

3. The burner flame shall be applied vertically at the middle of the lower edge of the specimens for both 3 seconds and 12 seconds.

SECTION C

Man-Made Fiber Filling Materials

I. Requirements

1. The average flame spread of all specimens shall not be less than 10 seconds.

2. The minimum flame spread of any individual specimens shall not be less than 7 seconds.

3. Man-made fiber fillers shall meet these requirements when tested both with and without any attached woven or non-woven materials such as scrims, cheese cloth, etc.

4. Man-made fiber fillers shall meet these requirements when tested in both machine (or linear) and transverse directions.

II. Test Procedure

1. Scope
   This procedure is intended for use in determining the resistance of resilient man-made fiber filling materials to flame spread, when tested using a modified version of Commercial Standard 191-53.

2. Test Specimen
   Test specimens shall be rectangles of fillers 6½ × 3 inches and in the thickness in which the fillers are to be used. A minimum of 5 specimens shall be tested.

3. Apparatus
   3.1 Cabinet. A test cabinet fabricated in accordance with the requirements of Commercial Standard 191-53 shall be used.
   3.2 Burner and Gas. The burner and gas specified in Commercial Standard 191-53 shall be used.
   3.3 Specimen Holder. A modified stainless steel specimen holder fabricated in accordance with the requirements of Figure 117B shall be used.

4. Summary of Method
   4.1 All specimens shall be tested, and conditioned for a minimum of 24 hours, at 70 ± 5°F and less than 55 percent relative humidity.
   4.2 The specimen in its holder shall be supported at an angle of 45 degrees.
   4.3 The burner flame, adjusted to a length of 5/8 inches, shall be applied to the specimen near the lower edge for 5 seconds.
   4.4 The time required for the flame to proceed up the batting a distance of 5 inches shall be recorded.
   4.5 The cabinet door shall remain shut during testing.

III. Definitions

1. Flame Spread: The time in seconds from application of the burner until the specified burn end point is reached.

2. Self-Extinguishing Time: The time in seconds from application of the burner until the specimen flame extinguishes, provided the flame front has not reached the specified burn end point.

IV. Test Results

1. The time of flame spread of individual specimens shall be noted. Average flame spread shall be determined.

2. If a specimen burn does not reach the specified end point the Self-extinguishing time shall be noted.

SECTION D

Resilient Filling Materials: Cigarette Resistance

I. Requirements

1. All resilient filling materials shall resist combustion from cigarettes.

2. The maximum char length of any specimen shall not exceed 2 inches in any direction from the cigarette.

II. Test Procedure

1. Specimens no less than 12 × 12 inches and in the thickness of intended use shall be tested.

2. Cigarettes, meeting the cigarette specifications of DOC FF 4-72, shall be burned on the surface, at the center of the specimen.

3. Specimens shall be tested with cigarettes both un-

covered, and covered with one layer of sheeting material.

4. Sheeting materials shall meet the sheet specifications of DOC FF 4-72, shall be laundered once before use, and shall not be less than 12 × 12 inches in size.

5. A minimum of 3 specimens both covered and uncovered shall be tested.

6. All test materials shall be conditioned for at least 24 hours prior to testing at 70 ± 5 °F and less than 55 percent relative humidity.

III. Test Results
1. The char dimensions of each specimen shall be measured to the nearest 0.1 inches.

SECTION E

Upholstery Fabrics

1. Fabrics which do not meet the Class 1 requirements of U.S. Department of Commerce commercial standard 191-53 shall not be used on articles of upholstered furniture.

2. Both surfaces of the fabric shall be tested to determine conformance with C.S. 191-53.

FLAMMABILITY TEST FRAME
FLEXIBLE FOAMS

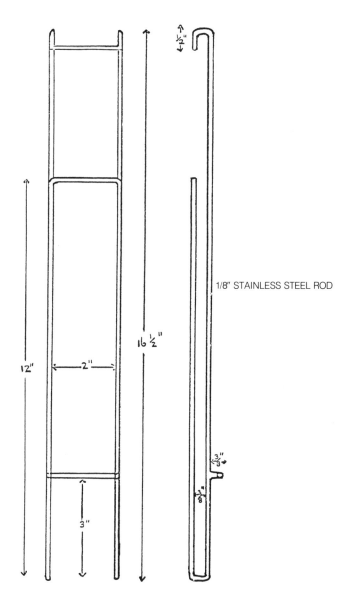

1/8″ STAINLESS STEEL ROD

FIGURE A   FIGURE B

FLAMMABILITY TEST FRAME—MODIFIED CS 191-53

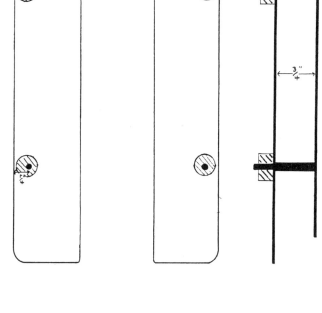

C PART 1632: STANDARD FOR THE FLAMMABILITY OF MATTRESSES (AND MATTRESS PADS) (FF 4-72)*

AUTHORITY: Sec. 4, 67 Stat. 112, as amended, 81 Stat. 569-70; 15 U.S.C. 1193, unless otherwise noted.

SOURCE: 40 FR 59940, Dec. 30, 1975, unless otherwise noted.

Subpart A—The Standard

§ 1632.1 Definitions.

In addition to the definitions given in section 2 of the Flammable Fabrics Act as amended (sec. 1, 81 Stat. 568; 15 U.S.C. 1191) and the procedures under that act for setting standards (16 CFR Part 1607), the following definitions apply for the purpose of this standard.

(a) "Mattress" means a ticking filled with a resilient material used alone or in combination with other products and intended or promoted for sleeping upon. This definition includes, but is not limited to, mattress pads, adult mattresses, youth mattresses, crib mattresses including portable crib mattresses, bunk bed mattresses, convertible sofa bed mattresses, corner group mattresses, daybed mattresses, roll-a-way bed mattresses, high risers, and trundle bed mattresses. This definition excludes sleeping bags, pillows, mattress foundations such as box springs, liquid and gaseous filled tickings such as water beds and air mattresses, upholstered furniture such as chaise lounges, drop-arm love seats, press-back lounges, push-back sofas, sleep lounges, sofa beds (including jackknife sofa beds), sofa lounges (including glide-outs), studio couches, and studio divans (including twin studio divans and studio beds), and juvenile product pads such as car bed pads, carriage pads, basket pads, infant carrier and lounge pads, dressing table pads, stroller pads, crib bumpers, and playpen pads. See § 1632.6, Glossary of terms, for definition of the above.

(b) "Ticking" means the outermost layer of fabric or related material that encloses the mattress core and upholstery materials.

(c) "Core" means the main support system that may be present in a mattress, such as springs, foam, or hair block.

(d) "Upholstery material" means all material, either loose or attached, between the ticking or between the ticking and the core of the mattress, if a core is present.

(e) "Tape edge" (edge) means the seam or border edge of a mattress.

(f) "Quilted" means stitched through the ticking and one or more layers of upholstery material.

(g) "Tufted" means buttoned or laced through the ticking and upholstery material and/or core.

(h) "Mattress prototype" means mattresses of a particular design, sharing all materials and methods of assembly, but excluding differences in mattress size. If it has been shown as a result of prototype qualification testing that a material has not influenced the ignition resistance of the mattress prototype, substitution of another material for such material shall not be deemed a difference in materials for purposes of prototype definition. If it is determined or suspected that a material has influenced the ignition resistance of the mattress prototype, a dimensional or other change in that material shall be deemed a difference in materials for purposes of prototype definition unless it is previously shown to the satisfaction of the Consumer Product Safety Commission that such dimensional or other change will not reduce the ignition resistance of the mattress prototype.

(i) "Mattress type" means mattresses sharing a method of assembly, such as tufted, multineedle continuous quilt, deep panel quilt, and smooth top, and all materials affecting cigarette ignition, but excluding differences in mattress size. More than one mattress prototype may be included in a single mattress type, provided each prototype has the same method of assembly.

(j) "Production unit" (unit) means a quantity of mattresses of one mattress type. This quantity is predetermined by the mattress manufacturer subject to the maximum number specified in the applicable parts of § 1632.4(b) *Specimen and Sampling.* No mattress completed while other mattresses of the same type are in production shall be excluded from the production unit to which such other mattresses are assigned.

(k) "Surface" means one side of a mattress which is intended for sleeping upon and which can be tested.

§ 1632.2 Scope and application.

(a) This standard provides a test method to determine the ignition resistance of a mattress when exposed to a lighted cigarette.

(b) All mattresses, as defined in § 1632.1(a), are subject to the requirements of this standard.

(c) Mattresses which are subject to the coverage of the Motor Vehicle Safety Standard, No. 302, subject: "Flammability of Interior Materials—Passenger Cars, Multipurpose Passenger Vehicles, Trucks, and Buses" (36 FR 290), issued by the National Highway Traffic Safety Administration, are excluded from coverage under this standard, unless also intended or promoted for uses included in § 1632.1(a).

(d) One of a kind mattresses, such as nonstandard sizes or shapes, may be excluded from testing under this standard pursuant to rules and regulations established by the Consumer Product Safety Commission.

§ 1632.3 General requirements.

(a) *Summary of test method.* The method involves the exposure of the mattress surface to lighted cigarettes as the standard igniting source in a draft-protected environment and the measurement of the ignition resistance of the mattress. These exposures include smooth, tape edge, and quilted or tufted locations, if they exist on the mattress surface. Two-sheet tests are also conducted on similar surface locations. In the latter test, the burning cigarettes are placed between the sheets.

(b) *Test criterion.* Testing the mattress surface in accordance with the testing procedure set forth in § 1632.4 *test procedure,* individual cigarette test locations pass the test if the char length on the mattress surface is not

---

*Reproduced with permission from Code of Federal Regulations, Title 16, Part 1000 to End, Revised as of January 1, 1976.

more than 5.1 cm (2 in) in any direction from the nearest point of the cigarette. In the interest of safety, the test operator should discontinue the test and record a failure before reaching the 2 in. char length if, in his opinion, an obvious ignition has occurred.

§ 1632.4 Test procedure.

(a) *Apparatus*—(1) *Testroom.* The testroom shall be large enough to accommodate a full-scale mattress in a horizontal position and to allow for free movement of personnel and air around the test mattress. The room shall be equipped with a support system (platform, bench, etc.) upon which a mattress may be placed flat in a horizontal position at a reasonable height for making observations. For thin, flexible mattresses and mattress pads, the top surface of the support system shall be nonmetallic. The test area shall be draft-protected and equipped with a suitable system for exhausting smoke and/or noxious gases produced by testing. The testroom atmospheric conditions shall be greater than 18° C (65° F) and at less than 55 percent relative humidity, except for production testing.

(2) *Ignition source.* The ignition source shall be cigarettes without filter tips made from natural tobacco, 85 ± 2 mm long with a tobacco packing density of 0.270 ± 0.020 g/cm^3 and a total weight of 1.1 ± 0.1 gm.

(3) *Fire extinguisher.* A pressurized water fire extinguisher, or other suitable fire extinguishing equipment, shall be immediately available.

(4) *Water bottle.* A water bottle fitted with a spray nozzle shall be used to extinguish the ignited portions of the mattress.

(5) *Scale.* A linear scale graduated in millimeters, 0.1 inch, or ¹⁄₁₆-inch divisions shall be used to measure char length.

(6) *Other apparatus.* In addition to the above, a thermometer, a relative humidity measuring instrument, a knife or scissors, and tongs are required to carry out the testing.

(b) *Specimen and sampling*—(1) *General.* The test criterion of section 1632.3(b) shall be used in conjunction with the following mattress sampling plan, or any other approved by the Consumer Product Safety Commission that provides at least the equivalent level of fire safety to the consumer (see Subpart B of this Part). Alternate Sampling plans submitted for approval shall have operating characteristics such that the probability of unit acceptance at any percentage defective does not exceed the corresponding probability of unit acceptance of the following sampling plan in the region of the latter's operating characteristic curves that lies between 5 and 95 percent acceptance probability. If such alternate sampling plan involves testing of components of mattresses or materials used in mattresses, its submittal shall be supported by clear evidence of the necessary correlation of the re-

sults of such testing with those results from testing as prescribed hereunder.

(2) *Mattress sampling.* The basic mattress sampling plan is made up of two parts: (1) Prototype qualification and (2) production testing. In addition, a batch sampling plan is given which may be used for small production quantities, when shipping requirements prohibit the use of the basic plan, or for other reasons at the discretion of the manufacturer.

(i) *Basic sampling plan.* A production unit in the basic sampling plan shall consist of not more than 500 mattresses of a mattress type or the quantity produced in 3 consecutive calendar months, whichever is smaller. This unit size may be increased to the quantity produced in 3 consecutive calendar months or less: *Provided,* That it is either documented that each of the materials contributing to the cigarette ignition characteristics of all the mattresses in the unit came from a single manufacturing lot of such material or 50 consecutive production units, at least 20,000 mattresses, have all been accepted in production testing as set forth in § 1632.4(b)(2)(i)(B).

(A) *Prototype qualification.* (1) For prototype qualification, the term "manufacturer" shall mean (a) with respect to a company having one manufacturing facility, that company, (b) with respect to a company having two or more manufacturing facilities, either that company or one or more of its manufacturing facilities as it elects, or (c) with respect to a company that is part of a group of companies that have elected to share in a prototype design, either that group of companies or a portion of that group or (a) or (b) above, as that company elects.

(2) Each "manufacturer" shall select enough of each mattress prototype from preproduction or current production to provide six surfaces for test (three mattresses if both sides can be tested or six mattresses if only one side can be tested). Test each of the six surfaces according to § 1632.4(d) *Testing.* If all the cigarette test locations on all six surfaces satisfy the test criterion of § 1632.3(b), accept the mattress prototype. If one or more of the cigarette test locations on the six surfaces fail the test criterion of § 1632.3(b), reject the mattress prototype.

(3) If it has been elected to include more than one company and/or more than one manufacturing facility in the term "manufacturer" for purposes of prototype qualification, each such company and each such manufacturing facility shall select enough additional prototype mattresses from its own preproduction or current production to provide two surfaces for test. Test each of the two surfaces according to § 1632.4(d) *Testing.* If all the cigarette test locations on both surfaces satisfy the test criterion of § 1632.3(b), accept the mattress prototype for that company or manufactur-

ing facility. If one or more of the cigarette test locations on the two surfaces fail the test criterion of § 1632.3(b), reject the mattress prototype for that company or manufacturing facility.

(4) Mattress prototype qualification may be repeated after the manufacturer has taken action to improve the resistance of the mattress prototype to ignition by cigarettes through mattress design, production, or materials selection. When mattress prototype qualification is repeated as a result of prototype rejection by the "manufacturer", such qualification shall be conducted as if it were an original qualification. When the mattress prototype qualification is repeated as a result of prototype rejection under the provisions of the preceding paragraph or as a result of production unit rejection, such qualification shall be performed as if the producer of the failing mattress were a company having one manufacturing facility.

(5) Each mattress prototype must be accepted in prototype qualification prior to shipping any mattresses to customers and prior to producing significant quantities of mattresses. If the "manufacturer" is one manufacturing facility, the first production unit manufactured immediately after successful prototype qualification or the production unit from which the mattresses were selected for the successful prototype qualification not to exceed 500 mattresses, may be accepted and shipped to customers without further testing if all mattresses in the production unit are the same as the prototype except for size.

(B) *Production testing.* For production testing, the term "manufacturer" shall mean each manufacturing facility. Random selection for production testing shall be accomplished by use of random number tables or equivalent means as determined by the Consumer Product Safety Commission. If it is desired to use only mattresses of a specified size (e.g., "twin") for testing, the drawing may be repeated until sufficient mattresses of that size have been selected. A production unit, except for the first production unit following successful prototype qualification as specified in § 1632.4(b)(2)(i)(A), is either accepted or rejected according to the following plan:

(1) *Normal sampling.* From each unit, randomly select enough mattresses to provide two surfaces for test (one mattress if both sides can be tested or two mattresses if only one side can be tested). Test each of the two surfaces according to § 1632.4(d) *Testing.* If all the cigarette test locations on both surfaces meet the test criterion of § 1632.3(b), accept the unit. If two or more individual cigarette test locations fail the test criterion of § 1632.3(b), reject the unit. If only one individual cigarette test location fails the test criterion of § 1632.3(b), select enough additional mattresses to provide four additional surfaces for test. Test each of the four

additional surfaces according to § 1632.4(d) *Testing.* If all the cigarette test locations on the four additional surfaces meet the test criterion of § 1632.3(b), accept the unit. If one or more of the individual cigarette test locations on the four additional surfaces fail the test criterion of § 1632.3(b), reject the unit. Unit rejection shall include all mattresses in the particular unit under test. Unit rejection also results in the loss of prototype qualification for all prototypes included in the unit under test. The loss of prototype qualification applies only to the company or manufacturing facility that produced the rejected unit.

(2) *Reduced sampling.* (i) The level of sampling required for mattress production acceptance may be reduced provided the preceding 15 consecutive units of mattresses, at least 500 mattresses, have all been accepted using the normal sampling plan. In this case, the production quantity for reduced sampling may be increased to up to two units, still not to exceed the production of 3 consecutive calendar months.

(ii) From this production quantity, randomly select enough mattresses to provide two surfaces for test. Test each of the two surfaces according to § 1632.4(d) *Testing.* If all the cigarette test locations on both surfaces meet the test criterion of § 1632.3(b), accept this production quantity. If two or more individual cigarette test locations fail the test criterion of § 1632.3(b), reject this production quantity. If only one individual cigarette test location fails the test criterion of § 1632.3(b), accept this production quantity.

(iii) Rejection shall include all mattresses in the production quantity under test. Rejection also results in the loss of prototype qualification for all prototypes included in the production quantity under test. The loss of prototype qualification applies only to the company or manufacturing facility that produced the rejected unit.

(ii) *Batch sampling plan.* (A) *General (1)* For the batch sampling plan, the term "manufacturer" shall mean each manufacturing facility.

(2) A production unit in the batch sampling plan shall consist of not more than 250 mattresses or the quantity produced in one period of 30 consecutive calendar days, whichever is smaller.

(B) *Batch unit qualification and acceptance (1)* Select enough mattresses from the initial production of the unit to provide four surfaces for test (two mattresses if both sides can be tested or four mattresses if only one side can be tested). Test each of the four surfaces according to § 1632.4(d) *Testing.* If all the cigarette test locations on the four surfaces meet the test criterion of § 1632.3(b), accept the unit. If one or more of the four surfaces fail the test criterion of § 1632.3(b), reject the unit.

(2) After rejection, unit qualification and acceptance under this batch sampling plan may be repeated after the resistance of the mattress to ignition by cigarettes is improved by the manufacturer taking corrective action in mattress design, production, or materials selection.

(3) Acceptance of any production unit under this batch sampling plan shall not have any effect on prototype qualification or unit acceptance of any other production unit.

(3) *Disposition of rejected units.* Rejected units shall not be retested, offered for sale, sold, or promoted for use as a mattress as defined in § 1632.1(a) except after reworking to improve the resistance to ignition by cigarettes and subsequent retesting in accordance with the procedures set forth in § 1632.4(b)(2)(i) *Basic Sampling Plan.*

(4) *Records.* Records of all unit sizes, test results, and the disposition of rejected units shall be maintained by the manufacturer, in accordance with rules and regulations established by the Consumer Product Safety Commission.

(5) *Preparation of mattress samples.* The mattress surface shall be divided laterally into two sections (see fig. 1), one section for the bare mattress tests and the other for the two-sheet tests.

(6) *Sheet selection.* The sheets shall be white, 100 percent combed cotton percale, not treated with a chemical finish which imparts a characteristic such as permanent press or flame resistance, with 170–200 threads per square inch and fabric weight of 115 ± 14 gm/m² (3.4 ± 0.4 oz/yd²), or of another type approved by the Consumer Product Safety Commission. Size of sheet shall be appropriate for the mattress being tested.

(7) *Sheet preparation.* The sheets shall be laundered once before use in an automatic home washer using the hot water setting and longest normal cycle with the manufacturer's recommended quantity of a commercial detergent, and dried in an automatic home tumble dryer. The sheet shall be cut across the width into two equal parts after washing.

(8) *Cigarettes.* Unopened packages of cigarettes shall be selected for each series of tests.

(9) *Compliance marketing sampling plans.* Sampling plans for use in market testing of items covered by this standard may be issued by the Consumer Product Safety Commission. Such plans shall define noncompliance of a production unit to exist only when it is shown, with a high level of statistical confidence, that those production units represented by tested items which fail such plans will, in fact, fail this standard. Production units found to be noncomplying under these provisions shall be deemed not to conform to this standard. The Consumer Product Safety Commission will publish such plans in the FEDERAL REGISTER for public comment prior to

their enactment.

(10) *Postponement of production testing.* Temporary suspension of production testing may be granted on a case-by-case basis by the Consumer Product Safety Commission in those instances where an individual manufacturer proves, under rules prescribed by CPSC, that he cannot acquire access to either in-house or independent testing facilities for production testing. In the event of such a suspension, the manufacturer would still be obligated to produce a mattress which meets all other requirements of the standard.

(c) *Conditioning—(1) Prototype and batch.* The mattresses, washed sheets, and cigarettes shall be conditioned in air at a temperature greater than 18° C (65° F) and a relative humidity less than 55 percent for at least 48 hours prior to test. The mattresses, washed sheets, and cigarettes shall be removed from any packaging and supported in a suitable manner to permit free movement of air around them during conditioning. The mattress meets this conditioning requirement if the mattress and/or all its component materials, except the metallic core, have been exposed only to the above temperature and humidity conditions for at least 48 hours prior to testing the mattress.

(2) *Production.* Mattresses to be tested according to § 1632.4(b)(2)(i)(B) *Production testing* shall be exempt from conditioning as specified in § 1632.4(c)(1). However, the mattresses shall not be exposed to any environmental conditions which promote resistance to cigarette ignition. Sheets and cigarettes in their normally used condition (dry) shall be used.

(d) *Testing—(1) General.* Mattress specimens selected for testing in prototype and batch sampling shall be tested in a testroom with atmospheric conditions of a temperature greater than 18° C (65° F) and a relative humidity less than 55 percent. If the test is not performed in the conditioning room, the mattress shall be tested within 1 hour after removal from the conditioning room.

(i) Light and place one cigarette at a time on the mattress surface. (If previous experience with the same type of mattress has indicated that ignition is not likely, the number of cigarettes which may be lighted and placed on the mattress at one time is left to the test operator's judgment. The number of cigarettes must be carefully considered because a smoldering or burning mattress is extremely hazardous and difficult to extinguish.) If more than one cigarette is burning at one time, the cigarettes must be positioned no less than 6 inches apart on the mattress surface. Each cigarette used as an ignition source shall be well lighted but not burned more than 4 mm (0.16 in) when placed on the mattress. (Fire extinguishing equipment must be readily available at all times.)

(ii) If a cigarette extinguishes before

burning its full length, the test must be repeated with a freshly lit cigarette on a different portion of the same type of location on the mattress surface until either (a) the number of cigarettes specified in § 1632.4(d)(1)(iii) have burned their full lengths, (b) the number of cigarettes specified has extinguished before burning their full lengths, or (c) the number of cigarettes specified have resulted in failures according to § 1632.3(b) *Test criterion.*

(iii) At least 18 cigarettes shall be burned on each mattress test surface, 9 in the bare mattress tests and 9 in the 2-sheet tests. If three or more mattress surface locations (smooth surface, tape edge, quilted, or tufted areas) exists in the particular mattress surface under test, three cigarettes shall be burned on each different surface location. If only two mattress surface locations exist in the particular mattress surface under test (tape edge and smooth surface), four cigarettes shall be burned on the smooth surface and five cigarettes shall be burned on the tape edge.

(2) *Bare mattress tests—*(i) *Smooth surfaces.* Each burning cigarette shall be placed directly on a smooth surface location on the test surface on the half reserved for bare mattress tests. The cigarettes should burn their full lengths on a smooth surface without burning across a tuft, or stitching of a quilted area. However, if this is not possible because of mattress design, then the cigarettes shall be positioned on the mattress in a manner which will allow as much of the butt ends as possible to burn on smooth surfaces. Report results for each cigarette as pass or fail as defined in the test criterion.

CAUTION: Even under the most carefully observed conditions, smoldering combustion can progress to the point where it cannot be readily extinguished. It is imperative that a test be discontinued as soon as ignition has definitely occurred. Immediately wet the exposed area with a water spray (from water bottle), cut around the burning material with a knife or scissors and pull the material out of the mattress with tongs. Make sure that all charred or burned material is removed. Ventilate the room.

(ii) *Tape edge.* Each burning cigarette shall be placed in the depression between the mattress top surface and the tape edge, parallel to the tape edge on the half of the test surface reserved for bare mattress tests. If there is no depression at the edge, support the cigarettes in place along the edge and parallel to the edge with straight pins. Three straight pins may be inserted through the edge at a 45° angle such that one pin supports the cigarette at the burning end, one at the center, and one at the butt. The heads of the pins must be below the upper surface of the cigarette (see fig. 2). Report results for each cigarette as pass or fail as defined in the test criterion.

MATTRESS PREPARATION

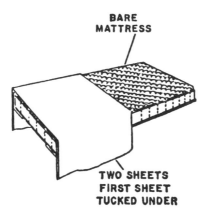

BARE MATTRESS

TWO SHEETS
FIRST SHEET
TUCKED UNDER

FIGURE 1

CIGARETTE LOCATION

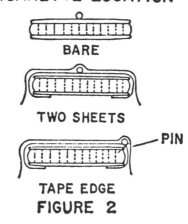

BARE

TWO SHEETS

— PIN

TAPE EDGE
FIGURE 2

(iii) *Quilted location.* If quilting exists on the test surface, each burning cigarette shall be placed on quilted locations of the test surface. The cigarettes shall be positioned directly over the thread in the depression created by the quilting process on the half of the test surface reserved for bare mattress tests. If the quilt design is such that the cigarettes cannot burn their full lengths over the thread, then the cigarettes shall be positioned in a manner which will allow as much of the butt ends as possible to burn on the thread. Report results for each cigarette as pass or fail as defined in the test criterion.

(iv) *Tufted location.* If tufting exists on the test surface, each burning cigarette shall be placed on tufted locations of the test surface. The cigarettes shall be positioned so that they burn down into the depression caused by the tufts and so that the butt ends of the cigarettes burn out over the buttons or laces used in the tufts on the half of the test surface reserved for bare mattress tests. Report results for each cigarette as pass or fail as defined in the test criterion.

(3) *Two-sheet tests.* Spread a section of sheet smoothly over the mattress surface and tuck under the mattress

on the second half of the test surface, which has been reserved for the two-sheet test. Care must be taken that hems or any other portion of the sheet which is more than one fabric thickness, is neither directly under nor directly over the test cigarette in the two-sheet test.

(i) *Smooth surfaces.* Each burning cigarette shall be placed directly on the sheet covered mattress in a smooth surface location as defined in the bare mattress test. Immediately cover the first sheet and the burning cigarettes loosely with a second, or top sheet (see fig. 2). Do not raise or lift the top sheet during testing unless obvious ignition has occurred or until the cigarette has burned out. (The extinguishment of the cigarette may be determined by holding the hand near the surface of the top sheet over the test location. If neither heat is felt nor smoke observed, the cigarette has burned out.) If ignition occurs, immediately remove the sheets and cigarette and follow the cautionary procedures outlined in the bare mattress test. Report results for each cigarette as pass or fail as defined in the test criterion.

(ii) *Tape edge.* (A) Each burning cigarette shall be placed in the depression between the top surface and the tape edge on top of the sheet, and immediately covered with a second sheet. It is important that the air space be eliminated, as much as possible, between the mattress and the bottom sheet at the test location before testing. Depress the bottom sheet into the depression using a thin rod or other suitable instrument.

(B) In most cases, the cigarettes will remain in place throughout the test; however, if the cigarettes show a marked tendency to roll off the tape edge location, they may be supported with straight pins. Three straight pins may be inserted through the bottom sheet and tape at a 45° angle such that one pin supports the cigarette at the burning end, one at the center, and one at the butt. The heads of the pins must be below the upper surface of the cigarette (see fig. 2). Report results for each cigarette as pass or fail as defined in the test criterion.

(iii) *Quilted locations.* If quilting exists on the test surface, each burning cigarette shall be placed in a depression caused by quilting, directly over the thread and on the bottom sheet, and immediately covered with the top sheet. It is important that the air space be eliminated, as much as possible, between the mattress and the bottom sheet at the test location before testing. Depress the bottom sheet into the depression using a thin rod or other suitable instrument. If the quilt design is such that the cigarettes cannot burn their full lengths over the thread, then the cigarettes shall be positioned in a manner which will allow as much of the butt ends as possible to burn on the thread. Report results for each cigarette as pass or fail as defined in the test criterion.

(iv) *Tufted locations.* If tufting exists on the test surface, each burning cigarette shall be placed in the depression caused by tufting, directly over the tuft and on the bottom sheet, and immediately covered with the top sheet. It is important that the air space be eliminated, as much as possible, between the mattress and the bottom sheet at the test location before testing. Depress the bottom sheet into the depression using a thin rod or other suitable instrument. The cigarettes shall be positioned so that they burn down into the depression caused by the tuft and so that the butt ends of the cigarettes burn out over the buttons or laces used in the tufts. Report results for each cigarette as pass or fail as defined in the test criterion.

§ 1632.5 Mattress pads.

(a) *Testing.* Mattress pads shall be tested in the same manner as mattresses according to § 1632.4 *Test procedure* except for laundering.

(b) *Laundering.* (1) Mattress pads which have had a chemical fire retardant treatment or contain any chemically fire retardant treated components, shall be tested in accordance with § 1632.4 *Test procedure* in the condition in which they are intended to be sold, and after they have been washed and dried 10 times according to the procedure prescribed in method 124–1969 of the American Association of Textile Chemists and Colorists washing procedure 6.2 (III), with a water temperature of 60°±2.8° C (140°±5° F), and drying procedure 6.3.2(B). Maximum load shall be 3.46 kg (8 lb) and may consist of any combination of test items and dummy pieces. Alternately, a different number of times under another washing and drying procedure may be specified and used, if that procedure has previously been found to be equivalent by the Consumer Product Safety Commission.

(2) Such laundering is not required of mattress pads which are not intended to be laundered, as determined by the Consumer Product Safety Commission.

(3) Mattress pads which are not susceptible to being laundered and are labeled "dryclean only" shall be drycleaned by a procedure which has previously been found acceptable by the Consumer Product Safety Commission.

(c) *Labeling.* (1) *Treatment label.* If a mattress pad has had a chemical fire retardant treatment or contains any fire retardant treated components, it shall be labeled with the letter "T" pursuant to rules and regulations established by the Consumer Product Safety Commission.

(2) *Care label.* All mattress pads which have had a chemical fire retardant treatment or contain any fire re-

tardant treated components shall be labeled with precautionary instructions to protect the pads from agents or treatments which are known to cause deterioration of their flame resistance. Such labels shall be permanent and otherwise in accordance with rules and regulations established by the Consumer Product Safety Commission.

(3) *Temporary requirement for noncomplying mattresses.* (i) Mattresses which do not comply with all the provisions of this standard and are manufactured during the 6 months following the effective date of this standard shall, prior to introduction into commerce, be prominently and conspicuously labeled with the following statement:

WARNING: This mattress does not meet the Consumer Product Safety Commission Flammability Standard for Mattresses (FF 4–72, as amended). It may be subject to ignition and hazardous smoldering from cigarettes.

(ii) Such label must be affixed to the mattress in such a manner so as to remain on or affixed thereto until its sale or delivery to the ultimate consumer. The label must be displayed on the mattress at the place of retail sale and the statement on the label must be prominently and conspicuously displayed on the invoice or other sales papers that accompany the mattress through commerce from the manufacturer to the final point of sale to a consumer.

(iii) This label must be at least 250 cm² (approximately 40 in²) with no linear dimension less than 12.5 cm (approximately 5 in). The wording of such label shall appear on a contrasting background with the letters in the heading WARNING no less than 1.2 cm (approximately ½ in) in height.

§ 1632.6 Glossary of terms.

(a) *Basket pad.* Cushion for use in an infant basket.

(b) *Box spring.* A bedspring that consists of springs attached to a foundation and enclosed in a cloth covered, upholstered frame.

(c) *Bunk beds.* A tier of beds, usually two or three, in a high frame complete with mattresses (see fig. 3).

(d) *Car bed.* Portable bed used to carry a baby in an automobile.

(e) *Carriage pad.* Cushion to go into a baby carriage.

(f) *Chaise lounge.* An upholstered couch chair or a couch with a chair back. It has a permanent back rest, no arms, and sleeps one (see fig. 3).

(g) *Convertible sofa.* An upholstered sofa that converts into an adult sized bed. Mattress unfolds out and up from under the seat cushioning (see fig. 3).

(h) *Corner groups.* Two twin size bedding sets on frames, usually slipcovered, and abutted to a corner table. They also usually have loose bolsters slipcovered (see fig. 3).

(i) *Crib bumper.* Padded cushion which goes around three or four sides inside a crib to protect the baby. Can

also be used in a playpen.

(j) *Daybed.* Daybed has foundation, usually supported by coil or flat springs, mounted between arms on which mattress is placed. It has permanent arms, no backrest, and sleeps one (see fig. 3).

(k) *Dressing table pad.* Pad to cushion a baby on top of a dressing table.

(l) *Drop-arm loveseat.* When side arms are in vertical position, this piece is a loveseat. The adjustable arms can be lowered to one of four positions for a chaise lounge effect or a single sleeper. The vertical back support always remains upright and stationary (see fig. 3).

(m) *High riser.* This is a frame of sofa seating height with two equal size mattresses without a backrest. The frame slides out with the lower bed and rises to form a double or two single beds (see fig. 3).

(n) *Infant carrier and lounge pad.* Pad to cushion a baby in an infant carrier.

(o) *Mattress foundation.* Consists of any surface upon which a mattress is placed to lend it support for use in sleeping upon.

(p) *Mattress pad.* A thin, flat, mat or cushion for use on top of a mattress.

(q) *Pillow.* Cloth bag filled with resilient material such as feathers, down, sponge rubber, urethane, or fiber used as the support for the head of a person.

(r) *Playpen pad.* Cushion used on the bottom of a playpen.

(s) *Portable crib.* Smaller size than a conventional crib. Can usually be converted into a playpen.

(t) *Press-back lounges.* Longer and wider than conventional sofa beds. When the lounge seat is pressed lightly, it levels off to form, with the seat, a flat sleeping surface. The seat slopes, in the sitting position, for added comfort (see fig. 3).

(u) *Push-back sofa.* When you push on the back of the sofa, it becomes a bed. Lift the back and it is a sofa again. Styled in tight or loose cushions (see fig. 3).

(v) *Roll-a-way bed.* Portable bed which has frame which folds in half with the mattress for compact storage.

(w) *Sleep lounge.* Upholstered seating section is mounted on a sturdy frame. May have bolster pillows along the wall as backrests or may have attached headrests (see fig. 3).

(x) *Stroller pad.* Cushion used in a baby stroller.

(y) *Sofa bed.* These are pieces in which the back of the sofa swings down flat with the seat to form the sleeping surface. All upholstered. Some sofa beds have bedding boxes for storage of bedding. There are two types: the one-piece, where the back and seat are upholstered as a unit, supplying an unbroken sleeping surface; and the two-piece, where back and seat are upholstered separately (see fig. 3).

(z) *Sofa lounge—(includes glideouts).* Upholstered seating section is mounted on springs and in a special frame that permits it to be pulled out for sleeping. Has upholstered backrest bedding box that is hinged. Glideouts are single sleepers with sloping seats and backrests. Seat pulls out from beneath back and evens up to supply level sleeping surface (see fig. 3).

(aa) *Studio couch.* Consists of upholstered seating section on upholstered foundation. Many types convert to twin beds (see fig. 3).

(bb) *Studio divan.* Twin size upholstered seating section with foundation is mounted on metal bed frame. Has no arms or backrest, and sleeps one (see fig. 3).

(cc) *Trundle bed.* A low bed which is rolled under a larger bed. In some lines, the lower bed springs up to form a double or two single beds as in a high riser (see fig. 3).

(dd) *Twin studio divan.* Frames which glide out (but not up) and use seat cushions, in addition to upholstered foundation to sleep two. Has neither arms nor back rest (see fig. 3).

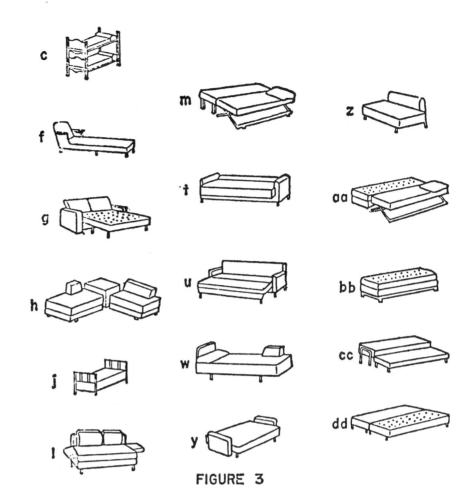

FIGURE 3

D CONSUMER PRODUCT SAFETY ACT REGULATIONS*

PART 1105—SUBMISSION OF EXISTING STANDARDS; OFFERS TO DEVELOP STANDARDS; AND THE DEVELOPMENT OF STANDARDS

AUTHORITY: Secs. 7 and 9, Pub. L. 92—573, as amended Pub. L. 94—284, 86 Stat. 1212—15, as amended 90 Stat. 505—506; 15 U.S.C. 2056, 2058.

SOURCE: 39 FR 16213, May 7, 1974, unless otherwise noted.

§ 1105.1 General policy considerations.

(a) The general policy under which the procedures in this Part 1105 are issued is that the interest and participation of the public is vital for carrying out the functions of the Consumer Product Safety Commission. Commission activities and deliberations are open to the public and afford any interested person the opportunity to participate and be heard. Accordingly, standards development activities by offerors will be open to the public and will afford the opportunity for any interested person to participate in the development of standards.

(b) The major objective of the Consumer Product Safety Act ("act") is to reduce unreasonable risks of injury associated with the use of consumer products. This objective may be achieved through the development and promulgation of mandatory "consumer product safety standards" where they are considered necessary to eliminate or reduce the risk of injury. A consumer product safety standard is a standard which will consist of (1) requirements as to performance, composition, contents, design, construction, finish, or packaging, or (2) requirements that a consumer product be marked with or accompanied by clear and adequate warnings or instructions, or requirements respecting the form of warnings or instructions, or (3) any combination of (1) and (2). Requirements other than those relating to labeling, warnings, or instructions, shall whenever feasible be expressed in terms of performance requirements.

(c) Under the act, consumer product safety standards may originate in three ways. First, the Commission, after publishing a "notice of proceeding" in the FEDERAL REGISTER, is authorized to publish as a proposed standard an existing standard which has been previously issued or adopted by a qualified public or private agency or organization. Second, the Commission is authorized to accept offers from one or more persons or organizations to develop a standard. Third, the Commission may under certain circumstances independently develop a standard.

(d) Since safety standards are intended to eliminate or reduce unreasonable risks of injury associated with consumer products, the Commission, in issuing this Part 1105, seeks the involvement of all interested persons, the general public, and especially ultimate consumers. Ultimate consumers and their representatives, as well as all other interested persons, are invited and encouraged to become involved by submitting offers to develop standards and by participating in the development of standards by other offerors.

(e) Persons who are not members of an established organization may form a group for the express purpose of submitting offers and developing standards; such groups are referred to in these rules as "ad hoc associations."

(f) Public involvement will be encouraged through the use of extensive public notice. In addition to providing notice in the FEDERAL REGISTER, the Commission will issue a press release at the initiation of a proceeding. This release will invite any person to either submit an existing standard or offer to develop a standard. A press release will also be issued at the time an offer is accepted. This second press release will invite all interested persons to participate in the development of a standard and will describe the method by which interested persons, including ultimate consumers, may participate.

(g) The Commission will maintain a list of all persons and organizations that have expressed an interest in either being offerors or in participating in the development of standards. Copies of the FEDERAL REGISTER notice of proceeding, press release, and/or other relevant documents will be transmitted by the Commission to appropriate persons and organizations on the list that have expressed an interest in being offerors. Copies of the FEDERAL REGISTER notice of proceeding and the notice of acceptance of any offers will be transmitted by the Commission to appropriate persons and organizations on the list that have expressed an interest in participating in the development of standards.

(h) The act enables the Commission to contribute to the offeror's cost in developing a standard in any case in which the Commission determines that a contribution is likely to result in a more satisfactory standard. The Commission views this provision of the act as a means by which a variety of organizations will be able to develop standards. The Commission also views this provision as a means by which the Commission can assist a cross section of interested persons, including consumers, to participate in the development of standards.

(i) The act provides that the invitation for the submission of offers to develop a standard shall state the period of time during which the standard is to be developed. Congress anticipated that this period would normally end 150 days after the publication of the invitation. The act also provides that the Commission may extend or shorten the period for development if it finds for good cause that a different period of time is appropriate either at the time of the invitation or at a later time. The Commission expects to receive standards that will, if adopted, appropriately reduce the unreasonable risks of injury to the public. The Commission will adopt a reasonable approach to determining the amount of time necessary to develop standards. The Commission believes, however, that as a general rule the public interest is best served by the development of standards in the shortest possible time commensurate with the objectives of the act and in conformance with the requirements contained in this Part 1105.

[39 FR 16213, May 7, 1974, as amended at 42 FR 58400, Nov. 9, 1977]

§ 1105.2 Summary of time sequence for the development of standards.

The notice of proceeding inviting the submission of existing standards and the submission of offers to develop standards will specify a period of time during which the standard is to be developed and submitted to the Commission. The act specifies that this period will end 150 days after the publication of the notice in the FEDERAL REGISTER, unless the Commission for good cause finds, and includes such finding in the notice, that a different period is appropriate. Under the act, persons must submit existing standards or offers to develop standards to the Commission within 30 days after the date of publication of the notice of

---

*Reproduced with permission from the Code of Federal Regulations, Title 16, Part 1000 to End, Revised as of January 1, 1976.

proceeding in the FEDERAL REGISTER. The Commission will evaluate the submissions and publish a summary of the terms of any accepted offer or offers as soon as possible, usually within 60 days after the date of publication of the notice of proceeding. In submitting an offer to develop a standard, each offeror is required to include a realistic estimate of the time required to develop the standard, including a detailed schedule for each phase of the development period. In accepting an offer and publishing a notice of the summary of the terms of each accepted offer, the Commission will either reaffirm the original period of time for the development of the standard, or, for good cause stated, establish and publicize a new period of time for the development of the standard. The standard, with all required accompanying information, must then be submitted to the Commission within the specified time, unless the Commission grants an extension and publishes a notice in the FEDERAL REGISTER stating its reasons for the extension.

[39 FR 16213, May 7, 1974, as amended at 42 FR 58400, Nov. 9, 1977]

§ 1105.3 Commencement of proceedings.

(a) A proceeding for the development of a consumer product safety standard shall be commenced by the publication of a "notice of proceeding" in the FEDERAL REGISTER which shall:

(1) Identify the product and clearly describe the nature of the risks of injury associated with the product;

(2) State the Commission's determination that a consumer product safety standard is necessary to eliminate or reduce the specified unreasonable risks of injury associated with the product;

(3) Include information with respect to any existing domestic, foreign, or international standard known to the Commission which may be relevant to the proceeding, including information as to any deficiencies that the Commission recognizes in each identified standard that may make it not totally acceptable as a proposed rule;

(4) Provide information concerning the availability of Commission material relating to: (i) The specific nature of the risks of injury associated with the product, (ii) the basis for the Commission's determination concerning the need for a mandatory standard, and (iii) additional information relating to the development of a mandatory standard which may be helpful to potential offerors;

(5) Include an invitation for any standards-writing organization, trade association, consumer organization, professional or technical society, testing laboratory, university or college department, wholesale or retail organization, Federal, State, or local government agency, engineering or research and development establishment, ad hoc association, or any company or person, within 30 days after the date of FEDERAL REGISTER publication of the notice:

(i) To submit to the Commission an existing standard as the proposed consumer product safety standard; or

(ii) To offer to develop a proposed consumer product safety standard;

(6) Include, to the extent known at the time the notice of proceeding is published, any requirement for additional information which is to be submitted to the Commission with either an existing standard or a standard to be developed by an offeror; and

(7) Specify the period of time during which the standard is to be developed and submitted to the Commission.

(b) The Commission will, for the purpose of providing greater public awareness of its actions, issue a press release concerning the initiation of the proceeding. The press release will summarize the information contained in the FEDERAL REGISTER notice, including the invitation to any interested organization or person to submit an existing standard or to offer to develop a proposed consumer product safety standard.

(c) The Commission will transmit a copy of the FEDERAL REGISTER notice, press release, and/or other relevant documents to appropriate persons and organizations, on a list maintained by the Commission, that have expressed an interest in being offerors for one or more standards.

§ 1105.4 Submission of existing standards.

(a) Any standards-writing organization, trade association, consumer organization, professional or technical society, testing laboratory, university or college department, wholesale or retail organization, Federal, State, or local government agency, engineering or research and development establishment, ad hoc association, or any company or person may submit a standard previously issued or adopted by any private or public organization or agency, domestic or foreign, or any international standards organization, that contains safety-related requirements which the person believes would be adequate to prevent or reduce the unreasonable risks of injury associated with the product identified by the Commission.

(b) Any submission of an existing standard should:

(1) To the extent possible, meet the requirements for standards developed by offerors contained in § 1105.8 as specified in each notice of proceeding;

(2) Identify the specific portions which are appropriate for inclusion in the proposed rule; and

(3) Be accompanied, to the extent that such information is available, by a description of the procedures used to develop the standard and a listing of the persons and organizations that participated in the development and approval of the standard.

(c) If the Commission determines that (1) there exists a standard which has been issued or adopted by any Federal agency or by any other qualified agency, organization, or institution, and (2) such standard if promulgated under the act would eliminate or reduce the unreasonable risks of injury associated with the product, then the Commission may, in lieu of accepting an offer to develop a standard under § 1105.6, publish the existing standard as a proposed consumer product safety standard.

§ 1105.5 Submission of offers.

(a) Any standards-writing organization, trade association, consumer organization, technical or professional society, testing laboratory, university or college department, wholesale or retail organization, Federal, State, or local government agency, engineering or research and development establishment, ad hoc association, or any company or person may submit an offer to develop a proposed consumer product safety standard. Each offer shall include a detailed description of the procedure the offeror will utilize in developing the standard. Each offer shall also include:

(1) A description of the plan the offeror will use to give adequate and reasonable notice to interested persons (including individual consumers, manufacturers, distributors, retailers, importers, trade associations, professional and technical societies, testing laboratories, Federal and State agencies, educational institutions, and consumer organizations) of their right and opportunity to participate in the development of the standard;

(2) A description of the method whereby interested persons who have responded to the notice may participate, either in person or through correspondence, in the development of the standard; and

(3) A realistic estimate of the time required to develop the standard, including a detailed schedule for each phase of the standard development period.

(b) Each offeror shall submit with the offer the following information to supplement the description of the standard development procedure:

(1) A statement listing the number and experience of the personnel, including voluntary participants, the offeror intends to utilize in developing the standard. This list should distinguish between (i) persons directly employed by the offeror, (ii) persons who have made a commitment to participate, (iii) organizaions that have made commitments to provide a specific number of personnel and (iv) other persons to be utilized, although unidentified and uncommitted at the time of the submission. The educational and experience qualifications of these personnel relevant to the development of the standard should also be included in the statement. This list should include only those persons who will be directly involved in person in the development of the standard; and

(2) A statement describing the type of facilities or equipment which the offeror plans to utilize in developing

the standard and how the offeror plans to gain access to the facilities or equipment.

(c) Persons who are not members of an established organization may form a group for the express purpose of submitting offers and developing standards. These groups are referred to as "ad hoc associations." An offer by an ad hoc association may be submitted by an individual member if the offer states that it is submitted on behalf of the members of the association. The individual member submitting the offer shall submit to the Commission a notarized copy of a power of attorney from each member of the association authorizing the individual member to submit an offer on behalf of each other member.

[39 FR 16213, May 7, 1974; 39 FR 18093, May 23, 1974]

§ 1105.6 Acceptance of offers.

(a)(1) If the Commission (i) does not decide to publish an existing standard as a proposed consumer product safety standard or (ii) decides to publish an existing standard as a proposed consumer product safety standard which does not address all of the specified unreasonable risks of injury associated with the product, the Commission will as soon as possible, usually within 60 days of the date of publication of the notice of proceeding in the FEDERAL REGISTER, accept one or more offers to develop a proposed consumer product safety standard.

(2) Acceptance of an offer will be based on a determination by the Commission that an offeror is technically competent, is likely to develop an appropriate standard within the period specified in the notice of proceeding or within the period determined by the Commission to be necessary and appropriate for the development of the standard, and will comply with all of the requirements of the Commission for the development of the standard.

(3) An offeror will be considered to have technical competence if the offer submitted indicates to the satisfaction of the Commission (i) that the offeror has demonstrated a thorough understanding of the problem, (ii) that the offeror has provided a rational approach to the solution of that problem, and (iii) that persons with appropriate technical expertise or experience will be utilized in the development of the standard either as employees, consultants, or volunteers.

(b) Prior to accepting an offer to develop a standard, the Commission may require minor modifications of the offer as a condition of acceptance.

(c) The Commission shall publish in the FEDERAL REGISTER the name, address, and organizational affiliation of each person whose offer it accepts and a summary of the terms of each accepted offer including the date established for the submission of the standard.

(d) The Commission, at or near the

time of the FEDERAL REGISTER acceptance notice, will issue a press release which:

(1) Identifies each person (name, address, and organizational affiliation) whose offer has been accepted;

(2) Summarizes the terms of each accepted offer including the date established for the submission of the standard; and

(3) Invites all interested persons to participate in the development of the standard and informs them of how they may participate.

(e) The Commission will transmit to appropriate persons and organizations, on a list maintained by the Commission, that have expressed an interest in participating in the development of one or more standards a copy of the FEDERAL REGISTER notice of proceeding as well as the notice of the acceptance of any offers.

(f) All persons submitting offers to develop standards whose offers have not been accepted will be notified in writing by the Commission. If requested by an offeror, the reasons for the nonacceptance of the offer will be supplied.

(g) If the Commission does not accept an offer to develop a proposed consumer product safety standard, the Commission may independently develop a proposed consumer product safety standard. Notice of this decision will be published in the FEDERAL REGISTER.

(h) In any case in which the sole offeror whose offer is accepted is a manufacturer, distributor, or retailer of the consumer product proposed to be regulated by the consumer product safety standard, the Commission may independently proceed to develop a proposed standard during the development period.

§ 1105.7 Development of recommended consumer product safety standards.

(a) The offeror shall comply with all Commission requirements for the development of standards and with all terms of the acceptance and shall cooperate with Commission liaison personnel assigned to monitor the development of the standard.

(b) In developing a standard, the offeror shall use the method agreed upon for interested persons to participate in the development of the standard and shall fully consider all of the suggestions and contributions of the respective participants. The offeror, after considering all suggestions and contributions, shall draft a standard. The draft standard shall be sent to all participants for their review and concurrence or nonconcurrence. Unanimity among all participants shall not be a prerequisite to the submission by the offeror to the Commission of a standard which, in the offeror's judgment, optimally meets the terms of the offer accepted by the Commission.

(c) The offeror shall maintain complete written records of the development of the standard. These records

shall include:

(1) The names, addresses, and titles if any, of all persons contacting the offeror for the purpose of participating in the development of the standard;

(2) All written comments and any other information submitted by any person in connection with the development of the standard, including the dissenting views of participants and comments and information with respect to the need for the standard;

(3) A discussion describing the base for resolution by the offeror of all of the substantive issues raised during the development of the standard;

(4) A statement of the economic and environmental factors considered during the development of the standard; and

(5) Records of all other matters relevant to the development and evaluation of the standard. These records shall be submitted to the Commission at the termination of the development period. The Commission will make these records available for public inspection and will supply copies upon request, subject to the provisions of the Freedom of Information Act (5 U.S.C. 552), section 6 of the Consumer Product Safety Act (15 U.S.C. 2055), and regulations relating to the availability of Commission records.

(d) The offeror shall provide monthly progress reports containing a summary of progress made, the work under way, the significant problems encountered and the work remaining to be accomplished. These reports shall be transmitted to the Technical Analysis Division, Office of Standards Coordination and Appraisal, Consumer Product Safety Commission, Washington, D.C. 20207. The offeror shall cooperate fully with the Commission and permit the inspection of its facilities and development activities by duly authorized representatives of the Commission for the purpose of determining whether satisfactory progress is being made toward the completion of the standard. The offeror shall be considered to be making satisfactory progress if the Commission concludes that the standard may reasonably be expected to be completed in accordance with the provisions of the accepted offer by the end of the development period.

(e)(1) If it appears to the Commission that an offeror is not making satisfactory progress, the offeror will be given the opportunity (i) to demonstrate ability and willingness to complete the development of the standard by the end of the development period, or (ii) to justify the need for an extension of the development period.

(2) The Commission, after consideration and due notice, may (i) terminate the offeror's role in the development process and require the offeror to submit to the Commission all information, records, and documents which pertain to the development of the standard, or (ii) extend the development period and publish notice of

such extension in the FEDERAL REGISTER, with the justification for the extension. If the Commission terminates the offeror's role in the development process, the offeror shall remit all funds contributed by the Commission which have not been expended.

(f) If the Commission determines that no offeror whose offer was accepted is making satisfactory progress, the Commission may terminate the development proceeding, publish a notice of the decision to terminate in the FEDERAL REGISTER, and independently develop a proposed standard.

(g) The offeror shall submit with the standard, test instruments or devices constructed or acquired to perform compliance tests if the Commission determines that these instruments or devices are necessary for the evaluation of the standard. In such a case, the instrument or device shall be sold to the Commission at the offeror's cost or loaned to the Commission for the evaluation of the standard. Further, the offeror shall in any circumstance submit detailed descriptions or plans and specifications for the acquisition or construction of these instruments or devices.

§ 1105.8 Recommended consumer product safety standards developed by offerors.

(a) Recommended standards must be suitable for promulgation under the act. To be considered suitable, a standard shall be written in a manner appropriate for use as a Federal mandatory standard as specified in the format established by the Commission. The format for each standard will be made available by the Commission on or before the acceptance of an offer. Recommended standards shall be supported by test data or other documents or materials which the Commission requires. Recommended standards shall also, if the Commission considers it to be appropriate, contain suitable test methods and reasonable testing programs. Test methods for the measurement of compliance with proposed standards shall be reasonably capable of being performed by the Commission and by persons subject to the act or by private testing facilities. Testing programs shall, if the Commission considers it to be appropriate and so states in the FEDERAL REGISTER notice of the acceptance of the offer, include sampling plans.

(b) Recommended standards shall consist of:

(1) Requirements as to performance, composition, contents, design, construction, finish, or packaging; or

(2) Requirements that a consumer product be marked with or accompanied by clear and adequate warnings or instructions or requirements respecting the form of warnings or instructions; or

(3) Any combination of (1) and (2).

(c) A recommended standard shall be supported by:

(1) An analysis demonstrating that each of the requirements is reasonably

necessary to prevent or reduce the unreasonable risks of injury identified in the notice of proceeding; and

(2) An analysis explaining why the recommended standard is in the public interest.

(3) An analysis of the extent to which elderly and handicaped persons may be adversely affected by the recommended standard.

(d) Each requirement of a standard, other than requirements relating to labeling, warnings, or instructions, shall whenever feasible be expressed in terms of performance. Whenever the requirements are not expressed in terms of performance, an explanation shall be provided to support the use of the nonperformance requirements.

(e) The offeror shall, in submitting a recommended standard, include data and information to demonstrate that compliance with the standard would be technologically practicable. The offeror shall also submit, to the extent that it can reasonably be obtained by the offeror, data and information on the potential economic effect of the standard, including the potential effect on small business and international trade. The economic information should include data indicating (1) the types and classes as well as the approximate number of consumer products which would be subject to the standard; (2) the probable effect of the standard on the utility, cost, and availability of the products; (3) any potential adverse effects of the standard on competition; and (4) the standard's potential disruption or dislocation, if any, of manufacturing and other commercial practices. Further, the offeror shall include information, to the extent that it can reasonably be obtained by the offeror, concerning the potential environmental impact of the standard.

[39 FR 16213, May 7, 1974, as amended at 42 FR 58400, Nov. 9, 1977]

§ 1105.9 Contributions to the offeror's cost.

(a) The Commission may, in accepting an offer, agree to contribute to the offeror's cost in developing a proposed consumer product safety standard in any case in which the Commission determines:

(1) That a contribution is likely to result in a more satisfactory standard than would be developed without a contribution; and

(2) That the offeror is financially responsible.

(b) In order to be eligible to receive a financial contribution, the offeror, in addition to furnishing the information required under § 1105.5, must submit:

(1) A request for a specific contribution with an explanation as to why the contribution is likely to result in a more satisfactory standard than would be developed without a contribution;

(2) A statement asserting that the offeror will employ an adequate accounting system (one in accordance

with generally accepted accounting principles) to record standard development costs and expenditures; and

(3) A request for an advance payment of funds if necessary to enable the offeror to meet operating expenses during the development period.

(c) The Commission, in publishing the terms of the accepted offer, shall include a statement of the purpose and amount of the Commission's contribution.

(d) The offeror whose offer has been accepted shall, for a period of three years after final payment under the development agreement, maintain records which fully disclose the total cost and expenditures for the project and such other records which will facilitate an effective audit. The Commission and the Comptroller General of the United States, or any of their duly authorized representatives, shall have access, for the purpose of audit and examination, to any books, documents, papers, and records relevant to the development of the standard.

(e) The Commission, based upon a finding after an informal hearing that all or part of the Commission's contribution has been or is being misused, may seek reimbursement of that part of the contribution which has been or is being misused and shall have the right, after providing due notice, to terminate the development agreement and to discontinue payments towards the contribution. For the purpose of this Part 1105, "misuse of a contribution" means a use other than that agreed upon in writing by the parties.

(f) The items of cost toward which the Commission may contribute are those allowable direct and indirect costs allocable to the development project (as set forth in the applicable subparts of Part 1-15 of the Federal Procurement Regulations (41 CFR Part 1-15)). The Commission may contribute to the costs of assuring adequate consumer participation in the development of the standard. The Commission may make its contribution in advance and without regard to 31 U.S.C. 529.

(g) The items of cost toward which the Commission will not contribute include:

(1) Costs for the acquisition of any interest in land or buildings; however, the Commission may contribute toward the lease or rental of land or buildings;

(2) Costs for the payment of salaries in excess of the salaries paid by the offeror to individuals at the time immediately preceding the offer, except for longevity and other routine increases which may accrue during the development of the standard;

(3) Costs for the payment of items in excess of the offeror's actual cost;

(4) Costs for items having a usable lifespan in excess of the development period, except that a contribution may be made toward the proportionate

value of the item during the development period determined by subtracting the item's estimated market value at the termination of the development period from the actual acquisition cost (the cost of items purchased by the Commission under § 1105.7(g) cannot be included in the Commission's contribution); and

(5) Costs determined not to be allowable under generally accepted accounting principles and practices or Part 1-15, Federal Procurement Regulations (41 CFR Part 1-15).

(h) Offerors who have received contributions from the Commission shall submit to the Commission a full accounting of these contributions and shall remit all amounts not expended within 60 calendar days after the offeror submits the standard.

[39 FR 16213, May 7, 1974, as amended at 42 FR 58400, Nov. 9, 1977]

NOTES

INTRODUCTION

1. Harry Anderson, "The Corporate Image," *Interior Design* 32, no. 10 (October 1961): 141.

2. Sherman R. Emery, "Contract Design: A Study in Growth," *Interior Design* 36, no. 10 (October 1965): 161. Italics indicated by S.C. Reznikoff.

CHAPTER 1

1. Reprinted with permission from Justin Sweet's *Legal Aspects of Architecture, Engineering and the Construction Process*, copyrighted © 1977 by West Publishing Co., St. Paul, p. 739.

2. American Society of Interior Designers, "Instruction Sheet for Interior Design Services Agreement" (New York, 1978, Document B 171a), p. 2, paragraph 1.4

3. Reprinted with permission from *Guidelines for Improving Practice* (Washington, D.C.: Victor O. Schinnerer and Co., 1978).

CHAPTER 2

1. "The Cynical Consumers," *Human Behavior Magazine*, August 1977, p. 49. Copyright © 1977. Reprinted with permission.

2. U.S. Department of Commerce, *Interagency Task Force on Product Liability*, vol. 1 (Washington: 1977), pp. 2–10.

3. Norman Polsky, "Report to Business and Institutional Furniture Manufacturers Association on MAAC II," 1977.

CHAPTER 3

1. *Fire Protection Handbook*, 14th ed. (Boston: National Fire Protection Association, 1976), Appendix D, A-30, 31.

CHAPTER 4

1. John S. Martel, "Safeguards in Specifying New Products," *Guidelines for Improved Practice* (Washington, D.C.: Victor O. Schinnerer & Company, 1971.

2. *Paxton v. Alameda County*, 259 Pac. 934. 938 (1953).

3. John Vilett, "The Relationship between the Performance Concept and the Systems Concept," *Performance Concept in Building*, NBS Special Publication 361, vol. 1, 1972, p. 208.

4. *The PBS Building Systems Program and Performance Specification for Office Buildings*, 3rd ed. (Washington, D.C.: General Services Administration, 1975), p. D50.

CHAPTER 5

1. *Fire Protection Handbook*, 14th ed. (Boston: National Fire Protection Association, 1976), p. 46.

2. Ibid.

3. Drawing by Ib Ohlsson, *Newsweek* magazine, June 13, 1944, p. 24.

4. "Design Approach to Fire Safety in Buildings," *Progressive Architecture*. Copyrighted by the Reinhold Publishing Company. Reprinted from the April 1974 issue.

5. "Flammability Testing for Carpeting," National Bureau of Standards, NBS Report NBSIR 78-1436, April 1978.

6. H. J. Roux, "The Scope and Limitations of Fire Testing," unpublished paper presented at the Fifth International Fire, Security and Safety Exhibition and Conference, London, England, 1978, pp. 5–7.

7. U.S. Department of Housing and Urban Development, Office of Policy Development and Research, "Fire Safety Systems Analysis for Residential Occupancies," vol. 1 (March 1977), pp. 48–50.

CHAPTER 6

1. *Office Building by System: The PBS Building System Program*, General Services Administration, Public Building Service, Washington, DC, 1977, p. 17.

2. This period of time may be extended to forty years, which is considered the average life span of a building.

3. *Life Cycle Costing Workbook: A Guide for the Implementation of Life Cycle Costing in the Federal Supply Service* (Washington, D.C.: General Services Administration, Value Management Division, 1977), pp. vi–25.

CHAPTER 7

1. *Standard for the Surface Flammability of Small Carpets and Rugs*, FF 2-70 (Washington, D.C.: U.S. Government Printing Office,) Section 1631.34, paragraph a.

2. Ibid., Section 1631.62, paragraph c.

3. Reprinted by permission of Allied Chemical Company.

4. William G. Klein, "Static Electricity: Problems and Solutions in Computer Facilities," unpublished paper, United Technical Products, Inc., Westwood, Mass., 1978, pp. 1–8.

5. "Why Use Carpet in Hospitals," J & J Industries, Inc., 1976.

6. *Carpet Specifier's Handbook*, 2nd ed. (Dalton, Ga.: Carpet and Rug Institute, 1977), p. 18.

7. Carpet Cushion Council, "The Supporting Facts about Carpet Cushion," 1977.

8. Housing and Urban Development, *Standard for Detached Carpet Cushion*, UM 72, 1979.

9. Burlington Carpet Division, Burlington Industries, Inc., Technical Services Department, "Measuring and Estimating Made Easy."

10. Ibid.

11. Ibid.

12. Ibid.

13. Burlington Carpet Division, Burlington Industries, Inc., Technical Services Department, "Carpet Workroom and Installation Manual," p. 8.

14. Burlington Carpet Division, Burlington Industries, Inc., Technical Services Department, "Installation Instructions for Direct Gluedown of Conventional Back Fabrics."

15. "Carpet Workroom and Installation Manual," pp. 12–14.

16. *Carpet Specifier's Handbook: Specification, Selection, Installation, Maintenance*, J & J Industries, Inc., revised May 1978, pp. 24–26.

17. "20-Day Maintenance Plan," Racine Industrial Plant, Racine, Wisc., 1978.

18. *Carpet Specifier's Handbook*.

CHAPTER 8

1. A. Philips Cramp, et al., "Preliminary Study of the Slipperiness of Flooring," NBS, COM-75-10059, Washington, D.C., July 1974, p. 1.

2. *The PBS Building Systems Program and Performance Specification for Office Buildings*, 3rd ed. (Washington, D.C.: General Services Administration, 1975).

3. "Resilient Flooring," CSI Monograph, Puget Sound CSI Chapter, Specification Series 09650, 1971.

4. "Maintenance of Vinyl Asbestos and Asphalt Tile Floors for Commercial, Institutional and Industrial Buildings" (Washington, D.C.: Resilient Floor Covering Institute, 1975).

5. Richard Perrell, FCSI, "The PAGS System of Architectural Guide Specifications," Scottsdale, Arizona.

6. "Technical Article: Specifying Acrylic/Wood Flooring," *Contract Interiors*, June 1975, pp. 98–99.

7. Radiation Technology, Incorporated, Bulletin RV 1073, Rockaway, N.J.

Chapter 9

1. Richard C. Perrel, FCSI, *The PAGS System of Architectural Guide Specifications*, Scottsdale, Arizona, 1977.

2. "Guide to Measuring for Wallcovering," Wallcovering Manufacturers Association, Springfield, N.J.

3. "Comparative Table of Wood Species." Reprinted with permission of the Architectural Woodwork Institute, Arlington, Va.

4. "Installation of Hardwood Plywood," *How to Sell Hardwood Plywood* (Arlington, Va.: Hardwood Plywood Manufacturers Association, 1975).

5. "Architectural Woodwork Interiors, Wall and Ceiling Treatments." Reprinted by permission of the Architectural Woodwork Institute, Arlington, Virginia, 1975, pp. 22–23.

6. Ibid., p. 19.

CHAPTER 10

1. S. Robert Hastings and Richard W. Crenshaw, "Window Design Strategies to Conserve Energy," NBS Building Science Series, NBS-BSS-104, Washington, D.C., 1977.

2. "Woven Woods and Window Shades by Graber," Graber Form No. 3219-00, p. 8.

3. "Window Magic," Levelor Blinds and Shades, Levelor Lorentzen, Inc., 1976.

4. "Kirsch Compact Architrac with Accordian-Fold Snap on Tape and Carrier System," Kirsch Company, Sturgis, Mich., 1976, p. 5.

5. These headings are also known as "Ripplefold," manufactured by The Kirsch Co.

6. Trade names "Neat Pleat" by Graber and "Archifold" by The Kirsch Co.

CHAPTER 11

1. Consumer Product Safety Act, Commission Organization and Functions, 16 CRF, Section 1000.1, The Commission, paragraph a, Washington, D.C., 1978.

2. *Arizona Republic*, Phoenix, Arizona, January 16, 1979, p. A–10.

3. Agency name changed in 1979.

4. Fire and Thermal Burn Program Staff, "Briefing Paper on Upholstered Furniture Flammability Standard" (Washington, D.C.: Consumer Product Safety Commission, October 1978).

5. Ibid.

6. Consumer Product Safety Act Regulations, Subchapter B, Part 1105.1, paragraph c. *Code of Federal Regulations*, 1009.3, revised January 1, 1978.

7. Fire and Thermal Burn Program Staff, "Briefing Paper on Upholstered Furniture Flammability Standard."

8. Margaret Neily, "Technical Update, Technical Practicability, Proposed Standard for the Flammability (Cigarette Ignition Resistance) of Upholstered Furniture" (Washington, D.C.: Consumer Product Safety Commission, October 1978.)

9. Ibid.

10. Ibid.

11. Fire and Thermal Burn Program Staff, "Briefing Paper on Upholstered Furniture Flammability Standard."

12. Neily, "Technical Update."

13. Nester B. Knoephfler and Julius P. Neumeyer, "Summary of Presentation to CPSC Staff Concerning Mythyborate Vapor Phase Process" (New Orleans, La.: Southern Regional Research Center, 1978), pp. 1–2.

14. Produced for upholstery liners and carpet liners.

15. Marketed under the trade name "Vonar," produced by The E.I. du Pont de Nemours and Company, Inc., Wilmington, Del.

16. Damant and Young, "Smoldering Characteristics of Fabric Used as Upholstered Furniture Coverings," Laboratory Report Number SP 77-1, State of California, Bureau of Home Furnishings, January 1977.

17. Chester J. Barecki, *Ignition of Bus Seats*, paper presented at a meeting of NFPA, May 1976; and *Theater Chair Burn Test: A Technical Report*, E. I. du Pont de Nemours & Company, Inc., Wilmington, Del.

18. "Statistical Analysis of the Upholstered Furniture Interlaboratory Study," Appendix L, Technical Rational, BES/CPSC, June 1976.

19. Ibid.

20. NBS Laboratory Tests on UFAC Welt Cord and Foam Test Methods, August 1978.

21. Patricia Fairall, "Technical Analysis of Industry Voluntary Upholstered Furniture Flammability" (Washington, D.C.: CPSC, October 1978).

22. Fire and Thermal Burn Program Staff, "Briefing Paper on Upholstered Furniture Flammability Standard."

23. Charles Smith, "Profile of Selected Groups Supplying Fabrics and Cushioning Materials to the Upholstered Furniture Industry," 1978, p. 4.

24. Federal Trade Commission, Docket Number C-2596, Washington, D.C., Nov. 4, 1974, p. 11.

25. "Briefing Paper on Upholstered Furniture Flammability Standard."

CHAPTER 12

1. *The PBS Building Systems Program and Performance Specifications for Office Buildings*, 3rd ed. (Washington, D.C.: GSA, PBS, 1975), pp. F1–3.

2. Ibid., p. F4

3. *Task-Lit Systems Furniture Energy Conservation Demonstration Project*, PCB-IPD-76-02-DHUD (Washington, D.C.: General Services Administration, Public Services, June 18, 1976), p. 66.

4. *Energy Conservation Design Guidelines for Existing Office Buildings*, 2nd ed. (Washington, D.C.: General Services Administration, Public Building Service, 1977), pp. 4–13, 4–16.

5. General Services Administration, Design Action Center.

6. *Energy Conservation Design Guidelines for Existing Office Buildings*, pp. B23–28.

7. *The PBS Building Systems Program and Performance Specifications for Office Buildings*, p. G5.3.

8. Knoll International, Inc., "Economics of Task Lighting," *Knoll Task Lighting*, 1976, pp. 12–15.

9. Ibid.

10. *The PBS Building Systems Program and Performance Specifications for Office Buildings*, p. D40.

11. *Task-Lit Systems Furniture Energy Conservation Demonstration Project*, pp. 39–40.

12. *Guide to Office Products, Furniture: Introductory Notes* (Hackensack, N.J.: Buyers Laboratory, Inc., 1977).

13. Vecta Contract, Dallas, Tex.

14. Fixtures Mfg., Corporation, Kansas City, Mo.

15. *Architectural Casework Details* (Arlington, Va.: Architectural Woodwork Institute, 1969), pp. 2–3.

16. *Factory Finishing of Architectural Woodwork* (Arlington, Va.: Architectural Woodwork Institute, 1970), p. 8.

17. *Specifying Wood Cabinets: Unfinished*, CSI Specification Series, 06411, The Construction Specifications Institute, 1970.

18. *Guide to Office Products, Furniture: Introductory Notes.*

19. Ibid.

20. Ibid.

CHAPTER 13

1. *Specific Building Firesafety Criteria*, General Services Administration, PBS P 5920.9 CHGE 10, May 5, 1978, Washington, D.C., p. 3-1.

2. Ibid.

3. *Building Firesafety Criteria*, General Services Administration, PBS P 5920.9 CHGE 8, December 1977, Washington, D.C., p. 4-1.

4. London Transport Board, "Second Report of the Operational Research Team on the Capacity of the Footways," Research Report no. 95, London, August 1958.

CHAPTER 14

1. *Design Criteria: New Public Building Accessibility*, General Services Administration and the Public Buildings Service, May 1977; and *Technical Handbook for Facilities Engineering and Construction Manual*, Part 4, Facilities Design and Construction, Section 4.12, Design of Barrier Free Facilities, Department of Health, Education, and Welfare, August 1978.

2. Ibid., p. 7.

3. Ibid., pp. 1, 2.

4. Ibid., p. 55.

5. Public Law 90-480, Subpart 101-19.604 "Exceptions," paragraphs a-d, as amended 1968.

CHAPTER 15

1. Victor O. Schinnerer and Co., Washington, D.C.

2. *Project Manual: Procedures and Techniques*, vol. 1, CSI Manual of Practice (Washington, D.C.: Construction Specifications Institute, 1975).

CHAPTER 16

1. Victor O. Schinnerer and Co., Washington, D.C.

2. *Project Manual: Procedures and Techniques*, vol. 1, CSI Manual of Practice (Washington, D.C.: Construction Speci-

fications Institute, 1975), chap. 11, p. 6.

3. Ibid.

4. *The PBS Building Systems Program and Performance Specifications for Office Buildings*, 3rd ed. (Washington, D.C.: General Services Administration and Public Building Service, 1975), Section A.

5. *Project Manual: Procedures and Techniques*, chap. 11, pp. 12–13.

6. Ibid.

7. *Guidelines for Improving Practice* (Washington, D.C.: Victor O. Schinnerer and Co., 1978).

8. See performance checklist in Chapter 4.

GLOSSARY

CHAPTER 4: QUALITY CONTROL: PERFORMANCE EVALUATION OF MATERIALS

Attributes: A list of qualities or properties that a subsystem or a component must have if they are to function according to the owner's needs.

Building system: A set of coordinated subsystems suitable for many building types, performing the major function of a building. Though it runs contrary to common usage, "system" refers to the whole building, not the major integrated components, which are termed "subsystems."

In-system: All the parts that go to make a subsystem or the building system itself.

Intercept: A term used to define the point at which two items intersect on the vertical and horizontal lines of a matrix.

New product: May refer to a time-tested product which (a) has not previously been used in a particular geographic area or (b) is being used in a new way.

Performance criteria: The set of detailed statements of verifiable requirements that must be met in order to fulfill user needs.

Product: The basic unit of construction, whether it be a material or an item of equipment; the usual level at which prescriptive specifying is carried on. Performance criteria can be introduced in specifying a product, but performance specifying is more effectively carried on at a level of subsystem.

Standards: Criteria that have been formulated and published and against which subsystems or products have been tested. Though subsystems or products may be tested to check their conformity to standards, it is sometimes deemed sufficient for the manufacturer responsible to certify that standards have been met.

Subsystem: An assembly of products manufactured to perform as specified, designed to fit the building system as a whole and the other subsystems. Ideally a subsystem is designed, manufactured, tested, and installed as a unit. Example: a ceiling/lighting subsystem; an office subsystem.

Systems building: Design and construction which uses highly organized subsystems or assemblies of products, suitable for many building types, designed to provide universal fit and to generate economies in overall building time and cost.

Test: A check of a component for conformity to performance criteria (including standards). Testing may be performed in the prototype stage, during manufacture, at the site during and after installation, and after project completion, or at any combination of these times. Testing may also be specified on either a sampling or a one-by-one basis. Testing may be performed by the design professional, the owner, a testing consultant, public agencies, or the manufacturer (with appropriate certification).

CHAPTER 5: QUALITY CONTROL: FIRE PERFORMANCE TESTING

Combustible: A material or structure which can burn. Combustible is a relative term; many materials which will burn under one set of conditions will not burn under others; e.g., structural steel is noncombustible, but fine steel wool is combustible. Does not indicate ease of ignition, burning intensity, or rate of burning, except when used with the word "higher."

Fire damage: The duration of a fully developed fire and the average fire temperature of the gases generated. The more ventilation the higher the fire temperatures.

Fire hazard (hazardous): Materials of more than average combustibility or materials that are dangerous because of their fire potential, instability, or toxicity. Also may describe the fire vulnerability of a property based on the fireload or fuel in the occupied space.

Fireload: Amount of combustibles present in a given situation, usually expressed in terms of weight of materials per square foot.

Fire prevention: Refers primarily to measures directed toward avoiding the inception of fire.

Fireproof: Officially *discontinued* in NFPA publications. No material is immune to the effects of fire of sufficient intensity and duration.

Fire protection: In the general sense this term includes everything related to the prevention, detection, and extinguishment of fire. In its specific sense, fire protection refers to the methods of providing for fire control or fire extinguishment.

Fire resistance: See listing under Chapter 11.

Fire retardant: See listing under Chapter 11.

Flameproof: A misleading term. The use of this term is discouraged in favor of "flame retardant" or "flame resistant."

Flame resistant: See listing under Chapter 11.

Flammable: A combustible material that ignites very easily, burns intensely, or has a rapid rate of flamespread. Flammable is used in a general sense without reference to specific limits.

Flashover: The phenomenon of a developing fire (or radiant heat source) producing radiant energy at wall and ceiling surfaces. The radiant feedback from those surfaces gradually heats the contents of the fire area, and when all the combustibles in the space have become heated to their ignition temperature, simultaneous ignition occurs.

Fuel: The amount of combustibles present in a fire situation.

Highrise buildings: Classified on the basis of height differences and correlated with the degree of life safety hazard present. Group 1: buildings of six stories or less with a height of up to 80 ft (24 m). These buildings can be completely evacuated within five minutes. Group 2: buildings with at least six stories but not exceeding 25 stories, with a height between 80 and 264 ft (24 and 83 m). These buildings have stack-effect potential and are beyond the reach of the fire department aerial ladders, but could be evacuated within a reasonable amount of time. Group 3: buildings exceeding 25 stories or 264 ft (83 m). These buildings fit all the classic parameters of a highrise building as set forth in the General Services Administration definition.

General Services Administration definition: (1) beyond the reach of fire department aerial ladder equipment; (2) requiring unreasonable evacuation time; (3) capable of creating significant stack effect; (4) requiring the fire suppression efforts to be executed internally.

It should be noted that these classifications do not account for special cases where immobile occupants are present, e.g., hospitals.

Interior finish: Defined by National Fire Protection Association as those materials that form the exterior/interior surfaces of wall, ceiling, and floors. Variations of this basic definition are found in some building regulations where counter tops, built-in cabinets, and even doors are included in the definition. Many codes, such as NFPA No. 101, Life Safety Code, exclude trim and incidental finish on the basis that it comprises less than 10 percent of the wall and ceiling areas. Free-hanging drapery that covers most or all of a wall surface may be considered interior finish. Surface coatings such as paint or varnish may also be included. Some authorities include the lining or coverings of ducts, shafts, and plenum spaces, as well as batt and blanket insulation, if the back faces a stud space through which fire might spread.

Pyrolysis: Decomposition as a result of heat.

Radiant flux: The minimum energy necessary to sustain flame propagation (see *Flashover*).

Smoke load: The total smoke which could be liberated by the combustion of furnishings and interior finishes in a compartment under prescribed exposure conditions.

Specific optical density (DS): Optical density measured by the percent of light transmission passed through the smoke. A photometric device is used to measure the light transmission. DM means the maximum optical density.

Sprinkler systems: The objective of a life-safety sprinkler system is not necessarily to effect final extinguishment of a fire, but to allow time for the occupants to excape by confining the fire to the room of origin. The system is composed of relatively small diameter copper pipe. The weight of this system is only one-third that of a conventional system. The sprinkler heads require a water pressure of approximately 30 psi and protect an area ranging from 160 to 225 sq ft (15 to 21 sq m). Automatic sprinkler systems are the most effective method that can be used to reduce the loss of life by fire. In a study of 661 highrise fires, sprinklers controlled 654 of the fires. This would mean a 98.9 percent satisfactory performance. When sprinkler systems are used in a commercial building, there is often a waiver of certain code requirements, resulting in more liberal interior materials standards, e.g., lower flame-spread rating for floor- and wallcoverings.

Toxic gases: The gases produced as a result of combustion. Toxic gases account for more fire death than all other causes combined. Gases produced by a fire depend on many variables such as the chemical composition of the burning material, the amount of oxygen available for combustion, and the temperature. The most common toxic gases are carbon monoxide, carbon dioxide, hydrogen sulfide, sufur dioxide, ammonia, hydrogen cyanide, hydrogen chloride, nitrogen dioxide, acrolein, and phosgene. The concentration of these gases in smoke is measured in PPM (parts per million).

Ventilation: In a fire situation, refers to insufficient air being provided to the involved room or area to fully burn the gases that are being generated. This results in excess distillation of the gases being driven off the ''fuels.'' When air does enter the space, combustion of the gases occurs.

CHAPTER 7: FLOOR SYSTEMS: RUGS AND CARPETS*

Abraded yarns: Continuous filament yarns in which filaments have been cut or abraded at intervals and given additional twist to produce a certain degree of hairiness. Abraded yarns are usually plied or twisted with other yarns before using.

Absorption: The ability of a fiber, yarn, or fabric to attract and hold gases or liquids within its pores.

Acrylics: In the carpet industry, refers to acrylic and modacrylic fibers. Acrylic fiber is a polymer composed of at least 85 percent by weight of acrylonitrile units. Modacrylic fiber is a polymer composed of less than 85 percent but at least 35 percent by weight of acrylonitrile units. Acrylics come only in staple form and are noted for their high durability, stain-resistance, and woollike appearance.

American Oriental: A term applied to loommade American carpets of the Axminster or Wilton weave which have been manufactured in the color and pattern designs of Oriental rugs. Being without sizing, these American-made carpets are soft and pliable and can therefore be folded like an Oriental. The sheen or lustre distinguishes this type of American carpet from the other weaves.

Antistatic: Ability of a fabric to disperse electrostatic charges to prevent the build-up of static electricity.

Average stiffness: Average weight in grams per denier that will stretch fiber 1 percent.

Axminster: One of the basic weaves used in making carpets. The pile tufts in this weave are mechanically inserted and bound to the back in a manner similar to the hand knotting of Oriental rugs, making possible almost unlimited combinations of colors and patterns.

BCF: Bulked continuous filament nylon. The highly bulked fibers have a trilobular or triskelion cross section, which gives them greater covering power than round, cross-section fibers possess.

*Provided by the Carpet and Rug Institute.

Backing: Material that forms the back of the carpet, regardless of the type of construction. (1) Primary back: in a tufted carpet, the material to which surface yarns are attached. May be made of jute, kraftcord, cotton, woven, or nonwoven synthetics. (2) Secondary back: also called "double backing." Any material (jute, woven, or nonwoven synthetics, scrim, foam, or cushion) laminated to the primary back.

Back seams: While all carpet seams are located on the back or underside of the carpet, those made when the carpet is turned over or face-down are called "back seams," while those made with the carpet face-up are called "face seams."

Bank: A setting machine yarn creel.

Beam: Large, horizontal cylinders or spools. The warp yarns are wound on beams located back of the line of weave. The woven fabric is wound on a beam located usually in front, just below the line of weave.

Bearding: Long fiber fuzz on loop pile fabrics. Caused by fiber snagging and inadequate anchorage.

Beat-up: (1) The action of the lay and reed when forcing the filling to fell off the cloth. (2) The point in the timing cycle of the above operation. (3) The number of tufts per inch of length in a warp row of pile. Used in connection with Axminster, chenille, and other carpets not woven over wires. Synonymous with "wire" in Wilton, velvet, etc.

Bent needles: (1) Needles in the tufting machine permanently pushed out of place causing a streak or grinning; they run lengthwise because of off-standard tuft spacing across the width. (2) A needle in the Jacquard that is out of alignment with punched holes in pattern cards.

Binding: A strip sewed over a carpet edge to protect against unraveling and/or to change its appearance.

Binding yarn: Cotton or rayon yarn running lengthwise of the woven fabric, used "to bind" the pile tufts firmly; often called "crimp warp" or "binder warp."

Bleeding: Loss of color when wet due to improper dyeing or from the use of poor dyestuffs. Fabrics that bleed will stain fabrics in contact with them when wet.

Blend: A fabric containing a mixture of two or more fibers or yarns, or a combination of two or more fibers spun into a yarn.

Breaking strength: Ability of a fabric to resist rupture by evenly applied tension. Expressed as pounds of force applied to 1 in. width in warpwise or fillingwise direction.

Brussels: A term formerly, but now rarely, used to describe a loop pile or round-wire carpet woven on the Wilton loom.

Brussels pitch: From 252 to 256 dents per 27 in. (68.6 cm) in width.

Buckling: A carpet that does not lay flat on the floor and contains ridges. Can be caused by uneven beam tension, dimensional instability, and putting together mismatched carpet. Failure to stretch wall-to-wall installations sufficiently will also contribute buckles. (See also *Puckering*.)

Bulking: Processing yarn, usually by mechanical means, to fluff it up and give more coverage with the same weight. Also known as texturizing and lofting.

Burling: An inspection process following carpet construction to correct loose tufts, etc.; also the process of replacing missing tufts by hand.

Cam loom: A loom in which the shedding is performed by means of cams. A velvet loom.

Carpet: The general designation for fabric used as a floor-covering. It is occasionally used incorrectly in plural as "carpets" or "carpeting." The preferred usage today is "carpet" in both singular and plural form. It may be used as an adjective, as in "carpeted floors."

Carpet cushion: Any kind of material placed under carpet to provide softness when it is walked on. Not only does it provide a softer feel underfoot, it usually provides added acoustical benefits and longer wear life for the carpet. In some cases the cushion may be attached to the carpet when it is manufactured. Also referred to as "lining," "padding," or "underlay," "carpet cushion" is the preferred term.

Catcher threads: Warp threads in chenille Axminster carpets which attach the chenille fur to the carpet backing structure.

Chain: (1) The binder warp yarn that works over and under the filling shots of the carpet. (2) Axminster loom: the endless chain that carries the tube frames. (3) Dobby loom: the endless chain of pattern selector bars.

Chain binders: Yarns running warpwise (lengthwise) in the back of a woven carpet, binding construction yarns together in a woven construction.

Chenille: A pile fabric woven by the insertion of a prepared weft row of surface yarn tufts in a "fur" or "caterpillar" form through very fine but strong cotton "catcher" warp yarns and over a heavy woolen backing yarn.

Cockling: A curliness or crimpiness appearing in the cut face pile as a result of a yarn condition.

Commercial matching: Matching of colors within acceptable tolerances or with a color variation that is barely detectable to the naked eye.

Construction: The methods by which carpet is made, combining the pile fibers to the backing materials. The term is applied to woven, tufted, and knitted carpet.

Continuous filament: Continuous strand of synthetic fiber extruded in yarn form, without the need for spinning which all natural fibers require.

Count: (1) A number of identifying yarn size or weight per unit of length or vice versa, depending on the particular system being used. (2) Count of fabric is indicated by the number of warp ends and filling ends per inch.

Crab: A hand device usually used for stretching carpet in a small area where a power stretcher or knee kicker cannot be used.

Crimping: Processing of yarns, usually by heat, steam, or pressure, to introduce and/or set a wavy texture and give increased bulk.

Crocking: The excess color rubbing off as the result of improper dye penetration, fixation, or selection.

Cropping: The passage of carpet under a revolving cylinder fitted with cutting blades to obtain a level surface and a uniform height of pile.

Cross-seams: Seams made by joining the ends of carpet together.

Cushion-back carpet: A carpet having a cushioning lining, padding, or underlay material as an integral part of its backing.

Dead: The pile yarn in a Wilton carpet (usually figured) which remains hidden in the backing structure when not forming a pile tuft.

Deep-dyed: Dye penetration in carpet fibers which permits clear, true carpet colors that retain their brillance for the life of the carpet.

Delustered nylon: Nylon whose normally high sheen is reduced by surface treatment.

Denier: Unit of weight for the size of a single filament. The higher the denier, the heavier the yarn. Denier is equivalent to the number of grams per 9,000 m (30,000 ft).

Density: The amount of pile packed into a given volume of carpet, usually measured in ounces of pile yarn per unit volume.

Density height: The square of the density multiplied by the pile height; a criterion by which the potential wearlife of different carpet grades can be compared theoretically. The assumption is made in the use of this criterion that the fibers in the materials being compared are of equal quality and all other factors are constant. For example, if a carpet has a density of 32 and a pile height of .25 in. (6.4 mm), a 25 percent increase in the pile height would mean a corresponding 25 percent increase in the durability of the carpet. However, if the density of the carpet were increased by 25 percent, the durability would have been increased by 66 percent.

Differential dyeing fibers (dye-variant fibers): Fibers, natural or manufactured, so treated or modified in composition that their affinity for dyes becomes changed, i.e., to be reserved, dye lighter or darker than normal fibers, depending upon the particular dyes and methods of application employed.

Dimensional stability: Tendency of a fabric to retain its size and shape; may be brought about by chemical treatment or mechanical means: e.g., a secondary backing adds dimensional stability to carpet.

Dope dyed: Same as spun dyed and solution dyed, this applies to synthetic fibers only. The coloring materials are added to the solution before extruding through a spinneret to form the filament.

Double back: A woven or nonwoven material adhered to the backing of some carpet as additional reinforcement to provide greater dimensional stability and improved tuft bind. Also known as scrim back.

Drop match: When the design in a carpet must be dropped in the next combining width of carpet to maintain the pattern.

Drugget: A coarse, heavy imported fabric, felted or plain woven, usually of all wool. The designs are either woven into a fabric or printed.

Dye beck: A large vat into which roll lengths are submerged for piece dyeing.

Dyeing: The process of coloring materials: impregnating fabric with dyestuff.
  1. Solution dyed: Synthetic yarn which is spun from a colored solution; the filament is thus impregnated with the pigment.
  2. Stock dyed: fibers are dyed before spinning.
  3. Yarn (or skein) dyed: yarn dyed before being fabricated into carpet.
  4. Piece dyeing unfinished carpet: carpet dyed "in a piece" after tufting or weaving but before other finishing processes such as latexing or foaming.
  5. Cross dyeing: method of dyeing fabrics with dyestuffs which have different affinities for different types of yarns.
  6. Space dyeing: process whereby different colors are "printed" along the length of yarn before it is manufactured into carpet.
  7. Continuous dyeing: the process of dyeing carpet in a continuous production line, rather than piece dyeing separate lots. Most often done on Kusters continuous dyeing equipment which flows on dyestuffs, as distinguished from submerging carpet in separate dye becks.
  8. Print dyeing: roller printing employs embossed cylinders to deposit the design on the face of the carpet. Several rollers in tandem, each printing a different color, produce multicolored patterns. Screen printing employs flat templates, or screens, through which dyes are forced on the carpet pile. Each color in a multicolor design requires a separate screen.
  9. Random multicolor dyeing: achieved with a random dye applicator, or TAK random pattern machine. The TAK machine disperses regulated amounts of dye on carpet already dyed in a single ground color, or even on totally undyed goods. Several TAK dyers in tandem can apply several different colors at preset intervals to achieve pattern effects.
  10. Worldtronic system: electronically controlled coloring system that makes use of a special dye bath to produce different colors within the same bath.
  11. Controlled color spacing: while yarn is fed through the needle, dye is applied along its length in different colors. Color sequence is carefully controlled. Carpet produced with this method of dyeing looks woven instead of tufted.
  12. Jet dyeing: continuous carpet roll feeds under jet dye heads at 24 ft (7 m) per minute. A computer programs a sequence of jet dye squirts. This system is also known as the Millitron system. Carpets can be printed in patterns with little waste.

Electrostatic flocking: The process used for the majority of flocked commercial carpets. Specially treated fibers are charged by an electrostatic field. When the charged fibers encounter the object to be coated, they are moving vertically at a high speed and they become firmly embedded in the adhesive.

Embossed: In carpet, the type of pattern formed when heavy twisted tufts are used in a ground of straight yarns to create an engraved appearance. Both the straight and twisted yarns are often of the same color.

Face seams: Seams, either sewed or cemented, that are

made without turning the entire carpet over or face-down. They are made during installation where it is not possible to make back seams.

Filament: A single strand of any kind of fiber, natural or synthetic. In textile use, filaments of natural fiber must be spun into yarns, and synthetic filaments are extruded as yarns.

Filler: Fuller's earth or clay, or similar material, used in the mix of latex and attached cushion.

Finishing: A final process through which fabrics are put in order to prepare them for the market; such as bleaching, scouring, calendering, embossing, rapping, mercerizing, waterproofing, or mothproofing.

Foam rotary shampooing: A shampooing method which reduces drying time to 30 to 60 minutes. The new equipment consists of a foamer attachment (a self-contained solution tank and foam builder) which fits on any rotary machine. One man does the shampooing and another removes the heavy dirty suds with a wet vacuum.

Full roll: An unbound cut of carpet, described in the carpet industry as being over 30 ft (9 m) in length and by the width of the production run from which it was cut.

Fusion bonded: Makes use of two backing fabrics that run parallel with a small space between the two. The backing has an adhesive on the facing sides. By implanting a multi-fold fiber between the backings, a sandwich is formed. At the end of production line, a blade slices through the middle fiber web, producing two identical carpets. Most of the fusion bonded carpet has a special backing applied, and then it is cut into carpet tiles.

Fuzzing: Hairy effect on fabric surface caused by wild fibers or slack yarn twist or by fibers slipping out of yarn or contour in either service or wet cleaning. It is corrected by shearing in manufacturing and by the professional cleaner. Carpet of continuous filament yarn is fuzzed by filament snagging and breaking.

Gauge/Pitch: The number of ends of surface yarn counting across the width of carpet. In woven carpet, pitch is the number of ends of yarn in 27 in. of width: e.g., 216 divided by 27 is 8 ends per inch. In tufted carpet, gauge also means the number of ends of surface yarn per inch counting across the carpet; e.g., 1/8 gauge equals 8 ends per inch. To convert gauge to pitch, multiply ends per inch by 27; e.g., 1/10 gauge is equivalent to 270 pitch, or 10 ends per inch × 27. One-eighth gauge is 8 ends of yarn per inch × 27, or 216 pitch.

Greige goods (Pronounced "gray goods"): Term designating carpet just off the tufting machine and in an undyed or unfinished state.

Grin: A term used to indicate the condition where the backing of the carpet shows between the rows of pile tuft; e.g., some carpet may show the backing when laid over the nosing of a step.

Ground color: The background color against which the top colors create the pattern or figure in the design.

Hair: Animal fiber other than wool or silk.

Hand: The "feel" of a carpet in the hand, determined by such factors as pile height, quality and kind of fibers, type of construction, type of backing, and dimensional stability.

Heather: A multicolored effect provided by intimately blending fibers of different colors prior to spinning carpet yarn.

Heat set: Stabilization of yarns to ensure no change in size or shape; the process of heat-setting in an autoclave, using super-heated steam under pressure.

Heddle frame: The frame on which the heddles are mounted.

Hessian: Plain cloth, usually of jute, containing single yarns of approximately the same count in warp and weft.

High density: A term to describe a material with heavier than normal weight-per-unit volume.

High-density foam: Rubber product applied as a liquid foam, then cured, to form an integral part of the carpet back. The minimum standards are weight of 38 oz/sq yd, thickness of 1/8 in. (3.2 mm), density of 25 lb/cu ft.

High low: A multilevel pile, sometimes combining cut and looped surface yarns.

Hooked rugs: Yarn or strips of cloth inserted into a pre-woven cloth stenciled with a pattern. Usually a hand or single needle process. Modern tufting is mechanized hooking.

Hopper: The assembly that engages the pile wire head, drawing it from the front of the wire set and returning it under the pile shed.

Hot melt: A blend of polymer and filling applied in a heated state to a carpet back in order to lock in surface yarns and provide lamination.

Indoor/outdoor: Obsolete term, see *Outdoor carpet.* The first carpet produced for outdoor use was named indoor/outdoor carpet. Over a period of time this term was erroneously thought, by retailers and consumers, to indicate "that if it is okay for outdoor use it has superior qualities indoors." Since this statement is generally incorrect, the carpet industry wants to avoid perpetuating this term.

Ingrain carpet: A double-faced pileless carpet using colored filling yarns to make the design. The fabric is reversible, and the designs and colors on the face and back will also be in reverse positions. This type was also called Scotch or Kidderminster.

Jacquard: The pattern control on a Wilton loom. A chain of perforated cardboard "cards" punched according to the design elements, which when brought into position activates this mechanism by causing it to select the desired color of yarn to form the design on the pile surface. The unselected colors are woven "dormant" through the body of the fabric.

Jacquard cards: Punched cards (usually laced together) which are presented to the Jacquard in sequence, for the selection of lifting of the pile ends as required for patterning.

Jaspe: Irregular stripes of two hues, shades, or values of the same color used to produce a particular effect on the pile yarn of plain or even designed fabrics. Various jaspe effects can be produced by varying the twist of the yarn.

Jerker bar (tufting): The guide or thread jerker which takes up slack tufting yarn during the upstroke of the needle and controls the amount supplied for the backstroke.

Jute: A fibrous skin between the bark and stalk of a plant native to India and the Far East. Shredded and spun, it forms a strong and durable yarn used in carpet backing to add strength, weight, and stiffness.

Kemp: Coarse, brittle white fiber occurring frequently in "nonblooded" carpet wools. These fibers do not accept dye, and consequently an excess could be prominent and undesirable.

Knee kicker: A short tool with gripping teeth at one end and a padded cushion at the other, used in making small stretches during carpet installation.

Knitting: A method of fabricating a carpet in one operation, as in weaving. Surface and backing yarns are looped together with a stitching yarn on machines with three sets of needles.

Laminated: Fabric composed of layers of cloth joined together.

Latex: A milky, rubbery fluid found in several seed plants and used to seal the back of carpet and provide lamination. May be used on tufted or woven carpet.

Latexing: The application of a natural or synthetic latex compound to the back of carpet.

Leno weave: Weave in which warp yarns, arranged in pairs, are twisted around one another between "picks" of weft yarn.

Level loop: A construction in which the carpet face yarns are tufted or woven into loops of the same pile height.

Lip: The chain and/or stuffer left on the edge of carpet after it has been cut.

Loopers: The thin, flat, steep components that move beside the inserted needles and hook the tufting yarn into loops.

Lustering: Finishing process produces luster on yarns and cloth.

Match, set or drop: In a set-match carpet pattern, the figure matches straight across on each side of the carpet width; in a drop-match, the figure matches the design midway; in a quarter drop-match, the figure matches one-quarter of the length of the repeat on the opposite side.

Mending (Picking): A hand operation carried out on carpet before finishing to remove any knots and loose ends of yarn, to insert pile tufts where missing, and to replace and repair backing yarns as required.

Metallic fiber: A manufactured fiber composed of metal, plastic-coated metal, metal-coated plastic, or a core completely covered by metal. The most important characteristic of metallic fiber in carpet is to reduce build-up of static electricity.

Mil: A unit commonly used for measuring the diameter of textile monofilaments—1/1,000 in.

Mill end: The remainder of a roll carpet, generally described in the carpet industry as being over 9 ft (2.8 m) in length, but under 21 ft (6.5 m) in length, by the width of the roll from which it was cut.

Modacrylics: Refer to *Acrylics.*

Molded rubber back: A new kind of carpet backing. Liquid rubber is coated on the carpet back and then rolled out with an embossed roller.

Monofilament: A filament large and strong enough to be used directly as a yarn for making textiles through any established process.

Moresque: Single strands of different colors of yarn twisted or plied together to form one multicolored yarn.

Multifilament: Yarns made of many filaments plied or spun together. The finer the filaments spun together, the softer and more luxurious the yarn and textiles made from it.

Nap: The pile on the surface of a carpet or rug.

Narrow carpet: Fabric woven 27 in. (68.6 cm) and 36 in. (9.4 cm) in width.

Needle: (1) *Jacquard loom;* the horizontal wires, rods, or plungers, the forward and backward movement of which is controlled by the pattern punch cards. One end is placed into a needle board and the ends extend slightly beyond the board surface. The other end projects into a leveling board, padder, needle box, or spring box. The forward and backward movements position the last cord knots to be picked up by the last board, lifting board or comberboard, or the hooks to be picked up by the griff remain in the grate. (2) *Axminster loom:* refers to the metal rod used to insert a short filling yarn. (3) *Knitting:* the hooks that make the loops. (4) *Tufting:* The needle with an eye to punch the pile yarn through the backing material. (5) *Needlepunching:* the needle that stitches the fibers to a base fabric.

Needlepunching: Layers or batts of loose fiber are needled into a core, or scrim, fabric to form a felted or flat-textured material. A needlepunched fabric can be embossed, printed, or laminated to a cushion, or otherwise finished.

Noil: A by-product in worsted yarn manufacture consisting of short wool fibers, less than a determined length, which are combed out.

Nonwoven: A fabric made up of a web of fibers held together by a chemical or fibrous bonding agent.

Nosing: The front dividing line of a step, where the top of a riser joins the front of a tread.

Olefins: Any long chain synthetic polymer composed of at least 85 percent by weight of ethylene, propylene, or other olefin units.

Outdoor carpet: Carpet that has been specially engineered so that all elements of the product will resist the ravages of the sun, rain, and snow. Outdoor carpet is generally made of all synthetic material. Special attention has been paid to sun fade degradation of the pile fiber.

Padding: See *Carpet cushion.*

Piece-dyed: Entire carpet immersed in dye bath. Used for dyeing tufted carpet.

Pigmented yarns: A dull or colored yarn spun from a solution to which a pigment has been added.

Pile: The upright ends of yarn, whether cut or looped, that form the wearing surface of carpet or rugs.

Pile crush: Bending of pile by constant walking or the pressure of furniture.

Pile density: The number of tufts both across and lengthwise the carpet. In tufted carpet the measure across the carpet is called needles per inch, or gauge. Lengthwise is called stitches per inch.

Pile height: The height of pile measured from the surface of the back to the top of the pile.

Pile setting: Brushing done after shampooing to restore the damp pile to its original height. A pile lifting machine or a pile brush is used.

Pile wire: A metal strip or rod over which the yarn is woven to produce a pile.

Pilling: A condition in certain fibers in which strands of the fiber separate and become knotted with other strands, causing a rough, spotty appearance. Pilled tufts should never be pulled from carpet, but may be cut off with a sharp scissors at the pile surface.

Pitch: See *Gauge*.

Plain or flat weave: A fabric with a flat surface in plain, twill, or fancy weaves, having a printed, stenciled, or "woven in" design, and generally reversible.

Plied yarns: Two or more strands, ends, or plys either twisted or otherwise cohesively entwined, intermingled, or entangled into a heavier yarn.

Plush finish: A dense cut pile carpet in which the surface has a solid "mirrorlike" appearance. The ends of each tuft tend to merge into a common surface.

Ply: The number of strands of yarn twisted together to form a single yarn, as in "2-ply" or "3-ply."

Polyester: A manufactured fiber in which the fiber-forming substance is any long chain synthetic polymer composed of at least 85 percent by weight of an ester of a dihydric alcohol and terephthalic acid (p-HOOC-C_6H_4—COOH).

Polymer: In synthetics, the basic chemical unit from which fibers are made. Polymer is made of large complex molecules formed by uniting molecules (monomers).

Polypropylene: High-molecular weight paraffin fiber made by the polymerization of propylene (FTC classification Olefin).

Power stretcher: An extension-type version of the knee kicker, with more teeth arranged in a head which can be adjusted for depth of bite, or used to stretch larger areas of carpet that cannot be handled by the knee kicker.

Primary backing: The material on which the carpet is constructed. The material to which the visible secondary backing is anchored. Usually jute or polypropylene.

Prime urethane cushion: A carpet cushion made from virgin polyether urethane foam slab stacks.

Printed carpet: Carpet with surface patterns applied by means of dyes used on engraved rollers, wood blocks, or screens.

Printing: The process of producing a pattern with dyestuffs on carpet and rugs. May be done by several methods, such as screen printing (e.g., on Zimmer equipment, which may be flat bed or rotary screen printing), or on roller equipment operating on the relief-printing principle (e.g., Stalwart equipment).

Puckering: A condition in a carpet seam, due to poor layout or unequal stretching, etc., wherein the carpet on one side of the seam is longer or shorter than that on the other side, causing the long side to wrinkle or develop a pleated effect.

Quarter drop match: See *Match*.

Random-sheared: Textured pattern created by shearing some of the top or higher loops and leaving others looped.

Repeat: The distance from a point in a pattern figure to the same point where it occurs again, measuring the fabric lengthwise.

Residual shrinkage: Amount of shrinkage remaining in a fabric after the decrease in dimensions has been determined by preshrinking; decrease in dimensions of a fabric after washing or dry cleaning.

Resilience: The ability of a carpet fabric or padding to spring back to its original shape or thickness after being crushed or walked upon.

Reverse coloring: The process whereby the dominant background colors and the top colors of a fabric are reversed. It can be done in Wilton weaves by changing the yarn colors of each frame.

Rows or wires: The number of lengthwise yarn tufts in 1 in. (2.5 cm) of carpet. In Axminster or chenille, they are called "rows;" in Wilton and velvet, they are known as "wires."

Rug: Soft floor coverings laid on the floor but not fastened to it. As a rule, a rug does not cover the entire floor.

Saxony finish: A dense cut pile carpet, usually made of heavy yarns that have been plied and heat set, so that each tuft end has a distinguishable appearance.

Scrim back: A double back made of light, coarse fabric, cemented to a jute, kraftcord, or synthetic back in tufted construction. (See *double back*.)

Sculptured: In carpet, this refers to a type of pattern formed when certain tufts are eliminated or pile yarns are drawn tightly to the back to form a specific design in the face of the carpet. The resulting pattern simulates the effect of hand carving.

Secondary backing: The extra layer of material laminated to the underside of the carpet for additional dimensional stability and body. Usually latex foam, jute, polypropylene, or vinyl.

Seconds: Carpets or rugs rejected for having certain imperfections, flaws, or deviations of weave and marked as "seconds" or "imperfect" by the manufacturer.

Self-tone: A pattern of two or more shades of the same

color. When two shades are used in a pattern or design, it is called "two-tone."

Selvage: The edge of a carpet so finished that it will not ravel or require binding or hemming.

Serging: Also known as "oversewing," this is a method of finishing the edge of carpet. It is customary to serge the side and bind the end.

Set or drop match: In a set-match carpet pattern, the figure matches straight across on each side of the narrow carpet width; in a drop-match, the figure matches midway of the design; in a quarter drop-match, the figure matches one-quarter of the length of the repeat on the opposite side.

Shading: An apparent change of color in carpet pile caused as light is reflected in different ways when pile fibers are bent; not a defect, but a characteristic especially of cut pile fabrics, including upholstery and clothing.

Shag: A low-density type of carpet of cut and/or loop pile construction wherein the pile surface texture has a random tumbled appearance. This effect is created in use by the random layover of the pile yarn in all directions, as distinguished from the normal upright position of the pile in plush carpet.

Shearing: The process in manufacture in which the fabric is drawn under revolving cutting blades as in a lawn mower, in order to produce a smooth face on the fabric.

Shooting or sprouting: Individual strands of yarn protruding above the surface of the pile. These may be extra long ends of tufts which were not sheared at the mill, pieces of backing material which have risen above the surface, loose ends which were not secured firmly, or occasionally the untwisting of the tightly twisted tufts in a twist weave carpet. This condition of sprouting or shooting does not mean that the fabric is coming apart, for it does no damage. It is only necessary to clip or shear these loose ends even with pile surface. The sprouting yarns should not be pulled out.

Short roll: An unbound cut of carpet, generally described in the carpet industry as being over 21 ft (6.5 m) in length, but under 30 ft (9 m), by the width of the roll from which it was cut.

Shot: The number of weft yarns in relation to each row of pile tufts crosswise in the loom. A 2-shot fabric is one having two weft yarns for each row of pile tufts; a 3-shot fabric has three weft yarns for each row of tufts.

Shuttle: In weaving, a boat-shaped, wooden instrument which holds the bobbin from which the weft yarns unwind as the shuttle passes through the warp shed.

Side seams: Seams running the length of the carpet, adding to the width. Also called "length seams."

Sizing: Operation consisting of applying starch, gelatin, oil, wax, or any other ingredient onto yarn to aid the process of fabrication or to control fabric characteristics. Warp sizing is usually referred to as "slashing."

Smyrna: A reversible, double-plied rug, woven from chenille fur strips without the backing characteristic of the chenille weave. The binding yarns are wool, cotton, jute, or paper.

Soil retardant: Agent applied to carpet pile yarns to resist soiling.

Specific gravity: Ratio of the weight of a given volume of the fiber to an equal volume of water taken as standard at stated temperatures.

Spinning: (1) *Chemical spinning:* The process of producing manufactured fibers, including the extrusion of the spinning liquid through a spinneret into a coagulating medium and the winding of the filaments onto bobbins or in cake form. (2) *Mechanical spinning:* twisting together and drawing out short fibers into continuous strands of yarn.

Splush finish: A term used to describe a semidense cut pile carpet, about halfway in appearance between a shag and a plush. The tufts lay less irregularly than a shag, but not as regular as a plush.

Sponge cushion: A carpet cushion made of chemically blown sponge, including both waffle or flat surfaces.

Sprouting: See *Shooting*.

Stabilizing: Treating a fabric so that it will not shrink or stretch more than a certain percentage.

Staple: Fiber in the natural, unprocessed state, usually in short lengths, which must be spun or twisted into yarn, as opposed to continuous filament.

Staple fiber: The short lengths into which filament yarns are cut to enable them to be spun on conventional spinning machinery.

Staple nylon: Nylon composed of specially engineered fibers cut into short staple for spinning yarns.

Stop marks: A mark across the width of tufted carpet caused by off-standard feed relationship of either yarn or cloth feed or both on the start up on the machine.

Stria or striped: A striped effect obtained by loosely twisting two strands of one shade of yarn with one strand of a lighter or darker shade. The single yarn appears like irregular stripes.

Stuffers: Extra yarns running lengthwise through a woven fabric to increase weight and strength.

Tabby weave: A type of weaving used to give a staggered diagonal pattern across the weft yarns. Most commonly used in loomed carpet construction.

Tak dyeing: Another new process in which dye is applied over a continuous dyed fabric by a controlled "sprinkle" technique. This allows more color and pattern interest in tufted carpet.

Take up: The difference in distance between two points of a yarn as it lies in the fabric and the same two points when the yarn has been removed and straightened, expressed as a percent of the extended length. Similar to extended length used in tufting except that extended length is linear and the base is 1 in. (2.5 cm) of carpet.

$$\frac{\text{Extended length} - \text{woven length} \times 100}{\text{Extended length}} = \% \text{ take up}$$

(See also *Crimping*.)

Tenacity: Stress applied to produce a particular elongation in a fiber. The breaking tenacity is the stress required to elongate a fiber to the breaking point.

Tensile strength: Breaking strain of yarns or fabrics. High tensile stength means strong yarns or fabrics.

Thermal conductivity: The measurement of heat flow through a material.

Thick and thin yarns: Specialty yarns of varying thickness.

Tip-shearing: Texture pattern created in the same way as random-shearing, but generally less definite than random-sheared.

Tone on tone: A carpet pattern made by using two or more shades of the same hue.

Top colors: Colors of the yarn used to form the design, as distinguished from ground color.

Total weight: Weight per square yard of the total carpet pile, yarn, primary and secondary backings, and coatings.

Tuft bind: The force required to pull a tuft from a cut pile floorcovering or to pull free one leg of a loop from a looped pile floorcovering.

Tufted carpet: Carpet or rug fabric that is not woven in the usual manner, but formed by the insertion of thousands of needles that punch tufts through a fabric backing on the principle of the sewing machine.

Velvet finish: The surface of a dense cut pile carpet, produced usually on a tufting machine or velvet loom. See also plush, splush, and saxony finish.

Vinyl: A synthetic carpet back which may be applied in either a hard or cushioned form.

Vinyl foam cushioning: A new kind of carpet cushioning made from a combination of solids and liquids. It is claimed that vinyl foam cushioning will not decompose.

Warp: A series of threads or yarns (usually delivered from a beam) running lengthwise in the carpet. Usually consists of chain, stuffer, and pile warp.

Warp pile: An extra set of warp yarns woven into a fabric to form an up-right pile.

Weft or woof: The threads running across a woven fabric from selvage edge to selvage edge, binding in the pile and weaving in the warp threads.

Weighting: Finishing materials applied to a fabric to give increased weight.

Woolen yarn: A rather soft, bulky yarn spun from both long and short fibers that are not combed out straight but lie in all directions so that they interlock and produce a feltlike texture.

Worsted yarn: Made of long staple carpet fiber combed to parallel the fiber and remove the extremely short fibers.

Woven backing: Backing produced by a weaving process using natural fiber, such as jute, cotton duck, or synthetic yarns.

Yarn: A continuous strand for tufting, weaving, or knitting:

(1) *Continuous filament yarn:* yarn formed into a continuous strand from two or more continuous filaments. (2) *Spring yarn:* yarn formed from staple by spinning or twisting into a single continuous strand or yarn.

CHAPTER 9: INTERIOR WALL FINISHES

Abrasion resistance: A quality of withstanding mechanical action, such as rubbing, scraping, or scrubbing which may tend to remove material progressively from a surface.

Appreciable change: A change that is noticeable in comparing the tested specimen with a sample of the original specimen under standard viewing conditions.

Area: The length multiplied by the width determines the area.

Blocking resistance: A quality of resisting adhesion or sticking between any surfaces which touch under uniform loading and temperature conditions for a specified time.

Bolt: A rolled length of wallcovering containing an area specified by the wallcovering manufacturer.

Breaking strength: A measure of the force necessary to break a web when subjected to a pulling force in the plane of the web.

Cloth-backed: Wallcovering having a backing of woven or knitted yarns.

Coating adhesion: A measure of the strength of the bond between the surface coating and the backing or substrate of a wallcovering.

Cold cracking resistance: A quality of resisting cracking of the coated or decorative surface when a wallcovering is folded while exposed to temperatures as prescribed in the test method.

Colorfastness: A quality of resisting change or loss of color resulting from exposure to light.

Crocking resistance: A quality of resisting transfer of color from a wallcovering surface by rubbing with a dry cloth of contrasting color.

Embossed: Wallcovering having a three-dimensional design impressed in the surface by pressure with or without heat.

Fabric-backed: Wallcovering having a backing of woven or knitted yarns or a nonwoven structure of randomly distributed textile fibers.

Flammability: A quality of resisting the propagation of flame under prescribed test conditions.

Flexographic: A process by which the decorative surface of a wallcovering is machine printed by the transfer of images from raised portions of a flat plate or roll.

Flocked: Wallcovering in which a part or all of the design results from short textile fibers standing more or less on end and bounded by adhesive to the wallcovering.

Grain: An embossed design impressed on a wallcovering.

Hand printed, hand screened: Wallcovering upon which the decorative surface is applied by hand rather than machine.

Heat aging resistance: A quality of resisting deterioration of the coated or decorative surface when a wallcovering is exposed to elevated temperatures over an extended period.

Length: the linear measurement of a roll.

Lining: Wallcovering used to prepare a wall or ceiling surface for hanging a patterned wallcovering or for other decorative treatment.

Lot: a designation to indicate similarity of production.

Mildew resistance: A quality of resisting microbial growth either on the back while drying after hanging or on the decorative surface when exposed to moisture under use conditions.

Peelability: A quality which describes a wallcovering from which the decorative surface may be dry-peeled from the substrate, leaving a continuous layer of the substrate on the wall, when the wallcovering has been installed and peeled according to the manufacturer's instructions.

Piece roll: A bolt of wallcovering containing more than one continuous length.

Prepasted: Wallcovering having a factory-applied adhesive on the back surface for adherence to a hanging surface after the adhesive has been activated.

Rotogravure: A process by which the decorative surface of a wallcovering is machine printed by the transfer of images from the valleys of an engraved or etched cylinder.

Run: Sometimes called a making or batch. The collective rollage produced at one time on a single machine, all of which would be expected to have the same overall appearance and physical characteristics.

Screen printed: Wallcovering upon which the decorative surface is machine printed by a flat or rotary screen process.

Scrubbability: A quality of withstanding scrubbing with a brush and a prescribed detergent solution.

Shrinkage: A decrease in dimensions occurring when a wallcovering is exposed to moisture.

Stain resistance: A quality of showing no appreciable change in appearance after application and removal of certain specified materials.

Standard roll: A standard roll as a unit of measure is 36 sq ft (3.3 sq m).

Strippability: A quality which describes a wallcovering which can be dry-stripped after having been installed and stripped according to manufacturer's instructions, leaving a minimum of product residue on the wall, without damage to the wall surface.

Tear strength: A quality of resisting the propagation of an existing tear.

Wallcovering: A flexible product designed to cover walls and ceilings for decorative and/or functional purposes.

Washability: A quality of withstanding occasional sponging with a prescribed detergent solution to remove surface soil.

Width: The cross-direction measurement after trimming for hanging.

PAINT COATING TERMS

Alkali: A caustic substance such as lye soda or lime. Alkalies or strong alkali solutions are highly destructive to oil paint films.

Back priming: Applying a coat of paint to the backside and edges of woodwork and exterior siding to prevent moisture absorption.

Binder: A film forming oil or resin.

Chalking: Powdering of the paint film on the film surface. Mild chalking may be desirable. Heavy chalking should be removed prior to repainting.

Clear finish: A material which is transparent in nature. Usually referred to if and when an application of the material is applied overall on a finished surface.

Coating system: A combination of specific coating materials and their sequential application to an appropriately prepared surface to impart color or protect the surface.

Dry film thickness: Thickness of applied coating or coatings when dry. Thickness is usually expressed in mils (1/1000 in.).

Eggshell: A luster between semigloss and flat which resembles that of an eggshell.

Emulsion paint: A paint, the vehicle of which is an emulsion of binder in water. The binder may be oil, oleoresinous varnish, resin, or other emulsifiable binders.

Enamel: A paint made with varnish or lacquer for a vehicle. The paint is characterized by an ability to form an especially smooth film.

Epoxy resins: A synthetic resin usually made from bisphenol A and epichlorhydrin.

Filler: A pigmented composition for filling the pores or irregularities in a surface preparatory to application of other finishes.

Flat: A finish having no luster or gloss.

Fungicide: A substance poisonous to fungi; retards or prevents fungi growth.

Latex paint: A paint containing a synthetic resin used as a binder for emulsion (water-thinned) paints.

Oil stain: A coating material with an oil binder plus dyes or pigments, but formulated so that normal applications do not deposit an opaque film.

Oil varnish: A varnish which contains resin and drying oil as the basic film-forming ingredients and is converted into a solid film primarily by oxidation.

Oleoresinous: A vehicle for varnishes and paints consisting of drying oils and resins.

Paint: A pigmented liquid composition which is converted to an opaque solid after application of a thin layer. Generally considered as all coating materials used in the act of painting.

Pigment: Solid coloring agents used in the preparation of paint and substantially insoluble in the vehicle.

Resin: A material, usually a solid or viscous liquid, used as part or all of the film-forming phase of paints, varnishes, and lacquers.

Sealer: A paint, varnish, or resinous product used to prevent excessive absorption of finish coats by the substrate; also applied to prevent bleeding or bonding chalked masonry surface before painting.

Semigloss: The glossiness of a finish that is between eggshell and a high or full gloss.

Shellac: A purified lac resin dissolved in an organic solvent (usually alcohol) and used to seal (fill) wood or as a varnish.

Shop coat or shop painting: Coating applied in the fabricating shop or plant before shipment.

Stain: A thin liquid composition, usually transparent, used to change the color of a surface without leaving a film of significant thickness.

Undercoat: In a multicoat system, any intermediate coat or a first or primer coat.

Varnish: A liquid composition which is converted to a transparent or translucent solid film after application as a thin layer. When a varnish is pigmented, it is usually called an "enamel."

Vehicle: The liquid portion of a paint. Anything dissolved in the liquid portion of the paint is part of the vehicle.

CHAPTER 11: FABRIC AND UPHOLSTERY FLAMMABILITY

Abutment: The horizontal crevice formed when the vertical side or back panels meet horizontal panel or seat cushions in upholstered furniture.

Afterglow: Glow in a material after the removal of an external ignition source or after the cessation (natural or induced) of flaming of the material. (See also flame, glow, and smoldering.)

Backcoating: A finishing technique that involves coating the underside of a fabric with a layer of polymeric or other material to improve dimensional stability, wearing quality, and resistance to seam slippage and raveling. Some backcoatings may serve as a heat barrier.

Barrier (heat): A liner used immediately below a fabric to prevent flaming or smoldering heat to ignite the upholstery filling below. This liner or heat barrier may be neoprene, polyester/cotton blend, polyester fiberfill, or aluminized liner. May be applied as a backcoating.

Burnout: Test terminology meaning that a cigarette has burned its entire length.

Butt end: The unlighted end of a cigarette.

Cellulosics: Fabrics made from natural plant fibers. Example: cotton, linen, hemp, jute, and ramie. Manufactured cellulose is made from wood pulp and cotton linters. Example: rayon.

Char: The material remaining from incomplete combustion.

Contract fabric: A fabric engineered to withstand heavy use in commercial and institutional installations. Characterized by a tight weave construction, high yarn count, and large percentage of thermoplastic fiber content. Frequently back-coated and treated for soil and flame resistance. Performance tested for abrasion, fading, and flame resistance. Colors are usually intense primaries or darker shades and neutrals (limited amount of tints and pastels). Patterns usually limited to stripes, plaids, and geometric shapes.

Convertable sofa: An upholstered sofa that converts into an adult-size bed. The mattress unfolds out and up from under the seat cushion.

Deck: See *seat support system.*

Fabric classification: In flammability testing the classification may be based on the ability of a fabric or group of fabrics to withstand ignition from either (1) a nonflaming source or (2) an open flame. Classification may also be based on specific construction, finish application, fiber content, and nominal weight per unit area. Coated fabrics with different chemical formulas and methods of application are usually considered fabric types in testing situations.

Fire: As related to textile flammability, destruction of materials by burning, in which the associated flames are not constant in size and shape and which results in a relatively high heat flux. (Compare with "flame.")

Flame: As related to textile flammability, a hot luminous zone of gas or matter in gaseous suspension, or both, that is undergoing combustion, that is relatively constant in size and shape, and that produces a relatively *low heat* flux. (Compare with "fire.") Examples are a match flame, candle flame, or a Bunsen gas flame.

Flame resistance: The property of a material whereby flaming combustion is prevented, terminated, or inhibited following application of a flaming or nonflaming source of ignition, with or without subsequent removal of the ignition source. Note (1) Flame resistance can be an inherent property of the basic material or product, or it may be imparted by specific treatment. Note (2): The degree of flame resistance exhibited by a specific material during testing may vary with different test conditions.

Flame resistant (adj.): Having flame resistance. Note (1): "Flame resistant" is the government-mandated description for certain products that meet established governmental conformance standards or specifications when the product is tested by a specific method. Note (2): Where no conformance standards exist, "flame resistant" is a relative term and is used to compare one material to another.

Flame retardant (adj.): Undefined. This term should not be used as an adjective except in the terms "flame-retardant treated" and "flame-retardant treatment."

Flame-retardant treatment: A process for incorporating or adding flame retardant(s) to a material or product. Note: The term "flame-retardant treatment" does not apply to textiles that are inherently *flame resistant.*

Furniture mockup: A representation of production furniture that utilizes the same upholstery fabric and upholstery filling assembled in the order used in the finished production furniture. Fabric representing the same fabric class (type) may be substituted, if permitted in the test standard.

Glow: Visible, flameless combustion of the solid phase of a material. (See also *afterglow* and *smoldering*.) Note: A solid may both glow and give all combustibles that burn in the gas phase (i.e., flame), but the two are not necessarily interdependent.

Inflatable furniture: Gas- or liquid-filled furniture which may be a chair, lounger, or other type of furniture used for seating or sleeping.

Loose seat cushion: A removable or interchangeable, attached or unattached, part of an upholstered furniture item upon which one sits.

Main support system: The frame or other supporting structures in the furniture item. Usually constructed of wood, plastic, or metal.

Mockup testing: See *Furniture mockup*.

Production furniture: All upholstered furniture manufactured or reupholstered for sale.

Reupholstered furniture: Furniture that has been reworked to replace any material such as upholstery fabric, cushioning or upholstery filling and is intended for sale by the reupholsterer or person contracting with the reupholsterer. This does not include minor repairs to the surface or frame.

Seat support system: The supporting medium for loose seat cushions.

Slipcover: A removable, fitted cover (fabric or related material) used on upholstered furniture.

Smoldering: Combustion without flame that may burn for a relatively long time while generating smoke, toxic gases, and heat.

Smolder resistance: The property of materials in which non-flaming combustion is prevented, terminated, or inhibited following the application of a flaming or nonflaming source of ignition.

Standard fabric: A term designating fabrics that represent the minimum performance characteristics of their respective type (classification).

Surface location: The designated area used for placement of the ignition source (cigarette) in mockup furniture flammability testing. Surface locations include horizontal crevices, seat cushions, tops of armrests, the top of back cushions, and loose seat support systems.

Thermoplastic fabrics: Materials that tend to become soft or moldable when heat is applied. Example: vinyl, nylon, olefin, polyester.

Tight seat: Any fixed or integrated part of the upholstered furniture item upon which one sits.

Tufted: An upholstery term referring to a surface treatment created by buttons which are laced through the upholstery fabric or upholstery filling.

Upholstery fabric: The outer layer of fabric or related material used to enclose the main support system and upholstery filling used in the furniture item. (Slipcovers are not included in this definition.)

Upholstery filling: Padding, stuffing, or filling material used

in a furniture item. May either be loose or attached, enclosed by an upholstery fabric, or located between the upholstery fabric and support system.

Upholstered furniture: A unit of interior furniture with a resilient surface, in whole or part, with a fabric or related material, that is intended for use in homes, offices, or other places of assembly and is intended for seating or reclining. Upholstered furniture not normally included in flammability regulations are inflatable furniture; ottomans not intended or promoted for use in modular seating groups; any chair or stool which has an upholstered seat and upholstered back (and/or sides) which are separated by 1 in. (2.5 cm) or more. Example: secretarial posture chair.

Welt edge: The seam or border edge of a cushion, pillow, arm, or back of a furniture component.

CHAPTER 14: SPECIFICATIONS FOR BARRIER-FREE PUBLIC INTERIORS

Accessible: A means or condition of approach, admittance and use, intended for use by physically handicapped people.

Ambulant disabled: People who have physical disabilities that do not necessarily restrict walking.

Balcony: An interior or exterior portion of seating, circulation, or work space which is raised 4 ft (1.2 m) or more above a floor or ground level.

Barriers: Physical or functional obstructions to the intended use of a space.

Built-up level: An elevation change in floor level of one or more risers not exceeding 4 vertical feet. Note: Less than three risers are not recommended as vertical access to built-up levels.

Chairbound: A person or persons who are confined to a wheelchair during the working day or who elect to use a wheelchair for ease of movement.

Communication and identification system: A standard organization of signs and cuing for purposes of identifying circulation routes, spaces, and hazards to physically handicapped people.

Corridor lobby: A wheelchair turnaround space in corridors; where seating is provided, it qualifies as a rest stop.

Corridor rest stops: Seating and wheelchair parking at specific intervals along a corridor.

Cues or cuing: Materials or components which communicate information by nonliteral means, including textures, color, graphics, and audible signals.

Equipment: Fixed or nonfixed building hardware and accessories. Example: mirrors, dispensers, or lighting fixtures.

Exception: A term indicating an accessible alternative to a requirement.

Flush: Within ⅛ in. (3.2 mm) maximum protrusion from surrounding surfaces.

Governing codes: Any codes applicable to a project, including basic federal criteria documents and state and city codes.

Hazards: Protrusions, obstructions, changes in materials or levels, exposed structural or mechanical components, or the effects of inclement weather which are likely to cause personal injury, confusion, or discomfort.

Leisure run stairs: Stairs having unusually shallow slope or small ruse-to-run ratio.

Loop circulation: Passageway for one-way circulation.

Mounting height: The distance from the floor to the top edge or surface of an object, except as noted.

Physically disabled or handicapped: Any individual who despite a physical disability, can be expected, without assistance from another person, to visit and utilize a building, including its services; the disabled; the handicapped; people with physical disabilities.

Public conveniences: Facilities for public use, such as rest rooms, telephones, and drinking fountains.

Ramping device: A permanent or temporary inclined plane usually ramping a small level change [½ in. (12.7 mm) or less] such as metal plate attached to a threshold.

Required accessible areas: Specified areas which must be physically accessible and functionally usable by physically disabled people.

Semi-ambulant disabled: People with partial mobility impairments, such as difficulty in walking, difficulty in breathing, strength, stamina, balance, and coordination problems.

Shall: A manditory regulation; indicates that an item must conform to a standard.

Should: Recommendations or that which is advised but not required.

Stairway: Three or more risers shall constitute a stairway.

Steps: One to three consecutive treads or risers.

Vertical access: Means of traveling from one floor level to another. Example: ramps, stairs, elevators, and other lifts. Escalators are usually not considered as vertical means of access for physically handicapped people.

Workstation: Floor areas, furniture and/or equipment used by employees for periods of time longer than one-half hour.

SELECTED READINGS

Almy, Richard. "Vinyl Flooring." *The Construction Specifier* 13, no. 8 (January 1961): 38–40.

American Society of Heating, Refrigerating, and Air-Conditioning Engineers, Inc. "Fenestration," Chapter 26. In *Handbook of Fundamentals*. New York, 1977.

Architectural Woodwork Institute. "Architectural Casework Details." Arlington, Va., 1969.

————. "Architectural Woodwork Interiors, Wall and Ceiling Treatments." Arlington, Va.

————. "Factory Finishing of Architectural Woodwork." Arlington, Va., 1970.

Armstrong Cork Company. *Fire Test Methods*. Lancaster, Pa., 1978.

————. *Floors: Product Information and Technical Data*. Lancaster, Pa., 1978.

Baker, Fischetti, William, and Young. *State and Local Efforts to Eliminate Architectural Barriers to the Handicapped*. Washington, D.C.: National League of Cities and Department of Health, Education, and Welfare, 1967.

Baker, Val M. "Resilient Flooring and Misplaced Responsibility." *The Construction Specifier* 14, no. 7 (December 1961): 47–48.

Barecki, Chester J. "Ignition of Bus Seats." Paper presented at a meeting of the NFPA, May 1976.

————. *Theater Chair Burn Test: A Technical Report*. Wilmington, Del.: E. I. du Pont de Nemours & Company, Inc.

Bayes, Kenneth, and Franklin, Sandra, eds. *Designing for the Handicapped*. London: George Godwin, Ltd., 1971.

Belles, Donald W. "The Radiant Flooring Panel Test Method." Unpublished paper presented at NEOCON 9, 1977.

Benjamin, I. A., and Adams, C. H. *Proposed Criteria for Use of the Critical Radiant Flux Test Method*. National Bureau of Standards IR 75-950, December 1975.

————, and Davis, S. *Flammability Testing for Carpet*. Washington, D.C.: Center for Fire Research for Applied Technology, National Bureau of Standards, April 1978.

Berman, S. M., et al. *Energy Conservation and Window Systems*. Washington, D.C.: U.S. Department of Commerce, PB-243-117, 1975.

BES/CDSC. "Technical Rationale: Proposed Standard for the Flammability (Cigarette Ignition Resistance) of Upholstered Furniture." May 1976.

Bugbee, Percy. *Principles of Fire Protection*. Boston: National Fire Protection Association, 1978.

Burlington Industries, Inc. "Carpet Maintenance Manual." Burlington Carpet Division, Technical Services Department, 1977.

————. "Carpet Workroom and Installation Manual." Burlington Carpet Division, Technical Services Department, 1977.

————. "Installation Instructions for Direct Glue-down of Conventional Back Fabrics." Burlington Carpet Division, Technical Services Department, 1977.

Carpet Cushion Council. *The Supporting Facts about Carpet Cushion*. 1977.

Carpet and Rug Institute. *Carpet Specifier's Handbook,* 2nd ed. Dalton, Ga., 1976.

Christian, W. J., and Waterman, T. E., "Fire Behavior of Interior Finish Materials." *Fire Technology,* August 1970.

Churchman, C. West. *The Systems Approach*. New York: Dell Publishing Co., Inc., 1968.

Collins, Belinda Lowenhaupt. *Windows and People: A Literature Survey, Psychological Reaction to Environment with and without Windows*. U.S. Department of Commerce, National Bureau of Standards Building Science Series 70, June 1975.

Con, J. M. *Carpets from the Orient*. New York: Universe Books, 1966.

Construction Specifications Institute. *Project Manual: Procedures and Techniques*. CSI Manual of Practice, vol. 1. Washington, D.C., 1975.

————. *Specifying Resilient Flooring*. Specification Series 09650, Washington, D.C., 1971.

Consumer Product Safety Commission. "Briefing Paper on Upholstered Furniture Flammability Standard." Washington, D.C.: Fire and Thermal Burn Program Staff, October 1978.

Cramp, A. Philip, et al. *Preliminary Study of the Slipperiness of Flooring*. Washington, D.C.: National Bureau of Standards COM-75-10059, 1974.

Damant and Young. "Smoldering Characteristics of Fabric Used as Upholstered Furniture Coverings." Laboratory Report Number SP 77-1, State of California, Bureau of Home Furnishings, January 1977.

Denyes, W., and Quintiere, J. *Experimental and Analytical Studies of Floor Covering Flammability with a Model Corridor*. Washington, D.C.: National Bureau of Standards IR 73-199, May 1973.

European Flooring Institute and the European Wallcovering Association. *Fire Hazard Evaluation for Flooring and Wallcoverings*. December 1975.

Fairall, Patricia. "Technical Analysis of Industry Voluntary Upholstered Furniture Flammability." Washington, D.C.: CPSC, October 1978.

Federal Register. *Standards for Surface Flammability of Carpets and Rugs, DOC-FF-1-70* 35, no. 74 (Apr. 16, 1970): 6211.

Ferguson, John B. *Summary of Flame Spread and Smoke Generation Tests Conducted for Operator Breakthrough.* National Bureau of Standards Technical Notes, 1973.

Formenton, Fabio. *Oriental Rugs and Carpets*, New York: McGraw-Hill Book Company, Inc., 1972.

Foster, Bruce E., ed. *Performance Concept in Building.* Vols. 1–2, Special Publication 361, Washington, D.C.: National Bureau of Standards, 1972.

Fung, C. W.; Suchomel, R.; and Oglesby, P. L. *NBS Corridor Fire Tests: Energy and Radiation Models.* National Bureau of Standards Technical Note 794, October 1973.

————. "The NBS Program on Corridor Fires." *National Fire Protection Association Fire Journal,* May 1973.

General Services Administration. *Design Criteria: New Public Building Accessibility.* Public Buildings Services, PBS(PCD):DG5, May 1977.

————. *Energy Conservation Design Guidelines for New Office Buildings,* 2nd ed. Public Buildings Services, July 1975.

————. *Energy Conservation Guidelines for Existing Office Buildings,* 2nd ed. Public Buildings Services, February 1977.

————. *Floor Covering Vinyl, Surface (Tile and Roll) with Backing.* L-F-475A, Interim Amendment-2, FSS, Washington, D.C., February 9, 1971.

————. *Guide for Space Planning and Layout.* Public Buildings Services 7610-145-0168 (undated).

————. "Lessons Learned: Systems Furniture Evaluation Study." Design Action Center, April 1978.

————. *Life Cycle Costing Workbook: A Guide for the Implementation of Life Cycle Costing in the Federal Supply Service, General Services Administration.* Washington, D.C.: Value Management Division, FSS, GSA, 1977.

————. *Office Building by Design.* Washington, D.C., 1977.

————. *The PBS Building Systems Program and Performance Specification for Office Buildings,* 3rd ed. Washington, D.C., 1975.

Gimer, Richard H. "Outline of Remarks." Unpublished speech, NEOCON, Chicago, 1978.

Greco, J. T. "Carpeting vs. Resilient Flooring: A Comparative Study in a Metropolitan Hospital." *Hospitals* 39 (1965): 55–58.

Hardwood Plywood Manufacturers Association. "How to Sell Hardwood Plywood." 1975.

Hartzell, L. G. *Development of a Radiant Panel Test for Flooring Materials.* Washington, D.C.: National Bureau of Standards, 1974.

Hastings, S. Robert, and Crenshaw, Richard W. *Window Design Strategies to Conserve Energy.* National Bureau of Standards, Building Sciences Series 104, June 1977.

J & J Industries, Inc. *Carpet Specifier's Handbook.* Dalton, Ga., 1978.

————. "Why Use Carpets in Hospitals." Dalton, Ga.

Jenson, Rolf P. E., ed. *Fire Protection for the Design Professional.* New York: Cahners Publishing Co., Inc., 1975.

Kashiwagi, T. "Experimental Observation of Flame Spread Characteristics over Selected Carpets." *JFF Consumer Product Flammability* 1 (December 1974): 367–389.

Kelly, William T. *New Consumerism: Selected Readings.* Columbus, Ohio: Grid, Inc., 1973.

Klien, William G. "Static Electricity: Problems in Computer Facilities." Westwood, Mass.: United Technical Products, 1978.

Knoephfler, Nester B., and Neumeyer, Julius P. "Summary of Presentation to CPSC Staff Concerning Mythyborate Vapor Phase Process." New Orleans, La.: Southern Regional Research Center, 1978.

Lee, T. G. *Smoke Density Chamber Method for Evaluating the Potential Smoke Generation of Building Materials.* Washington, D.C.: National Bureau of Standards Technical Notes, 1973.

————, and Huggett, Clayton. *Interlaboratory Evaluation of the Tunnel Test (ASTM-E-84) Applied to Floor Coverings.* Washington, D.C.: National Bureau of Standards, 1973.

Levelor Lorentzen, Inc. "Window Magic." New Jersey, 1976.

Litsky, B. Y., and Litsky, W. "Investigations on Decontamination of Hospital Surfaces by the Use of Disinfectant-Detergents." *American Journal of Public Health* 58 (1968): 524–543.

Loftus, J. J. "Interlaboratory Program for the Evaluation of a Proposed Flammability (Cigarette Ignition Resistance) Test for Upholstered Furniture." Washington, D.C.: National Bureau of Standards, March 1976.

Lumex, Inc. *Environments for the Elderly.* New York, 1979.

McGuire. *The Spread of Fire in Corridors.* National Research Council of Canada, Division of Building Research, December 1967.

McMullan, Joseph V. "Islamic Carpet." *Metropolitan Museum of Art Bulletin.* New York: Metropolitan Museum of Art, June 1970.

Mazzini, Ferdinando. *Tappeti Orientali.* Livorno: Societa Editrice Tirrena, 1954.

"Measuring Rate of Heat, Smoke and Toxic Gas Release." *Fire Technology* 8, no. 3 (August 1972): 237–245.

National Bureau of Standards. "NBS Laboratory Tests on UFAC Welt Cord and Foam Test Methods." Washington, D.C., August 1978.

National Commission on Fire Prevention and Control. *America Burning: The Report of the National Commission on Fire Prevention and Control.* Washington, D.C., 1973.

National Fire Protection Association. *Fire Protection Handbook,* 14th ed. Boston, 1976.

————. *Life Safety Code.* Boston, 1976.

National Paint, Varnish, and Lacquer Association, Inc. "The Selection of Paint." Washington, D.C.: Technical Division, 1967.

Neily, Margaret, "Technical Update, Technical Practicability, Proposed Standard for the Flammability (Cigarette Ignition Resistance) of Upholstered Furniture." Washington, D.C.: CPSC, October 1978.

Parker, William J. *Comparison of the Fire Performance of Neoprene and Flame Retardant Polyurethane Mattresses.* Washington, D.C.: National Bureau of Standards, 1973.

Perrell, Richard C., FCSI, SCIP. *PAGS System of Architectural Guide Specifications.* Phoenix, Az., 1979.

Pilsworth, R. "Carpet in Hospitals." *British Hospital Journal and Social Service Review* 79 (1969): 922.

Polsky, Norman. "Multi-Association Action Committee (MAAC) for Product Liability Reform." A report to the MAAC Committee, 1977.

Prunella, Warren, and Smith, Charles L. *Upholstered Furniture Preliminary Economic Assessment of a Cigarette Ignition Standard.* Hazard Identification and Analysis, October 1978.

Public Buildings Services. "Interior Planning and Design Guidelines for Open Planned Offices: Firesafety Criteria." Washington, D.C., April 1978.

Quintiere, J. *The Application and Interpretation of a Test Method to Determine the Hazard of Floor Covering Fire Spread in Building Corridors.* International Symposium, Fire Safety of Combustible Materials, Edinburgh, Scotland, October 1975, pp. 355–367.

———, and Huggett, C. *An Evaluation of Flame Spread Test Methods for Floor Covering Materials.* Special Publication 411. Washington, D.C.: National Bureau of Standards, 1974, pp. 59–89.

Racine Industrial Plant, Inc. "Twenty Day Carpet Maintenance Plan." Racine, Wisc., 1978.

Resilient Floor Covering Institute. *Maintenance of Vinyl Asbestos and Asphalt Tile Floors for Commercial, Institutional and Industrial Buildings.* Washington, D.C., 1975.

Roux, H. J. "The Scope and Limitations of Fire Testing." Unpublished paper presented at the Fifth International Fire, Security and Safety Exhibition and Conference, London, England, 1978.

Rylander, R., et al. "Bacteriological Investigation of Wall to Wall Carpeting." *American Journal of Public Health* 64, no. 2 (1974): 168.

Shaffer, J. G.; Migit, D.; and Ket, I. "The Microbiological Profile of Two Hospitals of Differing Structures." *Hospitals* 39 (1965): 71–77.

Sharry, John A., ed. *Life Safety Code Handbook.* Boston: National Fire Protection Association, July 1978.

Smith, Charles. "Profile of Selected Groups Supplying Fabrics and Cushioning Materials to the Upholstered Furniture Industry." 1978.

Society of the Plastics Industry, Inc. "Answers to Questions Frequently Asked about Plastics." New York, 1977.

"Specifying Acrylic/Wood Flooring." *Interiors,* June 1975, pp. 98–99.

Sweet, Justin. *Legal Aspects of Architecture, Engineering and the Construction Process.* St. Paul, Minn.: West Publishing Co., 1977.

Tu, M., and Davis, S. *Flame Spread of Carpet Systems Involved in Room Fires.* Washington, D.C.: National Bureau of Standards IR 75-1013, June 1976.

U.S. Bureau of Mines. "Static Electricity in Hospital Operating Suites." Report 520, Washington, D.C.

U.S. Consumer Product Safety Commission. *Tabulation of Data from National Electronic Injury Surveillance System.* Washington, D.C., 1977.

U.S. Department of Commerce. *Fire Protection for Architects and Interior Designers.* Washington, D.C.: National Fire Prevention and Control Association, National Fire Academy, 1978.

———. *Interagency Task Force on Product Liability,* vol. 4. Legal Study, ITFPL, Washington, D.C., 1977.

U.S. Department of Health, Education, and Welfare. *Technical Handbook for Facilities Engineering and Construction Manual.* Part 4: Facilities Design and Construction: 4.00 Architectural Section, 4.12 Design of Barrier-Free Facilities, Office of the Secretary, Department Technical Handbook Series, Department Staff Manual Series, January 1975 (revised August 1978).

U.S. Department of Housing and Urban Development. *Fire Safety Analysis for Residential Occupancies.* Washington, D.C.: Office of Policy Development and Research, March 1977.

U.S. Department of Labor. *Occupational Safety and Health Standards: Safety and Health Regulations for Construction.* Washington, D.C., 1970.

Veterans Administration. *Accommodations for the Physically Handicapped.* Washington, D.C., October 1973.

Wald, William. "Relevant Test Devised for Carpet Flammability." *Contract,* 1977.

Wilman, C. W. *Electricity.* London: The English Universities Press Ltd., 1964.

Wilson. "Evaluating Trade-offs: An Introduction to the L-Curve Measurement for Fire Safety." NFPCA Conference, Los Angeles, 1976.

INDEX

inspection, 127
installation, 126
    mechanical devices for, 127
plywood core types, 123
selection guide for, 124, 125
sizing, 125
species selection, 115–122
    appearance, 115
    availability, 122
    cost, 115
    dimensional stability, 122
    hardness, 122
    size limits, 122
specification guidelines for, 128–129
spines and moldings, 127
storage and handling, 126
veneer matching, 122. *See also* Veneers
wall subsurfaces, 126
wood species, comparison of, 126
People cost, 44–45
"Performance Concept in Buildings, The," 27, 45
Performance systems. *See* Materials, performance evaluation of
Product liability
    defined, 17
    and designers, self-protection by, 18
    duty to warn of, 18
    express warranty, 17
    industry custom in, 18
    misuse of, 18
    and product-related injury, 17
    punitive damages, 18
    state of the art, 18
    and statute of limitations, 17–18
    strict liability, 18
    subsequent modification, 18
    tort laws, 17
    and "useful life" concept, 18
Public Building Service, 44
Public Building Service (PBS) Building Systems Program and Performance Specification for Office Buildings, 44
Public interiors, barrier-free
    accessibility, 206–209, 216–217
    circulation
        horizontal, 209
        in offices, 214
        passage through open office, 215
        vertical, 209, 211, 213
            elevators, 211
            handrails, 211
            lobbies, 211
            ramps, 211
            stairs, 211
    communications for, 208–209
        lighting, 209
        safety information, 209
        signage, 209
        sound cues, 209
        tactile cues, 209
        wall graphics, 209
    comparative reach in, 216
    compliance with standards for, 218
    criteria for, 214–216
    dining areas in, 216–217

food service, 217
and disabled people, 206
dormitories in, 217
drinking fountains, 213
flooring transition strips, 207
general requirements for
    doors, 206–207
    floor covering, 207–208
    furniture, 208
    hardware, 207
    walls and partitions, 206
    windows, 206
lobby information desk, 212
open offices, 214–216
rest stops in, 210
seating (*See also* Furniture, general office; Seating)
    armrests, 208
    assembly, 218
    built-in, 208
specifications for, 206–218
spectator spaces, 217
telephones, public, 213, 214
thresholds, 207
turning space requirements in, 210
vending machines, 217
vestibule
    door swing, 207
    floor surfacing, 212
work surfaces, 215

Quality control. *See* Fire performance testing; Materials, peformance evaluation of; Value management

Racine Industrial Plant, 82
Regulations and standards (*See also* Codes)
    building codes, 21
    buildings, classification of, 21
    code uniformity, lack of
        county, 22
        federal, 22
        health departments, 22
        insurance, 22
        municipal, 22
        overlap, 22
        state, 22
        zoning, 22
    compliance. *See* Risk management and code compliance
    federal agencies, 20
    federal codes, 19
    fire codes, 21
    model codes, 19
    occupancy loads, 21
        and type of occupancy, 21
    state and local legislation, 19
Risk management and code compliance, 23–24
    general checklist, 23
    levels of compliance, interpretation of, 23
    proof of compliance
        documentation, 23
        onsite inspection, 23
        testing laboratories, 23
    questionable regulations, 23
    summary of, 24
    terminology, clarity of, for, 23

Edited by Sarah Bodine and Susan Davis
Designed by Jay Anning
Set in 9 point Times Roman